SPY/COUNTERSPY

SPY/COUUNTERSPY

An Encyclopedia of Espionage

VINCENT and NAN BURANELLI

MCGRAW-HILL BOOK COMPANY

New York St. Louis San Francisco Auckland
Bogotá Hamburg Johannesburg London
Madrid Mexico Montreal New Delhi
Panama São Paulo Singapore
Sydney Tokyo Toronto

Library of Congress Cataloging in Publication Data

Buranelli, Vincent.
  Spy/counterspy.

  Bibliography: p.
  Includes index.
  1. Espionage—Dictionaries. I. Buranelli, Nan,
date.   II. Title.
UB250.B87   327.1'2'0321   81–23666
ISBN 0–07–008915–9   AACR2

  234567890   DODO   89876543

ISBN 0-07-008915-9

The editors for this book were Thomas Quinn and Christine Ulwick,
the designer was Naomi Auerbach, and the production
supervisor was Teresa F. Leaden. It was set in
Souvenir Light by ComCom.
Printed and bound by R. R. Donnelley & Sons Company.

Contents

ABOUT THE AUTHORS

Vincent Buranelli is a professional historian and biographer. After serving in the U.S. Army during World War II, he studied at Downing College, Cambridge, receiving a Ph.D. He has written seven books and numerous articles and papers.

Nan Buranelli, a former member of British intelligence, has written for such publications as *The New York Times, Womensports, The Rotarian,* and *The People's Almanac*. Under a pseudonym, she has written a widely read syndicated column.

Preface

The spy is one of the classical figures of the human experience, known to every age, community, and culture from prehistoric times to our own because his or her talents meet a special need. At any given moment, past or present, somebody, somewhere, wants to know vital secrets of a real or potential enemy, and one way to make the discovery is through the art and science of espionage. That is the practical reason for the perdurable interest in spies. The psychological reason is that the profession has an inherent appeal in its combination of extreme danger, chilling suspense, and crafty undercover operations.

The spy story, whether fact or fiction, is therefore also timeless, as the relevant passages in the Bible and the popularity of contemporary thrillers indicate. For an author, fiction is the easier type, since it comes from the imagination. Fact is more recalcitrant, if only because espionage is, by definition, secret.

Spies operate in a murky twilight world of cover names, hidden objectives, pretended motives, clandestine assignations, official denials, and violent endings—a cloak-and-dagger world, to use the inevitable cliché. To describe that world from the outside and after the deeds are done is a vexing problem, one that frequently resists solution. The history of espionage is filled with gaps. It is a stage on which "Alias" and "Anon." are often featured actors in the play. Worse than that, major performances have gone unrecorded. The greatest spies may be unknown and unsuspected.

This conclusion could stand as a matter of logical inference, but it has the support of objective evidence to prove the point. Spies masked at the time of their espionage activities have been unmasked later on. The identity of Robert Townsend, leader of the Culper Ring in New York during the American War of Independence, remained a mystery for a century and a half, until a comparison of handwriting revealed the truth to a twentieth-century scholar.

One can only speculate about the motives for continued secrecy in such

cases. Is it reticence extending even beyond the grave? Is it fear of the consequences to the spy's family? Is it a feeling that spying is disreputable, the
betrayal of trustful people, and a determination not to be typed as a spy in
the public mind? Is it a desire to be as mysterious in the future as in the past?
These questions no doubt have answers as various as the spies themselves.

All this about secrecy having been said, the opposite problem remains to
bedevil the historian of espionage. There is an embarrassment of riches, for
spies have been among the most determined autobiographers, only too willing
to tell everything, and more than everything, about themselves. How many of
them have been anxious to hold the reader's attention by adding "artistic
verisimilitude to an otherwise bald and unconvincing narrative"!

Much spying has been and is done by individuals acting alone, so that their
testimony cannot be checked against the report of a second witness. Even a
second witness is no guarantee of the truth, since the two may contradict one
another—Sandor Rado and Alexander Foote could not agree on fundamental
facts regarding the espionage network to which they had both belonged in
Switzerland during World War II. The single spy is, nonetheless, the really
difficult spy, the one with freedom to exaggerate the importance and hazards
of the mission and the coolness, skill, and tenacity that enabled the spy to
achieve a triumphant success.

Problems proliferate for the reader. How much of these autobiographies
can one believe? That depends on how much can get past common sense. We
ourselves have in this encyclopedia been stopped most often by phony dia-
logue, by, as the *New Yorker* would say, statements we doubt ever got stated.
Did that witty repartee and those astute observations really occur to the spy
on the spur of the moment when confronted by suspicious colleagues, blun-
dering intruders, or counterespionage agents? It might be pleasant to believe
so and to refrain from undermining a good story by examining it too closely.
The way of the skeptic is hard, but skepticism has its own claims. We have
had to drop overboard entertaining fictions by Belle Boyd and Gustav Steinhauer.

Still, suitably winnowed, the books of real spies, however embroidered with
fanciful language and exaggerated performance, are useful to the historian. All
the more so are the works that come without the embroidery. Some former
secret agents who write of their experiences can be taken as basically truthful
in what they say (bearing in mind that they do not say everything they know
and at times prevaricate willingly or not; this is, after all, spying). That spymasters Allen Dulles and Mansfield Cumming are trustworthy in this sense, probably not even their harshest critics would deny. Books such as theirs are
therefore especially helpful to the researcher trying to find out what really
happened.

The above remarks concern the primary sources, the spies themselves. The secondary sources are the biographers of spies and the historians of espionage, the men and women who have sifted the evidence and produced studied accounts of who, what, where, when, and how. These are guides to the material, indispensable for encyclopedists working to a text of 400 articles and 200,000 words. Yet, private judgment remains the final criterion. We have used our firsthand knowledge wherever possible, and plausibility after that, especially when we found, as often happened, disagreement between authorities. We believe Mata Hari was a spy, but with some hesitation because it has been denied by some specialists with more knowledge of the details than we have.

If Mata Hari must be included in any espionage encyclopedia, how many other spies can claim a place beside her? Most of the known spies are necessarily excluded, for they add up to many more than there is room for in this volume. The French resistance of World War II produced thousands of spies whose names are in the public domain, so that only an encyclopedic treatment of the resistance itself could cover them all. Add this example to others nearly as striking (e.g., the number of Soviet spies in the west during the Cold War), and the somewhat intimidating dimensions of the problem come into focus.

We have been spared much of this dilemma by confining ourselves to modern history—beginning in Elizabethan England with Francis Walsingham, the first great spymaster of the Western world and arguably the greatest of them all. Everything that went before is ruled out. Except at this moment, you will not meet Rahab the Harlot and the Hebrew spies she sheltered in Jericho (Joshua, 2:6). It is appropriate to let Sun Tsu put in an appearance here; it is the only chance to be noticed we have allowed the Chinese sage and philosopher of espionage.

Time offers a dogmatic, although natural and convenient, dividing line between those who may enter and those who must be barred. Space is intractable, divided according to a subjective criterion—the knowledge of the writer. This encyclopedia is worldwide in the sense that it ranges from Norway to China. It is not, and could not be, worldwide if that definition implies equal consideration for all lands, something completely beyond anybody's competence. To the question of why most countries are ignored, we reply with Doctor Johnson, "Ignorance, madam, pure ignorance." If there were remarkable spies in Java in 1800, they are not named because we know nothing about them. The orientals who claimed our attention are those about whom books have been written in, or translated into, English, French, or German and, moreover, books available to us.

In the text that follows, there are too many Americans in comparison with Europeans, too many Europeans in comparison with other westerners, and too many westerners in comparison with the rest of the world. This imbalance is not something that calls for apology. Every historian of the world is in the same position, limited by the egocentric predicament to an angle of vision that takes in the local areas of the globe (nation, continent) more clearly than those further away. Will Durant calls his enterprise *The Story of Civilization,* but it is in fact the story of western civilization with occasional excursions further afield, as the titles of his individual volumes show: *The Renaissance, Rousseau and Revolution, The Age of Napoleon*—what have these to do with Japan or India? Durant says much more about the Roman Empire than about the Chinese Empire that existed at the same time.

We have cast our net as widely as possible, short of allowing in nonentities just because they happen to be exotic or fill a lacuna on the map. That is as much as can be, or need be, said.

Within the defined boundaries of our subject, and faced with the need to choose from a multitude of candidates, we at the start made one list of the mandatory and another of the possible entries. All of the former naturally survived and became part of the text, but only a minority of the latter. We used various criteria in making our selections in difficult cases, sometimes preferring one spy to another equally acceptable for the sake of geographical or temporal balance (not too many from Russia or the Jacobite movement) or because some unique twist of espionage was involved (Casanova spying on British sailors instead of on compliant women) or to let a stage performer take a bow (Josephine Baker rather than some others in the French resistance).

In at least one instance, a plain failure had to be chosen over many successful secret agents. Nathan Hale ranks among the most inept of all spies, and yet, certainly for Americans, an espionage encyclopedia without him would be an egregious solecism. Nathan Hale is here.

No one else would draw up a list identical to ours, and given another chance we might make other choices where marginal subjects are concerned. We see our final list as analogous to the titles of the "great books" and to be defended in a similar way. It is sufficient if specialists agree on 75 percent of the choices while disagreeing on the remainder, and we believe that at least 300 of our entries would be allowed to stand by most historians of espionage, and we take that to be clinical.

We have tried to make each article coherent and complete as far as it goes, but, the emphasis being on espionage, and everything else being background material, a startling shift of perspective takes place regarding some of our personalities. George Washington appears as a spymaster who did a few other things on the side.

A question that imposes itself on anyone who writes this broadly of espionage is the identity of the greatest spy. Does one stand out preeminently in the roll call of great spies?

We have discussed this question off and on and have emerged at the end with agreement on the criteria at least. For us the greatest spies are those who risk their lives on hazardous missions, discover and report to their headquarters information of the first importance on momentous issues, and do it without being unmasked by those they spy against.

Many spies fail to fulfill one or another of these criteria. Richard Sorge is often called the greatest spy because he reported clandestinely from Tokyo to Moscow in 1941 that Japan would not attack the Soviet Union, thus enabling Stalin to bring an army from Siberia for use against the Germans; but Sorge was caught and executed by the Japanese. Oleg Penkovskiy sent secretly from Moscow the information on Soviet rockets that enabled President Kennedy to make Nikita Khrushchev back down at the time of the Cuban missile crisis in 1962, but Penkovskiy ended up before a Russian firing squad. Kim Philby, who spied for the Soviet Union while an agent of British intelligence, got away to Moscow, but only after being exposed. Consequently, these three great spies fail to make the grade as *the* greatest.

We ourselves are divided on the question of who fits our definition best. One of us gives the palm to Wilhelm Stieber, the German spymaster whose personal espionage work in Austria and France was instrumental in the victories of Bismarck's Germany over those two nations. The other prefers Robert Townsend, operating in revolutionary New York under the nose of General Sir Henry Clinton and the guns of his army of occupation.

Which puzzles would we like to see cleared up? Well, who was "355," the woman who worked with Townsend in the Culper Ring and still eludes identification? Who was the Tory spy who in 1775 wrote in bad French from Concord to General Thomas Gage in Boston? Who was the spy on the raft at Tilsit in 1807 when Emperor Napoleon conferred with Tsar Alexander I?

Perhaps the most interesting of all such questions concerns Lazare Carnot, the French Revolution's "Organizer of Victory." Was Carnot really the spy in the Committee of Public Safety who passed information to royalist go-betweens and therefore to the British who were at war with his armies? The claim that he was boggles the imagination, which is, of course, no argument for leaving him out; on the contrary, he would add piquancy to the text. Regretfully, we concluded after studying the problem that there is no hard evidence to support the contention. Carnot is not here.

Still, piquancy exists, along with excitement, mystery, suspense, and, yes, humor (Velvalee Dickinson, the "Doll Woman" of New York, detected using as false return addresses the actual addresses of unsuspecting women who bought her wares through the mail; Montgaillard, the amusing rogue who played all sides from the French Revolution of 1789 to the fall of the Bourbons in 1830).

The world of espionage is difficult to explore, but what characters, in every sense of the word, do we not meet along the way!

Vincent and Nan Buranelli

CRITICAL APPARATUS

The articles in the text of this encyclopedia belong to four general categories:

1. People (Abel to Zimmermann)
2. Events (*Amerasia* to Watergate)
3. Organizations (Abwehr to Special Operations Executive)
4. Techniques (Agent to U-2)

Each article is introduced according to the same formula of title, dates (where appropriate), and brief definition.

Where a cover name is better known than a real name, we use the cover name (e.g., "Gordon Lonsdale" rather than "Konon Trofimovich Molody.") Code names are cited separately only when they are of exceptional interest.

Where dates are doubtful, we use the most plausible followed by a question mark. We also use the age of seventy as a round figure for calculating presumed death dates when there is no evidence to suggest a closer approximation.

Where a definition would allow a number of near synonyms as its key word, we have selected the one that seems to fit the case most accurately (e.g., we choose among "spy," "secret agent," "conspirator," and so on). Gavrilo Princip could be classified as a spy or a secret agent, but he is properly termed a conspirator, the assassin of the Austrian archduke in 1914, thereby setting in motion the events that led to World War I.

All the bibliographical references mentioned after the articles are in English, with two exceptions, on Sandor Rado and Wilhelm Stieber, where untranslated German works are listed because there is nothing in English to rival them in fundamental importance. Asterisks indicate the most useful titles to begin with when there are multiple choices.

the study of espionage

Guides to the Subject

A lexicon: U.S. Department of Defense, *Dictionary of Military and Associated Terms,* Joint Chiefs of Staff Publication No. 1, U.S. Government Printing Office, Washington, D.C., 1972.

A general bibliography: Paul W. Blackstock and Frank L. Schaf, Jr., *Intelligence, Espionage, Counterespionage, and Covert Operations: A Guide to Information Sources,* Gale Research Company, Detroit, 1978.

A specialized bibliography: Myron J. Smith, Jr., *The Secret Wars: A Guide to Sources in English* (three vols.), ABC-Clio, Santa Barbara, Calif., 1980–81.

An encyclopedia: Ronald Seth, *Encyclopedia of Espionage,* New English Library, London, 1972.

An analytical introduction: Allen Dulles, *The Craft of Intelligence,* Harper and Row, New York, 1963.

A technical treatise: David Kahn, *The Codebreakers: The Story of Secret Writing,* Macmillan, New York, 1967.

A general history: Richard Wilmer Rowan and Robert G. Deindorfer, *Secret Service: Thirty-Three Centuries of Espionage,* Hawthorn Books, New York, 1967.

A bird's-eye-view: Jock Haswell, *Spies and Spymasters: A Concise History of Intelligence,* Thames and Hudson, London, 1977.

A collected biography: Fitzroy Maclean, *Take Nine Spies,* Atheneum, New York, 1978.

Introductory Books in French and German

Alem, Jean-Pierre, *L'Espionnage à travers les âges,* Stock, Paris, 1977.

Buchheit, Gert, *Die anonyme Macht: Aufgaben, Methoden, Erfahrungen der Geheimdienste,* Akademische Verlagsgesellschaft Athenaion, Frankfurt am Main, 1969.

Gheysens, Roger, *Les Espions: Un panorama de l'espionnage de notre temps,* Elsevier Sequoia, Bruxelles, 1973.

Gunzenhäuser, Max, *Geschichte des geheimen Nachrichtendienstes (Spionage, Sabotage und Abwehr) Literaturbericht und Bibliographie,* Bernard & Graefe, Frankfurt am Main, 1968.

Puy-Montbrun, Déodat du, *Les Armes des espions,* Balland, Paris, 1972.

SPY/COUUNTERSPY

Abel, Rudolf *(1902-72)*   Russian spymaster in the United States.

Abel was born into a comfortable family of tsarist Russia and received a good education, especially in modern languages, that helped him to become a success in Bolshevik Russia. During the 1930s he went into Soviet intelligence and rose to be a language instructor for the NKVD (People's Commissariat for Internal Affairs, as the KGB was known from 1934 to 1946). During the World War II conflict between Germany and Russia (1941–45), he served as an intelligence officer on the German front.

The Center, Moscow's intelligence headquarters, put Abel through specialized training (1945–47) and then, when he was a colonel in the service, sent him to Canada with a forged passport. In 1948 he slipped across the border into the United States, where he began meeting the agents of his network who were already in place, recruiting more agents, and preparing for future assignments. In 1950 he lived in New York using the cover name "Emil R. Golfus." Posing as an artist and photographer, which he could do since he had some talent with the brush and the camera, he installed himself in a studio in Brooklyn from which, as resident director, or spymaster for the Soviet Union, he reported to Moscow and received instructions back by shortwave radio. His duties included monitoring the United Nations, as well as American affairs he could cover from his base in Brooklyn.

Abel, known to his agents only through cover names, communicated with them by means of drops in public places. Two of his agents, Morris and Leona Cohen, were skillful operatives on whom he particularly relied. They fled in 1950 out of fear that they might be discovered and arrested, and later turned up in England using the names Peter and Helen Kroger. They returned to spying for the Soviet Union. This time they were caught and sentenced. Abel, meanwhile, remained unknown to American counterespionage. In 1953 he received a visit from Reino Hayhanen, another agent of the Center, who had been instructed to act as Abel's cut-out, or front man. The partnership never flourished because Hayhanen drank, chased women, and, worst of all, failed to perform his espionage assignments.

A year after Hayhanen's arrival in New York, Abel was urging him to return to Moscow. In 1955 Abel himself went home for a rest, and was appalled when he came back to New York to find his subordinate guilty not only of incompetence but also of appropriating Center funds to pay for his pleasures.

Abel now pressed Hayhanen to go to Moscow, which Hayhanen at last agreed to do. He left in 1957, got as far as Paris, defected to the U.S. Embassy, and talked to an agent of the CIA (Central Intelligence Agency). His testimony caused Abel to be arrested in New York. Abel's studio was searched, and his spy apparatus was discovered.

Interrogated, Abel admitted only to being a Russian who had entered the United States illegally. But Hayhanen's evidence was reinforced by that of an American, Master Sergeant Roy Rhodes (identified by Hayhanen), who confessed that he had spied for the Russians while working at the motor pool of the American Embassy in Moscow. Abel was found guilty of espionage.

Abel's American lawyer, James Donovan, argued against a capital sentence on the ground that America might one day need the Russian spy to exchange for an American spy in Russia. The court agreed, and the argument proved prophetic in 1962 when Donovan arranged the deal by which Abel was exchanged in Berlin for Francis Gary Powers, the American U-2 pilot who had been knocked down by a Russian rocket over the Soviet Union.

Abel returned to Moscow, headed the Anglo-American desk at the Center, and before his death published memoirs that tell a little of the truth (while concealing a lot more) about his time in New York.

See also CENTER, THE; DONOVAN, JAMES; HAYHANEN, REINO; KROGER, PETER AND HELEN.

FURTHER READING: *James B. Donovan, *Strangers on a Bridge: The Case of Colonel Abel* (1964); Ronald Seth, *Unmasked! The Story of Soviet Espionage* (1965); Louise Bernikow, *Abel* (1970).

Abwehr   German military intelligence.

The word "Abwehr" is a shortened form of the German title meaning "foreign information and counterintelligence department." The organization dates from 1866, when the Germans established an intelligence bureau to carry out espionage against Austria before the war between the two powers, which Germany (Prussia) won, partly because of better intelligence. The bureau was expanded during the four years leading up to the Franco-Prussian War (1870–71). Wilhelm Stieber, a spymaster of genius, directed thousands of agents in France before hostilities began, one reason why the Germans won so quickly. World War I (1914–18) was the last gasp for the old system, although Walther Nicolai ran it with credit before the German defeat.

The Abwehr, as it was now called, revived with the German armed forces during the 1920s. In 1928 it took over all military intelligence for the German army, navy, and air force. When Adolf Hitler became chancellor of Germany (1933), he expanded intelligence work along with his armed forces. Admiral Wilhelm Canaris, becoming head of the Abwehr in 1935, led its three departments (espionage, sabotage, and counterespionage) into World War II. Canaris, a conspirator against Hitler, harmed the German war effort more than he helped it. He allowed his subordinates to send information to the Allies, and his second-in-command, Hans Oster, reported to them regularly on German strategy and battle plans.

The failures of the Abwehr caused Hitler to break up the organization in 1944. Canaris and Oster were both arrested and executed for their part in the July Plot, a conspiracy to assassinate the dictator.

See also CANARIS, WILHELM; NICOLAI, WALTHER; OSTER, HANS; STIEBER, WILHELM.

FURTHER READING: Paul Leverkuehn, *German Military Intelligence* (1954); André Brissaud, *The Nazi Secret Service* (1974); *David Kahn, *Hitler's Spies: German Military Intelligence in World War II* (1978).

Agent, Notional   A nonexistent secret agent; a fiction used by an intelligence organization in a deception campaign.

See DOUBLE-CROSS SYSTEM.

Agent, Secret   A person acting clandestinely as a spy or saboteur; same as an undercover agent.

See SABOTAGE; SPY.

Agent Provocateur A person who instigates incriminating overt acts by individuals or groups under suspicion by the police.

See COUNTERSPY.

Akashi, Motojiro *(1860?-1919)* Japanese army officer and spy in Russia before the Russo-Japanese War.

Akashi was one of the Japanese who rose from humble origins by joining the armed forces of the mikado, the emperor of Japan. As a youth in Tokyo, Akashi came to the attention of the Black Dragon Society, the patriotic organization that was planning for Japanese expansion in the Far East. The Black Dragon Society sent him to military school, supported him when he joined the Japanese army and as he rose to prominence in the officer corps, and gave him instructions when he entered the intelligence service.

By 1900 Akashi was a colonel. His first espionage assignments took him as a military attaché to the Japanese embassies in France, Switzerland, and Sweden. In 1904, as Japan prepared to launch the attack on Russia that would precipitate the Russo-Japanese War (1904–05), Akashi received orders to go to St. Petersburg, the capital of the Russian empire, and agitate among the revolutionaries scheming for the overthrow of the tsar, the hope in Tokyo being that disorder inside Russia would make the Japanese victory easier.

With the Japanese Embassy for a base and the title of military attaché for a cover, Akashi surreptitiously met the leaders of radical groups and promised them financial support if and when they moved against their government. He also collected information from them about the tsar's armed forces. The tsarist police never noticed that he was engaged in this kind of undercover work or that he spied on officials of the tsar's regime.

Sent to Tokyo in the diplomatic pouch of the Japanese ambassador, Akashi's reports were integrated into the overall scheme for the coming war. The Japanese attack took the Russians by surprise and struck at the weak points in the Russian armed forces, two good reasons for the lightning Japanese victory.

Akashi went back to Russia in 1906 after the conflict was over. Now he operated in Central Asia, attempting to provoke anti-Russian insurrections among the non-Europeans in this region of the tsar's empire. The scheme failed, even though Akashi was not the only Japanese spy in the area, because whole peoples could not be moved as easily as a few revolutionaries.

Returning to Tokyo, Akashi helped plan Japanese strategy during World War I (1914–18), when he served as assistant chief of the general staff. The capture of German-held Tsingtao on the Chinese coast (1914) caused the warlords in Tokyo to think of expanding Japanese military power onto the mainland. Akashi took part in the early planning for this move, although he did not live to see its culmination in 1931 when Japan invaded Manchuria.

FURTHER READING: J. L. Spivack, *Honorable Spy* (1939); *Ronald Seth, *Secret Servants: A History of Japanese Espionage* (1957); Shumpei Okamoto, *The Japanese Oligarchy and the Russo-Japanese War* (1971), describes the strategy to which Akashi contributed through his espionage in Russia.

Albani, Alessandro *(1692-1779)* Italian cardinal, art collector, and spy in Rome for the British government against the Jacobites, supporters of the Stuart claimants to the throne of Britain.

Born in Urbino, Albani was a nephew of Pope Clement XI, whom he served in various capacities, including commanding a regiment in the papal army, before taking ecclesiastical orders in 1712. Albani entered the papal diplomatic corps in 1720, served in Vienna, and later represented Austrian interests at the Vatican. Pope Innocent XIII made him a cardinal in 1721.

The most sensitive issue of European politics at this time was the Jacobite movement, which had taken form after James II lost the British throne in 1688, at the time of the Glorious Revolution. His son, the "Old Pretender," having failed to regain the throne by force in 1715 (at the "Fifteen," as the British called the attempt), established himself in Rome and became the center of constant intrigues by the Jacobites, who considered him James III, rightful king of England, Scotland, and Ireland.

The London government maintained spies in Rome to watch and report on the Jacobites. One such spy was Philip von Stosch. Another was Cardinal Albani, Stosch's friend.

Albani functioned effectively as an undercover agent because he knew the Old Pretender, had a corps of informants in Jacobite circles, and saw the reports of papal nuncios concerning Jacobites elsewhere in Europe. Albani collected art, which gave him a good cover when he met British travelers, many of whom came to him for Roman antiquities or Renaissance paintings. Some of Albani's reports went directly to London. Others he put into letters to Horace Mann, the British resident in Florence.

At first Albani's concern was to note the whereabouts of the Old Pretender, who in his travels around Europe might have tried to raise another military force with which to invade Britain. Then the son of "James III," Charles Edward, the "Young Pretender" ("Bonnie Prince Charlie"), became a problem, for he was known to be preparing an expedition. In 1744 Albani reported to Mann that the Young Pretender was rarely seen in public and that the members of the Jacobite court in Rome had ceased to talk freely, so that something must be about to happen. What happened was the "Forty Five," when Bonnie Prince Charlie landed in Scotland in 1745, raised the Jacobite standard, and marched south to defeat in England.

The Young Pretender fled back to the Continent, where he gradually declined into dissolute idleness. In 1766 Albani wrote to Mann announcing the death of the Old Pretender in Rome. At Mann's request, Albani pressured the pope into suppressing the Jacobite royal title.

Thereafter, Albani had little undercover work to do, and he gave his time to his duties as a cardinal and his pleasures as an art collector.

See also MANN, HORACE.

FURTHER READING: John Doran, *Mann and Manners at the Court of Florence, 1740–86* (1876), has an account of Albani's spywork for Horace Mann; Charles Petrie, *The Jacobite Movement* (1959); *Lesley Lewis, *Connoisseurs and Secret Agents in Eighteenth Century Rome* (1961); David Daiches, *Charles Edward Stuart: The Life and Times of Bonnie Prince Charlie* (1973).

Allied Intelligence Bureau *(1942-45)* Spy, sabotage, and propaganda organization based in Australia during World War II.

When General Douglas MacArthur of the United States reached Australia in 1942 as the tide of Japanese conquest washed over the Philippine islands, where he had been in command of the American-Filipino forces, he realized he needed a new kind of intelligence agency to plan for his coming counterof-fensive against the triumphant enemy. The remnants of defeated Australian, American, British, and Dutch forces had to be unified for espionage campaigns no less than for military campaigns.

This was the origin of the Allied Intelligence Bureau (AIB), with headquar-ters in Melbourne. It included five departments: sabotage, British espionage, Dutch espionage, propaganda, and the Australian Coast Watchers on the islands near or behind the Japanese lines. The head of the AIB was Colonel C. G. Roberts, director of Australian military intelligence.

The men of the AIB preceded MacArthur's advance from the islands north-east of Australia, through New Guinea, and on to the Philippines. They re-ceived information from the Coast Watchers by radio, mounted sabotage operations, monitored Japanese broadcasts, and filled the air with propaganda messages designed to encourage the conquered peoples and discourage their conquerors.

The activities of the AIB thus became an essential part of the Allied drive across the South Pacific to Japan. With the liberation of the Philippines, the organization had fulfilled the purpose for which it had been founded, and it passed into history.

See also COAST WATCHERS.

FURTHER READING: *Allison Ind, *Allied Intelligence Bureau: Our Secret Weapon in the War against Japan* (1958); Eric Feldt, *The Coast Watchers* (1959); D. C. Horton, *Fire over the Islands: Coast Watchers of the Solomons* (1970).

Amerasia Case *(1945)*   American scandal concerning the removal of clas-sified documents from government offices in Washington.

The magazine *Amerasia,* as the title implied, was a forum for discussing the relations between the United States and the Far East. Edited by Philip Jaffe, *Amerasia* first appeared in 1937 and continued to be published through the period of World War II (1939–45); among its contributors were Emmanuel Larsen, who worked in the U.S. State Department, and Andrew Roth of naval intelligence. The magazine defended an American policy of relying more on the Chinese Communists and less on the nationalists of Chiang Kai-shek.

In 1945 a secret British report on Thailand appeared in the magazine, and the only possible source was the files of the OSS (Office of Strategic Ser-vices). After the British government protested to Washington about the breach of confidentiality, OSS agents raided the *Amerasia* office and found classified documents from the State Department and other government bu-reaus. A subsequent raid by the FBI (Federal Bureau of Investigation), on orders from President Harry Truman, turned up many more documents that no one at *Amerasia* was authorized to remove from the offices where they were kept.

Jaffe, Larsen, and Roth were arrested along with several others, including John Service, an expert on China who served as a political adviser at the State Department. The case created a scandal, not only because of the removal of classified documents, but also because the Cold War was beginning and the reality of Communist espionage in Washington was undeniable. No evidence indicated, however, that the *Amerasia* group had passed secret information to a foreign government, and only Jaffe pleaded guilty to possessing classified documents. Larsen pleaded *nolo contendere* and was fined along with Jaffe. The charge against Roth was dismissed on a motion of the government, while Service and the others were cleared by a grand jury.

The *Amerasia* case led to a congressional investigation of Soviet espionage in Washington. At the same time, it gave a handle to Senator Joseph McCarthy, who in 1950 launched his notorious campaign against those whom he termed "Communists in government." McCarthy condemned Service for supporting the Chinese Communists against Chiang Kai-shek. In 1951 the State Department dismissed Service, who sued and in 1957 received reinstatement. By then both McCarthy and *Amerasia* were gone.

FURTHER READING: Frederick Woltman, *The Amerasia Case* (1950); John Stewart Service, *The Amerasia Papers: Some Problems in the History of U.S.-Chinese Relations* (1971); *E. J. Kahn, Jr., *The China Hands: America's Foreign Service Officers and What Befell Them* (1975).

American Black Chamber *(1919-29)*   Celebrated cryptological group headed by Herbert O. Yardley.
   See YARDLEY, HERBERT O.

André, John *(1750-80)*   British officer and espionage chief executed as a spy during the American War of Independence.

Born in London of Swiss-French parentage, André grew to be a talented young man who wrote verse, enjoyed music, and performed in amateur theatricals. Disappointed in love, he bought a commission in the army of King George III and in 1774 was posted to Canada, where invading Americans, now in rebellion against the crown, captured him in 1775.

After being freed in a prisoner exchange, André served as an officer under Sir William Howe in Philadelphia (1777) and under Sir Henry Clinton in New York City (1778). Clinton, needing information on the American enemy, ordered Captain André to recruit spies who could go behind the lines of the Continental army along the Hudson River and report on what they saw. André thus became a spymaster running an espionage network. The network was made up mainly of Loyalists, posing as Patriots, who wanted a restoration of royal rule in America. André dealt with dozens of agents, including the most successful female spy of the war, Ann Bates, who visited General George Washington's headquarters and spied on him, his staff, and his soldiers.

André was less successful at counterespionage. Although he rounded up some Patriot spies in New York City, he never uncovered the Culper Ring, which operated in Manhattan and on Long Island under the direction of his opposite number on the American side, Major Benjamin Tallmadge.

Nothing of any great significance developed for André as spymaster until May 10, 1779, when a Loyalist courier, Joseph Stansbury, arrived with the startling news that an American general, Benedict Arnold, stood ready to betray the Americans and come over to the British side. An undercover correspondence began in which, using cover names, André called himself "John Anderson" and Arnold used various aliases, such as "Mr. Moore" and "Monk."

They wrote in codes, one of which was a number system in which the first of three numbers referred to a page, the second to a line, and the third to a word on the line, in William Blackstone's *Commentaries on the Laws of England.* Since André and Arnold both owned copies of this standard work, each could open it and decode a message from the other.

Arnold wanted money and a general's rank under Clinton, but, being without a command at the time, he had too little to offer in return, and Clinton refused. The André-Arnold correspondence lapsed when André, promoted to major, accompanied Clinton's expedition to Charleston, South Carolina, in 1780. The city fell, and André, returning with Clinton to New York City, resumed the correspondence. Arnold now made a substantial offer—West Point, to the command of which Washington had assigned him, in exchange for £20,000 and the rank of general.

Clinton was interested, for West Point would give him control of the lower reaches of the Hudson River, which would be a severe blow to Washington and the Patriot cause. Clinton therefore permitted André to meet Arnold covertly to discuss the details, but ordered André to stay outside the American lines to avoid being caught and to stay in uniform to avoid being treated as a spy if he should be caught. André disobeyed both these orders, with fatal consequences to himself.

André went up the Hudson on a British sloop and met Arnold in a nighttime rendezvous at Haverstraw on September 21, 1780. André agreed to Arnold's financial and military demands, and Arnold, explaining how the British could take West Point by assault, handed over plans to the stronghold. André was satisfied that Arnold, as commanding general, could and would disperse the garrison at the critical moment.

By the time the conference ended, it was too late for André to return to his ship. He incautiously accepted an offer to go behind the American lines and spend the night at a farmhouse. In the morning, the ship had to drop down the Hudson when fired on by American guns. André decided at this point to return to the British lines by land, and to escape notice he exchanged his uniform for civilian dress. Concealing the plans of West Point in his boot, he set out on horseback for New York City.

He was accompanied part of the way by Joshua Hett Smith, whom Arnold had provided as an escort. Smith dropped off at the Croton River, and André rode on alone, making detours to bypass American positions, until he was stopped near Tarrytown by three American militiamen, John Paulding, David Williams, and Isaac van Wart. He showed them a pass made out by General Arnold to John Anderson, but, finding the West Point plans in his boot, they took him to the nearest American outpost. The officer in charge, Colonel John Jameson, assuming that his commanding general, Arnold, should interrogate the prisoner, ordered André to be taken to Arnold's headquarters at West Point.

Not long afterward, Major Benjamin Tallmadge, the American espionage chief, arrived at the outpost. Knowing that Arnold had asked free passage through the American lines for John Anderson and being informed about the John Anderson pass and the West Point plans carried by the prisoner, Tallmadge suspected Arnold of collusion with André. He persuaded Jameson to have André brought back. Jameson still insisted on sending word about the prisoner to Arnold, who, thus warned that the game was up, escaped down the Hudson to New York City.

Learning of Arnold's treason and André's capture, Washington ordered André held for trial by a special board of American generals. Meanwhile, the prisoner was placed in Tallmadge's custody. André's defense at his trial was that he could not truly be considered a spy since he had come through the American lines in uniform. He explained how he had been unable to return to his sloop in uniform, and he argued that he should not be held responsible for getting out of uniform, since he was virtually a captive trapped behind the American lines.

The board rejected his plea, found him guilty of being a spy, and judged that his execution would be justified. Washington, concurring, paused long enough to offer André in exchange for Arnold. Clinton refused, and André died on the scaffold. Tallmadge, who had come to admire André as a soldier and a human being, was among the many in both armies who lamented his fate.

See also ARNOLD, BENEDICT.

FURTHER READING: Carl Van Doren, *Secret History of the American Revolution* (1941); *James T. Flexner, *The Traitor and the Spy* (1953), is an account of Arnold and André; J. E. Morpurgo, *Treason at West Point: The Arnold-André Conspiracy* (1975).

Arcos Affair **(1924-27)**   Scandal concerning a Soviet espionage agency in London.

The establishment of diplomatic relations between Britain and the Soviet Union in 1924 involved commerce as well as politics, and the Russians dispatched to London a trade organization called "Arcos." Staffed by a much larger number of personnel than the existing trade justified, Arcos had a second, secret function, which was espionage. Some members did little if anything except spy on British industry and the armed forces. The information gathered went to Moscow in the diplomatic pouch, for Arcos, like the Soviet Embassy, enjoyed diplomatic immunity.

Arcos espionage continued without raising any suspicions on the part of the British authorities until 1926, when a general strike threatened to paralyze Britain. The Soviet Communist party, backing disorder in a capitalist country, sent more than £250,000 through Arcos to the strikers. This blatant interference by foreigners in a British domestic problem caused a hue and cry in the British press; the trade unions representing the strikers returned the money to Moscow, and MI5 (Military Intelligence 5, British counterespionage) began keeping Arcos under surveillance.

Two cases of Arcos espionage came to light in 1926. A technician serving in the Royal Air Force, arrested and found in possession of classified documents, confessed that he intended to deliver them to Arcos, for which he had been working for some time. An employee of an aircraft factory was caught in much the same way. These three incidents of 1926 proved too much for the British government to overlook, and it withdrew the diplomatic immunity under cover of which Arcos had been operating.

In 1927 a top-secret paper on RAF bombing tactics vanished from its file. MI5 and the Special Branch of Scotland Yard reported that, judging from their investigations, the paper had been delivered to Arcos. The police therefore raided the headquarters of the Russian trade organization. They did not find the document in question, but they did seize many others that exposed Arcos as an espionage agency hiding behind its trade accreditation. London immediately ordered Arcos personnel to go home and broke off diplomatic relations with the Soviet Union.

FURTHER READING: David Dallin, *Soviet Espionage* (1955); *Ronald Seth, *Unmasked! The Story of Soviet Espionage* (1965); Gordon Brook Shepherd, *The Storm Petrels: The Flight of the First Soviet Defectors* (1977), has a mention of the Arcos Affair.

Arnold, Benedict *(1741-1801)*   American Patriot, outstanding general, and notorious traitor of the American Revolution.

Born in Connecticut, Arnold served (1757) in the French and Indian War before becoming a druggist and merchant in New Haven. Standing for the defense of American rights against British oppression as the revolution approached, he joined his colony's militia in 1774, and after the fighting began at Lexington in 1775, he took part in the American siege of British-occupied Boston. His first important service as a military man was at Fort Ticonderoga, where he helped capture that British stronghold on New York's Lake Champlain.

General George Washington gave Arnold command of the eastern wing of an American invasion of Canada, whereupon Arnold led his troops on an epic trek through the Maine wilderness to Quebec. He joined forces with the western wing under Richard Montgomery, but an attempt to storm Quebec failed, Montgomery was killed, and in 1776 Arnold retreated from Canada, again showing exemplary patriotism, fortitude, and leadership.

In 1777 Arnold, by now a brigadier general, marched up the Mohawk Valley and broke the British siege of Fort Stanwix. Saratoga followed, where Arnold's valor on the battlefield contributed dramatically to the American victory over General John Burgoyne, who had moved south from Canada in the hope of winning a decisive engagement for King George III.

Washington had enough faith in Arnold to give him command of Philadelphia in 1778, following the British evacuation of the city. But Arnold began to nurse grudges against the Americans. In financial straits because of high living, he needed a promotion and resented having to wait for approval by the Continental Congress. Accused of irregularities in his command, he demanded a court-martial. He married Margaret Shippen, a Loyalist who supported his decision to go over to the king's side. The breaking point came in 1779, when the court-martial found him guilty and Washington reprimanded him.

Arnold was already in covert communication with Major John André, the British spymaster in New York City. Now Arnold wrote to André more frequently, using such cover names as "Mr. Moore" and "Monk" (the latter a reference to General Monk, who after the death of Oliver Cromwell, summoned Charles II from exile to restore royal government in England). André used the cover name "John Anderson," and the pair hid Arnold's treason behind coded messages.

When Washington assigned Arnold to West Point in 1780, Arnold offered to betray this American stronghold on the Hudson to the British for £20,000 and the rank of general. Arnold and André met by night at Haverstraw on September 21, 1780, and André made promises in the name of Sir Henry Clinton, the British commander in New York City. Arnold gave André the plans of West Point. These plans were later found in André's boot when he was stopped by American militiamen on his way back to New York City, causing him to be held as a suspect.

Ironically, a warning about John Anderson (as André identified himself to his captors) was dispatched to the commanding general at West Point, Arnold himself. This warning enabled Arnold to slip away from his quarters and have himself rowed to the British vessel from which André had come. Shortly afterward, Arnold was safely at Clinton's headquarters in New York City. André was hanged by the Americans on the charge of being a spy.

Granted a general's rank by Clinton, Arnold formed a regiment, raided Virginia, and devastated New London in his native Connecticut. He went to England after the decisive American victory at Yorktown in 1781, engaged in business, failed to obtain a military commission during the Wars of the French Revolution, and spent his final years in obscurity.

See also ANDRÉ, JOHN; WASHINGTON, GEORGE.

FURTHER READING: Carl Van Doren, *Secret History of the American Revolution* (1941); *James T. Flexner, *The Traitor and the Spy* (1953), is an account of Arnold and André; Brian Richard Boylan, *Benedict Arnold: The Dark Eagle* (1973).

Ashby, Turner *(1828-62)*   Confederate cavalry commander and spy during the American Civil War.

Born at Rose Bank, the family estate in Virginia, Ashby came of a line of soldiers going back to the American Revolution. He was privately educated, took to farming the estate, and in 1859, hearing of John Brown's raid on Harper's Ferry, led a mounted band of his friends and neighbors to the area. They arrived too late to be of assistance in putting down the revolt, but they stayed on guard along the Potomac as Brown followed his path to the gallows.

Although Ashby disliked secession, he remained loyal to his state when Virginia joined the Confederacy in 1861. As an accomplished horseman, he naturally went into the cavalry, but no one could have anticipated the military ability he now displayed. General Stonewall Jackson wanted daring, resourceful cavalry commanders, and Ashby became one of his best. Jackson also wanted a reliable espionage system. Ashby became part of that system.

Early in 1861, Ashby went behind the Union lines, using the cover story that he was a horse doctor—he knew so much about horses that the story was entirely credible. Reaching Chambersburg, Pennsylvania, he surveyed the enemy troop encampment there, estimated their numbers and readiness for combat, and returned with the kind of information Jackson always wanted while planning a battle.

Ashby served in General J. E. B. Stuart's cavalry that, by threatening the Federals at Harper's Ferry, kept them from interfering with General Joseph E. Johnston's move east to throw his forces into the battle of Bull Run (1861). Promoted to lieutenant colonel, Ashby took command of the Seventh Virginia Cavalry.

Meanwhile he had organized a spy ring to gather information about the Union army. His informants failed him in 1862 at Kernstown, Virginia, when Jackson suffered a repulse because the main Union force had not been discovered. Later that year, Ashby reported correctly to Jackson the plans and strength of the Federals at Front Royal, Virginia, which enabled

Jackson to plan his tactics, advance confidently, and win a decisive victory.

Ashby's success with the cavalry and with espionage led the Confederates to promote him to general. The Federals put a price on his head. Shortly afterward, while covering Jackson's operations in the Shenandoah Valley, Ashby was shot and killed in a skirmish with Union cavalry.

See also JACKSON, STONEWALL.

FURTHER READING: *Clarence Thomas, *General Turner Ashby* (1907); Harnett T. Kane, *Spies for the Blue and the Gray* (1954); John Bakeless, *Spies of the Confederacy* (1970).

Atlantic Wall Blueprint Affair (1943) French theft of a top-secret map of German fortifications along the Normandy coast.

As the Allies prepared to invade the Continent from England during World War II, the Germans built a system of defenses designed to prevent waterborne landings on the French side of the English Channel. Dubbed the "Atlantic Wall," the system extended from Brittany to the Low Countries; the most elaborate concentrations of underwater obstacles and beach defenses were at the most vulnerable points, close to the southern shore of England from which the Allied armada would sail. Normandy fell within this area, and here the Atlantic Wall was exceptionally strong.

The local network of the French resistance, the patriotic groups working against the German occupation, determined to aid the coming Allied invasion, and a primary aim was to obtain the plans of the Atlantic Wall so that the invaders would know how to break it. René Duchez, a housepainter and member of the network, succeeded in one dramatic episode. Employed in the redecorating of German headquarters in Caen in 1943, he noticed on the commanding officer's desk a large-scale folded map labeled "Special Blueprint —Top Secret." Seeing that the map concerned the Atlantic Wall, Duchez seized it while the commander was talking to an aide and hid it behind a mirror on the wall. On his return a few days later to resume painting the room, Duchez found the map undisturbed and carried it out of the building concealed among his paint brushes.

The German officer with whom he had made the arrangements for the redecoration had in the meantime been transferred out of Caen and replaced by another officer, so that the loss of the map at first went unnoticed. By the time the Germans began searching for it, the blueprint of the Atlantic Wall was on its way to London by way of Paris, Lorient, and a secret crossing of the Channel. The Allies were thus able to study the German defenses, to devise the best means of shattering them, and to train special units, such as the frogmen who were ordered to blow up underwater obstacles before the troops landed.

The Germans never suspected what had become of their blueprint. Their defenses therefore remained as described by the map, and the American First Army, landing at Utah Beach near Cherbourg on D-Day (June 6, 1944), quickly broke through and pushed inland. General Omar Bradley wrote later of Duchez's espionage coup: "Securing the blueprint of the German Atlantic Wall was an incredible feat—so valuable that the landing operation succeeded with a minimum loss of men and material."

See also FRENCH RESISTANCE.

FURTHER READING: Omar Bradley, *A Soldier's Story* (1951); *Ralph Collier, *Ten Thousand Eyes* (1958); Cornelius Ryan, *The Longest Day* (1974).

Azev, Yevno *(1869-1918)*   Russian police spy and double agent among revolutionaries opposed to the tsarist regime.

Born in Lyskovo, Russia, Azev was the son of a Jewish tailor who moved the family to Rostov on the Don River in the 1870s. Azev went to school in Rostov, worked as a salesman, and engaged in radical left-wing politics.

Noted in the police files as antitsarist, he fled to Germany in 1892, entered the university at Karlsruhe, studied engineering, and mingled with Russian students plotting the overthrow of the tsar. He joined the Social Democrats, the largest and most moderate of the Russian groups, but he also knew anarchists and terrorists who looked to violence as the path to the liberation of their homeland.

Unable to support himself financially in exile, and unable to return to Russia in view of the charges against him, Azev wrote to the Ochrana, the Russian secret police, offering to work as a spy in return for immunity. The Ochrana needed spies to infiltrate subversive Russian groups abroad. Azev's offer was accepted, and in 1893 he began espionage operations in Germany and Switzerland.

In 1901 Azev joined the Social Revolutionaries, an activist group dedicated to the use of terror; in time he became head of their combat section. Several assassinations were carried out with Azev's knowledge, including that of Grand Duke Sergei, governor general of Moscow. Azev's behavior was suspicious, since he did not warn the Ochrana to warn the victims, and there is some reason to believe that he thought the assassinations would benefit Russia. Still, he continued to send reports to the Ochrana, to which he betrayed some of his rivals among the Social Revolutionary leaders.

In 1906 Azev ordered the "execution" of Father Georgi Gapon, an unmasked police spy. Azev thus diverted attention from himself, but the leaks to the Ochrana continued after Gapon was gone, and in 1908 Azev was accused by a group of Social Revolutionaries. The case against him was so strong that he fled. He wandered around the Continent for years, was interned by the Germans during World War I, and died in the year the war ended.

See also GAPON, GEORGI; OCHRANA.

FURTHER READING: A. T. Vassilyev, *The Ochrana* (1930); *Boris Nicolaievsky, *Azeff, the Russian Judas* (1934); Fitzroy Maclean, *Take Nine Spies* (1978), has a chapter on Azev.

Babington, Anthony *(1561-86)* English Catholic undercover agent operating against the Protestant government during the Elizabethan era.

Babington belonged to a family of Catholics living in the English provinces who had to hide their religion because of the persecution to which Catholics were subjected by the Protestant government of Queen Elizabeth. After Queen Mary of Scotland, fleeing from the Protestant reformers in her country, sought sanctuary in England and was imprisoned by Elizabeth (1568), Babington served as a page to Mary's jailer. Numerous men became devoted supporters of Mary, and Babington, although a boy at the time, was the most ardent of them.

Posing as a Protestant, Babington accepted a place at Elizabeth's court in 1580, remained there for two years, and then traveled on the Continent, where he covertly joined Catholic Englishmen in Paris who were scheming against the religion and the throne of Elizabeth. Their scheme involved a Catholic rising in England to be coordinated with an invasion by a Spanish army. The upshot, if all went well, would be the replacement of Elizabeth by Mary as queen of England.

Babington threw himself into this scheme and became the most important conspirator upon his return to England. He carried letters to the queen of Scotland assuring her that she would be rescued, and he secured from her replies that he dispatched to the Catholic conspirators abroad. A number of the most important letters were in cipher, which Babington believed rendered the correspondence entirely safe.

However, Francis Walsingham, Elizabeth's spymaster, had maneuvered spies into Mary's entourage. Unknown to her and Babington, several letters in cipher were intercepted and decoded by Walsingham's cryptographers. Walsingham was thus in a position to introduce messages of his own into this correspondence and to keep the Babington plot developing until Mary and her champions were fatally compromised.

In 1586 Walsingham suddenly ordered the arrest of a conspirator, John Ballard, who confessed and filled in the last gaps in the government's case. Babington and five other conspirators fled and went underground. Walsingham's agents soon rounded them up, and they were lodged in the Tower of London. When they went on trial for treason, Babington blamed Ballard and begged Elizabeth for mercy, but nothing could save him from the block.

The irony of the Babington plot is that, intended to rescue Mary, it ensured her execution: one of the intercepted letters expressed her willingness to have Elizabeth murdered. The incriminating passage, possibly a Walsingham forgery, led to Elizabeth's signing of Mary's death warrant.

See also WALSINGHAM, FRANCIS.

FURTHER READING: J. H. Pollen, *Mary Queen of Scots and the Babington Plot* (1922); *A. G. Smith, *The Babington Plot* (1936); Antonia Fraser, *Mary Queen of Scots* (1969).

Baden-Powell, Robert *(1857-1941)* British founder of the Boy Scouts and spy on the Continent before World War I.

Baden-Powell was a native Londoner whose father was a professor of mathematics at Oxford. Educated at Charterhouse, a British public school, the son chose the army over the university and in 1877 joined the British hussars in India. For most of his military career, Baden-Powell moved among outposts of the British Empire, his greatest military feat being his defense (1900) of besieged Mafeking in South Africa during the Boer War.

His intelligence work began in 1888, at the time of the Zulu campaign following Britain's annexation of Zululand in black Africa. Two years later he shifted to the Mediterranean, where, from a base on the island of Malta, he made spy tours of the Balkans. This was when the tensions preceding World War I were building up and when British intelligence was still largely in the hands of inspired amateurs, since Mansfield Cumming had not yet founded MI6 (Military Intelligence 6, British espionage) in London. Baden-Powell was very much the inspired amateur of British espionage.

Posing as a lepidopterist for a cover story, and supposedly chasing butterflies with his net when he was out in the field, Baden-Powell toured areas of the Balkans then under the control of Austria. He scouted fortifications and military installations and hid the sketches of what he saw under the drawings of butterflies, thus rendering his spying innocent enough to pass the Austrian censor.

Later Baden-Powell carried out espionage missions in western Europe, on one of which he noticed and reported to London that the Germans were building naval installations at Hamburg that could accommodate large warships, an indication that the kaiser was putting his armed forces on something approaching a war footing.

Baden-Powell's book on his experiences appeared in 1915, when World War I had come and when the Allies (Britain and France) were using his espionage reports in a practical way against the Central Powers (Germany and Austria).

In spite of Baden-Powell's military and espionage achievements, he is best remembered for his founding of the Boy Scouts (1907), which became and remains an international institution. He received the Order of Merit in 1937 from King George VI and died during World War II, in which, as an octogenarian, he could not serve.

FURTHER READING: *Robert Baden-Powell, *My Adventures as a Spy* (1915); E. E. Reynolds, *Baden-Powell* (1957); Ronald Seth, *Some of My Favorite Spies* (1968), presents Baden-Powell as one of the author's favorites.

Baillie-Stewart, Norman *(1909-66)*　British army officer and spy for Germany.

Baillie-Stewart, born in London, was originally Norman Baillie Stewart Wright, his father being a Wright and his mother a Stewart. In 1910 his parents took him to India, where his father served in the Indian army of the British raj. Three years later he returned to England to begin his education, which continued during World War I (1914–18). He entered the Royal Naval College at Dartmouth in 1922, left because of illness in 1925, and later that year entered the Sandhurst military academy, from which he graduated in 1928 with a commission in the British army. At this time he changed his name to the more aristocratic double-barreled form, Baillie-Stewart.

In 1932 he visited Germany and, needing money for a lifestyle for which his military pay was insufficient, he agreed to spy for the Germans. He returned home, transmitted to Berlin information about the British armed forces, received payment for services rendered, and created suspicion by a lavish display of his sudden affluence. Arrested, tried, and found guilty, he received a five-year jail sentence. Held in the Tower of London, he became known in the British press as the "officer in the Tower."

In 1936, following his release, Baillie-Stewart went to Germany, where he remained during World War II (1939–45). Captured by British troops in conquered Germany and transported to London, he received another five-year sentence for pro-German activities. Released in 1949, he lived in Dublin thereafter.

FURTHER READING: Norman Baillie-Stewart (as told to John Murdoch), *The Officer in the Tower*, (1967).

Baker, Josephine *(1906-75)*   Black American-born spy for France against Germany during World War II.

Baker came from St. Louis, Missouri, where her father was a businessman hard-pressed to make a living. She dropped out of school, became a dancer and singer, and by 1924 was a star on Broadway. Accepting an offer to appear in Paris in *La Revue Nègre* (1925), a musical review featuring black performers, she became an immediate hit with the French public, decided to stay permanently, and became a naturalized French citizen in 1937.

When World War II broke out in 1939, Baker volunteered to serve in the French Red Cross. With the fall of France and the German occupation in 1940, she became a secret agent, using her stage career as a cover. Later that year she met Allied agents at a clandestine rendezvous, told them what she knew of the Germans in France, and was urged to continue spying.

Her great espionage coup came in 1943 in North Africa, where she toured the French colonies as a singer and dancer. Reporting on the Germans and their French collaborators, she provided information useful to the Americans when they invaded North Africa. General George Patton sent a message of thanks: "To Josephine Baker who helped us so valiantly."

After performing and spying in the Middle East in 1943, she retired from espionage to France in 1944 to help celebrate the liberation of Paris. President Charles de Gaulle awarded her the Cross of Lorraine and the Freedom Medal in 1945.

After the war, Baker went back to being a star of the French stage. She returned to America several times, and took part in the civil rights demonstrations of the 1960s.

FURTHER READING: Edith Isaacs, *The Negro in the American Theatre* (1947); Blake Erlich, *Resistance: France 1940–1945* (1965); *Josephine Baker and Jo Bouillon, *Josephine* (1977); Lynn Haney, *Naked at the Feast: A Biography of Josephine Baker* (1981).

Baker, Lafayette *(1826-68)*   Secret agent and director of Federal intelligence during the American Civil War.

Baker, a descendant of one of Ethan Allen's "Green Mountain boys" of American Revolution fame, was born in western New York State, where his father had a farm. The family moved to Michigan in Baker's youth.

Of a restless disposition, he wandered through the east in search of work, reached San Francisco in the 1840s, saw the Gold Rush of 1849, and joined the Vigilance Committee, which patrolled the city in a successful effort to control crime on the Barbary Coast. At this stage of his life, Baker believed in the vigilante policy of ruthlessness toward suspects followed by summary justice for those found guilty, the type of activity for which he later became notorious during his espionage career.

The year 1861, when the Civil War began, found Baker back east. Moving from New York to Washington, he offered his services to the Federal government, making the point that as a former vigilante he understood undercover work. General Winfield Scott, commanding the Union army, sent him into the Confederacy as a spy.

Using the cover name "Sam Munson," Baker made his way through the rebel lines. Arrested and taken to Richmond, he was interrogated by President Jefferson Davis, who judged him a spy and ordered him held. Baker escaped and made his way back across the Potomac with information on the southern forces he had seen.

Pleased with the success of the mission, Scott recommended the spy to the secretary of war, Edwin Stanton, for whom Baker became a confidential agent, taking espionage assignments in Virginia and Maryland and counterespionage assignments in Washington, where southern agents proliferated.

In 1862 Baker replaced Allan Pinkerton as director of the Federal intelligence system. Now Baker's vigilante experience began to dominate his behavior. Considering all methods acceptable that helped him to do his job, he made false arrests, ignored search warrants, practiced blackmail, and hectored prisoners while interrogating them.

He had many suspects to work on, for his net fell widely enough to catch not only spies for the Confederacy but also deserters from the Union army and profiteers growing fat on windfalls from the war.

Baker's two most celebrated suspects were Belle Boyd and Wat Bowie. Neither would tell him anything despite his bullying manner. In 1862 Bowie escaped from jail in Washington, reached the Confederacy, and resumed his undercover work. In 1863 Boyd was released and sent back to the Confederacy.

The Baker network did what it was intended to do—cut the flow of military information from Washington to Richmond and carry out espionage assignments in the south. By the time the war ended in 1865, Baker was a general and a power in the Federal government.

Then came the worst blot on his record, the failure of his agents to learn about the plot to assassinate President Abraham Lincoln, compounded by their inexplicable failure to protect the President in his box at Ford's Theater. Although Baker directed the successful pursuit of assassin John Wilkes Booth, he never recovered his old prestige.

Still, Baker continued in his high-handed way until President Andrew Johnson, leveling an accusation that Baker maintained spies even in the White House, dismissed him from his government post. Baker's final public act was testifying at the impeachment hearings (1868), where he appears to have perjured himself by alleging the existence of imaginary documents in his attack on Johnson.

Baker's tenure as intelligence chief has caused him to be compared to other notable figures in the same field. In his own time he was called the "American Fouché" because of the sinister power he wielded in the state. Like Wilhelm Stieber, he ran a vast spy network on enemy soil. Today a parallel could be drawn between Baker and J. Edgar Hoover, both serving in Washington as directors of counterespionage, both accused of overzealous investigations that violated the legal and civil rights of suspects.

See also PINKERTON, ALLAN.

FURTHER READING: *Lafayette Baker, *History of the United States Secret Service in the Late War* (1867); Harnett T. Kane, *Spies for the Blue and the Gray* (1954); Lord Longford, *Abraham Lincoln* (1975).

Bancroft, Edward *(1744-1821)* American double agent who worked for the British government during the American War of Independence.

Born in Massachusetts, Bancroft received little formal schooling, but he possessed talents that enabled him to make himself a scholar, a writer, and a scientist. His youthful wanderings brought him in 1763 to a plantation in Guiana, South America, owned by Paul Wentworth, like himself a New Englander. Bancroft remained on the Wentworth plantation for three years, a period in which he gathered information for a book on Guiana.

Bancroft returned to New England in 1766, and in the following year he went to London, his permanent base thereafter. He pursued medical studies and was elected to the Royal College of Physicians. For researches in chemistry, he was elected to the Royal Society with the sponsorship of Benjamin Franklin, agent for Pennsylvania in London. Franklin also brought him to the attention of the *Monthly Review,* for which Bancroft became the leading contributor on American affairs.

Franklin, who represented American interests in London during and after the Stamp Act crisis (1765), employed Bancroft as an undercover agent reporting on what British officials and military men were saying about the troubles with the colonies. Holding a high opinion of Bancroft's ability and patriotism, Franklin, on returning home in 1775, recommended him to Silas Deane, the American agent who went to Paris in 1776 to gain French support for the Americans in their struggle for independence. Deane hired Bancroft as a secretary and assigned undercover work to him. Bancroft, moving back and forth between Paris and London, brought Deane information about secret British plans, strategy, troop movements, and naval operations. But Bancroft, who suffered from avarice and had no scruples, was working for money, not out of patriotism, and he consented to become a double agent when approached by a British spy, his old friend Paul Wentworth. Bancroft now served as an espionage agent in the pay of the crown while pretending to serve America. He took American payment for disinformation (false or trivial reports) prepared for him by Wentworth and Wentworth's superior in London, William Eden.

When Franklin and Arthur Lee joined Deane in Paris in 1776 and the three negotiated with the French government on behalf of America, Lee told his colleagues that he suspected Bancroft. Deane and Franklin refused to believe that Bancroft, to whom they had given implicit trust, could be betraying them.

Meanwhile, Bancroft was gathering sensitive information about American diplomacy in Paris and transmitting it to London, using the cover name "Dr. Edwards." His method was to write his messages in invisible ink, mask them with innocuous notes, place them in a bottle, and hide the bottle in a hole amid the roots of a tree in the garden of the Tuileries, a royal palace in Paris. A courier, often the secretary of the British ambassador, retrieved the messages and replaced the empty bottle for further communications from Bancroft.

Since he handled the correspondence between the American commissioners and the Continental Congress, Bancroft was able to keep Wentworth and Eden informed day-to-day about how the negotiations with the French government were going. He correctly reported on January 27, 1778, before the fact was announced publicly in Paris, that France had joined America in a military alliance.

Bancroft continued to be a trusted confidant of the Americans until the peace of 1783, when Great Britain recognized the independence of the United States. An intriguer by nature, Bancroft returned to espionage in 1789, carrying out a secret mission for France in Ireland, evidently reporting on the possibility of an Irish insurrection with French help against British rule. The scant records that mention this mission indicate that he was still playing the game of double agent and working for the British government clandestinely.

Eventually Bancroft gave up undercover conspiracy for laboratory research; he added to his public reputation by publishing notable works in science during his later years. The truth about his duplicity during the American Revolution did not come out until many years after his death, when historians put the known facts together and discovered that Bancroft had been perhaps the most successful double agent in the history of espionage.

See also DEANE, SILAS; WENTWORTH, PAUL.

FURTHER READING: B. Boies, *Edward Bancroft* (1908); *Lewis Einstein, *Divided Loyalties: Americans in England during the War of Independence* (1933); Richard B. Morris, *The Peacemakers: The Great Powers and American Independence* (1965).

Bates, Ann *(1750?-1800?)*   American Loyalist and spy for the British during the American War of Independence.

Bates, a Pennsylvanian, was teaching school in Philadelphia when she married an ordnance expert who repaired guns for the British artillery. Her marriage gave her both firm Loyalist convictions (if she did not possess them already) and a knowledge of military matters that stood her in good stead when she became a spy.

After the British, under Sir Henry Clinton, abandoned Philadelphia for New York City in 1778, Bates, anxious to follow her husband, secured a pass from the new American commander in Philadelphia by posing as a Patriot—an irony worthy of Voltaire because the commander was General Benedict Arnold, who had not yet thought of taking the British side himself.

Reaching New York City, Bates joined the spy network organized by John André, Clinton's espionage chief. She reported directly to Major John Drummond, who gave her the cover name "Mrs. Barnes," told her to pose as a peddler, and sent her to the military encampment at White Plains, New York, where the Continental army under General George Washington confronted the British.

Her sex and her cover story gave her much leeway, for a female with trifles to sell to the soldiers could move about freely. Even so, her inquisitiveness caused her to be stopped once and held until a woman could be brought in to search her. Another time, while trailing Washington's army on the move, Bates fled to escape arrest and talked her way through the American lines to freedom.

No difficulties or dangers prevented her from making four round-trip journeys from New York City to Washington's headquarters or from gathering information on American plans, troop movements, the strength of regiments, the number of field guns, the amount of supplies, and morale. All this she reported to Drummond, who passed it on to André, who passed it on to Clinton.

Her most important discovery, made through artful conversation with Patriot soldiers at the American camp, was that the Marquis de Lafayette, who had come to fight for the Americans and was now Washington's comrade in arms, had gone to Rhode Island to meet a French fleet newly arrived to join the Americans under the terms of the Franco-American alliance of 1778. This warning prompted Clinton to speed up his expedition to Newport, where he strengthened the British garrison that held the city for another year.

In 1778 Bates penetrated the American lines and crossed into Pennsylvania to meet an unidentified woman said to be a spy "in Connection with General Arnold." Since this was before Arnold began his treasonable correspondence with the British, it must be assumed that British agents were spying on him simply as a high-ranking and trusted American general. Bates found the other woman and conducted her to New York City by way of a Tory underground in New Jersey.

Drummond went home to England, but Bates continued her espionage activities. In 1779, under André's direction, she again made a daring journey to Pennsylvania to escort her female counterpart to New York City, by which time André wanted all the information he could get about Arnold, who was already committed to changing sides at the most favorable moment.

Bates naturally went along when her husband was assigned to care for the artillery in Clinton's 1780 campaign in South Carolina. André, accompanying Clinton, kept her on call for more undercover assignments, but it is not recorded that he again availed himself of her gift for espionage. She and her husband sailed for England in 1781, just before the American victory at Yorktown rendered superfluous any more spying on George Washington and his Continental army.

See also ANDRÉ, JOHN.

FURTHER READING: Alexander Flick, *The American Revolution in New York* (1926); *John Bakeless, *Turncoats, Traitors, and Heroes* (1959), has the best account of spy Ann Bates; A. A. Hoehling, *Women Who Spied* (1967), considers Bates, mistakenly, a double agent.

Batz, Jean de *(1754-1822)*   Royalist conspirator and secret agent during the French Revolution.

Batz, who belonged to an aristocratic family of Gascony and held the title of Baron, served in the army, read widely in history and economics, and wrote pamphlets critical of the royal financial system. In 1789 he attended the states-general, the nearest thing to a French legislature at that time, as a deputy of the nobility. The French Revolution started with this meeting. Batz held financial posts in the national assembly, the legislative body founded by the revolutionaries, at which time he urged King Louis XVI to take a stand in favor of the nobility against the third estate, the commoners of France.

Distressed to see revolution instead of mere reform, Batz began to serve the king on missions to the royalists who had fled from France. In 1792 Batz, too, chose exile in order to think and decide what to do. Being a man of action, he soon returned to Paris to work covertly against the revolution. He became the leading conspirator in the French capital, working for an overthrow of the revolutionaries and a restoration of the monarchy to most of its old functions. His desire for financial reforms had not weakened, but he felt it would be absurd to press the point when France was going through social and political turmoil.

A real-life Scarlet Pimpernel, Batz risked his head to help aristocrats escape from France. After the monarchy was overthrown in 1792, Louis XVI and Queen Marie Antoinette went to prison, and Batz formed an undercover ring in the hope of saving them. The members of the ring used codes and passwords in communicating with one another, and they agreed to act when the revolutionaries condemned the king and set his execution for January 21, 1793.

Batz decided to place his men at a strategic point along the route to the guillotine and to rush the king's carriage as it came past. However, arriving at the rendezvous to lead the attack, Batz found that most of his followers, losing their nerve at the last moment, had abandoned him. He tried to make up for this by calling on passersby to join the effort to rescue their king, but too few responded. Batz and his fellow conspirators fled. The king continued on to the guillotine.

Next, Batz turned his attention to the queen, devising further plans to save her. He may have taken part in the most celebrated attempt to rescue Marie Antoinette, the Carnation affair, but this time the principal conspirator was Alexandre de Rougeville. This plan also failed; time ran out for the queen, and on October 16, 1793, she followed the king to the guillotine.

Batz continued to intrigue against the French Revolution. Using his knowledge of finance, he conspired to ruin the paper money of the revolution by contriving fraudulent financial schemes, enticing into them members of the Convention, which ruled France in 1793, and then waiting for the schemes to collapse. This grandiose plan had almost no effect. In 1795 Batz joined the insurrection in Paris that was put down by General Napoleon Bonaparte, the rising military man who within a decade would become emperor of France.

Batz was arrested, imprisoned, interrogated, and released. He survived to see his royalism vindicated by the summoning of the king in exile, Louis XVIII, to the French throne (1814). The king fled on Napoleon's return from Elba, but he entered Paris again in 1815 when the victory over Napoleon at Waterloo made the throne secure. Batz received honors from the king for his enduring loyalty and in 1818 retired to his country estate to meditate and write about the turbulent times he had lived through.

See also ROUGEVILLE, ALEXANDRE DE.

FURTHER READING: *Meade Minnigerode, *Marie Antoinette's Henchman* (1936); Saul K. Padover, *The Life and Death of Louis XVI* (1939); Vincent Cronin, *Louis and Antoinette* (1975).

Bay of Pigs *(1961)*   Attempted rebel invasion of Cuba organized by the CIA.

When Fidel Castro assumed power in Cuba in 1959, he did so with the goodwill of the United States, where it was assumed that he would soon honor his promise to hold free elections. Instead, he introduced a Communist-style tyranny supported by summary executions and mass arrests. He destroyed democratic institutions, nationalized foreign-owned businesses without compensation, began a virulent anti-American propaganda campaign, and threatened to export his revolution to other nations in Latin America. Reacting to Castro's excesses, the American government ended the importation of Cuban sugar in 1960, and in 1961 President Dwight Eisenhower broke off diplomatic relations with Havana.

Meanwhile, many anti-Castro Cubans had fled from the island to Florida, where their leaders plotted to return in force and lead a rebellion against the dictator. Their appeals to Washington for help received a sympathetic hearing from Eisenhower, who ordered Allen Dulles, director of the CIA (Central Intelligence Agency), to formulate a contingency plan for a rebel invasion of Cuba. President John Kennedy took office in 1961 and, impressed with CIA arguments that the people of Cuba were eager to be rid of Castro, Kennedy ordered the plan to be executed. The rebels were trained by the CIA at secret bases and transported to Cuba, where they landed on the shore of the Bay of Pigs. However, Kennedy canceled American air cover that was supposed to protect the beachhead, which left it vulnerable to a counterattack by Castro's forces. There was no popular rising against Castro, and the invaders were quickly defeated. The survivors were captured, and the United States had to pay ransom for their release in humiliating circumstances.

The Bay of Pigs caused Castro to turn openly to the Soviet Union for aid, including weapons. He allowed Soviet premier Nikita Khrushchev to install offensive rockets secretly in Cuba, which Khrushchev did in spite of a promise to Kennedy that the Soviet Union would confine military shipments to Cuba to lesser hardware. This set the stage for the Cuban missile crisis (1962), when Kennedy forced Khrushchev to remove the rockets.

Kennedy accepted the blame for the Bay of Pigs operation, but he considered that Dulles had given him a faulty estimate of the chance for success, and he felt that the CIA had mismanaged the operation. Dulles denied the worst accusation brought by critics of the invasion—that CIA agents had conspired to carry out the landing even if the President were to order it abandoned—but the fiasco made the position of the director untenable, and Dulles resigned.

See also CIA; Cuban Missile Crisis; Dulles, Allen.

FURTHER READING: *Haynes Johnson, *The Bay of Pigs: The Leader's Story of Brigade 2506* (1964), states that CIA agents told the Cubans to go through with the invasion no matter what orders came from Washington; Allen Dulles, *The Craft of Intelligence* (paperback ed., 1965), says the CIA had no intention of disobeying orders; Peter Wyden, *Bay of Pigs* (1979), reviews the incident in the perspective of time.

Bazna, Elyeza (1905-71) Valet of the British ambassador and spy for the German ambassador in Turkey during World War II.

Bazna was an Albanian born in what is now Yugoslavia, which was at the time a province of the Turkish Ottoman Empire. His family moved to Ankara, which, after the fall of the empire as a result of World War I, became the capital of modern Turkey. In Ankara, Bazna took odd jobs until he found his vocation as a chauffeur, butler, and valet working at European embassies—the Yugoslav, the American, the German, and finally, in 1943, the British.

World War II had reached a crescendo when Bazna became valet to Ambassador Hughe Knatchbull-Hugessen, a man of such regular habits that the valet could keep track of him by the clock—breakfast, bath, reading the newspapers, departure for his office, and so on. The ambassador kept a dispatch box at his bedside, where it often remained while he was out of the bedroom.

Bazna took advantage of the ambassador's routine to make wax impressions of the keys to the box. After having new keys cut, he began opening the box at advantageous moments and photographing the documents it held. His motive was money, and he therefore took his first photographs to the client who was sure to be the highest bidder, the German ambassador, who happened to be the former German Chancellor Franz von Papen.

Intelligence officer H. C. Moyzisch recognized the worth of the films, which he brought to Papen's attention. Papen concurred with Moyzisch, agreed to pay Bazna for any more films that good, and nicknamed Bazna "Cicero" because what he offered was so eloquent.

During 1943 and 1944, Cicero took from the British Embassy to the German Embassy in Ankara a series of documents on film that allowed the Germans to discover some of the most closely guarded Allied secrets. Reports on British-American wartime planning were there, including descriptions of the great conferences—Churchill and Roosevelt at Casablanca; Churchill, Roosevelt, and Chiang Kai-shek at Cairo; and Churchill, Roosevelt, and Stalin at Tehran. British-Turkish negotiations could be followed step by step.

In short, Cicero recorded the most significant information moving from Ankara to London and from London to Ankara, and in the latter case this meant everything the British Foreign Office thought the British ambassador in Turkey ought to know.

Through Bazna, the Germans first learned of the cover name "Overlord," although they failed to connect it with the approaching second front, the Allied invasion of the Nazi-dominated Continent. Indeed, Hitler and his foreign minister, Joachim von Ribbentrop, failed to exploit the Cicero documents, either to revise German strategy or, in the case of Ribbentrop, to maneuver to bring the war to an end as quickly as possible.

In 1944 the Cicero episode ended abruptly. The Turkish foreign minister warned the British ambassador that there was a leak at the British Embassy. Papen, as Allen Dulles wrote after the war, sent a telegram to Berlin that was obtained and decoded by Allied intelligence, which thus learned of Cicero's undercover operations in Ankara. Finally, a secretary at the German Embassy defected to the Allies and revealed what she knew about Bazna.

The British ambassador fired his valet, who scarcely minded; having been paid a fortune by the German Embassy, he decided to retire and live luxuriously. Bazna was thunderstruck when informed at the bank that most of his banknotes from Berlin had been forged by the Nazis.

At least he gained notoriety from which to profit. He wrote his autobiography, had books written about him, and lived to see a film based on his life as a spy in the British Embassy in Ankara. Even then his real name hardly mattered. The fame belonged, as it still belongs, not to Bazna but to Cicero.

See also DULLES, ALLEN; PAPEN, FRANZ VON.

FURTHER READING: *Elyeza Bazna, *I Was Cicero* (1962); Allen Dulles, *The Craft of Intelligence* (1963); Fitzroy Maclean, *Take Nine Spies* (1978), has a chapter on Bazna.

BCRA *(1940-45)* Military intelligence of the Gaullist forces in London.

When General Charles de Gaulle escaped to Britain following the defeat of France in World War II, he urged the French people by radio to struggle against the German occupation. This summons helped to bring the French resistance into existence—small groups forming underground to oppose the invaders wherever possible. The British aided the French resistance through the SOE (Special Operations Executive), which sent agents and supplies to France by secret routes. De Gaulle cooperated with the SOE and worked with the resistance directly. The BCRA handled espionage and covert operations for him.

The acronym BCRA stood for the French title meaning "Central Bureau of Intelligence and Operations." Since the organization worked for de Gaulle's Free French armed forces, it was a "Second Bureau" (military intelligence) of the type familiar in the French army since the end of the Franco-Prussian War (1871). The BCRA was directed by "Colonel Passy" (actually André Dewavrin), who selected agents to go to France, met agents from France, and reported to de Gaulle on how the underground campaign against the Germans was going. The Gaullist leader inside France, Jean Moulin, unified mutually hostile factions in the underground until he was caught and executed by the Germans in 1943.

The men of the BCRA were part of the French resistance, at long range in London and at close range in France, through most of the war. At the end, they had the satisfaction of participating in the victory over the Germans following the Allied invasion of the Continent in 1944. The BCRA disbanded when the liberation of France left the organization without duties.

See also DEWAVRIN, ANDRÉ; FRENCH RESISTANCE; MOULIN, JEAN; SECOND BUREAU; SPECIAL OPERATIONS EXECUTIVE.

FURTHER READING: Philip John Stead, *Second Bureau* (n.d.); *Richard Collier, *Ten Thousand Eyes* (1958), contains material from the author's talks with Dewavrin; Charles de Gaulle, *War Memoirs,* 3 vols. (1955–60); David Schoenbrun, *Soldiers of the Night: The Story of the French Resistance* (1980).

Beach, Thomas *(1841-94)* British undercover agent who spied on Irish rebels in America.

Born in Colchester, England, Beach ran away from home, lived precariously in France, and made his way to the United States, where he served in the Union army during the Civil War under a French alias, "Henri le Caron." He was mustered out in 1865 with the rank of major.

It came to his attention that Irish rebels were raising money in America to support Ireland's fight for freedom. These were the Fenians, who took their name from the band that surrounded Finn MacCool, a legendary hero of early Irish history. The American branch of the Fenians, founded by John O'Mahoney in 1858, was bent on using America as a base for a campaign against British rule of their homeland.

Beach wrote to his family about the Fenians, and his father showed the letters to the British authorities. The British secret service, successful in planting double agents in the ranks of Irish rebels in Ireland, requested more information on what the American Fenians were doing. Beach wrote a series of reports, including one in which he predicted the 1866 Fenian invasion of Canada, which was thrown back by Canadian troops.

In 1867 Beach went to England, entered the British secret service as a professional agent, and returned to America, where he joined the Fenians as Major Henri le Caron. He rose to be a commanding officer in the organization.

To maintain his cover, he visited the White House with a loyal Fenian to make an appeal on behalf of Irish freedom to President Andrew Johnson. In 1869 Beach traveled to Canada with a commission from the Fenian leadership to see how another invasion could be launched across the border from the United States. He informed the Canadian authorities, who easily broke up the 1870 attempt along the Vermont border.

Beach continued to keep London aware of Fenian plans until 1877, when the death of O'Mahoney ended the movement in the United States for all practical purposes. Returning to England, Beach continued to inform on troublesome Irishmen, notably the great political leader Charles Stewart Parnell. Beach was involved in the scandal of the "Parnell Letter," which was supposed to have been written by the Irish leader in defense of Irish assassinations of British officials. The proof in 1890 that the document was a forgery compromised Beach, whose spy career came to an end.

FURTHER READING: *Thomas Beach, *Twenty-five Years in the Secret Service: The Recollections of a Spy* (1892); William D'Arcy, *The Fenian Movement in the United States* (1947); W. S. Neidhardt, *Fenianism in North America* (1975).

Beall, John *(1835-65)* Soldier and undercover agent for the Confederacy during the American Civil War.

Born on a farm in Virginia's Shenandoah Valley, Beall studied law at the behest of his family, left the University of Virginia without waiting for a degree, and found a vocation for himself when the Civil War broke out in 1861. He served briefly in the Confederate armed forces under General Stonewall Jackson until wounded and mustered out of the military.

Regaining his health, Beall took to privateering on Chesapeake Bay, capturing Union ships, conveying them to southern ports as prizes of war, and looting them of their cargoes. He was a daredevil who liked to take chances, one of which led to his being captured by Federal agents and held until a prisoner exchange restored him to the Confederacy.

In 1864 Beall was in Toronto planning his biggest coup with a band of southerners who had joined him. His plan was to seize a Federal warship on Lake Erie, storm ashore on Johnson's Island, and liberate Confederate prisoners of war who were being held there. At the last moment, Beall's men mutinied for fear of the odds against them, and he was forced to call off the attack.

Beall next plotted to wreck trains in northern New York State by tearing up the rails near Buffalo. Characteristically, he neglected to arm himself with crowbars and other tools required for success. All his attempts failed, and he was arrested, ironically, while waiting to board a train back to Toronto. Convicted of spying and sabotage, he was hanged on Governor's Island, New York.

It is a mere legend that John Wilkes Booth assassinated President Abraham Lincoln in retaliation for Beall's execution.

FURTHER READING: *Daniel B. Lucas, *Memoir of John Yates Beall* (1865); Philip Van Doren Stern, *Secret Missions of the Civil War* (1959); Oscar A. Kinchen, *Confederate Operations in Canada and the North* (1970).

Beaumarchais, Pierre Augustin Caron de *(1732-99)* French dramatist and secret agent for the French government, notable for his covert support of the American side in the American War of Independence.

Beaumarchais was born into the family of a Paris watchmaker named Caron. He entered the family business as a boy, invented a new watch mechanism before he was twenty, married a wealthy widow in 1756, and took the aristocratic name "de Beaumarchais" from an estate she owned. Three years later, now accepted at the court of Versailles, he was teaching music to the daughters of King Louis XV. During the years 1764 and 1765, he represented a Parisian financial house in Spain, where he absorbed the local color that later gave an authentic atmosphere to his two greatest dramas.

His earliest plays, however, which he wrote on his return to Paris, were failures. A complicated financial scandal enhanced his fame but damaged his position in the city (1774), and to recoup he agreed to become a secret agent of the French government, for which he carried out a number of undercover missions. One took him to London in 1775, where, using the cover name "Norac" (his family name spelled backwards), he successfully negotiated an agreement with the Chevalier D'Éon, who was blackmailing the king of France by threatening to reveal a contingency plan for a French invasion of England.

Beaumarchais put *The Barber of Seville* on the Paris stage in 1775. His *The Marriage of Figaro* followed in 1784. These two sparkling comedies ensured his high place in the French theater and in the literature of Europe.

Meanwhile, Beaumarchais had accepted his most important undercover assignment from the French government. Silas Deane, a representative of the American Continental Congress, arrived in France in 1776 looking for French support of the Americans in their expanding war with the British. Deane received a sympathetic hearing from the French foreign minister, but as France was not at war with Britain, the support had to be clandestine. This logic led to dealings with the best secret agent in France, Beaumarchais.

The negotiations culminated in an agreement that Beaumarchais would establish Roderigue Hortalez et Cie. (Hortalez and Co.) in Paris, ostensibly as an ordinary business firm but really as an organization for covertly channeling war supplies to the Americans. Two-thirds of the capital came from France and France's ally, Spain. Beaumarchais raised the rest from private French interests.

He had to pay for the supplies he drew from French magazines and arsenals, but he was supposed to recoup from American payments in goods such as tobacco and rice. Allowed to keep any profits that accrued at the end, he was also responsible for any debts. Hortalez was thus expected to make its own way financially even though working for the French government.

Beaumarchais organized an enormous seaborne traffic between France and America. In time he had nearly fifty ships leaving the seaports of Marseilles, Bordeaux, Nantes, and Le Havre, heading directly for the French West Indies to disguise their true destinations and then continuing on to American ports to unload their cargoes. The guns, ammunition, and clothing were then transferred by wagon to the Continental army under the command of General George Washington. These supplies arrived in time to assist the Americans at the battle of Saratoga (1777), the decisive victory that changed the course of the war.

Hortalez continued to send supplies, but the trade was not profitable because the ships chartered by Beaumarchais, which were supposed to load tobacco and rice at Charleston, usually made the return voyage with their holds empty. The war rendered it impossible for the Americans to gather such goods, but beyond that, most members of the Continental Congress knew nothing about the agreement with Beaumarchais (those who had a role in the agreement feared a Tory in their ranks would alert London). Beaumarchais therefore could not get the congress to honor its debts.

Hortalez showed increasing losses and might have been forced to cease its operations if more French loans had not been forthcoming. The company was simply too valuable in the twilight war of 1777 and 1778 for the foreign minister at Versailles to permit it to go bankrupt.

Everything changed in 1778, when France entered the war on the side of the Americans. Hortalez suddenly became a minor factor compared to the armed forces of the French crown, which went into action in the New World by land and by sea, contributing significantly to the victory at Yorktown (1781) that ensured American independence.

By then Beaumarchais had turned his ships to trading in sugar and other products of the West Indies, a trade so lucrative that Hortalez showed a profit when he disbanded the firm in 1783.

Beaumarchais returned to writing until he took part in another upheaval, the French Revolution, which broke out in 1789. Although he favored the revolution, he was distrusted by its leaders because of his wealth and his record of service to Louis XV and Louis XVI. Briefly imprisoned, he agreed to go on an undercover mission for the republic, which ordered him to spirit a large consignment of muskets out of Holland into France for use by the revolutionary armed forces. He went to Holland in 1792, failed in his mission, and returned in disgrace, but managed to survive the failure. Ruined by the revolution, he was struggling to rise above his debts when he died.

Nearly four decades later, in 1835, the Congress of the United States finally acknowledged the long-standing debt by paying his heirs the money still owing to him.

See also DEANE, SILAS.

FURTHER READING: Carl Van Doren, *Secret History of the American Revolution* (1941); *George Lemaître, *Beaumarchais* (1949); William Stinchcombe, *The American Revolution and the French Alliance* (1969).

Beauregard, Pierre *(1818-93)*   Military commander and spymaster for the Confederacy during the American Civil War.

Beauregard belonged to a creole family of New Orleans, where he was born and received his education. He obtained an appointment to the military academy at West Point, graduated, joined the engineering corps in 1838, and served in the Mexican War (1846–48). Distinguishing himself in the military, he advanced through the grades until in 1861, as a general in the U.S. Army, he was named superintendent of West Point, a post that ordinarily would have been the summit of his career.

He resigned after precisely five days to join the South in secession from the Union, and on April 12, 1861, commanded the troops that began the Civil War by firing on Fort Sumter in Charleston harbor. He served throughout the conflict that followed (1861–65).

While confronting the advance of Federal troops under General Irvin McDowell in 1861, Beauregard, who appreciated the worth of espionage, developed through Captain Thomas Jordan a spy network from Washington into Virginia. His best informant was Rose Greenhow, who lived in Washington and gathered information about McDowell's strategy from nearly everyone in her set who knew anything of significance. These were men who would talk willingly or could be discreetly pumped.

Greenhow reported through couriers on July 10 that McDowell would move south six days later, on July 16 that the Federals would head for Bull Run, and on July 17 that they would try to cut the railroad to keep General Joseph E. Johnston from moving east to the battlefield from the Shenandoah Valley. A vigilant spymaster, Beauregard correlated what Greenhow told him with what he was hearing from spies along the route toward Bull Run. They all corroborated her testimony, as did a captured Union soldier. Thus, there could be no doubt in Beauregard's mind about what McDowell was doing.

Beauregard placed a guard at the railroad so Johnston could move east at once. Beauregard also devised the strategy by which his Confederate force entrenched itself and held the front while Johnston's struck a flanking blow. McDowell's troops were driven back in wild retreat at the battle of Manassas, or Bull Run (July 21, 1861). Beauregard sent Rose Greenhow his thanks for services rendered.

Beauregard later served in the west, where he was in command when the Confederates lost the hard-fought battle of Shiloh (April 7, 1862) to the Federals under Ulysses S. Grant. Promoted for his stubborn military action at Shiloh, Beauregard assumed command of the Georgia-Carolina coast, but he had no adequate army when in 1864 General William Tecumseh Sherman made his devastating march to the sea, after which only mopping-up operations remained along the coast before the surrender of the Confederacy in 1865 at Appomattox.

Beauregard went into railroading after Appomattox, ran the Louisiana lottery, and quarreled in print with former leaders of the Confederacy who criticized his part in the Civil War.

See also GREENHOW, ROSE.

FURTHER READING: Pierre Beauregard, *Commentary on the Campaign and Battle of Manassas* (1891); *T. Harry Williams, *P. T. G. Beauregard: Napoleon in Gray* (1955); John Bakeless, *Spies of the Confederacy* (1970).

Becker, Johann (1912-70?)   German spy in Argentina during World War II.

Born in Leipzig, where he graduated from high school in 1930, Becker saw the chaos that shook Germany in the aftermath of World War I. He joined Adolf Hitler's Nazi party in the belief that only the Nazis could restore order, and he soon became a committed member of the movement. After Hitler took power as chancellor of Germany in 1933, Becker entered Nazi intelligence, which in 1937 planted him as a "sleeper" in Buenos Aires. A merely latent spy, he stood ready to become active on receiving the order from Berlin. Meanwhile he was just another German businessman in the Argentine capital.

The outbreak of World War II in 1939 caused Becker to be recalled to Germany for special training, and in 1940, now holding the official title of diplomatic courier, he was back in Argentina. After the German declaration of war on the United States in 1941, Becker again returned to Germany, went through another espionage course, and was ordered to Buenos Aires to organize a German spy network (1943).

Becker gathered information from many sources, one being Colonel Juan Perón, who talked injudiciously about Argentine intentions during the war (and became president of Argentina after the war). Reporting in particular on Allied ships entering and leaving South American ports, Becker transmitted secret messages to Berlin by shortwave radio and the diplomatic pouch of the German ambassador. The breaking of diplomatic relations between Buenos Aires and Berlin as Argentina entered the war against Germany in 1944 disrupted Becker's network. Known German spies were arrested, and Becker himself had to go underground.

He evaded the Buenos Aires police until 1945. Caught and imprisoned in that year, he made an enforced trip to Germany after the Allied victory, and he seems to have remained there.

FURTHER READING: Karl Bartz, *The Downfall of the German Secret Service* (1956); Ladislo Farago, *The Game of Foxes: The Untold Story of German Espionage in the United States and Great Britain during World War II* (1971); *David Kahn, *Hitler's Spies: German Military Intelligence in World War II* (1978).

Beer, Israel *(1912-68)*   Israeli double agent for the Soviet Union.

The facts about Beer's early life are in doubt, beginning with his name. Apparently born in Vienna, he went to Palestine as Israel Beer in 1938 and joined Haganah, the underground committed to Jewish self-defense, in which he served during the years preceding the establishment of the state of Israel (1948). He was a confidant of Israel's first prime minister, David Ben-Gurion. In 1955 Beer was commissioned to write the official history of Israel's struggle for independence.

In 1961 Israeli counterespionage agents, following a tip that Beer was spending more money than he made, arrested him after seeing him pass classified documents to a Soviet spy. The fact then came out that he had been a double agent for five years, during which time he had used his connection with the Israeli government to gather political and military information, which he passed on to his Russian contacts.

Sentenced to ten years, Beer died in jail.

FURTHER READING: Richard Deacon, *The Israeli Secret Service* (1977); *Dennis Eisenberg, Uri Dan, and Eli Landau, *The Mossad, Israel's Secret Intelligence Service: Inside Stories* (1978).

Behn, Aphra *(1640?-89)*   English novelist, England's first professional woman writer, and spy for King Charles II in the Low Countries.

The facts of Behn's early life are still obscure. She is thought to have been born Aphra Johnson in or near Canterbury. In 1663 her father, possibly related to Lord Willoughby, governor of the British territory of Surinam in South America, was appointed to a post there. He died en route. The family returned to England after six months in Surinam, the setting of Behn's most famous novel, *Oroonoko; or the Royal Slave* (1688). In Surinam she knew William Scot, whose father, Thomas Scot, had been executed for conspiring in the execution of King Charles I. They began an affair modeled on the high-flown sentiments in Honoré d'Urfé's fashionable novel *L'Astrée*. Aphra played Astrea to William Scot's Celadon, names they would later use as code names when both were spies.

Back in London in 1664, Aphra Johnson seems to have married a Mr. Behn, a merchant of German or Dutch extraction of whom nothing more is known. He may have died in the plague that ravaged London in 1665.

The revival of England's trade, following Charles II's restoration to the throne, and the commercial rivalry with the Dutch, led to war in 1665. The king and his ministers feared that English refugees in Flanders and Holland would conspire with the Dutch enemy.

William Scot, a republican like his father, had joined the army of rebellious English officers gathering in the Netherlands under Colonel Joseph Bampfield. Scot's brother-in-law acted as a go-between for the republicans in England and the refugees. Scot was therefore privy to the republican plans and those of their Dutch mentors. Playing a double game, he correctly informed Lord Arlington, Charles II's chief of intelligence, that a rising was being plotted in Yorkshire and the north. Arlington, struck by the possibilities offered by a spy familiar with the enemy camp, instructed two agents in Holland to negotiate with Scot. He betrayed them to the Dutch, later claiming that their incompetence had endangered him.

Through her friend Sir Thomas Killigrew, groom of the bedchamber to Charles II, Arlington recruited Aphra Behn, a fervent royalist and Scot's Astrea, into his intelligence service. He dispatched her now to Holland by way of Antwerp to "bring in" the slippery Scot, that is, to persuade him to change sides and come back to England. She was to offer him the king's pardon and a suitable reward.

She sailed in July 1666, carrying with her *Memorialls for Mrs. Affora,* a list of questions about the Dutch and republican plans to which Scot must supply the answers.

Behn spent many months in Antwerp, having been warned not to go to Holland lest she be seized by Bampfield. Scot contacted her there. Using a code of her own invention and referring to Scot as Celadon, she reported back to London all the information she could gather. Included, as a measure of his good faith, were Scot's answers to the *Memorialls* and a warning that the Dutch intended to blockade the Thames with their fleet and even to land at Harwich. For some reason the English government ignored the warning, with the result that the Dutch swept into the Thames nearly unmolested.

Behn felt betrayed. Her information had been disregarded. Since no money was forthcoming from Arlington, who was perhaps waiting to see which way Scot would jump, she had been forced to pawn her jewelry to keep herself, pay Scot, and buy information. Her means exhausted, she finally had to borrow money for her passage home in the spring of 1667. When she could not pay back the loan she was thrown into prison. Eventually her debts were paid by the government, and she was released. Thereupon she decided to earn a living not by espionage but by the pen. It was an unheard-of decision for a woman of that time. Despite fierce attacks on her morals and her work—bawdy Restoration comedy of the same type as was written by men—she became one of the most successful of contemporary dramatists. She wrote poetry and translations and published *Oroonoko,* the passionate, antislavery, autobiographical novel for which she is remembered, shortly before she died. She was buried in Westminster Abbey.

FURTHER READING: Frederick M. Link, *Aphra Behn* (1968); Maureen Duffy, *The Passionate Shepherdess: Aphra Behn, 1640–89* (1977); °Angeline Goreau, *Reconstructing Aphra: A Social Biography of Aphra Behn* (1980).

Berg, Moe *(1902-72)*   American baseball player, linguist, and secret agent in Europe during World War II.

Berg's first name was Morris, but to his friends, as to millions of American sports fans, he was always "Moe." Raised in Newark by parents who were Jewish immigrants from Russia, he played baseball in high school and then at Princeton, where he studied languages, graduating in 1923. He left the campus for the Brooklyn Dodgers, the first of several teams he played with, usually as a second-string catcher, in a career that lasted sixteen years.

Famed for his ability to master languages and protected by a good cover, that of a touring baseball player, Berg was recruited by the U. S. government for undercover work abroad. In 1934, while barnstorming through Japan with an American all-star team, he surreptitiously took films of Tokyo harbor, of warships at anchor, and of military installations along the shore. Eight years later, General James Doolittle scrutinized these films before the American bombing raid on Japan after the attack on Pearl Harbor.

In 1941 Berg abandoned baseball and went to Latin America on a fact-finding tour for Nelson Rockefeller, the coordinator of inter-American affairs. In 1943 Berg joined America's wartime espionage organization, the OSS (Office of Strategic Services), and was sent to Europe by its head, General William Donovan.

Berg carried out daring secret missions during the war. He parachuted into Yugoslavia in 1943 and came back with a report that Tito and the partisans were the most successful insurgents fighting the Germans, and should be supported by the western Allies (Winston Churchill approved the report and acted on it). Berg flew into occupied Norway in 1943, met Norwegian freedom fighters, and obtained the information that led to the destruction by Allied bombers of a Nazi heavy-water plant. Assigned to locate German atomic scientists, Berg went to Switzerland and Italy in 1944, one result of his mission being that the invading Americans knew where to find many scientists before the Russians could capture them. These Germans contributed to American atomic and space science after World War II.

While in Switzerland, Berg cooperated with Allen Dulles, then an OSS spymaster in Europe. The two men did not always get along because Dulles expected Berg to report everything to him, which Berg refused to do on the ground that he held an independent commission from Donovan. But whenever Dulles was involved with Berg in an assignment, during the last year of the war, they worked together successfully.

In 1946 Berg was offered the American Medal of Merit, the highest decoration that can be awarded to a civilian for wartime service. Berg refused it for reasons that have never been explained. He served for a time as a scientific adviser at the headquarters of the North Atlantic Treaty Organization, and there are hints that he carried out classified assignments for the U. S. government into the 1960s. The one certainty is that he worked at his languages and relaxed at the ballpark.

See also DONOVAN, WILLIAM; DULLES, ALLEN; OSS.

FURTHER READING: Stewart Alsop and Thomas Braden, *Sub Rosa* (1946), is an account of the OSS; Allen Dulles, *The Craft of Intelligence* (1963); *Louis Kaufman, Barbara Fitzgerald, and Tom Sewell, *Moe Berg: Athlete, Scholar, Spy* (1974).

Beria, Lavrenti *(1899-1953)*   Russian spymaster and victim of a struggle for power in the Kremlin.

Beria was born in what is now Soviet Georgia, the same region that produced his later mentor, Joseph Stalin. His family being of the peasant class, Beria had no advantages as a child, but he received an education in the local schools and then attended a technical college in Baku, from which he graduated in 1919.

By then he had already joined the bolsheviks, headed by Vladimir Ilyich Lenin, and he worked in their behalf during the Russian civil war (1918–20). Lenin gave him a job in Soviet intelligence in 1921, an appointment that placed Beria in his natural habitat, the area of espionage, conspiracy, blackmail, and violence. After Lenin's death in 1924, Beria supported Stalin, who in 1934 had him named a member of the central committee of the Communist party. Four years later Beria became head of the NKVD (People's Commissariat for Internal Affairs, as the principal department of Soviet intelligence was called from 1934 to 1946). One of his first assignments was to manage for Stalin the execution of Nicolai Yezhov, the former head of the intelligence apparatus.

Beria held this post longer than anyone else in Soviet history, during which time he made the NKVD an efficient and dreaded corps of spies, informers, and agents of mass terror among the Soviet people. He sent assassins abroad to murder Russians in exile who criticized the Stalinist terror in their homeland.

In 1941, the year of the German invasion of Russia, Beria was promoted to deputy prime minister, which made him one of the most important leaders of the Soviet war effort. He took charge of security behind the battle lines, a formidable assignment as the Germans neared Moscow, one he handled with extreme brutality toward Russians who wavered in the face of the enemy or failed to obey orders to the letter. He was among the most energetic Russian leaders for the rest of the war (1941–45).

Stalin named Beria a marshal of the Soviet Union (1945) and a member of the Politburo, the highest ruling body in the Soviet Union (1946). In this latter year, the NKVD became the MVD (Ministry of Internal Affairs, 1946–54), according to the Soviet habit of giving organizations new names when the old ones sound too sinister.

The death of Stalin in 1953 left Beria one of the three or four most powerful men in the Soviet Union, a fact ratified by his new title, minister of internal affairs. He seemed in a strategic position to outmaneuver Georgi Malenkov and Nikita Khrushchev, his colleagues in the so-called collective leadership in the Kremlin, and rise to be a dictator. Why and how he failed remains a mystery to the outside world, but apparently he was arrested when he arrived for a conference with Malenkov and Khrushchev, who, afraid of his power and his intentions, struck first. It was announced from the Kremlin that Beria had been tried and executed for criminal antiparty and antistate activities.

A number of his closest associates were shot at the same time, many lesser figures were demoted or dismissed, and the whole MVD apparatus shook under the impact of the purge. In 1954 the organization lost the sinister name it had had under Beria and became the KGB (Committee for State Security). *See also* KGB.

FURTHER READING: Robert Conquest, *The Soviet Police System* (1968); Gerald Kurland, *Nikita Sergeievich Khrushchev: Modern Dictator of the USSR* (1972); *Tadeuz Wittlin, *Commissar: The Life and Death of Lavrenty Pavlovich Beria* (1972).

Berlin Tunnel *(1955-56)*   Secret CIA listening post connecting East and West Berlin.

The idea for the Berlin Tunnel developed in 1954 when an East Berliner arrived in West Berlin with the Soviet plans for three cables carrying communication lines between East Germany and the Soviet Union. The plans revealed that the cables ran six feet underground close to the American sector of Berlin. Reinhard Gehlen, the director of intelligence for the German Federal Republic, brought this fact to the attention of Allen Dulles, head of America's CIA (Central Intelligence Agency), and Dulles, with the approval of President Dwight Eisenhower, decided to exploit the opportunity to tap the communication lines.

The U.S. Army Engineers covertly dug a tunnel 300 yards long and 15 feet deep from West Berlin to East Berlin, using the cover story that they were building a radar station. They put in a cement floor, reinforced concrete walls, and a ventilation system. The U.S. Army Signal Corps installed technical equipment in the intercept chamber at the eastern end, where CIA technicians could bug the communication circuits in the exposed cables.

The system began operation in 1955. The CIA agents listened to conversations between Moscow and the East German government, the Soviet Embassy in Berlin, and Russian army headquarters in Zossen, near Berlin. They heard political and military exchanges on the highest level regarding Soviet policy and the problems of East Germany.

The secret listening post was a triumph of espionage of which the Russians never did become aware. It came to an end because of a double agent, George Blake, who, while attached to British intelligence in West Berlin, was actually working for the Soviet Union. Blake alerted the Russians to the existence of the Berlin Tunnel, and they seized the part of it extending into East Berlin, which of course included the intercept chamber.

See also BLAKE, GEORGE; GEHLEN, REINHARD.

FURTHER READING: Heinz Höhne and Hermann Zolling, *The General Was a Spy: The Truth about General Gehlen and His Spy Ring* (1972), has an appendix on the Berlin Tunnel.

Berryer, Nicolas-René *(1703-62)*   French police chief and spymaster during the reign of King Louis XV.

Born in Paris, Berryer received a general education at school and studied law before following a family tradition and entering the bureaucracy of the old regime in France. In 1728 he served in the Paris city administration. Three years later he entered the Parlement of Paris, a legal body and not a parliament in the English sense. After representing the crown in Poitou (1743–47), he received a royal summons back to Paris to become lieutenant of police, a position in which he served for a decade (1747–57).

During those years he served principally the king's mistress, Jeanne Antoinette d'Étioles, Marquise de Pompadour, who wanted to protect herself against political enemies and possible rivals who might replace her in the affections of Louis XV. Berryer formed a network of spies who reported to him everything they could learn at the Versailles court or in Paris. He established a *cabinet noir* ("black chamber") where his agents opened all letters traveling through the French postal system. The letters were read, the contents noted, and the envelopes resealed so that the addressees would never know the letters had been tampered with.

Berryer continued his espionage operations until the king promoted him from police work and gave him a series of appointments, of which keeper of the seals (1761–62) was the most important (and the last, since he died in the latter year). Pompadour survived him by two years, still maintaining the authoritative position beside the king that Berryer had done so much to ensure.

FURTHER READING: Nancy Mitford, *Madame de Pompadour* (1953); G. P. Gooch, *Louis XV* (1956); *Alan Williams, *The Police of Paris, 1716–1789* (1979).

Bettignies, Louise de *(1880-1918)*   French spymaster for the British and French Allies in World War I.

Bettignies was the seventh of eight children of a well-to-do porcelain manufacturer. Born and raised in Lille, she was a natural linguist who became fluent in English, German, and Italian, which she put to practical use in teaching children of the European aristocracy.

After the outbreak of World War I in 1914, with the German offensive into northern France, Bettignies fled to England. There she impressed British intelligence officers with the accuracy of her reports on German military positions, and they asked her to go back to German-occupied Lille to gather information. At the same time, she was to organize escape routes for Allied prisoners of war. She returned to the Continent using the cover name "Alice Dubois."

Bettignies, aided by a confederate, Marie van Houtte (cover name "Charlotte"), established a busy and effective network of spies known as the "Alice Service," extending into occupied Belgium and neutral Holland. What she learned, she relayed to London. Escaped prisoners of war received forged documents from the Alice Service with which to cross through the German lines to safety. Perhaps the spy network's greatest triumph was its warning to the Allies that the Germans were preparing for the Battle of Verdun.

German counterespionage realized that the Alice Service was operating in the area, but for more than a year they were unable to do anything about it. Then, in September of 1915, Van Houtte was captured in Brussels, and Bettignies in Tournai a few weeks later. At their court-martial, neither would admit a connection with the Alice Service. In 1916, Van Houtte received a prison sentence. Bettignies was sentenced to death, then reprieved and sent to jail.

Bettignies fell sick in prison and died just before the armistice (1918). The French government awarded her a posthumous Croix de Guerre and brought her body back to Lille for a funeral with military honors. Admirers raised a statue to her memory, one of the few to honor a spy.

FURTHER READING: Edward Spiro, *Sisters of Delilah* (1959); *A. A. Hoehling, *Women Who Spied* (1967).

Black Hand *(1911-17)*   Serbian terror organization operating in the Balkans.

During the latter part of the nineteenth century, a demand arose in Serbia for union with its Balkan neighbors Bosnia and Herzegovina, both of which had large Serbian populations. This ambition was checked by the Austro-Hungarian Empire, which gained control of the two provinces in 1878 and in 1908 formally annexed them. Unable to change the map through peaceful, political means, some Serbs turned to violence. In 1911 Dragutin Dimitrijevic, a Serbian officer in military intelligence, founded an underground network called the Black Hand. His purpose was to fight an undercover war against the Austro-Hungarians and their supporters, in Bosnia especially but with tentacles extending elsewhere in the Balkans. He included among his enemies Serbs in Serbia who were lukewarm in their attitude to the formation of a Greater Serbia.

The Black Hand became a byword for terror in the Balkans. Operating in secrecy, extorting an oath of obedience from its members, and punishing brutally those who informed to the authorities, the organization sent its agents to commit sabotage and assassination. Commanding spies everywhere in the disputed areas, it created fear and even panic wherever its seal, the imprint of a hand in black ink, suddenly appeared in a public place or dropped from a letter mailed to a private individual. The Black Hand thus cowed whole segments of the population in the name of Serbian nationalism.

The organization was active in the Balkan Wars (1912–13), which extended Serbia's border to the south, into Macedonia. The problem of Bosnia and Herzogovina, however, remained unsolved. Dimitrijevic decided to solve it through terrorism, by the assassination of the Austrian Archduke Franz Ferdinand when he and the archduchess came to Bosnia in 1914. By order of Dimitrijevic, the Black Hand formed a band of assassins to carry out the order. One of the band, Gavrilo Princip, got close enough to the royal car to shoot both the archduke and the archduchess. Austria commenced hostilities against Serbia, and the collision of nations in World War I followed.

In 1916 Dimitrijevic was arrested on a charge of turning his terror organization against the Serbian government following its flight to Greece to escape invading armies. He was executed in 1917, and the Black Hand, deprived of its head and guiding spirit, lapsed into inactivity and eventual dissolution.

See also DIMITRIJEVIC, DRAGUTIN; PRINCIP, GAVRILO.

FURTHER READING: Wayne S. Vucinich, *Serbia between East and West: The Events of 1903–1908* (1954); Roberta Strauss, *The Desperate Act: The Assassination of Franz Ferdinand at Sarajevo* (1968); *Nesta H. Webster, *Secret Societies and Subversive Movements* (1972).

Black Orchestra *(1935-44)*   Conspiracy of German military men against Hitler before and during World War II.

When Adolf Hitler became chancellor of Germany in 1933, there were already generals who opposed him as an upstart adventurer. Two years later, as his tyranny became stronger and his violence toward his opponents and victims more ruthless, the opposition coalesced into a definite plot to remove him and end the Nazi regime.

"Black Orchestra" was a name coined by Hitler's agents—oddly, because it derived from the Russians, who used "musician" as a code word for a clandestine radio operator. "Orchestra" meant that a group was involved. "Black" was a reference to the anti-Hitler activities of the group.

The leader of the Black Orchestra, General Ludwig Beck, served for four years as chief of the German general staff (1935–38). The principal agent was Admiral Wilhelm Canaris, head of the Abwehr (Foreign Information and Counterintelligence Department), who sent covert warnings to the western Allies when Hitler revealed his plans at secret staff meetings—the decision for war (1937), the seizure of Austria (1938), the rape of Czechoslovakia (1938).

Each time, Canaris urged Britain and France to make a stand against Hitler so that the Black Orchestra would have an added argument to present to the German people in moving to replace him. Winston Churchill wanted to support the Black Orchestra, but Churchill was out of power, and the Allies refused to act.

Hitler's invasion of Poland (1939) brought on World War II, during which the Black Orchestra continued to conspire against the dictator. The final effort was the July Plot (July 20, 1944), when Count Klaus von Stauffenberg planted a bomb at Hitler's headquarters, only to have Hitler escape the blast with minor injuries. The failure led to savage Nazi reprisals that cost Beck, Canaris, and Stauffenberg their lives.

See also CANARIS, WILHELM.

FURTHER READING: *Hans Rothfels, *The German Opposition to Hitler* (1962); Roger Manvell and Heinrich Fraenkel, *The July Plot* (1966); Anthony Cave Brown, *Bodyguard of Lies* (1975).

Blake, George (1922-   )   British double agent for the Soviet Union.

Blake was a Dutch national of Jewish origin, born in Rotterdam as Georg Behar. World War II disrupted his life. The German invasion of the Low Countries in 1940 trapped him, and he was interned by the invaders. Escaping, he fought in the Dutch resistance for three years (1940–43). Then German counterespionage identified him; he learned that he was about to be arrested, and he slipped through German-occupied France, crossed the Pyrenees to neutral Spain, and continued by sea to Britain. There he volunteered to help with the war effort.

He was assigned to the Special Operations Executive (SOE), an organization responsible for sending undercover agents to the Continent to cooperate with resistance groups against the Nazis. Blake worked mainly as an interpreter. After D-Day (June 6, 1944), when the Allies crossed the English Channel and invaded France, he served at Allied headquarters on the Continent, and the end of the war found him with British naval intelligence in Hamburg.

By now a naturalized British citizen, Blake gained a place in the British diplomatic corps, and in 1947 he went as vice consul to the British legation in Seoul, South Korea. Once more an invading army trapped him, this one from North Korea in 1950, as the Korean War erupted. He spent the next three years in captivity.

During this period he was either brainwashed by the North Korean Communists or else shifted his thinking of his own free will. Either way, he returned to London a committed Communist after the end of the war in 1953 and the exchange of prisoners.

Blake was already a spy for the Soviet Union when he joined the headquarters of MI6 (Military Intelligence 6, British espionage) in London, thereby gaining access to information about broad intelligence strategy, as well as to tactical instructions for agents in the field. He continued to be in a highly sensitive post when MI6 sent him to West Berlin in 1955. Here for three years he handed top-secret information on the western Allies to Soviet agents at clandestine meetings.

His betrayal was particularly damaging because he was in touch with Reinhard Gehlen, the intelligence chief of the German Federal Republic, and therefore knew what Gehlen's agents were doing and reporting. Blake informed the Russians of their identity, with the result that some spies for the west suddenly disappeared in Eastern Europe and were never heard from again.

Blake also informed the Russians about the Berlin Tunnel, which the Americans dug from West Berlin to East Berlin for the purpose of tapping communications lines leading to Moscow. The Russians seized their end of the tunnel in 1956, thereby destroying a unique source of information for the Allies.

In 1959 Blake discovered that a Gehlen agent named Horst Eitner was, like himself, a double for the Russians. Fearful because Eitner knew so much about him, Blake applied to MI6 headquarters for a transfer. He returned to London and then was posted to Beirut, where he served during the years 1960–61.

Meanwhile, back in West Berlin, Eitner was found to be a double agent and arrested. He revealed the truth about Blake. MI6 sent to Blake in Beirut a noncommittal order to return to London for a routine interview, thus preventing him from becoming suspicious. He walked into a carefully prepared trap at MI6 headquarters, where he was arrested as soon as he arrived.

Blake's treason concerned matters so closely connected with British national security that part of his trial was held behind closed doors. He received a sentence of forty-two years, but served only six before he escaped. He reached sanctuary in Moscow, where his services to the Soviet Union were rewarded with a job in Soviet intelligence.

See also BERLIN TUNNEL; GEHLEN, REINHARD.

FURTHER READING: Norman Lucas, *The Great Spy Ring* (1966); *Edward Spiro, *The Many Sides of George Blake, Esq.: The Complete Dossier* (1970); Heinz Höhne and Hermann Zolling, *The General Was a Spy: The Truth about General Gehlen and His Spy Ring* (1972), has an account of Blake and Eitner.

Blowitz, Henri de *(1825-1903)*   Bohemian journalist and spy at the Congress of Berlin.

Blowitz, a member of the aristocracy, was born in the family chateau at Pilsen. After the classical education and continental travel common to one of his rank, he settled in France and became a naturalized citizen. Attracted to journalism, he began writing newspaper articles during the 1860s, the period of the Second Empire, when Napoleon III sat on the French throne. Blowitz took the democratic side in French politics, writing commentaries in defense of Republicans against Bonapartist candidates for seats in the national legislature.

His profound knowledge of events and his perceptive analyses of them brought him to the attention of editor John Delane of the *London Times,* who was looking for a reliable correspondent in Paris. Blowitz accepted Delane's offer in 1871, following the defeat of France in the Franco-Prussian War (1870–71). Four years later Blowitz was the leading correspondent for the *Times* on the Continent, so important that in 1878 he was shifted from Paris to Berlin to cover the Berlin Congress.

The two leading figures at this international conference were Otto von Bismarck, the German chancellor, and British Prime Minister Benjamin Disraeli. The purpose was to settle European tensions following the Russo-Turkish War (1877–78). The main issue was Bulgaria, which had been enlarged by the victorious Russians at the expense of the Turks, an outcome that alarmed both Britain and Austria because of the instability it caused in the Balkans.

Blowitz arrived in Berlin with the intention of breaking through the censorship covering the congress. To do so he had to become a spy able to outwit the corps of secret agents Bismarck maintained to trace leaks and arrest suspects. How Blowitz succeeded has never been completely explained, but he is known to have had an informant in one of the delegations.

Blowitz protected himself so carefully that he never met this informant secretly, never acknowledged their friendship when they met publicly, and never employed go-betweens to bring back oral or written information. The journalist and the informant used a simpler and safer method. They dined at the same Berlin restaurant, placing their hats on adjacent pegs. The hats were indistinguishable, so Blowitz simply took the wrong hat when he left the restaurant, returned to his hotel room, and extracted the message from the hat band.

Blowitz immediately telegraphed the contents of the papers to London in code, and the *Times* published some of the most confidential information from the talks between the principals at the Berlin Congress. Everyone there soon realized that Blowitz was obtaining the information from someone on the inside, and Bismarck ordered his agents to find out how. They failed because they never realized that Blowitz and his informant were exchanging hats in the restaurant.

Blowitz thus reported secrets of the highest importance, including an agreement to defuse the Balkan powder keg by reducing the size of Bulgaria. This was Disraeli's personal triumph in dealing with the Russians, and Blowitz so reported it.

More than anything else, Blowitz wanted a copy of the Treaty of Berlin as soon as it was ready. His usual informant could not obtain one, so Blowitz found a delegate with access to the document. This time Blowitz arranged a personal secret meeting, a safe thing to do because he was leaving Berlin immediately. He telegraphed the terms of the agreement to London and caught the train for Paris before they appeared in print.

Furious at the time, Bismarck had become philosophical about it when he met Blowitz in 1883. The chancellor asked Blowitz to explain his espionage methods during the Congress, but Blowitz refused, providing an early example of a journalist protecting his sources. He did explain the hat trick when he published his memoirs in 1903, but he still concealed the names of his two contacts, and they remain anonymous.

FURTHER READING: °Henri de Blowitz, *Memoirs* (1903); W. N. Medlicott, *The Congress of Berlin and After: Diplomatic History of the Near East Settlement, 1878–1880* (1938); Werner Haas, *Bismarck* (1973).

Blue, Victor *(1865-1928)*   American naval officer and spy during the Spanish-American War.

A North Carolinian with Annapolis training, Blue in 1898, at the outbreak of the Spanish-American War, was an officer aboard the gunboat *Suwanee* assigned to duty in Cuban waters. He carried out from his ship three spy missions behind the Spanish lines.

First, there was the problem of getting American supply vessels through the Spanish defenses along the Cuban coast. Blue took a small boat by night into the shore, made arrangements with General Gomez, commander of the Cuban forces in the Caybarien area, for a secret rendezvous, and returned with the information that enabled an American supply ship to make a safe run to the rendezvous.

Second, there was the problem of the American blockade of Santiago harbor. An attempt had been made to bottle up a Spanish squadron in the harbor by sinking a ship at the entrance. But were all the enemy vessels actually there? Some had been reported on the high seas. Blue volunteered to find out.

Again landing surreptitiously on the Cuban shore, and disguised as a Cuban, he struck out with a rebel guide toward Santiago. It was a dangerous trek through the Spanish lines in one of the most sensitive areas held by the Spaniards. It was also a grueling trek through the jungle, sometimes through swamps waist-deep in mud and water.

Finally reaching the hills overlooking Santiago, Blue saw the answer to his question—the sunken ship had gone down to one side of the harbor channel, leaving it partially open for marine traffic. Still, his count showed that all identified Spanish warships were there.

This was the message he carried back to the *Suwanee* on his successful return trip. It allowed American warships to guard Santiago secure in the knowledge that no enemy warships would attack them from the high seas.

Third, American sailors ordered to take small craft directly into the harbor had to know in advance where their target ships were anchored. To settle this point, Blue went on another spy mission. Escorted by a rebel party, he again reached the Santiago hills, where he plotted the position of the Spanish ships on a chart of the harbor. He made a safe return to the *Suwanee,* and his chart would have provided the information for a successful American invasion of the harbor. Such an operation proved unnecessary because the Spanish squadron made a bid to break through the American line of ships and was destroyed by them.

After 1898, Blue remained in the U.S. Navy; he commanded the battleship *Texas* in World War I and was a rear admiral when he retired in 1919.

FURTHER READING: °George S. Bryan, *The Spy in America* (1943), prints Blue's account of his espionage activities; Margaret Leech, *In the Days of McKinley* (1959); Donald Barr Chidsey, *The Spanish-American War* (1971), gives the background to Blue's spy work.

Blunt, Anthony *(1907-   )*   British art historian, intelligence officer, and double agent for the Soviet Union.

Blunt was born in Bournemouth, the son of a clergyman in the Church of England. When he was four years old, his father became chaplain to the British Embassy in Paris, and there Blunt early acquired his consuming interest in art, especially French art.

Educated in Britain at the Marlborough public school, he then had a brilliant career at Cambridge and was elected a fellow of Trinity College in 1932. At Cambridge he became disillusioned with British democracy for its failure to control the economic depression of those years and with his own social class for living in comfort while the masses lived in misery. An intellectual attracted by unfashionable ideas, unable to assess the Soviet Union accurately, Blunt became a Marxist and a member of a pro-Soviet underground in Cambridge. His most important Communist friends, in the light of their later espionage careers, were undergraduates Guy Burgess and Donald Maclean. All three were homosexuals, and Blunt shared rooms with Burgess for a while. A fourth convert to Communism, Kim Philby, was an associate of Blunt's at Cambridge. The four assured one another that only the Russians could or would oppose Hitler's Germany.

While still at Cambridge, Blunt paid a visit to Russia that hardened his commitment to the Moscow line. By the time he left Cambridge in 1937, he was prepared to spy for the Soviet Union. No opportunity appeared during the next four years, as he pursued his researches in art history. This changed with the coming of World War II (1939–45). Blunt went into the British army in 1939, escaped from France after the German victory of 1940, and shifted to MI5 (Military Intelligence 5, British counterespionage). He was drawn into becoming a double agent for the Russians by Burgess, then an espionage officer and an experienced spy who passed information to Moscow by way of Russian contacts in London. Blunt, a counterespionage officer, did the same for the rest of the war.

In 1945 Blunt returned to art history, becoming over the next three decades one of the world's greatest authorities in the field. He wrote several books that won critical acclaim. Two of his specialties—showing the breadth of his interest and knowledge—were the seventeenth-century painter Nicolas Poussin and Pablo Picasso. Blunt received high honors to go with his fellowship at Trinity College—surveyor of the king's pictures (1945), director of the Courtauld Institute of Art (1947), fellow of the British Academy (1950), knighted by the queen (1956), professor of art history at the University of London (1960), and adviser for the queen's pictures and drawings (1972).

In 1951 Blunt made a momentary return to undercover work against Britain. Informed by Burgess that Maclean was about to be arrested on charges of spying for the Soviet Union, Blunt got in touch with a Russian contact who arranged for Burgess and Maclean to escape to Moscow. The Russian ordered Blunt to go with them, but Blunt refused, knowing by now that Russia was not the workers' paradise he had once imagined and that Britain was a better place to live.

The years following the defection of Burgess and Maclean were filled with rumors about a "third man," who had alerted the pair to their danger. This third man proved to be Kim Philby, who had passed the information to Burgess while both were in Washington and who had also defected to Russia. There was also speculation about a "fourth man" who had helped the fugitives. Blunt, in view of his friendship with Burgess, was questioned, but he denied his culpability. In 1964, however, confronted with new evidence against him and feeling free to talk for reasons he never explained publicly, he made a secret confession at counterespionage headquarters. He admitted that he was indeed the fourth man of the Burgess-Maclean case. He was able to provide so much basic information about the Soviet spy system that the authorities agreed to give him his freedom in exchange for it.

Blunt continued his career in art without interruption until 1979, when his past as a double agent suddenly became public property via a book written by journalist and biographer Andrew Boyle. The evidence collected by Boyle proved that Blunt was the fourth man who had helped Burgess and Maclean escape. A national scandal resulted. Prime Minister Margaret Thatcher made a statement in the House of Commons explaining why Blunt had been freed in return for his confession. This did not satisfy the critics in Parliament and in the news media who demanded to know why Blunt had been allowed to hold respectable positions, including that of art consultant to the queen. Some university men in intelligence were accused of seeing to it that Blunt, being from Cambridge, was allowed to escape the penalties that would have been imposed on a spy lacking his background.

Blunt agreed to an interview with the press and gave his side of the story. His principal self-defense regarding Burgess-Maclean was that he chose to betray his country rather than his friends according to the formula enunciated by novelist E. M. Forster ("I hope I would have the guts to betray my country"). Blunt argued that the secret information he handed over to the Russians during the war had not harmed Britain because it was about the Germans, but he did not allude to the fact that in 1940 the Russians were allies of the Germans and quite possibly relayed to Berlin information used by the German air force during the Battle of Britain. Commenting in general on his activities as a double agent, Blunt agreed he had made a "disastrous, appalling mistake." He also said: "I did not betray my conscience." A London newspaper summed up the reaction of an exasperated public: "Damn your conscience!"

Blunt's honors vanished much more quickly than he had accumulated them. The queen stripped him of his knighthood, Trinity College revoked his fellowship, and he was expelled by the British Academy. Disgraced at the age of 72, Blunt retreated from the limelight and suffered in silence.

See also BURGESS, GUY; MACLEAN, DONALD; PHILBY, KIM.

FURTHER READING: Cyril Connolly, *The Missing Diplomats* (1952); Anthony Purdy and Douglas Sutherland, *Burgess and Maclean* (1963); Bruce Page, David Leitch, and Phillip Knightley, *The Philby Conspiracy* (1968); *Andrew Boyle, *The Fourth Man: The Definitive Account of Kim Philby, Guy Burgess, and Donald Maclean, and Who Recruited Them to Spy for Russia* (1979); Douglas Sutherland, *The Great Betrayal: The Definitive Story of Blunt, Philby, Burgess, and Maclean* (1981).

Bonvouloir, Julien Achard de *(1749-83)* French secret agent in America during the American Revolution.

Bonvouloir, of an aristocratic Norman family, served in the French army before going on the travels that in 1774 brought him to the British colonies in North America. He returned home, became known for his knowledge of those colonies, and in 1775 was sent back to America as a secret agent after the first armed clashes between the Americans and the British. His orders were to find out how serious the rebellion was, what the chances were of the Americans being reconciled to the British crown in the person of King George III, and what opportunities existed for the French to prevent this so that they might be revenged for the British conquest of Canada in the Seven Years' War (1756–63).

Posing as a Belgian merchant to conceal his French origins and sympathies, Bonvouloir talked to leading Americans, including members of the Continental Congress, such as Benjamin Franklin. The Americans soon realized from his indiscreet questions that he was a French secret agent, and they began to sound him out about the possibilities of receiving diplomatic, financial, and military aid from France.

Bonvouloir reported to Paris that the Americans were determined to win their freedom but that they needed help. His reports led the French government to decide to support the rebellion across the Atlantic, but he was considered too imprudent to be kept on as a secret agent. He therefore received a summons home in 1776. Five years later he went with the French artillery to India, where he died.

FURTHER READING: Carl Van Doren, *Secret History of the American Revolution* (1941); *Helen Augur, *The Secret War of Independence* (1955); William Stinchcombe, *The American Revolution and the French Alliance* (1969).

Bossard, Frank (1912-   ) British spy for the Soviet Union.

Bossard's early life, compounded of poverty, menial work, resentment, and ambition, determined much of his later life. He was the posthumous son of a Yorkshire carpenter, and his mother ran a general store until she remarried. Bossard was a shop clerk at the age of 14, and the university status he craved was never a financial possibility.

He did get into a technical college in 1933, where he studied radio technology. He had personal problems, however, and in the following year he served a jail sentence for cashing a forged check.

The coming of World War II enabled Bossard to serve in the Royal Air Force, with which he saw action in the Middle East, emerging in 1946 with the rank of flight lieutenant. He seemed to have escaped completely from his sordid past when, five years later, he obtained a government job and was posted as a technical expert to Bonn, West Germany. In 1956 he was recruited by British intelligence.

Despite his success—and perhaps because past resentments still weighed on him—he began to drink heavily. Summoned back to London and evidently subsiding into his old animosities, Bossard agreed to steal classified information when approached by a Russian secret agent with a proposal.

Bossard was in a position to be useful to the Russians because he had access to data on guided missiles. For four years he placed photographs of secret documents in drops around London, hiding places where Soviet agents could pick them up surreptitiously. He also collected instructions and money from these drops.

In 1965 Bossard was caught by agents of MI5 (Military Intelligence 5, British counterespionage) and arrested by the Special Branch of Scotland Yard. The circumstances were so sensitive that, for security reasons, they were not made public. The overt evidence against Bossard included a list of nine drops, ranging from hollow trees in the park to broken drainpipes on the highway.

Although not as well known as other British spies for the Soviet Union, such as George Blake, Harry Houghton, and Kim Philby, Bossard is said to have been in their class as a traitor because of the highly technical nature of the information he sold to the Russians. They valued the information enough to pay him the equivalent of $75,000.

FURTHER READING: John Bulloch, *MI5: The Origin and History of the British Counter-Espionage Service* (1963); *Norman Lucas, *The Great Spy Ring* (1966); Bernard Newman, *Spy and Counter-Spy: The Story of the British Secret Service* (1970).

Bowie, Wat *(1831-64)*   Spy and undercover agent for the Confederacy during the American Civil War.

Bowie changed character after the Civil War began. Originally Walter Bowie, son of a Maryland lawyer, he was a notably placid type as he studied law and began his own practice. In 1861 he suddenly became Wat Bowie, daring Confederate marauder. His commitment to the southern cause made the difference.

The first year of the war saw him repeatedly crossing the Potomac by night and entering Washington to gather information about the Union army. He also sounded out men with southern sympathies, many of whom he persuaded to go to the Confederacy and join its armed forces.

In 1862 Lafayette Baker, head of Federal intelligence, acting on the word of an informer, sent agents to arrest Bowie at the home of a lady he was visiting. Bowie, held in prison in Washington, refused to be cowed by Baker's harsh questioning, was sentenced to death as a spy, escaped from his cell with the connivance of a southern sympathizer, and crossed the Potomac to safety behind the Confederate lines.

In 1863 Baker's men again surrounded a house Bowie was in, only to have him slip through their fingers disguised as a slave girl. Bowie joined Mosby's Rangers, a crack Confederate outfit, becoming a cavalryman and a spy. Imprudent as well as courageous, Bowie was a daredevil who took too many chances.

In 1864 he tried his most daring scheme, an attempt to kidnap the governor of Maryland in Annapolis. Unable to get into the city because of the military guards around it, Bowie and his men were surprised by a posse, and in the ensuing gunfight he was shot dead.

See also BAKER, LAFAYETTE.

FURTHER READING: Lafayette Baker, *History of the United States Secret Service in the Late War* (1867); V. D. Jones, *Ranger Mosby* (1944), is an account of Bowie's commander; *John Bakeless, *Spies of the Confederacy* (1970).

Boxers *(1898-1901)*   Chinese secret society opposed to foreign influences in China.

The English term "Boxers" was a nickname for the Chinese who called themselves "Righteous Harmony Fists," by which they meant that they adhered to the old mandarin concept of body-mind control through athletics. Looking back to the great days of China, the Boxers resented the degradation of their country in their own time, a period when the western powers and Japan occupied entire areas under the "unequal treaties" extorted from the Manchu rulers in Peking during the nineteenth century. The dowager empress Tzu Hsi resented her powerlessness, too, and it was with her covert support that the Boxers began their campaign. The Boxers were anti-Manchu, but for the moment common interests brought the two sides together.

The Boxers constituted a secret society. They used membership initiations, oaths of fealty to the cause, and passwords to identify one another in public. Against the "foreign devils" in China they used espionage, extortion, and violence. Boxer spies swarmed among the Chinese in occupied cities, keeping the unreliable under surveillance, taking the lives of informers, and creating a climate of fear for all who were not wholeheartedly with them. The Boxers persecuted Chinese Christians, regarding their religion as an un-Chinese importation from the west.

Undercover violence came out in the open with the Boxer Rebellion, which began when the Boxers murdered the German minister in Peking (1900). The Boxers then besieged the foreign legations accredited to the Manchu court. The powers thus affronted formed an international expedition, which marched to Peking. The expedition broke the siege of the legations with the help of the dowager empress, who by now feared the Boxers more than she feared the westerners. The Boxers were dispersed by western guns (1901). They never reassembled into a recognizable movement. Their achievement was a legacy of resistance to foreign domination that helped bring on the revolution of 1911 and the overthrow of the Manchu dynasty in 1912.

FURTHER READING: *C. C. Tan, *The Boxer Catastrophe* (1955); Israel Epstein, *From Opium War to Liberation* (1956); Richard Deacon, *The Chinese Secret Service* (1974), has a chapter on the Boxers.

Boyce, Christopher John (1953-   )   American spy for the Soviet Union.

Boyce was born in Palos Verdes, California, the son of an employee of an aircraft company. He went to a parochial grammar school and then high school, from which he graduated in 1971. He attended Harbor Junior College (1972) and Loyola University (1972–73). Dropping out of Loyola he obtained a job in the TRW Defense and Space Systems Group at Redondo Beach, California, in 1974, where he had access to classified information concerning the manufacture of space satellites for the CIA (Central Intelligence Agency) —spies-in-the-sky whose principal function was to report what they "saw" in passing over the Soviet Union.

By then Boyce and his friend Daulton Lee had both been alienated from American democracy by the Vietnam War, Watergate, covert CIA operations in other countries, and a feeling, not uncommon in their generation, that the system was beyond salvation. In 1975 they decided to spy together for the Soviet Union.

Boyce began copying top-secret documents at TRW and turning over the copies to Lee, who delivered them to the Soviet Embassy in Mexico City. This conspiracy continued for over a year, until Boyce became suspicious that Lee was holding out on him regarding the money paid by the Russians for the information. Boyce, who also feared that Lee, a drug user, might betray him unintentionally, went to Mexico City in 1976, joined Lee, and met the

Russians himself. The difficulties were ironed out, and the conspiracy continued.

Lee was arrested in 1977 in Mexico City. Incriminating films were found on him, and he said he had received them from Boyce. Picked up by agents of the FBI (Federal Bureau of Investigation), Boyce confessed to having copied thousands of documents for the Russians. His trial ended in a prison sentence of forty years. Lee got a life sentence. Boyce escaped from jail in 1980, remained at large in the Pacific Northwest for over a year, and was recaptured by U.S. Marshals in 1981.

See also LEE, ANDREW DAULTON.

FURTHER READING: Robert Lindsey, *The Falcon and the Snowman: A True Story of Friendship and Espionage* (1979) ("falcon" refers to Boyce's interest in hawking; "snowman," to Lee's use of drugs).

Boyd, Belle *(1844-1900)*   Spy for the Confederacy during the American Civil War.

A Virginian, born in Martinsburg, Boyd was originally called "Isabelle," a form she shortened to "Belle" early in life. Her father, a prosperous store-keeper, sent her to Mount Washington Female College in Baltimore, from which she graduated in 1860 proficient in Latin, French, music, and horsemanship.

Her father, supporting Virginia's secession from the Union in 1861, served under Stonewall Jackson, and Belle Boyd met Jackson's spy chief, Turner Ashby, to whom she sent or carried information about the Federal forces she saw in the Martinsburg area. In 1861, while caring for the wounded after a Confederate retreat, she reported to Confederate commanders the numbers and direction of the advancing northerners. Allan Pinkerton, the head of Federal counterespionage, questioned her and ingenuously found no reason to hold her.

Arrested again in 1862, she was again released; she returned to Martinsburg, and went on to Front Royal to stay in a hotel owned by her aunt. The Federals having commandeered rooms in the hotel, Boyd overheard their plans to deal with Jackson. Rushing across to the Confederate lines, she personally delivered her message to Turner Ashby, which was essentially that the few Federals still in Front Royal could be overrun by a swift Confederate advance before the enemy had time to break the bridges. Jackson listened to her report, pushed forward, and took the town. After the battle, he sent her, she says, his thanks for "the immense service that you have rendered your country today."

The Federals arrested her once more in 1863. She was taken to Washington, where Lafayette Baker, who had replaced Pinkerton, interrogated her. Baker failed to extort the confession he wanted, and Boyd was released on provision that she remain in the Confederacy. She returned to Martinsburg. Confederate General Robert E. Lee swept north to defeat at Gettysburg, which ended the comparatively easy espionage work to which she had become accustomed.

In 1864 Boyd undertook one more mission on behalf of the South, sailing from Canada with dispatches from Richmond to be delivered in London. The assignment came to nothing, as the Confederacy collapsed. That year she published one of the less trustworthy memoirs of the Civil War, useful more for its revelation of her character than for its accuracy.

A natural actress, Boyd went on the London stage in 1866. Two years later she was starring in a comedy in New York. Her thespian career lasted through the decade, and later in her life she lectured on her experiences, some patently fictional, during the Civil War. Having been married three times, she left several children at her death.

See also PINKERTON, ALLAN.

FURTHER READING: Belle Boyd, *Belle Boyd in Camp and Prison, Written by Herself* (1865); *Louis A. Sigaud, *Belle Boyd, Confederate Spy* (1967); Oscar A. Kinchen, *Women Who Spied for the Blue and the Gray* (1972).

Brainwashing   A system of psychological techniques used to restructure the thought processes of individuals.

The term "brainwashing" is a figure of speech comparing the (metaphorical) scrubbing of the mind to the (actual) scrubbing of the body. The purpose is to persuade a subject to give up "dirty" ideas (i.e., those the brainwasher disapproves of) and replace them with "clean" ideas (i.e., those the brainwasher approves of).

In the broadest sense, brainwashing may mean simply the use of logical arguments to persuade an opponent that his or her opinion is wrong. Even primary education may fall under the definition, usually with an opprobrious meaning. Psychologists more properly apply brainwashing in the rehabilitation of criminals. None of these examples implies anything but humane methods. It is otherwise where spies, or potential spies, are concerned.

The Chinese Communists both invented the word and developed an effective system of brainwashing after they seized power in China, their purpose being to change enemies of the regime into allies. The Chinese system is therefore the classical form.

All espionage and counterespionage organizations have methods for cajoling or frightening people into a shift of loyalties. The Chinese system of brainwashing, weighted toward psychological rather than physical abuse, is less humane than the methods of the CIA (Central Intelligence Agency) but less brutal than those of the KGB (Committee for State Security, Soviet intelligence). Typically, subjects are held in small cells for a long period of time in complete silence except when visited by their preceptor, an agent who talks to them about the virtues of Marxism-Leninism and the evils of western democracy. Subjects are kept under constant surveillance to break down their mental resistance, and if it is considered necessary, they are pressured physically through curtailment of such things as food, sleep, and warmth.

Finally, the victims are compelled to attend meetings with experts in Communist ideology and prisoners already brainwashed. There they are harassed, humiliated, ordered to confess, and when they show signs of having Communist convictions, congratulated for their candor, wisdom, and sense of reality.

The psychological process, when successful, involves a weakening of the personality to the point where the individual willingly accepts the ideology as the truth that will, it is presumed, maintain his or her dignity. This personal change is reinforced by entrance into, and acceptance by, Communist society.

The transformation of a subject who remains within a Communist atmosphere may well be permanent. For one who escapes that atmosphere, the effects of brainwashing are usually transitory.

See also CIA; KGB.

FURTHER READING: Edward Hunter, *Brainwashing: The Story of Men Who Defied It* (1956); *C. P. Tung, *The Thought Revolution* (1966); Richard Deacon, *The Chinese Secret Service* (1974).

Brewster, Caleb *(1747-1827)* Patriot secret agent during the American War of Independence.

Born on the family farm at Setauket on the shore of Long Island Sound across from Connecticut, Brewster went to sea in his youth and remained a sailor for most of his life. He turned his nautical ability to the service of his country when he joined the American cause in 1776 as the War of Independence developed. For two years he roamed Long Island Sound, leading a flotilla of small boats in attacks on British shipping.

This activity brought Brewster to the attention of General George Washington's spymaster, Major Benjamin Tallmadge, who needed a secret agent operating in the sound on the final leg of an espionage route that began in New York City and ran all the way to Tallmadge's headquarters in Connecticut. The system began with Robert Townsend, who gathered information in New York and put it into coded messages. Courier Austin Roe carried the messages to Abraham Woodhull at Setauket. This espionage network was known as the "Culper Ring," in which Woodhull used the cover name "Samuel Culper, Senior," and Townsend, "Samuel Culper, Junior."

After reaching Setauket, the messages still had to cross the sound. Brewster joined the Culper Ring soon after its creation in 1777 to perform this function. His method was to bring his boat ashore surreptitiously in one of the coves near Setauket and then to signal his arrival to Woodhull. A Patriot woman named Anna Strong did the signaling for him. Her home looked toward Woodhull's across Little Bay, the two being so close that Woodhull could see her clothesline. A black petticoat on the line informed him that Brewster had landed. The number of black handkerchiefs beside it let him know in which cove Brewster was waiting. Woodhull took the Townsend messages to Brewster, who ferried them across to Tallmadge on the Connecticut shore.

The Culper Ring operated in this manner for five years (1778–83). Brewster was an essential member of the network, either eluding British patrol ships in the sound or else waging successful battles with them. He kept his part of the Culper route open until the British evacuation of New York in 1783.

After the war, Brewster got married. Still the sailor, he commanded revenue cutters for over twenty years, until 1816, when he retired to his Setauket farm.

See also CULPER RING; TALLMADGE, BENJAMIN.

FURTHER READING: *Morton Pennypacker, *General Washington's Spies on Long Island and in New York* (1939); John Bakeless, *Turncoats, Traitors, and Heroes* (1959), has an account of Brewster; Corey Ford, *A Peculiar Service* (1965), is the best book on Brewster and the Culper Ring.

Broglie, Comte de *(1719-81)* French ambassador to Poland and director abroad of the King's Secret, the personal intelligence apparatus of King Louis XV.

Charles François, comte de Broglie, was the scion of a family belonging to the high French nobility, distinguished in the royal service. Following the family tradition, Broglie in 1752 accepted appointment by Louis XV to the French Embassy in Warsaw. He assumed the post with conflicting sets of instructions. The French foreign minister, officially in charge of French foreign policy, told Broglie to support the Polish nationalists in their choice of a king for their vacant throne. But Louis XV ordered Broglie to conspire for the election of a French candidate, Louis François de Bourbon, prince de Conti.

Broglie's predicament derived from his place in the King's Secret, the confidential network of agents through whom Louis XV worked when he wanted to pursue a policy apart from that urged on him by his ministers, whom he did not want to contradict. Since Louis was trying to maintain French influence in Poland beyond anything dictated by French interests, he took into the King's Secret a personal emissary whom he could trust to ignore dispatches from the French foreign ministry that contravened his plans. Broglie was that emissary.

Broglie naturally obeyed the king rather than the French foreign minister. Ensconced at the French Embassy in Warsaw, the ambassador became the intermediary to whom French agents sent messages from all over Eastern Europe. Broglie condensed these messages, made abstracts and added advisory memoranda, and sent full reports to Louis XV that the ministers at Versailles never saw. The extant reports reveal a host of schemes, proposals, and initiatives—all for nothing, since Broglie was unable to control events in Poland, and Conti never gained the Polish throne. The Seven Years' War (1756–63) reversed the balance of power in Europe, and in 1772 Poland fell prey to her oppressive neighbors, Russia, Prussia, and Austria.

The fate of Broglie's Polish adventure is an outstanding example of how the King's Secret disrupted French foreign policy and expended French energy on impossible or useless objectives.

See also KING'S SECRET; LOUIS XV.

FURTHER READING: *Duc de Broglie, *The King's Secret* (1879); G. P. Gooch, *Louis XV: The Monarchy in Decline* (1956).

Brossolette, Pierre *(1903-44)* French journalist and spymaster during World War II.

Brossolette was a Parisian who belonged to a middle-class family, took a degree in history, and during the 1930s wrote for a socialist newspaper. In 1938 French radio dropped him as a commentator on international events because of his denunciation of the Munich agreement by which France and Britain allowed Adolf Hitler, then chancellor of Germany, to dismember Czechoslovakia. When the Germans conquered France in 1940, Brossolette, refusing to write for the controlled French press, opened a small bookshop in Paris. He conspired with the French resistance against the Germans (1940–42) and then escaped from France to Britain to join General Charles de Gaulle.

Brossolette entered de Gaulle's BCRA (Central Bureau of Intelligence and Operations) and worked with its director, "Colonel Passy," who was actually André Dewavrin. In 1943 Brossolette went secretly to Paris, where he met Dewavrin and F. F. E. Yeo-Thomas, a representative of the Special Operations Executive (SOE), the British organization aiding the French resistance. As a known socialist, Brossolette had the advantage of being able to talk to left-wing factions of the resistance. He persuaded most of them to cooperate with right-wing groups, and he became a leader of combined forces. After returning to London to report to BCRA, Brossolette received further instructions from Dewavrin and flew back to France accompanied by Yeo-Thomas. This time both were seized by the Gestapo (German secret police). Brossolette apparently committed suicide by jumping from a window to make sure he would not reveal resistance secrets while being interrogated.

See also DEWAVRIN, ANDRÉ; FRENCH RESISTANCE; YEO-THOMAS, F. F. E.

FURTHER READING: *Eric Piquet-Wicks, *Four in the Shadows* (1957), presents Brossolette as one of the four; Blake Erlich, *Resistance: France, 1940–1945* (1965); David Schorenbrun, *Soldiers of the Night: The Story of the French Resistance* (1980).

Bugging The use of electronic devices for the surreptitious monitoring of conversations.

See INTELLIGENCE, SCIENTIFIC.

Bureau Ha (1939-45) Semiofficial Swiss intelligence organization.

After General Henri Guisan was elected Switzerland's commander in chief in 1939 during the tension surrounding the outbreak of World War II, he found himself in a quandary regarding intelligence. He needed information about Nazi Germany, and he wanted to pass warnings on to Britain and France, but he feared to antagonize Adolf Hitler by official clandestine operations that could be brought home to the Swiss government. Guisan therefore turned to the Bureau Ha, a private organization the name of which derived from that of its founder, Captain Hans Hausamann.

Realizing that Hitler's Germany could be a threat to neutral Switzerland, Hausamann some years before the war gathered a group of former officers to work with him in a headquarters at Villa Stutz, on Lake Lucerne. When war came, the Bureau Ha already had agents operating in Germany, Austria, Scandinavia, France, and Italy. It was thus a professional intelligence department without official standing, so that Guisan could rely on it while remaining in a position to disown it if need be.

Two foreigners held a special place at the Bureau Ha. Captain Thomas Sedlacek, a Czech, alerted Allied embassies in Switzerland to German plans discovered by Hausamann's men. Rudolf Roessler, a German, gave Hausamann reports that came from Roessler's own sources in Berlin.

The collapse of France in 1940 left Switzerland in grave danger, surrounded by German forces or by those of Germany's ally, Italy. The German invasion of Russia in 1941 added another problem because German counterespionage knew about a Soviet network operating in Switzerland. The Bureau Ha, nevertheless, allowed Roessler to deliver information to this network, which transmitted it to Moscow by radio. Swiss counterespionage, prodded by the Germans, broke up the network in 1943, but by then the tide of the war had shifted against Germany, whose defeat came two years later. The critical years for Switzerland, and Swiss intelligence, were over.

See also GUISAN, HENRI; ROESSLER, RUDOLF.

FURTHER READING: *Jon Kimche, *Spying for Peace: General Guisan and Swiss Neutrality* (1962); Urz Schwartz, *The Eye of the Hurricane: Switzerland in World War II* (1980).

Burgess, Guy *(1911-1963)*   British writer, diplomat, and spy for the Soviet Union.

Born in Devonport, Burgess was the son of an officer in the Royal Navy. He wanted to emulate his father, and that was the reason why, after a year at Eton(1924–25), he went to the naval college at Dartmouth (1925–27). When an eye problem forced him to give up the navy, he returned to Eton and stayed until his graduation.

In 1930 Burgess went up to Cambridge, where he studied history and made friends in the homosexual and Communist undergrounds of the university. He met Kim Philby, Donald Maclean, and Anthony Blunt, three who shared his aversion to the political system that had produced the depression of the 1930s and his strong belief that the Soviet Union had the right alternative system. Burgess was especially close with Blunt, with whom he shared rooms. Burgess, Blunt, Philby, and Maclean committed themselves to work secretly for the Soviet Union. Before Burgess left Cambridge in 1935, Adolf Hitler had become chancellor of Germany, and the growing Nazi terror strengthened the Communist bias of the Cambridge Marxists. Burgess was one of those who strove to convert believing Communists into secret agents for the Soviet Union.

In 1935 Burgess launched what was to become a ten-year career in journalism, much of it with the news department of the British Broadcasting Corporation (BBC). At the same time, he carried out espionage assignments for the Russians. He passed on information from John Cairncross at the Foreign Office of the British government, and he twice (1937 and 1939) went to France to meet Philby, who was spying for the Russians while reporting on the Spanish Civil War (1936–39) for London newspapers. Burgess joined MI6 (Military Intelligence 6, British espionage) in 1939 and stayed there as a writer until 1941. These were the early years of World War II (1939–45). Philby, having returned from Spain and from covering the 1940 Allied disaster in France, was also at MI6; the two were able to renew their friendship and their plans for helping the Soviet Union.

Burgess went back to the BBC, staying there until he shifted to the Foreign Office in 1944 to handle the news for this highly sensitive department of the British government. For six years he had access to top-secret documents, the contents of which he reported to his Russian contacts. In 1950 he received an appointment as second secretary to the British Embassy in Washington, where he found Philby already ensconced as first secretary. The two were able to conspire the more easily in that Burgess lived in Philby's home—to the distress of Mrs. Philby, who loathed Burgess for his supercilious demeanor, loud behavior, habitual drunkenness, and homosexual reputation. Burgess also alienated the British ambassador, who in 1951 had him recalled to London. Before Burgess left Washington, Philby learned that their old Cambridge friend, Maclean, who had served at the embassy and was now with the British Foreign Office, was suspected (correctly) of being a spy for the Russians. Philby's advice to Burgess was to warn Maclean immediately on arriving in London.

Burgess did so. He also informed Blunt, a respected art critic and no longer a spy, but still able to get in touch with a Russian spymaster about the problem. The Russians ordered Burgess, Maclean, and Blunt to escape to Russia. Blunt refused. Burgess and Maclean fled, reaching Moscow, revealing themselves as defectors, and settling there permanently. Burgess died in the year that Philby, the "third man" of the scandal, followed them into exile in Russia (1963). His remains were transferred to England for burial. In 1979 Blunt was exposed as the "fourth man" of the Burgess-Maclean case.

See also BLUNT, ANTHONY; MACLEAN, DONALD; PHILBY, KIM.

FURTHER READING: *Cyril Connolly, *The Missing Diplomats* (1952); Anthony Purdy and Douglas Sutherland, *Burgess and Maclean* (1963); Bruce Page, David Leitch, and Phillip Knightley, *The Philby Conspiracy* (1968); Andrew Boyle, *The Fourth Man: The Definitive Account of Kim Philby, Guy Burgess, and Donald Maclean, and Who Recruited Them to Spy for Russia* (1979); Douglas Sutherland, *The Great Betrayal: The Definitive Story of Blunt, Philby, Burgess and Maclean* (1981).

Burton, Richard *(1821-90)* English explorer, orientalist, author, translator, and secret agent for the British in India and Arabia.

Born at Torquay, England, Burton was educated by tutors on the Continent, where his hypochondriac father, a retired colonel in the British army, wandered in search of good health. At nineteen Burton entered Oxford, speaking French, Italian, Spanish, Portuguese, German, and modern Greek.

After two years at Oxford, where he studied ancient Greek, Latin, and some Arabic, Burton, restless and unhappy in this academic atmosphere, persuaded his father to buy him a commission in the army of the East India Company. Once in India, he began studying with enthusiasm the languages of that country, as well as those of Persia, Turkey, and Armenia. Over the years he mastered twenty-nine languages and forty dialects.

In 1843 Burton was posted with his regiment to the Sind (now in Pakistan), newly occupied by General Sir Charles Napier, who used him in military intelligence. Burton would disguise himself and wander in the bazaars among people whose customs interested him as much as their languages, gathering information of great value to the occupying forces. He was one of the great amateurs of espionage.

Napier sent Burton to help survey the Sind canal system and collect information there on the mood of the people. Sometimes Burton worked in native dress alongside the men leveling the canals. Sometimes he took off on foot, clad in the rags of a dervish peddler, to wander among the wild tribes of the hills, often penetrating with his wares even into the harems. With his deep-set eyes and long black mustachios he looked non-British and had only to tint his skin with henna to complete the effect. His knowledge of native customs and dialects was such that he could fool both his fellow officers and the native tribes.

Napier, pleased with Burton's performance, asked him to take on, unofficially, the dangerous mission of gathering information in the three male brothels of Karachi, which were too near the soldiers' camp for the general's peace of mind. Burton agreed, on condition that his report would not be sent to headquarters in Bombay. Disguised as Mirza Abdullah El Bushiri, a half Persian, half Arab merchant, he disappeared into the back alleys of the city. His detailed descriptions horrified Napier, who closed the brothels down forthwith.

This episode ruined Burton's career as a soldier. When Napier was recalled, his successor, who disliked Burton, sent the lurid report to Bombay. Burton was reprimanded and left India in 1849, bitter and broken in health from his labors.

Restored to health by 1853 he set off again as Mirza Abdullah on a pilgrimage to Medina and Mecca to "study the inner life of the Muslim." In Mecca he penetrated as one of the faithful into the sanctuary itself, earning the green turban and title of Hajji, one who had made the great pilgrimage. All the while he took secret notes for his books and for his government's information. *A Pilgrimage to Al Madinah and Meccah,* published in 1855, is a classic to be compared with T. E. Lawrence's *The Seven Pillars of Wisdom.*

For the rest of his life Burton continued to pass on valuable political, geographic, and other information to the British government. He made expeditions to Somaliland and Harrar in Muslim Abyssinia; and to East Africa in search of the source of the Nile. In 1861 the Foreign Office appointed him consul of Fernando Po on the west coast of Africa; then of Santos, Brazil; of Damascus (where he explored, before Lawrence, the unknown areas of Palestine, Syria, and the Holy Land); and lastly of Trieste, where he devoted himself to his greatest work, a six-volume translation of the *Arabian Nights.* Shortly before he died, Queen Victoria awarded Burton the title of Knight Commander of St. Michael and St. George, for his services to the crown.

FURTHER READING: *Richard Burton, *Scinde, and the Races that Inhabit the Valley of the Indus* (1851); Seton Deardon, *The Arabian Knight* (1953); Fawn M. Brodie, *The Devil Drives: A Life of Sir Richard Burton* (1967).

Bussy, François de *(1699-1780)* French spy for Britain.

Bussy was the illegitimate son of a French noble, therefore of the family but not quite in it. Raised as an impoverished member of the aristocracy, he found high offices within his grasp but not the money to pay for the style he thought they required. He was hounded by debts, even when he served as secretary to the French ambassador in Vienna (1725–28) and when he became chargé d'affaires himself (1728–33).

Bussy returned to France in 1733 to enter the ministry of foreign affairs. While performing his official duties, he met Lord Waldgrave, the British ambassador, whom he had known in Vienna. By 1735 Bussy was selling Waldgrave secrets of French diplomacy. Bussy used the number 101 for a code reference in his treasonable correspondence. He held rendezvous with Waldgrave by night in the park at Versailles, where he handed over copies of documents and transmitted information orally. Diplomatic assignments took Bussy to London several times between the years 1737 and 1741. There he seized the opportunity to work out new terms for cooperating with the British government. He continued his spying at least until 1749, when he became the equivalent of an undersecretary at the foreign ministry.

Bussy spent the money he received from his espionage so lavishly that he created suspicion at the foreign ministry. His enemies charged that London must be the source of his added income. They never could prove their contention, but the situation caused him to become more circumspect. He ceased to spy during the 1750s. Sent to London in 1761 in an attempt to negotiate an end to the Seven Years' War (1756–63), Bussy both failed in his diplomacy and refused to go back to his espionage. He stuck to his refusal until his retirement in 1767.

FURTHER READING: Eveline Cruickshanks, "101 Secret Agent," in *History Today* (1969).

Canaris, Wilhelm *(1887-1944)*   Director of German military intelligence and conspirator against Adolf Hitler before and during World War II.

The son of a wealthy industrialist, Canaris was born near Dortmund and educated in its schools. He entered the naval academy at Kiel in 1905, served on a training ship in the Mediterranean, and accepted a permanent position in the German navy after receiving his commission. By the outbreak of World War I (1914), he was an officer on a light cruiser. His ship had to be scuttled when it was trapped by British warships in Chilean waters, but he escaped from internment and returned to Germany to be awarded the Iron Cross by the kaiser.

Promoted to captain, he undertook secret missions to Spain for naval intelligence (1916) and commanded a submarine in the Mediterranean (1917). After the war he rose through the grades to admiral and became head of the Abwehr, or German military intelligence, in 1935. Strongly opposed to Hitler and the Nazi regime from humanitarian and conservative motives, Canaris began conspiring against the dictator that same year. He joined a group of military men, known later to the Nazis as the Black Orchestra, who hoped to remove Hitler in a bloodless coup.

Canaris sent secret messages to the western Allies after Hitler's aggressions began, warning Britain and France to oppose him on the seizure of Austria (1938), the rape of Czechoslovakia (1938), and the invasion of Poland (1939). The Allies finally reacted to the Polish invasion, and World War II began.

Canaris and his director of sabotage, Erwin von Lahousen, helped plan German wartime operations, but both tried to hamper them. In 1940 a leak of information on German strategy to the Belgian representative at the Vatican caused Canaris to be investigated, but nothing was proved against him.

Three years later, suspected of sabotaging the German campaign in Italy, Canaris was again investigated by the Nazis. This time derogatory material on him came to light, but the matter rested there for reasons that have never been explained. The Abwehr, however, was disbanded early in 1944, Hitler's charge against it being inefficiency.

Although Canaris, now with another post in the armed services, refused to join the bomb plot of July 20, 1944—the attempt to assassinate Hitler that merely injured him—the former head of the Abwehr knew of the plot and, naturally, failed to report it. He was arrested, held in jail for a period, and then barbarously executed as Hitler, faced with destruction, wreaked vengeance on his enemies.

Canaris remains an example of a German who tried to destroy Hitler without destroying Germany and failed in the attempt.

See also ABWEHR; BLACK ORCHESTRA; LAHOUSEN, ERWIN VON.

FURTHER READING: Fabian von Schlabrendorff, *The Secret War against Hitler,* (1965); *Roger Manvell and Heinrich Fraenkel, *The Canaris Conspiracy: The Secret Resistance to Hitler in the German Army* (1969); André Brissaud, *Canaris: Biography of the Head of German Military Intelligence* (1974).

Carbonari *(1806-31)*   Italian republican underground.

The word "carbonari" means "charcoal burners." It was adopted as a name apparently because men of this profession, traveling around Italy from one job to another, already formed a loose kind of secret society. The founders of the political movement, however, were officers of the French forces that occupied southern Italy in 1806 during the Napoleonic Wars, when Joseph Bonaparte, Napoleon's brother, became king of Naples. The Carbonari established secret lodges where plans for a republic were drawn up and spies assigned to espionage duties in Naples and in the Neapolitan region. When Napoleon replaced King Joseph with Marshal Joachim Murat in 1808, the Carbonari continued their clandestine activities against the regime. The fall of Napoleon in 1815 caused hope in the lodges, but this was disappointed by the return of the Bourbon monarchy, which Napoleon had driven into exile, in the person of King Ferdinand IV. The conspirators led a rebellion against the Bourbons in 1820. The Austrians intervened to suppress the rebellion, and hope for a Neapolitan republic faded.

Meanwhile, the underground movement spread to northern Italy, which became riddled with Carbonari and police spies operating against one another amid the individual violence and mass fear that such confrontations always create. In 1831 the Carbonari inspired revolts in Bologna, Parma, and Modena —a final effort at republicanism easily put down by the authorities in those cities. Then the Carbonari disintegrated, first because violence clearly could not achieve their goal and second because Giuseppe Mazzini showed that political methods were more efficacious in the fight for the freedom of Italy.

FURTHER READING: Baron Bertoldi (?), *The Memoirs of the Secret Societies of Southern Italy* (1821); *Harold Acton, *The Bourbons of Naples, 1734–1825* (1956); Denis Mack Smith, *Italy: A Modern History* (1969), follows the Carbonari from their beginning to their end.

Carré, Mathilde (1908-70?) French double agent for Germany during World War II.

Carré, the daughter of an engineer named Belard, was born and educated in Paris and attended the Sorbonne during the 1930s. Following the German victory over France in 1940, she joined a French underground organization working for the Special Operations Executive (SOE), based in Britain. Her code name was "the Cat," and for a year she sent messages in code to headquarters in London; this information was used in planning clandestine SOE operations on the Continent.

In 1941 the Germans arrested Carré and "turned her around," persuading her to work for them. Her evidence allowed them to break up the spy network she belonged to. Since her betrayal was not known in London, her broadcasts across the Channel were still believed, although now they contained only messages the Germans dictated. In 1942, on orders from Berlin, she "escaped" by motorboat from Brittany and reached Britain, where she was supposed to spy on the Allies for the Germans. A French SOE agent, suspicious of her, reported his suspicion. Confronted, she confessed everything she knew about German intelligence.

However, as her accuser was seized by the Germans on the next mission that took him to France and as the leak was traced to Carré, her second turnaround was not accepted at face value. The British interned her for the duration of the war and then sent her back to Paris, where in 1949 a French court condemned her to death, a sentence that was commuted to life imprisonment. Released in 1954, she is remembered as the "Mata Hari of World War II."

See also SPECIAL OPERATIONS EXECUTIVE.

FURTHER READING: Mathilde Carré, *I Was the Cat* (1960); Jean Overton Fuller, *The German Penetration of SOE: France, 1941–1944* (1975); *Lauran Paine, *Mathilde Carré: Double Agent* (1976).

Casanova, Giacomo *(1725-98)* Venetian adventurer, writer, and undercover agent in the service of King Louis XV of France.

Born in Venice, the son of stage players, Casanova became an occultist dabbling in sorcery, one reason why the Venetian authorities imprisoned him in 1755. He made a daring escape in 1756, traveled to Paris, and met an old friend, Cardinal François de Bernis, whom he had known in Venice. Bernis, now the French foreign minister, drew him into the service of King Louis XV as an undercover agent for special assignments.

At that time, the British had a garrison in Dunkirk and used the harbor for their warships under the terms of the Treaty of Utrecht (1713). In 1757, with the Seven Years' War (1756–63) raging and France pitted against Great Britain, Bernis wanted to send a spy into Dunkirk who could report on the size and state of the British flotilla. Casanova accepted the assignment, went to Dunkirk, and ingratiated himself with a number of British naval officers by posing as a former officer of the Venetian navy. One captain took him out and showed him over the warship he commanded. As a result, Casanova returned to Paris with all the information Bernis had hoped for.

Later in 1757 Casanova encountered a mystery man of the time, Count Saint-Germain, in Paris. Saint-Germain was also an undercover agent for the government of Louis XV. The two met again at The Hague in 1759, when both were charged with secret missions to the Dutch government. Casanova had arranged a Dutch loan to France in 1758, but in 1759 he failed in his mission, as did Saint-Germain (we cannot ascertain what these missions actually were).

Both men resumed their wandering from one nation to another. Their paths crossed for the last time in 1763 at Tournai. Saint-Germain, a professed alchemist, tried, according to Casanova, to prove he could turn base metals into gold by accepting a coin from Casanova, making cryptic motions with it —and palming a gold piece off on him.

In the Low Countries, Casanova took the title "de Seingalt," which he used for the rest of his life. His was a vagabond life of love affairs and confidence games, but also of writing, music, and scholarship. At the nadir of his fortunes he served as a spy for the Venetian inquisitors of state (1774–82), when he informed on the practitioners of sorcery, of which he had once been one.

He ended as librarian to Graf von Waldstein, whom he joined in 1785 in the ducal palace at Dux, in Bohemia. Casanova, who had written poetry, opera, and history and had made a place for himself in science fiction with his futuristic romance, *Icosameron,* spent his years at Dux mainly on the memoirs that rank among the classics of this literary type.

See also SAINT-GERMAIN, COUNT.

FURTHER READING: Pierre Gaxotte, *Louis the Fifteenth and His Times* (1934); *Giacomo Casanova, *History of My Life* (1962); Bonamy Dobrée, *Three Eighteenth Century Figures* (1962), includes Casanova among the three.

Cavell, Edith *(1865-1915)* British nurse and secret agent in German-occupied Belgium during World War I.

Cavell, born in Norfolk into a middle-class family, decided to follow the example of Florence Nightingale, the heroic nurse of Victorian Britain, and in 1895 she entered the nursing profession. After service in British hospitals, she went to Belgium in 1907 to become matron of the Berkendael Medical Institute in Brussels, where she served with distinction for seven years.

Cavell remained at her post in 1914 when the Germans invaded and overran Belgium at the outbreak of World War I. The speed of the German advance trapped thousands of Allied soldiers—Belgian, French, and British—behind the lines. Many of these men went into hiding and tried to make their way to safety in France or in neutral Holland. A Belgian underground formed to help them with hiding places, food, and forged identity cards.

Some injured or sick soldiers arrived at the Berkendael Medical Institute, where Cavell had the responsibility for seeing that they were cared for. What was to be done with them when they were cured? Unwilling to turn them over to the Germans, she began keeping their presence at the medical institute a secret until they could slip into the underground. They were then directed clandestinely from house to house through German-occupied territory. Belgian guides at the end of the chain conducted them, often within earshot of the enemy, to points from which they could get through to the Allied lines.

It is estimated that 200 Allied soldiers were sheltered at the medical institute and saved from German prison camps during the years in which Cavell was a secret agent of the underground. German counterintelligence realized that Allied soldiers were escaping from Belgium, but the underground remained in operation until a member was arrested in 1915 while carrying a notebook with a list of names, including that of Edith Cavell.

A German court-martial found her guilty, and she was executed by a firing squad. Her reputed final words were a defense of universal humanitarianism: "As I stand here in the presence of Eternity, I find that patriotism is not enough."

FURTHER READING: Helen Judson, *Edith Cavell* (1941); *Rowland Ryder, *Edith Cavell: A Biography* (1975).

Cell   The lowest and most expendable group in an espionage network. *See* NETWORK.

Center, the   Moscow headquarters of the Soviet espionage establishment.

The Center is made up of two sections, the GRU (Chief Intelligence Directorate of the General Staff of the Red Army), or military intelligence, and the KGB (Committee for State Security), which handles all other Soviet espionage activities. The two sections have often been rivals in the past, but today the GRU is definitely the junior partner.

The GRU naturally had enormous leeway during World War II, when the critical problem was to obtain information on the German armed forces. The GRU was, for example, the section that handled the Rado spy ring in Switzerland, from which came a flood of Nazi battle plans during the Nazi-Soviet conflict of World War II. Leading operatives of the GRU receive military rank in the Soviet armed forces, and that was how Alexander Foote became a major when he joined the Rado ring.

Now, however, the KGB has the dominant role at the Center, because it is the civilian branch tied directly to the Russian leaders in the Kremlin, who have shown a determination not to let the Soviet armed forces acquire too much power. While the GRU has its own espionage agents, they must pass scrutiny by the KGB; however, the KGB can act on its own, without deferring to the GRU.

The Center has a director, under whom function the heads of the GRU and the KGB. In 1947 an attempt was made to unify the Center by bringing the rival sections together in one overall organization, but the attempt failed because the rivalry was too strong, and Stalin apparently thought the results would not be worth the trouble.

See also FOOTE, ALEXANDER; KGB.

FURTHER READING: David Dallin, *Soviet Espionage* (1955); *Ronald Seth, *Unmasked! The Story of Soviet Espionage* (1965); David Wise and Thomas B. Ross, *The Espionage Establishment* (1967), is a comparative study of espionage systems.

Chambers, Whittaker *(1901-61)*   American journalist, spy for the Soviet Union, and informer on Soviet spies in the United States.

The son of a journalist, Chambers was born in Philadelphia and raised in Lynbrook, New York, on Long Island. His early life was a mean one, in which his father disappeared for three years (1908–11) and did little to help the family on returning. Chambers graduated from high school in 1919. He entered Columbia University in 1920 but was forced to leave in 1922 for writing a blasphemous play. He led an aimless life in America and Europe until 1925, when he joined the Communist party in New York, rising to become an editor of the *Daily Worker.* He married Esther Shemitz, a Communist, in 1931, and with her encouragement joined a Communist underground group. In 1934 he moved to Baltimore under orders to act as a courier, known as "Karl," carrying copies of classified documents from Communist spies in the U.S. government to a Russian contact.

Growing disillusioned with Communism, Chambers decided to break with the party in 1937, and two years later the alliance of the Soviet Union with Nazi Germany prompted him to turn informer. He went to Assistant Secretary of State Adolf Berle and said that Berle's aide, Alger Hiss, was a Communist. Berle took no action, and Chambers returned to *Time* magazine, where he was a writer. In 1948 Chambers repeated his charge against Hiss before the House Committee on Un-American Activities, displaying much detailed knowledge about Hiss and his wife, Priscilla. Chambers attributed his knowledge to having lived with the Hisses during the 1930s, when Hiss brought classified documents home from the State Department, Priscilla typed copies, and Chambers delivered the copies to a Russian contact. Chambers backed up his story that Hiss was a spy for the Soviet Union by producing films of documents, four notes in Hiss's handwriting, and 65 copies typed on the Hiss typewriter. Later Chambers handed over the celebrated "Pumpkin Papers," documents he had hidden in a hollowed-out pumpkin in a field on his farm in Maryland.

Meanwhile, the committee had arranged a confrontation of the two men in which Hiss, after expressing doubt because the appearance of Chambers was changed by much dental work, finally identified his accuser as "George Crosley," a journalist he had met a few times in the 1930s. Hiss challenged Chambers to repeat the charge away from the committee, in some public place not covered by official immunity. Chambers did so on the radio program *Meet the Press.* Hiss sued for slander. The Justice Department brought Hiss before a grand jury, which indicted him for lying when he said he had not met Chambers in 1938 and had never given him State Department documents. The grand jury, while agreeing that Chambers could have learned so much about Hiss only by living in his house, made the typewritten copies the basis of their decision, holding that those dated 1938 had been typed on the Hiss machine in the Hiss home.

Alger Hiss went on trial in 1949, but a hung jury resulted (eight to four for conviction). A second trial in 1950 ended in a guilty verdict, and Hiss went to jail for perjury. Chambers professed no animosity toward Hiss, whom he described as a friend as well as a coconspirator during the 1930s and whom he said he had tried to draw out of the spy network after his own break with it. (Hiss naturally denied everything.) To justify himself, Chambers wrote his version of these events. Suffering from depression, he several times thought of committing suicide, but a new-found religious faith appears to have held him back until he died a natural death.

See also HISS, ALGER; HISS CASE.

FURTHER READING: *Whittaker Chambers, *Witness* (1952); Alger Hiss, *In the Court of Public Opinion* (1957), is Hiss's rebuttal of Chambers; Allen Weinstein, *Perjury: The Hiss-Chambers Case* (1979).

CHEKA *(1917-22)* Extraordinary Commission for Combating Counterrevolution and Sabotage (the name originally given to the Soviet intelligence system now known as the KGB).
See KGB.

Church, Benjamin *(1734-77?)* American doctor and spy for the British during the American Revolution.

Born in Newport, Rhode Island, and raised in Boston, Massachusetts, Church was the son of a clergyman. Educated at the Boston Latin School and at Harvard, from which he graduated in 1754, he studied medicine, went to London, came home with an English wife as well as a medical degree, and soon became a fashionable physician in Boston. He also gained a reputation as a literary man, especially as a versifier.

With the Stamp Act crisis of 1765, when the British government provoked resistance in the American colonies by laying a tax on stamps, Church began a double life that lasted for ten years. Outwardly, he was a Patriot who wrote and spoke against King George III and his ministers. Covertly, Church was a Loyalist spy reporting to the British governor of Massachusetts. He played the former role so well that he was accepted by a group of American spies watching the British in Boston (1773) and was elected a delegate to the Massachusetts Provincial Congress (1774), the Patriot alternative to the British administration in the colony.

After fighting broke out at Lexington and Concord (1775), Church reported regularly to General Thomas Gage, the British governor in Boston, on American preparations for further armed resistance. At the same time, Church served on the Patriot Committee of Safety and was chosen to be one member of the two-man delegation that officially welcomed General George Washington on his arrival to take command of the colonial forces besieging the British in Boston.

Now surgeon general of those forces, Church was in a position to send Gage top-secret information from Washington's military councils. He continued to do so until one of his couriers was caught, a woman attempting to slip into Boston with a message in code. She admitted that Church had given her the message to deliver. Decoded by Washington's cryptologists, it described the conditions, numbers, and weapons of the American forces.

A court-martial found Church guilty. Washington merely dismissed him from the service, but the Continental Congress ordered him to be imprisoned. In 1777, Church, exchanged for a captured American doctor, set sail for the British West Indies.

FURTHER READING: Allen French, *General Gage's Informers: New Material Upon Lexington and Concord, Benjamin Thompson as Loyalist and the Treachery of Benjamin Church* (1932); Carl Van Doren, *Secret History of the American Revolution* (1941); Burke Davis, *George Washington and the American Revolution* (1975).

Church Committee *(1975-76)* The Senate Select Committee on Intelligence, headed by Senator Frank Church of Idaho, that investigated the CIA. *See* CIA.

Churchill, Peter *(1909-72)* British spy in France during World War II.

Born in Amsterdam, Churchill was the son of a diplomat attached to the British Embassy. He was sent back to England to be educated, took his degree from Cambridge, and between the wars worked at jobs that varied from silver fox farming to the consular service. In 1939 he entered the British army just before the German invasion of Poland touched off World War II (1939–45). Churchill's experience on the Continent and his command of languages led to his being shifted to the Special Operations Executive (SOE), the organization formed in London to direct clandestine operations against the Germans following their sweep across Europe and conquest of France.

Given the code name "Raoul," and assigned to aid underground networks in the south of France, Churchill reached his destination four times, twice landing from submarines and twice parachuting from planes. In between, he slipped back to Britain to report on his progress. Most of his work was done in 1942, when he met secret agents of the French resistance, provided them with money, and radioed information to London. His radio operator was Odette Sansom, also of the SOE. In 1943 the Germans seized Churchill and Sansom on word from a French spy already in jail. Taken to Germany, they were separated, Sansom being sent to the women's camp at Ravensbruck, from which she was rescued by Allied soldiers near the end of the war. Churchill survived because the Germans thought he was related to Prime Minister Winston Churchill, and therefore of possible value in negotiating with the British government. Churchill, too, was liberated by Allied troops as Germany collapsed.

In storybook fashion, Churchill and Sansom married when they got back to London. However, they were divorced in 1955. Churchill remarried and went to the south of France, where he dabbled in real estate.

See also SANSOM, ODETTE; SPECIAL OPERATIONS EXECUTIVE.

FURTHER READING: Jerrard Tickell, *Odette: The Story of a British Spy* (1949); *Peter Churchill, *Duel of Wits* (1957); M. R. D. Foot, *SOE in France: An Account of the Work of the British Special Operations Executive in France, 1940–1944* (1966).

CIA Principal intelligence organization of the United States.

When President Harry Truman closed the Office of Strategic Services in 1945 on the ground that its intelligence operations were strictly a necessity of World War II and had no place in peacetime, it seemed that the United States would not need an overall spy system in the foreseeable future. The Cold War quickly showed otherwise as the Soviet Union pressed its campaign of espionage and subversion against other nations. Alarmed by the hostility of the Kremlin, Congress in 1947 passed the National Security Act, which established the CIA (Central Intelligence Agency) as a permanent part of the U.S. government.

The National Security Act placed the CIA under the control of the National Security Council (NSC), which made it an arm of the executive branch of government, although subject to congressional oversight. The director of the CIA, reporting to the NSC on the operations of his own organization, would at the same time act as a connecting link between all American intelligence bureaus, including those of the armed forces. The CIA was supposed to be responsible for overseas espionage, domestic counterespionage being left to the FBI (Federal Bureau of Investigation). Thus, the National Security Act said that the CIA would have "no police, subpoena, law-enforcement powers, or internal security functions." The document also stated, however, that the CIA would be expected "to perform such other functions and duties related to intelligence affecting the national security as the National Security Council may from time to time direct." This clause led to subsequent CIA operations in the United States, in spite of the general tenor of the National Security Act, which most members of Congress assumed ruled out domestic spying.

The CIA grew into one of the biggest and certainly the best known of the world's major intelligence organizations. Today it employs about 20,000 people, more than half at its headquarters in Langley, Virginia, and the rest at its offices in Washington and in other cities from Boston to Los Angeles. The Intelligence Division has charge of the gathering of information from a myriad of sources, such as newspapers, books, reports published by foreign governments, and the speeches of diplomats at the United Nations. The Research Division handles technical and scientific problems, and the Support Division handles connections between headquarters and operatives in the field. The Plans Division manages covert operations. This is the general structure of the CIA, which has gone through three major phases.

The postwar phase lasted from the passage of the National Security Act until Watergate (see below). There was at the start a rush to fill the intelligence vacuum, a problem for which Americans were not prepared, inexperienced as they were with peacetime espionage. The national feeling had been expressed by Secretary of State Henry Stimson in 1929 when he said, while ending

Herbert O. Yardley's cryptanalysis of foreign documents in code: "Gentlemen do not read each other's mail."

The aggressions of the Soviet Union put an end to this naïveté in Washington, especially the ruthless coup engineered by the MVD (Ministry of Internal Affairs, 1946–54), later the KGB (Committee for State Security, Soviet intelligence), in Czechoslovakia in 1948, which President Truman denounced as "an outrage." Other steps along the American path to disillusionment were the Soviet attack on Hungary (1956) and the Kremlin's repression of the "Prague spring" (1968), when the Czechs made a bid for greater freedom under the leadership of Alexander Dubcek. Reacting to such events, the U.S. government strengthened the CIA by adding the Plans Division in 1951 and the Domestic Operations Division in 1964. Congress, at the same time, failed to impose more stringent controls or to insist on a strict monitoring system with regard to CIA operations.

Acting in secrecy and sometimes with a large degree of freedom, the organization moved against Communist expansion. In so doing, it produced a record of successes and excesses. In 1948, while Admiral Roscoe Hillenkoetter was director (the first), the CIA participated in a letter-writing campaign to help persuade the voters of Italy to oppose Communist candidates in the elections of that year. In 1953, when General Walter Bedell Smith was director, CIA agents supported the uprising in Iran that overthrew Premier Mohammed Mossadegh, who seemed to be driving his country into chaos and therefore inviting Soviet intervention. The directorship of Smith's successor, Allen Dulles (1953–61), produced a flurry of activity. The CIA supported the enemies of a pro-Communist regime in Guatemala (1954); dug the Berlin Tunnel and tapped telephone messages between East Berlin and Moscow (1955–56); obtained, directly or indirectly, a copy of the secret speech in the Kremlin in which Soviet premier Nikita Khrushchev exposed the crimes of Stalin (1956); directed the espionage flights of the U-2 spy planes over the Soviet Union (1956–60); and produced intelligence reports on Vietnam that President John Kennedy used when he resolved to commit American noncombat forces to the battlefield (1961). Kennedy removed Dulles because the President felt that the CIA let him down by being so optimistic about the Bay of Pigs operation in Cuba, when Cuban exiles landed on the island and were easily rounded up by the troops of Premier Fidel Castro (1961).

Kennedy's confidence in the CIA revived in the following year, when John McCone was director. A CIA spy plane brought back pictures in 1962 of Soviet offensive missile sites in Cuba, proving that the Russians had broken their promise not to install such weapons. Kennedy confronted Khrushchev and forced him to back down (the Cuban missile crisis). In 1963 the assassination of President Kennedy again raised questions about the competence of the CIA, which possessed derogatory information about the alleged assassin, Lee Harvey Oswald, but lost track of Oswald at the critical moment. It was also McCone's CIA that in 1964 aided the rebels who overthrew and murdered Patrice Lumumba, premier of the Congo Republic. The next director of the CIA, Admiral William Raborn, served during 1965 and 1966 in comparative calm.

With Richard Helms as director (1966–73), the post-Watergate phase began for the CIA. The revelation that three of the burglars involved in the break-in at Democratic headquarters in Washington's Watergate complex in 1972 had been CIA agents caused some critics of the organization to denounce it as a tool of the White House. Although Watergate testimony proved that the CIA had resisted pressure from the Nixon administration, derogatory information about the CIA came from other sources. This continued under Director William Colby (1973–76), who took over following the brief tenure of James Schlesinger in 1973. The CIA was attacked for conspiring against leftist movements in other nations and was accused of plotting to assassinate leaders like Castro. It was shown to have used the loophole in the National Security Act to indulge in domestic spying on American citizens, as well as on foreigners in the United States. It stood accused of experimenting on unwitting subjects, sometimes with mind-altering drugs, of making secret agreements with universities and professors to carry out assigned projects, and of contributing "laundered" funds to professional associations unaware of the source of the money.

In this welter of activities, supplemented by inference, guesswork, and rumor, both the friends and the enemies of the CIA found the evidence they needed to justify their positions. Opponents of the CIA fastened on the derogatory material and condemned the organization. Some, including former CIA agents disillusioned by their experience, proposed that the agency be dismantled. Defenders of the CIA declared that the indictment was exaggerated and that the acts condemned were justified as attempts to prevent pro-Soviet regimes from coming to power. To the defenders, the genuine and proven misdeeds of the CIA were serious flaws. Spokesmen for the CIA generally argued that almost everything could be justified as a proper reaction to Soviet aggression and subversion. The candor of some spokesmen was impugned. Helms was accused in the Senate of lying when he denied that the CIA conducted covert operations in Chile against the Marxist government overthrown in 1973. Colby received the same treatment when he said he knew nothing of CIA conspiracies in Angola in 1975.

Given this heated dispute, both presidents and Congress decided to act. As early as 1966 President Lyndon Johnson had ordered an end to secret CIA financial backing for private groups. In 1975 President Gerald Ford prohibited assassination plots against foreign leaders and established the Rockefeller Commission to investigate the CIA; the Rockefeller Commission's report termed the institution essentially sound, although guilty of some unlawful acts that should not be repeated. Also in 1975 the Senate Select Committee on Intelligence began its hearings. It was called the "Church Committee" after Chairman Frank Church of Idaho, who asked at the start whether the CIA was "a rogue elephant running amok." In the end, Church agreed with his colleagues, who declared in their report (1976) that the characterization was unjustified even though tighter congressional controls should be imposed on the CIA. When President Jimmy Carter took office in 1977, he tended to agree with this verdict.

Three years later, he had changed his mind about the controls, as had congressional leaders and some former enemies of the CIA, which entered its third phase, the post-Afghanistan and post-Iran phase. The Soviet invasion of Afghanistan and the seizure of the American hostages in Iran in 1979 created a conviction that what America needed was a stronger CIA able to act more quickly because less hampered by controls. In 1980, Congress passed and Carter signed the Intelligence Oversight Act, which restricted monitoring rights in Congress to the Senate and House intelligence committees, provided for only eight congressional leaders to be informed in extraordinary circumstances, and allowed the President to withhold prior notification at times. The proponents of the changes claimed they had been vindicated when the fact became known that the CIA had, in nearly complete secrecy, provided the forged passports that in 1980 assisted the rescue under Canadian auspices of seven of the American hostages held captive in Tehran. Congress also began in 1980 the process of legislating against former agents of the CIA who released classified information they had acquired on the job or who endangered active agents by revealing their identities.

See also BAY OF PIGS; BERLIN TUNNEL; CUBAN MISSILE CRISIS; DULLES, ALLEN; FBI; OSS; U-2; WATERGATE; YARDLEY, HERBERT O.

FURTHER READING: David Wise and Thomas B. Ross, *The Espionage Establishment* (1967), has a generally negative chapter on the CIA as it was at the time; Lyman B. Kirkpatrick, Jr., *The Real CIA* (1968), is favorable to the organization; Victor Marchetti and John D. Marks, *The CIA and the Cult of Intelligence* (1974), is very critical; Philip Agee, *Inside the Company: CIA Diary* (1975), is a denunciation by an embittered former agent; °Ray S. Cline, *Secrets, Spies and Scholars: Blueprint of the Essential CIA* (1976), is a balanced book on the subject; Robert L. Borosage and John Marks (eds.), *The CIA File* (1976), has hostile comments by a number of critics and a defense by former Director William Colby; Harry Rositzke, *The CIA's Secret Operations: Espionage, Counterespionage, and Covert Action* (1977), is moderately critical; William Colby, *Honorable Men: My Life in the CIA* (1978), is a self-defense by a former director; Cord Meyer, *Facing Reality: From World Federation to the CIA* (1980), is laudatory.

Cicero   Code name of an Albanian spy for the Germans in Istanbul during World War II.

See BAZNA, ELYEZA.

Cipher   Secret writing based on the manipulation of symbols representing letters of the alphabet.

Ciphers contrast with codes, which represent entire words, phrases, or sentences, rather than single letters, and with ciphony ("enciphered telephony"), which involves the scrambling of telephone conversations. Ciphers and codes are often combined for double security, the coded message being sent in cipher, where great issues of international relations are concerned, especially in wartime.

Cryptology, the science of ciphers, has three parts: cryptography (the enciphering of messages), cryptograms (the enciphered messages), and cryptanalysis (the deciphering of messages). The system begins with a plaintext, which is the message in ordinary language, and then goes through the process of concealment before emerging at the end in the same plaintext as at the start. The concealment process takes two forms, from which the cryptographer may choose—transposition and substitution.

In transposition, all the letters in the message are retained but are shifted to different positions. Mere transposition is rarely used for really important matters—it can be broken too easily by inspection or trial and error. It has, however, appeared in strange places. The code name "Dora" of World War II was nothing more than an anagram (the simplest of transposition ciphers) of "Rado," the name of the Soviet spymaster in Switzerland.

In substitution, letters are represented by other letters or symbols. Julius Caesar is said to have communicated with his generals and political allies in a cipher that moved each letter three places forward in the alphabet, D standing for A, E for B, and so on. Francis Bacon invented a biliteral ("two letter") cipher using just A and B such that AAAAA stood for A, AAAAB for B, AAABB for C, AABAB for D, and so through the alphabet, the two letters providing all the necessary combinations. Nonalphabetic substitutions can use numbers, proofreaders' marks, musical notes, geometrical forms, or purely arbitrary signs such as straight lines at different angles, as on the face of a clock.

The simplest method of using a substitution cipher is to stick to a single, easily remembered system, say the Julius Caesar cipher, that is known to both the writer and the recipient of the message. If many messages are sent in this way, a cryptanalyst may be able to find the pattern and break the cipher; therefore, professional cryptographers constantly shift from one system to another. For example, if as in the Julius Caesar cipher the first message shifts each letter three places ahead, the second message could shift ten ahead, the third message seven, and the rest according to whatever logic has been agreed on at the start. The cryptanalyst then has to break a new cipher each time and has only one example to work on. This pattern is too simple for practical use, but it demonstrates the essential characteristic of advanced cryptography.

The most celebrated cipher in history is the Vigenère table invented by Blaise de Vigenère, a sixteenth-century French cryptologist. The alphabet is written out completely on each line of a square, except that each line begins one letter behind the one above it, the first line beginning A, B, C, the second B, C, D, the third C, D, E, and the last Z, A, B. The key tells the recipient which line a letter is in and how far across the line to go to find it. Since the lines are all different, each gives a different representation of every letter.

Concentric circles, each bearing the letters of the alphabet, can reveal a message when the interior circle is spun so as to bring its letters into alignment with those on the outside. A vastly complicated refinement uses rotors, with several wheels spinning independently around an axle. A system of rotors connected to electrical typewriters formed the basis of the German Enigma machine of so much consequence in World War II.

All such systems have become outmoded; today, use is made of computers capable of working out extremely abstract and complicated ciphers. In 1978 the National Security Agency of the United States established a "data encryption standard" according to which a key has to be fifty-six numbers long, an indication of the incredible complexity of the system, which in fact the Senate Select Committee on Intelligence termed "unbreakable." The description is probably one that will not last for long given the current pace of technological progress. All the "unbreakable" ciphers of the past have in fact been broken, and there is little doubt that computers will be devised that can read messages enciphered by other computers. Cryptographers and cryptanalysts may well leapfrog one another into the future.

See also CIPHONY; CODE; ENIGMA; SECRET WRITING.

FURTHER READING: *David Kahn, *The Codebreakers: The Story of Secret Writing* (1967); Abraham Sinkov, *Elementary Cryptanalysis: A Mathematician's Approach* (1968); Norman Bruce, *Secret Warfare: The Battle of Codes and Ciphers* (1973).

Ciphony   The technology of concealing or uncovering secret messages transmitted by telephone.

The word "ciphony," a conflation of "cipher" and "telephony," refers to a form of cryptology that concerns the spoken word. Since the telephone converts sounds into an electric current, whatever is said openly can be enciphered by tampering with the current. Similarly, deciphering is achieved by restoring the normal current.

A scrambler tampers with the current in various ways, of which common examples are masking the voice by adding noise to the sound, shifting frequencies to make the voice a mere squeak, and transposing syllables out of their normal order so that the result in gibberish. This is the cryptography of ciphony. The cryptanalysis is the development of a descrambler that will restore the current to its pristine form and render the talk intelligible.

A scrambler is used when it would be inconvenient for one or more speakers to resort to other types of enciphered speech. During World War II, an elaborate system of machines handled by a team of engineers distorted the transatlantic telephone conversations between Prime Minister Winston Churchill in London and President Franklin Roosevelt in Washington. The two wartime leaders discussed their plans without hesitation because they believed nobody listening in could make sense of what they said.

Unknown to them, the Germans were not only listening in but also understanding every word. A team from the research institute of the German post office, led by engineer Kurt Vetterlein, devised a descrambler in 1942. The Germans then were able to understand the Churchill-Roosevelt conversations as if they had been coming across in plain English. That was how the Germans learned of the 1943 Allied plan to knock Italy out of the war. The scrambling system was changed in 1944 and never cracked thereafter, but Vetterlein had achieved one of the great breakthroughs of German ciphony.

See also CIPHER.

FURTHER READING: E. Schroter, *Research on Speech Scrambling in Germany* (1946); David Kahn, *The Codebreakers: The Story of Secret Writing* (1967); *David Kahn, *Hitler's Spies: German Military Intelligence in World War II* (1978), has an account of Vetterlein's achievement in breaking the Churchill-Roosevelt scrambler.

Coast Watchers *(1942-44)*   Network of Australian spies on islands conquered by the Japanese during World War II.

The origins of the Coast Watchers went back to 1919, when the Australians established a new kind of security system on the offshore islands and in the broad underpopulated areas of the continent. Civil servants, soldiers, planters, missionaries, and local peoples belonged to this network and reported on conditions as they observed them.

In 1942, with the lightning advance of the Japanese through the South Pacific, many Coast Watchers remained near or behind the enemy lines. They now became a department of the Allied Intelligence Bureau (AIB). Lieutenant Commander Eric Feldt, of the Royal Australian Navy, headed the Coast Watchers, collating their reports for each campaign.

The Coast Watchers, often reporting clandestinely by radio close to the enemy lines, sent information about Japanese landings in the islands, troop strength, and the rendezvous of naval flotillas and air squadrons. The AIB used this information in planning the espionage and sabotage operations that preceded the victorious Allied military campaigns through Guadalcanal (1942), the Solomons (1943), and New Guinea (1944).

See also ALLIED INTELLIGENCE BUREAU.

FURTHER READING: °Eric Feldt, *The Coast Watchers* (1959); Malcolm Wright, *If I Die: Coast-watching and Guerrilla Warfare behind Japanese Lines* (1965); D. C. Horton, *Fire over the Islands: Coast Watchers of the Philippines* (1970).

Code Secret communication system based on symbols representing words, phrases, or sentences.

Codes contrast with ciphers, which represent letters of the alphabet, and with ciphony ("enciphered telephony"), which involves the scrambling of telephone conversation. A coded message may be put into cipher before being dispatched, thus increasing the difficulty of the task faced by a cryptanalyst trying to read the message. Codes can also be combined with ciphony, since codes, unlike ciphers, can make use of sound. Indeed, a mere knock on a door in a prearranged manner is among the commonest of codes. The "code words" of political rhetoric are understood by listeners to be surrogates for the words the speaker really has in mind. Code names beamed by radio into hostile territory cover the identity of spies operating there.

Codes can also be transmitted visually. A white flag in wartime signifies a request for a pause in the fighting, whether to parley or to arrange a surrender. Most road signs are nonverbal codes.

Nearly any message that can be codified at all can be codified in language (a fake advertisement may be spoken over the radio or published in a newspaper), and writing is the fundamental form. Open written codes are used every day in ordinary transactions for speed and economy, telegraphed messages being a good case in point. Every major business uses codes, open where secrecy is not required, otherwise its own confidential system.

Like ciphers, codes are based on transposition or substitution.

Transposition (distorted word patterns) is too transparent for serious codes. Substitution, on the contrary, is one of the safest types of codification. The key to substitution in high-level intelligence work is contained in a code book, copies of which are possessed by both the sender of the message and the recipient. If there is any danger that either of them might be arrested or kidnapped and their quarters searched, an arbitrary volume is generally selected to keep the fact that it is a code book from being recognized. A Bible, dictionary, or a popular novel is a standard choice, the written code references for each word of the message being to a page, a line, and a numbered position of the line (all of which are usually rendered more secure by systematic shifts, for example, by an addition of three to each, so that page two really means page five).

Wherever a code book seems safe from discovery, as in a national embassy or on a warship at sea, it is a deliberately made-up volume listing the code symbols and their meanings in ordinary language. This kind of code book therefore amounts to a secret glossary in which terms can be looked up and their definitions discovered. When the definitions are substituted for the terms in the codified message, the message can be read. Since long messages in code arrive at embassies and aboard warships, and since the symbols are many and complex, an expert in codes is always assigned to handle the code book.

The advantage of employing a code is that if a cryptanalyst discovers the meaning of a few sets of symbols, this does not enable him or her to break the entire code at once, as would be the case with a cipher. The danger of employing a code is that an enemy may obtain a copy of the code book and read all messages in the code. That is why code books are instantly changed if there is any suspicion that this has happened. It is why the defection of a code clerk from an embassy or other intelligence post causes consternation among his or her superiors.

See also CIPHER; CIPHONY; SECRET WRITING.

FURTHER READING: Dan Tylor Moore and Martha Waller, *Cloak and Cipher* (1962); *David Kahn, *The Codebreakers: The Story of Secret Writing* (1967); Norman Bruce, *Secret Warfare: The Battle of Codes and Ciphers* (1973).

Code Name   An alias or a symbolic designation used by a spy for security in transmitting messages that might be intercepted; always used by the operator of a clandestine radio.

Cohen, Eli *(1924-65)*   Jewish spy for Israel in Egypt and Syria.

Born in Alexandria, Egypt, Cohen was the son of an Orthodox Jewish merchant. His early education took place at home and in the synagogue, and it included a strong attachment to Zionism, the movement for a Jewish homeland in Palestine. He studied for three years (1946–48) at Cairo University, only to be expelled during the anti-Jewish rioting in Egypt that marked the establishment of the state of Israel in 1948.

Cohen went secretly to Israel in 1951, received espionage training, and returned to Cairo to serve as a spy. Three years later orders came from Israeli military intelligence for him and a number of other secret agents to sabotage American buildings in Egypt in an effort to disrupt American-Egyptian relations. Egyptian counterespionage cracked the Israeli spy by means of a double agent, provoking the Lavon affair in Israel (the scandal about who was responsible, named after the Israeli defense minister, Pinhas Lavon).

Cohen was arrested by the Egyptians, but convinced them he knew nothing about the sabotage. Arrested again in 1956, he was expelled from Egypt. In 1957 he reached Israel, where in 1960 he became a full-fledged agent of the Mossad (Central Institution for Intelligence and Special Assignments), the main department of Israeli intelligence.

Assigned to Syria, Cohen arrived in Damascus in 1962 posing as a businessman. For three years, while cultivating government officials and high-ranking military men, he covertly radioed information to Israel from his room. He noted Soviet weapons reaching Syria and even toured the Golan Heights, where he was shown the Syrian defenses in that vital area facing Israel.

Cohen's radio betrayed him in the end; Syrian counterespionage pinpointed his room as the source of clandestine broadcasts. He was arrested in 1965 and executed.

His information helped the Israeli armed forces capture the Golan Heights during the "six-day war" (1967).

See also LAVON AFFAIR.

FURTHER RADING: Ben Dan, *The Spy from Israel* (1969); Joshua Tadmor, *The Silent Warriors* (1969); *Zwy Aldowby and Jerrold Ballinger, *The Shattered Silence: The Eli Cohen Affair* (1971).

Cohen, Two-Gun *(1889-1970)* British director of intelligence for nationalist China until World War II.

Morris Cohen, the son of Polish Jews, was born in London. After a rowdy youth in which he spent some time in a reform school, he went to live with relatives in Canada, where he took jobs as a salesman and carnival barker, while at the same time indulging a penchant for gambling.

A meeting in Edmonton in 1910 with Sun Yat-sen, the leader of the Chinese rebellion against the last emperor of the Manchu dynasty, introduced Cohen to his true vocation. He began purchasing arms for the rebellion, which triumphed under Sun in 1911. Cohen, after service in World War I, migrated to China, where in 1922 Sun appointed him head of intelligence.

Western soldiers of fortune were not unknown in China. Cohen differed from the rest in that he was the trusted adviser of the head of the Chinese government, not a minor figure or doubtful character about whom little is known. The Chinese accepted him and acknowledged his authority as a reflection of Sun Yat-sen's.

Cohen's main work lay in counterespionage—watching enemies of the Sun regime, from warlords to anarchists. His spies operated in the provinces and cities, especially in the coastal ports of Shanghai and Canton, and one of his secret agents is said to have been Isaac Trebitsch Lincoln, the mystery man from the west who spent his last years in the Far East.

Cohen was a flamboyant man of action who led forays into rebellious areas, attacked the headquarters of conspirators, rounded up suspects by the dozen, and put prisoners through tough interrogations. By his own account, he also supervised executions. Wearing one pistol at his shoulder and another on his hip, he gained his nickname—"Two-Gun."

When Sun Yat-sen died in 1925, Cohen continued his intelligence work for Sun's successor, Chiang Kai-shek. The Japanese and the Communists were both becoming a threat to nationalist China, and Cohen reported on both. In 1931 he correctly predicted the Japanese invasion of Manchuria.

During World War II, Cohen, while on a mission in Hong Kong, was seized by the Japanese and jailed for the duration of the war. Replaced by Tai Li as Chiang's intelligence chief and having no place after the Communist victory in 1949, when K'ang Sheng headed Mao Tse-tung's espionage apparatus, Cohen returned to Canada. He was in China briefly in 1956 and 1966 under Madame Sun's patronage before going back to London, where he died.

See also K'ANG SHENG; LINCOLN, ISAAC TREBITSCH; TAI LI.

FURTHER READING: Sven Hedin, *Chiang Kai-shek, Marshal of China* (1940); *Charles Drage, Two-Gun Cohen* (1954); Richard Deacon, *The Chinese Secret Service* (1974).

Colepaugh, William *(1918-   )* American spy for Germany in the United States during World War II.

Born in Niantic, Connecticut, Colepaugh was of German descent on his mother's side of the family, a fact that may have determined his subsequent allegiance. He attended Admiral Farragut Academy in Toms River, New Jersey, and went to the Massachusetts Institute of Technology, where he failed his courses and had to leave. An admirer of Adolf Hitler, the chancellor of Germany who provoked World War II (1939–45), Colepaugh began to spy for the German consul in Boston, reporting on British vessels in the harbor before the United States entered the war in 1941.

Having received naval training at Admiral Farragut, Colepaugh went to sea during the conflict, serving in the U.S. Navy and, after being discharged, probably for his pro-German sympathies, on British and European merchant vessels. In 1944 he sailed to Lisbon, jumped ship, and made his way to German-occupied France. Expressing to the Germans a willingness to serve in their armed forces, he was sent to Berlin, and, after checking by German intelligence, assigned to a spy school in German-occupied Holland. There he met Erich Gimpel, another trainee, who would be his partner on an espionage mission to the United States.

They seemed to complement one another. Gimpel was a technician who could handle such apparatus as radios and cameras, while Colepaugh, a native American, was a good front man since he could speak for the pair and prevent suspicion from developing about his German partner. Their principal assignment was to estimate the effect of German propaganda on the coming presidential election campaign of 1944 between Franklin D. Roosevelt, running for a fourth term, and Republican challenger Thomas E. Dewey. It was thought in Berlin that this could be done by reading newspapers and other public sources. Colepaugh received the cover name "William Charles Cauldwell," while Gimpel called himself "Edward George Green."

Their training finished, they crossed the Atlantic from Kiel in a German submarine, which surfaced in Frenchman Bay, in Maine. The two were rowed ashore in a rubber boat. The boat returned to the submarine while they went to Bangor and took a train to Boston. Continuing on to New York City, they found an apartment and prepared to begin their espionage work. By now the principal reason for their mission had ceased to exist, for the American election was over and Roosevelt had won.

Colepaugh and Gimpel lost their taste for espionage almost as soon as they realized that whatever they learned could not have any effect on the course of the war, which Germany was clearly in the process of losing. Gimpel tried to do some spying, but Colepaugh soon dropped it and began to have a good time spending the money with which they had been supplied. Then he became frightened of the predicament in which he and Gimpel were trapped—two useless spies who nevertheless would face the death penalty if caught. At last he slipped away from Gimpel and got in touch with an agent of the FBI (Federal Bureau of Investigation), to whom he told his story. The FBI began a search for Gimpel, by now himself badly frightened by Colepaugh's disappearance. He was arrested as he stood at a newsstand in New York's Times Square.

Colepaugh and Gimpel were both tried for espionage, found guilty, and sentenced to death. President Harry Truman, America's chief executive after Roosevelt's death in 1945, commuted the sentences to life imprisonment.

See also GIMPEL, ERICH.

FURTHER READING: Karl Bartz, *The Downfall of the German Secret Service* (1956); *Erich Gimpel (with Will Berthold), *Spy for Germany* (1957); David Kahn, *Hitler's Spies: German Military Intelligence in World War II* (1978).

Colonel Passy Code name for General Charles de Gaulle's intelligence chief during World War II.

See DEWAVRIN, ANDRÉ.

Committee of Secret Correspondence *(1775-77)* Committee of the Continental Congress responsible for communicating with agents abroad during the American Revolution.

The Continental Congress, leading the thirteen colonies in their opposition to British rule, established the Committee of Secret Correspondence on November 29, 1775, after the outbreak of hostilities. Its most important members were Benjamin Franklin and John Dickinson, both of Pennsylvania, and John Jay, of New York. The Committee's purpose was to discover how much sympathy for the American cause existed in Britain and in foreign countries, and how that sympathy might be translated into practical assistance.

The men of the committee at first placed most of their hope in Arthur Lee, the secret agent of the Continental Congress in London who was in touch with pro-American British leaders, such as John Wilkes, the former lord mayor of the British capital. As the British government became increasingly anti-American, the committee expanded its activities to include correspondents in most of the European capitals, with emphasis on Silas Deane in Paris because the French, having been defeated by the British in the Seven Years' War (1756–63) and having thereby lost Canada, were anxious to gain revenge by aiding Britain's rebellious colonies to the south of Canada.

Deane alone represented the colonies in Paris at first, and through him the Committee of Secret Correspondence dealt with Pierre Augustin Caron de Beaumarchais, the secret agent of the French government who dispatched supplies to the Americans through his front organization, Roderigue Hortalez et Cie. When the Continental Congress strengthened American representation in Paris by sending Franklin and Lee to join Deane in 1776, these three commissioners reported back to the Committee of Secret Correspondence on the progress of negotiations with the French.

By 1777 the American Revolution had become the American War of Independence, secrecy was no longer necessary, and the Committee of Secret Correspondence gave way to the Committee of Foreign Affairs.

See also BEAUMARCHAIS, PIERRE AUGUSTIN CARON DE; DEANE, SILAS.

FURTHER READING: Edmund C. Burnett, *The Continental Congress* (1941); *Henry Steele Commager and Richard Morris, *The Spirit of 'Seventy-Six* (1958), is a source book; William Stinchcombe, *The American Revolution and the French Alliance* (1969).

Conrad, Thomas *(1838-1904)* Scout and spy for the Confederacy during the American Civil War.

Although a Virginian born in Fairfax and educated in the schools of his state, Conrad went north of the Mason-Dixon line to Pennsylvania to attend Dickinson College, from which he graduated in 1860. He was a teacher and a lay preacher in the Methodist church in Washington when the Civil War broke out in 1861, an event that found him supporting Virginia's secession from the Union.

Because of Conrad's avowed Confederate sympathies, Allan Pinkerton of the Union secret service arrested him. Released on parole, Conrad remained in Washington for nearly two months, during which time he plotted to assassinate General Winfield Scott because Scott, a Virginian, had defied their state and remained head of the Union army. The Confederate government, consulted about the plot, canceled it.

After being sent to Richmond under a prisoner exchange, Conrad joined the cavalry and became a scout and spy for General J. E. B. ("Jeb") Stuart. Conrad both campaigned energetically in the field and served the religious needs of his unit. He finally became chaplain of the Third Virginia Cavalry.

As a spy, he several times slipped through the Federal lines and reached Washington, where he ran an espionage ring that sent information from the Union capital to the Confederate government. Under this system, reports went by courier from Washington to Richmond and from Richmond to Confederate commanders in the field.

In 1862 Conrad had a double agent (who has never been identified) planted in the northern intelligence bureau run by Lafayette Baker, who had succeeded Pinkerton. Conrad thus obtained the Federal plans and troop strengths for the peninsular campaign, when Union General George B. McClellan tried to capture Richmond in a sea-and-land offensive. Alerted, Confederate General Robert E. Lee outmaneuvered McClellan and drove him back. A month later, Conrad's spy ring in Washington provided information about General John Pope that enabled Lee to rout the Federals in the second battle of Bull Run.

Conrad had a hand in the last great engagement of that year, when he discovered that General Ambrose Burnside intended to cross the Rappahannock and mount a drive on Richmond. Leaving Washington and crossing surreptitiously through the Union lines, Conrad carried his message to Lee, who then drew up the strategy for a counterstroke with Stonewall Jackson, one of Lee's commanders who placed much reliance on espionage. The two Confederate commanders dovetailed their efforts and won a shattering victory at the battle of Fredericksburg.

At the time of the battle of Gettysburg in 1863, Conrad for a few brief hours held the fate of Washington, if not of the Civil War, in the palm of his hand. He saw how the Federals rushed their soldiers out of the Union capital to General George Meade as the showdown with Lee approached. Civilians manned most of the defenses, so that a real military force could have easily disposed of them. Conrad rode out to find General Stuart. Had he found him, Washington almost certainly would have fallen to the Confederates. As Stuart said later: "I would have charged down Pennsylvania Avenue!"

Conrad could not locate the fast-moving Confederate cavalry commander. The moment passed, Washington was never threatened again, and the initiative after Gettysburg passed to the Federals.

Not long afterward, Baker became aware of Conrad's spy activities, and Conrad became aware of Baker's knowledge, which ended Conrad's espionage career in Washington. Conrad continued as a scout in the Confederate forces, suffering with them through campaigns that led irresistibly to Lee's surrender to General Ulysses S. Grant at Appomattox in 1865.

After the surrender, Conrad plotted to kidnap President Abraham Lincoln, a plot that might have cost him his life because he resembled John Wilkes

Booth, Lincoln's assassin. Fortunately for Conrad, the Federals got onto Booth's trail and stayed with it to the end.

Conrad returned to private life, served as a clergyman in Virginia, and relived his Civil War exploits in sermons, lectures, books, and private conversations with other veterans of the old days of Robert E. Lee, Jeb Stuart, and the Civil War.

See also BAKER, LAFAYETTE.

FURTHER READING: *Thomas N. Conrad, *Rebel Scout* (1904); Virgil Carrington Jones, *Gray Ghosts and Rebel Raiders* (1956); John Bakeless, *Spies of the Confederacy* (1970).

Coplon, Judith (1922-   ) American spy for the Soviet Union.

Born in Brooklyn, New York, Coplon was the daughter of a prosperous businessman. After high school (1934–38), she entered Barnard College (1939), where she studied Russian and developed romantic illusions about the Soviet Union. Graduating in 1943, she took a job with the Justice Department in New York. She was transferred to Washington in 1945 to work in the foreign agents registration section.

Under the law, persons representing foreign interests in the United States were required to register with the Justice Department. Since the FBI (Federal Bureau of Investigation) had responsibility for seeing that the law was obeyed, Coplon was able to read FBI reports on the conduct of diplomats and the identification of secret agents. She therefore knew what the FBI knew about Soviet espionage in the United States.

This information was so valuable that after Coplon began working as a spy for the Soviet Union, the KGB (Committee for State Security, Soviet intelligence) sent a special agent, Valentin Gubitchev, to America to work with her. Gubitchev's cover was a post with the Soviet delegation to the United Nations. Their method was for Coplon to take classified documents home, type copies, and carry the copies to New York for delivery to Gubitchev.

The first suspicion of Coplon arose when her superiors noticed that her reports had a systematic pro-Soviet bias. The suspicion increased when she asked to see top-secret papers not connected with her departmental work.

In 1948 the FBI, learning that some of its most confidential information was known in Moscow, traced the leak to Coplon. They confirmed her guilt by giving her spurious documents, the contents of which she transmitted to the Russians.

FBI agents shadowed her to New York in 1948 and 1949 and noted her meetings with Gubitchev in out-of-the-way places, where she handed over parcels. The agents sprang their trap in 1949, when Coplon delivered to Gubitchev a false document especially prepared in Washington for the occasion.

The pair of spies, American and Russian, were arrested on the spot. A search of Coplon's rooms turned up a mass of classified documents for which she had no clearance.

Placed on trial in 1950, both were found guilty. In spite of his UN position, Gubitchev could have been jailed, but the U.S. government decided to deport him to the Soviet Union. Coplon received a prison sentence that an appeals court overturned on a technicality involving wiretap evidence. After being freed, she married and settled into a placid domestic existence.

See also GUBITCHEV, VALENTIN.

FURTHER READING: *David Dallin, *Soviet Espionage* (1955); Ronald Seth, *Unmasked! The Story of Soviet Espionage* (1965); Pierre J. Huss and George Capozi, Jr., *Red Spies in the UN* (1965).

Counterespionage   The art and science of combating spies; also, an organization that practices counterespionage.

See COUNTERINTELLIGENCE; COUNTERSPY.

Counterintelligence   An organization that safeguards secret information against spies; also, the methods used in such activity.

See COUNTERESPIONAGE; COUNTERSPY.

Counterspy   A person, usually associated with a counterespionage organization, whose responsibility it is to expose or forestall enemy spies.

A counterspy is a shield, as a spy is a sword.

Since the best way to protect classified information is to stop in advance the spies who would steal it, counterspies are employed. Counterspies usually are professionals with special training in counterespionage, because their spy adversaries are professionals at espionage. Counterspies working at headquarters may perform simple functions, such as clipping newspapers and censoring mail, the purpose being to gather sufficient evidence to deduce what enemy espionage is doing or planning. Another method of thwarting the enemy within one's own lines is to keep suspects under surveillance. Then there is the use of monitoring devices to uncover clandestine radios. An *agent provocateur* is a counterspy who joins a spy or group of spies and then tempts them into incriminating acts, upon which arrests can be made.

The ideal counterspy is a double agent, a member of the rival intelligence system who influences its plans, learns the identity of its spies, and reports all this to the counterespionage organization. A counterspy may be sent to infiltrate the enemy's ranks. A safer technique is to find an agent already in place who can be persuaded to become a double agent. John Le Carré, author of spy thrillers, has popularized the word "mole," meaning a counterspy inside an intelligence organization, and in *Tinker, Tailor, Soldier, Spy* has described the near-demoralization of an intelligence organization's staff when it it suspected that one of them is a mole.

See also MOLE; SPY.

FURTHER READING: *Allen Dulles, *The Craft of Intelligence* (1963); U.S. Department of Defense, Joint Chiefs of Staff Publication No. 1, *Dictionary of Military and Associated Terms* (1972); Dusko Popov, *Spy/Counterspy* (1974).

Courier   A member of a network who conveys messages or delivers documents.

A courier is a link connecting persons in the spy network who for security reasons cannot communicate directly with one another. A photographer who has films of secret documents for the leader, a cut-out who must get an order to an agent in the field, a government official who is willing to pass information to the network but cannot afford to be conspicuous—these are types that need couriers to act as their go-betweens.

Couriers frequently do not know the meaning of the messages or the contents of the documents they deliver. It is not their business to know. Their business is to carry a message or a document from one individual to another without asking questions or losing time. In some cases, they do not even meet the sender or the receiver, but pick up a letter or a package at one drop and deposit it at another.

Although the work of couriers generally is not glamorous, can be performed without any particular intelligence or skill, and may involve nothing more than an occasional assignment, they are indispensable to a network of any complexity. When they go into action, it is often in critical circumstances—for example, when microfilm has to be moved immediately or when a defector must be informed about escape arrangements.

See also NETWORK.

FURTHER READING: *Whittaker Chambers, *Witness* (1952), describes the author's career as a courier for a Soviet network in Washington; U.S. Department of Defense, Joint Chiefs of Staff Publication No. 1, *Dictionary of Military and Associated Terms* (1972).

Cover Name An alias used by a spy to conceal his or her real name while working in the field.

See LEGALS AND ILLEGALS.

Cover Story A fictional explanation of a spy's activities on an espionage mission.

Every adequately prepared espionage mission has two reasons—a good reason and the real reason. The good reason is the spy's cover story. It enables the spy to pass unnoticed in the field of operation and to escape suspicion if challenged. A good cover story explains all the spy's activities on the mission, does not clash with what is known outside the mission, and is plausible to those who hear it. A cover name is usually part of a cover story when the spy is in a foreign country or in occupied territory, the alias being tailored to the particular situation so as to add credibility to the fiction. Ordinary vocations that necessitate travel make good stories—a spy may pose as a salesman, for instance. Defective cover stories are always dangerous. One of the worst examples concerns Francis Gary Powers and his U-2 flight: a spokesman in Washington said Powers must have lost his way! Since the spy plane was a thousand miles inside the Soviet Union, that particular cover story had no plausibility at all. Nobody believed it, least of all the Russians.

See also COVER NAME.

FURTHER READING: Allen Dulles, *The Craft of Intelligence* (paperback ed., 1965); Wolfgang Lotz, *A Handbook for Spies* (1980).

Covert Operation A deceptive, violent, illegal, or immoral activity resorted to clandestinely by one side to affect the affairs of another.

"Covert operations" used to mean almost exclusively sabotage in wartime.

Today the term is broad enough in meaning to include the "dirty tricks" of Watergate, the kidnaping of rebellious satellite leaders by the KGB (Soviet intelligence), and attempts by one nation to influence elections in another. When nations are at war, anything still goes. Enemy leaders may be murdered or kidnaped; dams may be blown up; factories may be burned. In peacetime, covert operations are generally frowned upon by the public, since they involve doing things outside the accepted norms of political and international behavior. The revelation of certain illegal and violent covert operations resorted to by the CIA (Central Intelligence Agency) at home and abroad during the 1960s and 1970s caused much criticism on the American domestic scene.

Yet, some covert operations are legitimate, besides being a fact of life in our time. All espionage systems use them when the conditions seem to call for stronger than normal operations to avoid a presumably disastrous event. Only the Americans, however, are so insistent about making the facts public. One good result of this openness is that some of the more excessive operations have been ruled out. One danger is that acts permitted under international law may be thought illegal by the public, and the CIA may be hampered in its work by fear of criticism. To strike a sensible balance is a fundamental task faced not only by the CIA but also by intelligence organizations in all the democracies.

See also CIA; KGB; WATERGATE.

FURTHER READING: *Harry Howe Ransom, *Central Intelligence and National Security* (1958); Allen Dulles, *The Craft of Intelligence* (1963); Lyman B. Kirkpatrick, Jr., *The U.S. Intelligence Community: Foreign Policy and Domestic Activities* (1973); F. H. Hinsley with E. E. Thomas, C. F. G. Ransom, R. C. Knight, *British Intelligence in the Second World War: Its Influence on Strategy and Operations,* Vol. One (1979), Vol. Two (1981).

Crabb, Lionel (1910-56) British frogman who disappeared while spying on a Soviet warship.

An adventurous Londoner from a working-class family, Crabb joined the British merchant marine in his youth and sailed to ports across the Atlantic and the Pacific. Leaving the service he traveled around the United States during the 1930s, spent some time in Singapore, and in China became a spy for Chiang Kai-shek, the leader of the Chinese in their resistance to aggression by Japan following the Japanese occupation of Manchuria (1931).

In 1939, the year in which World War II broke out, Crabb went to sea again in the British merchant marine, serving as a gunner on vessels running the gauntlet of German submarines in the Atlantic. He then went into the Royal Navy (1940), received a commission (1941), and served in a frogman unit in the Mediterranean, where he operated against Italian warships and naval installations until the surrender of Italy in 1943.

Receiving his discharge after the war in 1948, Crabb continued his frogman career as a civilian, serving in particular with the British fishing fleets in the North Sea. He rejoined the navy in 1952 and was promoted to lieutenant commander, thereby becoming the Commander Crabb of his subsequent career. He left the navy for good in 1955.

Meanwhile, Nikita Khrushchev had risen to power in the Soviet Union as premier and head of the Communist party. He was noted for the personal diplomacy of his tours of the world to talk to international leaders. Khrushchev, accompanied by Nicolai Bulganin, chairman of the Soviet council of ministers, arrived in Britain in 1956 to meet Prime Minister Anthony Eden. Khrushchev and Bulganin made the trip aboard the *Ordzhonikidze,* a Soviet cruiser of modern design, great speed, and easy maneuverability. The cruiser remained tied up at a jetty in Portsmouth harbor while the two Russian leaders went up to London.

Exactly what happened at Portsmouth remains a matter of conjecture, but the most plausible theory is that the British admiralty, anxious not to lose this opportunity to learn more about the Soviet warship, hired Crabb to carry out an undercover, underwater operation. According to this interpretation, the frogman submerged surreptitiously in Portsmouth harbor, swam to the vessel, and began to spy on it from below the waterline.

Crabb never returned from this mission. His disappearance caused a furor in the British press and questions in the House of Commons, where the prime minister would say nothing more than that Crabb was presumed dead. Eden refused to reveal who had issued the order to spy on the cruiser or precisely what the frogman was trying to discover. Some time later a body was taken from the water outside the harbor, where the current had carried it, and was said to be the remains of Commander Crabb, but as the body was headless and otherwise beyond identification, the claim caused another dispute in the news media. Experts on underwater activity declared that Crabb could have been carrying a bomb that exploded underwater and decapitated him. Another belief was that the Russians aboard the *Ordzhonikidze* detected Crabb near the ship and killed him with an explosive device. Inevitably, there were those who believed the Russians captured Crabb and had him concealed aboard the cruiser when it took Khrushchev and Bulganin back to the Soviet Union. Each of these versions still has its partisans.

One constant in the case is the humor often expressed about the underwater disappearance of a frogman named Crabb.

FURTHER READING: *Marshall Pugh, *Frogman: Commander Crabb's Story* (1956); J. Bernard Hutton, *The Fake Defector* (1970), believes Crabb was captured by the Russians, taken to Russia, and brainwashed into joining the Soviet navy.

Crosby, Enoch *(1750-1835)*   Patriot spy during the American Revolution.

Crosby belonged to New England and New York, for he was born on Cape Cod, grew up on a farm in New York's Putnam County, and became a shoemaker in Danbury, Connecticut. The news of the battle of Lexington in 1775 caused him to join a Connecticut regiment, in the ranks of which he marched to New York City. He took part in that year's invasion of Canada, survived the defeat and retreat, and, his enlistment up, returned to Danbury.

He reenlisted in 1776 when the British captured New York City. John Jay, head of New York's Committee of Safety, met Crosby in White Plains. Jay needed spies to go among the residents of Putnam, Dutchess, and Westchester counties to sound them out covertly and to identify those who were true Patriots supporting the American Revolution and those who were Loyalists at heart, possible traitors. At Jay's urging, Crosby became one of these spies, and the most successful.

He used his civilian profession for his cover story, traversing much of New York in the guise of an itinerant shoemaker known by the cover name of "John

Smith." Stopping at one village after another, calling in at big houses in the countryside, he repaired shoes and spied on New Yorkers suspected of Loyalist leanings. Surreptitiously, in haymows or camped out under the stars, he wrote secret messages to Jay, describing individuals and naming names. Because of Crosby, numerous suspects were arrested by the Committee of Safety, some of whom were cleared, others warned, and some jailed.

So many arrests occurred in places Crosby had passed through that at last a group of Loyalists figured out who was causing their problem. They trapped Crosby and gave him a severe beating. He recovered, but his usefulness as a Patriot spy was at an end, and he rejoined the Continental army.

Serving in upstate New York, he had Benedict Arnold for a commanding general. In 1780, Arnold's plot to surrender West Point to the British went awry, and Arnold's confederate, John André, was captured. Crosby was one of the soldiers present at André's execution.

After the American victory in the War of Independence, Crosby devoted himself to religion. He died a deacon in the Presbyterian church.

Crosby has a place in the history of American literature. Jay once described to James Fenimore Cooper a secret agent who had worked for him during the revolution, and Cooper took this man as a model for Harvey Birch, the hero of his novel *The Spy*. Jay's description makes it seem that the original of Harvey Birch was Enoch Crosby.

FURTHER READING: Frank Monaghan, *John Jay* (1935), notes Jay's espionage activities that included Crosby; George S. Bryan, *The Spy in America* (1943); *James Fenimore Cooper, *The Spy* (James H. Pickering, ed., 1971).

Cryptology The science of writing (cryptography) and reading (cryptanalysis) ciphered messages (cryptograms).

See CIPHER; SECRET WRITING.

Cuban Missile Crisis *(1962)* American-Soviet confrontation following the discovery by U.S. intelligence of Russian offensive rockets in Cuba.

In 1961 President John Kennedy had to accept responsibility for the Bay of Pigs fiasco, when Cuban rebels organized by the CIA (Central Intelligence Agency) were defeated in their attempt to overthrow Premier Fidel Castro and destroy his Moscow-oriented regime. Castro then asked Soviet premier Nikita Khrushchev for heavy weapons, including rockets. Agents of the CIA discovered that these negotiations were going on, whereupon Kennedy warned Khrushchev that while the United States could not object to small rockets to defend Cuba, the presence of big offensive rockets would be an intolerable provocation. Khrushchev, through his foreign minister, Andrei Gromyko, declared that he understood Kennedy's position and swore that no offensive Soviet rockets would be based in Cuba.

Kennedy accepted the promise, but he also ordered the CIA to monitor events in Cuba, where Soviet technicians moved in and began secret work at sites that were off limits to ordinary Cubans. American U-2 planes flew over Cuba—the same high altitude spy planes that had surveyed the Soviet Union itself for four years (1956–60). In 1962 a U-2 pilot brought back photographs that showed launch pads being constructed for Russian offensive rockets capable of reaching the United States and other nations of the western hemisphere.

Why Khrushchev broke his word and challenged Kennedy is an open question. Perhaps the Soviet premier believed he could get away with it because he believed that the Bay of Pigs showed that Kennedy preferred a defeat to a showdown. Something like this logic must have been in Khrushchev's mind, or he would never have offered his challenge in Cuba, an island on America's doorstep, vulnerable to American armed forces and impossible for Soviet armed forces to defend. Khrushchev received a rude shock when Kennedy released the photographs of the launch pads, threw a naval blockade around Cuba, and demanded that the Soviets remove the rockets.

The missile crisis erupted. Kennedy assembled powerful armed forces in Florida and declared that if the rockets remained, he would send these forces into Cuba to destroy them. Khrushchev hesitated, trying to find a way out that would not humiliate him. He offered a trade, saying he would remove the Russian rockets in Cuba if Kennedy would remove the American rockets in Greece and Turkey. Kennedy refused. The American President had an advantage over the Soviet premier to this degree, that he knew what was being said in the Kremlin. Reports reached him, probably by way of British intelligence, from Oleg Penkovskiy, a spy for the west in Moscow. Penkovskiy passed the information that Khrushchev, knowing Russia's inferiority to the United States in rockets, would not dare to start a nuclear war. The spy was right. Khrushchev backed down and removed the offensive rockets from Cuba.

Kennedy received credit for taking a sane, resolute stand in the missile crisis. Khrushchev provided ammunition for his enemies in the Kremlin, who overthrew him in 1964, calling him a clown and turning him into a virtual nonperson in the Soviet Union.

See also BAY OF PIGS; CIA; PENKOVSKIY, OLEG; U-2.

FURTHER READING: Elie Abel, *The Missile Crisis* (1966); David Detzer, *The Brink: The Cuban Missile Crisis, 1962* (1979).

Culper Ring   The most successful espionage network of the American War of Independence.

When General George Washington deployed his forces near British-occupied New York City in 1778, he ordered Major Benjamin Tallmadge to recruit spies who could be depended upon to report from Manhattan on Sir Henry Clinton, the enemy commander, and the condition of Clinton's army. Such was the origin of the Culper Ring, the title of which came from the cover names of two of its chief operatives—"Samuel Culper, Senior," who was Abraham Woodhull, and "Samuel Culper, Junior," who was Robert Townsend. Tallmadge, as spymaster of the network, called himself "John Bolton."

The chain of information linked up in different ways, depending on who was available at a critical moment, but usually it began with Townsend, a Manhattan merchant who could move through the city and along its docks without rousing suspicion. Townsend wrote about what he knew from personal observation and what he learned from Patriot informers. Some informers worked regularly within the network. Enoch Hale was one, an astute agent and committed Patriot out to avenge his brother, Nathan Hale, whom the British had executed for spying two years earlier.

Townsend gave his written messages to Austin Roe, a Long Island farmer, who then crossed the East River and rode to Setauket, on the northern shore of the island, where Woodhull lived. There Roe hid the papers in a wooden box buried in one of Woodhull's fields. Woodhull retrieved the papers and passed them on to Caleb Brewster, a boatman who crossed Long Island Sound and met Tallmadge at Fairfield, Connecticut. Tallmadge then took the papers directly to Washington's headquarters near the Hudson River.

Townsend protected his secret messages by using invisible inks, codes, and ciphers. One of the ciphers was a system that gave numbers to persons, places, things, and abstractions. Thus, "345" decoded as "information," "711" as "Washington," and "727" as "New York City." Only four written keys to the codes and ciphers were kept, one each for Washington, Tallmadge, Woodhull, and Townsend.

Washington wanted to know above all what Clinton's plans were. The members of the Culper Ring were therefore instructed to report at once on such things as British troop movements, the stockpiling of military supplies around Manhattan, and the arrival of warships in New York harbor. The American spies also sent warnings about Tory spies, individuals who posed as Patriots but visited Clinton's headquarters with suspicious frequency.

Washington valued the Culper Ring so highly that he ordered all Culper messages brought to him as soon as they arrived, and he impressed upon Tallmadge the necessity of concealing the identity of the members of the ring. When British raiders seized some Culper papers in a sudden attack, Washington warned his spymaster to maintain better security. The British identified one American spy as a result of this raid, but the network kept operating.

The roundabout route sometimes took too long with messages arriving too late to be useful. Washington himself at one point suggested switching to a shorter route by way of Staten Island instead of Long Island. This proved impossible because safe links in the information chain comparable to Roe and Woodhull could not be established on Staten Island.

The Culper Ring's greatest coup came in 1780, just after Jean Baptiste de Vimeur, comte de Rochambeau, arrived at Newport, Rhode Island, with a French army to add to the Patriot cause. Clinton, faced with this threat, decided to meet it by attacking the French at Newport before they could join Washington. Clinton intended to leave a few troops in New York City, which was not threatened by the Americans and would not be left alone for long, since he anticipated a quick victory and a quick return.

Townsend saw the preparations for embarkation—soldiers filing down onto the docks, supplies piled high, troop ships arriving. He gave Roe the message, which proceeded to Washington's headquarters by way of Woodhull, Brewster, and Tallmadge. Alerted, Washington had a document drawn up purporting to show that he intended to attack New York with 12,000 men. This document was allowed to fall into the hands of a Tory, who hastened to the British with it. Alarmed, Clinton recalled his invasion force and mounted guard in New York City while Rochambeau mustered his army for the campaign.

The Culper conspirators operated until the end of the war. The British never learned about the network, nor did the Patriots, except for a privileged few at American headquarters. The members of the ring were cloaked in a secrecy so successful and retreated after the war into an anonymity so complete, that only in the twentieth century did historians uncover the facts about the remarkable Culper Ring.

See also TALLMADGE, BENJAMIN.

FURTHER READING: Morton Pennypacker, *Geneal Washington's Spies on Long Island and in New York* (1939); John Bakeless, *Turncoats, Traitors, and Heroes* (1959), is a gallery of secret agents at work during the American Revolution; *Corey Ford, *A Peculiar Service* (1965).

Cumming, Mansfield *(1859-1923)*   British naval officer and founder of MI6.

Cumming, of a middle-class English background, went into the Royal Navy and served in outposts of the empire (Malaya, Egypt) during the last quarter of the nineteenth century. He was a captain in 1911 when he took on the task, assigned to him by the London government, of establishing a spy system comparable to those on the Continent. The result was MI6 (Military Intelligence 6, British espionage).

MI6 received responsibility for intelligence in foreign countries, leaving to MI5 (Military Intelligence 5, counterespionage) the duty of protecting British soil from enemy undercover agents. MI6 achieved some of its signal successes, and had some of its most colorful agents, during Cumming's tenure as head of the organization.

His operatives discovered that Gustav Steinhauer was in charge of German espionage in Great Britain during World War I. In 1916 Cumming's man in Athens was novelist Compton Mackenzie, whose mission was so secret that when he described it in a book published during the thirties, he was fined and the volume was removed from circulation.

At the time of the Bolshevik revolution in Russia, Cumming dispatched two daring agents to work against it—Sidney Reilly and Paul Dukes, both of whom slipped into Moscow in disguise but failed to persuade enough Russians that they would be better off without their new rulers in the Kremlin.

When Cumming retired, he left a particular tradition for his successors to follow—each head of MI6 has been known as "C" ever since Cumming adopted his initial for identification within, and mystification outside, the organization.

See also MI6.

FURTHER READING: Mildred G. Richings, *Espionage: The Story of the Secret Service of the British Crown* (1934); *Richard Deacon, *A History of the British Secret Service* (1970).

Cushman, Pauline *(1833-93)*   Actress and spy for the Union during the American Civil War.

Cushman, whose name was Harriet Wood before she went into the theater and chose something more euphonious, was a Creole from New Orleans but raised in Michigan, where her father ran a post at which he traded with the Indians. Eager for the bright lights of the city, she traveled east, went on the stage in New York, made a success in light comedy, and played on the theatrical circuit as far away as Louisville and New Orleans.

In 1863, with the Civil War raging and prodded by her Unionist sympathies, she became a spy while playing in Louisville. She served as an undercover agent for the North among soldiers of the South. As an actress, she has been compared to Belle Boyd, who, however, lacked her talent (and worked for the South against the North).

Cushman covered her espionage activities by pretending to be an excessive, vocal partisan of the Confederacy, which sounded plausible because she came from New Orleans. She enjoyed mingling with southerners who trusted her and confided in her (sometimes, she posed as a man). Louisville was in the hands of the Federals, but Kentucky being a border state, it sheltered many enemies of the North, and these were the ones she reported on.

Cushman's place in the theater enabled her to move from city to city without falling under suspicion. In Tennessee, she played Nashville, and she went on an assignment for the army of the Cumberland, Union forces under the command of General Ambrose Burnside. She slipped through the Confederate lines and reached Shelbyville, where Confederate General Braxton Bragg had his headquarters. Cushman cleverly fooled some junior officers, got them to give her a guided tour of Bragg's camp, and left with his battle plans in the sole of her shoe.

But on her way back to Nashville, she was stopped by Confederate sentinels and taken to General Bedford Forrest, who sent her on to Bragg, who subjected her to a military tribunal that found her guilty of spying. She might have been executed if a swift Union advance had not rescued her.

Cushman's espionage exploits gained her the applause of officers and men under Burnside's command. That applause followed her back to civilian life after the war, when she was billed around the country as the "Spy of the Cumberland."

See also BOYD, BELLE.

FURTHER READING: *Ferdinand L. Sarmiento, *Pauline Cushman, Union Spy and Scout* (1865); Mary Elizabeth Massey, *Bonnet Brigades* (1966), has a passage on Cushman; Oscar A. Kinchen, *Women Who Spied for the Blue and the Gray* (1972).

Cut-Out A member of a network who represents other members in their relations with one another.

The term "cut-out" refers to one of the most important operatives in espionage, an active worker out front who helps his coworkers to maintain their anonymity. A principal cut-out enables the leader of the spy ring to stay safely out of sight behind the scenes, manipulating operations from a distance and reporting to headquarters indirectly. Lesser cut-outs represent the principal cut-out or anyone else who, for the sake of security, must deal with other agents through an intermediary.

Besides acting as a go-between, the principal cut-out often has duties of extreme importance to the whole network. He often is entrusted with the recruiting of new members into the network, a difficult task because reliable candidates must be found who have access to classified information or can be useful in other ways. The principal cut-out may have to make a hard decision about whether to take on board a timid official in a strategic post or an alcoholic who happens to be a wizard with microfilm. He may have to decide who should be a spy and who a courier.

The opprobrium of the leader falls on the principal cut-out if he accepts an individual who fails on the job or betrays the organization. Just about the worst thing that can happen to a leader is to have an incompetent principal cut-out. The leader may then find himself explaining the situation to his superiors and glancing over his shoulder to see if enemy counterespionage agents are getting close.

See also COURIER; NETWORK.

FURTHER READING: *Alexander Foote, *Handbook for Spies* (1964), describes how the author reported to cut-outs in his own espionage work; U.S. Department of Defense, Joint Chiefs of Staff Publication No. 1, *Dictionary of Military and Associated Terms* (1972).

d'Antraigues, Comte *(1753-1812)*   French secret agent for the royalists during the French Revolution and the Napoleonic era.

Born in Montpellier, d'Antraigues belonged to an aristocratic family and inherited his title. He became an officer in the French army, and after abandoning his military career spent a year traveling and seeing the world. He was at home in Montpellier, reading, writing, and living the life of a French noble, when the French Revolution broke out in 1789. His feeling at the time was that the power of the king of France ought to be restricted and that the historic feudal rights of the aristocracy should be observed.

D'Antraigues adhered to this political theory when he served in the constituent assembly in Paris, the body that in 1789 began work on a new constitution for France. The deliberations were too democratic for him, and in 1790 he went into exile in Switzerland, where he now began to write in favor of King Louis XVI and against the revolutionaries. He was one of those who, as the revolution became more violent, urged the powers of Europe to intervene militarily against it.

In 1792 the Spanish ambassador to Venice, impressed with the royalist writings of d'Antraigues, offered him a post at the Spanish Embassy. D'Antraigues accepted, and for the next five years he handled the correspondence that poured into the embassy from royalist spies inside France and across the Continent. D'Antraigues collated the messages and wrote reports for the Spanish ambassador and, with the Ambassador's permission, for the comte de Provence, the exiled brother of Louis XVI. D'Antraigues also communicated secretly with Francis Drake, the British minister in Genoa.

Many of the messages came from the Paris Agency, a network of spies that operated in the French capital before, during, and after the reign of terror presided over by Maximilien de Robespierre and the group he controlled, the Committee of Public Safety. The most sensational message reaching Venice from the Paris Agency indicated that Lazare Carnot, who directed the armed forces of the revolution for the Committee of Public Safety, was actually a spy who leaked its decisions to the agency. This assertion, however, has not withstood scrutiny. It has even been argued that d'Antraigues manufactured the story in order to add greater authority to his reports.

He certainly exaggerated the difficulties of the Committee of Public Safety, giving the impression that quarrels between its members signaled a coming collapse of the revolution. His purpose was to encourage the royalists and to persuade the British government, through Drake, to finance conspiracies and rebellions against the men controlling France. D'Antraigues had some success in both of these endeavors, although neither led to a restoration of the French monarchy.

The fall of Robespierre in 1794 galvanized d'Antraigues, who believed that the new regime would surely summon the comte de Provence, who called himself King Louis XVIII, back to the throne. This did not happen. In 1795 d'Antraigues saw more hope in an insurrection in La Vendée, an area in the west of France. The British supported the insurrection, but it was suppressed after the rise of Napoleon to power.

D'Antraigues was in Venice in 1796 when the comte de Montgaillard, a turncoat adventurer, arrived with information about a royalist attempt to win over General Charles Pichegru, commander of French forces in the north, to the royalist cause. D'Antraigues wrote a report on the basis of what he heard from Montgaillard, and he had this report in his pocket when he was arrested by the French following Napoleon's occupation of Venice in 1797. Napoleon used the report to discredit Pichegru by sending it to the Directory, the five-man group then in power in Paris.

D'Antraigues escaped from captivity in Venice. He wandered around Europe, still writing in favor of royalism. He was in Dresden in 1804 when he heard that Napoleon had become emperor of France, making the royalist cause more difficult than ever. D'Antraigues did not live to see the triumph for which he had worked so long, the restoration of the French monarchy in 1814, for he was shot to death in London in 1812 by an assassin whose motive has never been discovered.

See also Paris Agency.

FURTHER READING: G. Lenôtre, *Two Royalist Spies of the French Revolution* (1924); *Harvey Mitchell, *The Underground War against France: The Missions of William Wickham, 1794–1800* (1965).

Darragh, Lydia *(1729-89)*   Patriot spy in Philadelphia during the American War of Independence.

Born in Dublin, Ireland, Darragh was a Quaker who emigrated to Pennsylvania, where she and her husband, William, joined the general meeting of Friends in Philadelphia. The coming of the American Revolution caused her and the rest of the Darragh family to violate the Quaker pledge of nonviolence. They became Patriots committed to resistance to the crown. One son even joined the Continental army commanded by General George Washington.

When the British under Sir William Howe occupied Philadelphia in 1777, one room of the Darragh house was commandeered as a place where Howe's staff officers could confer. Howe established his headquarters in a house opposite the Darragh house. The Darraghs thus had an unrivaled vantage point from which to observe the coming and going of military commanders, to check on who visited headquarters, and to listen to indiscreet talk between officers.

The Darraghs reported what they learned to Washington at Whitemarsh, his headquarters before he pulled back to Valley Forge. William Darragh wrote shorthand messages on tiny pieces of paper, which Lydia sewed between the buttons and the cloth on the coat of her teen-age son. The son traveled to Whitemarsh, where his soldier brother retrieved the pieces of paper, wrote out the messages, and took them to the commander in chief. Washington relied on the Darragh reports to tell him what the British and Hessians were doing in Philadelphia.

On December 2, 1777, a number of British officers arrived at the Darragh house, ordered the family to go to bed, and entered the commandeered room for a staff conference. Realizing that something significant was under discussion, Lydia Darragh eavesdropped by holding her ear to the wall of the adjoining room, and unknown to the conferees, she heard that plans were afoot for a surprise attack on the Continental army. The intention was to surround and destroy Washington's forces. The date of the attack was set for December 4.

The next day, there being no time for the button method of sending secret messages by way of her son, and her husband being more likely than she to be stopped by British outposts, Lydia Darragh set out from Philadelphia to deliver the warning herself. She carried an empty flour bag and told the guards at the British outposts she was on her way to the Frankford mill. Accustomed to seeing Philadelphia women heading for the mill, they passed her through the lines.

Darragh met American officers, to whom she gave her information, which was passed on to Washington's headquarters. The upshot was that Howe, marching from Philadelphia, found Washington prepared for him, realized the element of surprise was gone, and retreated to Philadelphia.

The British left the city in 1778 and never came back. The members of the Darragh family were expelled from the Society of Friends for taking part in the War of Independence and for failing to attend Quaker meetings.

FURTHER READING: *John Bakeless, *Turncoats, Traitors, and Heroes* (1959), has an account of Darragh; A. A. Hoehling, *Women Who Spied* (1967); John F. Reed, *Valley Forge, Crucible of Victory* (1969).

Dasch, George *(1903-70?)*   Leader of the Nazi saboteurs who landed surreptitiously in the United States from German submarines during World War II.

Of a Bavarian Catholic family, Dasch studied for the priesthood before deciding on a secular career. He served briefly in the German army in 1918 as World War I was coming to an end. The turmoil in Germany after the surrender caused him to leave for the United States in 1922, where he served in the Army Air Corps for a year, after which he held many jobs, varying from waiter to salesman, during the 1920s and 1930s.

In 1941, before America's entrance into World War II, Dasch returned to Germany. Abwehr II, the sabotage department of German military intelligence, picked him, as a repatriated German-American with military training, to lead a sabotage mission in the United States in 1942 following America's entrance into the war.

After special training by Abwehr II, Dasch and seven other saboteurs were transported across the Atlantic in two submarines. The Dasch group of four landed at Amagansett on Long Island in New York, while the other group came ashore near St. Augustine, Florida.

However, during the voyage, Dasch and another saboteur, Ernest Burger, decided that they could not serve Nazi Germany. They defected and told the FBI (Federal Bureau of Investigation) what they knew, which led to the arrest of the other six saboteurs.

Dasch and Burger saved their lives by confessing and testifying in court. They received jail sentences, while the rest were executed. The two informers were deported to Germany after the war.

See also NAZI SABOTEURS.

FURTHER READING: Louis de Jong, *The German Fifth Column in the Second World War* (1956); Charles Wighton and Gunter Peis, *Hitler's Spies and Saboteurs: Based on the German Secret Service Diary of General Lahousen* (1958); *Eugene Rachlis, *They Came to Kill: The Story of the Eight Nazi Saboteurs* (1961).

Deane, Silas *(1737-89)* American diplomat and secret agent in France during the American War of Independence.

A native of Connecticut and a Yale graduate, Deane worked as a teacher, lawyer, and businessman before getting caught up, during the years before the revolution, in the disturbances that made him a politician. In 1769 he served as a leader in his colony's nonconsumption campaign in opposition to the Townshend Acts, which were taxes placed on the thirteen colonies by the British government. In 1772 he entered the Connecticut legislature, where he criticized British policies toward America.

Deane was a delegate to the Continental Congress from 1774 to 1776, during which period he advocated continued resistance to King George III. His patriotic ardor and his ability led to his being named American commissioner to France in 1776, making him the first diplomat to represent all the colonies abroad. Ostensibly he was just a merchant interested in selling American goods and in using the money to buy products needed at home. His real mission, regarding which he received instructions from the Committee of Secret Correspondence in the Continental Congress, was to maneuver undercover for French help in the American War of Independence. The leaders of the rebellion wanted arms and clothing for 25,000 men and, if possible, a Franco-American alliance. Deane worked for both aims.

His chief contact in Paris was Pierre Augustin Caron de Beaumarchais, through whose front organization, Roderigue Hortalez et Cie., military supplies were channeled to America before France entered the war. Deane at the same time was responsible for sending to General George Washington a number of officers for the Continental army. Among them were some intriguers, who thought to make European-style military careers in the New World and who caused trouble after their arrival. But Deane also accepted several who remain famous in the annals of the War of Independence—Lafayette, Kalb, Steuben, and Pulaski.

In September 1776, Benjamin Franklin and Arthur Lee, recently a secret agent for the American colonies in London, joined Deane in Paris, and these three commissioners together negotiated with the French. Lee quickly came to distrust Deane and to suspect that Deane had been siphoning off for himself some of the money he had received from America. Lee warned Deane that

Edward Bancroft, whom Deane had hired as a secretary, was a spy for the British, which we know to be true but which Deane denied, apparently in good faith. Franklin wrote to the Continental Congress, supporting Deane against Lee.

The American commissioners signed an alliance with France in 1778. Shortly afterward, Deane received an order to return home, where he found himself under attack on charges of mishandling the funds with which he had been supplied while abroad. The accusation was based on testimony by Lee, who alleged that the aid provided by France had been a gift and that the American money had gone into the pockets of Deane and Beaumarchais.

That particular allegation could not be sustained because the French minister of foreign affairs stated that the French supplies had been purchased. However, Deane failed to produce vouchers detailing his expenditures in Paris, an irregularity quite possibly intended to cover some of his dealings, which were shady if not treasonable (he had exaggerated his expenses in certain cases and engaged in dubious financial transactions). He was exonerated in the end for want of evidence, but the case left him a ruined man.

Deane went back to Europe in 1780. In his anger over the way he had been treated, he wrote letters to American friends in which he denounced the rebellion and urged reconciliation with the crown. These letters were published in New York by James Rivington, outwardly a Loyalist editor but actually a double agent ever since the fortunes of war had turned in favor of the Americans. The Patriots now condemned Deane for a turncoat, and the outcry became strident in 1784 when he published his pro-British *Address to the Free and Independent Citizens of the United States.*

Deane spent the rest of his life as an exile in England and on the Continent. After the adoption of the Constitution by the United States of America, he finally decided to return home, only to die on board a passenger ship under circumstances suggestive of suicide.

After reexamining his career, Congress in 1842 absolved him of wrongdoing and awarded his heirs the sum of $37,000 in restitution.

See also BANCROFT, EDWARD; BEAUMARCHAIS, PIERRE AUGUSTIN CARON DE; COMMITTEE OF SECRET CORRESPONDENCE.

FURTHER READING: Carl Van Doren, *Secret History of the American Revolution* (1941); *Julian P. Boyd, "Silas Deane: Death by a Kindly Teacher of Treason?" in *William and Mary Quarterly* (1959); William Stinchcombe, *The American Revolution and the French Alliance* (1969).

Dee, John *(1527-1608)* English scientist, occultist, and government spy during the Elizabethan era.

Born in London and educated at Cambridge, which he left in 1546, Dee was a typical man of his time in his passionate concern for both the natural and the occult sciences, which had not yet been properly differentiated. He traveled on the Continent during the years 1547 to 1550, studying mathematics, astronomy, and geography, principally at the universities of Paris and Louvain, and dabbling in astrology, alchemy, and necromancy.

On his return to London in 1551, he began to teach and write on the new knowledge of the earth gained by the voyages of discovery since Columbus. A defender of the heliocentric cosmology of Copernicus, Dee yet remained so much a practitioner of the occult arts that in 1555 he was accused of using sorcery against Queen Mary because of her Catholicism (the court found him not guilty). Following Mary's death three years later, Dee drew up for Queen Elizabeth an astrological interpretation of the best day in 1558 on which to hold her coronation.

In 1562 he was back on the Continent pursuing the pseudoscience of numerology, which led him into the investigation of hermetic manuscripts supposedly descending from ancient Egypt. While attempting to decipher them, he consulted the cryptological works of Girolamo Cardano and Johannes Trithemius, two masters of codes and ciphers, and the science of coding and decoding secret writings continued to be a prime interest of his thereafter.

After Dee's return to England, his writings on cryptology brought him to the attention of Francis Walsingham when the latter was organizing a spy network to counteract conspiracies to rescue Mary Queen of Scots, then Elizabeth's prisoner in England. Walsingham discovered in Dee the type of scholar who would make a good spy. As a wandering researcher, Dee could travel without drawing attention to himself. As an occultist, he could play upon the credulity of rulers and statesmen. As a cryptologist, he could write in ciphers that would conceal the most significant contents of his letters. Dee, for his part, wanted government subsidies to continue his work. He joined Walsingham's corps of secret agents.

During the 1570s Dee pursued science and occultism on the Continent, and he combined both with espionage at Walsingham's behest. Dee spied in France while Elizabeth was dangling a marriage proposal, which she did for temporary political purposes, before the duke of Anjou. Dee is said to have helped the queen to withdraw the proposal diplomatically when he cast for the duke a horoscope deliberately riddled with sinister signs concerning the marriage.

Dee traveled on the Continent again during the years 1583 to 1589, practicing necromancy, the raising of apparitions in a crystal ball, with his fellow occultist Edward Kelley. Dee also spied for Walsingham after Mary's execution in 1587, when King Philip II of Spain was preparing to send his armada against England. Walsingham is known to have had a spy in Cracow, Poland, who almost certainly was Dee.

The armada suffered defeat in 1588, Walsingham died in 1590, and Dee spent his last years out of government service, studying, writing, and teaching (he served as warden of Manchester College in 1595). He outlived Queen Elizabeth by five years.

See also WALSINGHAM, FRANCIS.

FURTHER READING: John Halliwell (ed.), *The Private Diary of John Dee* (1842); *Richard Deacon, *John Dee: Scientist, Astrologer, Geographer, and Secret Agent to Elizabeth I* (1968); Peter J. French, *John Dee: The World of an Elizabethan Magus* (1971).

Defoe, Daniel (1660-1731) English novelist, journalist, and undercover agent for the British government.

Defoe, a Londoner, came of a Presbyterian family, and he therefore could not attend the fashionable schools then under the control of the Church of England. He received a good education, nonetheless, in one of the "dissenting academies" founded by his sect. In 1683 he went into trade, attempted to make a living, and endured both bankruptcy and a stay in a debtors' prison. Turning to journalism, he published widely read pamphlets on religion and politics.

In 1703 Defoe wrote to Robert Harley, a rising figure in the English govern-ment (then speaker of the House of Commons), offering to become a spy in England. Harley accepted for two reasons. First, Defoe could report from the counties on Harley's political friends and foes. Second, Defoe could watch the Jacobites—the partisans of the "Old Pretender," exiled on the Continent but styling himself James III, who hoped to regain the British throne lost by his father, James II, in 1688.

Defoe used trade as a cover for his spy work. Calling himself by cover names, usually "Alexander Goldsmith," he made a riding tour of England in 1704, meeting leading men in the counties and reporting to Harley by post about their political opinions. Defoe paid other spies to let him know what they saw or heard in towns, markets, and fairs, a veritable network of agents conducting domestic espionage for those in power. It is for this reason that Defoe has been termed the "father of the Secret Service" in England.

So satisfied was Harley (now a secretary of state), that in 1706 he dispatched Defoe to the north when the union of England and Scotland was being nego-tiated. This time Defoe was no mere spy. Harley instructed him to labor covertly in behalf of the union by defending it without seeming to do so while talking to Scots who held positions of influence. Defoe was to send a report every week in the form of an unsigned letter.

Again Defoe performed satisfactorily. He found Scottish sentiment in favor of joining England, and reported so to Harley, who pushed the negotiations forward to success in 1707.

Harley, after becoming head of the government (1710) and Earl of Oxford (1711), fell from power in 1714, but members of the new government con-tinued to employ Defoe as an undercover agent. The problem now was the Jacobite movement. The Old Pretender and his army were defeated in 1715, but the threat remained. The government of King George I, who had come from Hanover in Germany after the death of Queen Anne in 1714, used spies at home and abroad to keep the Jacobites under surveillance. That was the reason for employing secret agents to watch the "Young Pretender," Charles Stuart ("Bonnie Prince Charlie"), on the Continent.

Defoe's assignment after 1715 was to infiltrate Jacobite circles. His most skillful maneuver concerned Jacobite newspapers, which he undercut by join-ing them as an editor and writing ambiguous material that compromised them with their readers. He thus neutralized Nathaniel Mist's *Weekly Journal* during the years 1716 to 1720 without Mist ever becoming aware of what Defoe was doing.

Defoe ceased to be a government spy in 1720. He had begun a new voca-tion: in 1719 he had published *Robinson Crusoe*. Other novels followed, and by the time of his death he had won for himself a place among the great writers of English literature. It took time for the fact to be discovered that he was one of the great undercover agents of English politics.

FURTHER READING: Basil Williams, *The Whig Supremacy, 1714–1760* (1935), has an account of Defoe's activities; Richard Deacon, *A History of the British Secret Service* (1969); *James Sutherland, *Daniel Defoe* (1971).

---

d'Éon, Chevalier *(1728-1810)*   French adventurer who served as an under-cover agent for King Louis XV.

Belonging to the French provincial nobility, Charles Geneviève d'Éon de

Beaumont, known as Chevalier d'Éon, could have followed his family tradition of selecting the king's army for a career. He chose instead to become a figure of mystery by equivocating about his sex, dressing sometimes as a man and sometimes as a woman, something he could do because he had a slight figure, soft features, and no beard.

D'Éon's ability to pose as either sex gave him a good cover for espionage and diplomacy, and in 1755 Louis XV recruited him into the King's Secret, a group of agents who reported directly to the king. Louis needed an emissary to go to St. Petersburg, gain the confidence of Tsarina Elizabeth, whose foreign minister was pro-British, and discuss negotiations with France. By posing as a young woman, "Lia de Beaumont," d'Éon became a favorite of the tsarina and persuaded her to open a secret correspondence with Louis XV.

The king rewarded d'Éon with a commission in the royal dragoons. Now d'Éon wore a military uniform, rode with his regiment, and became an expert duellist. In 1762 Louis sent him to London to find out on what terms the British would end the Seven Years' War. D'Éon, this time as a man, managed to copy papers in the diplomatic portfolio of a drunken British official, papers that revealed to Versailles the wartime policies being developed by the British government.

After the peace in 1763, Louis sent d'Éon back to London with instructions to collect information on the British armed forces, the state of the coastal defenses, and anything else that might be useful to know in case France decided to land an invading army in England. D'Éon obtained documents, talked to unwary soldiers and statesmen, and kept coded records for transmission to the king of France. He was miffed at not being appointed the next French ambassador to London, but Louis salved his wounded vanity by naming him a minister plenipotentiary in Britain.

This was the period when d'Éon's sex became a subject of intense curiosity because he seemed to change his gender with his clothing. Londoners made bets on both sides in the coffeehouses, and the mystery would have been solved by forcible inspection except for d'Éon's skill with a rapier.

D'Éon remained on his undercover mission in England until the death of Louis XV in 1774. When Louis XVI ordered him home, d'Éon demanded money and immunity from his enemies. He threatened, should his terms be rejected, to sell to the British the letters, maps, plans, and official instructions in his possession. The situation created by d'Éon was too dangerous for usual diplomatic methods. The ablest undercover agent available for sensitive assignments was Pierre Augustin Caron de Beaumarchais, the dramatist who had worked successfully for Louis XV as a secret emissary. Beaumarchais was therefore dispatched to London to confer with d'Éon.

The pair came to an agreement. D'Éon would turn over the documents in return for a sum to pay his creditors, a pension for himself, and a royal guarantee that he could live safely in France. He also agreed to wear women's clothing exclusively, a provision that would effectively neutralize him as a politician or conspirator. Back in France, d'Éon lived up to this agreement until 1777 when, seen again in his dragoon's uniform, he received a royal order to resume female dress permanently.

From then on he lived as a woman. When he died in London, an autopsy put an end to the speculation about his sex. D'Éon was a man.

See also KING'S SECRET.

FURTHER READING: M. S. Coryn, *The Chevalier d'Eon* (1932); *Edna Nixon, *Royal Spy: The Strange Case of the Chevalier d'Eon* (1965); Cynthia Cox, *The Enigma of the Age: The Strange Story of the Chevalier d'Eon* (1966).

Deriabin, Peter *(1921-   )*   Russian intelligence officer for, and defector from, the Soviet Union.

Deriabin, the son of a Siberian farmer, rose in life by becoming a faithful Communist. During the 1930s he was a Young Pioneer and a member of the Komsomol, the Communist youth movement. He graduated from high school (1937), took his teacher's certificate (1938), and taught school until the outbreak of World War II (1939), when he was conscripted into the Soviet army.

When the Germans invaded Russia in 1941 and drove toward Moscow, Deriabin took part in the defense that saved the city. He served in the battle of Stalingrad in 1942 and in the following counteroffensive that forced the Germans to retreat from southern Russia. Shot during the Odessa campaign (1944), he recovered, but having been wounded several times, he was allowed to leave the army for a counterintelligence school in Moscow. After his graduation in 1945, he entered the NKVD (People's Commissariat for Internal Affairs, later known as the MVD; Russian intelligence) and received an assignment in Siberia, where he helped tighten Communist control, which had slackened during the war, over the people of the region.

In 1947 Deriabin obtained a transfer to Moscow. The five years he spent at the headquarters of Soviet espionage began his disillusionment with the Soviet system. As he later testified, he saw that duplicity and violence were built into it. He became completely disillusioned when, now a major in the MVD (Ministry of Internal Affairs), his next tour of duty took him to Vienna in 1953 as the security officer charged with spying on the Russian colony of officials and their wives in the Austrian capital. He was also responsible for directing espionage against the Austrians through a network of secret agents already in place.

The duties of a Soviet security officer repelled him, particularly when he realized that the British, French, and Americans did not spy in this way on their own people. He was impressed with the freedom and relative prosperity, despite their defeat in the war, of the Austrians, who lived much better than did the victorious Russians, a fact that contradicted what he had been told in Moscow about conditions in the west.

The realization that he could no longer serve the Soviet Union developed so rapidly that less than five months after arriving Deriabin defected to the Americans in Vienna (1954). Granted political asylum, he described the Soviet intelligence apparatus, and after reaching the United States, testified in Washington before the House Committee on Un-American Activities. He received close attention as the highest-ranking Soviet intelligence officer to defect to the west.

In 1959 Deriabin published *The Secret World,* an autobiography, an exposure of the KGB (Committee for State Security, as Soviet intelligence was now called), and a condemnation of the Soviet system and Communist ideology. In 1965, while working for the CIA (Central Intelligence Agency), he translated the controversial *Penkovskiy Papers,* supposedly written by Oleg Penkovskiy, a spy for the west who had been executed by the Russians in 1963. These documents were said to have been smuggled out of Moscow by a secret channel, a claim often disputed by western experts and a fortiori by the Russians. Deriabin, at least, considered them genuine.

See also PENKOVSKIY, OLEG.

FURTHER READING: *Peter Deriabin and Frank Gibney, *The Secret World* (1959); Oleg Penkovskiy, *The Penkovskiy Papers* (1965); John Barron, *KGB: The Secret Work of Soviet Secret Agents* (1974).

Dewavrin, André (1912-   )   French director of intelligence for the Gaullist forces during World War II.

In 1940 General Charles De Gaulle reached London as France fell to the German invasion. There he organized his Free French armed forces to struggle for the liberation of France. His intelligence department was the BCRA, an acronym for the French title meaning "Central Bureau of Intelligence and Operations." The mysterious "Colonel Passy" headed the BCRA—actually Colonel Dewavrin, who took his cover name from the name of a subway station in Paris. A prewar professor at the French military academy of Saint-Cyr and a veteran of the French force that fought vainly in the Allied campaign to save Norway from the Germans earlier in 1940, Dewavrin built the BCRA into an espionage corps offering direction to and cooperating with the resistance inside France. He worked with the Special Operations Executive (SOE), a British organization also assisting the French resistance.

Dewavrin had responsibility for sending secret agents to carry aid and information to underground groups in France. Spies who could escape from France and get to London reported to him on what they knew, surmised, or hoped for. Gathering information from these sources and from clandestine radios on the Continent, interpreting what he heard in German broadcasts and read in German publications smuggled out of France, and receiving reports from British intelligence, Dewavrin constructed a mosaic revealing what the Germans were doing in France and suggesting how they might be opposed by the underground patriotic networks. In 1943 he made a flying trip to France accompanied by F. F. E. Yeo-Thomas of the SOE. They slipped into Paris for personal meetings with resistance leaders, the best of whom was Jean Moulin, selected by Dewavrin with De Gaulle's approval to head a coalition of underground cells.

Later in that year Dewavrin assumed responsibility for BCRA activities in North Africa, in the French colonies from which the Germans had been driven by the Allied campaign of 1942 and 1943. Dewavrin became technical director of counterespionage in France in 1944 and took part in the Allied campaign across the Continent as chief of staff to General Joseph Koenig. Dewavrin served to the end of the war in 1945, after which he returned to being a soldier in peacetime.

See also BCRA; FRENCH RESISTANCE; MOULIN, JEAN; SPECIAL OPERATIONS EXECUTIVE; YEO-THOMAS, F. F. E.

FURTHER READING: Rémy (Gilbert Renault-Roulier), *Memoirs of a Secret Agent of Free France* (2 vols., 1948–50); *Richard Collier, *Ten Thousand Eyes* (1958), contains information from the author's postwar talks with Dewavrin; David Schoenbrun, *Soldiers of the Night: The Story of the French Resistance* (1980).

Dickinson, Velvalee *(1893-1960?)*   American spy for Japan during World War II.

The "Doll Woman" of espionage was originally Velvalee Blucher, born in Sacramento, California, and educated in its schools, graduating from Sacramento High School in 1911. After Sacramento Junior College (1914–16), she spent a year at Stanford University (1916–17), leaving without a degree. But she had acquired a hobby—dolls. She worked in San Francisco, married Lee Dickinson (head of a brokerage firm), and became interested in Japan through handling accounts for Japanese-Americans farming in California. The Dickinsons met Japanese diplomats from the consulate in San Francisco. They joined the Japanese-American Society, in which they became ardent proponents of better relations between the United States and Japan.

The failure of the brokerage firm (1935) caused the Dickinsons to leave for New York, where Velvalee Dickinson opened a doll shop three years later, dealing not only in toys for children but also in antiques and collectors' items of great value. The shop was a success that brought her a nationwide clientele. She carried on a mail-order business and corresponded with clients in many states.

The Dickinsons were at the same time maintaining their connections with Japan by attending Japanese functions in New York and meeting Japanese officials and military men attached to the consulate. At some time during these years the American couple agreed to become spies for Japan, a promise they made good after the 1941 Japanese attack on Pearl Harbor that started the war in the Pacific. During 1942 the Dickinsons toured the American west coast gathering information about warships of the U.S. Navy, especially those that limped into San Francisco or San Diego from Pearl Harbor for repairs.

When the couple returned to New York, Velvalee Dickinson used her doll shop as a cover for her espionage. She wrote to a Japanese agent in Buenos Aires using the names and addresses of women she found in her business correspondence, so that she herself was not mentioned. The dolls gave her a code behind which to conceal the true meaning of her words. Thus, "three new dolls" referred to three American warships transferred to the Pacific, and "a doll in a hula skirt" referred to a ship just in from Hawaii.

She continued this method of spying on her own after the death of her husband in 1943, and it worked until the Japanese replaced their agent in Buenos Aires and abandoned the address to which she had been writing. They failed to inform her of the change, so that she kept on sending letters as before. Now, however, the Argentine post office, unable to find the addressee, stamped the letters "Return to Sender."

As a result, a number of American women whose names and addresses she had used were astounded to find letters from Buenos Aires, signed with their own names, in their mail boxes. They reported the bizarre puzzle of the letters and the forged signatures to the authorities. Since all the letters concerned dolls, and since all the women had corresponded with the Dickinson doll shop in New York, that was where the trail ended. Agents of the FBI (Federal Bureau of Investigation) arrested the proprietor.

During Velvalee Dickinson's trial in 1944, the press dubbed her, naturally, the "Doll Woman." Sentenced to ten years, she was paroled in 1951 and persuaded to retire from espionage if not from the doll business.

FURTHER READING: Frederick L. Collins, *The FBI in Peace and War*, revised by Lester Dember (1943); *A. A. Hoehling, *Women Who Spied* (1967); Richard Wilmer Rowan and Robert G. Deindorfer, *Secret Service: Thirty-three Centuries of Espionage* (1967), has a passage on Dickinson.

Dimitrijevic, Dragutin *(1876-1917)* Serbian intelligence officer and founder of the Black Hand.

Dimitrijevic was born in Belgrade, then the capital of independent Serbia (and now the capital of Yugoslavia). He attended the military academy in his native city (1892–95), received a commission in the Serbian army, and began his rise to the rank of general in military intelligence. A passionate Serbian patriot, Dimitrijevic was also a Balkan-style terrorist. In 1903 he took part in the assassination of King Alexander, whom he held responsible for creating chaos in the government of Serbia. In 1908 Dimitrijevic opposed the annexation of neighboring Bosnia and Herzegovina, with their large populations of Serbs, by the Austro-Hungarian empire.

Three years later he founded the Black Hand, an underground organization committed to undoing the annexation and uniting Bosnia with Serbia. The Black Hand resorted to terrorism in Bosnia, using sabotage and assassination as weapons against Austrian officials and pro-Austrian Serbs. When Dimitrijevic became chief of intelligence of the Serbian general staff in 1913, he was able, with or without the knowledge of his superiors, to make the espionage resources at his command available to the Black Hand in Bosnia.

When Vienna announced in 1914 that the Archduke Franz Ferdinand and the archduchess would attend military maneuvers in Bosnia, Dimitrijevic plotted their assassination, which he, from Belgrade, ordered the Black Hand to carry out. The selected assassins included Gavrilo Princip, who shot the royal pair in Sarajevo. This act started the series of events that led to World War I.

Dimitrijevic remained in the Serbian army during the convulsive years 1914 to 1916, when troops from Austria-Hungary, Germany, and Bulgaria invaded Serbia. He traveled with the Belgrade government when it retreated across Albania into Greece. Suspected of conspiring to overthrow the government and accused of directing the Black Hand against it, he was arrested in 1916 and executed in 1917. Marshal Tito, president of Yugoslavia, rehabilitated Dimitrijevic in 1953.

See also BLACK HAND; PRINCIP, GAVRILO.

FURTHER READING: R. W. Seton-Watson, *Sarajevo* (1926); *Wayne S. Vucinich, *Serbia between East and West: The Events of 1903–1908* (1954); Harold J. Gordon and Nancy M. Gordon, *The Austrian Empire: Abortive Federation* (1974).

Disinformation False, misleading, or trivial information planted by an intelligence organization to deceive its rival.

Doihara, Kenji *(1883-1948)* Japanese soldier and spymaster in Manchuria and China during the period of Japanese expansion in the Far East.

Born in Tokyo, Doihara was a samurai, a member of the military class, and as such he received training in the aristocratic code of bushido. His parents knew the Japanese royal family, and his sister married a prince.

Doihara therefore had a smooth path upward when he decided on a military career. By 1904 he was a major in the Japanese army. That same year he went to Peking as adjutant to the military attaché at the Japanese Embassy, a post from which he watched the development of Tokyo's plans for intervention in China.

Fully committed to Japanese nationalism, Doihara used the slogan "Asia for the Asiatics" as an enticement to other nations of the Far East to support Japan against the great powers of the west. At the same time, he sought to weaken China by supporting the leaders of independence movements in the Chinese provinces.

Doihara realized that the key to Japanese intervention in China was Manchuria, the broad, sparsely populated area in the northeast that could be invaded both from the sea and from Japanese-occupied Korea. Impressing his superiors with his strategic thinking, he received permission to tour Manchuria clandestinely, which he did by adopting different disguises in different places, appearing as a peddler, teacher, traveler, and so on. His success among alien peoples, when it became known in the west after World War I, won him the title of the "Lawrence of Manchuria," a reference to the achievements of T. E. Lawrence in Arabia.

The Russian Revolution of 1917, by weakening Russian strength in the Far East, provided a golden opportunity for Japan to conspire against Manchuria, and the man already in place, Doihara, received larger authority and more money for his campaign. He now built an elaborate spy network, drawing his agents from among both White Russians who had fled from the Bolsheviks into Manchuria and Chinese who lived there. He systematically used brothels and opium dens to turn patrons and addicts into spies.

In 1926, backing subservient warlords in China, Doihara carried out an assassination campaign against the recalcitrant. In 1931 he arranged the burning of the Japanese barracks at Mukden that provided Japan with a pretext for invading Manchuria with a big army. In 1932 his suggestion was followed when the Japanese brought the last emperor of China out of retirement to reign in Manchukuo (as the Japanese renamed Manchuria). This was Henry Pu-Yi, puppet of Japan.

One proof of Doihara's genius for espionage came in 1938, when Chiang Kai-shek, leader of Chinese resistance to Japan, executed a number of Chinese generals because they were discovered to be Doihara's agents.

But World War II, from Pearl Harbor (1941) to Hiroshima (1945), undid all the achievements of the Lawrence of Manchuria. Japan lost the war, lost her conquests, and lost her hold on the mainland of Asia. Doihara, who had risen to become head of the Japanese air force in 1942, was accused after Japan's defeat of violating the laws of war. Convicted of being a war criminal, he went to the gallows.

FURTHER READING: *Joseph Gollomb, *Armies of Spies* (1939), has a chapter on Doihara in Manchuria; *Ronald Seth, *Secret Servants: A History of Japanese Espionage* (1967); David Kahn, *The Codebreakers: The Story of Secret Writing* (1967), explains Japanese codes of the type used by Doihara in his espionage work.

Donovan, James *(1916-70)* American lawyer and a central figure in the espionage revolution in which spies are exchanged instead of executed.

The son of a New York doctor, Donovan went through schools in the Bronx, attended Fordham University (1933–37), and in 1940 took a law degree at Harvard. After practicing as a trial lawyer in New York for three years, he went into the U. S. Navy (1943) as World War II raged, became an intelligence officer, and then joined the OSS (Office of Strategic Services) as a general counsel. In 1945 and 1946 he helped prosecute the Nazi war criminals at the Nuremberg Trials; he then returned to his law practice.

Donovan became involved in the espionage revolution following the arrest in 1957 of Rudolf Abel, the Russian spymaster who had directed an espionage network in New York. Donovan defended Abel in court and, after Abel's conviction, appealed against the imposition of the death penalty on his client, pointing out that the day might come when the United States could exchange Abel for an American convicted in the Soviet Union. The judge thereupon sentenced Abel to a prison term.

Donovan's foresight was demonstrated three years later when Francis Gary Powers was shot down while piloting a U-2 spy plane on an espionage mission over the Soviet Union. A Moscow court ordered Powers first to jail and then to a Soviet labor camp. This provided an opportunity for an exchange, which was worked out by Donovan and Wolfgang Vogel, an East German lawyer representing Abel's family, the members of which claimed East German citizenship.

Donovan and Vogel negotiated with the knowledge, encouragement, and guidance of their two governments, the upshot being that Donovan and Abel traveled to Berlin in 1962, where they met Vogel and Powers in the middle of the Glienicker Bridge connecting the democratic and Communist areas of the divided city. Donovan walked back across the bridge with Powers, and Vogel did the same with Abel. This scene symbolized the espionage revolution, the realization that, with espionage a continuing reality on both sides, captured spies were useful as exchange counters and therefore too valuable to be executed.

Also in 1962, Donovan arranged to ransom the Cubans who had invaded Cuba at the Bay of Pigs in an effort to overturn the government of Fidel Castro. The invasion failed, the invaders were captured by Castro's armed forces, and the American government, responsible for backing the fiasco, purchased the release of the captives. Donovan handled the details of the settlement, and then went back to a more staid practice of the law.

See also ABEL, RUDOLF; BAY OF PIGS; ESPIONAGE REVOLUTION; POWERS, FRANCIS GARY; VOGEL, WOLFGANG.

FURTHER READING: *James B. Donovan, *Strangers on a Bridge: The Case of Colonel Abel* (1964); Francis Gary Powers (with Curt Gentry), *Operation Overflight: The U-2 Spy Pilot Tells His Story for the First Time* (1970); E. H. Cookridge, *Spy Trade* (1971).

Donovan, William *(1883-1959)* American government official and director of the OSS during World War II.

Born in Buffalo, New York, Donovan was the son of a prosperous businessman. He attended the local high school (1896–1900), and then went to Columbia University, from which he obtained his B.A. (1905) and his law degree (1907). He worked as a lawyer, joined the U.S. Army during World War I (1917–18), and won both the Congressional Medal of Honor and his nickname, "Wild Bill."

Donovan returned to his legal practice after the war and spent the years 1925 through 1929 in the office of the attorney general in Washington. While heading a Wall Street firm in the 1930s, he ran unsuccessfully for governor of New York on the Republican ticket (1932). He toured Europe in 1940, after the outbreak of World War II, on a fact-finding mission for President Franklin Roosevelt, who in 1941 named him to the new post of coordinator of information. A year later Donovan's agency became the OSS (Office of Strategic Services), with responsibility for espionage and secret operations.

Donovan organized the OSS and ran it for the rest of the war, basing his practice on what he had learned while visiting London in 1941 about the British secret service and the Special Operations Executive (SOE). In Washington he received advice from a Canadian, William Stephenson, who represented British intelligence in the United States.

During the war, Donovan often went into the field to supervise his agents. He was present during the Allied invasion of Sicily (1943), the Normandy landings (1944), and the Allied invasion of Burma (1944). In each case he had agents behind the lines before the operation began.

With the end of hostilities in 1945, Donovan presided over the demise of the OSS and then went back to private life. When the Cold War between the Soviet Union and the west showed the need for a permanent civilian espionage system, he added his advice to the establishment of the CIA (Central Intelligence Agency) in 1947.

He became American ambassador to Thailand (1953–54) before retiring.

See also OSS; STEPHENSON, WILLIAM.

FURTHER READING: Stewart Alsop and Thomas Braden, *Sub Rosa: The OSS and American Espionage* (1946); *Corey Ford, *Donovan of OSS* (1970); R. Harris Smith, *OSS: The Secret History of America's First Central Intelligence Agency* (1972).

Double Agent   A man or woman who works for two opposing espionage organizations but is loyal to one and betrays the other.

See COUNTERSPY.

Double-Cross System *(1941-45)*   The use of double agents by British intelligence for large-scale deception of the enemy.

Twin triumphs of British intelligence in World War II were the breaking of Germany's top machine ciphers (Ultra) and the controlling of Germany's espionage system in Britain (the Double-Cross System). Together they contributed in important ways to the vast deception plan (Operation Bodyguard) mounted before D-Day in Europe (June 6, 1944) to conceal from the Germans the time and exact location of the Allied landings in France.

But the Double-Cross System was in action long before D-Day, and with considerable success. Run by MI5 (Military Intelligence 5, British counterespionage) with the collaboration of MI6 (Military Intelligence 6, British espionage) and other agencies, it seized Germany's agents as they arrived in Britain and "turned" many into double agents who reported back to the Abwehr (German intelligence) at the dictates of their new masters. Some spies became double agents by indoctrination, while others did it for money, patriotism, disenchantment with Hitler, or some other reason. They included Germans, Poles, Spaniards, Yugoslavs, French, and British—about forty in all. Essentially they fed disinformation, a nicely balanced mixture of truth and lies, to their former spymasters, either in Hamburg or in neutral Madrid or Lisbon where the two warring sides met. Most communicated with the Abwehr by radio, a few by secret writing, a very few by personal contact.

To coordinate this network, the XX Committee, or Twenty Committee (Double Cross = XX = Twenty), was established. This committee, chaired by J. C. Masterman, an Oxford professor, was composed of representatives of MI5, MI6, Home Defence, the Air Ministry, the War Office, the Admiralty, and the civil departments, to which were later added representatives from COSSAC (Chief of Staff Supreme Allied Command) and SHAEF (Supreme Headquarters Allied Expeditionary Forces). The head of the London Controlling Section (LCS) sat on the committee. It met weekly to decide what disinformation could safely be disseminated, with due regard to the needs of each agency and command.

Since Ultra was reading the Abwehr's ciphers, any agent of a mind to acquaint his German spymaster with the true situation courted detection. Ultra not only monitored the agents but was able to supply a picture of the view from the German side—the order of battle, location of units, and so on. This made clear the reasons for the questions the German spymasters were asking their agents. The answers supplied by the Double-Cross System could then be tailored to the Abwehr's questions, and the latter's faith in the agents reinforced.

In the course of the war, notional networks of subagents—existing only in the minds of the deceivers (and of the Germans)—were fabricated to assist the Double-Cross agents. In addition, notional units were moved, notional landings planned, notional ships sunk, and notional sabotage carried out. As D-Day for Overlord (the invasion of France) approached, the Double-Cross System was ready to play its role in Operation Bodyguard.

Bodyguard had two main tasks on the invasion front. Fortitude North called for the creation of a notional army in Scotland that would keep Hitler's forces in Norway tied up there, expecting an invasion. Here the Double-Cross System helped by reporting the arrival of various notional units and by establishing the location of a notional headquarters. But the XX Committee's principal effort was in Fortitude South, designed to make the Germans believe the invasion of France would come from southeast England and that the Allies would land at Pas de Calais rather than in Normandy. Double-Cross agents, in particular "Garbo" (a Spaniard named Luis Calvo), created for the Abwehr a false order of battle that featured two army groups, one notional (FUSAG, the First U.S. Army Group, under the colorful command of General George Patton), one real (the Twenty-first Army Group in southeast England). Their presence in the southeast distracted Hitler's attention from the real invasion force gathering in the southwest and west of England and in the Midlands and helped convince him that the main strike would be in the Pas de Calais area.

The Double-Cross System did not end with the invasion. When Hitler launched his secret weapon, the V-bombs, double agents saved thousands of lives by misleading the Germans about where the bombs were landing. The Germans were maneuvered into aiming them short of London, and many fell in open country or in the suburbs. And in the continuing battle at sea similar tactics kept U-boats out of waters that had been notionally mined.

See also ABWEHR; LONDON CONTROLLING SECTION; MI5; MI6; PLAYBACK SYSTEM; ULTRA.

FURTHER READING: *J. C. Masterman, *The Double-Cross System in the War of 1939 to 1945* (1972); Anthony Cave Brown, *Bodyguard of Lies* (1975); Ewen Montagu, *Beyond Top Secret Ultra* (1978); Ronald Lewin, *Ultra Goes to War* (1978).

Downing, George *(1624-84)*   English diplomat and spy in Holland for the government of Oliver Cromwell.

Born in Dublin, Downing was the son of a lawyer who took the family to the colony of Massachusetts in 1638. Downing graduated from Harvard in 1642, the year in which the great rebellion broke out in England. He returned home, served in the forces of Oliver Cromwell against King Charles I, and in 1645 went to Scotland as Cromwell's secret agent.

After serving in Parliament (1654–56), Downing became British resident at The Hague (1657), where he added espionage to his diplomatic duties, reporting back to John Thurloe, Cromwell's spymaster in London. Downing spied on English royalists in Holland and on Dutch officials during the period of strained relations between England and Holland following the First Dutch War (1652–54).

Downing told Samuel Pepys that his spies at The Hague included servants of Jan De Witt, head of the Dutch government. As a result, Downing was able to report to Thurloe both oral decisions taken by De Witt in confidential conversations with his colleagues and the contents of top-secret documents in De Witt's possession. This information, however, proved of little consequence because Cromwell died in 1658, his commonwealth collapsed, and the restoration of King Charles II occurred in 1660.

Always adaptable, Downing accepted the restoration, served the new monarch, was knighted by him, received the title of baronet in 1663, amassed a fortune, and willed to the English government some of the most valuable real estate in London (including Downing Street, where the residence of the prime minister is now located). Downing's grandson used part of his immense inheritance to found Downing College, Cambridge.

See also THURLOE, JOHN.

FURTHER READING: *John Beresford, *The Godfather of Downing Street* (1925); Samuel Pepys, *Diary* (Robert Latham and William Matthews, eds., 1975), gives Downing's account of his espionage activities as reported by Pepys; J. P. Kenyon, *Stuart England* (1978), gives the historical background to Downing's career.

Dreyfus, Alfred *(1859-1935)*   French army officer and central figure of the Dreyfus Affair, a scandal that shook France at the end of the nineteenth century.

Dreyfus was born in Alsace, the son of a wealthy Jewish businessman. When the Germans won the Franco-Prussian War and took Alsace from France in 1871, the Dreyfus family, opting for French citizenship, moved to Paris. Dreyfus went to military school, entered the French army, and by 1889 held the rank of captain. Three years later, he was assigned to the Second Bureau (military intelligence) of the general staff at the ministry of war in Paris.

A number of his colleagues, especially Major Hubert Henry, were anti-Semitic enough to dislike Dreyfus because he was a Jew. Aristocrats among the officers considered him ambitious in a vulgar bourgeois manner. Men who had only their soldier's pay resented his wealth. Dreyfus was therefore vulnerable when catastrophe struck.

In 1894 he was suddenly arrested and charged with high treason. The evidence against him was a note offering to sell secret French military plans to the Germans. The note had gone from an officer on the general staff to the German Embassy in Paris, where it should have been delivered to the military attaché, Colonel Maximilian von Schwartzkoppen. A French counterspy intercepted the document and brought it to the Second Bureau. Henry informed his superiors that the handwriting proved Dreyfus had written the note.

Dreyfus was summoned to a meeting with staff officers, told by Major Armand du Paty de Clam to write lines from the incriminating note, and then arrested on the ground that the handwriting was the same. Incarcerated, Dreyfus received repeated visits from Paty de Clam, who tried fruitlessly to make him confess his guilt. The major was in good faith about this, but his good faith was the same as Henry's in that he was an anti-Semite willing to believe the worst of a Jewish officer.

Dreyfus, taken before a court-martial behind closed doors, protested his innocence, but his military judges manipulated the evidence to find him guilty. He was marched in front of the troops for a ceremonial degradation in which the insignia were stripped from his uniform and his sword broken. Then he stayed in jail until he could be shipped to Devil's Island.

Dreyfus spent the years 1895 to 1899 in the dreadful penal colony off French Guiana. He lived in a small stone hut with barred windows, constantly watched by an armed guard outside the door. By day he was allowed to walk in a treeless area of about half an acre. The climate and the food were so bad that he suffered at times from fever and indigestion. He cut wood, studied English, and wondered if he would ever see France again.

Meanwhile, back in France, the Dreyfus Affair erupted. His family pressed for a review of his conviction. Evidence accumulated that he was the victim of a miscarriage of justice, and that Major Ferdinand Esterhazy was really the guilty officer on the general staff. Novelist Émile Zola defended Dreyfus in the open letter "J'Accuse," which denounced the military. Henry forged documents to prove Dreyfus guilty, but the forgeries were exposed, and Henry confessed. Esterhazy fled to England, where he, too, confessed.

In 1899 Dreyfus was brought home to France from Devil's Island. He did not gain immediate vindication in court, but the president of France pardoned him. Only in 1906 did a legal ruling find him not guilty on all counts and order his reinstatement in the army with his old rank of captain.

Dreyfus, who had been degraded in a military ceremony, was reinstated in a military ceremony. He went back to his military career, retired in 1907, and came out of retirement to serve as an officer of the French army during World War I.

See also DREYFUS AFFAIR.

FURTHER READING: *Alfred Dreyfus, *Five Years of My Life* (1901); Betty Schechter, *The Dreyfus Affair: A National Scandal* (1965); Louis L. Snyder, *The Dreyfus Case: A Documentary History* (1973); David L. Lewis, *Prisoners of Honor: The Dreyfus Affair* (1973).

Dreyfus Affair *(1894-1906)*   French espionage affair, and the great national scandal of the Third Republic.

In 1894 a French counterspy intercepted a message from an officer on the French general staff to the military attaché of the German Embassy in Paris, Colonel Maximilian von Schwartzkoppen. This was the celebrated *bordereau,* or memorandum of the type that usually accompanied official documents. The writer offered to sell French military plans so secret that only a handful of officers knew about them, and it was quickly determined that somebody at general staff headquarters in Paris was a spy in the pay of the Germans.

Suspicion fell on Captain Alfred Dreyfus, an officer of the Second Bureau (intelligence). Dreyfus was ambitious, rich, and a Jew, three reasons why some of his colleagues resented him. He was brought before a secret court-martial that broke the military code by withholding evidence from his lawyer. Alphonse Bertillon, the founder of the prevailing method of criminal identification through a listing of personal characteristics, testified that the handwriting of the *bordereau* matched the defendant's. The military men sitting in judgment, tinged with anti-Semitism and jealous of the army's reputation, found Dreyfus guilty. He was dismissed from the army in 1895 and in 1896 sent to Devil's Island, the penal colony off French Guiana in South America.

The matter might have ended there except that in 1896 another document stolen from the German Embassy reached the Second Bureau, this one written by Schwartzkoppen and addressed to Major Ferdinand Esterhazy of the French general staff. The contents showed that Schwartzkoppen and Esterhazy were in surreptitious communication.

Lieutenant Colonel Georges Picquart, head of the Second Bureau, realized that Esterhazy, not Dreyfus, was the spy on the general staff, a truth reinforced by a comparison of the original *bordereau* with Esterhazy's handwriting. Picquart took the evidence to his superiors, who to his astonishment warned him to stop his investigation. When he persisted, they transferred him to North Africa.

Doubts about the guilt of Dreyfus were now widely expressed in the Paris press and even in the military. The army, refusing to admit it had made a mistake and concerned to protect its image, began a cover-up. Major Hubert Henry, the new head of the Second Bureau, fabricated evidence against Dreyfus, pious forgeries by which he thought to save the general staff from public ridicule. Even the chief of the general staff, General Raoul de Boisdeffre, believed that a miscarriage of justice might have occurred, but he felt that to admit it would tarnish the military and cost it the confidence of the French people.

As a result of this attitude, the army received a series of shocks much worse than might have been caused by candor and justice. The cover-up became more tortuous and less plausible as new facts came to light.

In 1897 Picquart made his evidence available to a lawyer, who passed it on to the vice president of the French senate, Auguste Scheurer-Kestner, who told his colleagues that Dreyfus was innocent. Also in 1897, a Paris newspaper published letters written by, and damaging to, Esterhazy, who demanded a court-martial, got one, and was found not guilty by the military men who judged him. Picquart, who refused to testify for Esterhazy, was himself court-martialed, found guilty of releasing official documents to the lawyer, and dismissed from the army (1898).

The entrance of novelist Émile Zola into the affair made it an issue of the French conscience. In 1898 Zola wrote the most famous document of the Dreyfus Affair, the open letter entitled "J'Accuse," addressed to the president of France, Félix Faure, and published in the newspaper *L'Aurore*, edited by Georges Clemenceau. Zola flatly blamed Esterhazy regarding the *bordereau* and, naming names, charged the ministry of war with ordering the exculpation of the known culprit. Zola demanded justice for Dreyfus.

The minister of war, General Auguste Mercier, sued Zola for libel. Mercier and Boisdeffre were among those who testified that there had been no cover-up and that Dreyfus was guilty. Henry appeared against Zola, Picquart for him. The novelist was found guilty, appealed, and won a second trial, but fearing that he could not receive justice in France, he fled to England.

France was rocked by the Dreyfus Affair. Those for Dreyfus were mainly of the left, republicans and anticlericals bent on curtailing the power of the Catholic Church in politics. Those against Dreyfus were mainly of the right, traditionalists, Catholics concerned for the place of the church in France, and anti-Semites who wanted Dreyfus to remain on Devil's Island because he was a Jew. The two sides, however, were not always clearly differentiated. Charles Péguy, a prominent Catholic writer, was pro-Dreyfus.

Some observers feared for the nation itself as the dispute grew worse, for the Third Republic, founded in 1870 after the defeat of France in the Franco-Prussian War, had not put down deep roots among the French people. Many Frenchmen regretted the overthrow of the Second Empire of Napoleon III, while others hoped for the return of the Bourbons, the old ruling dynasty of France. A solid minority, perhaps more than that, would not have been unhappy to see the Third Republic founder on the rocks of the Dreyfus Affair.

While the conflict went on, a French army officer, ordered to examine the Dreyfus documents, found that some had been forged by Henry. Arrested, Henry confessed. Alerted, Esterhazy escaped to England.

In view of these developments, Dreyfus had to be brought home for a reexamination of his conviction. In 1899 an appeals court overturned the verdict of 1894. Then it found Dreyfus guilty with extenuating circumstances with regard to some of the forged evidence. This verdict was so absurd that the president of France, Émile Loubet, put a stop to the harassment of Dreyfus by granting him a pardon.

Dreyfus, refusing to let the matter rest there, began a campaign for full vindication. In 1904 an appeals court agreed to reopen the entire case, and after one more evaluation of all the evidence, it threw out the second verdict against him (1906). He was reinstated in the army with his proper rank. The Dreyfus Affair was over.

Its effects lingered on, poisoning French society, which remained divided despite the outcome, and weakening France in the grave crises of the twentieth century. Anticlericals were so bitter that in World War I, Clemenceau, now premier of France, declined to put Ferdinand Foch, a staunchly Catholic general, in charge of military operations until France stood on the brink of disaster. Anti-Semites were so bitter that they helped prepare the way for the Nazi occupation of France during World War II. Only under the leadership of

Charles de Gaulle did the French people appear finally to emerge from the shadow of the Dreyfus Affair.

See also DREYFUS, ALFRED; ESTERHAZY, FERDINAND; HENRY, HUBERT; PIC-QUART, GEORGES.

FURTHER READING: Fred C. Conybeare, *The Dreyfus Case* (1899); Alfred Cobban, *A History of Modern France* (1961), gives the historical background of the Dreyfus Affair; *Louis L. Snyder, *The Dreyfus Case: A Documentary History* (1973); David L. Lewis, *Prisoners of Honor: The Dreyfus Affair* (1973).

Drop A place of concealment where an agent leaves espionage items to be retrieved by other agents.

A drop may be anything from a locker in a train station to a girder of an underpass to a hollow tree. The primary purpose of a drop is to protect two or more members of an espionage ring by making it unnecessary for them to meet, with the attendant danger of rousing suspicion. One furtively leaves what he or she has obtained at the agreed-upon place, and the other furtively picks it up. When a meeting would be safe but cannot be arranged, the drop functions as a place each can use at a convenient moment.

The term "letter box" is often used for "drop," but the former properly refers to a human being acting as a drop, typically one who finds espionage items in his letter box and hands them over when the right person calls.

FURTHER READING: *Ladislas Farago, *War of Wits: The Anatomy of Espionage and Intelligence* (1954); Christopher Felix, *A Short Course in the Secret War* (1963); U.S. Department of Defense, Joint Chiefs of Staff Publication No. 1, *Dictionary of Military and Associated Terms* (1972).

Duebendorfer, Rachel *(1901-73)*   Polish spy for the Soviet Union in Switzerland.

The daughter of a Jewish family named Hepner, Duebendorfer was born in Warsaw and spent part of her childhood in Danzig, a city later seized by Adolf Hitler—his final aggression before he started World War II (1939–45). Duebendorfer became a Communist in her youth and in 1920 began underground activities as a Soviet agent. She married and divorced during the 1920s, and about 1932 she took Henri Duebendorfer, a Swiss mechanic, for her second husband. It was purely a marriage of Communist convenience, the purpose being to gain her citizenship in Switzerland, where she could carry on her activities on behalf of the Soviet Union. Her husband disappeared from her life almost immediately.

During the decade 1934 to 1944 she lived in Bern with Paul Boettcher, a German journalist who worked with her for the Russians. In 1941, Sandor Rado, Moscow's spymaster in Switzerland, acting on orders from his superiors, brought Duebendorfer into his network. He gave her the code name "Sissy," and used her as his principal cut-out, or go-between with the rest of the members. However, she had a certain amount of independence, for the Russians occasionally dealt with her directly, using a code known to her but not to Rado.

Duebendorfer's great coup was her recruitment in 1942 of Christian Schneider ("Taylor"), who became her own cut-out with Rudolf Roessler

("Lucy"), the network's most important source of information on the German armed forces. When in 1943 the Russians ordered "Sissy" to try to discover the identity of "Lucy," she had the temerity to refuse, possibly through fear that Roessler would cease to spy for her, possibly because she did not want to be bypassed in dealing with him.

The Roessler reports went through Duebendorfer by way of Schneider until 1943, when Swiss counterintelligence broke up the Rado network. Arrested in 1944, Duebendorfer escaped from jail in 1945, reached Paris, and after the end of the war went to Russian-dominated eastern Europe, where she remained until her death.

See also RADO, SANDOR; ROESSLER, RUDOLF.

FURTHER READING: Alexander Foote, *Handbook for Spies* (2d ed., 1964); Sandor Rado, *Deckname Dora* (1972); *Paul L. Kesaris (ed.), *The Rote Kapelle: The CIA's History of Soviet Intelligence and Espionage Networks in Western Europe, 1936–1945* (1979); Anthony Read and David Fisher, *Operation Lucy: The Most Secret Spy Ring of the Second World War* (1981).

Dukes, Paul (1889-1967) British spy in Russia after the Russian Revolution.

Born in London, the son of a clergyman in the Church of England, Dukes studied at Charterhouse in Surrey and after graduation went to St. Petersburg (modern-day Leningrad) to study music at the conservatory (1909). He was at the Mariinsky Theater working with conductor Albert Coates in 1916 when he accepted an offer to join the Anglo-Russian commission that had arrived in St. Petersburg to coordinate the military and political efforts of the two nations as World War I continued.

In 1918 Dukes agreed to spy on the Bolsheviks, who had seized power in the previous year. Using forged identification papers, "ST25" for his signature on espionage reports, and different disguises depending on where he was, he performed the remarkable feat of getting himself accepted by the Soviet Communist party, the Red Army, the CHEKA (Extraordinary Commission for Combating Counterrevolution and Espionage, 1917–22; Soviet intelligence), and the Comintern (i.e., the Communist International). He sent reports back to London from each of these organizations during the years 1918 and 1919.

His achievement did not hinder the Communists from fastening their grip on Russia, but it won him a knighthood from King George V. Dukes devoted the rest of his life to writing, lecturing, and practicing yoga.

FURTHER READING: Paul Dukes, *Red Dusk and the Morrow* (1932); *Paul Dukes, *The Story of "ST25": Adventure and Romance in the Secret Intelligence Service in Red Russia* (1939); Arthur E. Adams (ed.), *The Russian Revolution and the Bolshevik Victory* (1972), describes the historical events that Dukes tried to influence.

Dulles, Allen (1893-1969) Director of the CIA.

Dulles belonged to a family of Watertown, New York, with a tradition of public service (his brother, like their grandfather and uncle, became secretary of state). He received his early education at home, in Washington, and while traveling in Europe. Entering Princeton in 1910, he took his bachelor's degree in 1914 and his master's in 1916, the year of his entry into the diplomatic service. He served in Bern, Switzerland, where he learned the value of espionage (but turned down the chance to meet an exiled Russian revolutionary named Lenin). Dulles was at Versailles when the treaties ending World War I (1914–18) were being discussed. Later assignments took him to Berlin and Constantinople (Istanbul). He became head of the Division of Near Eastern Affairs at the State Department (1922), and attended the Geneva disarmament conference (1927).

Dulles resigned from the State Department and practiced law in New York during the 1930s. When the chancellor of Germany, Adolf Hitler, started World War II in 1939, Dulles supported American aid to Britain and France. In 1941 he accepted an offer from William Donovan to join the espionage organization Donovan was building, the Office of the Coordinator of Information, which in 1942 became the OSS (Office of Strategic Services). Donovan sent Dulles back to Bern as a spy and troubleshooter for the OSS. During the years 1942 to 1945 Dulles gathered information on Nazi Germany. As the Third Reich faced collapse, Dulles carried on secret talks with dissident Germans who wanted to get rid of Hitler and surrender to the Allies. The talks failed because the Allies adhered to their pledge to the Russians and refused to make a separate peace with Germany. Dulles did, nevertheless, have a guiding hand in the negotiations that led to the surrender of German and Italian forces in Italy as the war neared its end.

In 1945 Dulles became chief of the OSS in the American zone of occupied Germany. He was at the Potsdam Conference of that year, when he reported to President Harry Truman that Japanese diplomats in Switzerland were putting out peace feelers with regard to the war in the Pacific, proposing a Japanese capitulation short of unconditional surrender (the offer was rejected, and Truman ended the war with the atomic bomb). Truman disbanded the OSS in 1945, and Dulles returned to his legal career.

Two years later, provoked by Soviet Cold War aggression, Truman signed the bill establishing the CIA (Central Intelligence Agency), the espionage organization of which Dulles became deputy director in 1951 and director in 1953. He served until 1961, becoming in the process the most celebrated personality in the history of the CIA and to the world the prototypical American spymaster. His agents operated in many places at home and around the globe. They dug and used the Berlin Tunnel between West Berlin and East Berlin that enabled them to listen in on phone conversations to and from Moscow (1955–56). They operated the remarkable flights of high-altitude U-2 American spy planes that for four years (1956–60) crossed the Soviet Union safely above the range of Soviet fighters or rockets.

There were not only successes, however. Two disasters occurred to the CIA while Dulles was director. One was the U-2 flight of Francis Gary Powers in 1960, just before the summit conference in Paris where President Dwight Eisenhower was scheduled to meet Soviet Premier Nikita Khrushchev. It was argued afterward that Dulles should have suggested canceling this U-2 flight for fear of something going wrong at so sensitive a moment. The flight was not canceled, Powers was shot down by a Russian rocket, and Khrushchev used the incident as an excuse to break up the summit conference. In 1961 Dulles presented arguments to President John Kennedy that a landing by Cuban exiles in Cuba at the Bay of Pigs could succeed in overturning the regime of Fidel Castro. In fact, the invasion collapsed in a matter of hours, and Castro openly turned to the Soviet Union for support.

Dulles resigned from the CIA in 1961 as a result of the Bay of Pigs. He turned from the practice of intelligence to writing about it, and although he respected the veil of silence covering classified information, he did clarify to some degree the manner in which the two disasters came about. With regard to the Powers U-2 flight, Dulles said it was a necessary link in a chain of flights and that Khrushchev's angry reaction was a mere pretense—the Soviet premier, realizing he could gain no concessions on Berlin at the Paris summit conference, used the U-2 incident as an excuse to disrupt the talks. With regard to the Bay of Pigs, Dulles pointed out that Kennedy at the last moment removed the air cover on which the invaders of Cuba had been depending. Dulles did not, however, claim in retrospect that the invasion would have been a success if the original conditions had been met.

In his writings on intelligence, Dulles remained a champion of the CIA. He took pains to rebut the argument that its agents ever made policy or attempted to circumvent orders from the President. He derided the notion that the CIA and other intelligence establishments ever constituted an "invisible government" of the United States. He adhered firmly to his position that the CIA was a responsible organization and should be retained pretty much as he knew it.

See also BAY OF PIGS; CIA; DONOVAN, WILLIAM; OSS; POWERS, FRANCIS GARY; U-2.

FURTHER READING: *Allen Dulles, *The Craft of Intelligence* (paperback ed., 1965); Allen Dulles, *The Secret Surrender* (1966), concerns the capitulation of German and Italian troops in Italy at the end of World War II; David Wise, *The Politics of Lying: Government Deception, Secrecy and Power* (1973), contradicts the Dulles view of the CIA.

***Dunlap, Jack** (1928-63)*   American spy for the Soviet Union.

Born in Louisiana, Dunlap liked to pretend in later years that his family owned a plantation. His father was actually a manual laborer who at one time served as a bridgetender. Dunlap himself dropped out of high school during World War II and went to sea aboard a ship in the merchant marine.

In 1952 he joined the United States Army, saw service in the Korean War as it was winding down, and emerged with a military record that earned him a good-conduct medal. He remained in the Army after the war, serving in various units and rising to the rank of sergeant.

The Army assigned Dunlap to the National Security Agency (NSA) in 1958 as one of the support personnel of that top-secret organization. Beginning as a chauffeur to the assistant director of the NSA, he received a promotion to the responsible position of document expediter, meaning a clerk-messenger carrying classified documents between officials with the clearance to see them.

Some time in 1958 an agent for the Soviet Union approached Dunlap, offering to pay for the contents of documents he handled. Avid for money, Dunlap agreed, and during the period 1959 to 1963 he turned over some of the most secret information possessed by the NSA, his method being, apparently, to sneak the documents out and back in by concealing them under his shirt.

In 1960 it was noticed that Dunlap was spending much more money than his pay could account for, but the authorities did nothing until 1963, when, as his tour of duty neared an end, he asked to be released from the Army and attached to the NSA as a civilian. A routine check, including a lie detector test, revealed derogatory facts about him. An investigation followed, he was found to be living in suspiciously high style, and the Army transferred him out of the NSA.

Realizing that the Army and the NSA had him under surveillance, Dunlap committed suicide by pumping carbon monoxide into his parked car. Only when his widow reported finding a cache of classified documents among his effects did the full scope of his espionage activities come to light.

FURTHER READING: David Kahn, *The Codebreakers: The Story of Secret Writing* (1967); Dan Oberdorfer, "The Playboy Sergeant," in Allen Dulles (ed.), *Great True Spy Stories* (1968).

Dzerzhinsky, Felix *(1877-1926)* Polish-Lithuanian head of the spy and terror apparatus of the Soviet Union.

Although born in Vilna, Lithuania, and the son of a prosperous Polish farmer, Dzerzhinsky was a Russian citizen at birth, since both Lithuania and Poland belonged to the Russian empire. He became a political radical early in life, making common cause with the Russian underground plotting the overthrow of the tsar. Exiled to Siberia in 1897 for agitating against the government, he escaped in 1899, was arrested again in 1900, and escaped again two years later. He fled to Berlin, where he continued to conspire with Russian revolutionaries for the downfall of the tsarist regime.

Dzerzhinsky was in Poland in 1905 when the abortive revolution of that year broke out. Captured by the tsarist police, he served a seven-year sentence (1905–12), returned to political agitation, and was caught again and sentenced to nine years. He served this sentence until 1917, when the successful Russian Revolution brought his release. He became a leader of the Bolsheviks in Petrograd (now called Leningrad).

Vladimir Ilyich Lenin, leader of the Bolsheviks and head of the Communist state after the Bolshevik triumph, named Dzerzhinsky director of the secret police, first called the CHEKA (Extraordinary Commission for Combating Counterrevolution and Espionage, 1917–22) and then the OGPU (United State Political Administration, 1923–34). Dzerzhinsky was thus the founder of the spy and terror organization that has ever since, under different acronyms, of which KGB (Committee for State Security) is the latest, played a fundamental role in the Soviet government. He did not himself introduce the worst excesses of the OGPU, which came later during Stalin's dictatorship, but by resorting to brutal methods to keep the Soviet people cowed and by using secret agents against anti-Communist Russians in exile, he blazed the trail later followed by Stalin's henchmen to a policy of deceit, violence, and mass terror.

Dzerzhinsky was not the complete policeman they were, and he tended at the end to leave the OGPU to his subordinates while he concentrated on being an official in the Soviet economic system. As commissar of transport in 1921, he reorganized the railroads. He became director of the Economic Council in 1924 shortly before his death.

See also KGB.

FURTHER READING: Robert Conquest, *The Soviet Police System* (1968); *Boris Levytsky, *The Uses of Terror: The Soviet Secret Service, 1917–1970* (1971); Richard Deacon, *History of the Russian Secret Service* (1972).

Eden, William *(1744-1814)*   Head of the British secret service during the American War of Independence.

Eden was an English aristocrat who studied at Eton and Oxford before entering Parliament. He held a succession of government offices, culminating in his appointment to the Board of Trade and Plantations in 1776. He became deeply involved in American affairs before and after the outbreak of the American Revolution, during which one of his principal responsibilities was to keep under surveillance the American agents who arrived in Europe looking for diplomatic recognition, military supplies, and alliances.

To meet this responsibility, Eden organized an elaborate secret service. Between the years 1776 and 1778, he had spies in all the major capitals of the Continent, a network through which intelligence information filtered back to London, where Eden made abstracts for use by the British government in attempting to counteract the Americans.

His best agents in this work were naturally American Loyalists who knew the American scene and could pass as Patriots if they had to. Paul Wentworth of New Hampshire, Eden's right-hand man in London, had charge of espionage in Paris, the most sensitive spot in Europe, since the Americans hoped to bring France into the War of Independence on their side.

Wentworth recruited Edward Bancroft of Massachusetts, who became his most dependable spy in Paris. The Reverend John Vardill of New York planned one of the coups of Eden's spy network, the 1777 theft of a file of dispatches from the American commissioners in Paris to the Continental Congress in Philadelphia. An agent spirited the dispatches from their pouches at Le Havre and substituted blank paper for the transatlantic voyage.

Eden's main concern was to persuade the Americans to return to their allegiance to the crown, and he became alarmed as Bancroft's reports revealed the progress of the talks between the French government and the three American commissioners, Benjamin Franklin, Arthur Lee, and Silas Deane. In 1777 Eden sent Wentworth to Paris to make offers that might interrupt the negotiations, but Wentworth failed because of the British demands for American capitulation.

Eden became personally involved in negotiating with the Americans in 1778, after the Franco-American alliance had become a reality. He served as one of a three-man British commission that went to America, refused to accept American independence, and returned to London empty-handed.

After that, having established the British secret service in its modern form, Eden moved out of espionage into higher posts in the king's government, winning for his efforts the title of Baron Auckland.

See also BANCROFT, EDWARD; DEANE, SILAS; WENTWORTH, PAUL.

FURTHER READING: Lewis Einstein, *Divided Loyalties: Americans in England during the War of Independence* (1933); Carl Van Doren, *Secret History of the American Revolution* (1941); *Richard Deacon, *A History of the British Secret Service* (1969), has a chapter on Eden.

Edmonds, Emma *(1841-98)*   Soldier, nurse, and spy for the Union during the American Civil War.

Edmonds was a Canadian born in New Brunswick, the daughter of a farmer. Raised in a religious atmosphere, she read the Bible fervently, attended church regularly, and, early in life, decided to go to the United States and become a missionary.

Adopting masculine attire, she worked as a salesman of religious books, covering territory between New England and Michigan, where she was in 1861 when the Civil War broke out. Her hatred of slavery, which sprang from intense moral and religious convictions, led her to join the Union army posing as "Franklin Thompson."

She seems to have maintained this imposture for two years, although the memoir she published in 1865 portrays her as a nurse at the beginning of her field service and later switching to being a soldier. In any case, she was present at the first battle of Bull Run (1861), after which she did nursing among the wounded. She was in uniform, posing as a man, during the Peninsular Campaign (1862), the battle of Antietam (1862), and the battle of Fredericksburg (1863).

At the time of the Peninsular Campaign, she volunteered to go into undercover work, for she felt attracted to spying because of the excitement. Edmonds worked in dangerous circumstances, garbed as a man for the most part and liable to be shot if caught.

While Union General George McClellan was waging the fruitless Peninsular Campaign, Edmonds went as a spy to Yorktown, posing as a black man (she used burnt cork to turn her hands and face the right color). Put to work by the Confederates on the assumption that she was a slave, she labored on the fortifications of Yorktown, covertly made sketches, and hid the papers in the soles of her shoes.

Escaping, Edmonds carried her information back to Union headquarters, including a report that the Confederate command considered Yorktown indefensible. On a second mission, she "posed" as a woman, and again came back safely. McClellan took Yorktown, acting partly on her evidence, but he mishandled the Seven Days' Battle and was driven back by Confederate General Robert E. Lee.

In 1863 Edmonds' military unit was transferred to Kentucky. She writes of more spying in Louisville, after which she left the army for health reasons. Resuming women's dress, she married Linus H. Seelye and wrote her autobiography, which had a phenomenal sale.

In 1882, while applying for a soldier's pension, she necessarily confessed her imposture. The facts became known, her old comrades-in-arms supported her appeal (a few had guessed the truth at the time), and she received her pension. In the year of her death, she became the only woman to be openly received into the Grand Army of the Republic, the organization of Civil War veterans.

FURTHER READING: S. Emma E. Edmonds, *Nurse and Spy in the Union Army: Comprising the Adventures and Experiences of a Woman in Hospitals, Camps, and Battle-Fields* (1865); *Sylvia G. L. Dannett, *She Rode with the Generals: The True and Incredible Story of Sarah Emma Seelye, alias Franklin Thompson* (1960); Oscar A. Kinchen, *Women Who Spied for the Blue and the Gray* (1972).

Eichmann, Adolf *(1906-62)* German war criminal tracked down and seized by operatives of Israeli intelligence.

Born in Solingen, Germany, into a lower-class family, Eichmann went to Austria in his youth, found a job in Linz, and by 1930 was working for an oil company in Vienna. He became an anti-Semite, joined the Austrian Nazi party in 1932, and moved to Germany. Ironically, he rose in the party as an expert on the Jews. To further his career he learned both Hebrew and Yiddish, along with studying Jewish history, culture, and religion. In 1940, following the outbreak of World War II, he received a promotion to chief of the Jewish section of the RSHA (Reich Central Security Office), the combined police and intelligence forces of Adolf Hitler's Third Reich.

Eichmann attended the Nazi meeting of 1942 at which it was decided to move the Jews to concentration camps. He received responsibility for implementing Adolf Hitler's "final solution" of the Nazi "Jewish problem." Eichmann had charge of the death camps where victims were murdered in gas chambers or otherwise barbarously put to death. In 1944 he reported to Himmler that the number of dead amounted to six million.

By then Nazi Germany was clearly losing the war. When the end came in 1945, Eichmann was interned by the Americans, but he escaped in 1946 and fled to South America, settling under an assumed identity in Buenos Aires. He remained high on the list of German war criminals wanted by the Allied governments.

Simon Wiesenthal, devoted to the punishment of guilty Nazis, gave information to Israeli intelligence, which by 1960 knew where to find Eichmann. Under the personal direction of Isser Harel, the head of the Mossad (Central Institution for Intelligence and Special Assignments; Israeli intelligence), Israeli agents kidnaped Eichmann from a Buenos Aires street and transported him clandestinely to Israel. Found guilty in 1961 of crimes against humanity, he was hanged in 1962.

See also HAREL, ISSER; WIESENTHAL, SIMON.

FURTHER READING: Hannah Arendt, *Eichmann in Jerusalem: A Report on the Banaltiy of Evil* (1963); Moshe Pearlman, *The Capture and Trial of Adolf Eichmann* (1963); *Isser Harel, *The House on Garibaldi Street: The First Account of the Capture of Adolf Eichmann Told by the Former Head of Israel's Secret Service* (1975).

Emmet, Robert *(1778-1803)*   Irish patriot who conspired to overthrow British rule in Ireland.

Born in Dublin, the son of a physician, Emmet was a brother of Thomas Addis Emmet. Both, after graduating from Trinity College, Dublin, joined the United Irishmen when Wolfe Tone led that patriotic organization in a futile attempt to free Ireland. Following the failure of the rebellion of 1798, Thomas Addis went into exile in America. Robert went to France to plan another rebellion, acting on the Irish maxim that "England's difficulty is Ireland's opportunity." This time the "opportunity" was provided by Great Britain's war with Napoleonic France.

In 1800 Emmet was conspiring with Irish refugees in Paris. In 1802 he had an interview with Napoleon, who gave him an indication that a rupture of the Peace of Amiens (1802) was near and that a French army might invade England.

Emmet hurried home to Ireland, gathered other rebels around him, stored weapons for an insurrection, and exulted when the Peace of Amiens collapsed in 1803. He set July 23 as the day when he would begin the drive for Irish freedom in Dublin, hoping to spark similar rebellions throughout Ireland. But there were government spies in his organization, and when Emmet and his followers marched through the streets of Dublin, they were quickly dispersed.

Emmet fled into the Wicklow Mountains south of Dublin and then moved to a hideout near the home of his betrothed, Sarah Curran. She was the daughter of the Irish patriot John Philpot Curran, a lawyer who had defended the rebels of 1798. Curran's law partner, Leonard MacNally, also had defended the rebels but was actually a government spy.

MacNally learned from Sarah where Emmet was hiding, and informed on him. When Emmet was captured and put on trial, MacNally appeared in court for the defense. MacNally enjoyed the trust of Emmet, Curran, and Sarah, and no one blamed him when the defendant was condemned and executed.

Emmet is remembered among the romantic failures in the fight for Irish freedom, in this resembling Roger Casement, who appeared a century later. One of those who lamented Emmet's tragedy was the Irish poet Thomas Moore, who took this theme for his inspiration when he wrote his poignant verse, "She is far from the land where her young hero sleeps."

See also MacNALLY, LEONARD.

FURTHER READING: Raymond Postgate, *Robert Emmet* (1931); Roy Jenkins, *Sarah Curran* (1958); *Leon O'Broin, *The Unfortunate Mr. Robert Emmet* (1958).

Enigma   German cryptological machine of World War II.

The origin of the Enigma machine was international: the idea of using electrical impulses to construct ciphers occurred to different cryptologists in different countries. Edward Hebern of the United States (1915), Hugo Koch of the Netherlands (1919), Arthur Scherbius of Germany (1923), and Boris Hagelein of Sweden (1934) all made contributions to the invention. Scherbius gave it the name that stuck and that became celebrated in the history of cryptology—"Enigma." Moreover, the German armed forces adopted the Scherbius model and turned it into a battlefield weapon.

The final version of Enigma consisted of two electric typewriters connected by wires leading to and from a plugboard to which they were fixed by jacks. The central part of the machine was a series of rotors, each bearing twenty-six cryptographic signs, standing for the letters of the alphabet, and each capable of spinning independently of the others. The clerk who used the Enigma typed the plaintext on one typewriter. The second typewriter reproduced the message in cipher. In between came the electrical impulses that spun the rotors, lining up their letters in the proper order.

The problem for a cryptanalyst was the fact that a different sign represented a given letter each time it appeared in a message. That is, each time a key was struck, the rotors moved into different positions. The number of possible combinations in the alignment of the rotors depended on the number of rotors. The German Enigma could accommodate five, which made the number of possibilities astronomical. Because of this, the Germans considered their ciphers unbreakable. They therefore used the same system throughout the war.

The story of how Enigma was, in fact, broken is a complex one involving Polish, French, and British cryptologists. These Allies obtained a German model before the war. French intelligence received operating instructions from a double agent at the cipher center in Berlin. A complete Enigma was built by the Poles from information provided by a Polish worker who had held a job in a German factory turning out the machines. No human mind could read the enciphered messages, but possession of one model enabled the Allies to attack the problem of building a machine capable of so doing. The Poles were moving ahead in this field, and they had the theoretical part done when World War II broke out in 1939.

The German conquest of Poland threw the burden onto the French and British. The fall of France in 1940 interrupted this cooperative effort. The British went ahead on their own, and their Ultra system eventually solved the problem. The solution amounted to building a primitive computer capable of making the rapid calculations needed to read Enigma ciphers. This achievement enabled the British to decipher German wartime messages transmitted by radio and to discover battle plans almost as soon as they were broadcast to German commanders in the field. The war in the Pacific was affected in the same way when the Japanese Purple cipher, a variation of Enigma, was broken in Washington.

In the postwar world, Enigma led to the development of enormously complex electronic cryptological machines, and Ultra to the development of advanced computers that can solve their ciphers. The battle of machines continues.

See also CIPHER; PURPLE; ULTRA.

FURTHER READING: *David Kahn, *The Codebreakers: The Story of Secret Writing* (1967); Ronald W. Clark, *The Man Who Broke Purple* (1977); Brian Johnson, *The Secret War* (1978); Ronald Lewin, *Ultra Goes to War: The First Account of World War II's Greatest Secret, Based on Official Documents* (1978); *F. H. Hinsley (with E. E. Thomas, C. F. G. Ransom, and R. C. Knight), *British Intelligence in the Second World War: Its Influence on Strategy and Operations* (vol. 1, 1979; vol. 2, 1981).

Erickson, Eric *(1889-1960)*   Ostensible Swedish Nazi and actual spy for the western Allies against Germany during World War II.

Born in New York, Erickson spent his early life in the United States. The poverty of his family compelled him to leave school, and after a succession of jobs, he became an employee of Standard Oil in Texas, where he made sufficient money to finance an education at Cornell University, which he entered in 1917.

World War I interrupted his studies, but he returned from service in the U.S. armed forces to take his degree. He worked for oil companies in the Far East during the 1920s. Then he went to Stockholm, where he established his own oil business and became a naturalized citizen of Sweden.

After the outbreak of World War II, Laurence Steinhardt, the American ambassador to Moscow, persuaded Erickson, who could readily visit Nazi Germany as a businessman, to report on German synthetic oil production. During the years 1941 to 1944, Erickson made many trips to Germany, cultivated high-ranking Nazis, and even persuaded the Berlin government to establish an oil refinery in Sweden. After that, he watched German methods and laboratory work at close range.

Erickson posed as a fervent Nazi all this time, and thereby incurred intense dislike in Sweden just as he curried favor in Berlin. He reported clandestinely to Allied intelligence, Britain's MI6 (Military Intelligence 6) and America's OSS

(Office of Strategic Services), his chief contribution being the identification of major Nazi oil installations inside Germany.

Erickson completely fooled Walter Schellenberg, head of Nazi counteres-pionage. Whether Erickson fooled Admiral Wilhelm Canaris, head of Nazi military espionage, is not clear. Canaris is known to have worked against the Hitler regime, and he may deliberately have failed to act against Erickson.

Through this Swedish businessman, the Allies kept track of German syn-thetic oil production during World War II. The principal installations were bombed repeatedly by British and American air fleets, thus curtailing the production of the lubricant vital for the Nazi war machine, which ground to a halt in many places when its oil ran out.

After the fall of Nazi Germany in 1945, Erickson returned to being simply a Swedish businessman with oil interests. His popularity in Stockholm revived as the truth about his wartime activities became public.

See also CANARIS, WILHELM; MI6; OSS; SCHELLENBERG, WALTER.

FURTHER READING: Walter Schellenberg, *The Labyrinth: The Memoirs of Walter Schellenberg* (1956); *Alexander Klein, *The Counterfeit Traitor* (1958); David Kahn, *Hitler's Spies: German Military Intelligence in World War II,* (1978).

Ernst, Karl *(1871-1930?)* German secret agent operating in London until World War I.

Although born in Hoxton, England, Ernst was of German parentage, he married a German wife, and his fundamental sympathies were German. He opened a barber shop in London in 1899, where he became known to German officers, first to those who simply wanted a haircut and then to those who were looking for information about conditions in Britain.

In 1909 Ernst became part of a German spy ring reporting directly to Gustav Steinhauer, who had responsibility for the kaiser's espionage in the British Isles. Ernst agreed to serve as Steinhauer's "letter box" in London, receiving from him addressed envelopes to forward to other spies and writing to Ger-many to "Frau T. Reimers," which was Steinhauer's cover name. Ernst clipped stories from British newspapers dealing with the British armed forces. He pumped British customers whose hair he cut. All relevant information went to Steinhauer in Berlin for evaluation.

But too much correspondence came to the barbershop from Germany, and too many letters addressed to Berlin came from it; in 1911 Vernon Kell of MI5 (Military Intelligence 5, British counterespionage) asked the home secretary, Winston Churchill, to allow covert censorship of the mail to and from Ernst. Churchill agreed, and Kell began following leads until he discovered the iden-tity of most of the German spies in Britain. He and his partner in counteres-pionage, Basil Thomson of the Special Branch (Scotland Yard), were able to arrest these spies in 1914 when World War I started.

Karl Ernst was among the first to go on trial accused of espionage. The judge imposed on him a term of seven years, which kept him in jail throughout the war.

See also KELL, VERNON; STEINHAUER, GUSTAV.

FURTHER READING: Gustav Steinhauer, *Steinhauer: The Kaiser's Master Spy* (1924); *John Bulloch, *MI5: The Origin and History of the British Counter-Espionage Service* (1963); Rich-ard Deacon, *A History of the British Secret Service* (1969).

Espionage   The art and science of spying in the most general sense; also, a noun standing for an organization that practices espionage.
See INTELLIGENCE; SPY.

Espionage Revolution   The international practice of exchanging spies instead of executing them.

Throughout most of history it has been an accepted principle of international law that men and women caught spying may be executed, and the death penalty was imposed in the most notorious cases until the 1960s. The rivalry between the democracies and the Communist bloc that emerged as a consequence of World War II involved a growing number of secret agents operating on both sides. The nations began to see that getting their own spies back was more important than executing enemy spies, and so a new policy developed of holding those who were caught until opportunities for exchanges might arise.

James Donovan, a New York lawyer, explicitly made this point in 1957 when he suggested that Russian spy Rudolf Abel, convicted by an American court, be spared execution because someday an American spy might be captured in Russia, and both nations might want to negotiate a transfer. Donovan's foresight was demonstrated in 1960 when American U-2 pilot Francis Gary Powers was shot down while on an espionage flight over the Soviet Union. In 1962 Donovan and East German lawyer Wolfgang Vogel negotiated a transfer of Abel for Powers.

In 1964 Vogel worked with British representatives for the transfer of Gordon Lonsdale (a Russian spy captured in England) for Greville Wynne (a British spy captured in Hungary). In 1969 Vogel arranged the transfer of Peter and Helen Kroger (conspirators with Lonsdale) for Gerald Brooke (a prisoner in Russia who protested he was not a spy).

These deals established the current espionage revolution.
See also DONOVAN, JAMES; VOGEL, WOLFGANG.

FURTHER READING: James B. Donovan, *Strangers on a Bridge: The Case of Colonel Abel* (1964); David Wise and Thomas B. Ross, *The Espionage Establishment* (1967), has a chapter on the espionage revolution; *E. H. Cookridge, *Spy Trade* (1971).

Esterhazy, Ferdinand *(1847-1923)*   French intelligence officer and spy for Germany; involved in the Dreyfus Affair.

Esterhazy, of French birth, Hungarian ancestry, and somewhat murky past, began his military career by joining the French Foreign Legion and serving in North Africa. He shifted to the regular French army when the Franco-Prussian War (1870–71) created a sudden demand for officers. In 1881 a successful undercover mission brought him the rank of major with assignment to the Second Bureau (military intelligence) of the general staff at the ministry of war in Paris.

Esterhazy kept mistresses and in other ways lived expensively even though he had a family. He found that he could not pay his debts out of his officer's pay. His solution to this problem was to turn double agent for the Germans. Before his treasonable activities ceased, he transmitted much classified information to Colonel Maximilian von Schwartzkoppen, the military attaché of the German Embassy in Paris.

On September 1, 1894, Esterhazy delivered to the embassy a memorandum offering to sell five top-secret French military plans. A French counterspy intercepted this document and took it to the French ministry of war, where a search began for the spy, who could only have been on or associated with the general staff.

Major Hubert Henry of the Second Bureau recognized that the memorandum was on Esterhazy's stationery, but he apparently thought that Captain Alfred Dreyfus was the writer. The leading expert on criminal identification, Alphonse Bertillon, lent his authority to the same conclusion. Convicted by a court-martial, Dreyfus went to Devil's Island in 1895.

In 1896 the head of the Second Bureau, Lieutenant Colonel Georges Picquart, presented his superiors with proof, in another document filched from the German Embassy, that Esterhazy was the culprit. For his pains, Picquart was ordered to remain silent and transferred to North Africa.

Henry, who replaced Picquart at the Second Bureau, backed Esterhazy against Dreyfus and forged anti-Dreyfus documents. The army, afraid of what the truth might be, began a cover-up. Esterhazy, prompted by fear that the fact would become known, went to Schwartzkoppen in 1897 and asked him to say that the Germans had been dealing with Dreyfus, but Schwartzkoppen refused.

Esterhazy wrote emotional, threatening letters to the president of France, Félix Faure, who ignored them. When the Dreyfus family accused Esterhazy and when some of his past letters were published showing that he felt contempt for France, he boldly demanded a court-martial, in the belief that the army would not dare to convict him and admit the innocence of Dreyfus. Esterhazy's belief was correct. The court-martial found him not guilty.

But Émile Zola's open letter "J'Accuse" (1898) jolted the ministry of war, the army, and Esterhazy. Addressing the president of France, Zola condemned the conspiracy of the military and demanded justice for Dreyfus. Zola was tried for libel, and since the court he faced was biased against him, he fled to England. He had, however, made the Dreyfus Affair a matter of conscience for the French people, who divided into passionate factions for and against Dreyfus.

Henry tried to stop the scandal by forging documents ostensibly written by Dreyfus, but exposure of this fraud only made the scandal worse. When Henry broke down under interrogation and told the truth, Esterhazy, now under investigation by the army, fled to England. There he confessed to writing the original *bordereau,* although he put the blame on a superior officer who was conveniently dead. Understandably, Esterhazy never returned to Paris.

See also DREYFUS AFFAIR.

FURTHER READING: Alfred Cobban, *A History of Modern France* (1961), gives the historical background of the Dreyfus Affair; Betty Schechter, *The Dreyfus Affair: A National Scandal* (1965); *Louis L. Snyder, *The Dreyfus Case: A Documentary History* (1973).

Farnsworth, John (1893-)   American spy for Japan.

Born in Cincinnati, Farnsworth belonged to an average middle-class family. After high school, he gained an appointment to Annapolis (1911). He graduated in 1915, served on a destroyer during World War I (1917–18), and studied aeronautical engineering at the Naval Academy (1922) and the Massachusetts Institute of Technology (1923).

Farnsworth rose to the rank of lieutenant commander but was discharged from the Navy in 1927 for borrowing money from an enlisted man, who reported him to the authorities. Farnsworth began spying for the Japanese at some point during the next few years. His method was to cultivate old friends in the Navy, from whom he gathered information on tactics, new ships, and technological advances in gunnery and communications.

In 1934 naval intelligence discovered he was in possession (unauthorized) of a classified document on naval security. Kept under surveillance, he was found to be spending much more money than his known sources of income could account for. When evidence was discovered that he was getting the money from Japanese agents, he was arrested (1936) and imprisoned (1937).

The Farnsworth case led to tighter security measures in the Navy. It also produced a greater awareness in Washington that Japan was engaged in an espionage campaign against the United States, the meaning of which became clear in 1941, after the Japanese attack on Pearl Harbor.

FURTHER READING: *Alan Hynd, *Betrayal from the East: The Inside Story of Japanese Spies in America* (1943); Ronald Seth, *Secret Servants: The Story of Japanese Espionage* (1957).

Fauche-Borel, Louis (1762-1829)   French royalist undercover agent during the French Revolution and the Napoleonic era.

Fauche-Borel was at birth simply "Fauche." He later added the surname of his wife, creating the hyphenated form by which he was known in his maturity. He learned to be a printer in his father's shop in Neuchâtel, Switzerland, before establishing his own printing business there in 1786.

After the outbreak of the French Revolution in 1789, Fauche-Borel printed royalist attacks on the revolutionaries. In 1791 he published the Declaration of Pilnitz, in which the emperor of Austria and the king of Prussia threatened to restore King Louis XVI by force to his rightful place as absolute monarch of France. Fauche-Borel, continued turning out royalist documents from his printing shop for the next four years.

In 1795 he met the comte de Montgaillard, an adventurer and turncoat who at the time happened to be working for the royalists. Montgaillard persuaded Fauche-Borel to become a royalist undercover agent and introduced him to Louis Joseph de Bourbon, prince de Condé, who sent him to see General Charles Pichegru, victorious in the name of the revolution but known to be dissatisfied with its violence.

Fauche-Borel met Pichegru several times at his Strasbourg headquarters and went to Switzerland to obtain money for Pichegru's army from William Wickham, the British spymaster in Bern. But arrangements could not be worked out for Pichegru to come over to the royalists (he later did so, in the time of Napoleon, and paid for it with his life).

Montgaillard, angry that Fauche-Borel had acted independently and blaming

Fauche-Borel for the failure of the mission, denounced him to the revolutionaries in Paris, who thereupon issued an order for Fauche-Borel's arrest, which occurred in 1802 when the latter incautiously entered Paris to continue his undercover work. He was in prison in 1804 when the French minister of police, Joseph Fouché, found him and offered to have him released if he would become a spy for the emperor, Napoleon Bonaparte.

Pretending to accept the offer, Fauche-Borel went to Germany at Fouché's behest and promptly turned royalist again. In 1806 Fauche-Borel received a letter from Charles Perlet in Paris telling him that leaders of a secret committee of underground royalists would like to meet him. Fauche-Borel sent his nephew, Charles Vitel, to Paris, and Vitel was seized by Fouché's agents and executed (1807). The secret committee was a myth created at the Paris ministry of police in the hope of luring royalists like Fauche-Borel back to France, where they could be arrested.

Fauche-Borel went to Paris in 1814, after the fall of Napoleon, and he was there in 1815 during the Hundred Days, when Napoleon returned from his exile on Elba to meet disaster at Waterloo. When Perlet called him a Bonapartist spy, Fauche-Borel sued for libel and won (1816). Fauche-Borel resumed his printing business, but the past seems to have preyed on his mind, and he committed suicide.

See also FOUCHÉ, JOSEPH; MONTGAILLARD, COMTE DE; PERLET, CHARLES; WICKHAM, WILLIAM.

FURTHER READING: John Hall, *General Pichegru's Treason* (1915); *G. Lenôtre, *Two Royalist Spies of the French Revolution* (1924), presents Fauche-Borel as one of the pair; Hubert Cole, *Fouché, the Unprincipled Patriot* (1971).

FBI Agency responsible for national police and counterespionage operations in the United States.

Established within the Justice Department in 1908 as the Bureau of Investigation, the FBI (Federal Bureau of Investigation) gained its present title in 1935, by which time it had become one of the most familiar organizations in America. Today it has thirteen divisions, including Identification (founded in 1924), the Crime Laboratory (1932), the FBI Academy (1935), and Computer Systems (1954). Each division has expanded its operations since its foundation, and numerous subdivisions have been added (e.g., the Computerized Criminal History programs in 1971). From headquarters in Washington, the FBI administers fifty-nine regional offices at home and more than a dozen abroad. The function of these offices is to cooperate with local police and to investigate criminal activities within specific categories defined by Congress. The latter include such crimes as kidnapping, air hijacking, violations of civil rights, and espionage.

The FBI has the world's most comprehensive system of crime fighting. It is staffed by specialists in every field, and its departments rank among the most advanced in serology, toxicology, and neutron activation analysis (atomic analysis of substances). FBI files contain millions of documents, including forged checks, typing analyses, charred paper, and coded messages from espionage cases. More than 1 million fingerprints are recorded. The editorial department issues the *Law Enforcement Bulletin* every month and *Uniform Crime Reports* every year. The FBI Academy, in Quantico, Virginia, trains the agents who belong to the organization. Representatives of other law enforcement agencies come to the academy for conferences on crime statistics and the latest methods of investigation.

The current form of the FBI is substantially the work of one man—J. Edgar Hoover, who in 1924 became director with a mandate from Attorney General Harlan Fiske Stone to reorganize the institution, which had deteriorated during the scandals of the administration of President Warren Gamaliel Harding (1921–23). Stone's commission to Hoover took the FBI out of politics and instituted a merit system for the employment and promotion of agents. Hoover succeeded so well in bringing the FBI into line with Stone's orders that he received renomination by every subsequent President and remained in office until his death.

The prestige of the FBI rose in the 1930s, when the crime wave in the United States proved too much for state, county, and city police to handle. In 1932 Congress passed the "Lindbergh law" (following the kidnapping and death of the infant son of aviation pioneer Charles A. Lindbergh), which made this type of crime a federal offense and gave responsibility for its investigation to the FBI, whose agents were now allowed to carry guns. The agents soon became the celebrated G-men ("government men") of American folklore. In 1934 they assisted in the investigation that led to the arrest of Bruno Richard Hauptmann, who was executed for the Lindbergh kidnaping, and they trapped desperado John Dillinger, who was shot by an FBI agent while resisting arrest.

As the 1930s were the gang-busting years of the FBI, the 1940s were the years of counterespionage. In 1939 an executive order of President Franklin Roosevelt gave Hoover's organization responsibility for domestic security, that is, for investigating espionage, sabotage, and subversive activities within the United States. In 1940, after the outbreak of World War II (1939–45) but before American participation in the hostilities, Hoover and his agents worked with the British Security Coordination (BSC), an organization headed by a Canadian, William Stephenson, and responsible for combined Anglo-American counterespionage. The activities supervised by Hoover and Stephenson had to be clandestine because of America's official neutrality. In 1941, but before the Japanese attack on Pearl Harbor, the FBI arrested a ring of Nazi spies, all of whom went to jail.

After Pearl Harbor (1941), the FBI and the BSC cooperated overtly for the rest of the war. The roundup of Germans, Italians, and Japanese broadened, for all these groups came from nations at war with the United States, and therefore they belonged in the class of enemy aliens. In 1942 the FBI captured eight Nazi saboteurs who had landed in America from submarines (two turned state's evidence and the other six were executed). Many more spies and saboteurs were caught during the war. None did any significant damage to the American war effort. Some were "turned around" and became double agents working for the FBI against Germany.

Following the war, and with the development of the Cold War, the Soviet Union replaced Nazi Germany as the main American problem, a special problem because more leading Americans sympathized with Communism than had ever sympathized with Nazism, and the members of the American Communist party were almost automatically suspect. Many members of the party were arrested under the law forbidding anyone to conspire to advocate the overthrow of the U.S. government by force (this practice gradually ceased because the courts tended to find the charge too vague). In 1948 the FBI entered the case of Alger Hiss, who was already on its list of alleged Communist agents, but without contributing anything of importance to the trial in which Hiss was found guilty of perjury. Also in that year, a leak of secret information inside the FBI itself led its agents to place Judith Coplon under surveillance, and in 1949 she was arrested along with her Russian contact, Valentin Gubitchev.

Soviet spies, foreign and domestic, remained a danger; Moscow continued its espionage in the United States. The urgency, however, diminished as the Soviet Union alienated Americans who had been its partisans and failed to attract new recruits. The reasons for this shift in attitudes were dramatically illustrated in Moscow in 1956, when Premier Nikita Khrushchev exposed the crimes of former Soviet dictator Joseph Stalin.

The decade of the 1960s produced different problems for the FBI. During the Vietnam War, antiwar protesters demonstrated in the streets, often violently. Civil-rights advocates conducted the dramatic freedom rides into segregated areas, and were met with hostility that in a few cases ended in murder. Student radicals left bombs in public places, causing injuries and death to passersby. The Black Panthers preached revolution and engaged in gun battles with the police. The groups just mentioned tended to be on the left in American society, but some on the right also became problems for the FBI—the Ku Klux Klan, the American Nazi party, the States Rights party.

Faced with novel situations, and suspecting too often that some groups had foreign backing (e.g., Cuban money for student activists), Hoover approved a series of countermeasures that caused him and the FBI to be criticized and condemned by concerned laymen and politicians and by the news media. He ordered his agents in Cointelpro ("counterintelligence programs") to infiltrate these groups, to use wiretaps and buggings, to open mail covertly, to search premises without warrants, and to spread disreputable rumors about individuals. Although Hoover defended his orders as necessary given the danger to the nation, he disbanded Cointelpro in 1971, shortly after Congressman Hale Boggs of Louisiana used the phrase "secret-police tactics" in describing the dubious conduct of the FBI.

Hoover died in 1972. President Richard Nixon nominated L. Patrick Gray to be the new director, but it was shown at the Watergate Committee hearings that Gray had allowed the FBI to be used by members of the administration during the cover-up conspiracy, and he requested that his name be withdrawn (1972). Nixon replaced Gray with Clarence M. Kelley, who received confirmation by the Senate and served until President Jimmy Carter took office in 1977. The leading criminal case of the Kelley period was the kidnapping of Patricia Hearst by the Symbionese Liberation Army (1974), her apparent cooperation with this radical and violent group, and her arrest by FBI agents (1975).

Carter's nominee, William H. Webster, confirmed by the Senate, gave the FBI a new emphasis, moving the organization in a broader way into the investigation of white-collar crime and political corruption. The most spectacular results of the shift were the Abscam ("Arab scam") cases of 1980, when FBI agents posing as Arab businessmen caught a number of politicians, on both the national and the state level, who were willing to sell political favors for money. With regard to intelligence operations, Webster liquidated the last vestiges of the "dirty tricks" that had been used when Cointelpro was investigating subversive activities. Nor was the phrase "subversive activities" applied widely enough to cover, as it had on occasion in the past, left-wing politics and civil-rights movements.

While eradicating the excesses, Webster modernized the FBI according to the new mood of the nation. He made his agents more responsive to social problems. He encouraged members of minority groups to enter the FBI and to think of it as a career, and the agents accepted under his jurisdiction included both blacks and women. J. Edgar Hoover had been called an autocrat. Webster could not try to emulate Hoover, for the term of the director was now limited by Congress to ten years.

See also COPLON, JUDITH; HISS, ALGER; HOOVER, J. EDGAR; NAZI SABOTEURS; STEPHENSON, WILLIAM; WATERGATE.

FURTHER READING: Don Whitehead, *The FBI Story* (1956), is favorable to the organization; Fred J. Cook, *The FBI Nobody Knows* (1964), is unfavorable; Andrew Tully, *The FBI's Most Famous Cases* (1965), is favorable; *Pat Watters and Stephen Gilles (eds.), *Investigating the FBI: A Tough, Fair Look at the Powerful Bureau, Its Present and Its Future* (1973), is unfavorable; Federal Bureau of Investigation, *Know Your FBI* (1974), is favorable; *Richard O. Wright, *Whose FBI?* (1974), is favorable; Sanford J. Ungar, *FBI: An Uncensored Look behind the Walls* (1975), is unfavorable.

Felfe, Heinz (1918-   )   German double agent for the Soviet Union.

Born in Dresden, Felfe was the son of an official in the criminal investigation department of the city. He attended Dresden schools, and around 1936, after Chancellor Adolf Hitler had consolidated his hold on Germany, he joined the Nazi party.

The outbreak of World War II in 1939 found Felfe in the Nazi secret service. In 1943 he was on the staff of Heinrich Himmler, head of the Gestapo, the Nazi secret police. Felfe worked on the Swiss desk in 1943, operated against the Dutch resistance to the German occupation in 1944, and in 1945 was arrested by the British after the collapse of Hitler's Germany.

Freed in 1946, Felfe served as a secret agent for the British as the Cold War developed between the Allies and the Russians. In 1949 he became a government official of the newly established Federal Republic of Germany (West Germany). In 1951 he entered the Gehlen Bureau, the intelligence system headed by General Reinhard Gehlen.

Felfe worked in the Gehlen Bureau for ten years, rising to become chief of counterespionage on the Russian desk. In 1961, he was arrested on information provided by a defector from the German Democratic Republic (East Germany); Felfe was discovered to have been a spy for the Russians since 1951. The resulting scandal contributed to the fall of the government of Chancellor Konrad Adenauer in 1963.

Condemned by a court in 1963, Felfe served six years in jail before being exchanged for a number of West Germans imprisoned in East Germany and the Soviet Union.

See also GEHLEN, REINHARD.

FURTHER READING: *Louis Hagen, *The Secret War for Europe: A Dossier of Espionage* (1968); Bernard Hutton, *How Russians and Other Iron Curtain Spies Operate* (1969).

Fielding, Xan (1918-   )   British spy during World War II.

Fielding was born in India, where his father was an officer in the British administration that ruled the subcontinent. He received a good education at the Charterhouse public school and Oxford, followed by studies in Germany at the universities of Bonn and Munich. A poet and translator who knew several languages, he went into British intelligence in 1939 on the outbreak of World War II. He was trained by the Special Operations Executive (SOE), the British organization that dispatched undercover agents to parts of Europe occupied by the Germans. In 1941 he landed surreptitiously in Crete, where he served in the Cretan resistance against the Germans for two years. He then was recalled to London for another assignment.

Fielding now entered the French Section of the SOE. He parachuted into southern France to cooperate with spies and saboteurs in the Basses-Alpes region, one of his confederates being Christine Granville, also of the SOE. When Fielding and two other agents were captured by the Germans in 1944 and threatened with immediate execution, Granville saved them by pretending that Allied troops were so near that the prison camp would be seized at any moment. The German commandant believed her and canceled the execution order, and the three spies were still alive when the Allies finally arrived.

Fielding was liberated; he returned to England and resumed his literary work, which includes a volume about his experience as a spy in World War II.

FURTHER READING: *Xan Fielding, *Hide and Seek* (1954); M. R. Foot, *SOE in France: An Account of the Work of the British Special Operations Executive in France, 1940–1944* (1960); Madeleine Masson, *Christine: A Search for Christine Granville* (1975).

Fleming, Ian *(1908-64)* British journalist, novelist, and intelligence officer during World War II.

The son of a Scottish Member of Parliament, Fleming was born in London while his father was attending the House of Commons. He was educated at Eton (1921–26) before attending the military academy at Sandhurst (1926–27), which he left without taking a commission in the British army. Becoming a journalist, he represented the London *Times* and the Reuters news agency in Moscow (1929–33), where he gained the knowledge of the Russians he later put into his novels.

Fleming worked in the financial world of London (1933–39) until the outbreak of World War II in 1939 drew him into the British armed forces. He became an assistant to the director of naval intelligence, whom he accompanied to Washington in 1941. Fleming wrote a report on intelligence operations for the benefit of America's wartime espionage organization, the OSS (Office of Strategic Services), in 1942. Under the code name "17F," he worked with William Stephenson in the coordination of British and American undercover operations. Returning to London, Fleming commanded a unit of Royal Marines at the Allied invasion of German-occupied France in 1944, his assignment being to look for enemy codes, reports on new weapons, and whatever else he found that was important for his superiors to know about.

Discharged in 1945 following the surrender of Germany, Fleming went back to journalism. In 1953 he published the first of his James Bond thrillers, in which he drew extensively on his intelligence experience to provide a realistic atmosphere. Thus, the name of his terrorist organization, SMERSH, was not an invention but rather taken from the acronym for the lethal department of

Soviet intelligence. The series of thrillers made Fleming wealthy and enabled him to live in the style to which he made himself accustomed.

See also SMERSH; STEPHENSON, WILLIAM.

FURTHER READING: Kingsley Amis, *The James Bond Dossier* (1965), is mainly literary; Henry A. Zeiger, *The Spy Who Came in with the Gold* (1965); *John Pearson, *The Life of Ian Fleming* (1966).

Foote, Alexander *(1905-58)* British radio operator for a Soviet spy ring in Switzerland.

Born in Liverpool, Foote came of a working-class family. He tried various jobs in his youth, became left wing in his political sympathies, and in 1936 went to Spain to serve in the International Brigade on the side of the pro-Communist Loyalists and against the pro-Fascist rebels under General Francisco Franco, who won and became dictator of Spain (1939). Foote, who saw no action of any note during the Spanish Civil War, returned to England in 1939. At loose ends, he allowed himself to be recruited by a Soviet agent in London who sent him to Switzerland to join a spy network operating for the Russians against Nazi Germany, firmly under the control of Chancellor Adolf Hitler.

When the German invasion of 1940 overwhelmed France, the Russians decided to place more emphasis on their network in neutral Switzerland, since their operatives in Paris were severely restricted. The Center, Moscow's intelligence headquarters, ordered Foote, who maintained a clandestine radio in Lausanne, to work directly with Sandor Rado, the spymaster in Geneva. Following Hitler's attack on Russia in 1941, the Swiss ring began to receive increasingly urgent requests from the Center, and Foote, using the code name "Jim," was its principal radioman transmitting material from agents in Switzerland and Germany.

In 1942 Rudolf Roessler of Lucerne began delivering the most important reports of all. Concealing his identity behind go-betweens Christian Schneider ("Taylor") and Rachel Duebendorfer ("Sissy"), and dubbed "Lucy" by Rado, Roessler turned in information from sources that have never been publicly identified. Foote met Lucy when their work together was over, and only then did he learn that the spy was Roessler.

Foote's espionage career ended in 1943 when the Swiss arrested three of the network's agents, an incident that caused Rado to go underground. Swiss counterespionage agents converged on Foote in a dramatic scene during which he burned his papers and smashed his radio transmitter while they were breaking through the door of his apartment.

Foote spent nearly a year in a Swiss jail before being released (1944). He managed to locate some former agents of the disrupted network, but Rado was gone. The spymaster had fled to Paris, recently liberated from the Nazi occupation. Foote followed and met Rado in the French capital, where they both received orders to report to the Center in Moscow. In 1945 they flew from Paris in a Russian plane that touched down in Cairo, where Rado disappeared. Foote never saw him again.

Foote went on by himself, delivered a bundle of documents Lucy had given him, suffered through an exhausting interrogation at the Center, and finally convinced the director that he had been loyal to the Soviet Union throughout.

As a result, Foote was given another assignment and told to report to Soviet espionage headquarters in Berlin (1947).

Disgusted by the mentality at the Center, disturbed by pathological suspicions that he had been working for the British, if not the Germans, and by now aware that the Soviet Union had replaced Nazi Germany as the worst threat to freedom everywhere, Foote bided his time. He arrived in the Russian sector of Berlin, pretended to be faithfully mastering the final details of his new assignment, and escaped to the British sector, where he asked to be allowed to go home. He was checked out, and since he had never conducted espionage operations against Britain, his request was granted without any conditions. Foote spent his last years as an ordinary British citizen.

See also RADO, SANDOR; ROESSLER, RUDOLF.

FURTHER READING: *Alexander Foote, *Handbook for Spies* (2nd ed., 1964); Sandor Rado, *Deckname Dora* (1972); Paul L. Kesaris (ed.), *The Rote Kapelle: The CIA's History of Soviet Intelligence and Espionage Networks in Western Europe, 1936–1945* (1979); Anthony Read and David Fisher, *Operation Lucy: The Most Secret Spy Ring of the Second World War* (1981).

Fouché, Joseph *(1759-1820)*   French minister of police and spymaster during the Napoleonic era.

Born in Brittany and destined by his family for the Church, Fouché studied with the Catholic order of the Oratorians and became a teacher in Oratorian schools, a vocation he abandoned after the outbreak of the French Revolution in 1789. He joined the left-wing Jacobin Club in Nantes, and in 1792 the people of his district sent him to Paris to represent them in the National Convention, which was about to assume the government of France.

Fouché was a radical at first. In 1793 he voted for the execution of King Louis XVI and ordered atrocities committed against suspected royalists in Lyons. But fear of Maximilien de Robespierre, who presided over the reign of terror, led Fouché to join the plot that overthrew Robespierre in 1794. Fouché supported Napoleon, who on gaining control of France appointed Fouché his minister of police for two terms (1799–1802 and 1804–10).

Fouché set a pattern in the practice of espionage and counterespionage, one that has been followed, with embellishments, by all subsequent organizations of this type. His manner of recruiting spies and the means he used to ensure their loyalty are still basic. His employment of double agents and his handling of planted misinformation (disinformation) have been studied by a succession of great spymasters. His files on suspects may seem meager in an age of computers, but they were the best of their time.

Fouché learned from one bad mistake. In 1804, the year in which Napoleon became emperor of France, Fouché rescued a condemned royalist spy, Louis Fauche-Borel, from prison in return for Fauche-Borel's promise to become a Bonapartist spy operating against royalists abroad. Safely out of France, however, Fauche-Borel went over to the royalists again. This failure led Fouché to devise better procedures to ensure the loyalty of his agents. He used promises, money, and threats, especially threats of kidnapping or assassination of those who might seek sanctuary beyond the French frontiers.

In 1806 either Fouché or one of his henchmen created the idea that there was a secret committee made up of leading Frenchmen disgusted with Napoleon and covertly organized for a rising in the name of the king as soon as Louis XVIII, then in exile, arrived on French soil. Another Fouché agent, Charles Perlet, received orders to spread the word about the secret committee. So successful was this disinformation that royalists wrote to Perlet asking about the leaders who would come out of hiding to greet the king. Even the British government, at war with France, tried to get in touch with this imaginary anti-Bonapartist group.

Fouché lured royalist agents back to France, where he arrested them or kept them under surveillance, but to his chagrin Fauche-Borel was not among them. Fauche-Borel's nephew, Charles Vitel, did come back, and Fouché had him arrested and executed as a warning (1807).

Napoleon rewarded Fouché for his police and espionage achievements with the title of duke of Otranto (1809). Fouché, nonetheless, displayed less loyalty to the emperor than he (Fouché) demanded of his spies. Feeling that Napoleon would lose in the end, Fouché opened communications with the king in exile, and in 1814, after Napoleon's abdication, he hurried to Paris from a diplomatic post in Naples. Failing to gain a high position under King Louis XVIII because the royalists could not forget his vote for the execution of Louis XVI, Fouché joined Napoleon again after the latter's escape from Elba, but he scarcely had time to reopen his files on the royalists when the Hundred Days ended at Waterloo and the Emperor abdicated for a second time (1815), putting an end to the Napoleonic era.

Since Fouché had urged Napoleon's second abdication after Waterloo, he was received by Louis XVIII, who named him minister of police. Fouché began hunting Bonaparist conspirators against the monarchy. The extreme royalists, still unreconciled to the ogre who had been responsible for so many of their misfortunes, forced him out again. After that Fouché wandered around the Continent carrying with him wherever he went the sinister reputation of an intriguer, a turncoat, and a spymaster whose agents had once been the terror of France.

See also FAUCHE-BOREL, LOUIS; PERLET, CHARLES.

FURTHER READING: Emil Ludwig, *Napoleon* (1926), treats skilfully of the relationship between Napoleon and Fouché; Nils Forsell, *Fouché, the Man Napoleon Feared* (1928); *Hubert Cole, Fouché, the Unprincipled Patriot* (1971).

Fourth Man   British secret agent for the Soviet Union implicated in the Philby-Burgess-Maclean spy case.
See BLUNT, ANTHONY.

Fox, Montagu *(1750?-1800?)*   British double agent on the Continent during the American War of Independence.

Little that is certain is known about Fox, even his real name being a matter of conjecture, but for nearly two years he functioned as an adept double agent transmitting disinformation (false or trivial reports) to the enemies of his country. These enemies were France, Spain, and Holland, all three of which were drawn to war with Great Britain in the two years (1778–80) following the decisive victory of the Americans over the British in the battle of Saratoga

(1777). France and Spain declared war on Britain in the hope of seeing their traditional enemy lose its former colonies. Britain declared war on Holland mainly because the Dutch continued to trade with Britain's enemies.

It was in these circumstances that Fox appeared at The Hague in 1780, presenting himself to Dutch officials and to the French and Spanish ambassadors as a disaffected Englishman anxious to see the British government of Lord North overthrown and a general peace arranged. He said that he and his friends in London believed the best way to achieve this end was to ensure the defeat of the British navy by supplying its adversaries with information about its strategy, strength, and supplies.

Fox was accepted at face value by the French, Spanish, and Dutch diplomats because of documents he showed them, one being a plan for a British offensive against Spanish colonies in the New World. The French ambassador sent him to Versailles, where the French foreign minister, although with some doubts, allowed the intelligence operation to proceed.

Fox then moved between The Hague and London, each time returning with documents he claimed were from the files of the British admiralty. They covered, in particular, secret orders to admirals of naval squadrons preparing to go to sea.

This information, ostensibly of the highest importance, never proved of any use in naval operations—one of the best indications that Fox was actually purveying disinformation. When he produced a document in which the name of the Spanish minister of marine was misspelled, it became clear that he was a double agent working for British naval intelligence, which had been supplying him with forged documents on his trips to London. Evidently a clerk was responsible for the misspelling, which went unnoticed because Fox was pressed for time in getting back to the Continent.

The French government at once issued an order for his arrest, but Fox learned of it in time to escape. What became of him after that is unknown.

FURTHER READING: Ronald Seth, *The Spy in Silk Breeches: The Story of Montagu Fox, 18th Century Admiralty Agent Extraordinary* (1968).

Francks, Wolfgang *(1880?-1940?)* German spy for the Turks in Palestine during World War I.

Francks was born in Germany and became a wanderer in exile for many years. Not much more than that can be said confidently of his early life, but he must have been a man of varied talents because he was at different times a sheep rancher, a businessman, and a newspaper reporter. He appeared in places as widely separated as the Australian outback, Bombay, and Cape Town, and he became fluent in English.

The outbreak of World War I in 1914 brought him hurrying back to Germany to serve in the armed forces of his country. While with the artillery in 1916, he volunteered for intelligence work, received training in espionage, and was sent in 1917 to Turkish-controlled Palestine, where his command of English would be useful against the British, who from their base in Egypt were attempting to conquer the Turks and capture Jerusalem.

Donning a British colonel's uniform, Francks boldly slipped behind the British lines and entered their camps. When challenged, he talked his way through using the air and intonation of a British officer just arrived from headquarters on an inspection tour. He talked with those he met about tactics, weapons, and morale and is said to have inspected an artillery regiment accompanied by its commanding officer. He claimed that he tapped telephone wires, listened to conversations, and even filtered into the communications system orders contrary to those he had heard.

Francks moved through the lines several times, gathering information and bringing it back to Turkish headquarters. Sometimes he traveled by night through the desert, and at least once he landed by parachute. But remarkable as his espionage was, he could not prevent General Edmund Allenby from carrying through the successful British campaign of 1918 that wrested Palestine from the Turks. World War I ended shortly thereafter, and Francks went back to Germany.

FURTHER READING: Archibald Wavell, *Allenby in Egypt* (1945); *Richard Wilmer Rowan and Robert G. Deindorfer, *Secret Service: Thirty-three Centuries of Espionage* (1967), has a passage on Francks.

Frederick the Great (1712-86)   King of Prussia who acted as his own spymaster.

Frederick was a cynic who mounted the throne in 1740 with a powerful army, a full treasury, and a driving ambition to expand his kingdom at the expense of his neighbors. In particular, he coveted the province of Silesia, then a part of Austria. His father had pledged Prussian respect for the territories of Maria Theresa, the Austrian royal heiress, but Frederick had no intention of letting that pledge hamper his foreign policy.

In 1740 he started the War of the Austrian Succession (1740–48) by invading Silesia, which he conquered and annexed. Another attempt at territorial expansion, this time against Saxony, led to the Seven Years' War (1756–63). Frederick did not hold Saxony at the end of the war, but he used it as a counter in parleying with his fellow monarchs, who were forced to recognize his permanent possession of Silesia.

Frederick was a great general and a great spymaster, who always possessed more knowledge about his enemies than they possessed about him. Before the Seven Years' War, a spy working in the Saxon archives in Dresden informed him that Spain would not join the anti-Prussian coalition, an important point because the Spaniards at that time were a major factor in European diplomacy. On the basis of this information, Frederick decided to go to war when it suited him instead of waiting to be attacked. His success in this and other wars derived substantially from his theory and practice of espionage.

He rationalized his theory by dividing spies into four major categories: (1) unimportant people who would spy for small sums or paltry favors; (2) double agents who could be used to plant misinformation on enemies; (3) important people, such as generals and government officials, who could be bought for large bribes; and (4) agents coerced into cooperating by threats to themselves, their families, or their property.

Frederick did not include ambassadors in his list, evidently because he considered that these representatives of national governments would spy as a normal part of their duties.

On the basis of his theory of espionage, Frederick drew all four types into his undercover network. Thus, the helpful clerk in the Saxon archives fell into the third category. Frederick often gave a spy the task of providing a specific piece of information, as in the case of his man in Madrid, who was told to find out exactly what position the Spanish government would take in the event of a European war.

This king of Prussia ranks high among spymasters. Francis Walsingham worked on limited problems in Elizabethan England and had to react to events for the most part. In France during the reign of Louis XIV, François Le Tellier, marquis de Louvois, sent out spies with general instructions to find out whatever they could. But Frederick the Great concentrated on specific matters of state affecting whole nations. Besides, the others were minions of their monarchs, while he was a monarch himself. They acted only under sufferance. Cardinal Richelieu acted on the highest level of state policy, but never forgot that he was subordinate to his sovereign, King Louis XIII of France. Frederick acted for himself on what he learned from his spies, which gives him a special place among spymasters.

FURTHER READING: William F. Reddaway, *Frederick the Great and the Rise of Prussia* (1904); J. W. Thompson and S. K. Padover, *Secret Diplomacy: A Record of Espionage and Double-dealing, 1500–1815* (1937); *Louis L. Snyder, *Frederick the Great: Prussian Warrior and Statesman* (1968).

French Resistance (1940-45)   Patriotic underground struggle against the German occupation forces in France.

Wherever the German armed forces overran a nation during World War II, a resistance movement developed among the subjugated people: small groups came together after the disaster of defeat and occupation to oppose the invaders covertly because open opposition was out of the question. Many resistance organizations combined into clandestine networks that engaged in duels of wits with German counterespionage and in hit-and-run tactics against the German armed forces. Whenever possible, the British sent help in the form of agents and supplies, working through the Special Operations Executive (SOE), based in London. This happened in countries throughout Europe.

The term "resistance," however, applies preeminently to the movement in France, for several reasons. The French, formerly the rivals and now the victims of the Germans, were especially determined to gain whatever degree of revenge they could in any manner available to them; a very large proportion of the population went into the underground after the capitulation of France in 1940. As the most populous occupied nation, France produced the largest number of resistance fighters. The remote regions of the country and the people of urban areas both provided hideouts for secret agents. Also, France was just across the English Channel from Britain and was therefore in a position to receive assistance quickly from the SOE. Finally, the French resistance had an inspiring leader in Charles de Gaulle, who by radio from London encouraged his underground followers in France to keep up the struggle until the day he and his Free French forces would return to take part in the liberation of their country. De Gaulle kept in touch with the underground through his BCRA (Central Bureau of Intelligence and Operations, Free French intelligence), which was directed by André Dewavrin, who used the cover name "Colonel Passy."

Over the four years of its operation, the French resistance became increasingly strong, bold, and effective. Large networks had their own spies reporting on the Germans and on the Vichy French, the collaborators led by Marshal Philippe Pétain. Ostensibly running a government at Vichy in unoccupied France, but actually a captive of the Germans, Pétain called on the French to cooperate with the victors. The resistance responded by harrying the Germans and Vichyites, shooting enemy soldiers, sabotaging trains, arranging for agents from Britain to land by boat, plane, or parachute at secret rendezvous, and keeping London informed through a myriad of clandestine radios spotted across France. There were constant crossings of the Channel both ways and nighttime flights from Britain deep into France. Some agents came ashore on the Riviera from small boats and submarines. Others tramped across the Pyrenees from Spain.

The effectiveness of the resistance provoked a terror campaign by the Germans, who, when their soldiers were assassinated, took revenge by "thirty-for-one" executions among the local population. German counterespionage threw out dragnets in the cities and tracked spies into woods and country houses. Many members of the underground struggle were caught and tortured, shot, or sent to death camps in Germany. The terror campaign could not suppress the resistance, which was ready when the Allies made their cross-Channel invasion of France in 1944. Its operatives emerged from their hiding places to fight openly. They cleared the Germans out of some areas of France by themselves. They joined the Allies in the victorious thrust inland from the coast. They rose against the Germans in Paris and were a notable force in the liberation of the city.

The French resistance had no function after Germany surrendered. The survivors went home, resumed their civilian jobs, held memorial services and annual celebrations, and wrote books about what they had done during the war.

See also BCRA; SPECIAL OPERATIONS EXECUTIVE.

FURTHER READING: Ronald Seth, *The Undaunted: The Story of Resistance in Western Europe* (1956); Milton Dank, *The French against the French: Collaboration and Resistance* (1974); *David Schoenbrun, *Soldiers of the Night: The Story of the French Resistance* (1980).

Friedman, Elizebeth *(1893-1980)* American cryptologist who worked in espionage in two world wars.

Friedman was originally Elizebeth Smith of Huntingdon, Indiana, where she graduated from high school before going on to Hillsdale College in Michigan. She took her degree in English in 1916. Accepting a job at the Riverbank Laboratories near Chicago, she worked on codes and ciphers. She married a cryptologist at Riverbank, William Friedman, in 1917.

The United States entered World War I that year. The Friedmans went to Washington to do cryptological work for the government, and during the war (1917–18) Elizebeth deciphered German messages and documents for the Army, Navy, and Coast Guard.

Between the wars she did other types of cryptological work, such as breaking codes used by rumrunners clandestinely bringing liquor into the United States in defiance of Prohibition.

World War II brought Elizebeth Friedman back to government service (as it did her husband, who in 1940 broke the principal Japanese code). She handled enciphered messages for the OSS (Office of Strategic Services) from 1942 to 1945. She also broke the code of the "Doll Woman" of New York, Velvalee Dickinson, who spied for the Japanese and concealed her messages in letters she wrote abroad ostensibly advertising her dolls.

After the war the Friedmans continued to do cryptological work for the government and to work at special problems for their own amusement, one result being *The Shakespearean Ciphers Examined* (1957), in which they exposed fallacies in the argument that Francis Bacon wrote the plays of Shakespeare.

Widowed in 1969, Elizebeth Friedman retired as a cryptologist.

See also DICKINSON, VELVALEE; FRIEDMAN, WILLIAM.

FURTHER READING: David Kahn, *The Codebreakers: The Story of Secret Writing* (1967); *Ronald W. Clark, *The Man Who Broke Purple* (1977).

Friedman, William *(1891-1969)* American cryptologist who broke the principal Japanese code during World War II.

Born in Kinishev, Russia, Friedman was the son of a Jewish employee of the Russian post office. The family emigrated to the United States and settled in Pittsburgh in 1892, and Friedman graduated from Pittsburgh Central High School in 1909. He studied at the Michigan Agricultural College in Lansing (1910) and at Cornell University (1910–14), from which he graduated with a degree in genetics.

Friedman went to work in 1915 at the Riverbank Laboratories near Chicago, where he was drawn to cryptology. He married another cryptologist, Elizebeth Smith, in 1917, after which they devoted their lives to the art and science of breaking codes and ciphers. They worked for the government in Washington during World War I (1917–18); in 1918 he was stationed in France at the headquarters of General John J. Pershing, commander of the American expeditionary force.

Between the wars Friedman headed the Signal Intelligence Service. In 1939, the year in which World War II broke out, he began to concentrate on Purple, the principal Japanese code, considered by Tokyo to be unbreakable because of the astronomical number of electrically guided combinations. Friedman broke Purple in 1940, enabling the United States to read messages in that code during the war in the Pacific (1941–45), a notable contribution to the defeat of Japan. In 1941 he visited Bletchley, England, where British cryptologists had already broken the principal German code.

After the war Friedman and his wife worked for the government. In 1952 he became the first cryptologist of the newly formed National Security Agency (NSA). The Friedmans together published *The Shakespearean Ciphers Examined* (1957), in which they exposed fallacies in the argument that Francis Bacon wrote the plays of Shakespeare.

The high pitch of Friedman's cryptological work had caused him to suffer several nervous breakdowns, persistent depression, and painful physical symptoms, all of which contributed to his death. His achievement in breaking Purple makes him one of the great cryptologists of all time.

See also FRIEDMAN, ELIZEBETH; PURPLE.

FURTHER READING: David Kahn, *The Codebreakers: The Story of Secret Writing* (1967); William Friedman, "Cryptology," in *Encyclopaedia Britannica (1969)*; *Ronald W. Clark, *The Man Who Broke Purple* (1977).

Fuchs, Klaus (1911-   ) German scientist and spy for the Soviet Union in Britain and the United States.

The son of a Lutheran pastor, Fuchs was born at Beerfelden, near Heidelberg. As a child, he developed a strong moral conscience at home. His father, an advocate of the Social Gospel, was strongly anti-Nazi during the 1920s, and the son carried this feeling over into the following decade as Adolf Hitler rose to power, becoming chancellor of Germany (1933).

At the University of Kiel, believing that Communism was the proper and effective antidote to Nazism, Fuchs joined the Communist party. He remained a Communist during his years in Britain (1933–40), where he took his Ph.D. in Bristol and his Sc.D. in Edinburgh.

The British interned him as a suspect German in 1940 after the outbreak of World War II. Convinced of his hostility to the Nazis and deciding to make use of his scientific knowledge, in 1941 the British allowed him to take part in atomic research at the University of Birmingham. He became a naturalized Briton in 1942, the same year in which he began to spy for the Russians, handing over to them reports on his research and on that of his colleagues.

Fuchs convinced himself that this was the morally right thing to do. He believed that the Soviet Union, fighting Nazi Germany on the battlefield, had a right to know what the western Allies knew about atomic energy and its technology.

In 1943 Fuchs moved to the United States, where he worked at Columbia University in New York. He got in touch with Harry Gold, named by the Russians to be his courier. It was all so clandestine that neither Fuchs nor Gold knew the other's real name. Fuchs went on to Los Alamos, New Mexico, where the atomic bomb was being built under the code name of the "Manhattan Project," to which he contributed his scientific knowledge and from which he transmitted secret information to Gold.

Returning to England in 1946, Fuchs joined the staff of scientists at Harwell, the leading British center for the study of atomic energy. He continued to spy for the Russians until the following year, when, feeling that they were using him for their own purposes and not for the good of humanity, he ended his espionage career.

Fuchs might have remained simply one of the ablest scientists at Harwell except for a new development across the Atlantic in the United States. His past caught up with him in 1950 when the FBI (Federal Bureau of Investigation) informed the British government that there had been leaks from the British scientific group at Los Alamos during the war and after. Suspicion fell on Fuchs, who was arrested, tried, and sentenced. Released in 1959, he returned to Germany—to East Germany because he could no longer find a place for himself in the western democracies.

His testimony, meanwhile, had broken the Rosenberg case in the United States. Fuchs described his American courier, which led to the apprehension of Harry Gold, who implicated David Greenglass. The investigation culminated with the arrest of Julius and Ethel Rosenberg.

See also GOLD, HARRY; GREENGLASS, DAVID; ROSENBERG, JULIUS AND ETHEL.

FURTHER READING: *Oliver Pilat, *The Atom Spies* (1952); Alan Moorehead, *The Traitors* (1963); Rebecca West, *The New Meaning of Treason* (1967); H. Montgomery Hyde, *The Atom Bomb Spies* (1980).

Funston, Frederick *(1865-1917)*   American Army officer and spy during the Philippine insurrection.

Funston was born in Ohio, worked as a journalist in Kansas City, and for eight years (1888–95) served as a special agent for the Department of Agriculture in Washington. He was a botanist, accompanying expeditions to Death Valley, Alaska, and other wild places on the map of North America. In 1896 he went to Cuba to advise the Cubans in their rebellion against Spain. Wounded in the fighting, he was captured by the Spaniards but released and expelled from the island.

With the outbreak of the Spanish-American War in 1898, Funston joined the Kansas Volunteers, holding the rank of colonel, before being sent to the Philippines, the scene of his most notable achievement, which came after the defeat of Spain. The Filipinos, under the leadership of Emilio Aguinaldo, rose against the Americans. Aguinaldo established a secret headquarters in northern Luzon from which he directed the insurrection. Guerrilla warfare against the Americans spread across the islands.

Funston had to turn spy to deal with Aguinaldo. The American officer gathered information in Manila by keeping suspects under surveillance, and he recruited spies whose reports from the interior enabled him to pinpoint the area of Luzon where Aguinaldo was hiding. Then, in a daring expedition through the Philippine jungle, Funston surprised Aguinaldo and conveyed him back to Manila (1901).

Aguinaldo went to jail, but later he became reconciled to American authority in the Philippines. The islands developed economically and obtained independence after the American-Filipino alliance of World War II.

For his feat, Funston was promoted to brigadier general in the U.S. Army. In 1914 he commanded American troops at the capture of Vera Cruz, in Mexico. Rising in rank and reputation, he was slated to become commander in chief of the American expeditionary force in World War I. He suddenly died of a heart attack, and command of the expeditionary force went to General John J. Pershing.

FURTHER READING: *Frederick Funston, *Memories of Two Wars* (1911); George S. Bryan, *The Spy in America* (1943); Donald Barr Chidsey, *The Spanish-American War* (1971), gives the background to Funston's spy work.

Furusawa, Sachiko *(1887?-1950?)*   Japanese spy in the United States.

Born into a lower-class family in Tokyo, Sachiko moved up in Japanese society at the age of 15 by marrying an officer in the imperial navy. A few years later she came to California, divorced her husband, and married a physician named Takashi Furusawa, who established a practice in Los Angeles. Both Furusawas became active in Japanese-American groups. Meeting Japanese officials and military men, they gradually moved into espionage for Japan.

Sachiko Furusawa frequently went aboard visiting Japanese vessels, where she delivered messages on American warships in California seaports and received queries about the U.S. Navy that Tokyo wanted her to answer. She and her husband gathered information themselves and used their contacts in the Japanese-American community. This continued through the 1930s, for although the Furusawas created so much suspicion that the FBI (Federal Bureau of Investigation) kept a dossier on them, Washington did not want any move made against them when Japanese-American diplomatic relations were becoming more tense.

In 1941 the Furusawas suddenly left for Japan. They wanted to be safely out of the way if war came, which it did on December 7 of that year with the Japanese air assault on Pearl Harbor.

FURTHER READING: *Alan Hynd, *Betrayal from the East: The Inside Story of Japanese Spies in America* (1943); Ronald Seth, *Secret Servants: A History of Japanese Espionage* (1957); Dorothy Borg and Shumpei Okamoto (eds.), *Pearl Harbor as History: Japanese-American Relations, 1931–1941* (1973).

Gapon, Georgi (1870-1906)   Priest of the Russian Orthodox Church and spy for the tsarist police.

Born in Poltava in the Ukraine, Gapon received a religious education, attended an Orthodox seminary, and about 1895 took holy orders. He was assigned to a church in St. Petersburg (now Leningrad), where he espoused the Social Gospel while serving among the workers of the city, who, he thought, would have to agitate for an alleviation of their depressed and oppressed condition under the tsar.

Beginning in 1903, Gapon formed labor unions, acting in collaboration with the tsarist secret police, the Ochrana, which allowed him to do so because the tsarist government thought the unions might act as a safety valve for the pent up resentment of the workers. Instead, the unions triggered an explosion. The workers went on strike under Gapon's leadership, and he led a big crowd to the Winter Palace in St. Petersburg to petition the tsar. Violence began, troops fired on the crowd, and thousands were killed or injured on "Bloody Sunday" (January 22, 1905).

Gapon escaped abroad. Revered as a hero by the workers in Russia, unknown to them he lived an indolent life, often in Monte Carlo, little befitting a priest or a labor leader. Wishing to return to Russia safely, in 1906 he became a police spy for the Ochrana, on whose behalf he joined the Social Revolutionaries, who were conspiring against the autocracy of the tsar. He drew information for the Ochrana from the leaders of the Social Revolutionaries, one of whom was Yevno Azev, head of the party's combat section.

The Social Revolutionaries, finding that the Ochrana knew most of their plans in advance, traced responsibility to Gapon, who was executed on Azev's orders. The other party leaders did not know at the time that Azev was himself a spy for the Ochrana and therefore only too eager to deflect suspicion from himself by pinning the guilt on Gapon.

See also AZEV, YEVNO; OCHRANA.

FURTHER READING: A. T. Vassilyev, *The Ochrana* (1930); *Boris Nicolaievsky, *Azeff, the Russian Judas* (1934); Fitzroy Maclean, *Take Nine Spies* (1978), considers Gapon in the chapter on Azev.

GAPS *(1943-45)*   Italian underground operating against German and Italian fascists during World War II.

In 1943 Italy experienced a series of convulsive changes. The Allied invasion of Sicily from North Africa brought about the downfall of Benito Mussolini, the dictator who had held power for nearly a generation. Adolf Hitler, struggling to hold Italy, sent an airborne squad to rescue Mussolini from his Italian captors. Hitler then set Mussolini up as head of a fascist republic in north Italy, while at the same time dispatching German troops to control the peninsula and to confront the Allied forces that had landed from Sicily south of Rome. The new antifascist government asked the Allies for an armistice, received it, and joined them against Germany. The Germans countered by turning Italy, from the Allied beachheads to the Alps, into an occupied nation.

As the Allies drove toward Rome, GAPS (Patriotic Action Groups) formed behind the German lines. Started by the Communists and later by all kinds of antifascists, the GAPS used sabotage and assassination to weaken the enemy grip on their country. They transmitted military intelligence by clandestine radios to the advancing Allies. In Rome, they became strong enough to form brigades under the command of General Filippo Caruso, who in 1944 helped liberate the city by linking up with the troops of British General Harold Alexander, commander of the Allied campaign.

Meanwhile, Mussolini's fascist republic, siding with the Germans, became the scene of brutal conflicts between the GAPS and the security forces. The republic collapsed in 1945, Mussolini was captured and executed by Communist partisans, the fascists either changed sides or went into hiding, and the GAPS disbanded.

FURTHER READING: Ronald Seth, *The Undaunted: The Story of Resistance in Western Europe* (1956), has a chapter on the GAPS; *Charles F. Dalzell, *Mussolini's Enemies: The Italian Anti-Fascist Resistance* (1961); W. G. Jackson, *Alexander of Tunis as Military Commander* (1972).

Gehlen, Reinhard *(1902-79)*   German spymaster for Nazi Germany, the United States, and the German Federal Republic.

Born in Erfurt, Germany, Gehlen was the son of a German army officer who served in World War I, returned to civilian life after Germany's defeat in 1918, and went into the publishing business. When the victorious Allies permitted a small German army to be reestablished in 1920 as a barrier against the Russian Communists, young Gehlen noted the fact and the reasoning, which he would recall and exploit in 1945 after the German defeat in World War II.

Meanwhile, he had decided on a military career, and after graduation from an officers' candidate school in 1921, he joined the artillery. He entered the new War Academy in 1933, the year Adolf Hitler became chancellor of Germany. Leaving the War Academy in 1935, Gehlen began a career of rapid advancement. In 1939 he was an officer attached to a division during the Polish campaign that started World War II. In 1940 he joined the staff of the German high command and helped plan the campaigns against France and the Soviet Union.

In 1942 Gehlen became the head of military intelligence with Foreign Armies East, the German forces in Russia. He developed an excellent espionage organization, assembled massive documentation on the Russians, and turned in meticulous intelligence reports regarding Soviet operational plans, troop concentrations, and armament.

When Germany collapsed in 1945, Gehlen, now a lieutenant-general, used his memories of 1920 in deciding what to do: he would be ready when the Allies needed German help against Communist Russia. His bargaining chips were his espionage files on the Soviet Union and his agents in place in areas occupied by the Red Army.

Gehlen had his files microfilmed as the end of the war drew near. He then ordered the originals to be destroyed and the microfilms hidden in the Bavarian mountains, safely away from the Russian advance. When the Americans arrived, he explained to them what he had done.

By then the Cold War between the Allies and the Russians was in the making, and the Americans were as impressed with the help Gehlen could give them as he had surmised they would be. They not only gratefully accepted the information he offered but also placed him in charge of a new intelligence system aimed at the Soviet Union and its satellites.

Gehlen became as successful in working for the Allies as he had been in serving Hitler. In 1955, following the establishment (1949) of the Federal Republic of Germany (West Germany) under the leadership of Chancellor Konrad Adenauer, Gehlen became director of the Federal Intelligence Service, a post he held until his retirement in 1968.

Remarkable espionage triumphs for the Gehlen Bureau marked these years. Gehlen was able to report top-secret information regarding the German Democratic Republic (East Germany) because he had one agent, Hermann Kastner, who was a member of the cabinet in East Berlin, and another, Walter Gramsch, who served in the East German intelligence system. Gehlen learned from an informant that it would be possible to construct what later became known as the Berlin Tunnel, the underground passageway from West Berlin to East Berlin that the Americans dug and from which they tapped the communication lines to Moscow. A Gehlen agent is said to have obtained a copy of the 1956 speech in which Soviet Premier Nikita Khrushchev, under the tightest security, exposed the crimes of Joseph Stalin. In 1968 Gehlen correctly predicted the Soviet invasion of Czechoslovakia that put an end to the "Prague spring," the Czech hopes for a greater measure of freedom from Moscow's control.

Gehlen also had his failures. His agents provided him with no warning in 1961 that the Communist regime in East Germany was about to build the Berlin Wall and thus put an end to free movement around the city. In that same year, the chief of his counterespionage department, Heinz Felfe, was found to have been a spy for the Russians for a decade. The resulting scandal contributed to the fall of Konrad Adenauer, chancellor of the Federal Republic, in 1963.

Gehlen stayed on as head of the Gehlen Bureau for another five years, but with much diminished prestige. Then he retired and wrote a self-serving account of his three careers—Nazi, Allied, Federal—as a spymaster.

See also BERLIN TUNNEL; FELFE, HEINZ; GRAMSCH, WALTER; KASTNER, HERMANN; WOLLWEBER, ERNST.

FURTHER READING: *Reinhard Gehlen, *The Service: Memoirs of General Reinhard Gehlen* (1972); Heinz Höhne and Hermann Zolling, *The General Was a Spy: The Truth about General Gehlen and His Spy Ring* (1972); Edward Spiro, *Gehlen: Spy of the Century* (1972).

Gestapo *(1933-45)*   Secret police of Germany's Third Reich.

When Adolf Hitler became chancellor of Germany in 1933, he established the Gestapo (a contraction from the German words for "secret state police") to ensure control of his Third Reich by his Nazi (National Socialist) party. At first directed by Hermann Goering, the Gestapo passed into the control of Heinrich Himmler in 1934. Himmler made it a byword for Nazi terror and tyranny as he hunted down enemies of the Third Reich and opponents of Hitler.

In 1939 the Gestapo and the SD (Security Service, civilian intelligence) were combined with the criminal police in the RSHA (Reich Central Security Office), an overall police system under Himmler's control. Himmler's policemen and police spies operated within Germany and then in the captive areas of Europe overrun by the German armed forces during World War II (1939–45). These years saw millions of people shipped to labor and death camps, a reign of terror that continued until the armies of the western Allies and the Soviet Union overran Germany in 1945. The victors dismantled the Gestapo along with the rest of the Third Reich.

See also HIMMLER, HEINRICH.

FURTHER READING: Willi Frischauer, *Himmler* (1953); *Edward Crankshaw, *The Gestapo* (1956); Joachim C. Fest, *Hitler* (1974).

Gimpel, Erich *(1910-   )*   German spy in the United States during World War II.

Born in Merseburg, Germany, Gimpel went to a local school during World War I (1914–18) and then studied the technology of high-frequency electrical transformers. He went into the radio business and in 1935 held a job with a German radio company in Peru. The approach of World War II during the late 1930s made him turn to espionage in order to help Adolf Hitler, who was now chancellor of Germany. With the outbreak of the conflict in 1939, Gimpel made regular reports to the German legation regarding ships arriving in and leaving Lima harbor.

In 1942 Gimpel, interned by Peru when it entered the war on the Allied side, got back to Germany by way of neutral Sweden. He worked in a radio factory in Hamburg until it was destroyed during an Allied air attack on the city. Returning to espionage in 1943, he served as a courier between Berlin and Madrid, crossing through German-occupied France with secret messages from Hitler to President Francisco Franco of Spain.

Gimpel was then singled out by German intelligence for a spy mission to the United States, a two-man assignment in which William Colepaugh, an American, would be the spokesman for the pair, while Gimpel would be the technician, handling the radios, cameras, and other equipment. Colepaugh would fend off suspicion of his German partner, and both would accumulate information from newspapers and other public sources to transmit back to Germany. They were to concentrate in particular on the effect of German propaganda on the coming 1944 presidential election campaign between Franklin D. Roosevelt, running for a fourth term, and the Republican challenger, Thomas E. Dewey.

Gimpel and Colepaugh, after training at a spy school in German-occupied

Holland, left Kiel aboard a German submarine, which crossed the Atlantic and surfaced in Frenchman Bay, Maine. The two were rowed ashore in a rubber boat, which returned to the sub while they went to Bangor and took a train to Boston. Continuing on to New York, they found an apartment and prepared to begin espionage work using the cover names of "Edward George Green" (Gimpel) and "William Charles Cauldwell" (Colepaugh).

Their assignment had been bungled by their superiors in Germany, for the American election was already over (Roosevelt won). Gimpel and Colepaugh did some perfunctory spying, gathering information that both realized could have no effect on the course of the war, which Germany was clearly in the process of losing. Colepaugh became frightened, slipped away from Gimpel, and went to an agent of the FBI (Federal Bureau of Investigation) with his story. The FBI began a search for Gimpel, by now himself badly frightened by Colepaugh's disappearance. He was arrested as he stood at a newsstand in New York City's Times Square.

Gimpel and Colepaugh were both tried for espionage, found guilty, and sentenced to death. President Harry Truman, America's chief executive since Roosevelt's death in 1945, commuted the sentences to life imprisonment.

See also COLEPAUGH, WILLIAM.

FURTHER READING: Karl Bartz, *The Downfall of the German Secret Service* (1956); *Erich Gimpel (with Will Berthold), *Spy for Germany* (1957); David Kahn, *Hitler's Spies: German Military Intelligence in World War II* (1978).

Giskes, H. J. *(1896-   )*   German intelligence officer and director of counterespionage in occupied Holland during World War II.

Giskes was born into a Catholic family of the Rhineland. Joining the kaiser's army, he served in the Alpine Corps during World War I, after which he took an active part in opposition to a Communist coup in Germany and to the establishment of a separate Rhenish Republic under French auspices. He went into business for ten years (1924–34) and then accepted a commission in the new German army, founded by Adolf Hitler, who had become chancellor of Germany in 1933.

Giskes was in the Abwehr (military intelligence) when Hitler started World War II (1939). After the Germans overran most of the Continent in 1940, Giskes served in Paris before being transferred to The Hague in 1941 with the rank of major. A year later the capture of a radio operator working secretly for the British gave Giskes the inspiration to launch Operation North Pole, in which he used the radio operator to deliver false messages to London. Unaware of the truth, the British sent agents and supplies to be captured by the Germans. In 1943 escapees from German detention got back to London, sounded the alarm, and ended the deception campaign.

Operation North Pole was Giskes' great triumph in counterespionage. He served for two years (1943–45) in Holland, Belgium, and northern France as the war turned against Germany. Captured by the Allies in 1945 following their invasion of the Continent, he was held prisoner until 1948. He was never considered a war criminal because the Dutch authorities testified that his conduct in Holland had been "in accordance with international law and the unwritten laws of humanity."

See also NORTH POLE.

FURTHER READING: *H. J. Giskes, *London Calling North Pole* (1953); Pieter Dourlein, *Inside North Pole: A Secret Agent's Story* (1954); Phillipe Garnier-Raymond, *The Tangled Web* (1968).

Goertz, Hermann (1890-1947) German spy in Britain and Ireland before and during World War II.

Goertz, who came of a wealthy family of Lübeck, Germany, received his early education from English governesses, so he grew up fluent in English. He studied languages at the university before his military service as an aviator in World War I (1914–18). He started a law practice in Hamburg, but his linguistic ability drew him into espionage work, and in 1935 he accepted a mission to report on installations of the Royal Air Force (RAF) in Britain.

Using as a cover story the pretense that he was writing a travel book, and accompanied by a comely young woman whom he used as a decoy to distract attention from his undercover activities, Goertz sketched airfields and gathered notes in East Anglia and elsewhere.

However, his decoy did not prevent a member of the RAF from reporting him, and he was shadowed by MI5 (Military Intelligence 5, British counterespionage). Goertz and his companion managed to slip out of Britain, but some of his papers were found, and he was arrested when he was foolhardy enough to return. Given a jail sentence for espionage, he was deported to Germany before the outbreak of World War II in 1939.

General Erwin von Lahousen of Abwehr II, the sabotage section of German military intelligence, sent Goertz to Ireland in 1940 to try to rally members of the Irish Republican Army and other Irishmen hostile to Britain over the partition of Ireland. The mission proved a disaster. First, Goertz was dropped by parachute in the wrong place, Northern Ireland. Then, although he had sneaked safely across the border, he violated the basic espionage rule that demands discretion of secret agents. Giving himself away by blatantly approaching Irish leaders, he was arrested by the Irish security forces and interned for the duration of the war.

Released in 1946, rearrested in 1947, and facing deportation to West Germany, Goertz committed suicide by swallowing poison.

See also LAHOUSEN, ERWIN VON.

FURTHER READING: *Sean O'Callaghan, *Jackboot in Ireland* (1958); Charles Wighton and Günter Peis, *Hitler's Spies and Saboteurs: Based on the German Secret Service War Diary of General Lahousen* (1958); Enno Striphan, *Spies in Ireland* (1963).

Gold, Harry (1910-55) American spy for the Soviet Union.

Born in Bern, Switzerland, into a Jewish family named Golodnotsky, Gold was brought to the United States as a child. The family moved around the country, but Gold received most of his education in Philadelphia, graduating from high school in 1928. He studied chemistry at the University of Pennsylvania, and became a competent scientist. The sorrows of the Great Depression added to a radical left-wing bias made him a committed Communist.

By 1935, holding jobs in which he had access to industrial scientific information, Gold was spying for the Russians, and with Nazi Germany's invasion of Russia in 1941, he became one of the Kremlin's most important secret agents in America. Anatoly Yakovlev, who came to the United States in 1944 to take charge of a spy ring based in New York, appointed Gold the chief courier of the ring and gave him assignments to gather classified information from those who had it and would part with it for money or for ideological reasons.

Gold received data on rocket research from Morton Sobell of General Electric Laboratories. His most significant sources, however, were Klaus Fuchs, a nuclear scientist, and David Greenglass, a machinist, at the Los Alamos atomic installation in New Mexico. Gold met Fuchs and Greenglass individually, took their reports, and transmitted everything to Yakovlev in New York. Gold did not meet Julius and Ethel Rosenberg, although he later testified that he knew about them and their essential work for the spy ring.

This network remained operational until 1946, by which time World War II was over and the Cold War between the Russians and the west was rapidly developing. Then the network broke up when Fuchs went back to England to resume his work in British atomic science, while Greenglass received his discharge from the U.S. Army and returned to civilian life.

In 1950 British authorities, warned by the FBI (Federal Bureau of Investigation) in Washington, arrested Fuchs. Gold, described by Fuchs, was picked up shortly afterward in New York. Gold confessed, naming Greenglass, Sobell, and the Rosenbergs. His testimony became part of the government prosecution that ended with the execution of the Rosenbergs. Gold received a sentence of thirty years.

See also FUCHS, KLAUS; GREENGLASS, DAVID; ROSENBERG, JULIUS AND ETHEL; SOVIET AMERICAN NETWORK.

FURTHER READING: Oliver Pilat, *The Atom Spies* (1952); Alan Moorehead, *The Traitors: The Double Life of Fuchs, Pontecorvo and Nunn May* (1952); *H. Montgomery Hyde, *The Atom Bomb Spies* (1980).

Gouzenko, Igor *(1919-   )*   Russian secret agent in, and defector from, the Soviet Canadian Network.

Gouzenko, born in Rogachov, near Moscow, was the son of a tsarist soldier who vanished in the fighting that followed the Russian Revolution. He attended school in Rostov-on-Don and Verkne Spasskoye, where his widowed mother began teaching in 1926. His later education came from the Komsomol, the Communist youth movement, of which he was a member.

A student of art and architecture in Moscow (1937–38), Gouzenko was recruited in 1939 as a cipher clerk into the NKVD (People's Commissariat for Internal Affairs, 1934–46), the most important bureau of Soviet intelligence, today known as the KGB (Committee for State Security). After the German invasion of Russia during World War II, Gouzenko served as an intelligence officer at the front (1941–42).

In 1943 Gouzenko went to Ottawa to work as a cipher clerk in the Russian Embassy, where he became a member of the Soviet Canadian Network, the spy ring directed from Moscow and operating in Canada. Gouzenko remained at his post for two years. Then, impressed with Canadian freedom and disgusted by the Soviet conspiracy against the Canadians, he defected. The documents he brought with him from the embassy code room revealed Soviet espionage plots not only in Canada but around the world. In particular, Gouzenko revealed that the spy ring had stolen a mass of secret information on atomic research in Canada.

Gouzenko's defection broke up the Soviet Canadian Network, exposed Alan Nunn May, a British atomic scientist, as a spy for the Soviet Union, and forced the Russians to a drastic overhaul of their espionage system. Gouzenko and his family disappeared behind a veil of secrecy provided by the Royal Canadian Mounted Police.

See also NUNN MAY, ALAN; ROYAL CANADIAN MOUNTED POLICE; SOVIET CANADIAN NETWORK.

FURTHER READING: *Igor Gouzenko, *The Iron Curtain* (1948); Oliver Pilat, *The Atom Spies* (1954); Norman Lucas, *The Great Spy Ring* (1966); H. Montgomery Hyde, *The Atom Bomb Spies* (1980).

GPU (1922-23) The second name given to the Soviet intelligence system now known as the KGB.

See KGB.

Gramsch, Walter (1897-   ) Double agent for the German Federal Republic in the German Democratic Republic.

Born and raised in the kaiser's Germany, Gramsch went into the government bureaucracy after World War I (1914–18), rising to become a railroad executive. He served in the German army during World War II (1939–45), became involved in the plot to assassinate Adolf Hitler in 1944, and was arrested by the Gestapo, the Nazi state police. Released after the Nazi defeat, he stayed in East Germany, hoping that the government, despite the Russian occupation, would in some way resemble a democracy.

The forcible inclusion of all political parties in one Communist-dominated party in 1946 disillusioned him. He was also angry about a Communist investigation into his Nazi past, and although his part in the assassination attempt was enough to clear him, he began to spy for the west in 1946. Using his railroad experience, he rose in the transport administration of East Germany (after 1949, the German Democratic Republic). Part of his duties were in espionage, which made him a double agent for the German Federal Republic (West Germany).

His superior, Ernst Wollweber, became minister of state security in 1953— that is, head of the intelligence system. Gramsch therefore had access to government plans and other top-secret information during this time. The period was not long because in 1953 the West German director of intelligence, Reinhard Gehlen, learning that a double agent in his own office had fled to East Berlin, warned Gramsch to get to West Berlin before the Communists could arrest him. Gramsch obeyed the order, reached the Federal Republic, and went back into administration, this time for a democracy. His espionage career was over.

See also GEHLEN, REINHARD; WOLLWEBER, ERNST.

FURTHER READING: Edward Spiro, *Gehlen: Spy of the Century* (1972); *Heinz Hohne and Hermann Zolling, *The General Was a Spy: The Truth about General Gehlen and His Spy Ring* (1972).

Granville, Christine *(1915-52)*   Polish spy for Britain during World War II.

Born on the family estate near Warsaw, Granville was the daughter of a Polish aristocrat, Count Jerzy Skarbek, and grandaughter, on her mother's side, of a Jewish banker. She received her education from the nuns of a Warsaw convent and in 1938 married Georg Gizycki, a Polish writer and traveler. They were in Kenya in 1939 when World War II began with the German attack on Poland. Leaving her husband, she went to London to participate in the struggle against Nazi Germany. The British trained her for missions directed by the Special Operations Executive (SOE), the espionage organization established to encourage and assist resistance in the areas occupied by the Germans. British intelligence gave her the cover name "Christine Granville," by which she was known thereafter.

During 1940 and 1941 Granville, having slipped surreptitiously onto the Continent, worked underground with the resistance in Hungary and Poland. Betrayed to the Germans by an informer in 1941, she escaped through Greece and Palestine to Cairo, where she reported to SOE headquarters in the Middle East. Returning to London, she parachuted into France in 1942, where she became part of a spy ring that included Xan Fielding, another SOE operative. She shuttled back and forth between France and Italy, was twice arrested by the Germans, and twice convinced them that they had no reason to hold her. In 1944, as Germany collapsed, she saved Fielding and two other secret agents by convincing the Nazi commandant of a prison camp near Digne that the invading troops of the Allies would soon overrun the camp and hold him responsible for the fate of his prisoners. Her bluff worked until the Allies did arrive.

Granville became a couturière after the war and then worked as a stewardess aboard a liner on the route between London and Cape Town. In 1952 she was murdered by a rejected suitor.

See also FIELDING, XAN; SPECIAL OPERATIONS EXECUTIVE.

FURTHER READING: Xan Fielding, *Hide and Seek* (1954); M. R. Foot, *SOE in France: An Account of the Work of the British Special Operations Executive in France, 1940–1944* (1960); *Madelene Masson, *Christine: A Search for Christine Granville* (1975).

Green House   A brothel used by intelligence organizations for the intimidation and/or blackmail of selected patrons.

See STIEBER, WILHELM.

Greenglass, David *(1922-   )*   American spy for the Soviet Union.

Greenglass, like his sister Ethel (who married Julius Rosenberg), was born and raised in New York City. After a desultory educational career in which he failed the courses at the Polytechnic Institute of Brooklyn and attended night classes at Pratt Institute, he went into the U.S. Army in 1943, during World War II. The Army gave him technical training and posted him to various military installations where he could use what he had learned, his last assignment being at Los Alamos, New Mexico, where he served as a machinist for the Manhattan Project, which led to the development of the atomic bomb.

What Greenglass did during his Los Alamos period (1944–46) later became a matter of venomous dispute between him and his wife, on one side, and his sister and brother-in-law, on the other. The Greenglasses' version follows.

In 1944 Greenglass was drawn into a Soviet espionage network by the Rosenbergs, who were already major figures in the network with much experience in stealing, or persuading others to steal, classified information for delivery to the Russians. Playing his new role, Greenglass reported covertly on research at Los Alamos, his most important contribution to the Rosenberg spy ring being a description of the triggering mechanism for the type of bomb that devastated Nagasaki and brought the war with Japan to an end.

The Rosenbergs arranged a clandestine meeting between Greenglass and Communist courier Harry Gold, who carried information from Greenglass to Anatoly Yakovlev, the Russian head of the ring. Greenglass also gave secret data to his wife for transmission to the Rosenbergs when she visited New York. Greenglass also dealt directly with the Rosenbergs part of the time.

In 1946, the year in which the Cold War between the Russians and the west became a harsh reality, Greenglass received an honorable discharge from the Army. Fearful and remorseful, Greenglass refused to do any more spying for the Soviet Union through the Rosenbergs. Greenglass went into business with Julius Rosenberg, but the two quarreled, and in 1949 Greenglass went to work for himself.

Such was the version of events presented by Greenglass and his wife.

In 1950 the Greenglasses and the Rosenbergs were rounded up after the British authorities, acting on a tip from the FBI (Federal Bureau of Investigation), arrested Klaus Fuchs, a scientist and formerly a spy at Los Alamos. Fuchs talked, implicating Gold, who implicated Greenglass, who implicated the Rosenbergs and testified against them at their trial (1951).

The Rosenbergs denied everything incriminating in the Greenglass testimony, but the jury believed that testimony, and the judge sentenced the defendants to death. Greenglass received a jail sentence of fifteen years, while his wife went free, though she had to cope with the demoralizing effects of the scandal on her life.

See also FUCHS, KLAUS; GOLD, HARRY; ROSENBERG, JULIUS AND ETHEL; SOVIET AMERICAN NETWORK.

FURTHER READING: *Oliver Pilat, *The Atom Spies* (1952); Ronald Seth, *Unmasked! The Story of Soviet Espionage* (1965); Sanford J. Ungar, *FBI: An Uncensored Look behind the Walls* (1976).

Greenhow, Rose *(1817-64)*   Spy for the Confederacy in Washington during the American Civil War.

Rose O'Neal was born in Maryland into a family that took slavery for granted along with hospitality, horsemanship, courtly manners, and the other facets of genteel southern life. She lived with an aunt as a Washington belle before her marriage to Robert Greenhow, an official in the State Department, in 1835. She then became a Washington hostess and entertained practically everyone of importance in the nation's capital.

Her friend James Buchanan entered the White House in 1857, where for the next four years he watched the slavery crisis push the nation toward an armed conflict. Greenhow knew William Seward, secretary of state in President Abraham Lincoln's administration, which took office in 1861.

Now a widow, she turned her talents to finding out what she could about Union plans at her banquets, soirées, and "at homes." She proved to be so good at differentiating between gossip and fact, between the trivial and the significant, that Captain Thomas Jordan, organizer of a Confederate spy ring in Washington, made her its head when he resigned from the U.S. Army to enter the service of the Confederacy.

Greenhow used couriers to carry her messages to southern commanders. She was assiduous in accumulating information from spies for the Confederacy and talkative Unionists.

Her masterpiece of espionage concerned the battle of Bull Run in 1861, regarding which she sent three momentous messages in less than two weeks.

On July 10 she made use of a female courier, Betty Duvall, who carried coded notes in her luxuriant black tresses, held in place by a comb. In this case the message told Confederate General Pierre Beauregard that Union General Irvin McDowell would start his advance six days later. On July 16 she informed Beauregard that the advance would be from Arlington Heights and Alexandria toward Manassas on a stream called Bull Run. On July 17 she warned Beauregard that the Federals intended to cut the railroad to the Shenandoah Valley to prevent Confederate General Joseph E. Johnston from coming east for the battle.

Thus alerted, Beauregard secured the railroad line for Johnston and devised the battle plan by which the Confederates waited for McDowell to attack. At the critical moment of the fighting, Johnston's men struck the Unionists on the flank, breaking their line and driving them in a panic back toward Washington. So important was Greenhow's contribution to the battle of Bull Run that Beauregard sent her an expression of his gratitude.

She continued to send messages from Washington to the Confederates until Union counterespionage, directed by Allan Pinkerton, picked up her trail. She was arrested a month after Bull Run and held in prison before being released in 1862 and ordered to go into the Confederacy and stay there. Her fame was such that Jefferson Davis, president of the Confederacy, received her and described her as an indispensable contributor to the Confederate success at the start of the Civil War. Beauregard welcomed her personally and thanked her again.

Greenhow went to Europe, where she was presented to Napoleon III and Queen Victoria, and published an account of her unfortunate experiences at the hands of her Northern captors. She sailed for home in 1864, but her ship ran aground off the coast, and fearing capture by men of the Union blockade, she tried to escape ashore in a small boat. The boat capsized and she drowned.

See also BEAUREGARD, PIERRE; PINKERTON, ALLAN.

FURTHER READING: Rose O'Neal Greenhow, *My Imprisonment* (1863); *Ishbel Ross, *Rebel Rose* (1954); John Bakeless, *Spies of the Confederacy* (1970).

GRU Soviet military intelligence.

The GRU (Chief Intelligence Directorate of the General Staff of the Red Army) was established in 1920 by Leon Trotsky, the founder of the Red Army (but a nonperson in the Soviet Union since he was exiled by Joseph Stalin in

1929). From the first, the GRU acted as an instrument of the Soviet government as a whole, not merely as military intelligence in the limited western sense, and its directors have experienced the convulsive violence of Soviet history in the same way as civilian officials. Thus, its first head, General Jan Berzin, was shot in 1937 during Stalin's purge of his opponents.

The GRU is subordinate to the KGB (Committee for State Security, the nonmilitary side of Soviet intelligence), but this does not prevent rivalry between the two, especially when the generals become suspicious of civilian intentions and competence. That is why KGB agents abroad often have responsibility for keeping GRU agents under surveillance. Maintaining a more general control, the KGB has the right to approve or reject recruits for the GRU.

Abroad, the GRU has military attachés in Soviet embassies, and they often direct spy rings in host countries. The Soviet Canadian Network exposed by defector Igor Gouzenko was run by the GRU, which has had many great spies working for it, including the two greatest of World War II, Rudolf Roessler in Switzerland and Richard Sorge in Tokyo.

See also GOUZENKO, IGOR; KGB; TROTSKY, LEON.

FURTHER READING: *Igor Gouzenko, *The Iron Curtain* (1948); David Dallin, *Soviet Espionage* (1955); John Barron, *KGB: The Secret Work of Soviet Secret Agents* (1974).

Gubbins, Colin *(1896-1976)* Director of Britain's Special Operations Executive during World War II.

Born in the remote Scottish Hebrides, Gubbins grew up in an international atmosphere because his father was a diplomat of the British government. Gubbins attended the Cheltenham public school, followed by the Royal Military College at Woolwich, where he took his commission in the British army in 1914 as World War I was breaking out. He served in Belgium and France, winning the Military Cross for gallantry on the battlefield. After the war he saw service in Ireland (1919–22), when the British tried unsuccessfully to put down the rebellion that resulted in independence for Ireland. An intelligence officer in India until 1928, Gubbins shifted to the War Office in London in 1929. A decade later he was head of a British military mission in Poland when the German invasion touched off World War II (1939–45).

Captured by the Germans, Gubbins escaped from internment and reached Britain in time to be assigned to the expedition of 1940 that challenged the Germans in Norway. He led the rear-guard action, when most of the expedition escaped after the debacle. Then he helped draw up plans for the establishment of the Special Operations Executive (SOE), the undercover organization designed to cooperate with freedom fighters opposing the German occupation forces on the Continent. Gubbins became director of operations for the SOE in 1941, and in 1943 he became executive director of the organization. He was therefore in charge at the time of the SOE's greatest activity, when spies were sent into many nations and covert operations launched against selected targets under German control.

Prime Minister Winston Churchill ordered the SOE to "set Europe ablaze." Gubbins, his lieutenants, and his secret agents obeyed the order. Despite inevitable blunders and misfortunes, the SOE helped keep the hope of liberation alive in Europe at a time when it seemed that the German victory might be permanent. The underground networks supported by the SOE provided thousands of unofficial soldiers who joined the Allies following their invasion of France in 1944 and who participated in the liberation of the conquered nations. With the German surrender in 1945, Gubbins went back to being an officer in the regular army.

See also SPECIAL OPERATIONS EXECUTIVE.

FURTHER READING: *M. R. D. Foot, *SOE in France: An Account of the Work of the British Special Operations Executive in France, 1940–44* (1966); Edward Spiro, *Set Europe Ablaze* (1967).

Gubitchev, Valentin (1910?-   )   Russian spy at the United Nations.

Working at the United Nations in the 1940s, Gubitchev posed as a secretary to the Soviet delegation who specialized in construction engineering, a type of experience in demand since United Nations buildings were going up along New York's East River. Gubitchev's cover story was the more plausible in that he held a degree from the Moscow Institute of Architecture. His actual function in New York was to be the liaison man between American spy Judith Coplon and a representative of the KGB (Committee for State Security, Russian intelligence), in the United States.

In 1945 Coplon began working for the Foreign Agents Registration Section of the Justice Department in Washington, where she had access to classified information from the FBI (Federal Bureau of Investigation). After she began working with Gubitchev, she used to copy documents from her office, take the copies to New York, and deliver them to him at clandestine meetings. This went on until 1948, when the FBI, learning that some of its secret reports were reaching the Russians, traced the leaks to Coplon and began shadowing her to her rendezvous with Gubitchev. In 1949 the two were arrested, and Coplon was found in possession of incriminating documents that she intended to turn over to Gubitchev.

At their trials, they were found guilty. The Russians at the United Nations protested that Gubitchev was not a spy and that in any case he should be granted diplomatic immunity. The U.S. government denied both parts of the protest, but fearing retaliation against Americans in Russia, asked the court to give him a suspended sentence, after which he would be deported. The court agreed, and in 1950 Gubitchev was put aboard a Polish ship for the long voyage home.

He left Coplon in jail behind him, but her conviction was set aside by an appeals court on a technicality involving wiretap evidence.

See also COPLON, JUDITH.

FURTHER READING: *David Dallin, *Soviet Espionage* (1955); Ronald Seth, *Unmasked! The Story of Soviet Espionage* (1965); Pierre J. Huss and George Capozi, Jr., *Red Spies in the UN* (1965).

Guisan, Henri (1874-1960)   Swiss commander in chief and director of intelligence during World War II.

Guisan was born at Mézières, Switzerland, the son of a doctor, and educated in Lausanne. He took his baccalaureate degree in 1893, the year in which he received a commission in the artillery. He rose through the ranks and was a general in 1939, when the approach of World War II led to his being named commander in chief.

Intelligence became Guisan's responsibility, a difficult one as neutral Switzerland faced Nazi Germany. Guisan had at his disposal the official Swiss intelligence system under Colonel Roger Masson, but the commander in chief needed a special espionage organization not tied to the government. Switzerland being legally neutral but actually anti-Nazi, Guisan wanted to warn the Allies about German plans discovered by Swiss agents, while remaining free to repudiate the espionage in case of a protest from Berlin. He did so by using the Bureau Ha, a semiofficial private intelligence group headed by Captain Hans Hausamann.

The fall of France in 1940 complicated Guisan's problem, for the Germans and their ally, Italy, now surrounded Switzerland with their armed forces. The German invasion of Russia in 1941 produced a special difficulty because German and Soviet spies were at large in Switzerland. In spite of the dangers, Guisan permitted the Bureau Ha to warn both the western Allies and the Russians about German plans and strategy. Much of this information came from Rudolf Roessler, an expatriate German with remarkable, and still debatable, sources in Berlin. Roessler worked with the Soviet network directed by Sandor Rado in Geneva, an operation of which Guisan was aware and to which he turned a blind eye.

When German counterespionage recorded the broadcasts from Switzerland to Moscow, it put pressure on Guisan, who fended off German intervention in his country by twice meeting secretly with Walter Schellenberg, the head of Nazi intelligence (1943). Whatever Guisan said at these conferences, he convinced Schellenberg that Switzerland was not helping the Soviet Union directly. To justify the Swiss position, Guisan permitted Swiss counterespionage to track down and destroy the Rado network.

Meanwhile Allen Dulles, of the American OSS (Office of Strategic Services), had arrived in Bern for clandestine talks with dissident Germans who were seeking to overthrow Hitler and end the war. Guisan allowed these negotiations to proceed from 1942 onward (they came to nothing). In all this, Guisan had shown a genius for maneuvering between the fear of a German attack and the need for a German defeat, and he brought Switzerland safely through to the end of the war in 1945.

He then returned to being a private citizen, although one unique in his country—the pilot who had weathered the storm.

See also BUREAU HA; DULLES, ALLEN; ROESSLER, RUDOLF; SCHELLENBERG, WALTER.

FURTHER READING: *Jon Kimche, *Spying for Peace: General Guisan and Swiss Neutrality* (1962); Urz Schwartz, *The Eye of the Hurricane: Switzerland in World War II* (1980).

Hale, Nathan (1755-76) Patriot and spy of the American Revolution.

The son of a Connecticut farmer, Hale graduated from Yale in 1773, the year of the Boston Tea Party, when a group of American Patriots threw a cargo of British tea into Boston harbor. He was teaching school in 1775 when he heard of the battle of Lexington, an event that prompted him to join the Connecticut armed forces. Participating in the siege of Boston in 1776, he was promoted to captain. He moved south to New York with the Continental army under the command of General George Washington. Hale was then selected by Colonel Thomas Knowlton to be an officer in a crack outfit, Knowlton's Rangers.

The British under Sir William Howe invaded New York. Washington, retreating from Long Island to Manhattan and facing a crisis, decided to send a spy behind the enemy lines. Knowlton, ordered to find a spy, called for a volunteer, and Hale answered the call. Having had no espionage training, Hale was expected to use his good sense and natural prudence in carrying out the assignment.

Exchanging his military uniform for the garb of a schoolmaster, his profession in civilian life and therefore a plausible cover, he slipped through the British lines and began his spy mission. His activities cannot be precisely determined, but he was on Long Island on September 12 and in Manhattan ten days later, so presumably he made the crossing of the East River on the heels of Howe's troops, who invaded Manhattan on September 15.

Along the way Hale recorded military information in documents that were found on him when he was arrested on September 21. It was said at the time that a cousin betrayed him, which would mean that he imprudently revealed his mission while behind the enemy lines. Nor did he have his cover story ready, but frankly revealed his identity and his purpose. Probably it never occurred to him to practice the deception of a spy. At any rate, his naiveté and his fate forced Washington to upgrade American espionage to make it more professional.

Howe ordered Hale to be hanged forthwith, and the execution took place the day after his capture. During his last hours, Hale wrote letters to Knowlton and to his brother Enoch (who two years later, as a member of the Culper Ring, functioned as a more professional spy than Nathan). Nathan Hale's famous last words ("I only regret that I have but one life to lose for my country") were a quotation from a play popular in the eighteenth century, Joseph Addison's *Cato,* the plot of which turns on Roman patriotism.

FURTHER READING: *George Dudley Seymour, *A Documentary Life of Nathan Hale* (1933); Morton Pennypacker, *General Washington's Spies on Long Island and in New York* (1939); Martha Mann, *Nathan Hale, Patriot* (1969), is for juveniles.

Hall, Reginald (1870-1943) Director of British naval intelligence during World War I.

Hall came of a naval family of Wiltshire, and he followed the family tradition by entering the Royal Navy, where he specialized in gunnery, served on several warships, and by 1905 had reached the rank of captain. He was named director of naval intelligence in 1914. Arriving shortly after the outbreak of World War I, Hall organized Room 40 at the Admiralty, the legendary home of cryptographers who monitored German military and diplomatic messages in code.

"Blinker" Hall, so called from a twitch in one eye, departed from crusty British naval tradition by bringing in outsiders, particularly university men from Cambridge and Oxford, who joined imagination and practical ability. Hall made a point of developing liaison with other intelligence organizations. He exchanged information and ideas with Mansfield Cumming of MI6 (Military Intelligence 6, British espionage), Vernon Kell of MI5 (Military Intelligence 5, British counterspionage), and Basil Thompson of the Special Branch (Scotland Yard).

Ironically, Hall's naval intelligence did not enjoy such close relations with naval operations. In one of the bizarre episodes of the war, neither knew what the other was doing. Naval intelligence tricked the Germans into laying mines in an unused route through the North Sea off the Orkney Islands. Naval operations, needing a route for the voyage to Russia of Lord Kitchener, organizer of the British war effort, and believing the Orkney route to be safe, chose it for Kitchener's vessel, which hit a mine and was lost (1916). Hall was not necessarily to blame for the disaster, for the "deep water admirals" generally ignored the intellectuals of Room 40, and conceivably a report went from intelligence to operations that was overlooked. The episode is still shrouded in mystery.

After the war, Hall went into politics and was elected to Parliament, where he spoke for national preparedness during debates in the House of Commons. He traveled to the United States, where his advice was sought on intelligence cases and the detection of spies.

World War II found him too old for active service. He was merely a member of the Home Guard when he died.

See also HAMPSHIRE INCIDENT; ROOM 40.

FURTHER READING: H.C. Hoy, *40 O.B., or How the War Was Won* (1934); *Reginald Hall and Amos Peaslee, *Three Wars with Germany* (1944); William James, *The Codebreakers of Room 40* (1956).

Hampshire Incident *(1916)* Destruction of a British warship through a British espionage maneuver during World War I.

When the British cruiser *Hampshire* struck a German mine off the Orkney Islands in 1916, it was the result of a blunder inside the British Admiralty, where the operations division did not know what the intelligence division was doing.

Captain Reginald Hall, head of naval intelligence, deciding to trick the German navy and lure it into an unimportant area of the sea, had a radio message sent from a destroyer to the Admiralty in London declaring that a channel off the Orkneys had been swept clear of mines. The message was deliberately repeated four times.

German military intelligence picked up the message and decoded it, and Director Walther Nicolai felt, as Hall intended, that it must be of the utmost importance because of the repetitions and because it went straight to the Admiralty in London instead of to a shore station. Putting the facts together as he believed them to be, Nicolai inferred that the British navy would be doing something of extreme urgency in the mine-free Orkney channel. Therefore, a German minelayer was ordered into the area to seed the water with mines.

Hall may have failed to inform the operations division about what he was doing, or operations may have overlooked his report. In any case Lord Kitchener, the organizer of the British war effort, was bound for Russia aboard the cruiser *Hampshire* to encourage the tsar to continue the war against Germany. Kitchener's crusiser had to take the safest route to Russia, which operations believed to be the the the little-used channel off the Orkneys. By now, because of the skill of the intelligence division, this was one of the most dangerous routes in the world. The *Hampshire* sailed into the Orkney channel, hit a German mine, and sank with the loss of all on board.

See also HALL, REGINALD; NICOLAI, WALTHER.

FURTHER READING: Admiralty White Paper, *The Loss of H.M.S. Hampshire on 5th June, 1916. Official Narrative* (1926); *Donald McCormick, *The Mystery of Lord Kitchener's Death* (1959); Richard Deacon, *A History of the British Secret Service* (1969).

Hardinge, Henry (1785-1856)   British army officer who served as the duke of Wellington's espionage chief during the Napoleonic Wars.

Hardinge came of a Kentish family living in the country near London. After entering the British army and serving routinely, he found an outlet for his espionage talents when assigned to Wellington's staff at the time of the Peninsular War (1808–14) between Britain and France.

Napoleon, now emperor of France, having forced the king of Spain to abdicate in 1808, intended to hold the Iberian Peninsula under French control by placing Joseph Bonaparte, his brother, on the Spanish throne. Wellington's orders were to drive the French out of the peninsula. Wellington succeeded partly because Hardinge gathered, systematized, and reported information from British spies and Spaniards who brought in French military documents. These Spaniards acted either out of patriotism, since the Spanish people hated the French invaders, or because of the money they received at Wellington's headquarters.

One of Hardinge's British spies effected a coup by stealing the code book of Marshal André Masséna. This enabled Hardinge to read French dispatches in cipher and to give his commanding general the detailed information on French battle plans that led to notable Anglo-Spanish victories at Salamanca (1812) and Vittoria (1813).

This success at espionage contrasted with the ineptitude of the French, an odd situation because espionage in Paris was very good during these years under two ministers of police, Joseph Fouché and René Savary. The French had outstanding spies in Germany, led by Karl Schulmeister, but they never were served in the peninsula by undercover agents of any ability. To this, at least in part, may be attributed Wellington's success in winning the campaign.

Hardinge, now a colonel, played an espionage role at Waterloo in 1815. In charge of the British secret service, he gathered information from French royalists and others opposed to Napoleon. On June 6, 1815, he received a message stating that Napoleon intended to make a feint on the Maubeuge side of the battlefield and then launch the main French attack toward Mons between Lille and Tournai. Two days later the battle developed in precisely that manner. Wellington was prepared, and Napoleon ordered his troops into a disaster.

Hardinge was knighted for his espionage achievements. He went into Parliament, became secretary of war in 1828 when Wellington was prime minister, and after serving in Ireland and India, received the title of viscount.

See also WELLINGTON, DUKE OF.

FURTHER READING: °Godfrey Davies, *Wellington and His Army* (1954), has an account of Wellington's reliance on Hardinge; Richard Deacon, *A History of the British Secret Service* (1969).

Harel, Isser (1912-   )   Director of the Mossad, the main department of Israeli intelligence.

Born into an Orthodox Jewish family of Vitebsk, Russia, Harel's name was originally Isser Halperin. His father was a businessman who, expropriated by the Communist regime, moved the family to Latvia in 1922. Seven years later most of the family went to Palestine, and Isser joined them the next year.

An ardent Zionist, he enrolled in Haganah, the underground organization dedicated to Jewish self-defense, and in 1942, during World War II, he changed his name to Isser Harel, its Hebrew form. Harel served in the British auxiliary forces in the war against Nazi Germany, but all the while he was doing intelligence work for the Zionists against both the British and the Arabs in Palestine. In 1944, as the war drew toward its close, he became head of Haganah intelligence.

In 1951, following the establishment of the state of Israel, and as a result of Prime Minister David Ben-Gurion's reorganization of Israeli intelligence, Harel became the head of the Mossad, with responsibility for foreign espionage and covert activities. He built the Mossad into one of the best intelligence organizations in the world. He went into the field himself, most notably when he directed the capture of Nazi war criminal Adolf Eichmann in Buenos Aires in 1960.

Harel resigned in 1963 after a quarrel with Ben-Gurion concerning the behavior of Harel's agents, two of whom were caught in Switzerland and jailed for violating Swiss law. Harel was security adviser to Prime Minister Levi Eshkol in 1965 but resigned the next year after another disagreement. He retired into private life.

See also EICHMANN, ADOLF; MOSSAD.

FURTHER READING: °Isser Harel, *The House on Garibaldi Street: The Capture of Adolf Eichmann* (1975); Richard Deacon, *The Israeli Secret Service* (1977); Dennis Eisenberg, Uri Dan, and Eli Landau, *The Mossad, Israel's Secret Intelligence Service: Inside Stories* (1978); Stewart Steven, *The Spymasters of Israel* (1980).

Harnack, Arvid (1901-42)   German spymaster for the Soviet Union during World War II.

Harnack's family included notable German intellectuals, his father being the historian Otto Harnack, and his uncle the theologian Adolf Harnack. Born in Darmstadt, Germany, Harnack received much of his education at home. In 1926, after graduating from the University of Berlin, he went to the United States on a Rockefeller grant to study economics at the University of Wisconsin. Returning home, he completed his studies at the University of Giessen (1930), where he was influenced by the leftist Giessen School of economics.

He was already an anti-Nazi, and a visit to Moscow in 1932 made him a committed Communist. He agreed to spy for the Soviet Union, which he did for the following ten years. He met other anti-Nazi Germans, including Harro Schulze-Boysen, who was in the ministry of aviation. Since Harnack was in the ministry of economics, the two were able to transmit to Moscow information of great importance.

Harnack and his confederates, allied with Schulze-Boysen, became part of the European Red Orchestra, the coordinated Soviet spy system with branches in Belgium, Holland, France, and Switzerland. Following the German invasion of Russia in 1941, Red Orchestra radios for over a year reported to Moscow on the German armed forces. German counterespionage cracked the Brussels spy ring in 1942, and the trail led to Harnack and his confederates. Arrested, Harnack, like Schulze-Boysen, was executed for treason.

See also RED ORCHESTRA; SCHULZE-BOYSEN, HARRO.

FURTHER READING: Gilles Perrault, *The Red Orchestra* (1969); *Heinz Höhne, *Codeword: Direktor: The Story of the Red Orchestra* (1971); Paul L. Kesaris (ed.), *The Rote Kapelle: The CIA's History of Soviet Intelligence and Espionage Networks in Western Europe, 1936–1945* (1979).

***Hayhanen, Reino** (1920-61)* Russian spy for the Soviet Union in the United States.

Born in Petrograd (now Leningrad) three years after the Bolshevik revolution, Hayhanen belonged to a peasant family. He gained an education under Communism, taught school, and in 1939 was conscripted into intelligence work by the NKVD (People's Commissariat for Internal Affairs, 1934–46; former name of the KGB, Soviet intelligence). He served as an interrogator of prisoners during the Russo-Finnish War (1939–40).

Hayhanen continued intelligence work during the World War II conflict between Germany and Russia (1941–45) and in 1948 began a course lasting four years in which he mastered English, as well as espionage techniques, and rose to the rank of lieutenant colonel. In 1952 he arrived in New York using a forged passport, and a year later, under instructions from the Center, Moscow's intelligence headquarters, he became a cut-out, or front man, for resident director Rudolf Abel.

Hayhanen, however, could not get along with his wife. He began to drink heavily, became involved with other women, and ignored his spy duties at critical moments. As a result, Abel tried to persuade him to return to Moscow, especially after Abel returned from a trip to the Soviet capital and found that Hayhanen had made a mess of the espionage they were supposed to be conducting and had spent on himself some of the money allotted to them by the Center to pay for undercover work.

Hayhanen was reluctant to go to Moscow because he feared that Abel had compromised him at the Center. In 1957 he agreed to go, only to lose his nerve in Paris, defect to the U.S. Embassy, and ask for asylum. He talked to an agent of the CIA (Central Intelligence Agency), as a result of which the CIA brought him to New York, where he helped track Abel down.

A piece of microfilm found in Abel's studio enabled Hayhanen to identify Master Sergeant Roy Rhodes, who had spied for the Russians while working at the motor pool of the American Embassy in Moscow. Hayhanen and Rhodes drew a net around Abel at his trial, and Abel received a jail sentence from which he was rescued in 1962 by being exchanged for Francis Gary Powers, the American U-2 pilot then a prisoner in a Russian jail.

Hayhanen received sanctuary in the United States and vanished from public notice until he was killed in 1961 in an automobile crash on the Pennsylvania Turnpike.

See also ABEL, RUDOLF; CENTER, THE.

FURTHER READING: *James B. Donovan, *Strangers on a Bridge: The Case of Colonel Abel* (1964); Ronald Seth, *Unmasked! The Story of Soviet Espionage* (1965); Louise Bernikow, *Abel* (1970).

Henry, Hubert *(1846-98)* French army officer and principal conspirator in the Dreyfus Affair.

Born near Châlons, Henry escaped from the drudgery of his parent's farm by joining the French army (1865), in which he served during the Franco-Prussian War (1870–71), beginning as a sergeant major and winning a battlefield commission. He held military commands in North Africa and Southeast Asia, and was a major in 1891 when he received an appointment to the Second Bureau (military intelligence) of the general staff at the ministry of war in Paris.

Henry was the first officer to examine the document that launched the Dreyfus Affair in 1894. Although recognizing that the offer to sell French military plans to the Germans was written on the stationery of Major Ferdinand Esterhazy, Henry at this point seems to have honestly believed what he reported to his superiors, that Captain Alfred Dreyfus had done the writing. Henry found the belief easy to entertain: he was an anti-Semite and Dreyfus was a Jew. Later, to protect himself and the army, Henry forged documents to incriminate Dreyfus, against whom he testified at the court-martial that sent Dreyfus to Devil's Island, the French penal colony off the coast of French Guiana.

Henry's superiors were deceived, the chief of the general staff, General Raoul de Boisdeffre, among them. They later began to have doubts about the guilt of Dreyfus but felt bound to obstruct further investigation for fear of the effect on the military establishment. When the head of the Second Bureau, Lieutenant Colonel Georges Picquart, showed them proof of Esterhazy's guilt, they transferred Picquart to North Africa and replaced him with Henry (1896).

Henry continued to fabricate anti-Dreyfus material. In 1898 he testified against Émile Zola during the novelist's trial for libel after writing a condemnation of the military men involved in the cover-up. Picquart, who testified for Zola, fought a duel with Henry in which the latter was slightly wounded.

But Henry's forgeries eventually betrayed him. An officer ordered to scrutinize the relevant Dreyfus documents uncovered the fraud, and the minister of war could no longer shirk the responsibility of searching for the truth, whatever it might be. The minister interrogated Henry, who broke down and admitted his guilt. Boisdeffre, acknowledging that he had been duped, resigned as chief of the general staff.

Taken to prison and nearly incoherent from the strain, Henry committed suicide in his cell.

See also DREYFUS AFFAIR.

FURTHER READING: Alfred Cobban, *A History of Modern France* (1961), gives the historical background of the Dreyfus Case; Betty Schechter, *The Dreyfus Affair: A National Scandal*

(1965); Louis L. Snyder, *The Dreyfus Case: A Documentary History* (1973); David L. Lewis, *Prisoners of Honor: The Dreyfus Affair* (1973).

Henry, John *(1776-1840?)*   Irish adventurer and spy for the British government in the United States.

Henry's biography is filled with gaps. He seems to have been born in Ireland in 1776, and he emigrated to America as a young man to join a business in Boston owned by his uncle. Discovering that ordinary work did not appeal to him, he quit to go into the U.S. Army, and by 1798 he had risen to the rank of captain. Then he left the army, wandered through New England—using a personable appearance and a glib tongue to good advantage —and studied law, which struck him as the proper field in which to exercise his special talents.

Henry never took a law degree, but he left that fact unmentioned when he migrated to what was then Upper Canada and wangled his way onto the bench as a judge. The suspicion he provoked by his demeanor (he was termed "an Irish adventurer") probably forced him to abandon his legal career. In any case, he was back in the United States in 1808, when he began writing letters to Canada condemning American democracy.

Living in New England, Henry noted the hostility of the Federalist Party toward the government in Washington. New England shipping interests resented the embargo that kept the American merchant marine off the high seas while Britain was at war with the France of Emperor Napoleon Bonaparte. President Thomas Jefferson's aim was to prevent American ships from being seized upon trying to trade with either country. The New England Federalists, however, whose vessels remained in port, felt the economic pinch, and they blamed Jefferson and his Democratic-Republican Party.

Henry, writing to his Canadian friend Herman Ryland, stressed the doubts of the New England Federalists about the worth of an American government that damaged their economic interests. Ryland showed some of Henry's letters to Sir James Craig, the governor of Canada, who was so impressed with the political analysis that he asked Henry to become his secret agent in New England. The friction between the United States and Britain was becoming more intense, leading up to the War of 1812. Apprehensive about a possible American invasion of Canada, Craig wanted to have a spy reporting to him from the critical area of the United States centered on Boston. Henry's letters, followed by a personal interview in Montreal, convinced Craig that Henry was the man he needed. Henry agreed.

The Governor's spy moved through New England during the year 1809, when James Madison succeeded Jefferson as president of the United States. The anti-British sentiment in Washington continued under Madison, who protested against British violations of the rights of neutrals in the war against Napoleon. The Jefferson embargo continued into 1809. Henry therefore found much to report regarding the continuing opposition to the national policy in Federalist New England.

After talking to Federalists in government and business, Henry reported that they were pro-British, anti-Napoleon, and angry with Madison. He was pleased to tell Governor Craig that he found many New Englanders in favor of seceding from the United States and forming some kind of association with Britain. This, of course, was common talk in Boston and elsewhere in New England, but it was the talk of angry men and women who said much more than they really meant, and Henry made no headway when, following Craig's instructions, he subtly and obliquely advanced the idea that London would welcome an alliance between England and New England.

Craig sent Henry's reports on to London, where their reception was favorable enough to keep the spy mission going. Then Henry, upon asking Craig for the payment agreed upon, was told that he would have to take his case to London. Henry went to the British capital in 1811, only to be informed that Montreal was in charge. Disappointed and vengeful, Henry returned to the United States and at the beginning of 1812 turned over to the Madison administration copies of the reports he had sent to the Canadian Governor.

Madison, angry to learn that a spy for the British had been active in New England while peace negotiations between Washington and London were going on, presented the reports to Congress. When published, they contributed to the American fury that brought on the War of 1812.

FURTHER READING: *Documents from Henry, the British Spy* (1812), published in the *Boston Patriot;* Irving Brant, *James Madison: The President, 1809–1812* (1956); Alan Lloyd, *The Scorching of Washington: The War of 1812* (n.d.), has an account of Henry's spy mission in New England.

Heydrich, Reinhard (1904-42)   Spymaster in Germany's Third Reich.

Born in Halle, Germany, Heydrich was the son of a musician said to have been Jewish, an origin that Heydrich later tried to conceal behind exaggerated anti-Semitism. He clung to his musical heritage, and during the time of his criminal activities as a Nazi henchman of Adolf Hitler he would relax by playing the violin in family concerts.

Educated in Halle, he entered the German navy in 1922, rose to the rank of lieutenant, and in 1931 was dismissed for conduct unbecoming an officer in a breach of promise case involving a young girl. He met Heinrich Himmler at about the same time. In 1932 Heydrich joined the SS (Hitler's Elite Guard), which Himmler commanded, and which included a civilian intelligence department, the SD (Security Service). In 1934 Heydrich became deputy chief of the Gestapo, and took charge of a police system that included both the Gestapo and the SD. He assisted Himmler in the 1934 "blood purge" of the Nazi party—the wiping out of members Hitler considered a threat. In 1936 Heydrich assumed authority over the regular police. Three years later Heydrich rose close to the top of the Nazi hierarchy when a reshuffling of security organizations left him in command of the RSHA (Reich Central Security Office), which brought together in one system the Gestapo, the SD, and the regular police.

Heydrich wielded immense power over the German people and the peoples in lands conquered by the German armed forces during World War II (1939–45). In particular, Heydrich directed Hitler's "final solution," the mass murder of Jews in the Nazi death camps. Heydrich became deputy protector for Bohemia and Moravia (Czechoslovakia) in 1941. His brutality provoked a determined resistance movement, and in 1942 he was killed by a bomb thrown into his car near Prague. The Nazis took their revenge by executing the men and deporting the women and children of the town of Lidice, where the assassins were said to have hidden.

See also HIMMLER, HEINRICH.

FURTHER READING: Willi Frischauer, *Himmler* (1953); Charles Wighton, *Heydrich, Hitler's Most Evil Henchman* (1962); *G. S. Graber, *The Life and Times of Reinhard Heydrich* (1980).

Himmler, Heinrich *(1900-45)* German chief of police and director of state security in Germany's Third Reich.

Himmler, the son of a school teacher, was born in Munich and educated in a high school in Landshut. He served in the German army without distinction in World War I (1914–18), studied at the Munich Technological College (1918–19), and took a diploma in agriculture. While working for a farming company, he joined the Nazi (National Socialist) party, led by Adolf Hitler. Himmler participated in Hitler's first bid for power, the unsuccessful beer hall putsch of 1923 in Munich.

Himmler rose to prominence as Hitler's power grew. Nazi leader in Bavaria since 1926, Himmler in 1929 became head of the SS (Hitler's Elite Guard), within which he established an intelligence department, the SD (Security Service). Himmler became acting chief of the Gestapo (Secret State Police) in 1934, the year in which he shocked moderate Germans and foreign observers by directing the "blood purge" of the Nazi party, the massacre of Hitler's rivals. In 1936 Himmler became head of the combined Gestapo and SD, and three years later he assumed control of all police forces, including the RSHA (Reich Central Security Office), which included the Gestapo, the SD, and the regular police. He was thus in charge of every organ of civilian intelligence (to which he added military intelligence when the Abwehr was broken up by Hitler in 1944).

Himmler tightened the Nazi hold on Germany by employing a corps of undercover agents who spied on the German people, identifying dissidents, Jews, Communists, and others who disturbed the solidarity of the masses behind Hitler. Countless Germans learned to live in fear of a nighttime knock on the door by Himmler's agents, and many victims were hurried away to jail cells, torture chambers, or execution.

Himmler extended his terror system to countries invaded by the German armed forces during World War II (1939–45). His spies operated from France to Russia. Jews were rounded up everywhere and transported to death camps. The conquered peoples were whipped into line to labor for the German war effort. Resistance groups were infiltrated, their leaders were subjected to torture and murder, and local populations paid in "thirty-for-one" executions when German soldiers were killed. In 1942 Himmler ordered the destruction of Lidice, the Czech town where his aide, Reinhard Heydrich, had been assassinated.

In 1943, as the German armies faltered, Himmler became minister of the interior, with responsibility for stabilizing the home front, maintaining order among the war-weary people, and punishing defeatists. The increasing danger to the Third Reich made Himmler more violent than ever, and in 1944 he behaved like a deranged sadist in dealing with Germans convicted of complicity in the July Plot to kill Hitler (who was merely injured by the bomb planted at his headquarters).

In spite of his past loyalty to Hitler, Himmler decided to act for himself in 1945 when the defeat of Nazi Germany and the destruction of its leader had become inevitable. Himmler made several attempts to negotiate peace with the Allies. Rebuffed by them (and by Hitler, who nearly went mad with rage at the news of Himmler's treason), Himmler donned a disguise and tried to lose himself in the chaos as Germany collapsed. Captured and identified by British soldiers, Himmler poisoned himself.

See also ABWEHR; GESTAPO; HEYDRICH, REINHARD; RSHA; SD.

FURTHER READING: *Willi Frischauer, *Himmler* (1953); Edward Crankshaw, *The Gestapo* (1956); Bradley F. Smith, *Heinrich Himmler: A Nazi in the Making, 1900–1926* (1971).

Hirayama, Choichi *(1869-1924)*   Japanese spy in Siberia at the time of the Russo-Japanese War.

Hirayama came out of the poorest area of Tokyo, where he struggled to make a living as a ricksha boy transporting members of the affluent classes through the streets of the Japanese capital. To escape from his sordid living conditions, in 1897 he joined the Black Ocean Society, a nationalist organization committed to the defeat of Russia in the Far East.

The Black Ocean Society sent Hirayama to an espionage school in Sapporo, on the northern Japanese island of Hokkaido, where he mastered spy techniques and the Russian language. His first undercover assignment took him to the town of Iman in Siberia on the trans-Siberian Railroad, a strategic point from which to spy on the Russians. Using a general store for a cover, he became a valued member of the community in Iman, through which he moved without creating suspicion.

Hirayama watched Russian troop movements along the trans-Siberian Railroad. Just as important, he formed a liaison with a Russian officer's wife, who talked freely to him about Russian plans in the Far East. Other Japanese secret agents came to Hirayama's store with reports from other strategic points in Siberia, as did Chinese agents from Manchuria.

Collecting information on Russian tactics, troops, and weapons, Hirayama sent dispatches clandestinely to Tokyo, where they became part of Japan's overall planning for the Russo-Japanese War (1904–05), which was marked by decisive Japanese victories, especially in the siege of Port Arthur and the naval battle of Tsushima (1905).

This conflict created so much anti-Japanese feeling among the Russians in Iman that Hirayama, although not suspected of being a spy, was forced to leave. He did not return until the fighting was over, but he then regained sufficient popularity to stay until the outbreak of World War I in 1914.

Since Japan and Russia were now allies, Hirayama felt safe. Everything changed with the Russian Revolution in 1917. Anti-Bolshevik forces used his store for their military headquarters, which compromised Hirayama when the Bolsheviks won, and in 1921 he had to leave Siberia for good.

The Black Ocean Society assigned him to further espionage work in 1922 in Manchuria. Ill health forced him to return to Japan a year later. He lived in retirement thereafter.

FURTHER READING: *Ronald Seth, *Secret Servants: A History of Japanese Espionage* (1957); Reginald Hargreaves, *Red Sun Rising: The Siege of Port Arthur* (1957), has an account of Japanese undercover activities prior to the Russo-Japanese War.

Hirsch, Willi *(1908-61)*   German spy for the Soviet Union in the United States.

Hirsch, born into a poor family in Kassel, was sent to the United States in 1923 to live with relatives. Raised in Philadelphia, he became a salesman, engaged in left-wing politics during the Depression, and used the name "John Gilmore." In 1932 he married Dorothy Baker, also left wing and a member of the Friends of the Soviet Union. He edited the artwork for the group's magazine, *Soviet Russia Today.*

Following a trip to Moscow in 1936, Hirsch worked as a freelance journalist and spied for the Russians as he traveled around the United States. In Chicago in 1958 he met William McCuaig, to whom he recommended the same type of espionage as a profitable venture. McCuaig reported this to agents of the FBI (Federal Bureau of Investigation). They asked him to pretend to be interested and to let them know everything that developed.

Hirsch introduced McCuaig to Igor Melekh, a Russian translator at the United Nations whose chief assignment from Moscow was to run a spy network in New York. McCuaig met Melekh in New York City and in Newark, New Jersey, in 1959, always with fake material provided by the FBI. McCuaig reported in 1960 that the Russian was getting suspicious and that there was no longer any point in the double-agent maneuver. The FBI arrested Hirsch and Melekh. Hirsch's apartment yielded enough incriminating evidence for both men to be held, put on trial, found guilty, and sent to jail.

The Russians were holding two American Air Force officers who had been shot down in an RB-47 spy plane over the Barents Sea, and an exchange was worked out in 1961, after President John Kennedy took office. The Americans came home and Melekh went home. Hirsch, a German by origin and therefore not claimed by the Soviet Union, went to England, continued on to Prague, and ended in Moscow, where he died not long afterward. The exchange was a manifestion of the espionage revolution, whereby spies are traded instead of executed.

See also ESPIONAGE REVOLUTION; RB-47.

FURTHER READING: David Wise and Thomas B. Ross, *The Espionage Establishment* (1967), has a description of the Hirsch case; *E. H. Cookridge, *Spy Trade* (1971).

Hiss, Alger *(1904-   )*   American public figure, convicted perjurer, and alleged spy for the Soviet Union.

Hiss was born in Baltimore, where, when he was three years old, his father committed suicide. The tragedy seems not to have had a lasting effect on Hiss, who had a pleasant childhood that included education in Baltimore schools. He attended the Powder Point Academy in Duxbury, Massachusetts (1921–22) and then Johns Hopkins University (1922–26). After graduating from Harvard Law School in 1929, the year in which he married Priscilla Fansler Hobson, a divorcee, Hiss served for a year as law clerk to Supreme Court Justice Oliver Wendell Holmes.

Hiss practiced law in Boston and New York during the early 1930s before going into government work in Washington with the Agricultural Adjustment Administration (1933–35), the Nye Committee investigating the arms industry (1934), the Justice Department (1935–36), and the State Department (1936–

45). He was executive secretary of the Dumbarton Oaks Conference, which founded the United Nations in 1944, and he became the organization's secretary general at its charter Convention in 1945. At the Yalta Conference in 1945, when Roosevelt, Churchill, and Stalin conferred on political arrangements to be made at the end of World War II (the end came in Europe a few weeks later), Hiss worked directly under Secretary of State Edward R. Stettinius.

Despite this notable career in public service, Hiss was the subject of derogatory material in the files of the State Department and the FBI (Federal Bureau of Investigation). In 1939 Whittaker Chambers, a former member of a Communist underground in Washington, told Assistant Secretary of State Adolf Berle that Hiss belonged to the underground, as did his wife and his brother, Donald Hiss. Berle did nothing about the accusation, presumably considering it too absurd to be true in the case of an outstanding American like Alger Hiss. At about the same time, the American ambassador to Paris, William C. Bullitt, warned Hiss's superior at the State Department, Stanley Hornbeck, that French intelligence possessed information stigmatizing both Alger and Donald Hiss as Soviet agents. When Hornbeck questioned him about the report, Alger Hiss denied the charge, and Hornbeck accepted the denial. In 1944, interrogated by the FBI, Hiss said he had never had any sympathy with Communism.

When Igor Gouzenko, the code clerk at the Soviet embassy in Ottawa, defected to Canada in 1945, he reported that an assistant to the secretary of state in Washington was a Soviet agent. The trail, by process of elimination, seemed to lead to Hiss. The FBI kept Hiss under surveillance, but the investigation produced nothing incriminating. In 1946 a new secretary of state, James Byrnes, prompted by the rumors about Hiss, asked him if he had ever had Communist ties. Hiss said no, repeating his denial to the FBI.

Hiss left the State Department in 1946, upon agreeing to become president of the Carnegie Endowment for International Peace in New York, where he served until 1948. The chairman of the Carnegie Board, John Foster Dulles, raised the Communist question and was satisfied when Hiss assured him there was nothing to the talk. Then Chambers, appearing before the House Committee on Un-American Activities as a self-confessed former Soviet agent, named Hiss as a Communist who had worked with him in the 1930s. Hiss came before the committee to deny the charge. He insisted, as he had already done before a grand jury, that he had never met Chambers.

The committee, at first favorable to Hiss, was startled when Chambers demonstrated an intimate knowledge of the Hisses and their homes. He knew, for instance, that they were avid bird watchers around Washington who once had returned from a field trip very pleased at having spotted a prothonotary warbler. Chambers declared he knew all this because he had lived in the Hiss houses during the years 1934 to 1938, when Alger and Priscilla Hiss had both been active, as he had been, in the Communist movement. Chambers testified that Hiss in 1936 had given an old car to the Communist party. Hiss testified that he had given the car to Chambers in 1935. Chambers said he had known Hiss into 1938. Hiss said he had last seen Chambers in 1937.

The committee arranged a confrontation between the two men at which Hiss, after some hesitancy, which he attributed to changes in Chamber's appearance, identified Chambers as a journalist he had known briefly and casually in the 1930s under the name "George Crosley" (Chambers professed not to recognize the alias but said he might have used it). Hiss challenged Chambers to repeat the accusation outside the security of the committee hearings, threatening to sue him for slander if he did. Chambers took up the challenge on the radio program *Meet the Press* when he asserted: "Alger Hiss was a Communist and may be now." Hiss filed his suit.

The committee had already discovered that Hiss had transferred his old car in 1936 to a used-car company, from which it had passed into the hands of the current owner, William Rosen, who refused to explain how he had gotten it and was later found to be a member of the Communist party. Chambers now accused Hiss of espionage, charging that Hiss during the 1930s brought home classified documents from the State Department, that Priscilla Hiss typed copies of most of them, and that Chambers gave the copies to his spy contacts while Hiss returned the originals to the State Department files. As evidence, Chambers presented to the committee four papers in Hiss's handwriting, photographs of documents, and sixty-five typewritten sheets. The latest of these were dated 1938. Chambers afterward produced the "pumpkin papers," documents that he had hidden in a hollowed-out pumpkin on his Maryland farm.

This evidence was presented to a grand jury, which focused on the typewriter that Priscilla Hiss had allegedly used to type copies of the documents. The typewriter had vanished, and the FBI was unable to find it. This lacuna in the evidence did not prevent the grand jury from indicting Hiss on two counts of perjury—in denying he met Chambers in 1938 and in claiming he never handed him classified documents from the State Department. The indictment led to two Hiss trials.

The first, in 1949, ended in a hung jury, eight to four for conviction. The second, in 1950, ended with the conviction of the defendant. Much of the evidence was in the form of testimony by witnesses about events that had occurred more than a decade previously, but the decisive factor proved to be the typed copies of the State Department documents, for the jury agreed that this typing matched that on other pages typed by Priscilla Hiss. The defense found the typewriter, presented it in court, and argued that the Hisses had given it away before the dates on the documents, so that it must have been used by somebody else—possibly Chambers himself. The evidence of the witnesses who testified on this point indicated that the machine had been in the Hiss home at the time the documents were typed. The jury therefore found Hiss guilty of perjury.

Declaring himself a victim of "forgery by typewriter," Hiss appealed, was turned down by the appeals court, and went to jail. In 1953 the Supreme Court refused to review the appeal. After nearly four years as a model prisoner in the federal penitentiary at Lewisburg, Pennsylvania, Hiss was released, and he returned to private life. He went into business, received a divorce from his wife, remarried, and spent many years trying to prove that he had been a victim of a miscarriage of justice. In 1980 he presented evidence that the FBI, having wiretapped his phone for two years (1945–47), could have learned details of his private life and coached Chambers until he memorized them. This attempt, like all the others, failed to convince the courts that the verdict ought to be reexamined.

See also CHAMBERS, WHITTAKER; FBI; GOUZENKO, IGOR; HISS CASE.

FURTHER READING: Whittaker Chambers, *Witness* (1952); Alger Hiss, *In the Court of Public Opinion* (1957); Tony Hiss, *Laughing Last* (1977), is defense of Hiss by his son; *Allen

Weinstein, *Perjury: The Hiss-Chambers Case* (1979), is a balanced book on the subject, putting the guilt of Hiss almost beyond doubt.

Hiss Case (1948-   ) American espionage affair and national dispute regarding the guilt or innocence of Alger Hiss.

By the time Alger Hiss completed his testimony before the House Committee on Un-American Activities in 1948, he was the subject of debate between his partisans and those of his accuser, former Communist spy Whittaker Chambers. The debate became heated in 1950, when a jury found Hiss guilty of perjury, a verdict implying that Chambers told the truth when he described Hiss as a spy for the Soviet Union. Opinions on Hiss divided at nearly every point.

Hiss enjoyed a sterling reputation, as a number of character witnesses testified. He was a graduate of Harvard Law School who had clerked for Supreme Court Justice Oliver Wendell Holmes, had held high positions in the U.S. government and at the United Nations, and had become president of the Carnegie Endowment for International Peace. Chambers, by contrast, was a seedy, sordid person and a self-confessed liar and former spy. Intellectuals and Americans who regarded themselves as belonging to the upper crust defended Hiss because he was one of them. They looked down on Chambers, who at the same time came under fire from the Communists for being a renegade. Admirers of President Franklin Roosevelt defended Hiss because he had worked in the Roosevelt administration. Since Hiss was condemned by the House Committee on Un-American Activities, which included a Republican Congressman named Richard Nixon, critics of the committee for its investigations of the American left and of Nixon for his smear campaign (1950) against Helen Gahagen Douglas in California, rallied behind Hiss and declared him an innocent victim of a moment of hysteria in American public life.

The evidence on which the jury brought its guilty verdict against Hiss was attacked on various, often contradictory, grounds. Some observers agreed with Hiss that "forgery by typewriter" had been perpetrated—that either the copies of classified government documents had not been made on the Hiss typewriter or else that they had been made by Chambers when the machine was no longer in the Hiss home. It was seriously considered that a second typewriter might have been constructed to match the typing of the Hiss machine. Doubt that Chambers could have done this led to conspiracy theories, in which he supposedly had received help from an organization with technical capabilities. The CIA (Central Intelligence Agency), the FBI (Federal Bureau of Investigation), and even the Russian KGB (Committee for State Security, Soviet intelligence) were mentioned as possible conspirators. The FBI was the chief candidate for supplier of the information about Hiss that Chambers claimed to have acquired when he and Hiss both worked for a Soviet spy ring in Washington.

Supporters of Chambers were often midwesterners with no rapport with the aristocratic Hiss. They termed the character differences of the two men irrelevant, and declared Hiss all the worse for his good standing in government circles. Rightists who disliked Roosevelt's New Deal disliked Hiss for being part of it. Angry about the Yalta Conference of 1945, which they considered a capitulation to the Russians, they included Hiss, who had been one of the American party at Yalta, among those they denounced. Defenders of the House Committee and of Nixon praised both for their discovery of the evidence on which Hiss was convicted. They questioned whether one man (Chambers) could weave such a web around another (Hiss) and argued that Chambers knew so much about Hiss because the two had worked together so closely as spies. The pro-Chambers side scoffed at "forgery by typewriter" and at the conspiracy theories as obvious absurdities. They declared Hiss a perjurer properly convicted.

Men and women of this persuasion tended to adhere to it as time passed, but there were some defections from the Hiss defense. Adlai Stevenson was notable among the latter. Before Hiss went on trial, Stevenson, who had known Hiss while they both had worked for the government, testified as a character witness for the defendant. After the guilty verdict, Stevenson stated his acceptance of it as just. Stevenson was running for President in the campaign of 1952, but the liberals, who formed a substantial group of his followers, tended to accept his statement as an honest one, and there is no evidence that significant numbers deserted him on the issue.

Hiss himself kept fighting to clear his name, an extraordinary struggle lasting many years. Hiss admirers called the Hiss case "America's Dreyfus affair." They never did, however, win vindication for him; and therein lies the essential difference between Alfred Dreyfus and Alger Hiss.

See also CHAMBERS, WHITTAKER; HISS, ALGER.

FURTHER READING: Ralph de Toledano and Victor Lasky, *Seeds of Treason* (1950), is anti-Hiss; Alistair Cooke, *A Generation on Trial: U. S. A. vs. Alger Hiss* (1952), is undecided but suggests that Hiss could have been victimized; William Allen Jowett, *The Strange Case of Alger Hiss* (1953), is pro-Hiss, by the former lord chancellor of Britain; Fred J. Cook, *The Unfinished Story of Alger Hiss* (1958), is pro-Hiss; Ronald Seth, *The Sleeping Truth: The Hiss-Chambers Affair Reappraised* (1968), is pro-Hiss; John Chabot Smith, *Alger Hiss: The True Story* (Penguin ed., 1977), is strongly pro-Hiss; Tony Hiss, *Laughing Last* (1977), is pro-Hiss, by his son; Allen Weinstein, *Perjury: The Hiss-Chambers Case* (1979), is anti-Hiss, supported by massive research; Morton Levitt and Michael Levitt, *A Tissue of Lies: Nixon vs. Hiss* (1979), is strongly pro-Hiss, an attempted rebuttal of Weinstein.

Ho Shen *(1750-99)*   Chinese spymaster for the Manchus in the eighteenth century.

Ho Shen's place in Manchu China was, in western terms, comparable to that of Francis Walsingham in Elizabethan England and that of Joseph Fouché in Napoleonic France. In Chinese terms, Ho Shen was the Tai Li or K'ang Sheng of his time. He was the spymaster who sought out, tricked, arrested, and destroyed enemies of the regime.

The Manchu emperor, Chien Lung, ruled over China from the "Forbidden City" of Peking. Ho Shen came to his attention during the 1770s as an able soldier and administrator. Appointed captain of the imperial guard in 1780, Ho Shen rose in the bureaucracy until he became grand chancellor of the state, responsible, among other duties, for intelligence operations within the Chinese empire.

Two enduring dangers to the Manchu Dynasty had to be dealt with—palace intrigues and rebellions in the provinces. More recently, foreigners had become a problem, for merchants and missionaries from the west were arriving in increasing numbers.

Ho Shen established spy networks extending from Peking to the coastal areas and the interior provinces. He knew everything that went on inside the palace, and he knew enough about the provinces to foresee and forestall rebellions. Foreigners proved more difficult, but Ho Shen maintained secret agents in the seaports to spy on crews who came ashore, and he appointed brokers who passed on all foreign goods offered for sale in China. He also organized ideological campaigns to warn the Chinese people not to heed the missionaries.

His agents watched shops, brothels, and other public places in Shanghai and Canton, and warned him when foreigners started for Peking. Knowing their names, occupations, and purposes, he either admitted them, if he thought their presence legitimate, or else turned them away.

Next to the emperor, Ho Shen was for twenty years the most powerful man in China and was so totally associated with Chien Lung that he could not long survive the death of the Manchu ruler in 1799. Attacked by the envious and the vindictive and accused of fraudulently accumulating a fortune at the expense of the imperial treasury, Ho Shen committed suicide.

FURTHER READING: Herbert Giles, *China and the Manchus* (1912); C. P. Fitzgerald, *The Horizon History of China* (1969), places the reign of Chien Lung in the context of Chinese experience, past and present; *Richard Deacon, *The Chinese Secret Service* (1974).

Hollis, Roger (1905-73)   Director of British counterespionage and suspected double agent for the Soviet Union.

Hollis was born in Taunton in Somerset, the son of a clergyman in the Church of England who became a bishop. After attending Clifton College in Bristol, he entered Oxford in 1924, but withdrew before taking a degree and went into the tobacco business. Some years of working in China left him with a touch of tuberculosis, from which he recovered in a Swiss sanatorium.

In 1939 Hollis joined MI5 (Military Intelligence 5, British counterespionage), where he worked on the Russian desk during World War II (1939–45). Promoted through the grades, he became deputy director (1953) and director (1956). Knighted by the queen in 1960, he retired five years later and lived quietly in the country, causing no gossip except when he divorced his wife and married his secretary. When he died in 1973, his funeral was marked by admiring eulogies.

Then, in 1980, Chapman Pincher, an investigative reporter specializing in espionage, published a book in which he revealed that Sir Roger Hollis had been suspected of being a counterspy and of reporting everything he knew (which was practically everything known to British intelligence) to the Russians. The suspicion had been so strong that in 1970 Hollis had been brought to London and subjected to an interrogation under the tighest security precautions by Sir Martin Jones, his successor at MI5.

Hollis was accused of concealing the fact that he had associated with Communists at Oxford and in China. He was told that a multitude of leaks on the highest level at MI5 pointed to him as the probable source. Four major accusations were brought against him. In 1945, after representing MI5 at the debriefing of Soviet defector Igor Gouzenko in Canada, he did not tell his superiors about Gouzenko's statement that the Russians had a mole in MI5. In 1963 Hollis was one of a few at MI5 in a position to warn Kim Philby in Beirut that an MI5 agent was coming to question him. That same year, Hollis prevented information about the scandal involving John Profumo, Christine Keeler, and Yevgeni Ivanov from being passed on to the British prime minister.

In 1964 Hollis played a dubious role in supporting Sir Anthony Blunt when the latter was granted immunity from prosecution in return for a confession.

The interrogation failed to shake Hollis, who denied all the charges and was allowed to go free. However, some of those present believed that he had been a double agent, and that this explained the ineptitude of MI5 in dealing with the Russians during his years with the organization. The implications were staggering, for if the director of MI5 had spied for the Russians, then British counterespionage—indeed, much of the British intelligence establishment— had been at that time unwittingly working for the Soviet Union.

Pincher's book caused such a storm in the news media and among the public that Prime Minister Margaret Thatcher, as in the Blunt affair, had to make a statement in the House of Commons. She said the interrogation of 1970 and subsequent investigations had indicated that Hollis, whatever his misjudgments, had not been a spy. Support for her position came from George Young, formerly of MI6 (Military Intelligence 6, British espionage), who described Hollis as the wrong man in the wrong job. Graham Greene, author of spy thrillers, gave it as his opinion that the KGB (Committee for State Security, Soviet intelligence) planted disinformation against Hollis in order to create a scandal in Britain and suspicion of British intelligence among Britain's allies.

At the moment of this writing, the case of Sir Roger Hollis remains open, with the balance somewhat in his favor.

See also: BLUNT, ANTHONY; GOUZENKO, IGOR; MI5; PHILBY, KIM; PROFUMO, JOHN.

FURTHER READING: Chapman Pincher, *Their Trade Is Treachery* (1981).

Honeyman, John *(1730-1823)* Patriot spy whose information enabled General George Washington to win the battle of Trenton during the American War of Independence.

A Scotch-Irishman from Ulster, Ireland, Honeyman was dragooned into the British army and shipped to America to serve in the French and Indian War. Under General James Wolfe, he took part in the capture of Quebec in 1759. After being discharged from the army, he drifted south and lived for a while in Philadelphia. On the strength of a letter of commendation from Wolfe, Honeyman was accorded an interview by George Washington during the Second Continental Congress, when Washington was appointed commander in chief of the Continental army (1775). Washington was impressed with Honeyman, as their subsequent dealings indicate.

Honeyman bought land in Griggstown, New Jersey, and was farming there in 1776 when the Continental army came through in retreat after its defeat in New York. Honeyman went to American headquarters, met Washington again, and offered his services to the commander in chief. They agreed that Honeyman would become a spy posing as a Loyalist and using the cover story that he was a dealer in livestock selling horses and cattle to the British and to their Hessian allies. (This cover story worked so well that Honeyman's house in Griggstown was attacked by a Patriot mob, and only a letter from Washington made the town safe for the spy's wife and children. Washington at the same time called Honeyman a "notorious Tory" to keep him from being exposed as an American spy.)

Washington continued his retreat into Pennsylvania, and Honeyman assumed his new role, one that caused him to visit Trenton and note the lack of discipline on the part of the Hessians stationed there. Acting according to Washington's plan, Honeyman allowed himself to be captured by American pickets near Trenton and carried to American headquarters on the other side of the Delaware River. He and Washington then held a long, confidential discussion at which Honeyman clearly detailed the situation in Trenton.

Washington, who took a personal interest in his espionage system, had been gathering information from other sources, but Honeyman's report was the one that made him decide to cross the Delaware again, this time from Pennsylvania into New Jersey.

It was arranged for Honeyman to be imprisoned, to escape, and to reach Trenton, where Hessian sentries brought him to Hessian headquarters. There, the Patriot spy assured the commanding officer, Colonel Johann Rall, that the American army on the Pennsylvania side of the river was completely demoralized by its defeat and retreat. Rall believed this tale, allowed his troops to hold their Christmas celebrations without the usual security measures, and was totally unprepared for the American assault after Washington's crossing of the Delaware on Christmas night of 1776.

Honeyman, having made his place in history, slipped away from Trenton before the battle, and while he may have continued to spy for Washington, he never was called upon again to perform so dangerous a mission for his country. He had the satisfaction of seeing his good name restored among his New Jersey neighbors, which happened long before his death, since he lived to be a nonagenarian.

See also WASHINGTON, GEORGE.

FURTHER READING: Frank R. Stockton, *Stories of New Jersey* (1896), has a romanticized picture of Honeyman; Alfred Hoyt Bill, *The Campaign of Princeton* (1948), mentions Honeyman's contribution to the success at Trenton; Allen Dulles (ed.), *Great True Spy Stories* (1968), reprints Leonard Falkner's *American Heritage* article on Honeyman.

Hoover, J. Edgar (1895-1972) Director of the FBI.

The son of a scientist in the Coast and Geodetic Survey, Hoover was born in Washington, D.C. He attended Central High School (1909–13), worked at the Library of Congress, and studied law at George Washington University, from which he graduated in 1916. He took a master's degree in the following year and obtained a job with the Justice Department in the War Emergency Division (this being the period of World War I). In 1918 he transferred to the Bureau of Investigation, later to be renamed the Federal Bureau of Investigation (1935). He rose from head of the General Intelligence Division to assistant director (1921).

Hoover became director in 1924, a position he accepted only on condition that the bureau would be free of political control so that he could clean up the organization. The FBI had been abused by the politicians during the two scandalous years (1921–23) of President Warren Gamaliel Harding's administration. The overhaul conducted by Hoover resulted in the weeding out of incompetents, a merit system for promotions, and a strengthened position for the director, who was renamed to the post by every president thereafter.

Within a decade Hoover had made the FBI one of the world's foremost crime-fighting organizations, celebrated for its investigative techniques and for its cooperation with local law-enforcement agencies across the nation. The 1930s were the decade of FBI gang-busting. The 1940s were the decade of counterespionage: the control of German spies during World War II (1939–45) and of Soviet spies during the Cold War that followed. Throughout these years Hoover carefully constructed the image of the FBI as an organization protecting the American people from criminals and enemy agents. He appeared before congressional committees to explain and defend what the FBI and he himself were doing. He was called a forceful advocate by his supporters in Congress, of whom there were many, and a propagandist by hostile critics, of whom there were few. The latter tended to accuse him of exaggerating the achievements of the FBI and, in particular, of claiming the lion's share of the credit for cooperative investigations involving other agencies, such as the U.S. Secret Service and the Treasury Department.

In 1940 Hoover began working with William Stephenson of British Security Coordination—clandestine cooperation between America and British counterespionage during the period before America entered World War II. In 1942 Hoover conducted the interrogation of eight Nazi saboteurs who had come ashore from German submarines and been captured by agents of the FBI (two of the spies approached the American authorities voluntarily and thereby saved their own lives; the other six were executed). Hoover also directed the campaign against Germany in which German agents were "turned around" and persuaded or forced to act as double agents for the United States.

During the Cold War with the Soviet Union, the magnitude of Soviet espionage in the United States became apparent. Hoover received responsibility for keeping the members of the American Communist party under surveillance and investigating the loyalty of government employees. He did not, however, play an important role in the investigation of Alger Hiss, the former government employee who in 1948 was indicted for perjury. A leak of information from the FBI itself led in that year to the identification of Judith Coplon as a spy for the Soviet Union. In 1949 she and her Russian contact, Valentin Gubitchev, were arrested in New York.

As Hoover saw it, the United States was faced with a many-headed conspiracy of Russian agents and American subversives; he decided on a new type of counterespionage. He established Cointelpro ("counterintelligence programs") in 1956, a bureau campaign that involved domestic spying. Cointelpro engaged in many dubious practices, from wire tapping to infiltrating targeted groups. The Vietnam War (1961–74) impelled Hoover to turn Cointelpro against antiwar demonstrators, whom he considered a danger to the nation. He later added student radicals, antibomb protesters, the Black Panthers, and even civil-rights leaders who were pacifists (he ordered his agents to try to discredit the black apostle of nonviolence, Martin Luther King, Jr.).

Cointelpro provoked a storm of protest. Hoover was accused of violating constitutional rights and other civil rights in his domestic spying. His enemies said he was an autocrat who doctored the evidence to make himself look good; a neurotic who saw Moscow's controlling hand behind every protest movement; a conspirator who kept files on notable Americans with the intention of blackmailing them, at least implicitly, should he deem it necessary; and a bigot who refused to accept blacks or women as FBI agents. Hoover's defenders retorted that he made mistakes as any human being will; that Soviet espionage was what Hoover considered it, a real danger (as Alger Hiss and Judith Coplon proved); that the FBI files were for information, not blackmail; and that Hoover put FBI standards first in selecting his agents.

However this debate may be judged, it is a fact that Hoover bowed to the criticism when he disbanded Cointelpro (1971). Since then, no one in authority at the FBI has proposed returning to the domestic espionage Hoover had attempted to justify, and Congress has taken steps to see that it is not used again. Also, of course, blacks and women are now FBI agents.

One charge against Hoover can be turned into a defense—his autocratic nature made him so jealous of his prerogative that he would not submit to pressure from politicians. He therefore kept the FBI clear of the Watergate scandal when President Richard Nixon wanted to use the bureau's files for his own purposes. It was under Hoover's successor, Acting Director L. Patrick Gray, that the files were turned over and the FBI became implicated in Watergate.

See also COPLON, JUDITH; FBI; HISS, ALGER; NAZI SABOTEURS; STEPHENSON, WILLIAM.

FURTHER READING: Don Whitehead, *The FBI Story* (1956), is favorable to Hoover; J. Edgar Hoover, *Masters of Deceit: The Story of Communism in America and How To Fight It* (1958), is self-laudatory and ghost-written; Jay Robert Nash, *Citizen Hoover: A Critical Study of the Life and Times of J. Edgar Hoover* (1972), is unfavorable; Ralph de Toledano, *J. Edgar Hoover: The Man in His Time* (1973), is favorable; Cathy Perkus (ed.), *COINTELPRO: The FBI's Secret War on Political Freedom* (1975), is obviously, unfavorable; *Ovid Demaris, *The Director: An Oral Biography of J. Edgar Hoover* (1975), is a balanced volume of reminiscences by some of Hoover's friends and enemies; William C. Sullivan with Bill Brown, *The Bureau: My Thirty Years in Hoover's FBI* (1979), is very hostile.

Hortalez, Roderigue et Cie. *(1777-83)* Ostensibly, a French trading company, but actually an undercover organization established in Paris by the dramatist Pierre de Beaumarchais to help the Americans in the period before France joined them as an ally during the American War of Independence.

See BEAUMARCHAIS, PIERRE AUGUSTIN CARON DE.

Houghton, Harry *(1906-   )* British spy for the Soviet Union.

Houghton, born and raised in England, joined the Royal Navy in 1937 and served through World War II (1939–45), becoming a chief petty officer before he received his discharge in 1945. He went into clerical work, was posted to the British Embassy in Poland in 1951, and discovered that he could make money on the black market to pay for an expensive lifestyle.

Transferred to England, he got a job in the Admiralty Underwater Weapons Establishment at Portland. His Polish contacts drew him into spying for the Soviets. His girlfriend, Ethel ("Bunty") Gee, also worked in the naval station, and she continued to have access to classified material after Houghton was transferred to a repair unit in 1957.

By then both were in the pay of Gordon Lonsdale, a Soviet agent interested in Portland research on underwater detection technology. Houghton and Gee held clandestine meetings with Lonsdale, usually in London, and passed secret documents to him. He took the information to Peter and Helen Kroger for transmission from their London home to Moscow by shortwave radio.

This system of espionage continued until 1960, when a counterspy for the west in Polish intelligence, Michael Goleniewski, provided information pointing to Houghton as a spy for the Russians. This report and the observation that Houghton was spending much more money than he made from his Portland job caused MI5 (Military Intelligence 5, British counterespionage) to shadow him and Gee to their meetings with Lonsdale. The MI5 agents noted the covert handing over of envelopes and packages, and in 1961, when enough evidence had been collected, the Special Branch of Scotland Yard arrested the trio. The trail led back to the Krogers, in whose home evidence of espionage came to light, of which the shortwave radio was the most incriminating.

The five went on trial, were found guilty of spying, and received jail terms. Lonsdale and the Krogers were eventually exchanged for Britons held in Russia. Houghton and Gee were released in 1970 and got married the following year. In 1972 Houghton published his version of the Portland conspiracy, in which he had played so prominent a role.

See also KROGER, PETER AND HELEN; LONSDALE, GORDON.

FURTHER READING: *John Bulloch and Henry Miller, *Spy Ring: The Story of the Naval Secrets Case* (1961); Rebecca West, *The New Meaning of Treason* (1964); Harry Houghton, *Operation Portland: The Autobiography of a Spy* (1972).

IMRO *(1893-1934)* Macedonian terror organization operating in the Balkans.

The Macedonian question, which caused international turmoil from the 1890s until after World War I, was the result of nationalism in the Balkans. Macedonia lay north of Greece and south of Serbia and Bulgaria, but was held by Turkey, to the east. The three European powers each claimed parts of Macedonia; in 1893 a group of Macedonian patriots founded a secret society to fight for independence, or at least for autonomy within a projected Balkan confederation. The society was called IMRO (Internal Macedonian Revolutionary Organization). It proclaimed its objective in the slogan: "Macedonia for the Macedonians!"

IMRO's first overt operation was the dispatch of undercover agents into Turkish Macedonia to spy on the Turks and to encourage the Macedonians to oppose their overlords from Constantinople. The Turks, discovering that informers and conspirators lurked among the subject population, began a campaign of repression. Terror on both sides escalated into a war between Greece and Turkey (1897). The latter won, but the freedom-for-Macedonia campaign continued, and in 1902 IMRO instigated a rebellion by the Macedonians. The Turks suppressed the rebellion brutally, but had to face an increasing number of secret agents infiltrating from both Greece and Bulgaria. The undercover war led by IMRO became fiercer, marked by atrocities against the Turkish population and the assassination of Turkish officials.

A coalition of Greece, Bulgaria, and Serbia defeated Turkey in the First Balkan War (1912–13), and Turkey was expelled from most of Macedonia. The victorious partners then quarreled about sharing the Macedonian fruits of their victory. In the Second Balkan War (1913), Bulgaria attacked Greece and Serbia, only to be defeated by those nations supported by Rumania and Turkey. IMRO played a small role in these wars between nations, and it nearly vanished during World War I (1914–18), which resulted in the division of Macedonia among Greece, Bulgaria, and the newly created Balkan nation, Yugoslavia.

Reviving during the 1920s, IMRO renewed its terror tactics in Yugoslav Macedonia. The organization was involved in the overthrow of the Bulgarian government (1923), and later participated in bombings and assassinations there and elsewhere in the Balkans. It lost its power and disappeared because of factional infighting and because of opposition among former partisans tired of the violence.

FURTHER READING: E. C. Helmreich, *The Diplomacy of the Balkan Wars, 1912–1913* (1938); Elisabeth Barker, *Macedonia: Its Place in Balkan Power Politics* (1950); *Nesta H. Webster, *Secret Societies and Subversive Movements* (1972).

Inayat Khan, Noor *(1914-44)*   Indian spy in France during World War II.

The daughter of an Indian father and an American mother, Inayat Khan belonged to the Sufi faith, a mystical branch of Islam. She was born in Moscow, to which her father, a Sufi missionary, had brought the family. They had to leave Russia in 1915 because of the turmoil caused by World War I, and for the next five years they lived in the west, mainly in London. In 1920 the family settled in France, where Inayat Khan attended a women's college at Suresnes near Paris for six years (1922–28). She traveled in India (1928–29), studied music in Paris (1931–32), and took a degree in psychology at the Sorbonne (1938). During the 1930s she was active in the Sufi movement in France.

Inayat Khan escaped through Bordeaux in 1940 as France was overwhelmed by the German invasion of World War II (1939–45). Reaching London, she volunteered for war work, which took her into the Women's Auxiliary Air Force in 1940 and three years later into the Special Operations Executive (SOE), the British organization that cooperated with the French resistance against the Germans. Trained as a radio operator, and given the code name "Madeleine" to use in clandestine broadcasts, she was taken by plane to a secret landing place in France. Making her way to Paris, she established herself in an apartment under the noses of the Germans. There she met resistance leaders and became their undercover radio operator. She reported to London on the safe places for weapons to be dropped by parachute, the fate of SOE agents in France, and covert operations by the resistance against the Germans.

The spy mission of Inayat Khan continued until she was betrayed, apparently by a Frenchwoman who sold information to the Germans about the apartment with the clandestine radio. Refusing to identify her resistance contacts after her arrest, she was taken to the German death camp at Dachau and executed.

FURTHER READING: M. R. D. Foot, *SOE in France: An Account of the Work of the British Special Operations Executive in France, 1940–1944* (1966); E. H. Cookridge, *Inside SOE* (1967); *Jean Overton Fuller, *Noor-un-nisa Inayat Khan (Madeleine)* (1971).

Industrial Espionage   Clandestine gathering of information in the world of business.

The basic reason for industrial espionage is the competition between firms for a share of the market. It may make the difference between profit and loss, or even solvency and bankruptcy, for the management of one firm to know what a competitor is doing in the way of new products, market research, or pricing. The use of spies is one way of keeping up with the competition, and this explains the widespread practice of industrial espionage in business.

Most industrial spies are enticed by money into double-dealing, although personal resentment can also be a factor, as when an employee feels unfairly treated by management and gets revenge by carrying trade secrets to a competitor. Sometimes one firm will send a spy to get a job with another, thus planting a double agent in a sensitive position, able to pump other employees, watch the executive offices to see who comes and goes, or surreptitiously ransack the files for the latest facts and figures regarding production.

While industrial espionage uses most of the techniques known to ordinary espionage—miniature cameras, electronic bugging devices, covert meetings with the "enemy" in out-of-the-way places—spying on a company is much less dangerous than most undercover work because there are fewer laws covering it. In many cases, no crime is involved no matter how much information is stolen. If the confidential plans of a car manufacturer or a fashion house are copied by a spy, and the spy is caught, the result may be, not a jail term but merely the loss of a job.

Industrial espionage usually becomes more dangerous when international cartels are involved, if only because of national laws governing the cooperation of citizens with foreign countries. Industrial espionage is most dangerous when it touches on national security, a comparatively recent development of our technological age. Today, nations are vitally concerned to know what other nations are doing in such areas as nuclear research and space exploration, so that industrial espionage can overlap with more general espionage. In fact, the industrial side of espionage is becoming the most important factor in the spying of nations on each other. It is more important, for instance, to know what kind of rockets a nation has on the drawing board than the strength of its armed forces. Naturally, this extension of military eespionage involves all the usual motives of espionage, including ideology.

Espionage leads to counterespionage, in industry as everywhere else. Firms with secrets to guard keep them in places accessible only to authorized personnel, plant disinformation (misleading reports on what they are doing), hire counterspies to watch for leaks and intruders, warn employees not to talk indiscreetly, and prosecute spies whenever they can. Where nations are competing, stronger methods are taken against those found guilty of industrial espionage, not excluding the death penalty.

FURTHER READING: *Peter Hamilton, *Espionage and Subversion in an Industrial State: An Examination and Philosophy for Defence of Management* (1967); Philip Hickson, *Industrial Counter-Espionage* (1968); Jacques Bergier, *Secret Armies: The Growth of Corporate and Industrial Espionage* (1975).

Intelligence An organization that gathers information, both openly and secretly, usually about a foreign power but in some cases concerning friends abroad or citizens at home; also, a term for such information.

See ESPIONAGE; SPY.

Intelligence, Scientific   Highly technical espionage, counterespionage, and covert operations.

The work of the spy and counterspy in our time is one more example of how science affects life. Most of the sciences are involved—physics (e.g., laser beams in communications systems), chemistry (sensitive acids for analyzing documents), biology (nearly undetectable poisons), medicine (the polygraph), electronics (bugging apparatus), photography (the microdot). Spy ships, planes, and satellites are loaded with scientific equipment, from radar for locating physical objects to ciphony devices that scramble radio conversations. Computers make and break incredibly complex ciphers. Machines can open and reseal letters without leaving a trace. Men and women on surveillance missions can plant miniature television sets in pictures or flower arrangements; on a lethal covert operation an assassin may dispose of a victim in a crowd by using a silent gun small enough to be concealed in the palm of one hand.

Anything that conveys a message of any kind, from a cipher to a radar beam, can be scientifically monitored. Anything that can be scientifically monitored can be scientifically protected. There is therefore a give-and-take in scientific intelligence comparable to the development of offensive and defensive weapons, a never-ending spiral.

Scientific intelligence came of age during World War II (1939–45). The Battle of Britain in 1940 was won to a substantial degree by superior British cryptology (Ultra) and the ability of British scientists to disrupt the radio beams used by German pilots to stay on course to their targets (the "battle of the beams"). Later in the war, the Germans developed rockets, and the Americans built the atomic bomb. British Prime Minister Winston Churchill aptly termed the scientific side of the conflict "the wizard war," since the major achievements remained outside the comprehension of the lay public.

The implications for future peacetime research were so momentous that even before the fighting ended in 1945 the victors sent intelligence experts into Germany to find the top German scientists. Those in the east were captured by the Russians, who put them to work on scientific projects in the Soviet Union. Those in the west surrendered to the Allies, and many agreed to continue their research for the democracies.

The biggest catch fell to the Americans in the person of Wernher von Braun, who had been technical director of the rocket research center and proving ground at Peenemünde and had been mainly responsible for developing the V-2 rocket, with which the Germans bombarded London toward the end of the war. Von Braun came to the United States, where he worked on rockets and headed the team that sent Explorer I, America's first space satellite, into orbit in 1958. He was the central figure in the space program, which enabled America to put a man on the moon in 1969.

Like other areas of scientific investigation, scientific intelligence gained enormously from the impetus given to research by the conditions of wartime. Scientists make startling discoveries and construct complex machines that influence espionage, counterespionage, and covert operations. Computers and space satellitles, for instance, are now taken for granted, while growing ever more sophisticated. Scientific intelligence continues to be the province of the wizards.

See also CIPHER; CIPHONY; MICRODOT; NAZI BUZZ BOMBS; POLYGRAPH; PUE-BLO; SPY-IN-THE-SKY; ULTRA; U-2.

FURTHER READING: John M. Carroll, *Secrets of Atomic Espionage* (1966); Robert M. Brown, *The Electronic Invasion* (1967); Boris T. Pash, *The Alsos Mission* (1969), concerns the American search for German scientists at the end of World War II; Brian Johnson, *The Secret War* (1978); *R. V. Jones, *The Wizard War* (1978).

Intelligence, Strategic Development of information regarding the strength and intentions of foreign nations either actually or potentially hostile.

Strategic intelligence is a product of the twentieth century, the century of total war. A nation engaged in a life-and-death struggle conscripts all of its resources, both human and material, and it should learn as much as possible about the resources of its enemies. Ideally, this information ought to be obtained in peacetime so that preparations can be made in case war should break out. However, whether in peace or war, strategic intelligence takes for its subject all the elements that contribute to an understanding of what a nation or coalition of nations can or may do.

These elements are economic, technological, scientific, social, political, psychological, and military in the broadest sense. The departments of ordinary intelligence gather the particular facts, which are integrated and passed on to a higher level for analysis and evaluation. When a decision for or against action has to be made, this is almost always the responsibility of the head of government after consultation with his closest advisers. They in turn receive briefings from experts who have examined the material, and who express their opinions on which of the possibilities available to the power under discussion should be considered most likely to be realized in the circumstances.

Nongovernmental groups, such as think tanks and college sociology departments, often develop strategic intelligence in a purely abstract way. The highly regarded International Institute for Strategic Studies in London not only is independent of the British government but also publishes reports that are distributed internationally, reports to which many governments subscribe.

The effectiveness of strategic intelligence, like all intelligence, is dependent on how it is used. The collapse of France in 1940 happened partly because the French government and high command did not make proper use of the information on Germany reported by strategic intelligence. The Allied invasion of the Continent after D-Day (June 6, 1944) was a success largely because the Allies had good strategic intelligence and exploited it skillfully against the Germans.

FURTHER READING: Washington Platt, *Strategic Intelligence Production: Basic Principles* (1957); *Harry Howe Ransom, *Strategic Intelligence* (1964); Central Intelligence Agency, *National Basic Intelligence Factbook* (1980), is a discussion of how the CIA develops strategic intelligence on other countries.

Invisible Ink Writing fluid that conceals messages by rendering them imperceptible under ordinary conditions.

Successful use of invisible ink depends on the recipient of the message knowing where the message is, what type of writing fluid has been used, and how the writing can be made visible on the page. Invisible ink belongs to a unique branch of secret writing in that the message is usually in plaintext because it is intended to escape notice by unauthorized readers. The danger is that if the existence of the message is discovered, it can be easily read (unlike a visible cipher or code that has to be broken).

The use of invisible ink is one of the oldest forms of secret communication. It was known in ancient times that writing in milk, lemon juice, or a solution of sugar in water remains imperceptible until heated, when the words emerge. The development of chemistry in modern times produced a number of new possibilities, such as blue vitriol (copper sulphate), lead nitrate, and cobalt chloride, each of which when mixed with water produces an invisible ink. Some chemicals react to heat, others have to be treated with chemical reagents. Blue vitriol responds to a wash of sodium iodide. Either heat or a chemical reagent can be applied to cobalt chloride, which has the added advantage of appearing under treatment and then disappearing again, so that it can be employed when a message has to be transmitted from one recipient to another.

Today ultraviolet rays and photographic techniques are used, but invisible ink has virtually vanished from espionage. Methods for discovering its presence have become too reliable for safety, and the microdot (i.e., miniature photography) is both easier to use and more secure.

FURTHER READING: *Herbert S. Zim, *Codes and Secret Writing* (1946); Dan Tyler Moore and Martha Waller, *Cloaks and Ciphers* (1962); Norman Bruce, *Secret Warfare: The Battle of Codes and Ciphers* (1972).

Jackson, Stonewall (1824-63)   Confederate commander and spymaster during the American Civil War.

Thomas Jonathan Jackson was born in Clarksburg, then in Virginia (now in West Virginia). An orphan and poorly educated, Jackson had the intelligence and character to win an appointment to the military academy at West Point in 1842. Taking his commission in the artillery, he served in the Mexican War (1846–48) and then was for ten years a teacher of artillery tactics at Virginia Military Institute.

When Virginia seceded from the Union in 1861, Jackson went with his state and became an officer in the Confederate army. At the battle of Bull Run (1861) he gained the familiar epithet "Stonewall" for his unyielding resistance to Union troops. He also saw how the espionage of Rose Greenhow in Washington helped General Pierre Beauregard.

Operating in the Shenandoah Valley, Jackson had a great spy in his cavalry commander, Turner Ashby, to whom he once said: "The kind of information I desire from behind the Union lines is the position of the enemy's forces, his numbers and movements, what generals are in command and their headquarters, especially the headquarters of the commanding general."

Jackson gathered all the information he could get before every battle. At Kernstown in 1862 he suffered a minor repulse because his spies failed to notice the main Union force in the area. After that, his espionage data were generally correct, and he exploited them masterfully. At Front Royal in 1862 he talked personally with the redoubtable Belle Boyd, who crossed the lines to tell him about the direction of the Union advance and the numbers on the march toward him. He accepted her report and won his battle.

Ashby and many other spies kept him aware of Union strategy during his brilliant Shenandoah campaign of 1862 and 1863. All the while, Jackson told those around him as little as possible about his own strategy. Even Ashby was sometimes taken by surprise when Jackson gave an order for a military operation.

Jackson remained closemouthed in the field because he felt that, with so many spies on both sides, no commander could be safe in telling his staff more than they needed to know. His practice justified itself in that no Union spy ever betrayed him to a Union commander as Confederate spies betrayed a succession of Union commanders to him.

The result was a series of great victories, crowned by Fredericksburg (1862) and Chancellorsville (1863). That last battle ended the epic of Stonewall Jackson: he was mistakenly shot by his own pickets and died shortly afterward.

See also ASHBY, TURNER.

FURTHER READING: Allen Tate, *Stonewall Jackson* (1928); Harnett T. Kane, *Spies for the Blue and the Gray* (1954); *John Bakeless, *Spies of the Confederacy* (1970).

***John, Otto** (1909-   )* Director of internal security for the German Federal Republic and double agent for the Soviet Union.

Born in Treysa, in the German province of Hesse, John was the son of a civil servant, and therefore grew up with a family tradition of public service. After graduating from school in Treysa (1928), he attended Frankfurt University (1929–33), studying law and becoming anti-Nazi as he watched the rise of Adolf Hitler to power in Germany.

John knew about the July Plot to assassinate Hitler during World War II. Escaping to Spain after its failure (1944), he returned to defeated Germany in 1946, resumed his legal career, and served as a translator at the Nuremberg Trials (1945–46) of Nazi war criminals.

In 1950 John became director of the Federal Internal Security Office in Bonn, where for four years he had responsibility for the control of Soviet espionage in the Federal Republic. In 1954 he disappeared while in East Berlin during a celebration of the tenth anniversary of the July Plot. When he reappeared under Communist auspices and made antiwestern propaganda statements, it was assumed that he had been a double agent working for the Russians all along.

Later that year John suddenly returned to the Federal Republic, declaring that he had been kidnapped by Russian agents, had been forced to make pro-Soviet pronouncements under duress, and had escaped as soon as he could. A Federal court disbelieved him and sentenced him to jail. He was released in 1958 but no longer employed in a responsible position.

FURTHER READING: Willi Frischauer, *The Man Who Came Back: The Story of Otto John* (1959); *Otto John, *Twice through the Lines* (1969).

K'ang Sheng *(1903-   )* Director of intelligence for Communist China after World War II.

K'ang Sheng's name was originally Chao Yun, which he repudiated after becoming a Communist because it reminded him of his bourgeois origins in Shantung Province, where his father was a rich and powerful landlord.

At Shanghai University in the early 1920s, K'ang Sheng joined a Communist cell and on graduation went to work for the Communist party as a labor organizer. He was in Shanghai during the years 1925 to 1933, but he apparently did not meet either of the operatives for the Nationalist Chinese who were there at the time, "Two-Gun" Cohen and Tai Li.

In 1933 K'ang Sheng was sent to Moscow by the Chinese Communist leader, Mao Tse-tung, to study Russian intelligence. Returning home, he entered the Chinese Communist intelligence organization known euphemistically as the Social Affairs Department, and by 1940 he was its head. During World War II he directed a network of spies against both the invading Japanese and the Chinese nationalists led by Chiang Kai-shek.

K'ang Sheng thus entered into a duel with his opposite number on the nationalist side, Tai Li. When Tai Li was killed in 1945 in an explosion on an airplane, K'ang Sheng was suspected by the Americans in China of having ordered one of his secret agents to plant a bomb, but they never found any proof that such was the case.

When Chiang Kai-shek and his nationalist followers fled to Taiwan in 1949, K'ang Sheng, as Mao Tse-tung's intelligence chief, became one of China's most powerful men. He went to Moscow several times during the 1950s to resume his contacts with the KGB (Committee for State Security), as the Russians now called their main intelligence agency.

However, relations between the two Communist giants deteriorated rapidly. In 1960, at an international Communist meeting in Moscow, K'ang Sheng made the first public Chinese attack on the Soviet Union.

After that, one of K'ang Sheng's duties was to conduct counterespionage operations against the KGB in China. At the same time, his spies were active in attempting to obtain information about Russian atomic installations, as well as about those in the west. In particular, he lured Chinese nuclear scientists home from abroad to add their knowledge to China's drive to build an atomic bomb.

Throughout, K'ang Sheng's loyalty was to Mao Tse-tung, whose favor enabled him to consolidate his position. He was elected to the Chinese Communist party secretariat in 1962, and four years later he played a prominent part in the Cultural Revolution, which convulsed Mao's China.

After Mao's death, K'ang Sheng faded from view, and western sinologists found it difficult to determine his fate under the post-Mao government of China.

See also COHEN, TWO-GUN; TAI LI.

FURTHER READING: David Wise and Thomas B. Ross, *The Espionage Establishment* (1967); Edward R. Rice, *Mao's Way* (1972), is a study of Mao Tse-tung's regime that gives the background to K'ang Sheng's career; *Richard Deacon, *The Chinese Secret Service* (1974).

Kao Liang *(1930?-   )* Chinese Communist newsman, diplomat, and secret agent in the Third World and at the United Nations.

One of the younger men to occupy an important position during the Mao Tse-tung era in China, Kao Liang became a correspondent for the China News Agency. He used this position as a cover for his more important assignments, which were in diplomacy and espionage. During Mao's lifetime, he was the most important Chinese intelligence operative abroad both as an individual spy and as a director of espionage networks.

Wherever Kao Liang went under his press credentials, he engaged in undercover diplomacy, searching out possible converts to the Chinese point of view. He also engaged in espionage, gathering information by legal and illegal means that he reported back to his superiors in China.

In the uncommitted nations of the Third World, he lived in high style, spending much money, entertaining lavishly, and succeeding in creating a favorable impression among many government officials in foreign capitals. He always had funds with which to offer covert support to pro-Chinese movements. He worried the KGB (Committee for State Security, Russian intelligence) and the American CIA (Central Intelligence Agency), both of which kept him under surveillance.

Implicated in conspiracies and expelled from India (1960) and Mauritius (1964), Kao Liang achieved his greatest success in eastern Africa, where his intrigues helped bring on the pro-Chinese revolution in Zanzibar in 1964. He thus obstructed Russian influence in that part of the Third World and thereby increased his prestige enormously in Peking.

Kao Liang came to the United Nations in 1971 as a member of Communist China's first delegation to the international organization. He there became an effective opponent of the Soviet Union, just as he had been in Africa.

FURTHER READING: David Wise and Thomas B. Ross, *The Espionage Establishment* (1967); *Richard Deacon, *The Chinese Secret Service* (1974); Warren Weinstein (ed.), *Chinese and Soviet Aid to Africa* (1975).

Kastner, Hermann *(1886-1957)* Cabinet member in the government of the German Democratic Republic and secret agent for the German Federal Republic.

Born in Saxony as the son of a prosperous landowner, Kastner had a good education, took a law degree at the University of Leipzig, and became a professor of law. During the Nazi period (1933–45), which included World War II, he made a reputation as a lawyer who defended anti-Nazis in court. He was arrested by the Gestapo, the Nazi state police, but he survived the Nazi regime and remained in Saxony, which was under Russian occupation following the German surrender.

As an experienced lawyer, Kastner went into the ministry of justice in East Berlin before transferring to the economics commission in 1948, the year in which, disillusioned with Communism, he began to spy for the west. The establishment of the German Democratic Republic (East Germany) and the German Federal Republic (West Germany) in 1949 made him a secret agent for the latter against the former. On being promoted to deputy prime minister he attended secret sessions presided over by Walter Ulbricht, first secretary of the Communist party of East Germany and therefore the real head of the government.

Kastner's system was to bring home top-secret documents, such as minutes of cabinet meetings, copy them, and return the originals surreptitiously. His wife concealed the copies in her clothing and drove from East Berlin to West Berlin, passing through the checkpoint without challenge because her husband was a member of the government and she had a special pass.

Kastner performed his duties in the East Berlin administration so proficiently and seemed so devout a Communist that he received strong backing from the Russians. In the thaw following the death of Stalin in 1953, it was even thought that Kastner might replace Ulbricht. Rioting among the East Germans, however, made it impossible to remove Ulbricht, a hard-liner who asked the Russians to suppress the demonstrators.

The question of Kastner's future became academic when a double agent defected from the Federal Republic and imperiled its agents in the Democratic Republic. West German intelligence chief Reinhard Gehlen warned Kastner, who at first refused to believe he was in danger, but on being promised a government post in West Berlin, he slipped across the border to safety.

See also GEHLEN, REINHARD.

FURTHER READING: Edward Spiro, *Gehlen: Spy of the Century* (1972); *Heinz Höhne and Hermann Zolling, *The General Was a Spy: The Truth about General Gehlen and His Spy Ring* (1972).

Kaunitz, Wenzel von *(1711-94)*   Austrian statesman and spymaster during the reigns of Archduchess Maria Theresa and Emperor Joseph II.

Kaunitz was born in Vienna, the son of a member of the Aulic Council, the highest deliberative body of the Holy Roman Empire. After studying and traveling as a fashionable Austrian aristocrat, he also joined the Aulic Council (1735), where he served for five years. In 1740 he went into the diplomatic service of Maria Theresa, who had inherited the Austrian throne from her father, and carried out assignments in Italy and the Netherlands before becoming ambassador to France (1750–53).

In 1753 Kaunitz began his great career as Austrian chancellor and chief adviser to Maria Theresa. He was the prime mover in the "diplomatic revolution" of 1756, when King Louis XV placed France on the side of Austria against the Prussia of Frederick the Great. As a result, the French, during the Seven Years' War (1756–63), wasted in central Europe the strength they should have turned against their rival overseas, Great Britain.

During forty years in power, Kaunitz developed an excellent espionage system to use in the international game of chess he played with rival powers. He placed his greatest reliance on a vast and intricate organization that censored the mail, for which purpose he established postal stations at central points of the Holy Roman Empire. Letters passing through these postal stations were carefully opened, read, and resealed before being allowed to proceed to their addressees. Those containing diplomatic or military information were copied so that Kaunitz could read their contents in Vienna.

Kaunitz also used secret agents to gather material. It was said that at one time all Prussian couriers but one who passed through the Holy Roman Empire were spies for Austria and that Kaunitz often read the dispatches addressed to Frederick the Great before Frederick did. Frederick, aware of the problem, sometimes used counterspies to pass misleading messages to Kaunitz. The king of Prussia employed secret agents more skilfully than Kaunitz did, one reason for Prussia's success against Austria.

All significant secret information that reached Vienna was recorded in five copies, one each for Kaunitz, Maria Theresa, her sons Joseph and Leopold, and Prince Stahremberg, who served in the strategic Austrian Netherlands (Austria at that time held what is now Belgium). Wide margins were left on these copies, which allowed the recipients to write comments. Austrian policy thus had a firm basis of expert opinion while Kaunitz was chancellor.

He continued to serve when Joseph II became emperor in 1765. The French Revolution undermined the international system Kaunitz had founded, for Austria allied herself with Prussia against the revolutionaries in Paris, and Kaunitz had to resign in 1792. He left an example of success in diplomacy and espionage for the next great Austrian statesman, Clemens von Metternich, who had the problem of dealing with Napoleon Bonaparte.

FURTHER READING: James Bryce, *The Holy Roman Empire* (1911); S. K. Padover, *The Revolutionary Emperor: Joseph the Second, 1741–1790* (1934); *Karl Roider (ed.), *Maria Theresa* (1973).

Kell, Vernon *(1873-1942)* British army officer and first director of MI5.

Born in Yarmouth, England, Kell had a cosmopolitan upbringing. His mother was half Polish, and he spoke Polish as well as English. He also mastered French, German, and Italian during childhood visits to the Continent. Entering Sandhurst, the British West Point, in 1892, he emerged from his training with both an officer's commission and the ability to serve as an interpreter on military missions abroad. He went to Moscow in 1898, where he learned Russian, and to China in 1900, where he took part in the western suppression of the Boxer Rebellion, the Chinese insurrection against the "foreign devils," the imperialists in China.

Returning to London, Kell joined the German Section of the War Office in 1902 with the rank of captain, and in 1907 he gained a place on the Committee of Imperial Defence. The British government, concerned about German spies in England and Scotland, established MI5 (Military Intelligence 5) in 1909, with Kell as its director. MI5, also called the "security service," became Britain's counterespionage organization, with responsibility for the British Isles and the British Empire.

Since MI5 had no power to make arrests, a function that devolved on Scotland Yard, Kell cooperated with Basil Thomson of the Special Branch at Britain's famous crime bureau. Kell also worked with Mansfield Cumming of MI6 (Military Intelligence 6, British espionage) and with Reginald Hall of naval intelligence.

In 1911 Kell went to the home secretary, Winston Churchill, asking for modification of the law requiring that a special warrant be obtained before private mail could be opened. Churchill allowed censorship of letters addressed to individuals on an MI5 list of suspects, and the interception of messages became a basic part of Kell's counterespionage strategy.

Prior to the outbreak of World War I in 1914, Kell and his men had been keeping suspect Germans under surveillance, reading their mail, and compiling dossiers on them. Accordingly, most of the German spies in Great Britain were arrested within days of the British declaration of war. Berlin sent more spies, but most were captured, many jailed, and a few executed. The most important among the last was Karl Lody, who had entered Britain using an American passport provided by German intelligence, had spied on military installations in Scotland, and was arrested in Ireland.

Successful in World War I, Kell stayed with MI5 until 1940. Adhering to old-fashioned counterespionage methods and out of touch with the times, he failed to meet the test of World War II (1939–45). In 1939 a spy sent to Germany the information that enabled a German submarine commander to penetrate the British naval base at Scapa Flow, torpedo the battleship *Royal Oak,* and get away unscathed. The spy of Scapa Flow was never caught, nor was the secret agent who blew up a munitions factory in Essex. Largely because of these two failures, Kell was forced into retirement.

See also MI5.

FURTHER READING: Winston Churchill, *The World Crisis* (rev. ed., 1942); *John Bulloch, *MI5: The Origin and History of the British Counter-Espionage Service* (1963); Richard Deacon, *A History of the British Secret Service* (1969); Jock Haswell, *British Military Intelligence* (1973).

Kent, Tyler *(1911-   )* American code clerk and double agent for Germany during World War II.

Kent was born in Mukden, Manchuria, where his father, an American diplomat, was serving. The family was wealthy and traveled, and Kent received his early education from governesses and tutors. He attended the exclusive St. Albans private school in Washington, D.C. (graduated 1927), followed by Princeton (1928–32), where he took a degree in history.

Accepted by the United States diplomatic service in 1933, he was assigned to the American Embassy in Moscow. Six years later he accepted the post of code clerk at the American Embassy in London. There he met Anna Wolkoff, a refugee from Communist Russia and a frank admirer of Nazi Germany.

Wolkoff persuaded Kent to take classified documents from the code room where he worked and allow her to copy them. During 1940, the worst year of World War II for the British, she passed information to the Germans. Since Kent handled cables between London and Washington, he was even able to provide Berlin with copies of the coded messages between Prime Minister Winston Churchill and President Franklin D. Roosevelt.

Suspicious of Wolkoff because of her pro-German bias, the Special Branch of Scotland Yard arrested her and Kent in 1940. The authorities found in his room a cache of official documents that he was not authorized to remove from the embassy—the most incriminating evidence in the case.

Kent went on trial and received a sentence of seven years. Deported at the end of the war in 1945, he returned to America and dropped out of sight.

See also WOLKOFF, ANNA.

FURTHER READING: Bernard Newman, *Epics of Espionage* (1950), has a chapter on Kent and Wolkoff; *John Holland Snow, *The Case of Tyler Kent* (1962); David Kahn, *The Codebreakers: The Story of Secret Writing* (1967), has a passage on Kent as a code clerk.

KGB The main bureau of the Soviet intelligence system, and one of the principal instruments by which the Kremlin controls the people of the USSR.

KGB (Committee for State Security) is merely the most recent name of an organization that has existed since Vladimir Ilyich Lenin reorganized the tsarist police system after the Bolshevik revolution of 1917. The Russians have a habit of changing the name of an office or department when the old name sounds too sinister (the word "commissar" is no longer used in its original sense), and the KGB is the most complete example of this process of coining euphemisms to cover cruel and enduring realities.

The CHEKA (Extraordinary Commission for Combating Counterrevolution and Espionage, 1917–22) was the original organization. Its head, Felix Dzerzhinsky, obeyed his mandate from Lenin to make the CHEKA a weapon of the Bolshevik regime against the Russian people, as well as against noncommunist nations. Dzerzhinsky introduced the brutality and terror, including summary justice and secret executions, that have remained a hallmark of the organization ever since.

The CHEKA was renamed the GPU (State Political Administration, 1922–23), which itself was renamed after the formation of the Union of Soviet Socialist Republics (USSR). The new acronym was OGPU (United State Political Administration, 1923–34). Of all the titles, this became the most sinister. Headed by Dzerzhinsky until his death in 1926, the OGPU extended its power throughout Soviet society and was largely responsible for overseeing Stalin's enforced collectivization of land, during which millions of Russians met with violent deaths.

The NKVD (People's Commissariat for Internal Affairs, 1934–46) was the next name. Under the leadership of Genrikh Yagoda, the NKVD became a massive state enterprise, controlling industries, labor camps, printing presses, and police forces. It was an octopus with tentacles extending from Moscow to the remotest villages, and except for Joseph Stalin, Yagoda was the most feared man in the Soviet Union. Stalin, however, always suspicious of any power but his own, had Yagoda shot in 1936 and replaced him with Nicolai Yezhov. Stalin had Yezhov shot in 1938.

Lavrenti Beria took over and remained in command as the NKVD became the MVD (Ministry of Internal Affairs, 1946–54). Following Stalin's death in 1953, the new leadership (Malenkov, Khrushchev, and others), fearing Beria and believing he was about to seize power, struck first. They had him arrested, and he was shot in Moscow's Lubyanka Prison, to which he had sent so many victims to be executed.

In 1954 the organization assumed the name KGB. Today it is the most important division of the Center, Moscow's intelligence headquarters. The GRU (Chief Intelligence Directorate of the General Staff of the Red Army) handles military espionage, but is subordinate to the KGB.

The KGB differs from western intelligence systems in its broad powers at home and abroad, in its use by the government against the Russian people, and in the systematic use of cruel and ruthless measures, particularly by the KGB department known as SMERSH ("death to spies"), which handles such things as the assassination abroad of Soviet defectors.

See also BERIA, LAVRENTI; DZERZHINSKY, FELIX; YAGODA, GENRIKH.

FURTHER READING: Robert Conquest, *The Soviet Police System* (1968); *John Barron, *KGB: The Secret Work of Soviet Secret Agents* (1974); Aleksei Myagkov, *Inside the KGB* (1977); Harry Rositzke, *The Eyes of Russia* (1981).

***Khokhlov, Nicolai** (1922-   )* Russian intelligence officer and defector to the west.

Khokhlov was born in Nizhnii Novgorod (now Gorki), the son of a printer who joined the Red Army and fought for the Communists during the civil war (1918–20) that followed the Bolshevik revolution of 1917. His parents were divorced, and when Khokhlov was a child his stepfather took the family to Moscow. Entering the Komsomol (Communist youth movement) in 1938, he began his rise through the Soviet system. In 1941 he was taken into the ministry of state security, which was concerned with espionage beyond the borders of the Soviet Union.

After the German invasion of Russia in 1941, Khokhlov served with guerrillas operating behind the enemy lines. In 1945 he went to Rumania on the heels of the advancing Red Army, where one of his duties was to organize undercover activities against the western Allies in case they should advance that far. The Russians, meanwhile, fastened their hold on the occupied nation. He later testified that in 1942 he refused an order to go to Ankara and assassinate Franz von Papen, the German ambassador to Turkey.

After the war Khokhlov worked in the MVD (Ministry of Internal Affairs, 1946–54), which is now the KGB (Committee for State Security, the main bureau of Soviet espionage). Since his duties principally concerned German affairs and since he was a trusted officer with the rank of captain, he was selected for a secret, sensitive assignment in West Germany in 1953 by SMERSH ("death to spies"), the terror department of the MVD. (Technically, SMERSH was disbanded in 1946, but it continues to function under another name.) The assignment was to go to Frankfurt, West Germany, and assassinate Igor Okolovich, the director of the anti-Soviet Society of National Unity. Okolovich was causing so much disaffection among Russian officials and soldiers in East Germany and Austria by his speeches and writings that Moscow decided to have him violently removed. The order for the assassination was given by the two leaders of the Soviet Union, Georgi Malenkov and Nikita Khrushchev.

Khokhlov and two East Germans received specialized training in assassination techniques, which included the use of an apparently ordinary pack of cigarettes that was actually an electric gun that fired pellets filled with potassium cyanide, a highly toxic substance that causes death shortly after it enters the bloodstream. The plot was for the three assassins to take advantage of any situation they might find or create after approaching Okolovich, shoot him noiselessly, and decamp before anyone else realized what had happened.

The plot failed because Khokhlov's conscience refused to let him go through with it. Arriving in Frankfurt, he went to the intended victim with the whole story and then defected to the Americans, who were happy to grant him political asylum. He was the first SMERSH agent to come over to the west and reveal the facts about the terror organization of Soviet espionage.

See also SMERSH.

FURTHER READING: *Nicolai Khokhlov, *In the Name of Conscience* (1959); Ronald Seth, *The Executioners: The Story of SMERSH* (1967); John Barron, *KGB: The Secret Work of Soviet Secret Agents* (1974).

King's Secret   Intelligence organization run by King Louis XV of France.

Louis XV established the King's Secret in the 1740s because some of the foreign policies he pursued contradicted the aims of certain ministers in his government. Rather than clash with his ministers, Louis circumvented them by recruiting men to serve him outside the ordinary diplomatic channels. He allowed his ministers to go forward with plans he apparently supported while using the King's Secret to promote plans of which they knew nothing or had to guess at when their efforts abroad were inexplicably fruitless.

The King's Secret originated when Louis XV, fearing a collapse of French influence in Poland in the face of Russian aggression, decided to take advantage of Poland's elective monarchy. A candidate had to be found, and Louis placed his power and prestige behind a French candidate, Louis François de Bourbon, prince de Conti.

The primary member of the King's Secret promoting this policy was Charles François, comte de Broglie, who in 1752 became French ambassador to Poland. Receiving contradictory instructions—from the French foreign minister, backing a candidate chosen by Polish nationalists, and from the king, backing the French candidate—Broglie followed the instructions given to him by the king. The ambassador intrigued in favor of the French candidate, but the intrigue failed, Louis François was excluded from the Polish throne, and the French lost time and energy in eastern Europe that should have gone into meeting the British threat to the French in America and India.

Through the King's Secret, Louis XV disrupted French diplomacy during much of his reign. There were occasional diplomatic successes, as when Charles Geneviève d'Éon de Beaumont, chevalier d'Éon, acting for Louis personally, persuaded the Tsarina Elizabeth to take a pro-French line in her diplomacy. But in general, the King's Secret made French foreign policy incoherent, the king undoing one day what his ministers had done, seemingly with his approval, the day before. To this situation may be traced in large part the disasters suffered by France in the Seven Years' War (1756–63).

See also BROGLIE, COMTE DE; LOUIS XV.

FURTHER READING: *Duc de Broglie, *The King's Secret* (1879); G. P. Gooch, *Louis XV: The Monarchy in Decline* (1956); Edna Nixon, *Royal Spy: The Strange Case of the Chevalier d'Éon* (1965).

Koedel, Simon *(1881-1950?)* American spy for Germany in the United States during World War II.

Born in Bavaria, Koedel came of a poor family. Unable to climb out of his poverty, in 1903 he emigrated to the United States, where three years later he became a naturalized citizen. His loyalty to America melted away during the 1930s, when he spent a long period in Nazi Germany and came to admire Adolf Hitler.

After volunteering for espionage work, Koedel was sent back to the United States as a "sleeper," an inactive spy waiting to be activated at a strategic moment. That moment came for Koedel in 1939, the year in which World War II began. Ordered into action by his superiors in Berlin, he spent more than five years (1939–44) moving covertly around the United States, gathering information of value to the German war effort.

His main assignment concerned transatlantic shipping. In Washington he learned from the Maritime Commission about the size and capabilities of Allied seaports. In New York he slipped along the docks noting the vessels that were arriving and leaving. The reports he wrote reached Berlin in the diplomatic pouch of the German ambassador to the United States.

Eventually Koedel's luck ran out. He drew attention to himself, was arrested by agents of the FBI (Federal Bureau of Investigation) in 1944, and went to jail. The next year, as the war ended in Germany's defeat, he was deported to his homeland.

FURTHER READING: *Karl Bartz, *The Downfall of the German Secret Service* (1956); Ladislas Farago, *The Game of the Foxes: The Untold Story of German Espionage in the United States during World War II* (1978).

Koehler, Walter *(1894-1960?)*   German double agent for the United States during World War II.

Koehler may have been Dutch rather than German by birth, and his original name may have been Albert van Loop. In any case, living in Germany he became completely devoted to it as his homeland. He did espionage work for the kaiser's war machine during World War I, until its defeat in 1918, and joined the Abwehr (Foreign Information and Counterintelligence Department, German military intelligence) after the rise to power of Adolf Hitler in 1933.

Koehler spent some years in the United States during the 1930s, and he functioned as a "sleeper" (an inactive spy waiting to be activated) until 1942, when Berlin ordered him to find out what he could about American atomic research. He was to send his reports by radio.

By then, however, Koehler had become disenchanted with Nazi Germany. He began to collaborate with the FBI (Federal Bureau of Investigation), which set him up with a radio on Long Island in New York. The FBI provided him with disinformation (false information) to transmit to an Abwehr listening post in Germany.

This went on until the end of the war in 1945, after which Koehler retired into private life.

FURTHER READING: *Don Whitehead, *The F. B. I. Story* (1956); Ladislas Farago, *The Game of the Foxes: The Untold Story of German Espionage in the United States and Great Britain during World War II* (1971).

Krivitsky, Walter *(1899-1941)*   Polish secret agent for, and victim of, the Soviet intelligence establishment.

Krivitsky, of a Polish-Jewish family of the province of Galicia, then part of the Hapsburg Empire, was originally named Samuel Ginsberg. Angry over the poverty and anti-Semitism that oppressed his family, in 1912 he joined an underground political movement. Later the study of the works of Karl Marx made him a convinced Communist.

In 1917, at the time of the Russian Revolution, he joined the Bolsheviks, headed by Lenin, who gave him a place in Soviet intelligence. He changed his name, as did so many Bolsheviks, and became Walter Krivitsky.

After Lenin's death in 1924, Krivitsky faithfully served Joseph Stalin as the latter fastened an iron dictatorship on the Soviet Union. Krivitsky rose to be a resident director (espionage chief) in the Netherlands around 1935. When his friend Ignace Reiss, also a resident director in Soviet espionage, broke with Stalin in 1937, Krivitsky remained loyal to the dictator.

Krivitsky was the director of Russian spy networks in western Europe, with headquarters in Paris, when he heard that assassins dispatched by SMERSH ("death to spies"), the terror bureau of Soviet intelligence, had murdered Reiss in Switzerland. Ordered to return to Moscow, and now alive to Stalin's brutality

Krivitsky decided to defect. He was granted political asylum by the French, to whom he gave information on the Soviet espionage and counterespionage apparatus.

Fearful that a SMERSH assassin might be on his trail, Krivitsky moved around inside France and traveled to other nations. In 1941 he was found shot to death in a Washington hotel. The legal verdict was suicide, but the most plausible explanation consistent with the facts is that Krivitsky was a victim of Stalin's revenge.

See also REISS, IGNACE.

FURTHER READING: *Walter Krivitsky, *I Was Stalin's Agent* (1941); Ronald Seth, *The Executioners: The Story of SMERSH* (1967); Gordon Brook-Shepherd, *The Storm Petrels: The Flight of the First Soviet Defectors* (1977), has a chapter on Krivitsky.

Kroger, Peter *(1910-   ) and Helen (1913-   )* American spies for the Soviet Union.

Peter Kroger was originally named Morris Cohen and was the son of Jewish immigrants from Russia. He went to high school in New York City and then attended the University of Illinois, where he took a degree in science and became a Communist. In 1937 he served with the Loyalists in the Spanish Civil War, against General Francisco Franco.

Cohen taught school in New York, married Leona Petka, and served in the U.S. Army during World War II. Both Cohens were ardent partisans of the Soviet Union, for which they began to do espionage work. As the Cold War developed, they became a link between two Communist spy rings in the United States, that run by Rudolf Abel and that to which Julius and Ethel Rosenberg belonged.

The cracking of the Rosenberg network by the FBI (Federal Bureau of Investigation) in 1950 alarmed the Cohens, who dropped out of sight for some years. They surfaced in London in 1954, calling themselves Peter and Helen Kroger, the names by which they are remembered. Soon they were spying for the Russians again, using a bookstore in the Strand as a front. Their chief function was to receive information from other Soviet agents and radio it from their London home to Moscow.

They worked under the immediate direction of Gordon Lonsdale, a Russian who received his most significant material from Harry Houghton, who had a job in the Admiralty Underwater Weapons Establishment at Portland. Houghton's girlfriend, Ethel Gee, also became involved in the spy plot.

The Krogers began to collaborate with Lonsdale in 1955 and continued until 1961, when MI5 (Military Intelligence 5, British counterespionage), after noting the pattern of Lonsdale-Houghton-Gee clandestine meetings, had all three, and the Krogers as well, arrested by the Special Branch of Scotland Yard. All were sentenced to prison for spying. In 1969 the Krogers, exchanged for Gerald Brooke, a British professor held by the Russians, disappeared behind the Iron Curtain.

See also ABEL, RUDOLF; LONSDALE, GORDON; ROSENBERG, JULIUS AND ETHEL.

FURTHER READING: *John Bulloch and Henry Miller, *Spy Ring: The Story of the Naval Secrets Case* (1961); Rebecca West, *The New Meaning of Treason* (1964); Fitzroy Maclean, *Take Nine Spies* (1978), considers the Krogers in relation to Lonsdale.

Krupp Gas Shells *(1915)*   Target of French espionage in Germany during World War I.

In Ypres, Belgium, in 1915, the Germans introduced poison gas to the battlefield, releasing it in a cloud intended to drift across the lines and kill or disable Allied soldiers. This maneuver was successful at Ypres, but on later occasions shifting winds carried the gas back toward those who had released it. The Germans did not, however, abandon the weapon, and French intelligence learned that new methods were being tested at the Krupp armaments factory in Essen. Krupp therefore became a principal target of French espionage in Germany.

Charles Luciéto, using the cover story that he was a German traveling salesman, made his way to Essen, where he stayed at a hotel. As he describes it, he cultivated a security guard he met in a beer cellar and learned that Krupp was experimenting with gas shells to be fired into Allied positions, where the deadly cloud would be safely away from the German lines. Luciéto persuaded the guard to let him watch a test in which sheep were gassed without any danger to the gunners who fired the shells. The French spy even obtained a fragment of one of the shells, which he brought with him when he made his return trip through Germany across the Rhine to Paris.

Luciéto's espionage coup influenced battlefield tactics during the rest of World War I. French and British commanders at the western front furnished their soldiers with gas masks before Krupp could begin mass production of gas shells. The new weapon had no effect on the war, which ended with German defeat in 1918.

FURTHER READING: *Charles Luciéto, *On Special Missions* (1925); Ronald Seth, *Some of My Favorite Spies* (1968), has a chapter on Luciéto.

Kühn, Bernard *(1894-   )*   German spy for Japan in Hawaii before the attack on Pearl Harbor.

Belonging to a lower-class family, Kühn in 1912 joined the German navy, which offered him the best chance for a respectable career. He saw service at sea during World War I, and after his ship was sunk by the British (1915), he became a prisoner of war for the duration of the conflict. Following the German surrender in 1918, he returned home fluent in English, an ability that made him of value to the Nazis when Adolf Hitler became chancellor of Germany (1933).

In 1935 the German government assigned Kühn to Hawaii. His instructions were to spy for the Japanese, Orientals who could not gather information as easily among the Americans as a European. Kühn arrived in Honolulu with his family and then began to roam the islands posing as an historian, an ethnologist, and a linguist interested in Hawaiian culture. His daughter, Ruth, often accompanied him and helped him with his espionage. For five years Kühn reported to the Japanese consul in Honolulu on American defenses in Hawaii.

In 1939 the Kühns moved to Pearl Harbor. Here they watched ships of the U.S. Navy arriving in and departing from America's most powerful naval base. Through a system of window lights and other signals they transmitted their information to Japanese secret agents, such as Takeo Yoshikawa, ostensibly a secretary at the Japanese consulate, who in turn passed it on to Tokyo.

Collating the Kühn information with what they knew from other sources, the Japanese warlords, realizing that the striking power of the U.S. Navy was concentrated at Pearl Harbor, decided on the attack that devastated the American naval base on December 7, 1941.

During the attack, American agents noticed signal lights flashing from the Kühn house, and the German spies were caught red-handed. Father, mother, and daughter went to jail, Bernard Kühn saving his life by telling the American authorities what he knew about Japanese espionage. He received a sentence of fifty years.

See also KUHN, RUTH; PEARL HARBOR; YOSHIKAWA, TAKEO.

FURTHER READING: *Ronald Seth, *Secret Servants: A History of Japanese Espionage* (1957); Roberta Wohlstetter, *Pearl Harbor: Warning and Decision* (1962); David Kahn, *The Code-breakers: The Story of Secret Writing* (1967).

Kühn, Ruth *(1917-   )*   German spy for Japan in Hawaii before the attack on Pearl Harbor.

The daughter of Bernard Kühn, Ruth Kühn is said to have had an affair with Joseph Goebbels, the propaganda minister of Nazi Germany, and to have become an embarrassment to him by 1933, so that Goebbels was relieved at being able to assign her father to espionage work for the Japanese in Hawaii in 1935. After arriving in Honolulu, Ruth became her father's aide, traveling through the islands and reporting to the Japanese on the American defenses.

When the Kühn family moved from Honolulu to Pearl Harbor in 1939, Ruth Kühn opened a beauty parlor, where she tended to naval officers' wives and listened to their conversation. She reported everything of military significance that she heard to Bernard Kühn, who saw that the information reached the Japanese, who used it in planning for the Pearl Harbor attack of December 7, 1941.

During the attack, the Kühns were caught signaling to the enemy from a window of their house. Father, mother, and daughter went to jail in 1942. Released following the Allied victory in 1945, Ruth Kühn was deported to Germany and vanished into private life.

See also KUHN, BERNARD; PEARL HARBOR.

FURTHER READING: *Ronald Seth, *Secret Servants: A History of Japanese Espionage* (1957); Roberta Wohlstetter, *Pearl Harbor: Warning and Decision* (1962); David Kahn, *The Code-breakers: The Story of Secret Writing* (1967).

Lahousen, Erwin von *(1897-1955)*   Director of German sabotage operations and conspirator against Adolf Hitler before and during World War II.

Lahousen's full last name was Lahousen-Vivremont, indicating that his family was of French origin. His ancestors settled in eastern Europe in an area of Polish Silesia that belonged to the Hapsburg Empire at the time of his birth on the family estate. Privately educated before attending the University of Vienna, he grew up in an aristocratic Catholic tradition.

Lahousen served in the Austrian army during World War I (1914–18), later graduated from a staff college, and after rising through the grades took charge of Austrian intelligence in eastern Europe (1933). He cooperated with both French and German intelligence while Adolf Hitler was consolidating his power in Germany.

When Hitler seized Austria in 1938, Lahousen joined Admiral Wilhelm Canaris, head of the Abwehr (Foreign Information and Counterintelligence Department, German military intelligence). Canaris and his chief of staff, Hans Oster, were both anti-Nazi, and Lahousen began to conspire with them against Hitler. Lahousen was discreet. No suspicion attached to him at the beginning of World War II in 1939 when, as Germany's sabotage expert, he helped plan Hitler's invasion of Poland.

Also in 1939, Lahousen began to keep the war diary from which much information can be derived concerning German espionage during the next four years. The diary shows him as a man struggling with his conscience and seeing ever more clearly that Hitler had to be destroyed no matter what the cost to Germany, although he naturally hoped to minimize that cost.

Lahousen turned his ability and his position against Hitler, slowing his department's activities whenever he could. This explains, at least partly, the ineptitude of his sabotage operations against the western Allies. All of the agents he sent to Britain in the years 1939 to 1943 were caught (of course, he did not betray them, but his efforts on their behalf were half-hearted). Some became double agents for the British.

Lahousen's man in Ireland, Hermann Goertz, failed ludicrously (1940–41). The Nazi saboteurs who landed in the United States from submarines in 1942 were promptly rounded up and jailed or executed.

In 1944 Lahousen joined a plot to assassinate Hitler. Although the Abwehr had by now been virtually disbanded, Lahousen still had access to sabotage materials, and he provided Count Klaus von Stauffenberg with the bomb that exploded at Hitler's headquarters on July 20. Unfortunately, Hitler merely suffered injuries in the blast.

Canaris, Oster, and Stauffenberg were executed. Lahousen survived and lived to testify against the Nazi leaders who were prosecuted at the Nuremberg Trials (1945–46).

See also CANARIS, WILHELM; OSTER, HANS.

FURTHER READING: *Charles Wighton and Günter Peis, *Hitler's Spies and Saboteurs: Based on the German Secret Service War Diary of General Lahousen* (1958); Ladislas Farago, *The Game of the Foxes: The Untold Story of German Espionage in the United States and Great Britain During World War II* (1971); David Kahn, *Hitler's Spies: German Military Intelligence in World War II* (1978).

Lang, Hermann *(1902-   )*   American spy for Germany in the United States before and during World War II.

Although never a declared Nazi, Lang remained loyal to Germany, where he was born and raised. Emigrating to America, he became a naturalized citizen in 1927, after which he held responsible jobs that had to do with the advancing technology of the period. By 1937 he had become an inspector in a factory producing the Norden bombsight, a secret American invention permitting pinpoint accuracy in high-altitude bombing.

Also in 1937, Lang met Nikolaus Ritter, who had come to America from Germany to organize a network of secret agents for the Abwehr (Foreign Information and Counterintelligence Department, German military intelligence). Ritter was delighted to learn that Lang, who had access to Norden blueprints, was in a position to deliver copies to him. The two men became co-conspirators in this enterprise. Passing from the factory files to Ritter by way of Lang, the copies were smuggled piecemeal out of America and into Germany aboard ships of the Hamburg-Amerika line.

When Lang visited Germany in 1938, he received the thanks of both the Abwehr and the Luftwaffe (the German air force), since the Norden bombsight was superior to any developed in Germany. He returned to the United States pledged to do whatever else he could for Germany, which was under Adolf Hitler's control and on a course leading to war.

Lang's pledge came to nothing because he had nothing more to offer. The outbreak of World War II in 1939 found him still on the job at the bombsight factory, from which he had already stolen its great secret. During 1940 he still was one of Ritter's men in the United States and on call for undercover assignments. In 1941, Lang was arrested during a general roundup of suspected German agents in the United States by the FBI (Federal Bureau of Investigation). William Sebold, a double agent for the United States, had exposed Lang. Sebold testified at Lang's trial, which ended with Lang being given a jail sentence that kept him confined for the rest of the war.

When hostilities ended in 1945, Lang was deported to a devastated and divided Germany, quite unlike the arrogant power that had feted him only a few years before.

See also RITTER, NIKOLAUS; SEBOLD, WILLIAM.

FURTHER READING: *Charles Wighton and Günter Peis, *Hitler's Spies and Saboteurs: Based on the German Secret Service War Diary of General Lahousen* (1958); Ladislas Farago, *The Game of the Foxes: The Untold Story of German Espionage in the United States and Great Britain during World War II* (1971); David Kahn, *Hitler's Spies: German Military Intelligence in World War II* (1978).

La Reynie, Gabriel de *(1625-1709)*   French police chief and spymaster during the reign of King Louis XIV.

La Reynie belonged to a family of magistrates in Limoges, his birthplace, and he followed his father and grandfather into the legal bureaucracy in 1646. The family was also completely royalist, and La Reynie supported the king's cause during the civil war known as the Fronde (1649–53), as a result of which he came to the attention of Cardinal Jules Mazarin, the head of the French government during the childhood of Louis XIV.

Mazarin brought La Reynie to Paris, and in 1661, the year of the cardinal's death, La Reynie purchased an office in the *parlement* of Paris (a legal body, not a parliament in the English sense). La Reynie rose to prominence in the reign of Louis XIV, who created a new position for him, that of lieutenant of police (1667). La Reynie now had responsibility for physical and social conditions in Paris, overseeing hospitals and prisons, keeping the roads in repair, enforcing the regulations governing markets, and taking measures to prevent epidemics in the crowded city.

La Reynie became a spymaster because he also had charge of law enforcement. He built a network of secret agents who went underground to track criminals and conspirators, a system that soon made Paris the safest capital in Europe. His most celebrated case was the Affair of the Poisons, which he brought to a conclusion in 1679, after three years of intensive investigation. This case involved not only murder but also sorcery, and La Reynie, constructing files on the basis of evidence provided by his agents, proved that indictments could be brought against some of the most highly placed men and women in France, including Madame de Montespan, the king's mistress.

Since the trail led so clearly to Montespan, Louis XIV closed the public hearings, and nothing more was said about her. A number of the guilty fled from Paris. The chief figure of the scandal, Catherine Monvoisin, was executed (1680).

La Reynie ran his department and his spy network until his retirement in 1697. The first regular police officer in Europe, he has had many successors.

FURTHER READING: *Philip John Stead, *The Police of Paris* (1957); Oreste A. Ranum, *Paris in the Age of Absolutism* (1968); John C. Rule, *Louis XIV* (1974).

Lavon, Pinhas *(1904-76)*   Israeli Defense Minister and the principal figure in the Lavon affair.

Born in Warsaw, Poland, into a Jewish family of merchants, Lavon was educated in the synagogue before and during World War I (1914–18). He attended Lvov University in the 1920s, went to Palestine as a Zionist, worked the land, and participated in the foundation of the state of Israel in 1948. Entering politics, he succeeded well enough to become minister of agriculture and then minister of defense in the first cabinet (1948–53) of Prime Minister David Ben-Gurion.

In 1954, when Moshe Sharett was prime minister, Lavon became involved in the scandal that bears his name. A network of Israeli spies in Egypt was discovered by Egyptian counterespionage on information from a double agent among the Israelis. The trials of the spies caused an international furor because evidence came out that their mission was to commit sabotage that might embroil Egypt in a conflict with the United States.

Sharett appointed a commission to investigate responsibility for the operation. The commission could not resolve the question, Lavon was forced to resign in 1955, although he protested his innocence and blamed Israeli military intelligence. Lavon's partisans made a political issue of what they called the "Lavon affair," and another commission was handed the problem. This commission absolved Lavon (1960). Ben-Gurion, again prime minister, refused to accept the verdict or to reinstate Lavon, who gave up the struggle for official vindication and retired from Israeli politics.

See also LAVON AFFAIR.

FURTHER READING: Richard Deacon, *The Israeli Secret Service* (1977); *Dennis Eisenberg, Uri Dan, and Eli Landau, *The Mossad, Israel's Secret Intelligence Service: Inside Stories* (1978); Stewart Steven, *The Spymasters of Israel* (1980).

Lavon Affair (1954-61) Espionage and political scandal in Israel.

The Lavon affair took its name from Pinhas Lavon, defense minister in the cabinet of Prime Minister Moshe Sharett in 1954, when what was called a "security mishap" occurred in Egypt. Secret agents working for Israel were ordered to sabotage American buildings in Cairo and Alexandria in an effort to disrupt American-Egyptian relations. The agents bungled their assignments, and one proved to be a double agent, who betrayed the network to Egyptian counterespionage. A Cairo court sentenced two of the defendants to death, six received jail sentences, and one committed suicide.

The Lavon affair erupted over the question of who gave the order for this undercover operation. Lavon denied responsibility, which he placed on Israeli military intelligence acting without his knowledge. When he demanded an official inquiry, Sharett appointed a commission, which could not decide who was responsible. Lavon resigned from the cabinet (1955).

Now the espionage fiasco became a political issue. Lavon's supporters charged that there had been a cover-up and that both false testimony and forged documents had been used to discredit the former defense minister. Israeli chief of staff Moshe Dayan was accused of conspiring against Lavon. A commission of the legislature, before which Lavon appeared and strenuously defended himself, found no evidence that he had been victimized.

The Lavon affair, however, continued to disrupt Israeli politics, and in 1960 Prime Minister David Ben-Gurion appointed another commission to investigate the case. This commission decided that Lavon had not issued the order, but it failed to say who in military intelligence had done so. Ben-Gurion rejected this pro-Lavon verdict. However, the prime minister remained so vulnerable to Lavon's political partisans that he had to resign and reorganize his cabinet before returning to office (1961).

The Lavon affair died down. Lavon's guilt or innocence remains, nonetheless, a matter of dispute among Israeli politicians and the general public.

See also LAVON, PINHAS.

FURTHER READING: Moshe Dayan, *The Story of My Life* (1976); Richard Deacon, *The Israeli Secret Service* (1977); Dennis Eisenberg, Uri Dan, and Eli Landau, *The Mossad, Israel's Secret Intelligence Service: Inside Stories* (1978); *Jacques Derogy and Hesi Carmel, *The Untold Story of Israel* (1979), sees the Lavon affair as Israel's Dreyfus affair.

Lawrence, T. E. (1888-1935) British soldier with the Arabs and spy against the Turks during World War I.

Lawrence of Arabia was born in Tremadoc, Wales, but his family was Anglo-Irish. His parents, who were not married, eloped from Ireland to get away from his father's wife, changed their name from Chapman to Lawrence, and spent their first years together in Wales. In 1896 the family moved to Oxford, England, where Lawrence finished his schooling and went on to the university (1907–10), from which he graduated with an honors degree in history.

Turning to the archaeology of the Near East, he spent the years 1910 to

1914 at Carchemish, on the Euphrates, where a British team was digging at ancient Hittite and Assyrian sites. In his final year at Carchemish, the European tensions were building up that would bring on World War I, and since Turkey, then ruling Palestine and Arabia, was allied with Germany, the British wanted to know what to expect in the region should military operations become necessary. That was the reason behind Lawrence's first espionage mission. Lawrence, Leonard Woolley, and Captain S. F. Newcombe, using archaeological work for a cover, went into the Turkish-controlled Sinai, mapped the area as far south as Aqaba, and published *The Wilderness of Zin* (1914), an archaeological study. The espionage was reported in secret.

With the coming of the war, Lawrence went into the mapping department of the foreign office in London. He was transferred to military intelligence in Cairo in 1915, where he used his knowledge of Arabic dialects in interrogating prisoners of war. When the revolt of the Arabs against the Turks in Arabia broke out in 1916, Lawrence was sent there to try to coordinate the desert fighting with the British campaign against the Turks in Palestine. How he succeeded is the subject of his postwar masterpiece, *The Seven Pillars of Wisdom.*

The principal objective of the Arab revolt was Damascus, far to the north in Syria. Lawrence guided the Arabs to their first big victory, at Aqaba (1917), with which he had become familiar during his prewar espionage. After that, he led spy missions behind the Turkish lines, on one occasion riding all the way to Damascus and back. Another time, entering Deraa to see how strongly it was held, by his own account he fell into the hands of the Turkish garrison commander who had him tortured but could not make him confess his identity or his mission. Escaping, he returned to Deraa with a force of Arabs and captured the place.

The parallel military campaigns in Arabia and Palestine succeeded. The British captured Jerusalem from the Turks in 1917, and the Arabs captured Damascus from the Turks in 1918. Lawrence got as far as Damascus and then, feeling that the Arabs were about to be betrayed by the Anglo-French alliance, he asked to be allowed to go home. Receiving his discharge, he did much writing and speaking against the policy, approved in London, that ruled out Arab independence in Syria (which came under French control). Disillusioned because he could not deliver on his wartime promises to the Arabs, Lawrence threw everything away and joined the Royal Air Force as an enlisted man, although he held the rank of colonel in the British army. He also did a tour of duty in the Royal Tank Corps on the lowest level.

Returning to civilian life in 1935, he was killed shortly afterward when he lost control of his motorcycle while racing at high speed down an English country lane. He bequeathed to posterity the legend of Lawrence of Arabia and the problem of trying to explain his personality, his motives, and his exploits.

FURTHER READING: Lowell Thomas, *With Lawrence in Arabia* (1925); *T. E. Lawrence, *The Seven Pillars of Wisdom* (1926); Donald Stewart, *T. E. Lawrence* (1977).

Leclerc, Julien *(1762-1839)* Royalist spy during the French Revolution and the Napoleonic era.

Leclerc was born in Normandy into a family that was bourgeois in social status, monarchist in political allegiance, and Catholic in religion. He became a priest and would probably have spent his life taking care of a parish and, given his ability, possibly rising to be a bishop if the French Revolution had not intervened. The revolutionaries' defiance of King Louis XVI in 1789 prompted Leclerc to become a spy for the royalist cause.

Taking the cover name "Boisvalon," he wrote from Paris an enormous number of letters to royalists in exile, secretly enclosing messages about conditions in France. He himself gathered some of this information, and the rest came from other spies at large in Paris and the provinces. Leclerc was one of a large number of undercover agents opposed to the revolution who worked individually or in networks and traded messages when they met. Many of them reported to Leclerc because they knew their reports would reach the comte de Provence, who lived in exile and used the title King Louis XVIII after the execution of Louis XVI (1793) and the death of his son, Louis XVII (1795).

When the revolution ended and the five-man Directory became the French government (1795–99), Leclerc hoped that this regime would be a prelude to the restoration of the monarchy. Instead, the Directory proved to be but an interim government before the rise to power of Napoleon Bonaparte. Refusing to despair, Leclerc turned his espionage talents against the new ruler of France.

In 1803, when Napoleon marshaled an army on the northern coast for a possible invasion of England, spies close to the government, one a clerk in the ministry of war, kept Leclerc informed about the condition of the armed forces and about Napoleon's plans. Leclerc therefore moved into the area of the encampment to do what he could to forestall the invasion or to make sure it failed.

He traveled through the area in a carriage, looking like an abbé visiting his parishioners but really watching military and naval preparations or meeting secret agents who could tell him what he needed to know. At night, he wrote his reports and dispatched them across the Channel to London, using French fishermen who were able to rendezvous with British warships patrolling off the French coast.

The system involved a whole espionage apparatus. Leclerc wrote his secret messages in invisible ink between the lines of apparently harmless communications regarding a (nonexistent) French heir in London to an inheritance in France. Dark lanterns were used to signal from houses on land to fishing boats in the Channel and from the boats to British warships. If strangers or Napoleon's agents were too close for the espionage operation to proceed safely, a fire on a headland or a rocket in the sky signaled a cancellation. If a British vessel carried a letter from London to Leclerc, its flag, flown at half-mast, was lowered and raised three times.

The Leclerc network included dozens of men and women who were willing to let their houses, businesses, or cafés be used against Napoleon. One day, however, a fisherman betrayed the network. Many members were rounded up and either jailed or executed. Leclerc himself escaped, fleeing first to England, where he learned that the Napoleonic invasion had been called off, and then crossing over to Germany, where the most important of the royalist exiles lived. He continued to write for the cause after Napoleon became emperor of France (1804). The battle of Waterloo (1815) put an end to the empire. Leclerc returned to France in 1816, when King Louis XVIII sat on the throne.

FURTHER READING: *G. Lenôtre, *Two Royalist Spies of the French Revolution* (1924); Harvey Mitchell, *The Underground War against France: The Missions of William Wickham, 1794–1800* (1965).

Lee, Andrew Daulton (1952-   ) American spy for the Soviet Union.

The adopted son of a doctor in Palos Verdes, California, Lee went to a parochial grammar school and then high school, from which he graduated in 1970. After a brief time at a junior college, he dropped out and started taking drugs, becoming a pusher. Arrested in 1971, he received a suspended sentence in 1972 for possession of marijuana. Entering Whittier College, he soon dropped out, went back on drugs and in 1974 served a term in jail, from which he emerged to resume his drug habits.

In 1975 he learned that his friend, Christopher Boyce, had access to classified documents at the TRW Defense and Space Systems Group at Redondo Beach, California, which produced space satellites for the CIA (Central Intelligence Agency). Lee knew that Boyce, like himself, had been alienated from American democracy by the Vietnam War, Watergate, covert CIA operations in other countries, and a feeling, not uncommon in their generation, that the system was beyond salvation. In 1975 they agreed to spy together for the Soviet Union.

Lee knew Mexico City, and so they agreed to work through the Soviet Embassy there, as that would be safer than any contact with the Russians could be in the United States. In 1975 Lee made the arrangements in which Boyce copied secret documents at TRW and turned the copies over to Lee, who delivered them to the Russians in Mexico City. In 1976 Lee flew to Vienna to get further orders from a Russian agent. Back home, he resumed his trips to Mexico City with documents provided by Boyce. That same year, Boyce, suspicious that Lee was holding out on him regarding the money received from the Russians, went to Mexico City also and made Lee introduce him to them. Boyce was satisfied, and the conspiracy continued.

Lee, on his last visit to the Mexican capital, in 1977, was arrested outside the Soviet Embassy after throwing something through the iron railing. He was trying to catch the attention of those inside, but the Mexican police, thinking he might be a terrorist, searched him and found films of TRW projects. He was taken to the border and handed over to agents of the American FBI (Federal Bureau of Investigation).

Lee's trial ended in a sentence of life imprisonment. Boyce, whom he had implicated, got forty years.

See also BOYCE, CHRISTOPHER JOHN.

FURTHER READING: Robert Lindsey, *The Falcon and the Snowman: A True Story of Friendship and Espionage* (1979) ("falcon" refers to Boyce's interest in hawking, "snowman" to Lee's use of drugs).

Legals and Illegals Soviet distinction between two types of spies assigned to foreign countries.

All espionage systems make some use both of intelligence operatives covered by an official standing and of those who work as independents, but the Russians use the two types more systematically and on a much larger scale than anyone else. The terms "legals" and "illegals" were coined in Moscow and have been adopted in the west to refer to the Soviet spy apparatus.

Legals belong to legitimate Soviet institutions or groups abroad—embassies, United Nations delegations, trade missions, news bureaus, art exhibitions, theater casts, and the like. Legals carry out their ostensible assignments, hoping that this will conceal the spy work that is the real reason for their being in the host country. Legals can get into the host country without any trouble and, if caught, they have official protection, often diplomatic immunity. However, legals, being known, are circumscribed in their activities.

Illegals, sent by Moscow clandestinely, must slip into other nations without being noticed. Frequently they are provided with forged passports in the names of dead citizens of those nations, so as to have names that will pass scrutiny while obviating the danger of meeting the individuals being impersonated. Illegals have freedom of movement, but they have no official protection if caught and may be ignored by those who sent them. Even if the system of exchanging spies leads to their release, illegals generally spend some time in jail before that happens.

The two departments of Soviet espionage, the KGB (Committee for State Security, civilian intelligence) and the GRU (Chief Intelligence Directorate of the General Staff of the Red Army, military intelligence) both employ legals and illegals.

FURTHER READING: *Alexander Orlov, *Handbook of Intelligence and Guerrilla Warfare* (1963); David Wise and Thomas B. Ross, *The Espionage Establishment* (1967); John Barron, *KGB: The Secret Work of Soviet Secret Agents* (1974).

Le Queux, William *(1864-1927)*   British writer of spy and adventure novels and unofficial agent for British intelligence before and during World War I.

Born in London of a French father and English mother, Le Queux was educated privately in England and Italy, studied art in Paris, and became a London journalist. He served for two years (1891–93) as foreign editor of *The Globe,* a post that added to his international background a knowledge of European diplomacy and introduced him to many European statesmen.

In 1893 Le Queux quit journalism to devote himself to writing, specializing in detective stories and thrillers. As he traveled in search of material for his books, he became aware of espionage realities and began reporting what he found to influential persons in London. He also carried out unofficial assignments for British intelligence. In 1905, for instance, in Belgrade, then a hotbed of intrigue, he discussed the international situation, at the behest of the British foreign office, with his good friend King Peter of Serbia.

In 1908, alarmed at what he considered the apathy of the British public, Le Queux wrote *The Invasion of 1910,* which was published by Lord Northcliffe in *The Daily Mail.* It was a warning in fictionalized form of a coming war with Germany.

From then on Le Queux wrote regularly on the German menace. He claimed to have learned from a friend in the kaiser's espionage service that the kaiser was determined to start a war, a charge Le Queux supported by describing his own undercover operations—for instance, a visit incognito to a gun factory in Düsseldorf.

Protesting that he was being ignored by the British government, Le Queux published *Spies of the Kaiser* in 1910 in order to alert his compatriots to German intrigues in Great Britain. Actually, a year earlier, Vernon Kell had begun work as head of MI5 (Military Intelligence 5, British counterespionage) and was gathering material that would be used in rounding up German spies in Britain in 1914 on the outbreak of World War I.

Le Queux was notorious enough to the Germans to be guarded by Scotland Yard during the conflict. He did not do undercover work abroad, as did such other British writers as Somerset Maugham and Compton Mackenzie, but he did write and lecture almost incessantly on his favorite subject, German iniquity, until the end of the war in 1918.

Then Le Queux went back to being a spy novelist, traveler, and friend of the royal, the powerful, and the interesting.

His final contribution to intelligence came from his interest in wireless communications. He was among the first to experiment with transmitting messages by voice on the air and to foresee what a remarkable tool this could be in future espionage.

FURTHER READING: William Le Queux, *Spies of the Kaiser* (1910); *N. St. Barbe Sladen, *The Real Le Queux: The Official Biography of William Le Queux* (1938); Richard Deacon, *A History of the British Secret Service* (1967).

Leyds, Willem (1859-1940) Dutch government official and spymaster in South Africa before the Boer War.

Leyds was born in Java, then part of the Dutch empire. Educated in Holland, he took a doctor of laws degree at the University of Amsterdam in 1884, the year he met Paul Kruger, the president of the Transvaal Republic, who was touring Europe in an effort to gain support for the Dutch Boers in South Africa against encroaching British imperialism. Kruger offered a government post in Pretoria to Leyds, who in 1888 became state attorney in the capital of the Transvaal.

Besides his strictly legal duties, Leyds took over the Transvaal intelligence system, which he regularized and expanded as the tension between the Boers and the British in South Africa became worse. His principal concern during his nine years in office was to fend off military operations by the British in the Cape Colony against the Transvaal.

To that end, he founded a network of spies whom he sent into the Cape equipped with codes and ciphers that Leyds had devised himself. These spies reported on British intentions and on the feelings of the Cape Boers toward a possible war between the Cape and the Transvaal. Leyds, finding the Cape Boers solidly behind their ethnic comrades in the Transvaal, sent money through his secret agents to support Boer candidates in Cape elections.

At the same time, he mounted an undercover campaign to sway public opinion in Britain and on the Continent by manipulating the press. Sending funds through European banks to keep the operation clandestine, Leyds subsidized newspapers that favored the Boers. His agents read the major periodicals of London, Paris, and Berlin, noting the content of news stories, articles, and editorials and writing rejoinders to those that took a pro-British position.

Through the years 1888 to 1897, Leyds remained a close friend and associate of Paul Kruger, who finally decided that his state attorney would be more valuable in Europe than in the Transvaal. Appointed ambassador-at-large,

Leyds established his headquarters in Brussels and began arguing the pro-Boer position in a most effective manner in talks with European leaders. He could not, however, win anything stronger than sympathy or ward off the outbreak of violence in South Africa that led to the Boer War (1899–1902).

Leyds remained at his post in Brussels during the conflict, speaking out strenuously in favor of the Boers but watching helplessly from a distance as they suffered defeat and had to bow to British rule. When the Boer War ended in 1902, his function as a mouthpiece for the government in Pretoria was gone (Kruger himself fled into exile). Leyds retired to his native Holland, where he spent much of the nearly four decades left to him writing on the history and politics of the Transvaal.

FURTHER READING: *Douglas Blackburn and W. Waithman Caddell, *Secret Service in South Africa* (1911), has an account of Leyds as spymaster; Willem Leyds, *The Transvaal Surrounded* (1919); Eversley Belfield, *The Boer War* (1975).

Lincoln, Isaac Trebitsch *(1879-1943)*   Hungarian secret agent for Bulgaria, Turkey, Germany, and China.

Lincoln, whose original full name was Isaac Trebitsch, belonged to a Jewish family that was in business near Budapest on the Danube. His parents wanted him to be a rabbi, and he attended a Hebrew seminary before his secular interests, mainly money and women, led him to drop out and begin a wandering life, during which he changed his loyalties, both political and religious, several times.

In 1896 he was in London and a member of the Church of England. Three years later he was in Hamburg, and a Lutheran. Migrating to Canada, he not only reverted to Anglicanism but was ordained into the ministry (1902) by the archbishop of Montreal. He returned to England in the following year, gradually lost interest in his religious vocation, and switched to business and politics after meeting Seebohm Rowntree, who possessed both a fortune from the chocolate trade and a high post in the Liberal Party. Rowntree employed him from 1906 until 1909. Trebitsch changed his name to Lincoln in 1909 and became a naturalized Briton so that he could run for Parliament, to which he won a seat in 1910.

Bad investments cost Lincoln so much of the money he had accumulated in Rowntree's service that he could not afford to run in the next election. Declaring himself bankrupt, he turned to freelance journalism, covered Bulgaria and Turkey during the Balkan Wars (1912–13), and began a career in espionage, becoming a double agent for both Bulgaria and Turkey, without any real commitment to either.

He sold Bulgarian secrets to Constantinople and Turkish secrets to Sofia, until the Bulgarians discovered his treachery and jailed him. He was released through the intervention of Walther Nicolai, head of German military intelligence, which makes it evident that Lincoln had been working for the Germans, too.

Returning to London in 1914, on the outbreak of World War I, Lincoln received a place on the Hungarian desk of British censorship. He wanted to go into British intelligence, but his application was rejected. He then tried to ingratiate himself by reporting to MI6 (Military Intelligence 6, British espionage) on secret talks he claimed to have had with the head of German intelligence in Holland. The information Lincoln produced proved so worthless that MI5 (Military Intelligence 5, British counterespionage) grew suspicious. The French were already convinced that he was a spy for the Germans. In 1915 he left Britain even though nothing had been proved against him.

Lincoln went to the United States, where, by writing anti-British diatribes in the German-American press, he gave substance to the suspicion of him in London and Paris. Extradited to London in 1916, he was sent to jail, not, however, on spy charges but because he had forged a check in Rowntree's name. Deported to Hungary in 1919, after the war had ended, Lincoln went to Germany, where he became involved in the Kapp Putsch (1920), the monarchist plot to overthrow the Weimar Republic. The failure of the attempt caused him to leave Germany. He turned up in China in 1921 as a secret agent of Chinese intelligence, a post he held during the early 1920s, as the government in Peking struggled to control the warlords in the provinces. He is said to have worked at least part of the time under the direction of Morris ("Two-Gun") Cohen, who had come from Britain to run the intelligence system of nationalist China.

His Chinese experience gave Lincoln an interest in Buddhism, to which he became a convert. He remained an anomalous figure, spending part of his time in a Sri Lanka monastery (1926) and part in Europe buying arms for China (1927). He was known as the Abbot Chao Kung when he died in Shanghai in 1943 during World War II.

See also COHEN, TWO-GUN.

FURTHER READING: *Ignatius Timothy Trebitsch Lincoln, *The Autobiography of an Adventurer* (1931); David Lampe and Laszlo Szenasi, *The Self-Made Villain: A Biography of I. T. Trebitsch-Lincoln* (1961); Richard Deacon, *The Chinese Secret Service* (1974), has a chapter on Lincoln.

Lody, Karl *(1880?-1914)*   German spy in the British Isles during World War I.

Lody's background was German and American. He had been born in Germany and served in the German navy before taking a job with the Hamburg-Amerika line that kept him in New York most of the time between 1900 and 1914. He was fluent in English when he returned to Germany in 1914 to do what he could for the German war effort of World War I.

Gustav Steinhauer of German naval intelligence needed a spy for duty in Britain because the German network he had established before the war had been broken up by British counterespionage when the hostilities began. Lody volunteered, and stuck to his decision even though Steinhauer candidly warned him of the hazards—the skill of MI5 (Military Intelligence 5, British counterespionage) and the Special Branch of Scotland Yard; the fact that he would be on an island, with no chance to cross a neutral border to safety if anything went wrong; and the penalty (execution) imposed on spies under international law.

Lody entered England through the port of Southampton using a forged American passport and the cover name "Charles Inglis." From then on, he made too many naïve mistakes. Having arrived without a cipher that would conceal his espionage reports, he wrote openly to people with German names in Stockholm (in neutral Sweden). He bicycled around the Scottish coast asking too many questions about naval installations.

As a result, Vernon Kell of MI5 and Basil Thomson of the Special Branch put agents on his trail, which led to Ireland, where he was arrested and found to be in possession of incriminating documents. His espionage career had lasted just about two months, from September to November 1914.

While on trial, Lody impressed his judges with his courage, good manners, and bearing befitting an officer and a gentleman, but none of this saved him from being shot as a spy.

See also STEINHAUER, GUSTAV.

FURTHER READING: Gustav Steinhauer, *Steinhauer: The Kaiser's Master Spy,* (1930); *John Bulloch, *MI5: The Origin and History of the British Counter-Espionage Service* (1963); Richard Deacon, *A History of the British Secret Service* (1969).

London Controlling Section *(1941-45)* British secret organization responsible for the strategic use of disinformation.

Both sides used deception, or disinformation, as a weapon in World War II, sometimes in new and sophisticated ways. The Germans scored, for instance, with North Pole, the subversion of Dutch agents. The Allies had spectacular success with Bodyguard, their plan to mislead the Germans about the strategy of Overlord, the Allied invasion of Europe in 1944.

To handle deception, Prime Minister Winston Churchill and his advisers created, in 1941, the London Controlling Section (LCS), dedicated to the deployment on an almost global scale of "special means," all the secret, devious methods of underground warfare necessary for victory.

The Section was small, but under its controller, Colonel John Bevan, its power grew to be immense. It directed many Allied secret agencies in attacks on the Axis powers (Germany, Italy, and Japan). It spread over Europe, the Near East, and the Indian Ocean, with branches in Washington, Cairo, Algiers, and Delhi.

The LCS's plans for Overlord (1944) were worked out in conjunction with the American Joint Security Control and the Anglo-American Deception Unit of SHAEF (Supreme Headquarters of the Allied Expeditionary Forces). But its activities began in Africa in 1940, before America was at war. General Archibald Wavell formed A-Force, which became the Mideast arm of the LCS. A-Force built phantom armies with inflatable trucks and tanks, laid false roads and airfields in the desert, and dropped dummy paratroopers, as well as using real double agents and false wireless signals to hoodwink first the Italians and then the Germans. A-Force helped drive German General Erwin Rommel's forces out of Africa in 1943. It also helped mislead the Axis about the landings in Sicily and the Italian mainland. Before and after D-Day, Plan Zeppelin—the build-up of phantom armies that kept vital German forces tied down in the Balkans—was the work of A-Force.

The LCS took no part in tactical operations. These were carried out by the agencies linked to it, such as MI5 (Military Intelligence 5, British counterespionage), the Double-Cross Committee, MI6 (Military Intelligence 6, British espionage), Y Service (radio intelligence), the Special Operations Executive (SOE), the economic and political warfare agencies, and their American counterparts. By D-Day, the LCS was linked to a deception section at every Allied war planning staff.

See also DOUBLE-CROSS SYSTEM.

FURTHER READING: Sefton Delmer, *The Counterfeit Spy,* (1971); °Anthony Cave Brown, *Bodyguard of Lies* (1975); Ronald Lewin, *Ultra Goes to War* (1978).

Longinov, Yuri (1923-   )   Russian spy in Africa.

Born in Moscow, Longinov was the son of a Soviet bureaucrat, which helped him enter the bureaucracy himself. In 1936, while still at school, he studied languages, especially English, as a preparation for service abroad. After World War II, he attended Moscow University and then the Institute of International Relations (1951–52). Trained in espionage, he did his first tour of duty outside the Communist bloc in Rome in 1961, after which he spent four years (1963–67) in a number of European capitals.

Longinov's principal assignment took him to Africa in 1967, using a Canadian passport and the cover name "Edmund Trinka." He moved mainly between South Africa, Kenya, and Ethiopia, reporting to Moscow by radio about armies, rocket and nuclear capabilities, political leaders, and rebel movements. His constant traveling to sensitive areas created suspicion, and on his last visit to Johannesburg he was arrested by the South African police. Confronted with incriminating evidence found in his apartment, he confessed to being a spy for the Soviet Union and went to jail (1967).

The Russians wanted to get him back, and in the context of the developing "espionage revolution," whereby spies are exchanged instead of being executed or permanently imprisoned, this was a realistic possibility. Since Cape Town had no diplomatic relations with Moscow, a three-way deal was worked out involving the Federal Republic of Germany. The South Africans traded Longinov to the West Germans for a consignment of weapons. Bonn then traded the Soviet spy to the Russians for a number of West Germans held in jails in the Communist bloc. This triangular exchange returned Longinov to Moscow in 1969.

FURTHER READING: E. H. Cook, *Spy Trade* (1971).

Lonsdale, Gordon (1922-70)   Russian spymaster in Great Britain.

Lonsdale was born in Russia (his real name was Konon Trofimovich Molody). He lived for nine years with relatives in California and became fluent in English, which in later years enabled him to pass for a native of an English-speaking country. Returning to the Soviet Union in 1938, he committed himself to Communism, served in the Red Army during World War II, and joined the KGB (Committee for State Security, Soviet intelligence). Trained in special forms of espionage, he went to Canada in 1954 with a forged passport and the alias "Gordon Lonsdale."

In 1955 Lonsdale arrived in England posing as a Canadian businessman. Assigned by the KGB to obtain information on British underwater detection devices, he contacted an Englishman who worked in the Admiralty Underwater Weapons Establishment at Portland and would sell naval secrets for money— Harry Houghton, doubly useful because his girlfriend, Ethel Gee, also worked there and had access to classified documents.

The information that Lonsdale obtained from Houghton and Gee was of the utmost importance not only to Great Britain but also to the North Atlantic

Treaty Organization (NATO), which guarded Europe against the Russians. Lonsdale took the information to Peter and Helen Kroger, who relayed it by shortwave radio from London to Moscow.

This espionage ended in 1961 because MI5 (Military Intelligence 5, British counterespionage) had become suspicious of Houghton's meetings with Lonsdale. The Special Branch of Scotland Yard arrested the pair, along with Gee and the Krogers. The trial of the five defendants created a scandal in Britain, where angry questions were asked about why espionage at a major naval research station was so easy. The London government then introduced more stringent regulations at Portland and other installations where secret research was going on.

The five defendants in the Portland case received long prison sentences. In 1964 Lonsdale gained his freedom by being exchanged for Greville Wynne, an Englishman who had been caught spying in Russia. Lonsdale went back to Moscow, where he published, at the behest of the KGB, a mendacious account of his espionage career.

See also HOUGHTON, HARRY; KROGER, PETER AND HELEN.

FURTHER READING: *John Bulloch and Henry Miller, *Spy Ring: The Story of the Naval Secrets Case* (1961); Gordon Lonsdale, *Spy: Twenty Years in the Soviet Secret Service* (1965); Fitzroy Maclean, *Take Nine Spies* (1978), has a chapter on Lonsdale.

Lotz, Wolfgang (1921-   ) Israeli spy in Egypt.

Born in Mannheim, Germany, Lotz was the son of a Jewish mother and a gentile father who worked as a theatrical director. After his father's death and his own graduation from the Mommsen Gymnasium in Berlin (1933), Lotz accompanied his mother to Palestine, where they remained as Adolf Hitler became chancellor of Nazi Germany.

In 1937 Lotz joined Haganah, the underground committed to Jewish self-defense. Two years later he entered the British army to fight against Nazi Germany during World War II. Transferred to Egypt, he was there during the years (1941–42) when German Field Marshal Erwin Rommel won dazzling victories in the desert but failed to reach Cairo.

After the end of the war in 1945, Lotz returned to the Jewish underground in Palestine. He took part in the fighting with the Arabs that preceded the establishment of the state of Israel in 1948. After that, he went into Israeli intelligence, for which he became a spy in Egypt in 1960.

Posing as a Nazi refugee from defeated Germany, Lotz became familiar with other Germans in Egypt, who introduced him into government circles in Cairo. He was thus able to radio to Israel information on the Egyptian military and on the German rocket scientists working for Egypt.

Successful for five years, Lotz gave himself away when he was picked up by the Egyptians for questioning about his relations with other Germans in Cairo. He was sentenced to life imprisonment in 1965, but was exchanged in 1968 for Egyptian soldiers captured in the "six-day war" of 1967. His spy information had been used by the Israelis in their victory over the Egyptians.

FURTHER READING: *Wolfgang Lotz, *The Champagne Spy: Israel's Master Spy Tells His Story* (1972); Richard Deacon, *The Israeli Secret Service* (1977); Dennis Eisenberg, Uri Dan, and Eli Landau, *The Mossad, Israel's Secret Intelligence Service: Inside Stories* (1978).

Louis XV *(1710-74)*   King of France who personally directed an undercover organization, the King's Secret.

The idea of the King's Secret occurred to Louis XV in 1743, when he made it a prime objective of his foreign policy to maintain French influence in Poland. To achieve this, Louis backed a French candidate for the vacant Polish throne. Since the French foreign minister opposed this policy on the ground that France could gain nothing of substance, the king determined to bypass the minister by creating an alternative diplomatic system. He recruited his own agents, often men officially attached to the French foreign ministry, whom he sent abroad with instructions that contradicted their instructions from the French foreign minister. So began the King's Secret.

Its director abroad in 1752, at a critical moment for French diplomacy in Poland, was Charles François, comte de Broglie, the French ambassador to Warsaw. The French foreign minister thought he had the backing of the king for a policy of supporting the Polish nationalists on the question of a king for Poland. Unknown to the minister, the king had the French candidate ready. Broglie, unable to pursue two contradictory policies, pursued the king's.

The royal policy did not succeed, however; rather, it dissipated French strength during two decades. In 1772 Louis XV had to watch the partition of Poland between Russia, Prussia, and Austria. France by then had entered the Seven Years' War (1756–63) with divided councils and too many armies excluded, because of the King's Secret, from the conflict with the British. Defeat in war and the loss of French colonies at the peace in 1763 resulted.

During this reign, the king's "political mistresses" played a damaging role. Jeanne Antoinette d'Étioles, marquise de Pompadour, however, was probably no more than a minor figure in the "diplomatic revolution" of 1756 that made France an ally of Austria and a belligerent in quarrels in eastern Europe from which France could not benefit.

The King's Secret, however, did have its successes, as in the case of the Chevalier d'Éon, who represented Louis at the court of the Tsarina Elizabeth and initiated confidential communications between St. Petersburg and Versailles. But the successes of the royal undercover organization were minor compared to its catastrophic failures.

See also BROGLIE, COMTE DE; KING'S SECRET.

FURTHER READING: Duc de Broglie, *The King's Secret* (1879); *Pierre Gaxotte, *Louis the Fifteenth and His Times* (1934); Gordon Wright, *France in Modern Times* (1974), has an estimation of Louis XV and his diplomacy.

Louk, Mordecai *(1934-   )*   Israeli spy for Egypt.

Born in Spanish Morocco, Louk emigrated to Israel in 1949, worked as a carpenter, and joined the Israeli army. In 1961, while on military maneuvers, he defected to Egypt, where he received political asylum and was trained in espionage. Egyptian intelligence, realizing Louk could not conceal his identity in Israel, sent him to Europe to spy on Israelis and to identify Israeli secret agents.

Louk worked for two years (1962–64) in Germany, Switzerland, and Italy. Then, in a quarrel over money, he told his Egyptian superior in Rome that he intended to drop out of the spy network. In a bizarre series of events, a band of Egyptians seized Louk, drugged him, locked him in a trunk, and tried to ship him by air to Egypt. A customs official at the Rome airport heard his feeble cries and released him.

The Egyptians responsible were expelled from Italy. Louk returned to Israel, where in 1965 a court sentenced him to thirteen years for treason. When released, he went back to being a carpenter.

FURTHER READING: Richard Deacon, *The Israeli Secret Service* (1977); *Dennis Eisenberg, Uri Dan, and Eli Landau, *The Mossad, Israel's Secret Intelligence Service: Inside Stories* (1978).

Louvois, Marquis de *(1641-91)* French minister of war and spymaster during the reign of King Louis XIV.

Louvois, who was François le Tellier before becoming a marquis, inherited a high place in the royal government because his father had served both Louis XIII and Louis XIV as minister of war. In 1654 Louvois began to assist his father, whom he replaced in 1666 at the head of the French military establishment. Drastic reforms of the military were introduced in the years that followed —promotion according to merit, improvement of the commissariat, new weapons (e.g., the bayonet), and the wearing of uniforms.

As Louis XIV was Cardinal Richelieu's heir in the pursuit of French predominance in Europe, Louvois was Richelieu's heir in the use of spies. He had no master undercover agent to match François Leclerc du Tremblay, the Cardinal's right-hand man, but Louvois understood the necessity of keeping spies in the main cities of France and of foreign powers. He paid his agents well to send him information on everything from the behavior of his officers to the plans of France's enemies.

Amateurs were indispensable to his network. French travelers, writers, actors, and riding masters, all in demand across Europe, reported whatever they thought might be useful from the European courts where they stopped. Louvois even had hotel maids on his payroll.

The information Louvois requested was usually general rather than specific. He told his agents to pick up whatever they could and pass everything on to him for scrutiny. Louvois winnowed the wheat from the chaff and sometimes gained definite answers to definite problems.

His spies abroad enabled his sovereign to enter into war better prepared than the enemies of France. Domestic spying enabled Louvois to maintain discipline in the army that Louis XIV launched into battle with much success. The marquis fell from favor eventually, but the military force he had developed remained the best in Europe until Frederick the Great's Prussian armies went into the field.

FURTHER READING: Henry Offley Wakeman, *The Ascendancy of France, 1598–1715* (n.d.); *Will Durant, *The Age of Louis XIV* (1963); John C. Rule, *Louis XIV* (1974).

Lucy German spy in a network in Switzerland operating against Germany during World War II.

See ROESSLER, RUDOLF.

Macdonnell of Glengarry, Alastair Ruadh *(1725?-61)* Scottish clan chief and spy for the London government during the Jacobite movement.

Known as "Young Glengarry" until his father died in 1754 and he inherited clan leadership, Macdonnell belonged to one of the greatest highland clans fighting for the Jacobite cause—the restoration of the Scottish, and Catholic, Stuarts to the British throne. He supported Prince Charles Edward Stuart, the "Young Pretender," in the rising of 1745 (the "Forty-Five"), when the prince attempted to oust the Hanoverian dynasty.

Macdonnell was captured when the Forty-Five failed, thrown into the Tower of London, and held there until 1749. On his release he joined the exiled Jacobites on the Continent, where "Bonnie Prince Charlie" (the Young Pretender) was wandering incognito, trying to gain international support for his cause.

In 1750 Charles paid a secret visit to London to estimate his chances of success. Shortly afterward a group of his followers conceived the Elibank Plot, named for Lord Elibank, a Scottish peer. Macdonnell and Elibank's brother, Alexander Murray, with a handful of French officers and 400 highlanders were to attack St James's Palace in London and kidnap George II. The Scottish clans were to rise when this had been achieved and when troops from Sweden under Marshall Keith, a Jacobite leader, had arrived in Scotland. To coordinate operations, two exiled Jacobites, Dr. Archibald Cameron and the chief of Lochgarry, went to Scotland from the Continent. The move on the palace was to begin on November 10, 1752.

For an unknown reason, execution of the plot had to be postponed. Then in 1753 Dr. Cameron was arrested and hanged, though no evidence against him could be produced other than his participation in the Forty-Five, eight years earlier.

Skilled English and Continental government agents were constantly watching the Jacobites, but it was a Scottish Jacobite who betrayed the Elibank Plot. The spy was Alastair Ruadh Macdonnell, or "Young Glengarry," alias "Pickle" (his favorite cover name, from *Peregrine Pickle,* by Tobias Smollett, an author he admired), alias "Roderick Random," alias "Alexander Jeanson."

A handsome, arrogant man, fond of money and the good life, Macdonnell felt his past sacrifices for the Stuarts were insufficiently appreciated. He, his father, and his clan had nearly ruined themselves for the Jacobite cause. In spite of this, when he asked the titular king, the exiled James III, for money, Macdonnell received instead a useless copy of a warrant for a peerage, issued years before to his grandfather by the "Old Pretender." It was almost an insult. He knew that 40,000 louis d'or, which had arrived from France too late to help in the Forty-Five, were lying hidden in Loch Arkaig in Scotland for the prince's use. Macdonnell probably thought Charles should have been more generous, but in fact little of that money ever reached the prince.

Macdonnell turned his coat and from 1752 or earlier reported regularly to Henry Pelham, British secretary of state. His betrayal of the Elibank Plot, in which he participated while relating the entire scheme to its enemies, caused the Jacobites to abandon the conspiracy, their last real attempt to overthrow the Hanoverians. Macdonnell continued to report to London until 1760, the year before he died, and Prince Charles continued to wander (he spent nearly eighteen years so doing) before finally withdrawing to Rome on the death of his father in 1766.

Macdonnell's treachery was not discovered (though charges were made against him in his own time) for more than 100 years, when Andrew Lang published the story, drawn from Stuart papers, in *Pickle the Spy.*

FURTHER READING: *Andrew Lang, *Pickle the Spy* (1897); Charles Petrie, *The Jacobite Movement* (1950); Gordon Donaldson and Robert S. Morpeth, *A Dictionary of Scottish History* (1977).

***Maclean, Donald** (1913-   )* British diplomat and spy for the Soviet Union.

The son of a Scottish politician, Maclean was born in London when his father was a member of Parliament. He attended Gresham's School in Norfolk (1927–31), where his homosexual tendencies were not yet serious enough to give him problems. Going on to Cambridge in 1931, Maclean met Kim Philby, Guy Burgess, and Anthony Blunt (the latter two were also homosexuals) and joined them in looking for an alternative to the political system they blamed for the British economic depression of the period. Like the other three, Maclean became a Communist and an undercover agent for the Soviet Union.

Graduating from Cambridge in 1934 and eager for a job in the British Foreign Office, Maclean stilled the rumors about his ideology by publicly repudiating Communism. He got a job and worked his way upward. The year 1940 found him in Paris with his wife. They escaped back to Britain as the German offensive gathered momentum and the collapse of France became inevitable. Maclean worked in London until 1944, all the while reporting to the Russians classified information from the Foreign Office.

In 1944 Maclean received an appointment as first secretary at the British Embassy in Washington. He served on the Combined Policy Committee, which concerted the plans for the development of atomic energy by Britain, Canada, and the United States. Still a spy for the Russians, Maclean passed on to them what he learned at these sessions. He got away with it at the time, but the leak was later traced to him, the beginning of the espionage scandal of 1951.

Maclean's increasing homosexuality combined with the tension of spying caused his character to deteriorate. His London superiors recalled him in 1948, assigned him to Cairo in the hope that he would pull himself together, found they had made a mistake, and in 1950 removed him for heavy drinking and making a spectacle of himself.

Nevertheless, in 1951 he received the American desk at the Foreign Office in London, probably because, as was later charged, his superiors had been to the British universities, notably Cambridge, and wanted to take care of one of their own. Then investigations in London and Washington regarding leaks of Allied atomic research to the Russians began to focus on Maclean, since he was the one official who met all the qualifications required by the successful spy. The net began to close around him, a fact of which he was apprised by Burgess, just returned from a post in Washington, where Philby had alerted him to Maclean's peril. Burgess revealed the fact to Blunt at the same time, and Blunt, who had given up spying, reported to a Russian contact. The Russians ordered Burgess, Maclean, and Blunt to go to the Soviet Union. Blunt refused. Burgess and Maclean escaped, made their way to Moscow, and proclaimed themselves defectors.

Maclean's wife and children joined him in 1953, reaching Russia by a secret escape route from Switzerland. Another British defector arrived in Moscow ten years later—Kim Philby, the "third man" of the Burgess-Maclean case. Blunt was the only one of the Cambridge quartet of Soviet spies to remain in London, and in 1979 he was exposed as the "fourth man" in the case.

See also BLUNT, ANTHONY; BURGESS, GUY; PHILBY, KIM.

FURTHER READING: *Cyril Connolly, *The Missing Diplomats* (1952); Anthony Purdy and Douglas Sutherland, *Burgess and Maclean* (1963); Bruce Page, David Leitch, and Phillip Knightley, *The Philby Conspiracy* (1968); Andrew Boyle, *The Fourth Man: The Definitive Account of Kim Philby, Guy Burgess, and Donald Maclean, and Who Recruited Them to Spy for Russia* (1979); Douglas Sutherland, *The Great Betrayal: The Definitive Story of Blunt, Philby, Burgess and Maclean* (1981).

MacNally, Leonard (1754-1820) Irish lawyer, writer, and spy for the British government.

Born in Dublin, the son of a merchant, MacNally took a law degree and was serving in the Dublin law courts and writing plays on the side when he turned informer for the British government in 1794. Britain was at war with revolutionary France, and Irish rebels considered this the right time to strike for the freedom of Ireland. The British secret service therefore planted spies among them, one of whom was MacNally.

Joining the rebellious United Irishmen, led by Wolfe Tone, MacNally reported their plans to the Anglo-Irish administration in Dublin as the movement developed into the insurrection of 1798, which failed disastrously. MacNally used a special technique in his role of secret agent, representing in court clients whom he had betrayed. He thus gained the reputation of an Irish patriot, which enabled him to become one of the most successful spies of his time. He worked for money, and he commanded large sums from the Dublin authorities.

MacNally's principal achievement in undercover work was his betrayal of Robert Emmet, the Irish conspirator who, like Wolfe Tone before him and Roger Casement afterward, believed that Ireland should rebel when Great Britain was at war. Since the British were again at war with France in 1803, Emmet planned an Irish rising for that year.

The rising failed, and Emmet went into hiding. He stayed near the home of his betrothed, Sarah Curran, the daughter of MacNally's law partner. Sarah Curran naturally confided in MacNally regarding the whereabouts of Emmet. MacNally went to see Emmet, lulled him into a false sense of security, and told the police where to find the fugitive.

Arrested, Emmet faced a court on a charge of treason with MacNally for his defense attorney. The rebel went to the gallows, and his attorney went back to writing plays that are now forgotten. MacNally's patriotic reputation remained intact until the facts were discovered after his death.

See also EMMET, ROBERT.

FURTHER READING: Stephen Gwynn, *Irish Literature and Drama in the English Language* (1936), gives the Dublin background to MacNally's literary career; Frank MacDermott, *Theobald Wolfe Tone* (1939), gives the historical background to MacNally's espionage career; *Leon O'Broin, *The Unfortunate Mr. Robert Emmet* (1958).

Magic American cryptological system of reading messages in the principal Japanese cipher during World War II.

See PEARL HARBOR; PURPLE.

Malraux, André *(1901-76)* French writer, philosopher, politician, and spymaster against the Germans during World War II.

Malraux, the son of a banker, was born in Paris and educated at the Lycée Turgot (1916–19). He became a Parisian intellectual and art critic (1919–20). Traveling widely in the 1920s (Far East) and the 1930s (Arabia), he wrote about his experiences in books that won critical acclaim. In 1936 he went to Spain to aid the pro-Communist Loyalist forces opposing General Francisco Franco.

Entering the French army in 1939 as World War II began, Malraux commanded armored forces at the time of the German invasion in 1940 and the fall of France. He was captured by the enemy, escaped, and joined the French resistance, the underground that continued the struggle covertly. His cover name was "Colonel Berger," his area, Périgord in southern France. As a former officer in the French army, he took control of the local resistance network, directing its spies in their espionage missions and planning sabotage strikes against the Germans, who placed "Colonel Berger" on their wanted list. Malraux skillfully conducted his underground campaign for over three years. Captured by the Germans in 1944, he escaped soon enough to take part in the roundup of German soldiers, as their occupation of France collapsed under the blows of Allied forces moving inland from the invasion beaches.

In 1945 Malraux became minister of information in the government of Charles de Gaulle. The government fell in 1946, but a year later de Gaulle returned to power, and Malraux returned with him. Both were out of office after 1953; both returned in 1958, Malraux as minister of cultural affairs. De Gaulle's final retirement from public life in 1969 was also Malraux's.

FURTHER READING: *André Malraux, *Anti-Memoirs* (1968); Pierre Galante, *Malraux* (1971); David Schoenbrun, *Soldiers of the Night: The Story of the French Resistance* (1980).

Mann, Horace *(1701-86)* English diplomat, art collector, and spymaster for the British government in Florence during the Jacobite movement.

The son of a London merchant, Mann received a good education, became a friend of Horace Walpole, the writer and connoisseur, and in 1737 was appointed by Walpole's father, Prime Minister Robert Walpole, to a diplomatic post in Florence. Mann's principal assignment was to report on the Jacobites, who since the flight of King James II from England in 1688 had been plotting on the Continent. The "Old Pretender" (the son of James II, also known to his followers as James III) had failed at the "Fifteen," an attempt to regain the throne by force in 1715. But his son, Charles Edward, the "Young Pretender" ("Bonnie Prince Charlie"), nursed the ambition to invade Britain.

Mann was promoted to British resident in Florence in 1740, by which time he had organized a network of spies in Italy. Two leading figures had long been undercover agents for the British—Cardinal Alessandro Albani in Rome and Philip von Stosch, first in Rome and then in Florence. The Eternal City was the critical point because the Jacobite court was located there.

In 1743 Albani began writing to Mann about the movements of the Old Pretender and the Young Pretender. The cardinal warned in the following year that the Young Pretender dropped out of sight so frequently that some coup must be near, a warning validated by the "Forty-Five," the expedition of 1745 when Charles Edward tried to regain the British throne, only to be militarily defeated in England. The Young Pretender fled back to the Continent, drowned his disappointment in liquor, and allowed the Jacobite cause to decline.

When Albani reported in 1766 that the Old Pretender was dead, Mann at once urged him to do what he could to have the pope suppress the Jacobite royal title, since Charles Edward had no chance of ever becoming Charles III of England. Albani succeeded, and that ended the European importance of the British Jacobites. The Young Pretender was in Florence in 1775, but Mann had little to report on him except his debauched behavior. In 1785 Mann was astounded to hear Charles Edward tell a gathering in Florence that he had paid a secret visit to London in 1750, of which none of Mann's spies had been aware.

The collapse of the Jacobite movement allowed Mann to concentrate on his two delights, life in Italy and the collection of Italian artwork. He remains most familiar, however, for his long correspondence with Horace Walpole in England, thousands of letters covering forty years during which they never met.

FURTHER READING: *John Doran, *Mann and Manners at the Court of Florence, 1740–1786* (1876); Lesley Lewis, *Connoisseurs and Secret Agents in Eightenth Century Rome* (1961); David Daiches, *Charles Edward Stuart: The Life and Times of Bonnie Prince Charlie* (1973).

Marlowe, Christopher *(1564-93)*   English dramatist and government spy during the Elizabethan era.

The son of a Canterbury shoemaker, Marlowe revealed as a child a quick intelligence that gained him admission to the King's School in his native town. He went to Cambridge in 1581 and took his bachelor's degree in 1584. He would have been rejected for the master's degree in 1587 because he had been away from Cambridge for long periods, but the queen's government interceded on his behalf with the university authorities.

The intercession came about because Marlowe had been serving the government as a secret agent during his absences. Francis Walsingham of the queen's privy council had recruited a group of young men from Cambridge to join his undercover network in spying on Catholic conspirators who hoped to place Mary Queen of Scots on the throne of Queen Elizabeth, and Marlowe was one of his recruits.

Marlowe's assignments took him to Rheims, France, where the English Catholics in exile had their headquarters and planned their campaign to restore the Catholic religion to the throne in England, which Elizabeth had drawn into the Protestant camp during the conflicts caused by the Reformation. Posing as a Catholic, Marlowe entered the Catholic seminary in Rheims, where he spied on professors and students at the seminary. His secret reports to Walsingham covered Catholic plots for the reconversion of England and the identity of Catholic agents who would operate clandestinely in their homeland on behalf of the queen of Scotland.

It is not known whether Marlowe's reports from Rheims had any decisive effect on Walsingham's exposure of the plots against Elizabeth or on the execution of Mary in 1587, the year in which Marlowe wrote *Tamburlaine,* the play that established him among the great writers of English literature. *Dr. Faustus* (1591) and *Edward II* (1593) enhanced his reputation in the Elizabethan theater. But Marlowe was a daredevil and a low-life by inclination, and at the height of his dramatic powers he was killed in a squalid tavern brawl. *See also* WALSINGHAM, FRANCIS.

FURTHER READING: *Austin K. Gray, "Christopher Marlowe, Government Agent," in *Publications of the Modern Language Association* (1928); T. M. Pearce, *Christopher Marlowe, Figure of the Renaissance* (1934); A. L. Rouse, *Christopher Marlowe* (1965).

Marshall, William (1924-   ) British spy for the Soviet Union.

Marshall was born in London, where his father drove a bus. Intending to go into the British merchant marine, Marshall began training for such a career, only to drop out. He shifted to the study of radio technology, and became proficient enough to be assigned to the Royal Signal Corps (1948) and after that to the British diplomatic service with a posting to Moscow (1950).

Agents of the KGB (Committee for State Security, Russian intelligence) discovered Marshall's weakness—something of a misfit in ordinary society, he could be swayed by anyone who made a point of cultivating him. He soon had good friends in Moscow. By 1952, the year of his recall to England, he had begun to feel an attraction to Communism, since his pleasant Russian friends believed in it.

Attached to a radio installation in Buckinghamshire, Marshall got in touch with Pavel Kuznetsov of the Soviet Embassy in London. The pair made a deal by which Marshall would, for large sums of money, sell classified information to Kuznetsov.

The conspiracy did not last for long because the Special Branch of Scotland Yard was watching Kuznetsov, as it did all Russian diplomats, and MI5 (Military Intelligence 5, Brisish counterespionage) was watching Marshall, who fell under suspicion while flaunting his new wealth. Marshall-Kuznetsov rendezvous in London were observed, Marshall was seen covertly giving papers to Kuznetsov, and in due time the two were arrested, as they met clandestinely in St. George's Park.

Kuznetsov, as a Russian Embassy official immune to prosecution, returned to Moscow unscathed, except for his failure in London, which may have caused him some problems when he reported to the KGB. Marshall, as a British subject, received a sentence of five years.

FURTHER READING: John Bulloch, *MI5: The Origin and History of the British Counter-Espionage Service* (1963); *Norman Lucas, *The Great Spy Ring* (1966); Bernard Newman, *Spy and Counter-Spy: The Story of the British Secret Service* (1970).

Martin, William (1931-   ) American cryptologist and defector from the United States to the Soviet Union.

Born in Columbus, Georgia, Martin was taken at the age of fifteen to Ellensburg, Washington, where his father went into business. Martin finished his schooling in Ellensburg, made a name for himself in mathematics and chess, and in 1949 entered the Central Washington College of Education. A year later he joined the United States Navy, was assigned to cryptology, and was sent to Japan to work in the American headquarters at the Yokosuka naval base. There he met and worked with Bernon Mitchell, who subsequently defected with Martin.

Leaving the Navy, Martin in 1955 entered the University of Washington, where he studied mathematics. Completing the course in 1957, he accepted a job with the National Security Agency (NSA), where after special study at George Washington University, he became a cryptologist in 1958, the year Mitchell obtained the same type of position.

The pair discovered mutual affinities based on latent if not overt homosexuality. In 1958, unknown to their superiors, they joined the Communist party. In 1959 they traveled without authorization to the Cuba of Fidel Castro.

By then, they were expressing anti-American opinions. Each openly condemned the American U-2 flights over the Soviet Union, of which they were aware through their intelligence work.

In spite of their growing disaffection and the suspicion to which it should have exposed them, Martin and Mitchell remained with the NSA until 1960, when they suddenly vanished together. Turning up in Moscow, they held a news conference at which they attacked American intelligence policies, such as the breaking of the codes of friendly nations.

Since their work at the NSA had shown them that the KGB (Committee for State Security, Russian intelligence) was doing the same things and worse, the motives of Martin and Mitchell remained obscure. Their superiors at the NSA stated that homosexuality lay at the root of their problem.

This naturally raised the question of why the truth about Martin and Mitchell had not been discovered. The result was an overhaul of security and hiring practices at the NSA.

See also MITCHELL, BERNON.

FURTHER READING: *House Committee on Un-American Activities, *Report on Security Practices in the National Security Agency* (1962); Sanche de Gramont, *The Secret War: The Story of International Espionage since World War II* (1962); David Kahn, *The Codebreakers: The Story of Secret Writing* (1967).

Martin, William *(1943)*   Nonexistent officer invented and used by British intelligence to deceive German intelligence.

The Allied victory over the Germans in North Africa in 1942 posed the question of where to strike next, in Sicily or in Greece. The decision for Sicily had to be camouflaged as much as possible, and the best cover for the military invasion would be to induce German intelligence to believe that Greece would be the target. German armed forces would then be assigned to Greece, keeping them out of the battle for Sicily.

This meant planting disinformation (false information) pointing to Greece with German intelligence. "William Martin" played a role in this effort. British intelligence found a corpse, gave it a name and the rank of major in the British marines, and equipped it with a briefcase containing carefully forged documents. The corpse was taken by submarine to a point off the coast of Spain and released in the water where the tide would carry it ashore near Huelva. The belief in London was that the Spanish authorities, although officially neutral, would allow the Germans in Huelva, fascists like themselves, to see and copy the documents. The prediction was vindicated by the outcome.

Recovering the body from the water, the Spaniards revealed the contents of the briefcase to the German attaché. He learned that Major William Martin was a courier bound for the Mediterranean with top-secret letters to Allied commanders in that theater of war stating that Greece was next on the timetable of invasions. To add verisimilitude to this covert operation, British intelligence had placed personal items in the briefcase—letters from Martin's father and girlfriend, her snapshot, a receipt for a diamond engagement ring, and even the stubs of two tickets to a play.

Enhancing the realism, London ordered the British attaché in Huelva, who knew nothing of the plot, to inquire about the documents Major William Martin carried. The attaché received them from the Spanish authorities after the Germans had made copies that were then forwarded to Berlin. German intelligence took the disinformation seriously, and the German high command maintained more soldiers in Greece than were needed, while Sicily fell to the Allies.

FURTHER READING: Ewen Montagu, *The Man Who Never Was* (1952); Fitzroy Maclean, *Take Nine Spies* (1978), has a chapter on "William Martin."

Mata Hari *(1876-1917)*   Dutch spy for Germany against France during World War I.

Born in Leeuwarden, Holland, the daughter of a hatter, Mata Hari's true name was Margaretha Zelle. To get away from a home environment that oppressed her, in 1895 she impulsively married a Scottish officer, John MacLeod, who, serving in the Dutch colonial forces, took her to the Dutch East Indies, where they spent eight years (1895–1902).

The marriage failed, but Margaretha Zelle became enchanted with the east, especially with the dancing girls in the temples of Java. On returning to Holland in 1902, she separated from her husband (divorcing him in 1906), spent a couple of years in obscurity, and in 1905 suddenly appeared in Paris in the guise of a temple dancer from India. She now called herself Mata Hari, which she said meant "Eye of the Dawn."

Personally bewitching, with large dark eyes and a ready wit, she captivated Paris as she performed her exotic, erotic, nearly nude dances. During the next decade she appeared in theaters from Monte Carlo to Berlin, gaining a lurid reputation and a succession of masculine admirers who lavished money on her in return for her favors. She was among the high-priced courtesans of Europe.

By the time World War I broke out in 1914, Mata Hari, at 38, was having trouble creating the illusion of a sinuous, agile temple dancer. She was now living off wealthy men in several countries, some of them Frenchmen and Germans of authority.

Mata Hari was in Berlin when the war began. She went back to Holland and in 1915 was in Paris, where French counterespionage already had her under surveillance because of her German connections. French agents claimed to have discovered that she sent information to Berlin through neutral diplomats and that she reported the names of Allied undercover agents to the Germans in Brussels. But Paris did not have sufficient evidence to hold her.

In Madrid in 1916, Mata Hari had lovers at both the French and German embassies. The Germans sent a radio message to Berlin asking funds for Agent H21, whom the French identified as Mata Hari. Since the message went in a code the Germans knew the French had broken, it seems that the sender wanted her to be caught, perhaps because he suspected her of being a double agent working for France.

Instructed to go to Paris to pick up her money, Mata Hari was arrested. Placed on trial, she made a spirited defense, admitting she took money from the Germans but insisting it was for bedroom diversions, not espionage. The evidence went against her, and she was executed by a French firing squad.

In popular legend, Mata Hari is the most famous of spies and the best example of the *femme fatale* wangling secret military information from susceptible men.

FURTHER READING: *Thomas Coulson, *Mata Hari: Courtesan and Spy* (1930); Sam Waagenaar, *The Murder of Mata Hari* (1964); Fitzroy Maclean, *Take Nine Spies* (1978), has a chapter on Mata Hari.

Maugham, Somerset *(1874-1965)*   British novelist and secret agent during World War I.

Born in Paris and orphaned at the age of ten, Maugham went to the King's School in Canterbury, England, where he spent seven years (1884–91). After some months at the University of Heidelberg, he studied medicine at St. Thomas's Hospital in London and started out to make a career as a physician. However, the publication of a successful novel, *Liza of Lambeth* (1897), turned him from medicine to literature. He became the author of a succession of books that gave him a high place in twentieth-century letters, his masterpiece being *Of Human Bondage* (1915).

When World War I broke out in 1914, Maugham volunteered as an ambulance driver in France. A year later he joined MI6 (Military Intelligence 6, British espionage), which capitalized on his fluency in French and his cover story that he was simply a writer by sending him on an undercover mission to Switzerland. In 1917 he was switched to Russia, where a regime headed by Alexander Kerensky was struggling to remain in power following the removal of the tsar.

Maugham reached Petrograd (later Leningrad), where he met Kerensky and sent coded messages from the Russian leader to London by way of the British Embassy. When Maugham returned home, he carried a personal letter from Kerensky appealing for British help. Prime Minister David Lloyd George gave Maugham a (negative) reply to deliver to Kerensky, but the Bolshevik seizure of power in 1917 intervened to render academic any further communication with Kerensky (who had fled from Petrograd).

When Maugham went back to being a novelist after the war, he used his secret agent missions as material for his novel *Ashenden* (1928), which is about espionage. He was living on the Riviera at the outbreak of World War II (1939), but the German invasion of France in 1940 forced him to flee into exile for the duration of the conflict. Then he returned to the Riviera and to writing.

FURTHER READING: *Somerset Maugham, *Ashenden; or the British Agent* (1928); Frederic Raphael, *W. Somerset Maugham and His World* (1976).

McParlan, James *(1844-1919)*   Irish spy among the Molly Maguires of the Pennsylvania coal fields.

Born in County Armagh, Ireland, McParlan became a wanderer who, failing to find steady employment in Ireland or England, came to America in 1867. After working at various jobs, he finally found his niche in 1871 as an agent of Allan Pinkerton's National Detective Agency in Chicago.

Pinkerton's clients included mine owners in the Pennsylvania coal fields, where the workers, mainly Irish members of the violent secret society called the Molly Maguires, were causing strikes and committing mayhem in an effort to gain higher wages and better working conditions. Pinkerton needed an Irish Catholic to infiltrate the Molly Maguires, and in 1873 McParlan received the assignment.

He maneuvered his way into good standing in the society, took its oath, attended its lodge meetings—and reported on its leaders, plans, and activities. The years 1874 and 1875 saw an outburst of extreme violence in the coal fields, including several murders, and when the accused went on trial in 1876, McParlan broke his cover to testify against them in court.

This ended his usefulness in the coal fields, but he remained with the Pinkertons. In 1907, while head of the bureau in Denver, he handled the sensational murder of Frank Steunenberg, governor of Colorado. McParlan persuaded the chief suspect, Harry Orchard, to confess.

McParlan achieved international renown as an undercover agent. He is the original of the character Birdie Edwards in *The Valley of Fear,* perhaps Arthur Conan Doyle's best story.

See also PINKERTON, ALLAN.

FURTHER READING: Allan Pinkerton, *The Molly Maguires and the Detectives* (1877); *Wayne G. Broehl, Jr., *The Molly Maguires* (1964); James D. Horan, *The Pinkertons: The Detective Dynasty that Made History* (1968).

Metternich, Clemens von *(1773-1859)* Austrian statesman and spymaster during the early nineteenth century.

Metternich was born at Coblenz in the Rhineland, a part of the Holy Roman Empire. From his youth he intended to follow his father's footsteps into diplomacy in the service of Austria, the dominant state of the empire, and in pursuance of that aim he studied international relations at the University of Strasbourg (1788–90). Carrying out diplomatic assignments for Emperor Francis II while the French Revolution and Napoleon were shaking Europe, Metternich developed a hatred of revolutionary principles.

When he became Austrian foreign minister in 1809 and the most important Austrian statesman since Wenzel von Kaunitz, Metternich had to conceal his true opinions because the German states lay at the mercy of Napoleon, now Emperor of France, who had put an end to the Holy Roman Empire in 1806 after the crushing French victory at the battle of Austerlitz. By 1813, when Metternich was named a prince of the Austrian empire, the tide had turned. Napoleon was defeated and sent to Elba in 1814, while the victorious allies gathered at the Congress of Vienna (1814–15), which survived Napoleon's return and the Battle of Waterloo and rearranged the map of Europe.

All the principal participants at the Congress of Vienna spied on the others, but the representatives of Britain, Prussia, and Russia were amateurs compared to Metternich, who ran the best undercover organization and was operating in his own city. His chief of police, Franz Hager, maintained a list of visitors to Vienna, and secret agents followed those whom Metternich wanted kept under surveillance. Writers, journalists, landlords, and hotel servants were encouraged to come forward with information.

Metternich bribed men close to the diplomats at the congress. The most important unknown quantity was Tsar Alexander I of Russia, a despot of immense power and mystical ideas without whom no stable peace could be arranged. It was vital for Metternich to know Alexander's intentions, and he discovered them in advance of the formal discussions through two trusted acquaintances of the tsar, Konrad Bartsch, a Viennese editor, and Jean la Harpe, a French teacher.

Possessing much advance information about his colleagues, Metternich was able to ingratiate himself with them, anticipate their demands, play upon their weaknesses, and maneuver for their acceptance of his plan for a balance of power in Europe. Knowing Alexander's mind, Metternich placated the tsar by paying lip service to the proposal for a "holy alliance," a grandiose idea Alexander entertained for a new era when the nations would be guided by Christian morality.

After the Congress of Vienna, Metternich remained a leading political figure in Austria and in Europe, but his ideas became increasingly obsolete as revolutionary ideas gained ground. Neither diplomacy nor espionage (and he clung to both) could reverse the historical trend. In 1848 a revolution in Austria forced him into exile, and revolutions across the Continent toppled his international system. He spent the next decade lamenting the fate of the reactionary principles on which he had pinned his faith.

FURTHER READING: Harold Nicholson, *The Congress of Vienna* (1946); *Donald Eugene Emerson, *Metternich and the Political Police: Security and Subversion in the Habsburg Monarchy* (1968); Dorothy Gies McGuigan, *Metternich and the Duchess: The Public and Private Lives at the Congress of Vienna* (1975).

Mexican Spy Company (1846-48)   Espionage ring working for the Americans during the Mexican War.

When U.S. General Winfield Scott landed with his troops at Vera Cruz in 1847, during the Mexican War, he found himself on unfamiliar terrain, amid a hostile population, and uncertain about the position, strength, and plans of Antonio de Santa Anna, president of Mexico and commander of the Mexican army. Scott needed reliable military intelligence, and for that reason he ordered Lieutenant-Colonel E. A. Hitchcock to establish a secret service including natives of the Vera Cruz region of Mexico. Hitchcock thereupon organized the Mexican Spy Company.

The company numbered about 100, all Mexicans except for three American officers who commanded them. The real leader was a Mexican weaver named Dominguez, who, after being terrorized and robbed by an officer of the Mexican army, had turned savagely against all authority in his homeland and become a brigand preying on travelers in the Mexican provinces.

From there it was but a step to becoming a spy for the invading Americans. Many other members of the Mexican Spy Company told similar stories. But there were also those who worked simply for Yankee money.

As Scott advanced toward Mexico City, Dominguez led a party of his men into the capital on an undercover operation and sent back to Hitchcock reports on Santa Anna's preparations to fight the invaders. Scott used this information in winning a series of victories, crowned by that at Chapultepec, before occupying Mexico City in the decisive action of the Mexican War.

The Mexican Spy Company disbanded after a few critical months of service. Dominguez had earned so high a reputation for quick judgment and bold action that he was offered, but refused, a commission in the Mexican army. He and his men dropped out of sight.

This group provides a good example of how disaffected or mercenary citizens of a nation may be used by an invading army. Hitchcock and his Mexican Spy Company were comparable to John André and his Loyalist spies during the American Revolution and to Wilhelm Stieber and his French spies during the Franco-Prussian War.

FURTHER READING: Charles W. Elliott, *Winfield Scott: The Soldier and the Man* (1937); *George S. Bryan, *The Spy in America* (1943); Jack Bauer, *The Mexican War* (1974).

Microdot Photograph of a message reduced to microscopic size.

Soon after the invention of photography, the camera became an essential part of espionage because of the ease and speed with which it allowed documents to be copied. Miniature photography came into extensive use during the Franco-Prussian War (1870–71) when pigeons, each carrying dozens of small pieces of film, were released in besieged Paris and flew over the German lines to destinations in unoccupied France.

Technological advances in the twentieth century permitted further diminution of size until, during World War II, the Germans developed the microdot, a technique for reducing a normal-size page to a dot completely unreadable by the naked eye.

The microdot is useful in espionage because it can be hidden as a period ending a sentence of an innocuous message. Anyone alerted to its existence puts the microdot under a microscope and brings the true message into focus.

FURTHER READING: *G. W. W. Stephens, *Microphotography* (1957); Andrew Tully, *The Super Spies: More Secret, More Powerful than the CIA* (1969); David Kahn, *Hitler's Spies: German Military Intelligence in World War II* (1978).

MI5 The British security service, responsible for domestic counterespionage.

MI5 (Military Intelligence 5) is an organization roughly equivalent to America's FBI (Federal Bureau of Investigation). The big difference is that while the FBI can arrest suspects, in Great Britain that function devolves on the Special Branch of Scotland Yard. Otherwise, MI5, as the security service, has the same responsibility as the FBI for identifying spies, keeping records of their activities, and deciding when they should be exposed or arrested.

The head of MI5 is the director, who reports to the home secretary of the British cabinet. The greatest director, Vernon Kell, established MI5 in 1909 and headed it until 1940, showing exceptional skill in handling the spy problem, especially the German spy problem of World War I. Kell worked closely and successfully with Basil Thomson of the Special Branch.

MI5 usually operates in a highly secret manner, but it came to public attention in 1961 when the Portland espionage case broke, revealing that Soviet agent Gordon Lonsdale and a band of Communist spies had stolen classified information for delivery to Moscow. The Portland case created such a scandal that some of the anonymity surrounding MI5 had to be surrendered to mollify its critics and calm the British public.

In 1963 the Profumo scandal compromised MI5. John Profumo, secretary of state for war, was found to have indulged in an affair with a call girl who had a Russian intelligence agent among her admirers. The head of MI5, Sir Roger Hollis, who had known about the affair, was accused of not informing Prime Minister Harold Macmillan in time. Hollis lost his position and Macmillan's Conservative Party lost the next election.

See also HOLLIS, ROGER; KELL, VERNON; LONSDALE, GORDON; PROFUMO, JOHN; SPECIAL BRANCH; THOMSON, BASIL.

FURTHER READING: John Bulloch and Henry Miller, *Spy Ring: The Story of the Naval Secrets Case* (1961); *John Bulloch, *MI5: The Origin and History of the British Counter-Espionage Service* (1961); David Wise and Thomas B. Ross, *The Espionage Establishment* (1967); F. H. Hinsley with E. E. Thomas, C. F. G. Ransom, R. C. Knight, *British Intelligence in the Second World War: Its Influence on Strategy and Operations,* (vol. 1, 1979; vol. 2, 1981).

MI6 The British secret intelligence service responsible for espionage outside British territory.

MI6 (Military Intelligence 6) is the British secret service, but its functions are not those of the American Secret Service, the main duties of which are to guard the president of the United States and those around him. MI6 resembles America's CIA (Central Intelligence Agency), both being charged with the responsibility for spying on enemies and potential enemies of the nation.

The head of the British secret service reports to the foreign secretary of the British cabinet. MI6 has been in operation since 1911, when it was set up by Captain Mansfield Cumming as World War I approached. Assigned to espionage, the organization filled a vacancy in overall British intelligence; its sister service, the already existing MI5 (Military Intelligence 5) handled counterespionage. Cumming used his initial, "C," to identify himself to his subordinates, and the heads of MI6 have called themselves "C" ever since.

MI6 has had a checkered history. It discovered that Gustav Steinhauer was Germany's spymaster for Great Britain during World War I, and its agents reported from inside the kaiser's empire as the conflict raged. But during World War II it suffered the humiliation of having two of its operatives kidnaped by the Germans at Venlo in the Netherlands (1939), and partly as a result of this, the major responsibility for covert operations on the Nazi-occupied Continent was taken from MI6 and given to the newly established Special Operations Executive (SOE) in 1940.

The Cold War created for MI6 the problem of spying against the Soviet Union. MI6 showed great skill in handling Colonel Oleg Penkovskiy of military intelligence at the Center in Moscow, gathering information and documents from him before he was discovered and executed in 1963. Also in 1963, MI6 suffered a shock when one of its most important operatives, Kim Philby, turned up in Moscow boasting that he had spied for the Russians all during his years with the secret service. Philby's defection caused a reorganization at MI6.

See also CUMMING, MANSFIELD; PHILBY, KIM; SPECIAL OPERATIONS EXECUTIVE; STEINHAUER, GUSTAV; VENLO INCIDENT.

FURTHER READING: Michael Foot, *SOE in France: An Account of the Work of the British Special Operations Executive in France, 1940–1944* (1966); Bruce Page, David Leitch, and Phillip Knightley, *The Philby Conspiracy* (1968); *Richard Deacon, *A History of the British Secret*

Service (1969). F. H. Hinsley (with E. E. Thomas, C. F. G. Ransom, and R. C. Knight, *British Intelligence in the Second World War: Its Influence on Strategy and Operations* (vol. 1, 1979; vol. 2, 1981).

Mitchell, Bernon *(1929-   )* American cryptologist and defector from the United States to the Soviet Union.

Born in Eureka, California, Mitchell was the son of a lawyer. He attended high school in Eureka and in 1950 entered the California Institute of Technology, in Pasadena. A year later he joined the United States Navy, was assigned to cryptology, and was sent to Japan to work in the American headquarters at the Yokosuka naval base. There he met and worked with William Martin, who subsequently defected with him.

Leaving the navy, Mitchell in 1954 entered Stanford University, where he studied mathematics. Completing the course, in 1957 he accepted a job with the National Security Agency (NSA), where after special study at George Washington University, he became a cryptologist in 1958, the year Martin obtained the same type of position.

Homosexuality brought them together. In 1958, unknown to their superiors, they joined the Communist Party. In 1959 they traveled without authorization to the Cuba of Fidel Castro.

By then, they were expressing anti-American opinions. Each openly condemned the American U-2 flights over the Soviet Union, of which they were aware through their intelligence work.

In spite of their growing disaffection and the suspicion to which it should have exposed them, Mitchell and Martin remained with the NSA until 1960, when they suddenly vanished together. Turning up in Moscow, they held a news conference at which they attacked American intelligence policies, such as the breaking of the codes of friendly nations.

Since their work at the NSA had shown them that the KGB (Committee for State Security, Russian intelligence) was doing the same things and worse, the motives of Mitchell and Martin remained obscure. Their superiors at the NSA stated that homosexuality lay at the root of their problem.

This naturally raised the question of why the truth about Mitchell and Martin had not been discovered. The result was an overhaul of security and hiring practices at the NSA.

See also MARTIN, WILLIAM.

FURTHER READING: *House Committee on Un-American Activities, *Report on Security Practices in the National Security Agency* (1962); Sanche de Gramont, *The Secret War: The Story of International Espionage since World War II* (1962); David Kahn, *The Codebreakers: The Story of Secret Writing* (1967).

Mole A counterspy working within an intelligence organization and reporting secretly to its rival.

The major intelligence organizations of the world have all had high-ranking officers who proved to be moles. Michael Goleniewski of Polish military intelligence betrayed many Soviet spies to the American CIA (Central Intelligence Agency) before defecting to the United States in 1960. Anatoly Filatov was not so lucky. After reporting to the CIA from the foreign ministry in Moscow for two years, he was caught in 1978.

Moscow's moles of this period included William Whelan, who as a lieutenant-colonel in the U.S. Army was intelligence adviser to the chief of staff. Exposed and sent to jail in 1966, Whelan remains the highest-ranking American military man known to have spied for the Russians in Washington. The North Atlantic Treaty Organization (NATO) unearthed a mole in 1963, Georges Pâques, a French diplomat close to the leaders of the Paris government. The CIA was shaken in 1980 when it learned that one of its officers, David Barnett, had betrayed some thirty American secret agents to the KGB (Committee for State Security, Soviet intelligence).

The case of Yuri Nosenko shows how difficult it sometimes is to determine the true loyalty of an individual. Nosenko reached the United States in 1964, claiming to be a defector from the Soviet Union. He seemed a catch of immense importance because he had been a senior officer in the KGB. However, it was feared at the CIA that he was a plant, dispatched to Washington to spread the word that Lee Harvey Oswald, the assassin of President Kennedy, never had had any connection with the KGB while living in the Soviet Union. Nosenko was eventually cleared by the CIA in 1968.

Whenever an intelligence organization's spies abroad disappear, there is always the fear that they were betrayed by a mole inside the organization. Intelligence officers may reach different conclusions on that point. This happened at the CIA when James Angleton, head of counterespionage, became convinced that moles inside the CIA were mainly responsible for the discovery of America's moles in the Soviet bloc. Director William Colby held that leaks in the spy apparatus and mistakes by spies were the chief factors. The dispute became so intense that in 1974 Colby forced Angleton out of the CIA.

See also COUNTERSPY.

FURTHER READING: Edward Jay Epstein, "The Spy War: Where Are the Moles?" in *The New York Times Magazine* (1980).

Molly Maguires Secret society in the Pennsylvania coalfields during the nineteenth century; the object of espionage by the authorities.

See MCPARLAN, JAMES.

Monat, Pawel (1921-   ) Polish spy in the United States and defector from Communism.

Monat was born in Polish Galicia, an area between Germany and Russia and therefore perennially under foreign control during the course of European history. When he was eighteen, invasion came once again, in the form of a Russian army, following the Nazi-Soviet agreement that permitted German Chancellor Adolf Hitler to start World War II. Galicia fell within the Russian share of Poland, while the Germans took the rest (1939).

Of a middle-class family, Monat had finished his schooling when the Russians arrived. They put him in the Komsomol, the Communist youth organization, where he was subjected to propaganda and trained to be a faithful member of the Communist party. In 1940 he was drafted into the Soviet army, and a year later he saw his first fighting, as the Germans attacked the Soviet Union.

During World War II, Monat served in numerous battles, as the Nazi forces first advanced, then suffered defeat, and finally began to retreat from Russia and from eastern Europe. In 1943 he joined the Polish army formed by the Russians, who maintained strict control of it, and in 1944 he took part in the liberation of Warsaw.

After the war, Monat remained in the military, attended staff college, and in 1950 went into Polish intelligence. Trained in English as well as in general espionage, he was assigned to the American section of the bureau, where he kept watch on the armed forces of the United States. In particular, he drew up performance records during the Korean War (1950–53). Visiting the Communist side of the lines in Korea in 1952, he felt his first disillusionment with Communism because the reality he saw contradicted what he had been told about the technical proficiency of Communism and its human superiority over democracy.

In 1955 Monat came to the United States as military attaché at the Polish embassy in Washington, bringing with him instructions to roam around the country and report to Warsaw on persons and activities of special import to Polish intelligence. At Camp Lejeune, South Carolina, he spied on U.S. Marine landing maneuvers (1955). During the following year he watched rocket launchings at Cape Canaveral, air drills at Patrick Air Force base, and ships entering and leaving the Key West naval base.

Trained in the secrecy of Communist espionage and knowing by experience the iron rigidities of life in Communist countries, Monat was astounded at the ease with which he could travel in the United States. The friendliness of Americans and their freedom from fear impressed him. So did the free press, from which he took data that in the Communist bloc would be closely guarded government secrets.

Still, he remained faithful to the Soviet-dominated Warsaw regime through 1957, the year in which he received orders to set up a system of drops by means of which other Communist agents in the United States could secretly communicate with one another. One such drop was a crack between two shelves in the New York Public Library, where papers could be surreptitiously inserted and just as surreptitiously removed.

Monat returned to Warsaw in 1958. By now utterly disillusioned with Communism, he decided to defect as soon as he could. His chance came in 1959, when he persuaded his superiors in Polish intelligence to let him make a tour of inspection through the Communist bloc to check up on Polish military attachés. Allowed to go to Vienna to begin his tour, he went to the American Embassy and asked for political asylum. Returning to the United States, he disappeared into anonymity to protect himself from Communist revenge.

FURTHER READING: *Pawel Monat with John Dille, *Spy in the U. S.* (1961); Richard F. Staar, *Communist Regimes in Eastern Europe* (1971).

Montgaillard, Comte de *(1761-1835)* French adventurer and secret agent for whichever side seemed to be winning during the French Revolution and the Napoleonic era.

Montgaillard gave himself the title he used. His original name was Maurice Rocques, of an undistinguished family living in Languedoc. He joined the army under his assumed name, served in Martinique, returned to France, left the army, and moved in high circles of church and state, to which he gained entrance through a persuasive manner and a smooth tongue.

When the French Revolution began in 1789, Montgaillard, not realizing how successful it would be, took the royalist side, becoming a secret agent of King Louis XVI. He joined the flight of the royalists from France and in 1793 was condemned as an émigré by the revolutionaries in Paris.

He finally saw that the revolution could not be undone, and judging that there might be a place in it for him, Montgaillard made overtures to the new leader of the revolution, Maximilien de Robespierre. He returned to France in 1794, during Robespierre's reign of terror, and represented Robespierre in a mission to Austrian military headquarters to see if the allied powers would come to terms with the French Revolution.

The answer was negative. Montgaillard, fearing for his head if he returned to Paris, went to England. In London he passed as a faithful royalist, being convincing enough in this pose to be accorded an interview with Prime Minister William Pitt. In 1795 Montgaillard was back on the Continent at the headquarters on the Rhine of Louis Joseph de Bourbon, prince de Condé, a leading royalist who maintained his own army to fight the French republic.

Montgaillard supported an attempt by Condé to corrupt General Charles Pichegru, who had fought for the revolution until its violence disillusioned him. Unwilling to risk his own head, Montgaillard drew Louis Fauche-Borel, another royalist conspirator, into the scheme. Condé sent Fauche-Borel to see Pichegru, who, however, was not ready to move openly against the revolution. Fauche-Borel had both failed in the mission and acted independently of Montgaillard, who in consequence denounced him to the revolutionaries as a royalist spy.

Montgaillard moved about on the Continent, met the royalist secret agent Louis de Launai, comte d'Antraigues, in Venice, returned to Condé's head-quarters, and blackmailed the prince by threatening to publish some incriminating documents. Condé paid the blackmail.

Meanwhile, as the royalists languished in exile with no certainty of ever returning to France, Montgaillard decided to abandon them. While the five-man Directory governed France (1795–99) after the overthrow of Robespierre, Montgaillard turned up in Paris proclaiming his devotion to the principles of the revolution. He served as a government spy against the royalists, an activity he continued following Napoleon's rise to power in 1799. Montgaillard then worked for spymaster Joseph Fouché, minister of police under Napoleon.

Montgaillard's main service to the Bonapartist cause was a pamphlet he produced in 1804 denouncing the royalism of Pichegru. The general had been deported to French Guiana in 1797 for opposing the Directory. Escaping in 1798, he conspired with royalists in England and Germany before slipping covertly into France in 1804 to lead a plot against Napoleon, who was now emperor of France. Pichegru was arrested by Fouché's agents. Napoleon wanted Pichegru discredited, and Montgaillard, who in 1795 had tried to get Pichegru to come over to the active royalists, now castigated him for meditating treason to the revolution at that time. Soon after the pamphlet appeared, Pichegru either committed suicide or was murdered in his cell.

The fall of Napoleon and the restoration of the Bourbons to the throne of France caused Montgaillard to declare once more for royalism (1814). He wangled (or possibly blackmailed) a pension from King Louis XVIII, but this ended when the revolution of 1830 drove the Bourbons permanently from the throne. Montgaillard had no chance to profit this time, for no one trusted him any longer. He lived the rest of his days in misery after having over four decades shifted his allegiance enough times to rival the Vicar of Bray.

See also D'ANTRAIGUES, COMTE; FAUCHE-BOREL, LOUIS.

FURTHER READING: *John Hall, *General Pichegru's Treason* (1915); G. Lenôtre, *Two Royalist Spies of the French Revolution* (1924), has an account of Montgaillard's career as faithless undercover agent; Leo Gershoy, *The French Revolution and Napoleon* (1964), gives the historical background of Montgaillard's activities.

Moody, James *(1744-1809)*   American Loyalist, marauder, and spy for the British during the American War of Independence.

Moody, who was born in New Jersey, owned a farm there in the period of growing hostility between the colonies and the mother country. Although a Loyalist by conviction, he did not throw his support to the British in 1775 after the battle of Lexington, nor did the Declaration of Independence in 1776 prompt him to come out openly in favor of the crown. But in 1777, Moody refused to swear allegiance to the state of New Jersey, and this made him a marked man, hated by his Patriot neighbors and kept under surveillance by the state authorities.

Abandoning his farm, he escaped to the British lines and volunteered to serve in a brigade formed by another New Jersey Loyalist, Cortlandt Skinner, who planned operations against the rebels from his headquarters on Staten Island. Moody recruited Loyalists in New Jersey during 1777, an activity that caused the state authorities to confiscate and sell his property.

In 1778 Moody led a daring expedition into northern New York, far behind the American lines, to search for Colonel John Butler, a Tory frontier fighter with whom the British command in Philadelphia had lost communication. Moody found Butler and returned with a report that Butler was still in the field conducting hit-and-run attacks on Patriot towns, outposts, and military positions.

During the next year, Moody led raids throughout New Jersey, capturing Patriot officials, burning supply dumps, and driving off livestock. He also undertook spy missions, in one of which he slipped into General George Washington's camp to gather information. Moody's most dramatic undercover assignment, in 1780, was to kidnap Governor William Livingston of New Jersey, an attempt that failed because one of Moody's men talked about the mission after being captured by Patriots.

A statewide search for Moody began, and he was finally run to earth at Englishtown. Imprisoned, he escaped during a cloudburst, reached the security of the British lines, and resumed his marauding career. He made a habit of laying traps for American mail couriers in New Jersey and New York, at one point seizing dispatches from Washington to Jean Baptiste de Vimeur, comte de Rochambeau, commander of the French army in America. A plan by Moody to enter Philadelphia and make off with the official papers of the Continental Congress failed because the Americans got wind of it.

Moody was too notorious a figure to remain in America after Yorktown (1781). He went to London in 1782, where he wrote an account of his exploits. In 1784 he delivered an emotional and effective appeal to the British government for recompense as a Loyalist who had lost everything because of his devotion to the crown. The government made him an award, part of which was a grant of land in Nova Scotia, where he farmed until his death.

FURTHER READING: °Charles I. Bushnell (ed.), *Narrative of the Exertions of Lieut. Jas. Moody* (1865); Edward A. Jones, *Loyalists of New Jersey* (1927); John Bakeless, *Turncoats, Traitors, and Heroes* (1959), has an account of Moody.

Moravec, Frantisek *(1895-1966)*   Czech intelligence officer and defector from the Soviet bloc to the west.

Moravec was born near Prague when Bohemia was a province of the Austro-Hungarian empire. He entered Prague University in 1914, only to have his education interrupted by World War I (1914–18). Entering the Czech army in 1914 and assigned to the eastern front against the Russians in 1915, Moravec, like many other Czech soldiers preferring the Russians to the Austrians, went over to the enemy. He saw service with the forces of the tsar before the Russian Revolution of 1917 left him stranded with the Czech Legion in Russia. The Czechs, refusing to surrender to the Communists after their victory, seized the Trans-Siberian Railway and got out by way of Vladivostok.

Returning to Prague, Moravec found himself a citizen of a new nation, Czechoslovakia, which rose out of the postwar turmoil in central Europe. In 1928 he graduated from the military college in Prague, gained his commission, and went into military intelligence. The position of Czechoslovakia between Communist Russia and (from 1933) Nazi Germany tempted both tyrannies to use spies and underground movements against the Prague regime. As a result, Moravec and his colleagues in intelligence were compelled to concentrate most of their efforts on counterespionage. Moravec worked under difficult conditions, since Prague could not afford to antagonize either Moscow or Berlin.

He walked a narrow line until 1938, when German Chancellor Adolf Hitler, given a free hand by Britain and France, dismembered Czechoslovakia, leaving the free remnant only the ghost of a nation. Moravec, like his government, had no scope for action because of German pressure. He suffered the opposite pressure after World War II (1939–45), when the Russians were in control of Czechoslovakia. The 1948 coup by Russian undercover agents, who murdered Jan Masaryk, the Czech president, and installed a puppet regime to run the country, came as a surprise to Moravec, even though he was by then the director of military intelligence. The fact that he could be hoodwinked by the Russians and the iron control they fastened on Czechoslovakia, made him realize his personal danger. Seizing an opportunity to get out, he defected to the west, received political asylum in the United States, and revealed what he knew of the Russians and their covert operation that had destroyed freedom in Czechoslovakia.

FURTHER READING: Frantisek Moravec, *Master of Spies: The Memoirs of General Frantisek Moravec* (1975).

Morros, Boris *(1895-1963)*   American motion picture producer, spy for the Soviet Union, and counterspy for the United States.

Morros was born into a Russian-Jewish family of St. Petersburg (now called Leningrad). His father was a teacher and his mother a singer, so that he received a good education that included musical training. Mastering the cello, he appeared in public concerts as a boy and even played before the tsar. His musical career continued until the Russian Revolution (1917). In 1922 Morros left Russia for the United States, where he resumed his musical career and became associated with motion pictures. He joined Paramount in 1930 and five years later was the company's musical director in Hollywood.

Morros moved into the orbit of Soviet espionage because of his desire to visit Leningrad to see his parents. The Russians both allowed him to do this (1934) and threatened to stop him in the future if he refused to work for them. By 1936 he was permitting Communist agents to pose as Paramount talent scouts in Nazi Germany, against which Morros felt a bitter antipathy because of its anti-Semitism. He founded his own motion-picture company in 1939, the year in which Adolf Hitler started World War II.

Vassili Zubilin, the head of the NKVD (People's Commissariat for Internal Affairs, 1934–46; Soviet intelligence) in the United States, recruited Morros for espionage assignments in 1942. Zubilin, responsible for organizing a spy network, ordered Morros to cooperate with Alfred and Martha Dodd Stern, two prominent Americans. Stern was a wealthy businessman. His wife was the daughter of William E. Dodd, a former American ambassador to Hitler's Germany. She left Berlin a committed anti-Nazi, and a visit to the Soviet Union in 1938 made her a committed Communist. Critical of American democracy, the Sterns were known backers of Communist causes. Morros began to work with them in 1943.

A year later he met Jack Soble, who replaced Zubilin at the head of the network. Morros later dealt with Soble's brother, Robert Soblen (the pair were Lithuanian Jews who had adopted slightly different versions of the family name after leaving the Soviet Union). Jacob Albam joined the ring, as did George and Jane Zlatovsky.

The purpose of the ring was to protect Soviet spies through ostensibly innocent American organizations (e.g., Morros's company), to act as couriers, and to transmit secret information to Moscow. The members achieved little of any practical value, but worry and patriotism made Morros feel that the Soviet conspiracy had to be stopped. In 1947 he went to agents of the FBI (Federal Bureau of Investigation) in Los Angeles, confessed he had been a spy for the Soviet Union, and agreed to become a counterspy for the United States. He made several trips to Europe to meet the Zlatovskys in Paris and other Soviet spies in Vienna, Geneva, and Belgrade. In 1950 he went to Moscow, where he was interrogated and approved by his superiors in Soviet intelligence.

The death of Joseph Stalin, the Russian dictator, in 1953, and the execution of Lavrenti Beria, head of the Soviet secret police, drove Soble into a panic because he had been one of Beria's spymasters. Soble fled to Canada, where Morros, on FBI instructions, sought him out in 1954 and tried unsuccessfully to persuade him to return. Soble later came back to the United States because he needed money, but his spy ring was in a shambles, and in 1957 he was arrested along with Albam. All the members of the network were indicted. The Zlatovskys, however, were safe in Paris, and the Sterns, having fled to Mexico, continued on to Prague in Soviet-controlled eastern Europe. Soblen remained at large until 1960.

Morros appeared in court as a witness against the accused. Soble, his wife, and Albam received prison sentences. Soblen appealed to the Supreme Court, his appeal was rejected, and he fled to Israel in 1962. The Israeli authorities, charging that he had arrived with a false passport, put him on a plane bound for New York, but he committed suicide in London.

An echo of these old events sounded in 1979. The Justice Department asked a district court in New York to dismiss the charges against Alfred and Martha Dodd Stern because all of the witnesses who could testify against them, including Morros, had died. The judge ruled in favor of the dismissal. The Sterns, who in 1957 had been indicted for conspiracy to steal secret American information for the Soviet Union, were free to return to the United States after twenty-two years of exile.

FURTHER READING: *Boris Morros (as told to Charles Samuels), *My Ten Years as a Counterspy* (1959); Norman Lucas, *The Great Spy Ring* (1966).

Mossad   The main department of Israeli intelligence.

The word "mossad" means "institution" in Hebrew, and the full title of the Israeli organization is Central Institution for Intelligence and Special Assignments. The Mossad, handling external espionage, is roughly the equivalent of America's CIA (Central Intelligence Agency), a position it has held since 1951, when Prime Minister David Ben-Gurion reorganized Israeli intelligence and brought order into the various espionage, counterespionage, sabotage, and assassination groups that had existed since before independence. Three major agencies emerged from the reshuffling—the Mossad, Shin Beth (counterespionage), and military intelligence.

The Mossad, however, has a higher place in the Israeli government than the CIA does in the government of the United States. The Mossad often deals with other nations directly, especially those with which Israel has no diplomatic relations, and the head of the organization reports to the prime minister.

The best-known department of the Mossad is Special Operations, whose secret agents have conducted a fierce undercover campaign against enemies of Israel and fugitives who have committed crimes against the Jewish people.

In 1960 agents of the Mossad, led by Isser Harel, kidnapped Adolf Eichmann in Argentina and covertly transported him to Israel. Eichmann stood trial and was executed as a former Nazi who had been responsible for the murder of thousands of Jews at Auschwitz, the worst of the Nazi death camps, during World War II.

In 1972 Israeli agents took up the trail of the Arab terrorists who had murdered most of the Israeli team at the Olympics in West Germany. As a result, one Arab leader was blown up in his car in Beirut, another was shot to death in Rome, and a third was killed in Paris by an explosive device attached to his phone.

In 1976 agents of the Mossad staged the dramatic rescue of hostages being held at Entebbe, Uganda, after the hijacking of an Israeli plane. The Israeli rescue party flew into Entebbe, attacked the airport, herded the captives into the rescue plane, and flew out unscathed.

The Mossad has had its failures. Some of its agents have been killed by those of its principal rival, the intelligence department of the Palestine Liberation Organization. Occasionally, the Mossad has attacked the wrong person. This happened most notoriously in 1973 at Lillehammer, Norway, when Mossad agents murdered a Moroccan waiter in the mistaken belief that he was a PLO leader.

On balance, the Mossad is ranked by espionage experts among the half-dozen best intelligence organizations in the world.

See also HAREL, ISSER.

FURTHER READING: Christopher Dobson, *Black September: Its Short, Violent History* (1973), concerns the massacre of the Israeli Olympic team; David Timmin (with Dag Christensen), *Hit Team* (1976); *Dennis Eisenberg, Uri Dan, and Eli Landau, *The Mossad, Israel's Secret Intelligence Service: Inside Stories* (1978); Stewart Steven, *The Spymasters of Israel* (1980).

Moulin, Jean *(1898-1943)* French public official and spymaster during World War II.

The son of a scholar and educator of Béziers in the south of France, Moulin attended the schools of Béziers before entering the University of Montpellier in 1917. He served in the French army during 1918 and 1919, returned to the university, took a law degree (1921), and obtained a post in the local government of French Savoy (1922). Rising through the administrative system, he was prefect of Chartres when World War II broke out in 1939.

The collapse of France in 1940 led Moulin to attempt suicide rather than surrender to the victorious Germans. Failing in the attempt, he decided to use his position to undermine German control of the Chartres region, a decision that led to his removal from office in 1941 by the Vichy government of Marshal Philippe Pétain, who took orders from the Germans. Moulin then left France secretly, made his way to London, and offered his services to General Charles de Gaulle, leader of the Free French. De Gaulle and his director of intelligence, Colonel André Dewavrin, impressed with Moulin, sent him back to France to organize the principal factions of the French resistance into a unified force under the Gaullist banner.

Moulin landed by parachute near Arles (1942). A series of clandestine meetings around France (in Marseilles, Lyons, Avignon, and Paris) led to the coalescence of underground groups into the National Council of the Resistance (1943). Known as "Max," Moulin persuaded leaders of the resistance to form interconnected secret cells, to continue hit-and-run tactics against the Germans, and to prepare for overt action when the armies of the Allies returned to France. The success of this effort made Moulin one of the outstanding figures of the French resistance.

Moulin used an art gallery in Nice as a cover, which allowed him to move around France without suspicion. In 1943, however, following another secret trip from France to London and back, he was betrayed by one of his own men to the German secret police, the Gestapo. His captors tortured him barbarously in an effort to make him reveal the names of underground leaders. He refused to talk, and they executed him. The resistance continued along the lines Moulin had laid down, harassed the German occupation forces until 1944, and then joined the Allied armed forces following the invasion of France across the English Channel. After the war, Moulin was accorded a tomb in the Panthéon in Paris.

See also DEWAVRIN, ANDRÉ.

FURTHER READING: *Eric Piquet-Wicks, *Four in the Shadows* (1957), presents Moulin as one of the four; Milton Dank, *The French against the French: Collaboration and Resistance* (1974); David Schoenbrun, *Soldiers of the Night: The Story of the French Resistance* (1980).

Munday, Anthony (1560-1633)   English actor, dramatist, and government spy during the Elizabethan era.

The son of a London bookseller, Munday abandoned the family business in the 1570s to go on the stage. He began to write plays and poetry, the start of a career that made him a popular success in print and in the theater.

Munday became a spy at about the same time. He entered the service of Queen Elizabeth's great spymaster, Francis Walsingham, at a time when Elizabeth was holding Queen Mary of Scotland as her prisoner. Since Mary was a Catholic and Elizabeth a Protestant, certain English Catholics plotted to replace Elizabeth with Mary on the English throne, to which Mary had a claim because she belonged to the same royal line as Elizabeth and because Elizabeth was childless.

In 1578 Walsingham sent Munday to Rome as a secret agent. Munday spied on the English Catholics who either lived in Rome or passed through the Eternal City. Using an alias and pretending to be a Catholic, Munday gained entrance to the English College, where students were prepared for a return to England and an attempt to reconvert their homeland to the Catholic faith. He did so well in his studies that he became one of the group called "the Pope's scholars."

Munday all the while was sending secret reports to Walsingham in London. He named the Englishmen on the faculty at the English College and the students who would be going covertly to England as missionaries. He described the Catholic plans as he heard them and the financial and military backing the conspirators hoped to obtain from the leading Catholic powers, France and Spain.

Thus forewarned, Walsingham was able to have most of the men of the English College in Rome seized, imprisoned, and executed after they landed in England. Returning to London, perhaps in fear of being exposed in Rome, Munday took part in the hunt for these undercover missionaries during the years 1581 and 1582. He was especially valuable in this type of counterespionage because he knew many of the victims by sight.

In 1582 Munday wrote an account of his stay at the English College. In 1586 he gained a place at Elizabeth's court. He wrote voluminously for the stage thereafter and is thought to have had some influence on Shakespeare.

See also WALSINGHAM, FRANCIS.

FURTHER READING: *Celeste Turner, *Anthony Munday* (1928); A. L. Rowse, *The English Renaissance* (1974), gives the historical and cultural background in which Munday worked.

Munsinger Affair (1960-66)   Canadian sex-and-spy scandal involving members of the government.

The scandal derived its title from Gerda Munsinger, a German who had been born in Königsberg (now Kaliningrad in the USSR). Her family name was Heseler. Her father, a member of the Communist party, taught her the ideology of Marxism-Leninism, and in 1947 she became a spy for the Soviet Union, operating in West Germany. In 1952 she applied for a Canadian visa, only to be turned down on the basis of a report on her activities by the Royal Canadian Mounted Police (RCMP), which termed her a spy, prostitute, thief, and smuggler.

That same year she married a sergeant in the U.S. Army, Michael Munsinger. He could not gain her admission to the United States, and two years later they were divorced. However, she kept her married name, evidently because she was too notorious under her maiden name. In 1955 Gerda Munsinger managed to slip into Canada. There she became erotically involved with members of the government headed by Conservative Prime Minister John Diefenbaker. The highest ranking of her catches was Pierre Sevigny, the associate minister for national defence. In 1960 Sevigny sponsored her when she applied for Canadian citizenship.

This application brought her again to the attention of the RCMP, which reported to the prime minister that she was a security risk. Faced with expulsion, Gerda Munsinger went to East Germany in 1961. Sevigny resigned from the government in 1963, the year in which Diefenbaker lost a national election to Liberal Lester Pearson, who remained in office until 1967. Pearson had to deal with a spy for the Soviet Union named Victor Spencer. In 1966 Spencer was dismissed from his job with the post office and deprived of his pension. The Conservatives attacked the government for its handling of the case. The Liberals counterattacked by referring to Gerda Munsinger. Pearson ordered a commission to investigate the Munsinger affair, the facts became public, and the scandal resulted.

The commission declared that Sevigny had been a security risk even though no evidence was found that he had ever passed classified information to the Communist spy. It termed Diefenbaker "imprudent" for allowing Sevigny to remain in office despite the RCMP description of her activities. A number of reputations were damaged by the report, but the final verdict was that no one had been lured into becoming an unwitting espionage agent for the Soviet Union.

See also ROYAL CANADIAN MOUNTED POLICE.

FURTHER READING: *°Report of the Commission of Inquiry into Matters relating to One Gerda Munsinger* (1966); Nora and William Kelly, *The Royal Canadian Mounted Police: A Century of History, 1873–1973* (1973); Bruce Thordarson, *Lester Pearson: Diplomat and Politician* (1974).

MVD (1946-54) The fifth name given to the Soviet intelligence system now known as the KGB.

See KGB.

National Security Agency   The organization responsible for the communications systems of the United States government.

Established in 1952 within the Defense Department, the National Security Agency (NSA) reflects the highly sophisticated nature of communications in the modern world—a world of computers, space satellites, and electronic devices of extreme sensitivity.

When World War II began in 1939, the United States had a welter of cryptological services working largely in isolation from one another. The shattering Japanese attack on Pearl Harbor in 1941 made apparent the need for closer cooperation, and in 1949 the Armed Forces Security Agency unified the communications departments of the Army, Navy, and Air Force. This organization proved so successful that the government decided to bring all its cryptological bureaus and divisions under one tent.

The three armed services, the CIA (Central Intelligence Agency), the FBI (Federal Bureau of Investigation), and other bodies involved in the making and breaking of codes and ciphers thus began to cooperate through the NSA, which was housed in a new building in Fort Meade, Maryland.

The director of the NSA reports to an assistant secretary of defense, who in turn reports to the secretary of defense. Since the secretary of defense sits on the National Security Council, there is a direct line of communication from the NSA to the President of the United States.

The NSA is an enormous organization employing thousands of people at home and abroad. It is also one of the least known, because its activities are covered by a veil of secrecy. Unlike the CIA, it almost never comes to public attention.

One big scandal, however, has rocked the NSA. Two of its cryptologists, Bernon Mitchell and William Martin, defected to the Soviet Union in 1960 and revealed what they knew to the Russians, which forced an overhaul of security measures and hiring practices at Fort Meade.

FURTHER READING: *House Committee on Un-American Activities, *Report on Security Practices in the National Security Agency* (1962); David Kahn, *The Codebreakers: The Story of Secret Writing* (1967); *United States Government Organization Manual* (current ed.).

Nazi Buzz Bombs *(1943-44)*   The first missiles used in warfare and the objects of an international espionage campaign.

The buzz bomb (the V-1 of the German missile system) was an unmanned airplane driven by jet propulsion and carrying an explosive warhead. It had a range of over 100 miles, which made it an effective weapon to use against London from the coast of German-occupied France during World War II (1939–45).

The Germans maintained tight security over the development of the V-1. Then, in 1943, a missile being tested flew off course from its proving ground in Germany and landed on Bornholm, a Danish island in the Baltic Sea. A Danish officer photographed and sketched the debris. Since Denmark was occupied by the Germans, the Danes covertly transmitted this material to London, where it was studied by British scientists.

More information came from the Alliance International Service, a spy network made up of members of the French resistance. Marie-Madeleine Fourcade, the head of the network, directed agents who used the names of animals for cover names, from which her organization became known as "Noah's Ark." After the German victory over France in 1940, this network developed into one of the most active in France. The V-1 information reached Fourcade from Jeanne Rousseau, a member of a Paris underground network, who discovered that the Germans were testing flying bombs at Peenemünde and Zempin and that the launch sites would be on the Channel coast when the weapons became operational. Rousseau wrote a detailed and accurate report, which Fourcade sent secretly to London.

Two more French spies, Michel Hollard and André Comps, penetrated the launch-site system on the coast. They brought out information on the strange new installations, even noting that a catapult they saw was aimed in the direction of London. These facts, too, went to the British capital for study.

The Royal Air Force (RAF) began flying reconnaissance missions over the suspect areas of France and Germany. One plane brought back a photograph from Peenemünde in which intelligence officer Constance Babington-Smith identified a V-1 on its launch pad. The buzz bombs were clearly operational. Photos from the French coast showed the launch pads near completion.

The Germans were so far ahead that they were able to hurl their buzz bombs at London during the period 1943 to 1944. The bombs caused many casualties and much damage, in spite of heavy bombing of Peenemünde and the launch sites by British and American bombers. The threat ceased only after D-Day (June 6, 1944) when the Allies were able to overrun the sites.

By then, the Germans had developed their V-2 rocket, which had a history oddly similar to that of the V-1. A rocket veered away and landed in Sweden, from which information reached London about this new weapon. Spies reported that Peenemünde was also the proving ground. The RAF brought back photos of V-2s on their pads. Great bombing raids were mounted from British air bases. It all ended when the Russians captured Peenemünde in 1945.

See also INTELLIGENCE, SCIENTIFIC.

FURTHER READING: Constance Babington-Smith, *Air Spy: The Story of Photo Intelligence in World War II* (1957); George Martelli and Michel Hollard, *The Man Who Saved London: The Story of Michel Hollard* (1961); Marie-Madeleine Fourcade, *Noah's Ark* (1974); *R. V. Jones, *The Wizard War* (1978).

Nazi Saboteurs *(1942)*   Eight German undercover agents who landed surreptitiously in the United States from submarines during World War II.

In 1942, the year of Germany's greatest strength in the Atlantic during World War II, Abwehr II, the sabotage department of German military intelligence, mounted a campaign against the United States. The program was run by Lieutenant Walter Kappe, who had spent thirteen years in America and who therefore knew his enemy from personal experience.

Kappe chose his undercover agents from a list of repatriated German-Americans, ending up with two groups of four, each group to be transported across the Atlantic by submarine. George Dasch headed the group that included Ernest Burger, Richard Quirin, and Heinrich Heinck. Edward Kerling headed the group that included Hermann Neubauer, Werner Thiel, and Herbert Haupt.

Their two submarines made the voyage to America successfully, landing the Dasch group at Amagansett, on Long Island, not far from Montauk Point, and the Kerling group near St. Augustine, Florida. The eight carried guns, explosives, American dollars, and fake identification papers. Their orders were to slip inland and carry out sabotage operations—blowing up bridges, setting fire to factories, disrupting railroad lines, and doing whatever else they could to slow down America's contribution to the war.

The Nazi saboteurs did little more than get ashore, because Dasch and Burger betrayed the mission to the American authorities, and within a few days the other six were picked up by agents of the FBI (Federal Bureau of Investigation).

All eight went on trial and were convicted of being spies. Six were executed. Dasch and Burger saved their lives by turning state's evidence. They went to jail for the duration of the war and then were deported to Germany.

See also DASCH, GEORGE.

FURTHER READING: Louis de Jong, *The German Fifth Column in the Second World War* (1956); Charles Wighton and Gunter Peis, *Hitler's Spies and Saboteurs: Based on the Secret Service War Diary of General Lahousen* (1958); *Eugene Rachlis, *They Came to Kill: The Story of the Eight Nazi Saboteurs in America* (1961).

Network A spy ring made up of members related directly or indirectly through a common aim and a common leader.

A network is like a spider web in which the leader is the "spider," the cells are the "nodes" in the web, and cut-outs and couriers are the "strands" of the web. The figure of speech can be pushed further because, just as to touch any part of a spider web is to alert the spider, just so, should any agent be caught or defect, the leader will be alerted at once through channels of information he has developed, unless the network has been torn apart by a disaster, such as a mass roundup of its members.

A cell, the lowest unit of the network (except for the single agent), is composed of a small number of agents who receive assignments for which they are qualified. Specialists in bugging and photography work in cells, and the nature of their work subjects them to the danger of being caught red-handed. Hence, they almost never know about other cells, much less about the higher levels of the organization, and least of all about the leader. Because of this calculated ignorance, they cannot reveal anything fatal to anyone but themselves and such minor figures as couriers and lesser cut-outs.

The members of a network do not have to be inspired by the same motive. Some may do their spying for money, others for the sake of an ideology, still others out of desire for revenge. What unites them is the aim set by the leader of the network, who receives their information and decides how to use it.

See also COURIER; CUT-OUT.

FURTHER READING: *Ladislas Farago, *War of Wits: The Anatomy of Espionage* (1954), has a chapter on the organization of networks; U.S. Department of Defense, Joint Chiefs of Staff Publication No. 1, *Dictionary of Military and Associated Terms* (1972).

Nicolai, Walther (1873-1934) Director of German military intelligence during World War I.

Nicolai did not belong to the Prussian Junker (aristocratic) class that dominated the German armed forces in the nineteenth century, and he had to rise through sheer ability after winning his commission in the German army. He made his mark in 1896 when assigned to duties in Russia overtly as an observer of the tsar's armed forces and covertly as a spy. His report earned him promotion to captain and an appointment to the War Academy in Berlin in 1901, from which, on his graduation in 1904, he went back to espionage.

Nicolai spent more time in Russia before establishing an intelligence headquarters in Koenigsberg (Kaliningrad in the Soviet Union since World War II). Returning to the general staff in 1913 with the rank of lieutenant colonel, he became director of military intelligence (the Abwehr), the most famous to hold that post until Admiral Wilhelm Canaris in World War II.

Almost at once, Nicolai's organization was shaken by an espionage scandal in Austria, where it came to light that the chief of staff of the Austro-Hungarian command in Prague, Colonel Alfred Redl, was a double agent in the pay of the Russians. Austria was Germany's closest ally, the two nations periodically exchanged military information, and Nicolai had conferred with Redl on intelligence matters only four years earlier. The Redl affair forced the Germans as well as the Austrians to revamp their intelligence and their military strategy because their possible enemy, Russia, knew so much about both.

Nicolai repaired the damage and put together a number of successful spy networks, the members of which remain largely unknown. He made some use of the international adventurer Isaac Trebitsch Lincoln; in 1913 Nicolai used his influence to have Lincoln released by the Bulgarians, who had imprisoned him on a charge of being a double agent for the Turks.

World War I put Nicolai's department to its greatest test. Before it ended, he had hundreds of secret agents at work in France, Belgium, and Russia. Much of the information he received and systematized became part of the German planning that produced victories on the western front and in the east.

The German failure in Britain was not Nicolai's fault. The kaiser's naval intelligence had responsibility for the British Isles because of the Germans' concern about the British navy, and the man in charge was the bumbling Gustav Steinhauer, whose indiscretions enabled the British to track down his agents and jail most of them in 1914.

The most interesting of Nicolai's agents never went out on spy missions. This was a woman, Elsbeth Schragmüller, who in 1914 wrote to him asking for an assignment, an appeal to which he responded by giving her a place in the German censorship system in occupied Belgium. She did well enough to be assigned as a teacher to an espionage training school in Antwerp, and her graduates gave the Allies many problems before the war ended.

The revolution that erupted in defeated Germany ended Nicolai's espionage career and forced him out of the military into retirement (1919), along with many of the kaiser's officers. Nicolai agreed with those Germans who, claiming that Germany had been betrayed rather than defeated in World War I, called for a national policy of revival at home and revenge on the Allies. He advocated cooperation with the Communist regime in Russia in order to rebuild the German armed forces.

He saw in Adolf Hitler, the German leader who would overturn (as Hitler eventually did) the Treaty of Versailles. Nicolai, however, was never a Nazi, and he is said to have been one of the early victims of the Nazis.

See also SCHRAGMÜLLER, ELSBETH; STEINHAUER, GUSTAV.

FURTHER READING: *Walther Nicolai, *The German Secret Service* (1924); Armgaard Karl Graves, *The Secrets of the German War Office* (1914); Michael H. Cochran, *Germany Not Guilty in 1914* (1972), presents the historical background to Nicolai's career in espionage, largely agreeing with him that Germany was not responsible for the outbreak of World War I.

NKVD *(1934-46)* The fourth name given to the Soviet intelligence system now known as the KGB.
  See KGB.

North Pole *(1942-43)* Deception campaign in Holland run by German counterespionage during World War II.

In 1942, German counterespionage agents arrested Hubert Lauwers, a Dutch radio operator who had been sending clandestine messages to London from The Hague. Lauwers belonged to the Special Operations Executive (SOE), the underground organization directed from Britain with instructions to organize resistance to the Germans in the occupied nations of Europe. The capture of Lauwers and the rest of his spy ring occurred so quickly that the British did not become aware of it, a fact that enabled Major H. J. Giskes, head of German counterespionage in Holland, to arrange a "playback" campaign, which he called Operation North Pole.

Lauwers agreed to continue broadcasting to London under Giskes' direction. The Dutch operator surreptitiously inserted warning signals into the messages, but the British, failing to notice the warnings, took the messages seriously. The SOE, thinking that their underground in Holland was flourishing, dropped agents and more supplies by night at agreed-upon points. The parachutes floated down into the hands of the waiting Germans.

The radio in The Hague reported that the operation had been a success, that the newly arrived agents had joined the underground, and that the supplies were being used for sabotage. This set the pattern for a deception campaign in which the Germans instructed the British what to do, and the British did it. The SOE apparatus in Holland was thus under the control of the enemy against which it was supposed to be working. The Germans captured more than fifty agents, thousands of weapons, and thousands of pounds of explosives before Operation North Pole came to an end.

In 1943 two British agents imprisoned in Holland managed to escape. Crossing occupied France, they reached neutral Spain and made their way to London, where they broke the dismal truth to their superiors at SOE headquarters. There were no more British triumphs in Holland until the Allied invasion of the Continent in 1944.

See also GISKES, H. J.; PLAYBACK SYSTEM; SPECIAL OPERATIONS EXECUTIVE.

FURTHER READING: *H. J. Giskes, *London Calling North Pole* (1953); Pieter Dourlein, *Inside North Pole: A Secret Agent's Story* (1954); Phillipe Garnier-Raymond, *The Tangled Web* (1968).

Norwegian Heavy Water *(1942-43)* A covert operation designed to prevent Nazi scientists from building an atomic bomb.

When the Germans invaded and occupied Norway in 1940 during World War II (1939–45), they gained control of Norsk Hydro, an installation at Vemork in the mountains to the west of Oslo that specialized in the production of heavy water. Two years later Berlin demanded a vast increase in production at Norsk Hydro. The Allies were alarmed because of the importance of heavy water in nuclear research, and the fear grew that Nazi scientists might be developing an atomic bomb.

London therefore decided that a sabotage assault should be mounted against Norsk Hydro. The Special Operations Executive (SOE), charged with planning and carrying out covert operations on the Continent in cooperation with undercover groups fighting the Nazis, found a number of Norwegian refugees willing to undertake this mission. The SOE built a model of Norsk Hydro from information provided by a Norwegian chemist who had worked there. The men on the covert operation learned from the model how to move around inside the installation.

A spy dropped by parachute into the Vemork area radioed back to London reports on German security at the target of the attack. Four other men parachuted in to join the first; they were the covering party. The sabotage party failed in an attempt involving the use of gliders, which crashed in the mountains. Then, early in 1943 another parachute landing succeeded under the leadership of Knut Haukelid. Using skis to cross the mountains in the snow, the Norwegians reached Vemork, slipped into Norsk Hydro, planted explosives in the basement, and escaped just before the blast that tore apart the heavy-water apparatus.

The Germans repaired the damage, but after Allied bombing raids they decided to move the Norwegian installation to Germany. Knowing that their route would include a ferry crossing a lake to a railhead, Haukelid planned and led another attack. Slipping into Norway, he and a companion boarded the ferry when it was about to sail, with drums of heavy water for a cargo. The two saboteurs concealed explosives under boards in the bow and went ashore. The ferry blew up in the middle of the lake, carrying the drums of heavy water to the bottom.

It was discovered after the war that Nazi scientists had not been close to building an atomic bomb.

See also SPECIAL OPERATIONS EXECUTIVE.

FURTHER READING: "Knut Anders Haukelid, *Skis against the Atom* (1954); Thomas Gallagher, *Assault in Norway: Sabotaging the Nazi Bomb* (1974).

Nunn May, Alan (1911-   ) British atomic scientist and spy for the Soviet Union.

Born in Kings Norton near Birmingham, Nunn May, the son of a brass founder, won a scholarship to King Edward's School in Birmingham in 1924. He went to Cambridge in 1930, took a science degree in 1933, and went on to earn a Ph.D. in 1936. In that same year, he visited Leningrad as a lecturer, and returned to England a convinced Communist—perhaps already an undercover agent of Soviet intelligence.

A brilliant scientist, Nunn May was at Cambridge University in 1942 working under the direction of Professor John Cockcroft on highly secret research

(World War II was in a critical stage for the Allies at the time). In 1943 Nunn May went to Canada, and in 1944 he was added to the Cockcroft scientific team that had arrived in Canada to pursue atomic research.

By then Nunn May was part of the Soviet Canadian Network, a spy ring directed from Moscow and operating in Canada. The network used the code name "Alek" to cover Nunn May's identity. His reports had a high priority because he delivered information on the development of the atomic bomb, a field in which Russian science was far behind. Nunn May added American research to Canadian after trips to the United States, where he received briefings on the success of the Manhattan Project (which resulted in the development of an atomic bomb) in Chicago.

In 1945 Nunn May went back to England and joined the science faculty at King's College in London. Not long afterward, code clerk Igor Gouzenko defected from the Soviet Embassy in Ottawa, bringing with him information about the Soviet Canadian Network in general and about Nunn May in particular. Arrested in London, Nunn May received a ten-year sentence in 1946 and was released after serving six. In 1962 he left England to take the post of professor of physics at Ghana University.

See also SOVIET CANADIAN NETWORK.

FURTHER READING: Oliver Pilat, *The Atom Spies* (1952); Ronald Seth, *The Anatomy of Spying* (1963); Norman Lucas, *The Great Spy Ring* (1966); *H. Montgomery Hyde, *The Atom Bomb Spies* (1980).

Ochrana *(1881-1917)*   The secret police of tsarist Russia.

The Russian word "ochrana" means "guard," and the function of the Ochrana was to guard the tsar, his family, and his officials, both civilian and military. Such an organization originated during the time of Tsar Ivan the Terrible in the sixteenth century. The unstable tsar sent spies among the Russian people to report on critics of his regime, and the use of a secret police in one form or another never vanished from Russia after that. Alexander II relaxed the system, but his assassination by terrorists in 1881 brought it back in full force and entrenched more strongly than ever.

Such was the background of the Ochrana, founded by Alexander III shortly after the death of his father. Continuing terrorism and the multiplication of revolutionary movements in Russia led to the Ochrana's becoming the first powerful, institutionalized, and dreaded secret police force of the modern world. Although the Ochrana operated within legal limits, the laws were severe, and the organization had the right, for example, to exile prisoners to Siberia, a practice for which it became notorious.

The Ochrana maintained spies at home and abroad to keep suspected revolutionaries under surveillance. It employed *agents provocateurs* to lure antitsarist leaders into overt acts for which they could be arrested. Yevno Azev, who joined a band of revolutionaries in 1893 and seemed to encourage their terrorism, was actually a spy for the Ochrana.

Condemned by Russian intellectuals, such as novelist Leo Tolstoy, who described in his autobiography how the secret police shadowed him because of his liberal opinions, the organization nevertheless continued operating until the Russian Revolution (1917). When the Bolsheviks seized power, they published Ochrana records as part of their general condemnation of the tsarist regime. However, just as the Bolsheviks restored autocracy to the Russian government after ousting the moderates who overthrew the tsar, so did they restore the secret police, in each case making the system more efficient and ruthless than in the past.

The CHEKA (Extraordinary Commission for Combating Counterrevolution and Espionage) replaced the Ochrana, the difference being that while the tsarist secret police guarded the government against violence and had a legal status, the Communist secret police came into existence as the lawless servant of a lawless government, to support which it used mass terror against the Russian people.

See also AZEV, YEVNO; CHEKA.

FURTHER READING: *A. T. Vassilyev, *The Ochrana: The Russian Secret Police* (1930); Ronald Hingley, *The Russian Secret Police: Muscovite, Imperial Russian, and Soviet Political Security Operations* (1970); Lennard D. Gerson, *The Secret Police in Lenin's Russia* (1976).

OGPU *(1923-34)* The third name given to the Soviet intelligence system now known as the KGB.

See KGB.

Orlov, Alexander *(1895-1973)* Russian secret agent for, and defector from, the Soviet Union.

Orlov belonged to a Jewish family of Minsk, his real name being Leon Feldbin. He received a Jewish education but abandoned the family tradition in 1917 when he became an active supporter of the Russian Revolution. Serving in the Red Army, he fought in the Russian civil war (1918–20) that ended in victory for the Communists under the leadership of Vladimir Ilyich Lenin.

Orlov went into the legal apparatus of the Soviet government after the conflict was over, and became a prosecutor so energetic that he impressed Felix Dzerzhinsky, the head of the OGPU (United State Political Administration, 1923–34), the intelligence and security organization of the Soviet Union. Orlov joined the OGPU in 1924 and rose under Dzerzhinsky's direction, mastering espionage. He became a trusted secret agent and was allowed to handle assignments abroad. During the decade of 1926 to 1936 Orlov traveled through Europe recruiting Communist spies and establishing networks loyal to the Soviet Union.

The end of the decade saw the violence of the Spanish Civil War (1936–39), in which the republican government of Spain was backed by Joseph Stalin's Russia, and the nationalist insurgents, under General Francisco Franco, were supported by Adolf Hitler's Germany. Stalin wanted a liaison man between the Spanish and Soviet governments, and the assignment went to Orlov (who changed his name from Feldbin at this time). Arriving in Spain in 1936, Orlov worked to keep the republican regime loyal to the Soviet Union and organized spy networks and guerrilla groups to operate behind the nationalist lines.

As Franco's forces moved forward to victory, Orlov received an order from Moscow to ship the gold reserves of the republican government to Russia for safe keeping. The Spanish finance minister agreed to this proposal—first, to keep the gold out of Franco's hands, and second, in the belief that the Russians would faithfully return the treasure to Spain at the right time.

Orlov went to the seaport of Cartagena, to which the gold had been moved from Madrid as the nationalists pushed toward the capital. He found tons of the precious metal, worth hundreds of millions of dollars. Using crews from Russian merchant vessels in the harbor, he had the gold carried aboard four ships, which carried their cargoes across the Mediterranean Sea and the Black Sea to Odessa. The gold presumably was trucked from Odessa to vaults in Moscow.

After this remarkable achievement, Orlov began to have doubts about the system for which he worked. Stalin started his brutal purge of the "old Bolsheviks" in 1936, and many who were associated with them, or who were merely suspect to the dictator, went before firing squads. Secret agents abroad received orders to return home, and some did so only to be executed. Others, realizing what was happening in Moscow, defected rather than return.

In 1937 one of Orlov's cousins was shot on a charge of belonging to a group plotting to remove Stalin and return to what they considered pure Leninism. Orlov continued his espionage work in Spain, but he became increasingly worried about whether he was incriminated in the plot simply by being related to one of the plotters. He had had no patron in Moscow to speak for him since Dzerzhinsky's death. The breaking point came in 1938 when Orlov received a sudden order to report to intelligence headquarters in Moscow. Now really frightened, he sent his family to safety in France, then fled there himself and defected to the Canadian Embassy in Paris.

He reached Canada and then crossed the border into the United States, where he found a permanent haven, living for the most part in Cleveland under the name "Alexander Berg." In 1953 he published a book about Stalin's reign of terror. In 1955 he appeared before the Senate Subcommittee on Internal Security, to which he described the Soviet use of spies and assassins. In 1963 he published a manual exposing the general nature of the KGB, the successor of the OGPU, in which he had begun his espionage career. He lived thereafter in anonymity.

The Spanish gold has still not been returned to Spain by the Russians.

See also DZERZHINSKY, FELIX.

FURTHER READING: *Alexander Orlov, *The Secret History of Stalin's Crimes* (1953); Alexander Orlov, *Handbook of Intelligence and Guerrilla Warfare* (1963); Gordon Brook-Shepherd, *The Storm Petrels: The Flight of the First Soviet Defectors* (1977), describes Orlov as spy and defector.

OSS *(1942-45)*   America's principal espionage organization during World War II.

Since the United States had no overall espionage system at the start of the war in 1939, or even at the time of the attack on Pearl Harbor (1941), a system had to be established quickly. President Franklin Roosevelt gave the task to

William ("Wild Bill") Donovan, who organized the OSS (Office of Strategic Services) in 1942, with responsibility for espionage and other secret operations.

The latter function was the one for which the OSS became famous. Donovan allowed his 13,000 agents much leeway for personal initiative, and they distinguished themselves in places as far apart as North Africa (1942), China (1943–45), and Europe after the Allied landings in Normandy (1944). In Switzerland, Donovan's best espionage agent, Allen Dulles, met covertly with Germans and Italians in a position to help end the war (1944–45).

The end of the war came in 1945 in both Europe and the Pacific. That same year President Harry Truman closed the OSS, which had been strictly a wartime organization. It left a legacy on which its successor—the CIA (Central Intelligence Agency), which came into existence in 1947—could build.

See also CIA; DONOVAN, WILLIAM; DULLES, ALLEN.

FURTHER READING: *Stewart Alsop and Thomas Braden, *Sub Rosa: The OSS and American Espionage* (1964); Cory Ford, *Donovan of OSS* (1970); Anthony Cave Brown (ed.), *The Secret War Report of the OSS* (1976).

Oster, Hans *(1888-1945)* German intelligence officer and conspirator against Adolf Hitler before and during World War II.

Oster was born into a very devout Protestant family of Dresden, and he clung to this heritage throughout his life. This made him an opponent of the Nazi regime after 1933, when Adolf Hitler became chancellor of Germany. That same year, Oster moved from ordinary service in the armed forces into the Abwehr, German military intelligence, where he rose to the rank of general during the next decade.

Oster was one of three major figures in the Abwehr who conspired to overthrow Hitler, the other two being Admiral Wilhelm Canaris, head of the organization from 1935 on, and Erwin von Lahousen, director of the sabotage branch after 1938. Oster became chief of staff to Canaris, and the three men created a remarkable conspiracy against the regime within an intelligence department that supposedly served that regime.

Before the outbreak of World War II in 1939, Oster took the lead in attempting to bring together a group of German civilians and military men who hated the Nazis and feared Hitler would bring on a catastrophe for Germany and Europe. In 1940 Oster worked for the success of a plan to have the Vatican mediate between the Allies and a German administration to assume authority in Germany after the removal of Hitler. This plan failed because of opposition among the highest-ranking generals, who either would not act against the government while Germany was at war or else refused to violate their oath to Hitler.

Oster turned to the hope of a German defeat in the west that would force the generals to act. He sent warnings to Norway, Denmark, Belgium, and Holland of Hitler's planned invasions of 1940. The lightning German advances through these nations, followed by the victory over France, established Hitler's prestige among the loyal generals more strongly than ever, and undercut the opposition.

Hitler's attack on Russia in 1941 caused Oster to press harder for a direct move by the civilian-military conspirators, in the hope that Hitler could be arrested and replaced with a minimum of violence. This scheme came to nothing because too many of the high command refused to join.

The conspirators now turned to the only recourse that seemed to be open . . . — assassination. Several plans to kill Hitler were d . . . . them nearly succeeded. In 1943, a bomb smuggled aboard his plane failed to go off because the triggering device malfunctioned. In 1944, the conspirators in the July Plot succeeded in exploding a bomb at Hitler's headquarters, but the briefcase containing the bomb was moved away from where Hitler was standing, and he escaped with minor injuries.

Implicated in the July Plot, Oster was arrested by the Gestapo, the Nazi secret police, taken to a Nazi death camp, and executed.

See also CANARIS, WILHELM; LAHOUSEN, ERWIN VON.

FURTHER READING: Ladislas Farago, *Burn After Reading: The Espionage History of World War II* (1961); *Fabian von Schlabrendorff, *The Secret War against Hitler* (1965); Roger Manvell and Heinrich Fraenkel, *The Canaris Conspiracy* (1969).

Owens, Arthur *(1899-1960?)*   British spy for, and double agent against, Germany.

Owens was an anomalous figure who came under suspicion by both sides before his espionage career ended. Born in Wales into a poor family, he had enough ability to read science books on his own before taking a course in electrical engineering. During the 1930s, the period during which Adolf Hitler rose to become chancellor of Germany (1933), he traveled on the Continent as a salesman. Because of the Nazi threat, the British government wanted information from inside Germany, and Owens agreed to act as a spy while he was there. The code name "Johnny" covered this phase of his career.

By 1937 he was working for the Germans. He did so out of a Welsh nationalist prejudice against England and a desire for money. In 1939, Owens received clandestine training in radio espionage at a school in Hamburg, and he was prepared to start broadcasting from Britain later that year after World War II broke out.

However, British counterespionage became suspicious of him because of the triviality of the information he brought back from Germany. Arrested and interrogated, Owens cracked and agreed to become a double agent and broadcast disinformation (material the British wanted the Germans to believe). The orders he received from Germany were handed over to his British superior. Some of these orders concerned spies who, dropped into Britain by parachute, could be immediately rounded up.

Owens continued to work as a double agent until 1941, when British counterespionage became suspicious that he was still covertly sending information to Germany. However, the Germans also suspected him because of the arrest of a German agent in Britain whom Owens had been asked to assist. No longer trusted by either side, Owens went to jail in England for the duration of the war. He left for Ireland in 1945, where he is said to have lived and died under an assumed name.

FURTHER READING: Ladislas Farago, *The Game of the Foxes: The Untold Story of German Espionage in the United States and Great Britain during World War II* (1971); *Charles Whiting, *The War in the Shadows* (1973); David Kahn, *Hitler's Spies: German Military Intelligence in World War II* (1978).

Pack, Amy Thorpe *(1910-63)*   American spy for the Allies in Washington during World War II.

Born in Minneapolis, Amy Thorpe traveled widely in her childhood because her father was an officer in the Marine Corps whose tours of duty took him to such places as Cuba and Hawaii. When he retired from the Marines, her international education continued, as the family traveled in Italy, Switzerland, and France.

She made her debut in Washington in 1929, when she was the belle of the season—a willowy blonde with green eyes, a quick intelligence, a fascinating personality, and an enormous capacity for attracting men. A year later she married Arthur Pack, a secretary at the British Embassy, and went with him to Chile and Spain, where she did Red Cross work while the Spanish Civil War went on (1936–39).

In 1937 the Packs transferred to the British Embassy in Poland. Here her espionage career began. Men in the Warsaw government found her irresistible, talked volubly in her company, and divulged state secrets to her without thinking. Reporting this at the embassy, she was told to cultivate her contacts and bring back whatever information she could pump out of them. This information, which went to MI6 (Military Intelligence 6, British espionage) in London, included her prediction of the Munich Agreement of 1938, when Britain and France gave way to Hitler and let him carve up Czechoslovakia. She had seen a confidential German map showing the new borders.

Her husband being transferred back to Chile in 1939, the year World War II started, she wrote pro-Allied articles for Chilean newspapers until the local Germans protested to the Santiago government that she was too anti-German for a neutral nation, as Chile then was. Anticipating that she would have to leave Chile, she wrote to MI6 in London seeking a position on the basis of her work in Poland, and she received an encouraging reply.

Her opportunity arrived when she returned to Washington in 1940. She received a visit from an aide to William Stephenson, a Canadian who, based in New York, was coordinating British and American intelligence. Stephenson instructed his aide to judge her potential in espionage. The aide decided she would make a good spy, accepted her offer to become one, and dubbed her "Cynthia," the cover name she made famous.

Since America was not yet in the war, Washington still had its contingents of German, Italian, and Japanese diplomats. The city was a hotbed of rumors and conspiracies. Cynthia received orders to join the social whirl, to which she was accustomed, to use her magnetic personality to attract men, and to report to Stephenson's organization. She therefore took a house in Washington where she could have intimate meetings with carefully selected guests (male only).

Her first triumph was her captivation of the Italian naval attaché, who, as she told it later, revealed the identity of an official in the Italian Embassy who would, and did, steal the Italian naval code for her. She had it photographed and returned to him, and this pilfered information helped the British Mediterranean fleet sink major warships of the Italian navy.

Stephenson, who had arranged for her to be given this assignment, now called on her personally, and from this meeting came the most difficult and dangerous of her spy missions: to gain entrance to the French Embassy.

Since the fall of France to the Germans in 1940, the embassy had taken orders from the Vichy regime of Marshal Philippe Pétain. The French ambassador of that time was a defeatist who favored the Germans because he believed they would remain in possession of France indefinitely. He would not countenance any move against the Vichy regime he represented in Washington.

Stephenson wanted to know what plans Pétain had for the Vichy armed forces. Cynthia, who got into the French Embassy by posing as an American journalist, met the press attaché, Captain Charles Brousse, found him susceptible to her charms, entertained him at her house several times, and reported to Stephenson that he was strongly anti-German.

At the most propitious moment in their relationship, she told Brousse she was with American intelligence, fearing he might be alienated by her connection with British intelligence. He began giving her secret information about Vichy. Then Stephenson asked her to obtain the Vichy naval ciphers, which were vital (Cynthia, of course, did not know this) because of the coming American invasion of North Africa, an operation that would have a better chance of success if the Allies could decipher orders to the French fleet in the Mediterranean.

Brousse agreed to help her. They fooled a night watchman by asking him to let them use one corridor of the embassy as a place of assignation for several nights running. On one night, Cynthia surreptitiously let a locksmith in, and he unlocked the door to the code room and discovered the combination to the safe where the cipher books were kept. On the critical night, Cynthia entered the code room with the locksmith, removed the books from the safe, handed them out the window to a confederate, who had them copied, and returned them to the safe. No one else in the embassy knew about this espionage operation.

At the time of the American landings in North Africa in 1942, when the Germans invaded unoccupied France, the Allies were able to read the order to scuttle the French fleet. This kept it out of Hitler's hands and contributed to the success of the landings, as well as to the subsequent invasion of France, which toppled the Vichy regime.

After the war, Cynthia and Brousse married, her first husband having died and his first wife having obtained a divorce. They lived in a château at Castelnou in the Pyrénées until she contracted the cancer that killed her.

See also STEPHENSON, WILLIAM.

FURTHER READING: H. Montgomery Hyde, *The Quiet Canadian: The Secret Service Story of William Stephenson* (1964); *H. Montgomery Hyde, *Cynthia* (1965); Robert O. Paxton, *Vichy France: Old Guard and New Order, 1940–1944* (1972).

Papen, Franz von *(1879-1969)* German diplomat and spymaster during World War I and World War II.

Born the son of a wealthy Westphalian landowner, Papen was an aristocrat, a Catholic, and a monarchist. He went to military school, took his commission in the kaiser's army in 1907, and after six years served on the German general staff. Then he accepted the first of a series of diplomatic assignments, an appointment to the German Embassy in Mexico City, where he remained in the years 1913 to 1915, which saw the outbreak of World War I.

Papen was shifted to the United States in 1915 to be the German military attaché, with headquarters in New York. With the conflict raging between the

Central Powers (Germany and Austria) and the Allies (Britain and France), one of his duties was to prevent, as far as he could, American military supplies from reaching British or French ports. Since America was officially neutral but biased toward the Allies, another of Papen's duties was to work for the defeat of Germany's enemies without alienating the American people or causing a drastic shift of American opinion against the Central Powers.

Papen developed a strategy of buying American war supplies and of tying up the production of companies manufacturing them. The Bridgeport Projectile Company, the most successful of his efforts, with American management for a front, was actually German-owned. This company manufactured guns and ammunition. Under Papen's behind-the-scenes manipulation, Bridgeport ordered all the gunpowder it could get to keep any from reaching the Allies. Papen's company also took orders for its products from the Allies, and kept them waiting for deliveries that never came.

The rest of Papen's undercover work in the United States was disastrous for him, sometimes in comic circumstances. The commercial attaché of the German Embassy, Heinrich Albert, who provided the money from Berlin to pay for costly ventures, left a briefcase filled with incriminating documents on an elevated train in New York. An American secret service agent filched the briefcase, the "Albert papers" were published in a New York newspaper, and German prestige suffered a severe blow.

Papen quarreled with Franz von Rintelen, an agent sent from Berlin to commit sabotage in America. Papen considered Rintelen a wild man, and Rintelen considered Papen a fool. Papen asked Berlin to recall Rintelen; the request was transmitted in a code that was broken by the British, who arrested Rintelen on a Dutch (i.e., neutral) ship that stopped in a British port en route to Germany. Rintelen said afterward that Papen had deliberately betrayed him to be rid of him permanently. Papen denied it, but confessed he was glad he never saw Rintelen again.

This fiasco was typical of Papen's dealings with his espionage agents. He sent saboteurs to blow up the rails of the Canadian Pacific Railway to keep Canadian troops from sailing for France. The saboteurs, who failed in their mission, fell into the hands of the Canadian police. One of the saboteurs tried to blackmail Papen by threatening to reveal who had been behind the attempt. It is not clear from Papen's account whether the blackmail succeeded or not.

The danger in the threat was that Papen had violated American law by using the United States as a base for directing hostile activities against a friendly nation. He also stepped beyond legal limits when he had passports forged for German nationals who wanted to get through the British blockade of Germany, return to their homeland, and join the armed forces of the kaiser. Both the sabotage and the forgeries were bad mistakes, as Papen admitted when he came to write his memoirs.

Given his repeated missteps, Papen was bound to fail. Some of his undercover activities became known to the American government, which declared him *persona non grata*. He returned to Germany, and so ended his first venture into espionage.

Papen served in Palestine in 1918 with the Turkish forces trying to put down the Arab revolt guided by T. E. Lawrence (Lawrence of Arabia). This was another defeat for Papen, since the Arabs won. Back in Germany, he seemed to have recouped everything when he became chancellor in 1932, but it was actually the prelude to catastrophe. Adolf Hitler became chancellor in 1933, and Papen served the new regime at home and abroad, to his lasting regret when his eyes were opened to reality a decade later.

With regard to espionage, Papen's most important service came when he was ambassador to Turkey (1939–44). In 1943 he began dealing with Elyeza Bazna, an Albanian to whom he gave a famous code name—"Cicero." Bazna, valet to the British ambassador in Ankara, produced copies of secret documents from London, and Papen paid large sums for them (unknown to Papen, Nazi Foreign Minister Joachim von Ribbentrop sent him forged banknotes for the payoffs).

Papen received from Bazna and transmitted to Berlin information of the highest importance, especially records of the conferences between Winston Churchill and Franklin D. Roosevelt. However, neither Hitler nor Ribbentrop made intelligent use of the reports—in particular, they never associated the word "Overlord" with the second-front invasion (1944) of the Nazi-dominated Continent.

In 1944 the Turks discovered the leak at the British Embassy, although not the identity of the man responsible. An American agent, obtaining a copy of a telegram from Papen to Ribbentrop concerning Bazna, took it to Allen Dulles, the American representative of the OSS (Office of Strategic Services). According to Dulles, he notified British intelligence. Then a German secretary defected to the British carrying word about Bazna. The British ambassador fired the valet, and this espionage episode came to a close.

Papen returned for the second time in his life to a defeated Germany. He was found not guilty of war crimes by the Nuremberg tribunal in 1946, but a German denazification court sentenced him to a jail term. He spent his final years justifying his conduct to himself if not to the world.

See also BAZNA, ELYEZA; RINTELEN, FRANZ VON.

FURTHER READING: Tibor Koeves, *Satan in a Top Hat: The Biography of Franz von Papen* (1941); *Franz von Papen, Memoirs* (1952); Fitzroy Maclean, *Take Nine Spies* (1978), considers Papen's negotiations with "Cicero."

Paris Agency *(1791-97)* Royalist espionage network active in Paris during the French Revolution.

Undercover agents supporting the monarchy began operating in France from the start of the revolution in 1789. Their numbers and activities increased as the danger to King Louis XVI and Queen Marie Antoinette became more threatening, and in 1791 the Spanish ambassador in Paris, with the approval of Louis XVI, formed a spy ring to gather information that could be used either against the revolutionaries in France or to persuade the other powers of Europe to intervene militarily in behalf of the French monarchy.

Such was the origin of the Paris Agency, which continued to operate throughout the remaining years of the French Revolution. Its principal members were Sandrié Despomelles, a former officer in the king's army; Pierre Lemaître, a lawyer who had been in the king's finance council; François Sourdat, a magistrate from Troyes; and André Brottier, a priest and scholar. A number of lesser figures belonged to the Paris Agency, the composition of which varied as time brought recruits and removed leaders (Lemaître, for instance, was caught and executed in 1795).

These men worked first for the Spanish ambassador, who transmitted their messages to Madrid and to the Spanish Embassy in Venice, where the comte d'Antraigues, a French royalist on the embassy staff, ran a veritable clearing-house for antirevolutionary information gathered in France and across the Continent. D'Antraigues collated the messages he received and wrote interpretive reports for Spanish officials, British agents, and the exiled comte de Provence, who represented the French monarchy, taking the title King Louis XVIII after the execution of his brother Louis XVI in 1793 and the death of Louis XVII (the son of Louis XVI) in 1795.

The spies of the Paris Agency, with contacts in places ranging from the mobs in the streets to functionaries of the revolutionary government, produced all kinds of information, sometimes useful, sometimes not. According to d'Antraigues, one source was Lazare Carnot, who as a member of the Committee of Public Safety (1793–94) organized the revolutionary armed forces for the defense of the French republic against the hostile powers of Europe. Carnot would have been the most important of all their contacts, but it seems that d'Antraigues may have invented the connection.

Maximilien de Robespierre, the most prominent member of the Committee of Public Safety and the one most responsible for the reign of terror, fell from power in 1794. The men of the Paris Agency were disappointed that the revolution did not fall with him. The five-man Directory took over the government of France, ruled during the years 1795 to 1799, and instead of recalling King Louis XVIII to the throne prepared France for the rise to power of Napoleon Bonaparte.

The Directory put an end to the Paris Agency, which lingered on into 1797 until a pair of pretended recruits for the espionage network betrayed it to the authorities. The members at the time went into hiding or into jail. Attempts to revive the network failed.

The Paris Agency had no real function after 1797; the French Revolution was over and the Napoleonic era was about to begin. Even in its heyday its influence was negligible, for the reports it developed had no effect on the course of events; rather, they raised false hopes among the royalists abroad for the imminent collapse of the revolution, with all the disappointment and discouragement this entailed. Still, the members had risked their lives, particularly during the reign of terror, in behalf of a cause they believed in, and they had been adept enough at espionage to continue making their reports until the final catastrophe.

See also D'ANTRAIGUES, COMTE.

FURTHER READING: G. Lenôtre, *Two Royalist Spies of the French Revolution* (1924); *Harvey Mitchell,The Underground War against France: The Missions of William Wickham, 1794–1800* (1965).

Pearl Harbor (1941) Japanese espionage and military victory over the United States.

The attack on Hawaii was part of contingency planning in Tokyo long before the air strikes that devastated the Pearl Harbor naval base and plunged both Japan and America into World War II. As early as 1939 two German spies, Bernard and Ruth Kühn, were reporting on the movement of American warships into and out of Pearl Harbor. In 1941 Takeo Yoshikawa joined the staff at the Japanese Consulate and began the espionage activities that enabled him to provide Tokyo with an accurate description of conditions at the naval base on December 7, 1941, the day of the assault. The success of Yoshikawa and the Kühns represented a failure of American counterespionage.

This need not have been decisive because William Friedman of American intelligence in 1940 had broken Purple, the principal Japanese cipher, used for transmitting top-secret diplomatic messages. The Americans knew from the Purple traffic between Japan and the Japanese Embassy in Washington that the Tokyo government toward the end of 1941 was moving closer to war in the Pacific. The Americans knew the negotiations in Washington were called "the matrimonial question" in Japanese coded talk and that President Franklin Roosevelt was "Miss Kimoko" and Secretary of State Cordell Hull, "Miss Umeko."

From broken Japanese military ciphers, the Americans were familiar with the "winds messages." If an order to the Japanese armed forces read, "east wind rain," that meant an attack on the United States. "West wind clear" meant an attack on the British Empire. "North wind cloudy" meant an attack on the Soviet Union. Historians of World War II debate whether the "east wind rain" message was actually picked up by American intelligence, but that the Japanese were going to launch a military campaign, probably against the United States, was clear. The danger became imminent when Tokyo sent a Purple message to the Japanese ambassador in Washington ordering him to prepare to destroy the Purple machine at his embassy, a plain indication that Japan was about to go to war with the United States.

Quite suddenly the Japanese navy changed the ciphers and codes in which it communicated with its ships at sea. The Americans momentarily lost track of the Japanese Pacific fleet, the principal striking force of which was headed east across the Pacific toward Hawaii. On December 6, American cryptologists deciphered a series of Purple messages, the substance of which was a menacing rejection of American policy in the Far East. The final message in the series arrived early on the morning of December 7 for delivery by the Japanese ambassador to the secretary of state. The message declared that Japan was breaking off diplomatic relations with the United States. The time of delivery was 1:00 P.M. in Washington—7:30 A.M. Hawaii time.

All these intercepts belonged to a general system nicknamed "Magic" by the cryptologists because it revealed to them as quickly as to Japanese diplomats the intentions and decisions of the Japanese government regarding foreign affairs. An immense amount of top-secret information from Tokyo was available to the Americans because of Magic. Why, then, were they so unprepared for the Japanese assault on Pearl Harbor?

It has been argued, for one thing, that this information was embedded in an immense mass of messages regarding Japanese plans in the Pacific and the Far East, so that American cryptanalysts could not immediately determine what was significant and what irrelevant. Again, Hawaii was not mentioned as a target; it seemed more logical for the Japanese to strike at the Americans in the western Pacific (and, of course, they did invade the Philippines).

Then, with the Japanese declaration of war about to be presented in Washington on December 7, a warning to Hawaii was forestalled by circumstances. General George Marshall, American chief of staff, could not radio the warning because of atmospherics between the mainland and the islands. He decided against the telephone for fear that the Japanese would tap into the conversation and realize that their Purple code had been broken. As a result, the Marshall warning went by ordinary telegraph through San Francisco to an office in Hawaii, where a messenger on a motorcycle delivered it to General Walter Short, Army commander for Hawaii. So much time elapsed that the messenger arrived almost as the first Japanese planes were flying in from their carriers.

Many of Short's planes were destroyed on the ground, but the real disaster struck the naval forces of Admiral Husband Kimmel, who lost five battleships, either sunk or crippled. Two cruisers and three destroyers were also hit, along with a number of smaller vessels. Leaving more than two thousand American sailors dead or wounded, the Japanese planes, having suffered negligible losses, flew back to their carriers.

Short and Kimmel, accused of dereliction of duty, were relieved of their commands and ordered home. Roosevelt appointed a presidential commission to investigate, the Army and the Navy conducted their own investigations, and after the war Congress took up the problem. Unanimity of opinion could not be reached. Some investigators placed most of the blame on Washington for not alerting Kimmel and Short to the full gravity of the Japanese threat. Other investigators maintained that the two commanders received warnings so ominous that they should have deployed their forces. Friedman offered a plausible explanation when he blamed a "series of accidents" (e.g., the fate of the Marshall telegram) for the catastrophe.

The ability to read Purple and other Japanese ciphers helped restore the American advantage as the war progressed. At the battle of Midway (1942)—the turning point of the war with Japan—the victory of the rebuilt, reinforced U.S. Pacific fleet was partly due to good cryptology. The enemy strategy, the composition of the strike force, and the timing of the attack were all known. The Americans were therefore able to prepare for the naval engagement aware of exactly what they needed to do, while the Japanese sailed into the unexpected and therefore into defeat.

In 1943 American cryptanalysts learned that Admiral Isoroku Yamamoto, head of the Japanese navy and architect of the attack on Pearl Harbor, was going to make a flying tour of Japanese bases in the South Pacific. A trap was set, and his plane was shot down by an American fighter. The loss of Yamamoto was a severe blow to Japan.

See also FRIEDMAN, WILLIAM; KÜHN, BERNARD; KÜHN, RUTH; PURPLE; YAMAMOTO, ISOROKU; YOSHIKAWA, TAKEO.

FURTHER READING: *Roberta Wohlstetter, *Pearl Harbor: Warning and Decision* (1962); Ladislas Farago, *The Broken Seal: The Story of "Operation Magic" and the Pearl Harbor Disaster* (1967); Edward Van Der Rhoer, *Deadly Magic: A Personal Account of Communications Intelligence in World War II in the Pacific* (1978); W. J. Holmes, *Double-Edged Secrets: U. S. Naval Intelligence in the Pacific during World War II* (1979).

Penkovskiy, Oleg *(1919-63)*   Russian intelligence officer and double agent for the west against the Soviet Union.

Born in Ordzhonikidze, in the Caucasus, Penkovskiy was the son of a tsarist army officer who fought against the Communists in the Russian civil war (1918–20). This family history was used by the Russians to blacken his reputation after they discovered that he was a spy for the west. Penkovskiy attended a secondary school in Ordzhonikidze, from which he graduated in 1937. After training at the Kiev Artillery School (1937–39), he received his commission just in time for World War II (1939–45), but before the Germans attacked Russia (1941).

Penkovskiy served gallantly in the Ukraine during the early German victories in 1941 and in the triumphant Soviet campaigns through Poland and Germany in 1944. Wounded more than once, he received several Soviet decorations and awards for his performance on the battlefield.

After the war, Penkovskiy studied at the Frunze Military Academy in Moscow (1945–48) and in 1949 went into the GRU (Chief Intelligence Directorate of the General Staff of the Red Army), Soviet military intelligence. He was a full colonel when assigned as a military attaché to the Soviet Embassy in Ankara, Turkey, in 1955, where he engaged in espionage against the host country. Back in Moscow, he served in GRU headquarters (1956–58), after which he underwent special training in military engineering (1958–59).

Penkovskiy at this point seemed among the most trustworthy officers in Soviet intelligence. Actually, he was becoming progressively disillusioned with the Soviet system, especially with the leadership of Premier Nikita Khrushchev. Penkovskiy feared that Khrushchev might trigger a nuclear war.

In 1961 Penkovskiy made his first move against Khrushchev and the Soviet system. Greville Wynne, a British businessman, was in Moscow to arrange for a trade delegation to visit London. Penkovskiy was scheduled to head the delegation, so he and Wynne held talks on the subject. Seizing the opportunity, Penkovskiy said he would like to get in touch with western intelligence. Wynne, who had done undercover work for the British government during World War II and after, made the arrangements on his return to London.

As a result, Penkovskiy met secretly with British and American intelligence officers after he arrived with the Russian trade delegation in the British capital. He convinced these westerners that he was sincere, and he agreed to become a double agent. Ostensibly a faithful officer of the GRU, he transmitted to the west classified information of the highest importance.

During 1961 and 1962 Penkovskiy cooperated with Wynne in Moscow and with intelligence officers in the west. He reported on the strategy and tactics of Khrushchev. He handed over top-secret documents on Soviet plans, espionage, armaments, rockets, and space satellites.

One piece of information had an immediate impact on world affairs. His reports on the number and size of Soviet rockets let U.S. President John Kennedy know that, despite Khrushchev's boasting, the Russians were too weak in rocketry to think of starting a war. This knowledge contributed to Kennedy's decision in 1962 to confront Khrushchev regarding Soviet offensive missiles in Cuba. Khrushchev bowed to Kennedy's demand and withdrew the missiles.

Realizing that classified information of the highest importance was leaking from Moscow to the west, Soviet intelligence began a feverish search for the source, and the trail led to Penkovskiy, who was arrested in Moscow in 1962. Wynne was picked up in Budapest. Convicted after a trial in 1963, Penkovskiy was said by the Russians to have been shot immediately afterward. Wynne served nearly a year of a prison sentence before being exchanged in 1964 for Gordon Lonsdale, a convicted Soviet spy imprisoned in Britain.

Penkovskiy left behind one tantalizing mystery: Was he the author of the

Penkovskiy Papers, the exposure of Soviet intelligence, and indeed of the Soviet Union itself, published under his name in 1965? Wynne, for one, thought the answer was in the affirmative, and so did Peter Deriabin, a former officer in the Russian intelligence apparatus who defected to the west and translated the *Penkovskiy Papers.* A commonly accepted theory is that, while the basic information came from Penkovskiy, the text as published was prepared by the CIA (Central Intelligence Agency) in Washington.

See also WYNNE, GREVILLE.

FURTHER READING: *Oleg Penkovsky, *The Penkovskiy Papers* (translated by Peter Deriabin, 1965); Greville Wynne, *The Man from Moscow* (1967); Fitzroy Maclean, *Take Nine Spies* (1978), has a chapter on Penkovskiy.

Perlet, Charles *(1769-1828)*   Royalist agent during the French Revolution; Bonapartist agent during the Napoleonic era.

Born in Geneva, Switzerland, to middle-class parents, Perlet learned to be a printer, migrated to Paris, and did well at his trade, publishing a journal of his own along with books, pamphlets, and periodicals. With the coming of the French Revolution in 1789, Perlet, a royalist by conviction, used his press to publish writings apparently neutral but actually favorable to the King and hostile to the revolutionaries. This proroyalist strategy finally got Perlet into trouble, and in 1797, during the period of the five-man Directory that governed France when the violence of the revolution was over, he was exiled to a penal colony in French Guiana.

Allowed to return home during the Consulate (1799–1804), when Napoleon Bonaparte was the most powerful man in France, Perlet found his business in ruins. Looking for another means of making a livelihood, he decided to become a Bonapartist spy, and in 1804 he joined the corps of agents maintained by Napoleon's spymaster, Joseph Fouché, minister of police.

Perlet's main assignment, in which his printing experience figured, was to propagate the false belief that a secret committee of royalists was working underground in France for the overthrow of Napoleon. The Bonapartists wanted to entice royalists to return to France, where they could be arrested. Most of all, Fouché wanted to lure into a trap Louis Fauche-Borel, an agent who had betrayed him.

Perlet wrote to Fauche-Borel in 1806, urging him to come to France and meet leaders of the secret committee who were supposedly waiting to meet him. Fauche-Borel's nephew, Charles Vitel, went in his place in 1807, only to be arrested at once and executed. No big fish swam into Fouché's secret-committee net, but Perlet did arouse much interest among royalists, some of whom wrote to ask for details about the mythical underground group.

After the restoration of King Louis XVIII, who replaced Napoleon on the French throne (permanently, in 1815), Perlet wrote that Fauche-Borel was a Bonapartist spy. Fauche-Borel sued Perlet for libel and won (1816). Discredited, Perlet returned to Geneva and resumed printing, financing himself partly by blackmailing Louis XVIII, about whom he held documents so embarrassing that the French government purchased them for a substantial sum.

See also FAUCHE-BOREL, LOUIS; FOUCHÉ, JOSEPH.

FURTHER READING: *G. Lenôtre, *Two Royalist Spies of the French Revolution* (1924), presents Perlet as one of the pair; Leo Gershoy, *The French Revolution and Napoleon* (1964), gives the historical background to Perlet's espionage activities; Hubert Cole, *Fouché, the Unprinci-pled Patriot* (1971).

Petrov, Vladimir (1907-66)   Russian secret agent for, and defector from, the Soviet Union.

Born as Vladimir Shorokhov in a Siberian town of tsarist Russia, Petrov was the son of a peasant. He attended a local school during World War I (1914–18) and in 1919 went to work for a blacksmith. Four years later he joined the Komsomol, the Communist youth movement, in which he finished his schooling.

In 1930 he joined the Soviet navy, at which time he called himself Vladimir Proletarsky to show his solidarity with the proletariat. The navy trained him to be a cipher expert. As such he returned to Moscow in 1933 and joined the OGPU (United State Political Administration, 1923–34), the main department of Soviet intelligence, which today is called the KGB (Committee for State Security).

After service in China (1937) and Moscow (1938), he became head of the OGPU cipher section. In 1943 he arrived in Stockholm under the name Vladimir Petrov, with the rank of major, and with responsibility for espionage at the Soviet Embassy. Back in Moscow (1947–51), he handled espionage assignments so expertly that in 1951 he was appointed to the Soviet Embassy in Canberra, Australia, a sensitive post because the Soviet Union had decided to launch a major spy campaign against Australia.

Petrov and his wife, Evdokia, also a trained cipher clerk, worked together in this campaign, one that proved unsuccessful because too few Australian sources of information could be developed. Under criticism in Moscow for their failure, the Petrovs became resentful. Then, in 1953, Lavrenti Beria, head of the Soviet security and intelligence system, was suddenly arrested by his colleagues in the Kremlin and executed. Beria was charged with having conspired to seize power.

Somehow implicated in the Beria affair and ordered home to Moscow, the Petrovs decided to defect. They asked the Australians for political asylum in 1954 and delivered a damaging blow to Soviet intelligence by handing over secret documents concerning the Russian spy conspiracy in Australia and espionage activities elsewhere.

See also BERIA, LAVRENTI.

FURTHER READING: Commonwealth of Australia, *Report of the Royal Commission on Espionage, 22nd August, 1955* (1955); *Vladimir Petrov and Evdokia Petrov, *Empire of Fear* (1956); Ronald Seth, *Unmasked! The Story of Soviet Espionage* (1965).

Philby, Kim (1912-   )   British intelligence officer and double agent for the Soviet Union.

Philby's real name was Harold Adrian Russell Philby. His parents called him "Kim," after Rudyard Kipling's fictional character, during his early years in India, where he was born at Ambala when his father held a position in the Indian civil service. His father, explorer and scholar St. John Philby, sided with the colonial peoples of the British Empire against British rule, a fact that may partially account for the son's subsequent betrayal of Britain.

Sent to England to be educated, Kim Philby attended Westminster School in London (1923–28) and went to Cambridge in 1929, where he remained until his graduation in 1933. During his college years he became friendly with Guy Burgess, Donald Maclean, and Anthony Blunt. All four, coming from well-to-do homes, were disturbed by the contrast between the comforts of their class and the suffering of the lower classes during the depression of the 1930s in Britain. All four were intellectuals fond of extreme ideas and credulous about reports of equality and justice in the Soviet Union. They were therefore vulnerable to the arguments of Communist spokesmen who insisted that Britain's political and social problems could be solved, as Russia's were supposedly being solved, by application of the tenets of Marxism-Leninism. Philby, Burgess, Maclean, and Blunt became members of a Communist cell in Cambridge. Philby was one of those who agreed to serve as a secret agent for the Russians.

After leaving Cambridge in 1933, Philby worked as a journalist in London, deliberately choosing moderate publications in order to conceal his left-wing opinions and espionage activities. In 1934 he married an Austrian Communist, Alice Kohlmann. He shared her conviction that only the Soviet Union would oppose Germany, now led by Adolf Hitler. In the guise of a right-wing reporter, Philby went to Spain in 1937 to cover the civil war (1936–39) from the side of the profascist forces of General Francisco Franco, rather than joining the pro-Communist loyalists. He continued to spy for the Russians, twice holding rendezvous in France with Burgess, who was his courier. Franco's victory in 1939 caused Philby to return to London.

During World War II (1939–45) Philby reported on the British expeditionary force in France until the shattering German invasion of 1940. Escaping back to Britain from Dunkirk, he entered MI6 (Military Intelligence 6, British espionage). That made him a spy of enormous importance to the Soviet Union. Burgess, in MI6 during the years 1939 to 1941, also spied for the Russians. Philby and Burgess renewed their friendship and exchanged confidences about their activities.

In 1944 Philby received an appointment to the Russian desk at MI6, where he systematically deceived his superiors by suppressing information damaging to Moscow. He occasionally went into the field on top-secret missions, one of which took him to Turkey in 1946. Three years later he arrived in Washington as first secretary of the British Embassy. Functioning as a liaison between MI6 and America's CIA (Central Intelligence Agency), he provided the Soviet Union with a double agent in the very heart of Anglo-American intelligence.

Burgess took the post of second secretary at the embassy in 1950, but his obnoxious behavior in Washington caused him to be recalled in the following year. Meanwhile, Philby had learned that Maclean, now at the British Foreign Office in London, was under suspicion of being a spy for the Russians. Philby therefore warned Burgess that on his arrival in London he should alert Maclean. Burgess and Maclean, aided secretly by Blunt, defected to the Soviet Union.

The Burgess-Maclean scandal brought Philby himself under suspicion, since he was a close friend of Burgess, who had lived in his house in Washington despite the resentment of Philby's wife. Moreover, Philby's intelligence work kept him aware of Maclean's peril. Recalled to London in 1951, Philby faced the suspicion that he was the "third man" of the scandal, the one who had informed the pair of fugitives in time for them to escape. He had the coolness to withstand a lengthy interrogation at MI5. His answers were clever enough to confuse the issue, and he remained with MI6 for over a decade, despite the suspicion in some quarters that he was guilty. In 1955 a member of Parliament, Marcus Lipton, named Philby as the third man of the Burgess-Maclean case. Philby's superiors responded by posting him to Beirut, where he remained during the years 1956 to 1963, still working undercover for the Soviet Union.

Incriminating information concerning his past, from Cambridge to Beirut, accumulated at MI6 headquarters in London. Still, in circumstances that remain controversial, the intelligence organization made no move against him. One theory is that his superiors hoped that he would follow Burgess and Maclean into exile to avoid a lurid trial that would show them guilty of stupidity, if not of dereliction of duty. Another theory is that those superiors, being mainly from Cambridge (or Oxford) themselves, could not really believe that a colleague with their background was a double agent working for the Russians.

In 1963 Philby, finally frightened that he might be recalled and confronted with incontrovertible evidence, made a move that broke the case open and proved he was indeed the third man: he defected to the Soviet Union. Moscow granted him political asylum and gave him a place in Russian intelligence, which he had served so faithfully for so many years. He remained in Moscow, meeting an occasional newsman or historian from the west and boasting in speech and print of the damage he had done to his country.

See also BLUNT, ANTHONY; BURGESS, GUY; MACLEAN, DONALD.

FURTHER READING: Harold Adrian Russell Philby, *My Silent War* (1968); *Bruce Page, David Leitch, and Phillip Knightley, *The Philby Conspiracy* (1968); E. H. Cookridge, *The Third Man* (1974); Andrew Boyle, *The Fourth Man: The Definitive Account of Kim Philby, Guy Burgess, and Donald Maclean, and Who Recruited Them to Spy for Russia* (1979), identifies Blunt as the "fourth man" of the Burgess-Maclean case; Douglas Sutherland, *The Great Betrayal: The Definitive Story of Blunt, Philby, Burgess and Maclean* (1981).

Picquart, Georges *(1854-1914)* French intelligence officer and principal military advocate of justice for Captain Alfred Dreyfus.

Picquart was, like Dreyfus, a native of Alsace whose family adhered to French nationality after the Franco-Prussian War (1870–71), when France lost the province to Germany. Picquart, choosing the French army for a career, rose through the grades until he became head of the counterespionage section at the ministry of war in Paris. This was in 1895, when the Dreyfus Affair was developing into a national scandal.

Dreyfus had been convicted of treason and sent to Devil's Island, the French penal colony off French Guiana, where he might have remained had not Picquart discovered evidence of his innocence. A document filched by a French counterspy from a wastebasket at the German Embassy in Paris showed that Major Ferdinand Esterhazy, also of the French general staff, was in secret communication with the embassy's military attaché. Then a handwriting comparison revealed that the fundamental document in the anti-Dreyfus dossier, the offer to sell French military plans to the Germans, had been written by Esterhazy.

Appalled by Esterhazy's treason and the fate of Dreyfus, Picquart took the evidence to General Raoul de Boisdeffre, chief of the general staff. Boisdeffre referred him to the acting chief of staff, General Charles Gonse. To Picquart's astonishment, Gonse told him to forget the whole subject. When Picquart persisted, arguing vehemently that the blame should be placed where it belonged, he received a transfer from Paris to Tunis. He was replaced by Major Hubert Henry, who was involved in the cover-up as a forger of documents and a conspirator against Dreyfus.

While in North Africa, Picquart had a heated exchange of letters with Henry, whom he suspected of complicity in the plot. Picquart presented his evidence to a lawyer, who in turn discussed it with Auguste Scheurer-Kestner, vice president of the French senate. Scheurer-Kestner believed the evidence exonerated Dreyfus, and said so to the other senators.

Esterhazy was accorded a court-martial, which exculpated him for a time; Henry appeared for the defense, but Picquart refused to do the same. Picquart then faced a court-martial that accused him of revealing official documents to the lawyer. He was found guilty and sentenced to sixty days' arrest. This did not prevent him from testifying in behalf of novelist Émile Zola, accused of libeling prominent military men when in his open letter "J'Accuse," he demanded an end to the cover-up and justice for Dreyfus and Esterhazy alike (1898).

The army cashiered Picquart, who fought a duel with Henry in which the latter suffered minor cuts. The minister of war had Picquart tried again on the old charge of revealing official documents. Found guilty, Picquart went to jail, but he was released in time to testify for Dreyfus, who had returned to France in 1899 and begun the legal battle that ended in 1906 with his complete vindication.

The military conspirators were discredited, and Picquart was reinstated in the French army in 1899. He entered the first cabinet of Premier Georges Clemençeau as minister of war in 1906 and served until 1914, when he died of injuries sustained in a fall from a horse.

See also DREYFUS AFFAIR.

FURTHER READING: *D. W. Brogan, *The Development of Modern France, 1870–1939* (1940), considers the French army in politics at the time of the Dreyfus affair; George Chapman, *The Dreyfus Case: A Reassessment* (1955); Louis L. Snyder, *The Dreyfus Case: A Documentary History* (1973); David L. Lewis, *Prisoners of Honor: The Dreyfus Affair* (1973).

Pinkerton, Allan *(1819-84)*   Scottish-born lawman, private detective, and director of intelligence for the federal government during the American Civil War.

Pinkerton was born in Scotland and, as the son of a Glasgow policeman, grew up with an interest in law enforcement. He emigrated to Illinois in 1842, became a cooper, and one day while chopping wood accidentally discovered a gang of counterfeiters. By helping to capture the gang, he started along the path toward a law-enforcement career that saw him become deputy sheriff first of Kane County (1846) and then of Cook County (1847).

Pinkerton joined Chicago's police force in 1850 as its first detective. Resigning two years later to go into business for himself, he founded one of the most celebrated of all organizations in the field of crime investigation—Pinkerton's National Detective Agency. His clients were mainly railroad companies, which hired him to prevent hijacking and other forms of robbery and to solve crimes already committed.

In 1861 the federal government, aware of a plot to assassinate Abraham Lincoln in Baltimore en route to Washington, commissioned Pinkerton to protect the President-elect. Pinkerton sent operatives to Baltimore and, acting on their information, escorted Lincoln aboard a night train for a secret run through the Maryland city to the national capital.

With the beginning of the Civil War in 1861, Pinkerton created an intelligence system for an old friend, General George B. McClellan, who commanded the army's Ohio Department. Adopting the cover name "E. J. Allen," Pinkerton traveled covertly through the south and reported back to McClellan on the conditions he found there. He accompanied McClellan to Washington when the general assumed command of the army of the Potomac.

Pinkerton now organized a network of espionage agents who penetrated the Confederacy in search of political and military information. He also organized a counterespionage system for the Washington area.

His most effective spy, who eventually lost his life, was Timothy Webster, one of those who had investigated the Baltimore plot against Lincoln. Directing counterespionage, Pinkerton tracked down and arrested Rose Greenhow, who was transmitting information from her home in Washington to the Confederacy. He interrogated Belle Boyd, but failed to discover her significance as a spy for the South.

Being so close to McClellan, personally and professionally, Pinkerton would not remain at his post after McClellan failed in the field and was replaced in 1862. Lafayette Baker took over federal intelligence, while Pinkerton spent the rest of the Civil War in other types of service, principally in investigating the claims of businessmen against the government.

In 1865, with the end of the war, Pinkerton returned to his detective agency, which he expanded by hiring more operatives and opening branches in New York and Philadelphia. The nation began to hear about "the Pinkertons" and their success in combating crime. Their masterpiece was the solution of a theft from the Adams Express Company that netted the thieves, temporarily, more than half a million dollars.

Many subsequent cases involved labor disputes, in which Pinkerton's men became proficient at industrial espionage, intervened in behalf of management against strikes, and gained an odious reputation among workers. Operative James McParlan lived in the lodges of the violent Molly Maguires in the Pennsylvania coal fields, gathered evidence, and in 1877 testified against their leaders at trials from which that group never recovered.

Pinkerton spent his last years writing books about his detective agency, thereby providing material for private-eye thrillers.

See also BAKER, LAFAYETTE; MCPARLAN, JAMES; WEBSTER, TIMOTHY.

FURTHER READING: *Allan Pinkerton, *The Spy of the Rebellion* (1883); Philip Van Doren Stern, *Secret Missions of the Civil War* (1959); James D. Horan, *The Pinkertons: The Detective Dynasty That Made History* (1968).

Playback System Use of converted double agents to transmit disinformation by radio to their former directors.

Playback in its widest sense is an old maneuver in espionage, for captured spies have often been persuaded, by cajolery or force, to send misleading messages through the channels connecting them to their directors. The modern meaning of the term, however, emerged with the use of radio. Clandestine operators transmit messages to their headquarters. Hence, if an operator can be captured and "turned around" without his headquarters becoming aware of the fact, he can be used by his captors to send disinformation. The side imposed upon is then victimized by its own espionage apparatus.

World War II produced three notable examples of the playback system. British counterespionage turned around the German agents who, under the Double-Cross System, radioed disinformation back to Germany during most of the war and in 1944 helped to deceive the Germans about where the Allies would land on the French coast on D-Day. In Holland, the Germans captured and turned around so many secret agents from London that the Dutch underground was actually run by the Germans. The Germans also waged a playback campaign against the Russians after breaking up the Red Orchestra, the network of Soviet spy rings in Germany, Belgium, Holland, and France.

See also DOUBLE-CROSS SYSTEM; NORTH POLE; RED ORCHESTRA.

FURTHER READING: *H. J. Giskes, *London Calling North Pole* (1953); Heinz Höhne, *Codeword: Direktor: The Story of the Red Orchestra* (1971); John C. Masterman, *The Double-Cross System in the War of 1939 to 1945* (1972).

Polygraph   An instrument used to determine whether or not a speaker is telling the truth.

Commonly known as a lie detector, the polygraph is based on a theory of psychophysical behavior. The theory states that (1) lying causes conflicts in the mind of the speaker; (2) these mental conflicts cause emotional reactions, such as fear and anxiety; (3) the emotional reactions cause bodily changes in respiration, perspiration, blood pressure, and pulse rate; and (4) the bodily changes can be measured scientifically and objectively.

The polygraph does the measuring. It generally comprises a pneumograph around the chest that reports on the subject's breathing, a cuff around the upper arm recording blood pressure and pulse rate, and electrodes on the hands to follow variations in sweating. The gadgets are connected to a needle that produces marks on a moving paper band.

If the needle traces a steady pattern across the paper as questions are asked and answered, the subject is considered free from significant mental conflicts and therefore is presumed to be telling the truth. Conversely, if the needle varies widely from the norm when a question is answered, the subject is considered to be lying at that point.

The polygraph is widely used in intelligence work. For example, in business counterespionage it is used to uncover and control employee theft and white-collar crime. Often, accused men and women will ask for a lie-detector test in the conviction that it will exculpate them.

The instrument, nonetheless, remains controversial because it is not completely accurate. Sometimes the needle fluctuates because the subject feels upset by emotions not associated with the fear and anxiety that spring from lying. To cite a typical case, embarrassment can cause a truthful reply to jar the needle. Moreover, if the subject has to be prepared for the test, the tester's explanation may introduce an uncontrolled element into the proceedings.

The doubtfulness of the results is one reason why courts have generally been reluctant to permit the polygraph to be used. Another reason, frequently advanced in the United States, concerns constitutional safeguards against invasion of privacy. Since the lie detector penetrates the innermost thoughts of a human being, it is condemned as the ultimate invasion of privacy, and is said, therefore, to be unconstitutional and something to which no citizen should be unwillingly subjected.

The polygraph thus remains a useful tool when its scientific limits are understood and its legal problems respected.

FURTHER READING: Fred Edward Imbau, *Lie Detection and Criminal Investigation* (1948); *Robert J. Ferguson and Allan L. Miller, *Polygraph in Court* (1973).

Pontecorvo, Bruno (1913-   ) Italian physicist and alleged spy for the Soviet Union.

Pontecorvo came of a Jewish family in Pisa. Despite the fact that his father was a prosperous businessman, Pontecorvo opted for Communism early in life. A gifted scientist, he took a Ph.D. in physics in 1934, became a teacher at Rome University, and did laboratory work under the guidance of Professor Enrico Fermi, later to be a principal figure in America's Manhattan Project, which built the atomic bomb.

In 1936 Pontecorvo went to Paris on a fellowship, where he continued his research under Professor Frédéric Joliot-Curie, a committed Communist, at the Collège de France. With the fall of France to the German invasion in 1940, Pontecorvo escaped through Spain and Portugal to safety in the United States. He rejoined Fermi, who had left Italy earlier because he could not accept the fascist regime and was at Columbia University.

Pontecorvo moved to Canada in 1943 when invited to join the staff of the Anglo-Canadian atomic project with its research facilities at Chalk River. The suspicion about him focuses on this period, when the notorious Soviet Canadian Network was stealing atomic secrets at Chalk River and passing them on to Moscow. However, nothing was ever proven against him, and he was not mentioned in the documents turned over to the Canadian authorities by Igor Gouzenko, the code clerk who defected from the Soviet Embassy in Ottawa and exposed the activities of the Soviet Canadian Network.

Completing his work in Canada, Pontecorvo went to England to join the staff at the Harwell nuclear installation (1949). The sudden arrest of his colleague at Harwell, Klaus Fuchs, and the revelation that Fuchs had clandestinely given top-secret information to the Russians, may have frightened Pontecorvo, who in that same year (1950) took his family to the Continent, using the story that they were on vacation. All of them dropped out of sight, creating a mystery as to what had become of them.

The truth emerged in 1955, when Pontecorvo appeared at a news conference in Moscow, declared that he had chosen the Soviet Union because he wanted to work on atomic energy for peaceful purposes, and announced that he and his family were Soviet citizens. This news conference appeared to justify the worst interpretation of his behavior and to suggest that he had indeed been a spy while holding responsible research positions at atomic laboratories in the west. The suspicion deepened when he received the Order of Lenin in 1963 and was elected a full member of the Soviet academy of sciences.

Nevertheless, Pontecorvo confessed to nothing, and much checking at his stops in the United States, Canada, and Britain failed to turn up anything illegal in his past. In 1978 he visited Italy, where he received a welcome befitting an eminent native son. The trip was difficult to explain on the assumption of his guilt, and the question remains open.

FURTHER READING: Alan Moorehead, *The Traitors* (1963), considers Pontecorvo guilty; *Norman Lucas, *The Great Spy Ring* (1966), stresses the point that nothing has been proven against Pontecorvo.

Powers, Francis Gary *(1929-77)* American pilot of a spy plane shot down over the Soviet Union.

Born in Kentucky, Powers was the son of a coal miner who as the result of an accident became a shoemaker. Powers received his schooling in the town of Bourdyne and attended Milligan College, from which he graduated in 1950. He entered the U.S. Air Force, which trained him as a fighter pilot. In 1956, holding the rank of captain, he was transferred to an espionage campaign in which selected pilots flew U-2 spy planes over the Soviet Union to monitor Russian military exercises, atomic explosions, and any other activities that could pose a threat to the nations of the west. Many U-2 flights had taken place between American bases in Norway and Pakistan over a period of four years, and some pilots had become confident enough of successful flights to call the route a "milk run."

The CIA (Central Intelligence Agency), which ran the U-2 campaign under the cover story that the pilots were working for the National Aeronautics and Space Administration (NASA), gave Powers nearly three months of training with U-2s in the Nevada desert and then attached him to an American base at Incirlik, Turkey. Here he remained for four years, gaining experience in flying reconnaissance planes along the Turkish-Soviet border (1956–60). He was ordered to Peshawar, Pakistan, in 1960 and briefed for a flight across the Soviet Union. He was told that he would be safe if he flew at 68,000 feet because no Soviet plane or rocket could reach that altitude. He was to land at an American base in Norway.

Powers took off and flew directly into Soviet air space. He was nearly over the city of Sverdlovsk when his U-2 was rocked by an explosion, and his engine quit. Unable to right his plane or use its destruct mechanism, Powers ejected himself and parachuted to the ground. He was seized by local inhabitants and held until the police arrived. Taken to Moscow, he went on trial as a spy, confessed the facts about his mission, and received a sentence of three years in prison and seven years in a labor camp.

Soviet Premier Nikita Khrushchev used the incident as the basis of a propaganda attack on the United States. He stated that a Russian rocket had knocked down the U-2 (contradicting what Powers had been told at Peshawar) and warned that American bases on foreign soil would be bombed if they sent any more spy planes over the Soviet Union.

In Washington, where no proper cover story had been formulated (a violation of an elementary espionage principle), an attempt was made to lie out of the crisis, one story being that an American weather plane might have strayed into Soviet air space as far as Sverdlovsk. At last, President Eisenhower decided to tell the truth. He had not, however, known about this particular flight, which came at an embarrassing time, when he was about to meet Khrushchev at a summit conference in Paris. The CIA director, Allen Dulles, had known and he declared that the Powers flight was justified by America's need to be kept informed about the Soviet Union on a continuing basis.

Khrushchev, who had never protested to Washington about previous U-2 flights, used this one as an excuse to break up the Paris summit conference. His motives have never been publicly explained, but presumably he realized he could not gain any substantial concessions from Eisenhower and at the same time was concerned about the criticism of his colleagues in the Kremlin (who four years later overthrew him, alleging he was guilty of "hare-brained schemes").

Powers remained in a Russian jail until 1962, when he was exchanged for Rudolf Abel, a Soviet spy captured in the United States. Leaving the Air Force and the CIA, Powers went into civil aviation with Lockheed and continued as a pilot until he was killed in a crack-up.

See also ABEL, RUDOLF; DULLES, ALLEN; U-2.

FURTHER READING: James B. Donovan, *Strangers on a Bridge: The Case of Colonel Abel* (1964), describes the exchange of Abel for Powers; *Francis Gary Powers (with Curt Gentry), *Operation Overflight: The U-2 Spy Pilot Tells His Story for the First Time* (1970); Ray S. Cline, *Secrets, Spies, and Scholars: Blueprint of the Essential CIA* (1978), describes the U-2 spy campaign from the standpoint of the CIA.

Poyntz, Juliet (1887-1937?) American spy for, defector from, and victim of the Soviet intelligence apparatus.

Of a respectable American family and a graduate of Barnard College, Poyntz became a member of the Communist party in New York during the 1920s. She represented the party unsuccessfully in campaigns for the assembly and the board of aldermen. As a fervent partisan of the Soviet Union, she traveled to Moscow in 1934, received training in espionage, and returned to the United States with orders to spy for the Russians and recruit other Americans who would do the same.

Poyntz conferred clandestinely with Soviet agents and followed their instructions until 1936, the year in which Joseph Stalin, now dictator of Russia, conducted the notorious trials in Moscow at which he began eliminating the "old Bolsheviks" of the Russian Revolution. Appalled by the spectacle, Poyntz abandoned espionage, left the Communist party, confessed her disillusionment, and began to write hostile criticism of the cause to which she had so lately been devoted.

In 1937 she suddenly vanished without a trace. Carlo Tresca, a left-wing socialist with a knowledge of Communist tactics, declared that she had been kidnapped by Soviet agents to prevent her from revealing any more facts about Russian spies in America.

FURTHER READING: David Dallin, *Soviet Espionage* (1955); Ronald Seth, *Unmasked! The Story of Soviet Espionage* (1965); Richard Deacon, *A History of The Russian Secret Service* (1972).

Princip, Gavrilo (1895-1918) Serbian conspirator whose assassination of the Austrian archduke and archduchess led to World War I.

Born in Bosnia, a province of the Austro-Hungarian empire, Princip came of a patriotic Serbian family opposed to domination by Vienna and anxious for a union of Bosnia with Serbia. Princip finished his elementary education and entered a high school in which many pupils held radical political opinions derived from their parents. He mingled with conspirators in the school underground and became a member of the Black Hand, a secret society founded in Serbia in 1911 by Dragutin Dimitrijevic to struggle for the liberation of Bosnia. For a year or so Princip and his friends spied on Austrians and pro-Austrian Bosnians. Then, in 1914, Vienna announced that Archduke Franz Ferdinand and his wife would pay a ceremonial visit to Bosnia.

Dimitrijevic, now chief of intelligence of the Serbian general staff, plotted the assassination of the archduke in Sarajevo by a band of Black Hand conspirators. Princip, then 19 years old, was one of the band. He fired the shots that killed the archduke and the archduchess as they drove through Sarajevo. The crime caused Austria to declare war on Serbia. Germany supported Austria, Russia supported Serbia, and international alliances and national fears led France and Britain to join Russia against Germany. The great nations of Europe and eventually the United States became embroiled in World War I.

Princip was seized by the Austrians and held in jail during the war. He died of tuberculosis in 1918, the year in which the conflict ended, and thus he could not know about the one consequence of his assassination of the archduke that he would have considered most important—the postwar union of Serbs and Bosnians in the new nation of Yugoslavia. Princip remains memorable because never before or since has a character so trivial touched off a human tragedy so cataclysmic.

See also BLACK HAND; DIMITRIJEVIC, DRAGUTIN.

FURTHER READING: *R. W. Seton-Watson, *Sarajevo* (1926); Roberta Strauss, *The Desperate Act: The Assassination of Franz Ferdinand at Sarajevo* (1968); Walter Laquer and George L. Mosse, *Nineteen-Fourteen: The Coming of the First World War* (1970).

Prior, Matthew *(1664-1721)*   English poet and spymaster on the Continent during the reign of King Louis XIV of France.

Born in Dorset into a middle-class family, Prior was fortunate enough to meet Charles Montagu, later the earl of Halifax, when both attended the Westminster School in London. Both went on to Cambridge, where Prior became a fellow of St. John's College in 1688, the year of the Glorious Revolution, when James II fled into exile on the Continent and conspiracies by his supporters, the Jacobites, became a primary concern of the new king of England, William III.

Prior, who had begun writing poetry, chose diplomacy for his vocation, and with Montagu's friendly assistance, he rose rapidly in government service. Assigned to The Hague, Prior became a secretary to the diplomats who signed the Treaties of Ryswick (1697) ending the War of the Grand Alliance, between the France of Louis XIV on the one side and England, Holland, Spain, and the Holy Roman Empire on the other.

Among the peace terms was one by which Louis XIV agreed to abandon James II and recognize William III as king of England. The Jacobites in France, however, continued to conspire on behalf of their exiled monarch, and Prior, on being named secretary to the English ambassador in Paris, was assigned to keep them under surveillance and report on them to his superiors in London.

He organized a network of spies who frequented the Jacobite court in exile at Rheims. His agents included, by his own description, an Englishman named Bailey who was "a cunning fellow," an Irishman named Brocard who posed as a salesman of "things English," and three Frenchwomen, "my widow Langlois and her two daughters."

During Prior's term in Paris (1697–99), his spies also reported on the French government, for the motives of Louis XIV had to be evaluated as he moved toward the final conflict of his reign, the War of the Spanish Succession (1701–13), by which he placed his great-grandson on the throne of Spain. The poet returned home to England and entered Parliament, where he served until 1701, the year in which James II died and the Jacobite movement increased its activities under his son, the "Old Pretender" and under *his* son, the "Young Pretender."

After William III died in 1702, Prior held posts in the government administration during the early years of the reign of Queen Anne. In 1710 Robert Harley, in control of the English government, employing another writer, Daniel Defoe, to spy on the Jacobites in England, also employed Prior to report on the Jacobites abroad. This was one of Prior's assignments when he served in Paris again during the years 1712 to 1714. Another was to assist with the negotiations that produced the Treaty of Utrecht (1713), ending the War of the Spanish Succession.

The death of Queen Anne in 1714 finished Prior's public career. His Tory friends fell from power, and he went to jail rather than inform on them. Released, he resumed writing poetry, some of which he gathered into a volume published in 1718. The authorities did not ask him to assist them with his knowledge of the Jacobites at the time of the "Fifteen," the attempt of the Old Pretender to regain the English throne in 1715. Prior did not live to see the "Forty Five," the fruitless invasion of Scotland by the Young Pretender in 1745.

FURTHER READING: *C. K. Eves, *Matthew Prior: Poet and Diplomat* (1939); Charles Petrie, *The Jacobite Movement* (1948); Richard Deacon, *A History of the British Secret Service* (1969).

Profumo, John *(1915-)* British cabinet minister and central figure of an espionage scare.

As his name indicates, Profumo was of Anglo-Italian origin. His father, a member of the Italian aristocracy, settled in London and mingled with the British aristocracy. Profumo therefore enjoyed a good education that took him to Harrow and Oxford. In 1940 he became the youngest member of Parliament. This being the period of World War II, Profumo went into the British army, becoming an officer and rising to the rank of brigadier by the end of the war in 1945. He became a successful businessman before regaining his seat in Parliament in 1950. He married actress Valerie Hobson (1954) and then held high places in the Tory government of Prime Minister Harold Macmillan and was appointed secretary of state for war (1960).

In 1961, while a guest of Lord Astor, Profumo met Christine Keeler, a former show girl whose chief talent seems to have been performing nude onstage. Profumo and Keeler began a tawdry romance, meeting secretly at the London apartment of a fashionable osteopath named Stephen Ward, with whom she lived. Ward was a known Communist sympathizer and a friend of Yevgeni Ivanov, an intelligence officer at the Soviet Embassy in London. Ward occasionally carried unofficial messages from Ivanov to British authorities—and Ivanov, too, had meetings with Chrstine Keeler at Ward's apartment.

The British security service warned Profumo about Ward, a garrulous individual who might be indiscreet in talking to Ivanov. Although Profumo did not know about Keeler and Ivanov, he decided to break his liaison with her, which he did toward the end of 1961. Nearly a year later Keeler became involved with two West Indians, who had a fight over her, and one was bound over for trial in 1963. The circumstances reached the press, from the reporting of which there emerged a picture of Keeler and other girls of her type living sordid lives as members of a call-girl ring run by Ward. She told her story to a newspaper, naming Ward, Profumo, and Ivanov (the Russian immediately left for Moscow).

Because a cabinet minister was involved, the newspaper postponed printing her account until it could be checked. Profumo, denying everything, tried to have it stopped completely. However, as reporters turned their attention to Ward, the osteopath tried to defend himself by threatening to tell a tale about the Profumo-Keeler connection that could "bring down the government." He mentioned at the same time that Keeler had sold to the press an intimate letter from Profumo. Questions were asked in the House of Commons, and the secretary of state for war came under so much pressure that he could not evade having to make a personal statement to the members of Parliament. On March 22, 1963, he stated solemnly and categorically before the bar in the Commons that he had never indulged in any improprieties with Christine Keeler. His statement satisfied the prime minister and most Tories and socialists.

The focus of attention now shifted to Ward, who faced prosecution for living off the earnings of prostitutes. Desperately trying to save himself, he sent a letter to the prime minister stating that Profumo had lied in the House of Commons. Once again the pressure was on Profumo. This time it proved too great for him to bear. The newspapers asked what kind of people this cabinet minister associated with. The possibility of a security leak from Profumo to Keeler to Ivanov was discussed. Besieged by reporters whenever he appeared in public and his defense sounding increasingly improbable, Profumo wrote a letter to Macmillan on June 4, 1963, confessing that he had lied and resigning from the government.

Profumo retreated from the glare of publicity into social work in London. He was accompanied by his wife, who had known nothing about her husband and Christine Keeler until the scandal broke. Keeler married and lived less and less in the public eye. Ward, facing a guilty verdict in court on the prostitution charge, committed suicide. Macmillan asked Lord Denning to investigate the Profumo affair and make a report. Denning absolved the prime minister, but Macmillan, victimized by Profumo and badgered in Parliament, resigned his office a month later.

See also Profumo Affair.

FURTHER READING: *Lord Denning, *Lord Denning's Report: Presented to Parliament by the Prime Minister by Command of Her Majesty, September 1963* (1963); Iain Crawford, *The Profumo Affair: A Crisis in Contemporary Society* (1963); Ludovic Kennedy, *The Trial of Stephen Ward* (1965).

Profumo Affair *(1963)*   British espionage scare involving a cabinet minister.

When John Profumo, secretary of state for war, resigned from the British government in 1963, he did so because he had lied in the House of Commons about his relations with call girl Christine Keeler. A second problem remained unresolved—whether or not he had been a security risk because Keeler by her own testimony had also been the paramour of a Soviet intelligence officer named Yevgeni Ivanov. The sudden return of Ivanov to Moscow six months earlier made it seem that the Russian had left Britain before he could be implicated in an espionage case.

Prime Minister Harold Macmillan appointed Lord Denning to conduct an investigation. The Denning report, published only three months after Profumo's resignation, formulated the problem as follows.

Profumo had known both Keeler and her "protector," Stephen Ward, a fashionable osteopath (who subsequently committed suicide just before being found guilty on a charge of living off prostitutes). Ward also had known Ivanov, who, like Profumo, had met Keeler in Ward's London apartment. The Profumo-Keeler-Ivanov link created the danger that the Russian intelligence officer might have persuaded the call girl to pump the British secretary of state for war and that she might have been a conduit through which classified information about the British armed forces could have moved from London to Moscow. Furthermore, Ivanov was known to have used Ward unofficially to relay Soviet views to British authorities regarding certain international problems. Ivanov tried to find out through Ward when and if the United States would provide West Germany with atomic weapons. At the time of the Cuban Missile Crisis (1962), Ivanov urged the British government through Ward to call a conference on Cuba where the issue might be settled favorably to the Soviet Union. It was widely believed that if Ivanov had used Ward directly in the interests of the Kremlin, he could scarcely have resisted the temptation to use Profumo indirectly through Christine Keeler.

Denning interviewed all the principals in the crisis (except, of course, Ivanov). He pursued rumors when he felt they were plausible, and he looked into the charges of a cover-up in the British government, perhaps by the prime minister himself—charges that arose naturally because Profumo's lie in the House of Commons had shaken public confidence where cabinet ministers were concerned.

The Denning report came out three months after Profumo's resignation from the government. The report absolved the former secretary of state for war of the accusation that he had been a security risk while in office. Profumo, Denning concluded, had never discussed government secrets with Keeler, nor had she asked him about them, nor had Ivanov asked her to ask. Ivanov may have feared that Keeler would tell Profumo about his questions. In any event, the Russian intelligence officer was so discreet with the call girl that Denning even questioned whether there had been an erotic liaison between them at all.

Declaring that there had been neither espionage nor a cover-up in the Profumo affair, the Denning report gained general acceptance by the British people and the news media. Macmillan's political opponents in Parliament still accused him of incompetence, of not knowing what was going on, and of believing Profumo too readily. In the following month the prime minister, a casualty of the scandal, resigned.

See also PROFUMO, JOHN.

FURTHER READING: *Lord Denning, *Lord Denning's Report: Presented to Parliament by the Prime Minister by Command of Her Majesty, September 1963* (1963); Iain Crawford, *The Profumo Affair: A Crisis in Contemporary Society* (1963).

Pueblo (1968)   American spy ship captured by the North Koreans.

After the Korean War (1950–53), when the need became pressing for the United States to know what aggressive Communist nations were doing and when technological advances gave espionage an added dimension, the U.S. Navy converted a number of small ships into floating electronics installations. One of these spy ships was the *Pueblo,* assigned to monitor North Korea.

Commander Lloyd M. Bucher had orders to cruise outside North Korean territorial waters but close enough to land to intercept radio messages and maintain other types of electronic surveillance. On January 23, 1968, a North Korean warship suddenly appeared, stopped the *Pueblo,* and sent a boarding party to take control of the American vessel. Bucher ordered the destruction of his code books, but many confidential papers and much secret equipment were seized. The North Koreans took the *Pueblo* to shore, and Bucher and his men were held prisoners.

This incident caused an international crisis that simmered for almost a year. The North Koreans claimed they had seized the *Pueblo* in their territorial waters. The United States insisted, supported by Bucher's testimony, that the vessel had been in international waters. However, nothing could be done about the hard fact that the Americans from the *Pueblo* were in a North Korean jail, and eventually, to gain their release, Washington admitted the espionage and apologized.

FURTHER READING: *Lloyd M. Bucher and Mark Rosovich, *Bucher: My Story* (1970); Victor Gallery, *The Pueblo Incident* (1970); Trevor Armbrister, *A Matter of Accountability: The True Story of the Pueblo Affair* (1970).

Purple   Principal Japanese cipher during World War II.

In 1937 Japan began using a code unknown to American cryptologists. It worked like the Enigma machine, a copy of which the Japanese had obtained from the Germans, to which technical improvements had been added. The Japanese called it "Alphabetical Typewriter 97." The Americans called it "Purple" for reasons that remain unclear but probably followed from the use of colors as code words.

Like Enigma, Purple involved two typewriters connected by a plugboard from which a complex system of electrical wires ran into each machine. The code clerk turned four rotors bearing letters to a given alignment and typed the plaintext on one typewriter. As he did so, the second typewriter automatically typed the same message in code. The rotors moved automatically, shifting the alignment of letters so that the code varied as the typing continued.

The plaintext was obtained by the reverse method, by typing on the second machine and sending the electrical impulses back along the wires and rotors to the first.

The problem for American cryptologists was to build a Purple code machine that would decipher the coded messages picked up from Japanese broadcasts. This was so difficult that the Japanese considered their code unbreakable. However, after a year of work, William Friedman of the Signal Intelligence Service found the solution. Purple machines were built by the Americans, Japanese military orders on the highest level were read, and this cryptological achievement contributed to the defeat of Japan in World War II.

See also ENIGMA; FRIEDMAN, WILLIAM.

FURTHER READING: William Friedman, "Cryptology," *Encyclopaedia Britannica* (1969); David Kahn, *The Codebreakers: The Story of Secret Writing* (1967); *Ronald W. Clark, *The Man Who Broke Purple* (1977).

Rado, Sandor (1899-1981) Hungarian spymaster for the Soviet Union in Switzerland.

The son of a prosperous Jewish businessman, Rado was born and educated in a suburb of Budapest. He joined the Communist party while attending the University of Budapest, and in 1919 he supported the Russian-backed dictatorship of Béla Kun during the few months of its existence. Rado spent the early 1920s in Moscow, where he married Helene Jensen, also a convinced Communist and later his partner in espionage for the Soviet Union.

Rado became a professional geographer and cartographer after studying both sciences at the University of Jena. He returned to Moscow for briefing in intelligence work (1931), became the Kremlin's man in Germany (1932–33), and escaped first to Vienna and then to Paris in 1933 following Adolf Hitler's rise to chancellor of Germany. In 1936, acting on orders from the GRU (Chief Intelligence Directorate of the General Staff of the Red Army, Russian military intelligence), Rado went to Switzerland to assume control of a spy network. His code name in communicating with Moscow was "Dora" (an anagram of his real name), and for a cover he ran a business in Geneva that made and sold maps.

Rado's network included Rachel Duebendorfer ("Sissy"), his cut-out, or go-between, who was based in Bern and allowed him to remain behind the scenes while she made the necessary contacts, and Alexander Foote ("Jim"), Rado's principal radio operator, who transmitted information to Moscow from Lausanne. As he was "Dora" to his Russian superiors, Rado was "Albert" to the members of his team. The German conquest of France in 1940 made Paris much more difficult for clandestine Communist operations, and the Russians therefore upgraded their network in neutral Switzerland. Following Hitler's attack on the Soviet Union in 1941, the Rado group became a principal source for the Russians on all aspects of the German campaign.

Rudolf Roessler began to work for Rado in 1942. Roessler kept himself concealed behind cut-outs Christian Schneider ("Taylor") and Duebendorfer, and Rado never learned his true identity while they were cooperating. Rado gave Roessler the code name "Lucy" because Roessler worked in Lucerne, and through this intelligence chain Roessler sent to Moscow some of the most important espionage reports of the war.

Rado ran his spy network successfully as part of the Red Orchestra, as the Germans called the system of Soviet spy networks in western Europe, until 1943, when the Swiss arrested three of his agents. He went underground and escaped a Swiss dragnet by moving stealthily from one hideout to another with the assistance of the Swiss Communist party.

In 1944 Rado fled to Paris after its liberation from the German occupation. There he met Foote. The pair were ordered to Moscow to brief the Center, Moscow's espionage headquarters, about the fate of their spy ring, to plead their cases, and to hear an official verdict on their conduct. They left Paris in 1945 on a Russian plane and stayed in the same hotel room after touching down in Cairo.

There Rado vanished, and Foote never saw him again. The Russians, keeping track of Rado, demanded his extradition, won it from the Cairo authorities, and sent an officer to escort him forcibly to Moscow. How Rado survived his interrogation at the Center remains unexplained, but he went to jail because of the fiasco in Switzerland. According to one rumor, Rado's incarceration was arranged by Lavrenti Beria, the head of the Russian secret police, whose son had disgraced himself in Switzerland and been sent home by the director of the network.

In any case, Rado dropped out of sight for some years. Then he surfaced in Budapest in 1955, became a teacher of cartography at Budapest University, and in 1971 published his autobiography in his native language. Translated into German (1972), it is a self-serving account of his espionage years in Switzerland but useful whenever it can be checked according to logic, psychology, or outside sources.

See also DUEBENDORFER, RACHEL; FOOTE, ALEXANDER; RED ORCHESTRA; ROESSLER, RUDOLF.

FURTHER READING: Alexander Foote, *Handbook for Spies* (2d ed., 1964); *Sandor Rado, *Deckname Dora* (1972); Paul L. Kesaris (ed.), *The Rote Kapelle: The CIA's History of Soviet Intelligence and Espionage Networks in Western Europe, 1936–1945* (1979); Anthony Read and David Fisher, *Operation Lucy: The Most Secret Spy Ring of the Second World War* (1981).

Rake, Denis (1901-   )   British spy in France during World War II.

Born in Brussels, where his father was a journalist and his mother an opera singer, Rake grew up bilingual in English and French. He became a stage performer as a child, part of the time with a circus. In 1915, following the World War I conquest of Belgium by the Germans, he escaped with his mother to England. Remaining there for the rest of the war, he returned to the stage between the wars, appearing mainly in light comedies and operettas. He joined the British army in 1939 on the outbreak of World War II and served as an interpreter in France until the victorious German sweep of 1940.

Escaping back to Britain, Rake in 1941 went into the Special Operations Executive (SOE), formed to aid the resistance in France against the German conquerors. When an SOE radio operator in Lyons was caught by the Germans, Rake received orders to replace him. Rake went by way of Gibraltar, from which he reached the Riviera by boat. He traveled north to Lyons, where, housed in various sites under the protection of patriotic Frenchmen, he radioed

London about the conditions he found and relayed messages from local resist-ance leaders. Lyons was in unoccupied France, the area run for the Germans from Vichy by Marshal Philippe Pétain. Warned that Vichyite police were on his trail, Rake transferred to Paris in the occupied zone, then to Limoges in the unoccupied zone.

The Vichyites arrested Rake in Limoges, along with two leaders of the resistance. The captives were released by their French captors when the Ger-mans took over the unoccupied zone in 1942. Rake got back to London, returned to France, and continued clandestine broadcasts until the Germans were driven out by the Allied invasion of France in 1944. He retired to London in 1945, worked at various jobs, and eventually wrote his memoirs.

FURTHER READING: Maurice Buckmaster, *They Fought Alone: The Story of British Agents in France* (1958); M. R. D. Foot, *SOE in France: An Account of the Work of the British Special Operations Executive in France, 1940–1944* (1966); *Denis Rake, *Rake's Progress* (1968).

RB-47 *(1960)* American spy plane shot down while monitoring the Soviet Arctic.

The RB-47 on this mission carried a crew of six and flew from a base in England to the Barents Sea in the Arctic, off the northern coast of the Soviet Union. Loaded with communications equipment, the plane was supposed to make an electronic survey of the coast and the coastal waters and to return with information about Russian installations and activities in the area. On July 1, 1960, a Soviet fighter plane attacked the RB-47 and shot it down. The wreck-age landed in the water. The Russians picked up and imprisoned two survivors, Captain Freeman Olmstead, the co-pilot, and Captain John McKone, the navigator.

President Dwight Eisenhower, declaring that the spy plane had been over international water, demanded the return of Olmstead and McKone. Soviet Premier Nikita Khrushchev retorted that the plane had intruded into Soviet air space and that the two prisoners would not be released. Khrushchev had a special reason for adopting this attitude—he did not want to help Richard Nixon, the Republican candidate for President in 1960, who, following the Russian capture of pilot Francis Gary Powers, had defended America's U-2 spy flights over the Soviet Union.

Two developments made Khrushchev change his mind. A few months after the RB-47 incident, two spies for the Soviet Union, Willi Hirsch and Igor Melekh, were arrested and imprisoned in the United States, and in 1961 President John Kennedy took office. Both sides wanted their captives returned, and in one of the early instances of the espionage revolution by which spies are exchanged instead of executed, Olmstead and McKone were traded for Hirsch and Melekh.

See also ESPIONAGE REVOLUTION.

FURTHER READING: David Wise and Thomas B. Ross, *The Espionage Establishment* (1967), has an account of the RB-47 case; *E. H. Cookridge, *Spy Trade* (1971).

Red Orchestra *(1939-43)* Coordinated spy rings in western Europe work-ing for the Soviet Union during World War II.

The name "Red Orchestra" was coined by German counterespionage. Since the Russians used the term "musician" as a code word for one of their clandestine radio operators, the Germans used "orchestra" when a group was involved. "Red" referred to the fact that the spies were transmitting information to Moscow.

The Red Orchestra (*Rote Kapelle* in German) has been described differently by different writers, depending on how many Soviet spy rings are counted. To include them all is to extend the clandestine organization from Yugoslavia to Spain, at least. Britain has been associated with the Red Orchestra because a German-Jewish refugee named Ruth Kuczynski is said to have run a London branch with access to the inner circles of Prime Minister Winston Churchill's wartime government. Actually, the Germans applied the name originally to the network in occupied Belgium, following the German victories of 1940, and then extended it to two other occupied nations, Holland and France, as well as to Germany itself. An important network, but safe from German counterespionage, operated in Switzerland.

The director in Moscow had charge of the Red Orchestra. His principal lieutenant in the field was Leopold Trepper, the *grand chef* (big chief) of western Europe. Arriving in the west in 1939, Trepper surreptitiously met spies already in place, recruited new ones, organized networks, and tightened up discipline. He himself worked in Belgium and France. His movements as he traveled between networks cannot be precisely detailed. Through couriers he had occasional liaison with the Red Orchestra spymasters in Germany and Switzerland, Harro Schulze-Boysen and Sandor Rado, respectively.

When the Germans invaded Russia in 1941, Moscow ordered the Red Orchestra to expand its reports on the German armed forces, which the espionage rings did for over a year, becoming in the process a significant part of the Soviet resistance to the invasion. German counterespionage, picking up masked radio signals, tracked down a transmitter in Brussels in 1941 and another in 1942. The radio operator arrested in the second case, Johann Wenzel, talked so freely that the Germans were able to disrupt and disperse the Red Orchestra spy rings in Germany, Belgium, Holland, and France. Trepper was among those captured.

Part of the Red Orchestra then experienced a strange reincarnation as an anti-Soviet system. The Germans "turned around" Trepper and some of his former agents, and persuaded them to form a "playback" campaign in which they resumed transmitting by radio to Moscow, except that now they broadcast under German direction. The playback campaign continued into 1943, and then ceased because Moscow demanded hard information about the German armed forces. The generals in Berlin decided that the game was not worth the information, Moscow soon realized what the change in radio reports meant, and the Red Orchestra lapsed for good.

See also RADO, SANDOR; SCHULZE-BOYSEN, HARRO; TREPPER, LEOPOLD.

FURTHER READING: Gilles Perrault, *The Red Orchestra* (1969); *Heinz Höhne, *Codeword: Direktor: The Story of the Red Orchestra* (1971); Leopold Trepper, *The Great Game: Memoirs of the Spy Hitler Couldn't Silence* (1977); Paul L. Kesaris (ed.), *The Rote Kapelle: The CIA's History of Soviet Intelligence and Espionage Networks in Western Europe, 1936–1945* (1979).

Redl, Alfred *(1864-1913)*   Director of Austrian espionage and double agent for the Russians before World War I.

Redl was born in Lemberg (now Lvov, in the U.S.S.R.), where his father, a former officer in the Austrian army, had a job as a railroad official. The son entered military school in 1882, joined the armed forces of Emperor Franz Joseph of Austria on graduating, rose through the grades, and by 1899 was an observer stationed with the Russian army.

In 1900 Redl entered the department of military intelligence in Vienna, where he became noted for modernizing counterespionage by means of fingerprints, hidden cameras that photographed suspects and caught them off guard, and techniques such as the use of bright lights to confuse prisoners under interrogation. Redl wrote explanatory articles for military publications and lectured on his methods to staff officers of the Austrian army.

In 1902 he became a double agent working for the Russians. His motive was money, which he needed to pay for a sybaritic homosexual life.

When the Vienna foreign office discovered in 1903 that the Russians knew Austria's contingency war plans, Redl (who had delivered them to St. Petersburg) received an order to find the traitor. The Russians permitted Redl to denounce several lesser spies in order to save himself. He was too valuable to them to be allowed to fall under suspicion in Vienna.

This "achievement" helped to gain Redl the post of director of espionage in 1907. Two years later he conferred in Berlin with Walther Nicolai of German intelligence and brought back information about the kaiser's army to pass on to his Russian paymasters. In 1912 Redl received a promotion to colonel and assignment as chief of staff to a general commanding an army corps in Prague. Here Redl continued his concealed life style and his espionage for the Russians.

Back in Vienna, his successor in the espionage department, Maximilian Ronge, followed his methods and improved upon them, in particular by expanding the postal censorship.

In 1913 Ronge received from Nicolai in Berlin two envelopes addressed to "Nikon Nizetas" at the general post office in Vienna. The envelopes had already been in Vienna, had not been picked up, and had been returned to their place of mailing in Germany.

Since the sender could not be located, the envelopes were opened and found to contain large sums of money, together with the addresses of espionage centers in Paris and Geneva. Nicolai sent these envelopes and their contents to Ronge for an investigation of "Nikon Nizetas."

Ronge returned the envelopes to the Vienna post office, placed detectives on guard, and waited to see who would call for them. Two more letters arrived for the cryptic addressee, one with a message obviously in code: "Regarding your proposals, they are all acceptable." It was signed "F. Dietroch."

At last the addressee arrived for his mail—Colonel Alfred Redl! He was "Nikon Nizetas," and "F. Dietroch" was his Russian contact. The identification seemed impossible to Ronge at first, but Redl, on being tracked to his hotel, cornered in his apartment, and confronted with the facts, confessed. He accepted a pistol proffered to him as the only honorable way out and committed suicide.

His papers revealed an astounding career of betrayal covering more than a decade. He had transmitted to the Russians thousands of secret documents that had crossed his desk, protected Austrians who spied for Russia, and destroyed Russians who spied for Austria.

One of his thefts from his own records affected history in the year after his death. He had handed over Austria's contingency plan for military operations against Serbia, next to the Austro-Hungarian empire and the home of conspirators and terrorists demanding Balkan freedom. The Austrian plan would go into effect in case of war. The Serbians learned about it from the Russians.

When terrorist Gavrilo Princip assassinated Archduke Franz Ferdinand in 1914, the Austrians put their plan into operation. The Serbians, knowing the plan, were able to hold the Austrians off until what Vienna thought would be a minor military operation developed into a shattering collision of the great powers, and World War I devastated the Continent.

Redl's treachery thus had enormous consequences. Like Kim Philby in British intelligence and Oleg Penkovskiy in Soviet intelligence, but even more than they, he remains a good example of a double agent at or near the top of his country's espionage system.

See also Nicolai, Walther.

FURTHER READING: *Maximilian Ronge, *The Treachery of Colonel Redl* (1921); Walther Nicolai, *The German Secret Service* (1924); Fitzroy Maclean, *Take Nine Spies* (1978), has a chapter on Redl.

Reilly, Sidney *(1874-1925?)*   British secret agent before, during, and after World War I.

Although Reilly was a mystery man who invented romantic stories about himself, his origins have been traced to Odessa, where he was born the illegitimate son of a Jewish doctor. He got away from his past (including his original name, Sigmund Rosenblum) as soon as he could. After studying chemistry in Vienna (1890–93), he went to Brazil, where he worked for some years with safaris penetrating the Amazon jungle. Arriving in London in 1896 with recommendations from a British officer he had known in Brazil, Reilly got a job with British intelligence. He married a wealthy widow, and in 1899 changed his name to Sidney George Reilly.

His travels took him to the Far East in 1902, where he may have been working for the Russians and Japanese, as well as for the British, and from which he reported correctly to London that the Manchu dynasty of China could not last much longer (it fell in 1912).

Back in England, Reilly seems to have mingled business and espionage during the decade 1905–1915. His travels took him to Germany, France, and Russia as those nations hurtled toward World War I (1914–18). In 1917, MI6 (Military Intelligence 6, British espionage) sent Reilly secretly to Germany on several assignments. By his own account, he once donned a German uniform, boldly walked into an officers' mess, and heard talk about a coming offensive on the western front. He also, again by his own account, joined the kaiser's entourage and learned of the plan for unrestricted submarine warfare.

After the war, British intelligence turned its efforts against the Communist regime that had seized power in Russia in 1917. A number of spies, Reilly among them, slipped into Moscow to work for an overthrow of the Bolsheviks. Protected by cover names and disguises, Reilly moved among the Bolsheviks as a Bolshevik and among the counterrevolutionaries as a counterrevolutionary. Since he received part of his funds from Bruce Lockhart, the head of a special mission from London, Reilly was caught in the so-called Lockhart plot, which Soviet intelligence alleged was a British scheme to murder Vladimir

Ilych Lenin and Leon Trotsky, the Soviet leaders. Reilly escaped from Russia before he could be arrested with Lockhart (who was expelled).

Reilly went back to Russia on missions of which little is known. He appeared in Warsaw in 1921, participating in an anti-Bolshevik congress of Russian refugees led by Boris Savinkov. The congress was a futile gesture that had no effect on events in the Soviet Union, except to make the Soviet political police more brutal toward opponents of the regime.

Reilly's name has been linked to the "Zinoviev letter" of 1924. Gregory Zinoviev was the head of the Communist International when it was alleged that a letter from him to the British Communist party called for action against the Conservatives and support of the Labour government. The whole thing was a hoax perpetrated in London to damage the Labourites in the 1924 election. Reilly was accused of inspiring, if not writing, the Zinoviev letter. No proof of this has ever been found.

Reilly went to Russia once more as a spy in 1925. This time he did not return. It has been said that he stayed because he had been a counterspy for Soviet intelligence all along, but he was almost certainly shot as a genuine British spy.

FURTHER READING: *Sidney George Reilly, *The Adventures of Sidney Reilly, Britain's Master Spy* (1931), published by Reilly's widow, is a memoir that mingles fact and fiction; Robin Lockhart, *Ace of Spies* (1967), is a biography by Bruce Lockhart's son; Edward Van Der Rhoer, *Master Spy: A True Story of Allied Espionage in Bolshevik Russia* (1981), claims Reilly was a counterspy for the Russians.

Reiss, Ignace *(1899-1937)*   Polish secret agent for, defector from, and victim of the Soviet intelligence establishment.

Reiss, like his friend Walter Krivitsky, came of a Polish-Jewish family in the province of Galicia, part of the Hapsburg empire. He was originally named Ludowik Poretsky. His parents were cultured, and he received a good education at home before attending school in Lvov before and during World War I (1914–18).

Attracted to radical politics at an early age, Reiss joined the socialists in Vienna in 1917. Two years later he moved further to the left, becoming a member of the Polish Communist party. He went to Moscow in 1920, supported the Bolsheviks, and in 1922 returned to Lvov as a secret agent for the Soviet Union.

Caught and imprisoned, Reiss escaped, fled to Moscow (1929), and in 1932 entered the OGPU (United State Political Administration, 1923–34; Soviet intelligence) He became resident director (espionage chief) of the OGPU in France, serving the cause of international Communism as Joseph Stalin rose to supreme power in the Soviet Union.

Stalin's destruction of the "old Bolsheviks" of the Russian Revolution in 1936 shook the faith of Reiss, who in the following year broke with the dictator and wrote a letter denouncing his crimes. Ludowik Poretsky now changed his name in order to hide from the agents of SMERSH ("Death to Spies"), the terror bureau of Soviet intelligence. Ludowik Poretsky became Ignace Reiss, the name by which he has been known ever since.

His attempts at concealment failed. Stalin's assassins tracked him down and murdered him in Switzerland. His fate triggered the defection of Krivitsky, who also was murdered by Stalin's agents.

See also KRIVITSKY, WALTER.

FURTHER READING: Ronald Seth, *The Executioners: The Story of SMERSH* (1967); *Elisabeth K. Poretsky, *Our Own People: A Memoir of "Ignace Reiss" and His Friends* (1970); Gordon Brook-Shepherd, *The Storm Petrels: The Flight of the First Soviet Defectors* (1977), has a chapter on Reiss.

Resident Director A head of a Soviet spy ring operating against a targeted country.

A resident director is a person named by the Center, Moscow's espionage headquarters, to control a network at a base abroad. Every espionage organization selects its spymasters very carefully, but Moscow has a special problem because of the danger of defection to the west. Every would-be resident director is checked thoroughly for firm Communist beliefs, party loyalty, and willingness to obey orders from the Center, no matter what they might be.

Usually the resident director resides in a country adjacent to, rather than in, the targeted country. The reason is that the chances of and penalties for being caught are not so great, since any nation is primarily concerned with its own security, not that of a neighbor. It is much more dangerous for a resident director who operates in the targeted country itself.

A resident director rarely is a Russian because of the complications for Moscow if the resident director is caught. He rarely is a native of the country he operates in because he might be identified or suffer from patriotic scruples that would not bother a foreigner.

Having set up his secret headquarters in the place to which he has been assigned, the resident director becomes the focal point of information and instructions coming in and going out. The Center keeps in touch with him not only through the ordinary channels of communication but also, occasionally, through members of the local Communist party. He reports back to the Center on everything from network expenses to unreliable agents that are being either sent home or eliminated.

Rudolf Abel was the most important resident director ever to be caught, and, significantly, he was a Russian who lived in the country against which he was conspiring, the United States. Sandor Rado, a Hungarian operating against Nazi Germany from Switzerland, showed how a resident director could compromise himself in Moscow by failing to keep sound financial accounts. Vladimir Petrov, in Australia, was the most important resident director to defect to the west.

See also ABEL, RUDOLF; CENTER, THE; PETROV, VLADIMIR; RADO, SANDOR.

FURTHER READING: Vladimir and Evdokia Petrov, *Empire of Fear* (1956), is an expose of Soviet espionage; *Ronald Seth, *Unmasked! The Story of Soviet Espionage* (1965); Louise Bernikow and Burt Silverman, *Abel* (1970), is an account of Rudolf Abel as undercover resident director in New York.

Revere, Paul *(1735-1818)* American spy and courier for the Patriots of Massachusetts during the American Revolution.

Revere, celebrated for the ride about which Henry Wadsworth Longfellow wrote a poem marred by historical inaccuracies, was born in Boston of Huguenot parents. After learning the trade of silversmith from his father, Revere served (1756) in the French and Indian War, and then returned to Boston, where he became a great silversmith. Politically, he was a Patriot from the start of the quarrel between the American colonies and Great Britain.

In 1770 he did the copper plate "Boston Massacre" that spread the familiar anti-British myth of what happened when a detachment of the king's soldiers clashed with a stone-throwing mob. As a member of the Sons of Liberty, Revere took part in the Boston Tea Party in 1773, when a band of Americans threw a cargo of British tea into Boston harbor, after which he rode to New York to announce the news. When the British government imposed the Intolerable Acts, including the closing of Boston harbor, Revere carried a Massachusetts appeal for support to the middle Atlantic colonies. Later he delivered the Suffolk Resolves, calling for defiance of the crown, to the Continental Congress in Philadelphia.

Revere was a skilled and energetic horseman who performed many missions for the Provincial Assembly of Massachusetts, one of them in 1775 to Portsmouth, New Hampshire, where his warning enabled a band of Patriots to break into a fort there and seize a store of arms and gunpowder before British soldiers arrived.

As the hostility deepened, Revere participated in spy activities in Boston under the cover of his silversmith's shop. He became a leader of America's first real espionage ring, the members of which filtered through the streets of the city, noting the number of British troops, their arms, their disposition, and their morale. This information went to the Committee of Safety, established by the Provincial Assembly and led by John Hancock.

Revere and his Patriots were thus spying on the British in Boston while Loyalist agents such as Benjamin Thompson were spying on the Americans outside Boston.

Laboring at his silversmith's trade and doing undercover work on the side, Revere remained on call as one who would leap into the saddle whenever the Committee of Safety had orders, warnings, or information to deliver. On April 16, 1775, he rode to Concord to warn that the British might march to seize the military stores in the town. He also warned John Hancock and Samuel Adams, leaders of the Massachusetts resistance, that they were in danger of being arrested. This was the occasion when Revere told William Conant, a Patriot living across the Charles River, that if the British moved, their route would be signaled from Boston by lantern from the steeple of North Church —"one if by land, two if by sea."

Revere's historic hour struck on April 18, when a flotilla of small boats in the Charles indicated that Gage was sending his men across to the other side to begin their march to Concord. The Committee of Safety ordered Revere and his fellow courier, William Dawes, to sound the alarm. Dawes rode along Boston Neck, the land route to Concord. Revere helped hang two signal lanterns in the belfry of North Church (he was not "on the opposite shore," as Longfellow has it). Then he took the water route, having himself rowed across the Charles by night in a boat with muffled oars. He went to the Conant house and obtained a horse for his ride. Galloping past the homes of the citizens, Revere gave the stentorian cry that echoes through history: "The British are coming!"

At Cambridge he eluded a British patrol and rode on with Dawes and Samuel Prescott, who had joined them. Revere got to Lexington, where he warned Hancock and Adams, but there he was stopped and arrested. Dawes got away but had to turn back. Prescott pounded on to Concord.

The three had fulfilled their mission. The word was out. Armed Patriots swarmed along the British line of march. The American War of Independence began at Lexington that morning.

Revere's captors released him, and he rode back to Boston. Although he saw some military service in the years that followed, he did nothing to enhance his reputation, but then anything would have been anticlimatic after "the midnight ride of Paul Revere." He printed the first Continental money and engraved seals for America and the state of Massachusetts. After the war was over (1783), he resumed his work as a silversmith, turning out some of the finest pieces ever done in the United States. He ran a copper mill, made defensive plating for American warships, one of which was the *Constitution* ("Old Ironsides"), and helped Robert Fulton construct boilers for steam vessels.

FURTHER READING: *Esther Forbes, *Paul Revere and the World He Lived In* (1942); Arthur B. Tourtellot, *Lexington and Concord* (1963); Walter M. Whitehill, *Paul Revere's Boston* (1975).

Richelieu, Cardinal *(1585-1642)*   French statesman and spymaster during the reign of King Louis XIII.

Richelieu, whose name was Armand Jean du Plessis, was born in Paris into a family of the French provincial nobility, seigneurs of Richelieu in Poitou. He entered the Church, became bishop of Luçon in 1607, and seven years later represented the clergy of his district at the last States-General to be summoned by the king of France before the French Revolution.

Gaining a place at court and backed by Marie de Medici, mother of King Louis XIII, Richelieu became secretary of state for foreign affairs (1616). His career was interrupted in 1617 when Marie fell into disfavor for meddling in political affairs. He returned to power in 1621 with the support of François Leclerc du Tremblay, a Capuchin friar at court, who would become his most trusted adviser. Richelieu became a cardinal in 1622, and in 1624 he rose to be chief minister to Louis XIII, a post he held for the rest of his life.

Richelieu organized a spy network inside France because of his many enemies who resented his place at the king's side and conspired to ruin him. Richelieu placed his secret agents wherever in the kingdom he suspected intrigues were germinating. His caution saved him at the most critical juncture of his career, when his spies alerted him in 1630 to the fact that the queen mother and some conspirators around her were trying to persuade the king to dismiss him. Richelieu appeared suddenly at the meeting, turned the tables on his enemies, convinced the king that he should be retained, and never lost the royal favor after that. Such was the "day of dupes," celebrated in French history.

Richelieu's foreign policy was to raise France to preeminence in Europe at the expense of the Hapsburgs. The Cardinal kept a network of spies transmitting information from the centers of power on the Continent. Most of all, he relied on his closest adviser and principal undercover agent, Tremblay, who soon became famous in European councils as "Father Joseph" and Richelieu's "Gray Eminence."

Richelieu sent Tremblay to the minor states of the Holy Roman Empire to stir up trouble for the Hapsburg emperor, Ferdinand II. During the Thirty Years' War (1618–48), the two French Catholic ecclesiastics intrigued against

Catholic Austria wherever they could. Richelieu, through his agents, helped the Protestant king of Sweden, Gustavus Adolphus, to invade the empire. Tremblay maneuvered the emperor into dismissing his best Catholic general, Albrecht von Wallenstein, in 1630.

Although the victories of Gustavus compelled the emperor to restore Wallenstein to his command in 1632, the damage had been done. The Protestant intervention planned and financed by Richelieu prevented the Hapsburgs from reimposing their old authority over the German states. Before the Cardinal's death, France was the premier European nation.

See also TREMBLAY, FRANCOIS LECLERC DU.

FURTHER READING: Henry Offley Wakeman, *The Ascendancy of France, 1598–1715* (n.d.); Aldous Huxley, *Gray Eminence* (1941); *G. R. Treasure, *Cardinal Richelieu and the Development of Absolutism* (1972).

Richer, Marthe *(1889-1950?)* French spy in Spain during World War I.

Richer was the daughter of a brewery worker in Blamont, in Lorraine, the family name being Betenfeld, indicating a German origin in the borderland between France and Germany. She received her early education in Blamont before entering a school in Nancy (1901), where she studied German for a year and obtained a certificate signifying her proficiency in the language. After three years of studying the art of the couturier, she established her own business in Paris (1906).

Fascinated by planes, Richer learned to fly and in 1913 became one of the first women in France to gain a pilot's license. She married Henri Richer in 1914, the year in which World War I began. When he was killed in action in 1915, she decided to fight against the Germans herself by volunteering for espionage work. Accepted by French intelligence, she was dispatched to Spain, where the Germans maintained a spy network headed by Baron Hans von Krohn of naval intelligence. Passing as a pro-German from Lorraine, Richer arrived in San Sebastian in 1916, moved freely amid the German colony in the Spanish seaport, met Krohn, and soon was living in Madrid as his mistress.

When he sent her to Paris on a spy mission regarding French armament production, she reported to French counterespionage and returned to Spain with instructions to remain with Krohn, to feed him misleading material prepared by her superiors, and to inform them about everything of military significance that she learned from the German spymaster. Given the code name "Alouette" ("Lark"), she carried on as a double agent for two years, at one point accompanying Krohn aboard a German submarine interned at Cádiz, which enabled her to describe this type of craft in a message to Paris.

In 1918 Richer abandoned Krohn as the war ended in Germany's defeat. Her espionage career ended at the same time.

FURTHER READING: *Marthe Richer, *I Spied for France* (1935); Richard Wilmer Rowan and Robert G. Deindorfer, *Secret Service: Thirty-three Centuries of Espionage* (1967), has a passage on Richer.

Rintelen, Franz von *(1877-1949)* German undercover agent in the United States during World War I.

Rintelen came of an aristocratic family, which gave him influential connections in Germany. His father was a banker with interests in the United States, so that Rintelen grew up speaking English fluently. He entered the German navy in 1903, rising rapidly through the grades. On the outbreak of World War I in 1914, he was a captain attached to the kaiser's naval high command.

America, although legally neutral, was actually pro-Allied, and the Germans decided to resort to undercover operations to prevent American war supplies from reaching the British and the French. Since these supplies moved by sea across the Atlantic, it was decided that at least one German agent in the United States ought to be a naval officer who understood ships and could sabotage them with professional skill.

Rintelen qualified in every respect. He was selected by his superiors to undertake the assignment.

Arriving in New York in 1915, Rintelen called on Franz von Papen, the German military attaché who had charge of undercover operations in the United States. The two men quarreled immediately, for Rintelen appalled Papen with his grandiose schemes for bombing American ships and committing arson against American warehouses. Papen, who had worked out less questionable covert activities with Heinrich Albert, the German commercial attaché, feared that Rintelen would compromise their whole campaign.

Rintelen refused to be dissuaded. Ignoring Papen, he went ahead with his own brand of espionage and sabotage, specializing in the use of technical devices he had developed or had had developed for him by a German scientist working in the United States. One device was a pipe divided by a copper plate into watertight compartments, the first filled with sulphuric acid and the other with picric acid. The sulphuric acid could be timed to eat through the copper, unite with the picric acid, and touch off a terrific explosion. Another device was a bomb triggered by the revolutions of a ship's propeller.

Rintelen claimed that he arranged through such time bombs for many American ships to be sunk or disabled on the high seas, a claim not sustained by merchant marine reports of 1915. Papen, a skeptic regarding Rintelen's boasts and considering him worse than useless, persuaded Berlin to recall him. Papen's message went out in a code broken by the British, and Reginald Hall, head of naval intelligence in London, had Rintelen removed from a Dutch ship (the Netherlands was a neutral nation) when it stopped at Southampton on the way to the Continent.

Rintelen believed that Papen deliberately planned to have this happen, which Papen denied, and after the war the two men exchanged angry accusations in which Papen was termed "a foolish and stupid intriguer" and Rintelen "a man of limited intelligence." There must have been something to be said for both descriptions: Berlin recalled Rintelen, and Washington expelled Papen not long afterward.

The British extradited Rintelen to the United States in 1917, and he spent the rest of World War I in the federal penitentiary in Atlanta, Georgia, after being convicted of sabotage. He returned to Britain, where he became a naturalized citizen.

See also PAPEN, FRANZ VON.

FURTHER READING: *Franz von Rintelen, *The Dark Invader* (1933); Franz von Papen, *Memoirs* (1952); David F. Trask (ed.), *World War One at Home: Readings on American Life, 1914–1920* (1969), gives the background to Rintelen's undercover conspiracies in the United States.

Ritter, Nikolaus *(1897-1960?)*   German spymaster responsible for espionage activities in the United States and Great Britain before and during World War II.

Born in the Rhineland, Ritter was the son of a university professor and therefore received a good education at home before attending local schools. He took his university degree in 1924 at Cologne. Turning from education to business (as the more profitable), he began to sell textiles in 1925. Two years later he went to America and managed a branch of his business in New York. The visit stretched into a career lasting a decade, until the bottom fell out of the textile market in 1937.

Returning to Germany in that year, Ritter used his fluency in English to gain a post in the Abwehr, German military intelligence, the head of which, Admiral Wilhelm Canaris, sent him back to America to organize German espionage in the United States. Ritter's greatest coup of 1937 concerned the Norden bombsight, a secret American invention permitting pinpoint accuracy in high-level bombing. His agent, Hermann Lang, an inspector in a factory producing the bombsight, made copies of the blueprints and turned them over to Ritter, who had them smuggled into Germany aboard ships of the Hamburg-Amerika line.

By the beginning of World War II in 1939, Ritter was a captain in the Abwehr with responsibility for espionage in Great Britain and America. He worked on Operation Sea Lion, the abortive German plan to invade England in 1940 after the fall of France. When Sea Lion was abandoned, Ritter waged an espionage war against Britain through his secret agents.

His campaign failed disastrously. None of his spies accomplished anything, and some, unknown to him, were "turned around" by British intelligence, becoming double agents reporting disinformation (plausible but false or trivial material) as part of the Double-Cross System developed in London.

However, Ritter made a fatal mistake in America, to which he sent William Sebold as a trusted agent in 1940. Sebold's emergence as a double agent for the United States against Germany and his court testimony against Lang and other German agents in 1941 compromised Ritter, who was transferred to duty with the Luftwaffe, the German air force.

After the end of the war in 1945, Ritter sought and found anonymity in private life.

See also DOUBLE-CROSS SYSTEM; LANG, HERMANN; SEBOLD, WILLIAM.

FURTHER READING: Karl Bartz, *The Downfall of the German Secret Service* (1956); *Günter Peis, *The Mirror of Deception: How Britain Turned the Nazi Spy Machine against Itself* (1976); David Kahn, *Hitler's Spies: German Military Intelligence in World War II* (1978).

Rivington, James *(1724-1802)*   British secret agent for the Americans during the American War of Independence.

His father being a London publisher, Rivington naturally went into the publishing business when he became old enough. He emigrated to America in 1760 to escape his debts and in the hope of finding better opportunities. However, although he established bookstores in New York, Philadelphia, and Boston within two years of his arrival, he lost two of them in 1766 because of an imprudent land scheme in which he became involved. He was forced to reorganize his business, and by 1768 he was again a solvent publisher in New York.

Rivington added a newspaper to his enterprises in 1773, in which he tried to be fair to both sides during the violence that preceded the American Revolution. After the outbreak of hostilities in 1775, a band of Americans, incensed by Rivington's inclusion of comments favorable to British policies in America, destroyed his press, an act of vandalism that caused him to flee to England in 1776. A year later he was back in New York, now under a British military occupation, with the title of the king's printer.

No longer neutral, Rivington founded a newspaper called the *Loyal Gazette,* later the *Royal Gazette.* As these names imply, he took a strong position in favor of King George III and against the American advocates of independence. The printer changed his mind as the balance of power in the war shifted against the British.

In 1779 he went into partnership in a coffeehouse with Robert Townsend, a pretended Loyalist who was actually a member of the Culper Ring, an espionage network operating in New York. The effect of the partnership on Rivington's political convictions is unknown, for Townsend was discretion itself with regard to his undercover activities, and it seems unlikely that Rivington would have known about them. Similarly, Townsend probably never knew about Rivington's change of heart. The implication is that the two partners were pretended Loyalists and real Patriots, and that the fact was unknown to either of them.

In any case, by 1781 at the latest Rivington was sending secret information from New York to General George Washington. Rivington also misled the British commander in New York, Sir Henry Clinton, by spreading false reports about Washington's strategy. Thus, Washington, heading for Virginia and the battle of Yorktown, kept Clinton immobilized by pretending to plan an attack on New York. Rivington published a report of this supposed military operation and helped convince Clinton that the report was true. Consequently, Clinton's forces stayed in New York, while their comrades were defeated at Yorktown (1781).

Rivington, still outwardly a Loyalist, was in danger from the Patriots while the British were evacuating New York in 1783. Washington's spymaster, Major Benjamin Tallmadge, entering the city to protect those who had served the American cause clandestinely, included Rivington among them. Rivington remained safe in New York until his death.

See also TOWNSEND, ROBERT.

FURTHER READING: *Catherine Snell Crary, "The Tory and the Spy: The Double Life of James Rivington," *William and Mary Quarterly* (1959); John Bakeless, *Turncoats, Traitors, and Heroes* (1959), discusses Rivington as an American spy; Corey Ford, *A Peculiar Service* (1965), is the fullest account of Rivington within the setting of his espionage activities.

Robertson, James *(1770?-1820)*   Scottish Catholic monk and British secret agent during the Napoleonic Wars.

Born in Scotland into a Catholic family, Robertson was taken as a youth to the Scottish Benedictines of Regensburg, Bavaria, where he eventually made his religious vows and became a monk of the order. His superiors sent him to Scotland on a religious mission in 1797, and he was there when Britain and France, led by Napoleon Bonaparte, went to war in 1801.

Robertson came to the attention of the British government in 1808, when a German-speaking secret agent was needed for an undercover mission through Germany to Denmark. Napoleon, now emperor of France, had forced Spain to garrison the Danish islands with some 15,000 men, his purpose being to have this military force out of the way while he conquered their homeland. The British, starting a campaign to drive the French from Spain back over the Pyrenees, wanted to transfer the Spaniards from Denmark to Spain, where they could take part in the campaign. London's undercover mission was to reach the Spanish general, the Marquis de la Romana, and arrange for the transfer aboard a British fleet.

Robertson, the monk from Regensburg, accepted the assignment. Doffing his clerical garb, he donned layman's clothing and went to the Continent posing as a salesman and using the cover name "Adam Rohrauer." His first stop was Heligoland, an island in the North Sea near the mouth of the Weser River, the site of a British military station where a secret service agent briefed him about conditions in the German states under French occupation, explained how British ships could sail covertly to the islands and take the Spaniards off, and gave him a boat for the short voyage to Hamburg.

Once ashore, Robertson ran a grave risk, for Napoleon's minister of police, Joseph Fouché, had a network of spies, French and German, in Germany. Robertson's cover name and cover story saved him. Speaking fluent German, he peddled his wares and at the same time learned that some sick and injured Spanish soldiers were in a hospital at Altona near Hamburg. Visiting the hospital, he spoke to the soldiers as a Catholic to Catholics, and they informed him that their general was on Fyn, largest of the Danish islands.

Robertson now moved into the hinterland, crossed Germany, and reached Fyn, where he persuaded the Marquis de la Romana to agree to a covert embarkation for Spain. They set a day for a rendezvous with a British flotilla.

Back in Heligoland, the Scottish Benedictine reported to the secret service agent, who arranged a successful rendezvous with the Spaniards. Most of the men were picked up and carried to Spain, where they helped the British commander Wellington win the Peninsular War (1808–14) against the French.

Robertson returned to London, lived for a time in Dublin, and in 1813 undertook for the British government diplomatic assignments that required fluent German but no risky espionage activity. Wellington employed him on diplomatic assignments in 1813, and in 1815 London bestowed a pension on him in recognition of his contribution to the victory over France.

Again wearing the habit of a Benedictine monk, Robertson returned to the monastery at Regensburg. He spent his final years writing a manuscript about his undercover exploits and doing humanitarian work among the blind and deaf of Bavaria.

See also WELLINGTON, DUKE OF.

FURTHER READING: *James Robertson, *Narrative of a Secret Mission to the Danish Islands in 1808* (Alexander Clinton Fraser, ed., 1863); Felix Markham, *Napoleon and the Awakening of Europe* (1965), describes the international setting of Robertson's espionage coup; Richard Deacon, *A History of the British Secret Service* (1969), has an account of Robertson the secret agent.

Roessler, Rudolf *(1897-1958)*   Anti-Nazi German spy in Switzerland.

Roessler was born in Kaufbeuren, a Bavarian town where his father held a post in the forestry department of the city government. The strongly Protestant faith of his parents influenced Roessler at home while he was receiving his education at the local schools. On the outbreak of World War I in 1914, he left high school to serve in the German army. Discharged following Germany's surrender in 1918, he moved to Augsburg and became a journalist. Ten years later he was in Berlin making his living as a newspaper critic and moving among theater people and café intellectuals.

Roessler's Berlin period (1928–33) ended because of the success of the Nazi movement, which he abhorred. He left for Switzerland when Adolf Hitler became chancellor of Germany (1933), and in 1934 he established a publishing house, the Vita Nova Verlag, in Lucerne. For the next five years, he ran his business as if he were simply one more political exile from Nazi Germany. Actually, he was in touch with anti-Nazi forces within Germany, and in 1939, as World War II approached, a Swiss espionage officer, Xavier Schnieper, persuaded Roessler to make his information available to Swiss intelligence.

The connection could not be official, because the Swiss feared it would be a provocation to their aggressive neighbor, Nazi Germany. Roessler therefore began to work for an intelligence organization nominally independent of the government, the Bureau Ha, so called because it had been founded by Captain Hans Hausamann. Roessler appeared regularly at Bureau Ha headquarters, where he reported his latest information from Berlin. His accuracy regarding Hitler's war plans made General Henri Guisan, commander of Switzerland's armed forces, rely on him to an increasing extent, especially after the German conquest of France in 1940, when the French army ceased to shield the Swiss from the Germans.

The mystery about Roessler was and is the identity of his sources inside Germany. He was able to provide details on Hitler's strategy sessions, on decisions regarding the deployment of the German armed forces, and on battlefield tactics and weaponry to be used in coming German campaigns. Roessler is even said to have obtained in advance the top-secret plans for Operation Barbarossa, the German invasion of Russia in 1941. Evidently Roessler had informants in or close to the German high command. It has been said that he once identified as his principal source General Hans Oster, second in command at intelligence headquarters in Berlin and a known conspirator against Hitler before and during the war, but the report remains dubious. Another suggestion is that much of Roessler's information about Germany came from London after British cryptanalysts broke the principal German code and began to read German orders broadcast in the code.

Whatever the explanation, Roessler received his information by radio and passed it on to the Swiss. At the same time, he received from the Bureau Ha information picked up by Swiss intelligence that Guisan wanted passed on to the Allies. In 1942 Roessler began to work for the Soviet spy network headed by Sandor Rado in Geneva, a practice that Guisan winked at as long as he could so that Moscow could be warned about Hitler's plans for the invasion of the Soviet Union. Roessler never allowed Rado to know his identity. He delivered his messages to a go-between, Christian Schneider (known as "Taylor"), who in turn delivered them to Rado's go-between, Rachel Duebendorfer ("Sissy"). Rado bestowed the code name "Lucy" on his unknown informant in Lucerne, and until the network ceased operating only Schneider knew that Lucy was Roessler.

German counterintelligence quickly learned that clandestine radios were transmitting information from Switzerland to Moscow. Berlin brought pressure on Guisan, who for fear of a German military move against Switzerland, ordered his own counterintelligence to disrupt the Rado network, which occurred with the arrest of some of its operatives in 1943. Although Rado escaped, Roessler was among those rounded up. He was jailed briefly as a face-saving measure for the Swiss and to pacify the Germans, found not guilty of espionage, and released. The German threat to Switzerland ended with Germany's defeat (1945).

After the war, Roessler went back to publishing in Lucerne, suffered financial reverses, and agreed to work for the Russians again, but without Swiss approval. Now he transmitted information on the Allied forces in Europe to espionage channels in Soviet-dominated Czechoslovakia. Most of the facts he gathered could be found in American, British, French, or Swiss newspapers, and he resorted to such hoary espionage practices as hiding documents in food parcels sent through the mail. One package was opened, counterespionage was alerted, and Roessler found himself facing a Swiss court. He went on trial in 1952, and received a sentence of one year. Afterward, he remained in Switzerland, which he was allowed to do because of his old association with Swiss security, and he resumed his publishing business until his death.

See also BUREAU HA; DUEBENDORFER, RACHEL; GUISAN, HENRI; OSTER, HANS; RADO, SANDOR.

FURTHER READING: Jon Kimche, *Spying for Peace* (2nd ed., 1961), is an account of espionage in Switzerland during World War II; Pierre Accoce and Pierre Quet, *A Man Called Lucy* (1966), is a book on Roessler that contains too many mistaken or arbitrary judgments; *Paul L. Kesaris (ed.), *The Rote Kapelle: The CIA's History of Soviet Intelligence and Espionage Networks in Western Europe, 1939–1945* (1979), is an account of the general system to which Rado's network belonged, with comments on Roessler; Anthony Read and David Fisher, *Operation Lucy: The Most Secret Spy Ring of the Second World War* (1981).

Room 40   Headquarters of British naval intelligence during World War I.

The British navy had long maintained an intelligence division when the outbreak of World War I created a crisis because the Germans were broadcasting in codes they considered unbreakable. Admiral Henry Oliver, head of the division in 1914, asked Alfred Ewing, an expert in codes, to gather a staff of experienced cryptologists and start working on the German codes. Oliver received a promotion in November, and Captain Reginald Hall, replacing him, moved Ewing's group into Room 40 in the Old Building of the Admiralty. From then on, "Room 40" stood for naval intelligence, its secrecy, its undercover work, and its startling achievements.

The achievements resulted partly from three windfalls. In 1914, after Russian warships sank a German cruiser, a drowned German sailor was recovered from the water still clutching a copy of the German naval code book, which the Russians made available to the British. Also in 1914, a British trawler fishing in the North Sea brought up a chest from a sunken German submarine, and the chest contained the German naval attaché code book, used by Berlin in communicating with its embassies abroad. In 1915 a trunk left behind by Wilhelm Wassmuss, the German consul in Bushire, Persia (modern Iran), when he escaped from British troops was opened in London and found to contain the German diplomatic code. These guides permitted Room 40 to make immediate translations of all documents in their codes.

The great coup for Room 40 came in 1917 when Hall's experts read the "Zimmermann telegram," the notorious German note that promised the states of the American southwest to Mexico if Mexico would become a belligerent with Germany. The transmission of this information to Washington was instrumental in bringing the United States into the war on the side of the Allies.

The final achievement of Room 40 was its report in 1918 that sailors of the German navy had mutinied. The kaiser, realizing that the end had come for him and his empire, fled into exile, and Germany surrendered.

See also HALL, REGINALD; WASSMUSS, WILHELM; ZIMMERMANN TELEGRAM.

FURTHER READING: H. C. Hoy, *40 O.B., or How the War Was Won* (1934); Reginald Hall and Amos Peaslee, *Three Wars with Germany* (1944); *William James, *The Code Breakers of Room 40* (1956).

Rosenberg, Julius *(1918-53)* **and Ethel** *(1915-53)*   American spies for the Soviet Union.

The Rosenbergs are united in history as in life because they were convicted and punished for their dual activities in one of the most notorious and damaging espionage rings active in the western democracies.

Both Rosenbergs, children of Jewish immigrants, were born and raised in New York. Ethel Greenglass, after graduating from high school, tried the performing arts—drama, music, and dancing—with minor success. She took office jobs, and became a left-wing radical involved in protests and strikes during the Great Depression. She met Julius Rosenberg at a workers' fundraising affair and married him in 1939.

Rosenberg came from a religious family, and his father sent him to Hebrew schools in the hope that he would become a rabbi. Instead, the son abandoned religion for Marxist philosophy and Leninist principles of revolution. He went to City College in New York, took a degree in electrical engineering, and emerged a card-carrying Communist. He married Ethel Greenglass in the year of his graduation, and the pair took up militant Communism.

In 1939 the Rosenbergs defended Stalin's pact with Hitler and agitated for American neutrality when Hitler started World War II. In 1941, following Nazi Germany's attack on the Soviet Union, the Rosenbergs demanded all-out American support for Stalin's Russia.

Meanwhile, Julius Rosenberg had in 1940 obtained a civilian job with the U.S. Signal Corps. Evidence brought out at their trial indicates that he and his wife were already spying for the Russians when her brother, David Greenglass, was assigned to the atomic installation at Los Alamos, New Mexico, in 1944, with access to classified information about the development of the atomic bomb.

According to Greenglass, the Rosenbergs drew him into their espionage ring, one that included scientist Klaus Fuchs, courier Harry Gold, and Soviet spymaster Anatoly Yakovlev. That Greenglass, at the instigation of the Rosenbergs, stole atomic data for the Russians is now generally accepted, as is the guilt of the Rosenbergs in gathering classified information from other sources.

Although Julius Rosenberg was so indiscreet in his pro-Soviet talk that the Signal Corps dropped him in 1945, no hint of treason had been alleged against him. He went into business with Greenglass in 1946, the year in which Greenglass, by his own testimony, refused to do any more spying for the Rosenbergs and the Russians. The brothers-in-law quarreled, and the parting of the ways came in 1949, when Greenglass walked out.

Everything collapsed for the Rosenbergs and Greenglass in the following year. The British authorities, alerted by the FBI (Federal Bureau of Investigation), arrested Fuchs, whose testimony started a chain of arrests leading from Gold to Greenglass to the Rosenbergs.

Gold and Greenglass received prison terms. Their testimony contributed to the guilty verdict at the trial of the Rosenbergs, who throughout the proceedings denied the charge that they had committed espionage but failed to convince the jury. Sentenced to death, the condemned couple appealed all the way to the Supreme Court, which declined to stay the execution. President Dwight D. Eisenhower refused to exercise executive clemency in their behalf, and the Rosenbergs were executed in 1953.

See also FUCHS, KLAUS; GOLD, HARRY; GREENGLASS, DAVID; ROSENBERG CASE; SOVIET AMERICAN NETWORK.

FURTHER READING: Oliver Pilat, *The Atom Spies* (1952); Ronald Seth, *Unmasked! The Story of Soviet Espionage* (1965); Louis Nizer, *The Implosion Conspiracy* (1973); *H. Montgomery Hyde, *The Atom Bomb Spies* (1980).

Rosenberg Case *(1951-53)* Furor surrounding the fate of the convicted spies Julius and Ethel Rosenberg.

Julius and Ethel Rosenberg received death sentences in 1951 on charges of spying for the Russians. The verdict came under attack from those who considered that the Rosenbergs were innocent, and the sentences were attacked by those who thought that the Rosenbergs were guilty as charged but did not deserve to die.

Mass rallies in U.S. cities and abroad featured speakers who demanded that the condemned pair be rescued from death row. Pleas for clemency reached the White House from the president of France, from Pope Pius XII, and from other influential Europeans, as well as from American politicians, clergymen, and other concerned citizens. Ambassadors reported from American embassies in many countries that the prestige of the United States would be damaged if the executions were carried out.

Those who sought to save the Rosenbergs often argued that their trial was an example of anti-Semitism in action, the couple being condemned because they were Jews. Those who argued thus ignored or termed irrelevant the fact that the judge and the prosecutor in the Rosenberg trial were also Jews.

Personalities became involved. David Greenglass, the brother of Ethel Rosenberg, was savagely denounced as a spy and a criminal. His appearance at the Rosenberg trial was attacked on contradictory grounds—that he either lied about the defendants or acted like a scoundrel in telling what he knew about his sister and brother-in-law.

Greenglass and Harry Gold, another spy and a witness against the Rosenbergs, received jail sentences. The cry went up that the Rosenbergs deserved nothing worse than the same treatment. Morton Sobell, a member of the espionage ring who stood trial with the Rosenbergs, went to jail. Why make exceptions of his two codefendants?

Those who believed in the justice of the verdict agreed with the court that the Rosenbergs had filled a unique directing role in the Soviet network and that, therefore, they were much worse than the others. Judge Irving Kaufman made the point that the Rosenbergs had been the most dangerous to America's national security of all who had conspired to pass classified information to the Russians. He concluded, therefore, that the harshest verdict on them was justified.

The American courts, up to the Supreme Court, validated that judgment. All of the Rosenbergs' appeals were turned down. Only President Eisenhower could have saved them. That hope ended when Eisenhower announced that he had reviewed the evidence, still agreed with the court, and would not intervene to stop the executions.

When the Rosenbergs were gone, their names did not fade into oblivion. Their partisans and their opponents continued to quarrel in print, and books still appear on one side or the other. The prevalent opinion remains today that the defendants were guilty, but even those who remain convinced that justice was done can feel the poignance of the defense of Julius and Ethel Rosenberg by their sons, who were young children when the executions took place in 1953.

See also GOLD, HARRY; GREENGLASS, DAVID; ROSENBERG, JULIUS AND ETHEL; SOVIET AMERICAN NETWORK.

FURTHER READING: Malcolm P. Sharp, *Was Justice Done? The Rosenberg-Sobell Case* (1956); *Louis Nizer, *The Implosion Conspiracy* (1973); Michael Meeropol and Robert Meeropol, *We Are Your Sons: The Legacy of Ethel and Julius Rosenberg, Written by Their Children, Robert and Michael* (1975); H. Montgomery Hyde, *The Atom Bomb Spies* (1980).

Rougeville, Alexandre de *(1761-1814)*   French royalist conspirator during the French Revolution.

Rougeville, born Alexandre Gonsse, son of a prosperous farmer of Artois, was given to telling interesting fictions about himself, one being that he had a right to the aristocratic title he used. He never served, as he claimed, on General George Washington's staff during the American War of Independence or on the staff of the brother of the king of France before the French Revolution. It is true that Rougeville somehow made his way into the royal entourage at Versailles, where he was one of the loyal group called "Knights of the Dagger" around King Louis XVI and Queen Marie Antoinette.

When the French Revolution began in 1789, Rougeville opposed it. When a mob stormed the Tuileries, a royal palace in Paris (1792), Rougeville defended the queen and led her to safety. The violence increased, and the royal pair, captured while trying to escape from France, were imprisoned. On January 21, 1793, Louis XVI was executed by order of the revolutionary tribunal, the dreaded court that hastened many of its victims to the guillotine.

From the beginning of the revolution, royalists had conspired in behalf of the king. There were royalist riots in the provinces and royalist intrigues in Paris. When the king and queen were imprisoned, many plans, all unsuccessful, were devised to rescue them. The death of Louis XVI left Marie Antoinette as the focus of royalist concern.

The transfer of the queen from her first prison to the Conciergerie galvanized her partisans, for this was the last stopping-point for accused persons before facing the revolutionary tribunal. Her life was now plainly in danger, and any rescue attempt would have to be made quickly.

Rougeville, who had by then already been involved in royalist conspiracies that had come to nothing, decided to take the lead in a supreme effort to get Marie Antoinette out of the Conciergerie, out of Paris, and out of France. His scheme became known as the "Carnation affair."

The precise details are probably beyond discovery, but on August 23, 1793, Rougeville gained entry into the queen's cell. Using a confident bearing and a smooth tongue, he got past her guards and dropped two carnations, attached to which she found a note reminding her that she had friends she could rely on. She pricked a return message with a pin on a piece of paper, indicating that she would be ready for anything at the critical moment.

Rougeville returned two days later. Again passing her guards, he had a hurried conversation with the queen in which they agreed on September 2 as the day on which Rougeville and his confederates would rush into the prison and escape with her.

Marie Antoinette, always unfortunate, had given her message to a guard she supposed to be loyal to pass on to Rougeville. The guard took it to the wife of the prison warden, who gave it to the inspector of prisons. The message reached the authorities, and on the day set by Rougeville for the queen's rescue, the way out was barred. That was the final chance for Marie Antoinette, who went to the guillotine on October 16, 1793.

Other heads rolled over the Carnation affair, but not Rougeville's. He escaped in the confusion. Remaining a royalist throughout the revolution and the Napoleonic era, he hailed the return of King Louis XVIII from exile just before Napoleon's abdication as emperor of France in 1814. Napoleon's agents had time to seize Rougeville and execute him.

FURTHER READING: *Thomas Carlyle, *The French Revolution* (1837), has an eloquent description of the efforts to save Marie Antoinette; Dorothy Moulton Mayer, *Marie Antoinette* (1968); Vincent Cronin, *Louis and Antoinette* (1975).

Rowan, Andrew *(1857-1943)* American army officer and secret agent during the Spanish-American War.

Born in Virginia, Rowan experienced the hardships of the Civil War (1861–65) and the rigors of Reconstruction, which followed the defeat of the Confederacy. Reconciled to the Union, he entered West Point in 1877 and received his commission in the U.S. Army in 1881. During the 1880s he served in the Bureau of Military Intelligence in Washington and in the American Embassy in Santiago, Chile, as military attaché.

The decision of President William McKinley to support the Cuban rebels against Spain in 1898 created a need in Washington to know what the rebels required to keep them from being suppressed by the Spanish troops on the island. Someone had to find and consult with Calixto García, the rebel leader. Colonel Arthur Wagner, chief of the Bureau of Military Intelligence, chose Rowan for this assignment.

Rowan traveled to Jamaica and was taken in a small boat to a covert nighttime landing in Cuba's Oriente Province. His cover story, should he be stopped by the Spaniards, was that he was an English hunter out after game in the Cuban jungle. Already alerted, a party of rebels met him on the beach and escorted him on a rugged four-day trip through a wilderness in which paths had to be hacked with machetes through the undergrowth.

Slowed by swamps and creepers, harassed by flies and mosquitoes, they slipped past Spanish scouts, sentries, outposts, and military encampments. Rowan took every opportunity to estimate the numbers, disposition, and armament of the forces of the king of Spain. He also gathered information from Cubans loyal to the rebel cause whom he met along the way.

The journey ended at Bayamo, where García had set up his headquarters from which to direct guerrilla warfare against the Spaniards. In hurried consultations, Rowan learned that guns and ammunition were García's fundamental needs, food and supplies being secondary. Rowan also learned from García details about Spanish troop movements, harbor defenses, and morale.

With the conference, Rowan had completed the first part of his assignment. The second part was to get out of Cuba without being caught. García gave him an escort back to the coast, where he took a boat to Nassau and from there reached Key West.

Rowan's spy mission to Cuba contributed to the successful American strategy in the Spanish-American War. He did two tours of duty in the Philippine Islands during the first decade of the twentieth century before leaving military service in 1909. His place in American history is that of the man who carried the message to García.

FURTHER READING: *Andrew S. Rowan, *How I Carried the Message to Garcia* (n.d.); George S. Bryan, *The Spy in America* (1943); Donald Barr Chidsey, *The Spanish-American War* (1971), gives the background to Rowan's spy work.

Royal Canadian Mounted Police Administrative department originally responsible for Canada's internal security, including counterespionage.

This celebrated organization began as the North-West Mounted Rifles (1873), changed almost immediately to the North-West Mounted Police (1873–1904), continued as the Royal North-West Mounted Police (1904–20), and gained its present title in 1920.

Established to maintain law and order in the Canadian west, the Royal Canadian Mounted Police (RCMP) patrolled an enormous terrain, extending from the American border to the Arctic. Its duties ranged from pursuing criminals to aiding settlers who arrived unprepared for the harsh winters or the rugged farming conditions. In 1898 the men of the RCMP moved into the Yukon to police the Gold Rush, as hordes of prospectors poured into the area hoping to strike it rich by panning the streams. The presence of the "Mounties" was a major reason why the Yukon gold camps were peaceful compared to the turbulence of the Alaskan camps over the mountains to the west.

The twentieth century saw the development of the RCMP into one of the world's notable crime-fighting organizations, equipped with laboratories for the scientific analysis of evidence, large fingerprint and other identification files, and an academy for training police officers. In 1942 one of its ships made the first crossing of the Northwest Passage from west to east. The RCMP grew into seventeen divisions operating throughout Canada except in the provinces of Ontario and Quebec. The commissioner runs the organization from his headquarters in Ottawa and keeps in touch with liaison officers in London and Washington. The force switched from horses to motorized vehicles during the 1960s, but conditions in the Arctic still require the use of dog sleds.

Counterespionage became a central concern following World War II, with the exposure of Russian espionage in Canada. Igor Gouzenko, the code clerk who defected from the Soviet Embassy in 1945, gave his story to the RCMP, which followed his leads and broke the case of the atomic spies who belonged to the Soviet Canadian Network. In 1960 the RCMP's discovery of the facts about the notorious Gerda Munsinger led to the Munsinger affair, a political scandal involving high-ranking members of the Canadian government.

Today the RCMP works with computers and other sophisticated technical equipment, but some of the glamour of the past remains, especially the reputation of the Mounties in scarlet tunics and whipcord breeches who "always get their man."

However, during the 1970s allegations were made that the RCMP had violated the civil rights of Canadian citizens during internal-security investigations. Some members of the organization were accused of illegal wiretapping and opening of mail, of forced entry into private premises in search of evidence, and of responsibility for such "dirty tricks" as making fraudulent calls for resistance to the Canadian government, ostensibly by the Quebec Liberation Front. A commission established in 1977 confirmed so many of the allegations that in 1981 the government took internal security and counterespionage responsibilities away from the RCMP and gave them to the newly formed Security Intelligence Service.

See also GOUZENKO, IGOR; MUNSINGER AFFAIR; SECURITY INTELLIGENCE SERVICE; SOVIET CANADIAN NETWORK.

FURTHER READING: *Nora and William Kelly, *The Royal Canadian Mounted Police: A Century of History, 1873–1973* (1973); H. Montgomery Hyde, *The Atom Bomb Spies* (1980); *Report of the McDonald Royal Commission* (1981).

RSHA *(1939-45)*   Main security department of Germany's Third Reich.

The initials RSHA stand for the German title meaning "Reich Central Security Office." Adolf Hitler, as chancellor of Germany and architect of World War II, organized all his police forces under Heinrich Himmler in 1939 in order to tighten security. The RSHA, the part of the system under Reinhard Heydrich, was made up of the Gestapo (the secret police), the SD (civilian intelligence), and the criminal police. It had responsibility for protecting Hitler's Nazi Third Reich, and its powers were virtually unlimited. Its Office VI, run by Adolf Eichmann, had responsibility for the "final solution," the Nazi attempt to exterminate the Jews of Europe.

Heydrich directed the RSHA until his assassination by Czech undercover agents in 1942. Himmler replaced him on an interim basis until Ernst Kaltenbrunner assumed control in 1943. Kaltenbrunner's authority broadened in 1944, when the Abwehr (military intelligence) was absorbed into his organization. After the defeat of Germany by the Allies in 1945, the RSHA was dismantled, and Kaltenbrunner lost his title (he was executed as a war criminal after the trials at Nuremberg in 1946).

See also ABWEHR; EICHMANN, ADOLF; GESTAPO; HEYDRICH, REINHARD.

FURTHER READING: *Telford Taylor, *The Nuremberg Trials, War Crimes and International Law* (1949); Willi Frischauer, *Himmler* (1953); G. S. Graber, *The Life and Times of Reinhard Heydrich* (1980).

Sabotage Clandestine damage to physical objects considered essential to the capabilities of an enemy or potential enemy.
See COVERT OPERATION.

Saint-Germain, Count *(1696?-1784)* Mystery man and undercover agent in the service of King Louis XV of France.

Saint-Germain's origins—his family and place of birth—are as unknown today as they were in his time. He used to hint that he was of European royalty, but he never satisfied the curiosity of his contemporaries by mentioning the branch or the nation. He appeared quite suddenly, an individual gifted in music, painting, languages, and occultism.

An early mention of him is by the English writer Horace Walpole, who in one of his famous letters places him in London in 1743, working as a musician and calling himself Count Saint-Germain. Two years later Saint-Germain was accused of being a spy for the Jacobites, partisans of the Stuarts who had been exiled on the Continent since James II fled from the throne of England in 1688 at the time of the Glorious Revolution. The "Old Pretender," who used the title James III, had failed to regain the throne by force in 1715. In 1745 his son was leading a second attempt, the "Forty Five." Fearful of a Jacobite rising in England, the British government rounded up suspected Jacobite spies, of whom Saint-Germain was one. He cooly defended himself when interrogated, and he was released for lack of evidence.

He dropped out of sight for over a decade (possibly, as occultists have always contended, mastering the mystic arts) and then arrived in Paris, where Giacomo Casanova, the Venetian adventurer, writer, and spy, met him in 1757. By then Saint-Germain was a confidant of Jeanne Antoinette d'Étioles, marquise de Pompadour, the mistress of Louis XV. He was also working for the king as an alchemist and an undercover agent. The king set up an alchemical laboratory for him in the hope that he could solve France's financial problems by turning base metals into gold. No gold was forthcoming, and the project was canceled.

In 1759 Saint-Germain went on a secret mission to The Hague. Exactly what the mission was remains debatable. He found Casanova there, also on a secret mission. Both men failed to achieve their objectives, whatever these may have been, and each decided not to return to Paris. Perhaps Saint-Germain could not go back because Casanova suspected him of playing a double game and warned the Dutch and French authorities. At any rate, the French government did ask the Dutch to arrest Saint-Germain, who learned about the request and fled to England.

The whole episode, however, may have been a maneuver by Louis XV and his ministers to get a secret agent into London during the Seven Years' War (1756–63) to report on the plans of the British government. Prime Minister William Pitt thought so, for he termed Saint-Germain a spy for the French and ordered him to leave England forthwith (1760).

Saint-Germain was considered in his subsequent wanderings to be a secret agent for various governments and individuals, something he could succeed at because he belonged to the occult underground of Europe, where he could both acquire information and find safety. All this is conjecture, because he hid what he was doing. He emerges into the light of history at the end of his career, serving (1779–84) as resident occultist to the mystical Karl, prince of Hesse.

See also CASANOVA, GIACOMO.

FURTHER READING: Pierre Gaxotte, *Louis the Fifteenth and His Times* (1934); *Giacomo Casanova, *History of My Life* (1962); Arthur E. Waite, *Alchemists through the Ages* (1970), traces the occult tradition to which Saint-Germain belonged.

Sansom, Odette *(1912-   )*   British spy in France during World War II.

Sansom was French by origin, the daughter of a banker in Amiens who went into the French army during World War I and was killed in 1916 at the battle of Verdun. Educated in a convent at Saint Sens, near Rouen, she married an Englishman named Roy Sansom in 1931, and they moved to England a year later.

After the fall of France to the invading Germans in 1940, she provided the British authorities with photographs of her area of the coast of northern France for use in bombing missions and secret landings from small boats or submarines.

In 1942 Sansom joined the Special Operations Executive (SOE), the British organization charged with supporting underground campaigns against the Germans on the Continent. Her code name was "Lise." She landed surreptitiously on the Riviera near Cannes and made her way inland to bring money and encouragement to clandestine French spy networks, and to act as a radio operator for them in reporting to London. Another SOE operative, Peter Churchill, was her superior in the underground. He found her so expert in her spy activities that he asked London to let her stay, and the request was granted.

In 1943 an arrested French spy informed on them, and they were picked up by the Germans, who transported them to Germany and sent Sansom to the women's camp at Ravensbrück, where she experienced the horrors of the Nazi system. Saved by the collapse of Germany in 1945, Sansom testified before a war-crimes court in Hamburg in 1946, identifying women she had seen mistreating prisoners at Ravensbrück (four of the defendants were sentenced to death for their crimes). Peter Churchill's name saved him—the Germans thought he was related to Winston Churchill, the British prime minister.

The death of Sansom's husband left her free to marry again. She became the wife of her wartime comrade-in-arms, Peter Churchill. Unfortunately, that was not the end of the story: they were divorced in 1955. Odette retained one tangible reminder of their exciting days together—the George Cross awarded to her by the British government for her bravery as a spy in France during the war.

See also CHURCHILL, PETER; SPECIAL OPERATIONS EXECUTIVE.

FURTHER READING: *Jerrard Tickell, *Odette: The Story of a British Agent* (1949); Peter Churchill, *The Spirit in the Cage* (1955); M. R. D. Foot, *SOE in France: An Account of the Work of the British Special Operations Executive in France, 1940–1944* (1966).

Savary, René *(1774-1833)*   French minister of police and spymaster during the Napoleonic Wars.

Born in the Ardennes region of eastern France, Savary was of the right age to profit from the rise of Napoleon Bonaparte. Joining the French army in

1790 after the outbreak of the French Revolution, Savary took part in the campaigns along the Rhine before being selected in 1798 to serve in the Egyptian campaign from which Napoleon returned to enter French politics. By 1800 Savary was one of the generals closest to Napoleon, who was now the most powerful man in France.

Savary remained loyal to Napoleon, who became emperor of France in 1804, through victory and defeat. He held military and diplomatic posts, was given the title duke of Rovigo in 1808, and in 1810 replaced Joseph Fouché as minister of police.

Savary gained this position because he had already done undercover work for Napoleon. In 1799 Savary met Karl Schulmeister, brought him into French espionage, and thereby provided France with the best spy of the period. In 1804, when Napoleon wanted to frighten French aristocrats plotting against him outside France, he ordered the execution of the duke of Enghien, who was living in Germany near the Rhine. A detachment of French soldiers kidnaped the duke and rushed him to Vincennes near Paris. Savary commanded the troops in the Vincennes area as Enghien was hurriedly tried, condemned, and disposed of by a French firing squad.

When Savary took over the ministry of police in 1810, he found that Fouché, embittered by his dismissal, had carried off most of the espionage files, apparently in the belief that Napoleon would have to recall him to clear up the mess at the ministry. This never happened, because Savary, finding one register of secret agents still in the files, was able with their help to reorganize the espionage system. He summoned all the agents he knew about to his headquarters, interrogated them about their duties and contacts, and followed the clues to other operatives. At the end, he had a nearly complete roster of the men and women who had served Fouché.

The new minister of police soon had networks of spies and couriers reporting to him about anti-Napoleon movements inside France and in foreign nations. This espionage organization, however, failed him regarding the most important plot. In 1812, while Napoleon was away on his disastrous Russian campaign, General Charles Malet led a band of conspirators in a rising against the emperor. Malet seized Savary and held him captive until a squad of soldiers put down the abortive rebellion.

Savary remained a staunch Bonapartist after Napoleon returned from exile on Elba in 1814, and he wanted to accompany the fallen emperor to St. Helena in 1815 (after Waterloo), but the victorious Allies would not permit it. Savary went into exile, came back to France, published his memoirs in 1828, and making his peace with the restored Bourbons, held a command in the French army at the time of his death.

See also FOUCHÉ, JOSEPH; SCHULMEISTER, KARL.

FURTHER READING: *Duc de Rovigo, *Memoirs* (1828); J.T. Headley, *Napoleon and His Marshals* (1847); John Bowle, *Napoleon* (1975).

Saxe, Marshal *(1696-1750)*   German soldier who became a marshal of France and a leading theorist of military intelligence.

Maurice de Saxe was the illegitimate son of the ruler of Saxony who became king of Poland with the title of Augustus II. After an aristocratic upbringing at his father's court, Saxe adopted arms as a career, his first service being with the coalition that opposed King Louis XIV of France in the War of the Spanish Succession (1701–13).

In 1711 his father gave him the title of count of Saxony, and in 1719, four years after the death of Louis XIV, Saxe switched to the French army (this being a period, before the rise of nationalism, when it was common for military commanders to change their allegiance for the sake of their careers). He spent nearly two years (1725–27) in Poland and Russia, was elected duke of Courland, and lost the title because of Russian opposition to him.

Back in France, Saxe returned to his military duties. His ability caused King Louis XV to promote him to general during the War of the Polish Succession (1733–35). The king named him a marshal of France (1744) and, the highest French military rank, a marshal-general of France (1747) during the War of the Austrian Succession (1740–48). Saxe's greatest victory was at Fontenoy (1745), against the British and their Continental allies.

Saxe holds a place in the history of espionage both because he used spies adroitly in each of his campaigns and because he wrote one of the best theoretical analyses of the art of military intelligence.

His prescriptions for successful espionage include the following: Spend as much money on spies as the situation requires. Recruit spies in the area near the coming battlefield, if possible, since they will be in a position to gather information more easily than strangers. Maintain spies everywhere in the enemy camp, especially at the commissariat, for the food being stored may reveal the type of campaign the opposing military cammander intends to wage. As a precaution against leaks, do not allow spies to be known to one another except when their assignments make this necessary. In dealing with spies, be constantly on guard against double agents who are really spying against you for the enemy.

Saxe on spies may sound banal today, but that is only because his ideas have been so completely absorbed into the modern theory and practice of espionage. In his time, and for long after, he was the foremost expert on the subject.

FURTHER READING: Maurice de Saxe, *Reveries or Memoirs Upon the Art of War* (1732); translated by L. H. Thornton, (1944); Basil Liddell Hart, *Great Captains Unveiled* (1928), has a chapter on Saxe; *J. M. White, *Marshal of France: The Life and Times of Maurice, Comte de Saxe* (1962).

Schellenberg, Walter *(1900-52)* German intelligence officer during World War II.

Schellenberg was born in Saarbrücken, where his father worked in the business of manufacturing pianos. After his education in his native city, Schellenberg studied at the University of Bonn, first medicine (1929–31) and then law (1931–33), in which he took his degree. He lectured on law at the university during 1934.

Meanwhile he had joined Adolf Hitler's Nazi party. Schellenberg's legal knowledge was helpful to the Nazis, and he was given a succession of positions. In 1939 he became deputy leader of espionage in the SD (Security Service) of the RSHA (Reich Central Security Office). In that first year of World War II, Schellenberg maneuvered a pair of British intelligence officers into a meeting in Holland where he was able to kidnap them and rush them across the border to internment in Germany (the "Venlo incident"). In 1940 Schellenberg went to Portugal in an attempt to kidnap the duke and duchess of Windsor, who were about to sail for the Bahamas, but this plot failed. Also in 1940 Schellenberg wasted much of his time drawing up a list of British leaders to be arrested after Operation Sea Lion (Germany's intended invasion of Britain, which never took place).

In 1942 Schellenberg became head of his espionage department. He now turned his attention to Switzerland, where a Soviet spy ring was transmitting to Moscow information on the German armed forces. The chief spy, Rudolf Roessler, had informants in Berlin whom Schellenberg vainly tried to discover. In 1943 Schellenberg met secretly with General Henri Guisan, Switzerland's commander in chief, who persuaded him that the Swiss government was not conspiring against Germany, so that a German violation of Swiss neutrality would not be justified. To prove his thesis, Guisan had Roessler and the rest of the spy ring arrested, and Switzerland remained safely neutral for the duration of the war.

In 1944, with defeat staring Germany in the face, Schellenberg advised Heinrich Himmler, the director of all German security forces, to negotiate a peace with the western Allies (Himmler tried and failed). The war ended in 1945, and Schellenberg was arrested. Condemned at Nuremberg as a war criminal, he received a sentence of six years in 1946, was released in 1950, and wrote his autobiography.

See also GUISAN, HENRI; HIMMLER, HEINRICH; SD; VENLO INCIDENT.

FURTHER READING: Walter Hagen, *The Secret Front: The Story of Nazi Political Espionage* (1954); *Walter Schellenberg, *The Labyrinth: The Memoirs of Walter Schellenberg* (1956); David Kahn, *Hitler's Spies: German Military Intelligence in World War II* (1978).

Schragmüller, Elsbeth *(1887-1940)* German espionage instructor during World War I.

Schragmüller was born into a well-to-do family in Westphalia. She studied privately and, traveling widely for the sake of her health, became fluent in French, English, and Italian before attending the University of Freiburg, from which she received her Ph.D. in 1913.

On the Freiburg faculty when World War I broke out in 1914, Schragmüller wrote persistent letters to Walther Nicolai, head of German military intelligence, asking for a place in his organization. Nicolai found her a post in the censorship in German-occupied Belgium, where her superiors noticed that she had a genius for intelligence work. They sent her to Baden-Baden for special training, and she completed the course with honors.

Her next appointment was to a spy school maintained by the Germans in Antwerp. Here she became the most successful of all the instructors on the staff. Her appearance helped, for she had mesmerizing blue eyes to go with a strong character and quick intelligence. Regarding espionage, she believed it should be more scientific, especially in the use of psychology.

Thus, she taught her students to make their spy contacts come to them if possible, rather than the reverse, because an agent handled thus would tend to be tired, ill at ease, and less able to guard against slips of the tongue or telling more than intended. Schragmüller also developed to a high point an old espionage maneuver called "the sacrifice," in which one spy is delivered to the enemy in order to save another of greater value. She imbued her students with the idea that they should resort to the sacrifice against their best friends, if necessary, and that they should be ready to accept its validity if used against them.

British and French intelligence knew of Schragmüller's presence at the Antwerp spy school, but they did not learn her name until the war was over. While it lasted, they called her "Fraulein Doktor" and "the beautiful blonde of Antwerp." Counterespionage agents of the French Second Bureau spent much of their time trying to run down her operatives in France.

This went on in the years 1914 to 1918. Then the war turned decisively against the Germans, who had to retreat from Belgium as the Allies advanced. Schragmüller abandoned her spy school and followed her defeated compatriots back to Germany.

After the war, she became a professor of history in Munich University, where she stayed until her death during World War II, a conflict in which espionage reached a degree of proficiency and ruthlessness probably never dreamed of by "the beautiful blonde of Antwerp."

See also NICOLAI, WALTHER.

FURTHER READING: *Walther Nicolai, *The German Secret Service* (1924); Nicholas Snowden, *Memoirs of a Spy* (1933); Richard Wilmer Rowan and Robert G. Deindorfer, *Secret Service: Thirty-three Centuries of Espionage* (1967), considers Schragmüller's spy career.

Schulmeister, Karl *(1770-1853)*   Alsatian master spy for the French during the Napoleonic Wars.

Schulmeister was the son of a Lutheran minister of Neu Freistett in Alsace on the banks of the Rhine. Educated for the church, young Schulmeister abandoned his religious vocation and became a smuggler carrying contraband cargoes across the river between France and Germany. To give himself a cover, he ran a store in Strasbourg, the main city of Alsace, where he talked to soldiers of the Alsatian shore patrol, learned their routes, and thus evaded them in his smuggling operations (which, after the outbreak of the French Revolution in 1789, included the smuggling of aristocrats out of France).

In 1799 Schulmeister met René Savary, an officer in Napoleon's army on the Rhine. Savary recruited Schulmeister, an Alsatian and therefore fluent in both French and German, for undercover missions in Germany, and by 1804 Schulmeister was the leading spy in the French network run by Joseph Fouché, minister of police for Emperor Napoleon Bonaparte.

In 1805 Napoleon sent Schulmeister to Vienna to lay the groundwork for the coming French campaign against Austria. Schulmeister arrived in the Austrian capital with the cover story that he was a Hungarian nobleman who had been expelled from France for defending the Austrian case against Napoleon. He wrote to General Karl Mack, commander of the Austrian forces on the Danube, offering to reveal secret information about Napoleon's Grand Army. Mack accorded him an interview and was sufficiently impressed to have him appointed to the Austrian general staff as head of military intelligence for the approaching battle.

This was one of history's classic examples of a secret agent for one power running an enemy's espionage system. Schulmeister kept Napoleon informed about Mack's strategy and the condition of the Austrian army, and he fed Mack disinformation (false reports) about Napoleon's strategy and the condition of the French army. From Schulmeister, Napoleon heard (correctly) that Mack was overconfident, and Mack heard (incorrectly) that Napoleon's troops were in a state of virtual rebellion. Schulmeister even bribed two Austrian officers to provide him with information he could not get himself.

The result was the battle of Ulm (October 20, 1805), which can scarcely be called a battle since Napoleon set a trap for Mack, surrounded his forces, and compelled him to surrender ignominiously.

In 1808 Schulmeister directed French intelligence at Erfurt in Prussia, where the emperor of France conferred with Tsar Alexander I of Russia. Napoleon ordered Schulmeister to spy on Alexander in order to find out what the tsar's advisers were telling him. Schulmeister organized a spy ring that included a Russian at the tsar's headquarters who took French gold in exchange for information. Schulmeister's reports strengthened Napoleon's hand, and Alexander signed an agreement giving France control of most of Europe.

Early in 1809 Schulmeister gained a military command in the French army. He took part in Napoleon's second Austrian campaign, distinguished himself in the fighting around Landshut, and, at the head of his soldiers, led the way to the capture of a bridge over the Isar River. In this last action, he suffered sword cuts on his face that left him permanently scarred.

After Napoleon's victory, Schulmeister became commissioner of police in Vienna, with the task of maintaining security during the French occupation. He carried out the task so efficiently and ruthlessly that a French observer said: "He inspires in the Viennese so much terror that he is by himself worth an army corps." The Viennese, of course, remembered Schulmeister as the "Hungarian nobleman" who had spied on them and tricked General Mack into the catastrophe at Ulm. They remained quiescent under this control, which lasted until the signing of the peace treaty.

This French triumph led in the long run to the downfall of Schulmeister. Napoleon married Marie Louise, an Austrian archduchess, in 1810. She resented Schulmeister's betrayal of her father, the Austrian emperor, in 1805, and his tyranny in Vienna in 1809. She used her influence to have him dismissed. Although Napoleon had valued Schulmeister's espionage work very highly, and had paid him well for it, the emperor gave in to the new Empress. Schulmeister had to retire from the military service. He hoped to receive that coveted Napoleonic decoration, the Legion of Honor, but Napoleon rebuffed him with the words: "Gold is the only suitable reward for spies."

Schulmeister bought an estate in Alsace and lived there until the defeat of Napoleon by combined Allied forces at the Battle of the Nations (1813). The Austrian commander, having invaded Alsace, ordered his artillery to pound Schulmeister's house into ruins in retaliation for Schulmeister's notorious activities in Austria.

Napoleon's bid to regain his crown on his return from exile on Elba in 1815 caused Schulmeister to declare openly for him. When the battle of Waterloo ended Napoleon's hopes, Schulmeister paid for his loyalty with a large fine, and then he lost the rest of his money in bad speculations. He was reduced to tending a tobacco stall in Strasbourg for the rest of his life, which amounted to more than three decades.

His epitaph is what Napoleon said of him in the days when they were both victorious in their respective fields—that Karl Schulmeister was "the emperor of spies."

See also SAVARY, RENÉ.

FURTHER READING: °Duc de Rovigo, *Memoirs* (1828), is Savary's reminiscences, including his account of Schulmeister; John Bowle, *Napoleon* (1975), describes the titanic career of the man Schulmeister served.

Schulze-Boysen, Harro (1909-42) German spymaster for the Soviet Union during World War II.

The double-barreled name reflected upper-class origins. Schulze-Boysen's father was a Schulze and his mother a Boysen, and at their marriage they determined not to lose the aristocratic implications of either name. So, their son was a Schulze-Boysen.

He was born in Kiel, where his father, a nephew of Grand Admiral Alfred von Tirpitz, held a command in the kaiser's navy. Schulze-Boysen went to school in Duisburg (1923–27) before studying law at the universities of Freiburg (1928–30) and Berlin (1930–31). A romantic believer in freedom—almost an anarchist—he was alarmed by the growth of Nazi power in Germany, and when Adolf Hitler became chancellor in 1933, Schulze-Boysen decided to oppose him wherever and whenever possible. Arrested for anti-Nazi activities in that year, he got off through family influence and soon afterward was able to find a job in the press department of the German air ministry.

In 1936 Schulze-Boysen began passing information to the Soviet Embassy in Berlin. Although he was not a Communist, he believed that only the Russians could stop Hitler. He gathered around him a band of conspirators, and he was in close association with Arvid Harnack, a committed Communist who headed another anti-Nazi group. Schulze-Boysen remained an unofficial spy for the Russians until 1941, when, following the German invasion of Russia, they recruited him for systematic espionage. His group, under the code name "Choro," became a unit of the Red Orchestra, the network of Soviet spy rings on the Continent.

Schulze-Boysen was of special value to the Russians because in 1941 he was promoted to liaison officer for the chiefs of staff of the German air force. In that capacity he was able to report on aircraft production, fuel reserves, the attrition of crews in combat, and command thinking on the strategy of air warfare. His agents filled in much of what he could not learn for himself about troop movements, promotion or demotion of German generals, and Hitler's whereabouts at critical moments. Most of this information was taken to Brussels by courier and radioed to Moscow through a Red Orchestra transmitter in the Belgian city because of the difficulty and danger of transmitting directly from Berlin to Moscow.

In 1941, while the Germans were pushing deep into Russia, Soviet intelligence committed the blunder of querying Brussels, using code names and addresses, about a temporary silence on the part of the Berlin networks. The Germans found this message when they cracked the Belgian branch of the Red Orchestra in 1942. The Brussels radio operator confessed. Putting all the information together, the Germans disrupted the Red Orchestra and arrested many of the agents, including Schulze-Boysen and Harnack, both of whom were executed.

See also HARNACK, ARVID; RED ORCHESTRA.

FURTHER READING: Gilles Perrault, *The Red Orchestra* (1969); *Heinz Höhne, *Codeword: Direktor: The Story of the Red Orchestra* (1971); Paul L. Kesaris (ed.), *The Rote Kapelle: The CIA's History of Soviet Intelligence and Espionage Networks in Western Europe, 1936–1945* (1979).

SD *(1931-45)* The intelligence department of the Nazi party in Germany's Third Reich.

The SD (Security Service) was established by Heinrich Himmler as the intelligence arm of the SS (Adolf Hitler's Elite Guard), which Himmler headed from 1929. The SD mushroomed into an enormous network of secret agents and police spies after Hitler became chancellor of Germany (1933). In 1934 it was united with the Gestapo (Secret State Police) under the command of Himmler's closest henchman, Reinhard Heydrich. Five years later the SD was placed in the RSHA (Reich Central Security Office), the overall security system directed by Heydrich.

The SD became the essential intelligence organ of Hitler's Nazi party, and as such it was responsible for the safety of Hitler, his subordinates, and the political apparatus by which he maintained his tyranny over the Third Reich. The SD had wide powers of investigation among the German people. It could arrest men and women considered dangerous or obnoxious by the Nazis, and it could send the condemned to the dreaded concentration camps, where labor was usually hard and life short.

The German victories of World War II (1939–45) allowed the SD to extend its authority into the occupied lands, where it rounded up Jews, Communists, "undesirables" in general, and selected prisoners of war for transportation to the Nazi death camps. This went on until the overthrow of Germany in 1945. The SD was dismantled, and membership in it was declared to be a crime by the Nuremberg tribunal that presided over the trials of the Nazi war criminals (1946).

See also HEYDRICK, REINHARD; HIMMLER, HEINRICH.

FURTHER READING: Walter Hagen, *The Secret Front: The Story of Nazi Political Espionage* (1954); *Andre Brissaud, *The Nazi Secret Service* (1974); G. S. Graber, *The Life and Times of Reinhard Heydrich* (1980).

SDECE Principal intelligence organization of France.

The SDECE (Department of Foreign Information and Counterespionage) was established in its present form in 1958, after a reorganization of French intelligence into two major branches, the second being the DST (Control of National Surveillance). The SDECE is thus, in American terms, the French CIA (Central Intelligence Agency), while the DST is the French FBI (Federal Bureau of Investigation).

The SDECE, dealing with intelligence on the highest level, is under the supervision of a government committee and ultimately responsible to the premier of France. It is divided into the three sections commonly found in national intelligence organizations: espionage, counterespionage, and covert operations. All three are supposed to keep their spy and counterspy activities beyond the borders of France, leaving the DST to operate within those borders, but the line has been as difficult to maintain in certain cases as with other espionage systems. All feel the temptation to spy on nationals at home whom they suspect of being dupes or agents of foreign intelligence.

The SDECE is said to be one of the most successful in fending off attempts to infiltrate its ranks. No undercover agent from a Communist country has yet been exposed in circumstances bad enough to create a national scandal. Like the British and their MI6 (Military Intelligence 6, British espionage), the French do not discuss the SDECE publicly in the manner of the Americans and the CIA. The SDECE is not to be confused with the Second Bureau, French military intelligence.

See also SECOND BUREAU.

FURTHER READING: David Wise and Thomas B. Ross, *The Espionage Establishment* (1967); Miles Copeland, *Without Cloak and Dagger: The Truth about the New Espionage* (1974).

Sebold, William (1902-   ) American double agent for the United States against Germany during World War II.

Born and raised in Germany, which he served as a soldier in World War I, Sebold transferred his loyalty to his adopted country when he moved to the United States and became a naturalized citizen in 1922. He worked as a mechanic, rising to a technical position with Consolidated Aircraft in San Diego.

Sebold visited Germany in 1939 to see his mother, and he fell into the clutches of the Gestapo, the dreaded political police directed by Heinrich Himmler. The Gestapo, which kept dossiers on born Germans in the United States, forced him to undergo espionage training by threatening to reveal that he had concealed his prison record in Germany when he went through the American naturalization process.

Sebold graduated from the spy school in Hamburg and was dispatched to America in 1940 by Captain Nicklaus Ritter, who ran the English-speaking desk of the Abwehr (Foreign Information and Counterintelligence Department, German military intelligence).

Sebold, hiding his true feelings from the Germans, got in touch with the American consul in Cologne. As a result, he was met aboard ship in New York harbor by agents of the FBI (Federal Bureau of Investigation), for which he began to work as a double agent. He handed over a list of spies Ritter had given him—names of Germans or German-sympathizers already doing undercover work in America for Hitler's Third Reich. With FBI assistance, Sebold radioed disinformation (plausible but false reports) back to Hamburg.

Having made the most of Sebold's defection from the German espionage system, the FBI in 1941 suddenly rounded up Ritter's American espionage network, including Hermann Lang, who had stolen the secret of America's Norden bombsight. Sebold testified against Ritter's agents when they came to trial that year, and his testimony both sent them to jail and caused Ritter to be retired by his superiors from espionage work. After the trial, Sebold went back to ordinary life.

FURTHER READING: Karl Bartz, *The Downfall of the German Secret Service* (1956); Ladislas Farago, *The Game of the Foxes: The Untold Story of German Espionage in the United States* and Great Britain during World War II (1971); *David Kahn, *Hitler's Spies: German Military Intelligence in World War II* (1978).

Second Bureau   French military intelligence.

The Second Bureau has the responsibility for interpreting intelligence reports, most of which come from the espionage and counterespionage departments of the Special Services (called the Fifth Bureau in wartime). Having made its interpretation of a given situation, the Second Bureau delivers reports to the French general staff for use in strategical and tactical decisions.

This system began after the Franco-Prussian War (1870–71), an analysis of which showed that the French debacle had resulted partly from the superior intelligence available to the German high command. Resolved that they should no longer be inferior in their knowledge of the enemy, the French founded the Second Bureau. It expanded in numbers, grew in proficiency, and became a safeguard of France in the last quarter of the nineteenth century. The reports it drew up concerning German strength before and during World War I (1914–18) were generally accurate and a contribution to the victory of France and her allies.

The Second Bureau was also mainly right about Germany after the war. During the 1920s, it correctly estimated that the Germans were evading the terms of the peace restricting the size of the German armed forces. After Adolf Hitler became chancellor of Germany (1933), the Second Bureau kept track of German strength from year to year as Hitler scrapped treaties and ordered his generals to rearm his Third Reich. In 1939 the Second Bureau predicted Hitler's attack on Poland. In 1940 it warned the French high command of the coming German offensive in the west and correctly predicted the vectors along which the attack would move. Sound information went to waste because the French generals could not or would not apply to the battlefields intelligence reports contradicting what they believed.

With the fall of France in 1940, the Second Bureau was reduced to a minor organization serving a rump army of 100,000 men under the control of Marshal Philippe Pétain, who at Vichy in unoccupied France headed a puppet government controlled by the Germans in occupied France. The members of the Second Bureau had to decide whether or not to serve Pétain (and therefore the Germans) in the real sense as well as ostensibly. Most of the men at the top decided in the negative and waited for the day when they could again fight the enemy.

Meanwhile, General Charles de Gaulle, leader of the Free French in London, founded his own Second Bureau—the BCRA (Central Bureau of Intelligence and Operations). The BCRA linked up with the French resistance, the undercover spies and saboteurs who worked against the German invaders. The descent of the Allied armed forces on France in 1944 allowed the Vichy Second Bureau to declare openly for de Gaulle. After the victory, the BCRA disbanded and the Second Bureau formerly of France and later of Vichy, returned to being military intelligence for a real General Staff of a real French Army.

See also BCRA; FRENCH RESISTANCE.

FURTHER READING: *Philip John Stead, *Second Bureau* (n.d.); Alexander Werth, *France: 1940–1955* (1966); David Schoenbrun, *Soldiers of the Night: The Story of the French Resistance* (1980).

Secret Writing   Cryptography in the broadest sense.

Cryptography means "hidden writing," so the term can be applied to any method by which a writer renders a message unintelligible to anyone not authorized to read it.

Since secret writing is used to conceal something from a third party, the identity and abilities of that party may have a decisive influence on a writer's selection of the particular form of communication. To an illiterate, all writing is secret writing. A foreign language is mystifying to anyone who does not know it. Shorthand intelligible to secretaries is meaningless to nearly everybody else. These forms of concealment, however, are rarely used in espionage because of the danger that the third party will find someone capable of reading the message.

The two familiar methods are those that keep the message from being seen and those that leave it visible but protected from prying eyes.

Of the first group, writing in invisible ink is well known. A page may appear to be blank, or concealed words may be written between the lines of an innocuous message. The secret writing becomes visible upon heating the page or washing it with a reagent. Another method is to use pinpricks on pages that can be seen only with a magnifying glass. Much employed in earlier periods, both invisible ink and pinpricks have largely given way in our time to the microdot, a form of miniature photography that allows a message to be reduced to microscopic size.

Of the second group of methods, the most important are ciphers (based on the alphabet) and codes (based on words, phrases, or sentences). These are staples of intelligence work. Games are often based on the distortion of words, as in pig Latin. Words may be staggered in the form used by Arthur Conan Doyle in his story "The Gloria Scott." The message in the story says: "The supply of game for London is going steadily up. Head-keeper Hudson, we believe, has now been told to receive all orders for fly-paper, and for preservation of your hen pheasant's life." Sherlock Holmes discovered the secret writing concealed in the message by reading the first and then every third word.

See also CIPHER; CODE; MICRODOT; INVISIBLE INK.

FURTHER READING: Herbert S. Zim, *Codes and Secret Writing* (1946); *David Kahn, *The Codebreakers: The Story of Secret Writing* (1967); Norman Bruce, *Secret Warfare: The Battle of Codes and Ciphers* (1973).

Security Intelligence Service   Canadian organization responsible for internal security, including counterespionage, replacing the Royal Canadian Mounted Police in this area.

See ROYAL CANADIAN MOUNTED POLICE.

Serov, Ivan (1905-   )   Last of the notorious Soviet spymasters.

Born at Sokal in western Russia, Serov came from a peasant family, served in the Red Army, and rose in the Soviet bureaucracy under the guidance of Georgi Malenkov, who would become the leader of the Soviet government after Stalin's death in 1953. During World War II (1941–45) Serov had charge of deporting hundreds of thousands of people from eastern Europe. He is also said to have ordered the Katyn Forest massacre, when the Russians murdered 15,000 officers of the Polish army.

In 1954 Malenkov named Serov head of the KGB (Committee for State Security), the newly reorganized Soviet intelligence organization that had been known as the MVD (Ministry of Internal Affairs, 1946–54). In 1956, after Malenkov had been removed from power, Serov went to England to prepare for a visit by the Soviet leaders, Nikita Khrushchev and Nicolai Bulganin. However, a furious British press attack on Serov ("Ivan the Terrible") forced his recall.

In 1958 Khrushchev removed Serov from the KGB for failing to detect a move by Khrushschev's political enemies against him. Serov slipped down the Soviet ladder of power and in 1963 disappeared.

Since then, the directors of Soviet intelligence have tended to stay out of the limelight.

See also KGB.

FURTHER READING: Ronald Seth, *Unmasked! Forty Years of Soviet Spying* (1965); Norman Lucas, *The Great Spy Ring* (1966); *Gerald Kurland, *Nikita Sergeievich Khrushchev: Modern Dictator of the USSR* (1972), describes how Khrushchev degraded Serov.

Seth, Ronald *(1911-   )*   British teacher, spy, and author of books on espionage.

Seth was born in the town of Ely in Cambridgeshire and received his higher education at nearby Cambridge University. After graduating he became a teacher. In 1935 he went to the University of Tallinn, in Estonia, to accept a professorship in English language and literature, remaining there until 1939, the year of the outbreak of World War II. Returning to England, he worked for the British Broadcasting Company (BBC) as an expert on the Baltic area and as an intelligence analyst during the Russo-Finnish War (1939–40).

After lecturing to officers of the Royal Air Force on the methods and uses of intelligence (1941), Seth went into the Special Operations Executive (SOE) in 1942 and received training for undercover missions in the German-occupied areas of the Continent. Dropped by parachute into Estonia, where he could make use of his experience there, especially his knowledge of the language, he got in touch with the Estonian underground, took part in spying on the Germans, and helped organize sabotage missions. However, he soon fell into the hands of the Germans, who held him for two years (1942–44), mainly in Germany and occupied France.

Seth said he was released in 1944 in order to act as a courier carrying peace feelers to London from Heinrich Himmler, the head of the Nazi secret police. The British authorities refused to take the mission seriously, but Seth remained free. He worked in the civil service after the war ended (1945) and then resumed teaching. In 1952 he became a writer of books on espionage, of which the following are especially notable: *Secret Servants: A History of Japanese Espionage* (1957); *Unmasked! The Story of Soviet Espionage* (1965); *The Spy Who Wasn't Caught: The Story of Julius Silber* (1966); *The Sleeping Truth: The Hiss-Chambers Affair Reappraised* (1968); *Encyclopedia of Espionage,* 2d ed. (1975).

FURTHER READING: Ronald Seth, *A Spy Has No Friends* (1952), is an autobiography.

Silber, Julius *(1875?-1933)*   German spy in England during World War I.

Born in German Silesia, Silber came of a family in straitened circumstances. He therefore dropped out of school to go into business, a career that took him to South Africa in the 1890s as an official of a German company. He became so fluent in English that he was able to serve as an interpreter during the Boer War (1899–1902) and later at British prison camps. He perfected his command of the English language in the dozen years (1902–14) that he wandered around the United States taking jobs where he found them.

In Washington when World War I broke out in 1914, Silber went to the German Embassy, volunteered to become a spy in England, was accepted, and got to his destination by way of Canada. His good record of working with the British in South Africa ingratiated him with them, and his command of German was invaluable to them. Since they needed men and women to censor the mail, they put him to work in the post office, where he handled, among his other tasks, innocuous messages that the British allowed to reach Germany by way of neutral countries.

Silber used the system for his espionage. Thus, as a censor he had the right to forward mail after reading it, and he often enclosed a note of his own before resealing an envelope and sending it on. When the British government stopped all mail for Germany in 1915, Silber sent "window" letters to himself. These were read before delivery to him. He then had stamped envelopes, and after removing the harmless letters and replacing them with spy notes, he would tag the envelopes "opened by the censor" and mail them to German sympathizers in neutral countries to be forwarded to Germany.

Another way Silber assisted Germany was by tampering with the mail between Britain and America. At least once, he smudged blueprints for a delivery of American arms. Another of his maneuvers was to route important mail through several censors, using technicalities such as a request for confirmation that a letter had received clearance.

This went on all during the war (1914–18), and in 1919 Silber left the British post office with a warm commendation from his superiors, who termed his work "exemplary." They were surprised when, after returning to Germany, he published an account of his espionage career in England. They were astounded when they checked and found his account correct.

FURTHER READING: *Julius Silber, *Invisible Weapons* (1932); John Bulloch, *MI5: The Origin and History of the British Counter-Espionage Service* (1963); Ronald Seth, *The Spy Who Wasn't Caught: The Story of Julius Silber* (1966).

Sleeper   A spy placed in a potentially operational area without an immediate assignment but waiting to be activated by an order from headquarters.

See SPY.

SMERSH   Department of Soviet intelligence that specializes in terror tactics outside the USSR.

SMERSH is an acronym for the Russian phrase meaning "death to spies." The organization constitutes the Section for Terror and Diversion of the KGB (Committee for State Security, Soviet intelligence), and it has existed in some form ever since the Bolshevik revolution of 1917. During World War II, the term SMERSH came into use, when it stood for terror against both the Germans and anti-Communist Russians. After the war, SMERSH began to concentrate on foreign countries. It developed sophisticated murder techniques that seem more appropriate in spy novels that in real life.

The term SMERSH ceased to be used in 1946, but the organization remains. The years 1950–1970 were its period of greatest activity, before the slackening of the Cold War.

The function for which SMERSH is most notorious in the west is the killing, kidnaping, blackmailing, or otherwise disposing of selected opponents of the Soviet regime who live abroad. To facilitate murder when the murderer must quickly escape, SMERSH invented an array of lethal gadgets and concoctions, from electric guns to poisons both highly potent and hard to detect. Its murder laboratory is one of the world's most effective research facilities.

Detailed information about SMERSH and its methods reached western intelligence mainly through KGB agents who defected, especially through Nicolai Khokhlov and Bogdan Stashinsky. Both testified to the organization's skill in scientific murder. Khokhlov, for instance, was armed with a miniature electric gun firing cyanide pellets, while Stashinsky had a small tube that sprayed prussic acid. These agents were horrified by their assignments and finally defected rather than obey their superiors.

The most celebrated victim of SMERSH was Leon Trotsky, who lost out in his duel with Joseph Stalin for power in the Soviet Union. Trotsky was murdered in Mexico in 1940 by a SMERSH agent acting under direct instructions from Stalin.

See also KHOKHLOV, NICOLAI; STASHINSKY, BOGDAN.

FURTHER READING: E. H. Cookridge, *Soviet Spy Net* (1955); *Ronald Seth, *The Executioners: The Story of SMERSH* (1967); A. I. Romanov, *Nights Are Longest There: SMERSH from the Inside* (1972).

Sokolov, Alexander (1919-   )   Russian spy in the United States.

Sokolov was born in Tiflis, the capital of Soviet Georgia, but he grew up in Paris, to which his father brought the family in 1922 in flight from the Communist regime dominating their homeland. Despite this background, Sokolov took part in left-wing politics while at school and continued this interest at the Sorbonne. In 1937 he joined the French Communist Party. Conscripted into the French army at the outbreak of World War II in 1939, he saw the debacle following the German invasion of France in 1940 and lived in Paris until its liberation by the Allies in 1944.

More of a Communist than ever, Sokolov went to Moscow in 1947, received espionage training, and by 1949 had become an agent of the GRU (Chief Intelligence Directorate of the General Staff of the Red Army, Soviet military intelligence) in East Germany. He returned to Russia in 1953, received more training, and in 1958 appeared in New York using the cover name "Robert Baltch." He and his wife became a spy team operating under the supervision of a Russian spymaster, Igor Egorov. The Sokolovs moved between New York, Baltimore, and Washington during the period 1959 to 1963, reporting on American military installations, arms factories, and proving grounds.

In 1961 the FBI (Federal Bureau of Investigation) caught a member of the spy ring, Kaarlo Tuomi, persuaded him to become a double agent working for the United States, and through him gathered enough information on the Sokolovs and Egorov to arrest them. The three benefited, however, from the espionage revolution, the growing tendency to exchange spies rather than execute or jail them. In return for the Sokolovs and Egorov, Moscow offered to hand over two American captives they were holding, Marvin Makinen, a student, and Walter Ciszek, a Catholic priest. Washington accepted the offer, and the exchange was made.

See also ESPIONAGE REVOLUTION.

FURTHER READING: David Wise and Thomas B. Ross, *The Espionage Establishment* (1967); *E. H. Cookridge, *Spy Trade* (1971).

Sorge, Richard *(1895-1944)* German spy for the Soviet Union in Japan before and during World War II.

Sorge's mother was Russian, and he was born near Baku. His father, a German mining engineer, was working in the Baku oil fields at the time.

The family moved to Berlin in 1898. Sorge attended schools in the German capital, became a fervent German nationalist, and in 1914 joined the kaiser's army as World War I erupted. Wounded twice while serving on the Eastern front, he was invalided out in 1916.

He then became a wandering student, attending the universities of Berlin, Kiel, and Hamburg. His political ideas took a radical turn, and in 1918, as Germany collapsed, he joined the German Communist party. Working as a journalist, he received an assignment to Moscow in 1925, a tour of duty that hardened him in his allegiance to the Soviet Union. In 1930 he began to work clandestinely for the GRU (Chief Intelligence Directorate of the General Staff of the Red Army, Soviet military intelligence).

That same year, Sorge went to Shanghai, where he served as a German journalist and as an undercover agent of the GRU. He formed a spy ring to report on China that included four men later associated with him in Tokyo —two Japanese newsmen, Ozaki Hatsumi and Miyagi Yotoku, a German radio operator, Max Klausen, and a Yugoslav photographer, Branko Voukelitch.

Sorge went to Japan in 1933. Still supposedly a patriotic German journalist, he became an assistant to Eugen Ott, military attaché at the German Embassy. He also joined the Nazi party, posing as a devoted follower of Adolf Hitler.

After a year of traveling in the United States, France, Austria, Czechoslovakia, and Russia, Sorge returned to Tokyo in 1935 and organized a spy ring, using his men from Shanghai and others in the Japanese capital. So proficient was the ring at stealing top-secret plans that Sorge could, on a visit to Moscow in 1936, report that Japan intended to move against China, not Russia. A year later, that prediction came true.

In 1938 Eugen Ott became German ambassador to Tokyo. He brought his old friend Sorge into the embassy to work on highly confidential issues regarding Germany and Japan. Ott knew that Sorge knew Ozaki Hatsumi, by now a close friend of members of the Japanese government. What Ott did not know was that Hatsumi was an agent of a pro-Soviet spy ring run by Sorge.

Seeing top-secret documents from Berlin at the German Embassy, Sorge was able to report on both Germany and Japan to his superiors in Moscow as World War II approached. Early in 1941 he correctly predicted that Hitler would attack Russia in June, a prediction ignored by Joseph Stalin, the Soviet dictator.

Sorge's most effective espionage coup (this time, Stalin believed him) was his prediction that Japan would enter the war in 1941 by striking against the United States in the Pacific rather than against the Soviet Union in Siberia. Thus informed, Stalin brought his Siberian forces west to join in the critical battles that turned the tide of the conflict with Hitler's Germany.

This was also Sorge's final espionage coup. Japanese counterespionage, suspicious of information leaks, tracked down and seized members of the Sorge ring. Yotoku implicated Sorge, who, confronted with incriminating documents found in his rooms, confessed.

He went on trial in 1943 and was executed in 1944. It took the Russians twenty years to acknowledge Sorge's contribution to their World War II victory; in 1964, they declared him a Hero of the Soviet Union. In 1965 they placed his image on a postage stamp now famous in philately.

FURTHER READING: Charles H. Willoughby, *Shanghai Conspiracy: The Sorge Spy Ring* (1952); Hans-Otto Meissner, *The Man with Three Faces* (1955); *F. W. Deakin and G. R. Storry, *The Case of Richard Sorge* (1967).

Soviet American Network *(1944-50)* Russian-directed spy ring operating in the United States during and after World War II.

The Russians ran a number of spy rings in the United States toward the end of World War II, including one at the University of Chicago and another at the University of California, but the true Soviet American Network was that based in New York, which included more successful spies and did more damage than any other.

In 1944 Anatoly Yakovlev arrived in New York with the title of Soviet vice-counsul and orders to develop a powerful network of secret agents already in place supplemented by others he might recruit. His most important agent was Klaus Fuchs, a German atomic scientist who, after working at British laboratories, had come to America in 1943 to help develop the atomic bomb. Fuchs by then was a spy for the Russians, to whom he delivered information about Allied nuclear research on a regular basis.

Yakovlev dealt with Fuchs through courier Harry Gold, an American chemist who for years had been an ardent Communist and a secret agent for the Soviet Union. This connection became of supreme importance when Fuchs moved from Columbia University to Los Alamos, New Mexico, where the atomic bomb was being developed. Fuchs was an observer at the first atomic explosion in 1945, by which time he had passed to Yakovlev, through Gold, information of fundamental importance on the theory of the bomb and the practical problems of building one.

David Greenglass, an American technician at Los Alamos, handed to Gold basic data on the triggering mechanism of the bomb. The most notorious American members of the network were Julius and Ethel Rosenberg (Ethel being Greenglass's sister). The subsequent prosecution of Julius Rosenberg pictured him as the mastermind who had led Greenglass into espionage for the Soviets. Morton Sobell, a codefendant with the Rosenbergs, worked for

General Electric in Schenectady, New York, where he reported to Gold on secret rocket research. These were the principal members of the group.

The Soviet American Network operated successfully during the period 1944 to 1946, when Yakovlev sent to Moscow sufficient information on scientific developments in the United States to enable the Russians to build an atomic bomb much more quickly than otherwise would have been the case. The Americans who fed Yakovlev the information were therefore not only guilty of treason but also responsible for altering the international balance of power in favor of the Soviet Union.

The network ceased operating in 1946, when Fuchs went back to England and Greenglass refused to do any more spying. However, the knowledge that there had been leaks at Los Alamos kept the case open for the FBI (Federal Bureau of Investigation), which in 1949 identified Fuchs as a spy. Alerted, the Special Branch of Scotland Yard arrested him in 1950. He confessed, implicated Gold, who on being arrested implicated Yakovlev and Greenglass, who in turn implicated his sister and brother-in-law, the Rosenbergs.

The Soviet American Network thus unraveled. Yakovlev escaped to Russia, but the Rosenbergs were executed, and the rest of the convicted spies went to jail.

See also FUCHS, KLAUS; GOLD, HARRY; GREENGLASS, DAVID; ROSENBERG, JULIUS AND ETHEL.

FURTHER READING: Oliver Pilat, *The Atom Spies* (1952); Norman Lucas, *The Great Spy Ring* (1966); Morton Sobell, *On Doing Time* (1974), is a self-serving autobiography by a member of the network; *H. Montgomery Hyde, *The Atom Bomb Spies* (1980).

Soviet Australian Network (1943-54)   Russian spy organization operating in Australia during and after World War II.

This network must be termed simply Russian (rather than Russian-directed, as were those in Canada and the United States) because the Soviets never enjoyed much success in recruiting Australians to spy for them. The failure was not for want of trying. The first members of the NKVD (People's Commissariat for Internal Affairs, 1934–46; Soviet intelligence) and the GRU (Chief Intelligence Directorate of the General Staff of the Red Army, Soviet military intelligence) sent from Moscow to Canberra in the midst of the war carried orders to work as usual through citizens of the nation they were operating against. Wartime espionage in Australia produced practically nothing of value to the Russians.

After the war, a few Australian Communists revealed information of minor importance, and in 1949 the knowledge that a leak existed caused the Australians to keep the Russians under surveillance. In 1951 Vladimir Petrov of the MVD (Ministry of Internal Affairs, 1946–54), as the NKVD was now called, arrived at the Russian Embassy in Canberra. Petrov had been given responsibility for improving the espionage system, but he had little more success than his predecessors, a fact that amazed his superiors in Moscow. They informed him in 1952 that he would be recalled. The recall was delayed into 1953, when the whole Soviet intelligence system was shaken by the sudden arrest and execution of its head, Lavrenti Beria. Petrov was fearful of returning home, and when he received his recall order in 1954 he decided to defect. Australia granted Petrov and his wife political asylum.

Moscow broke off diplomatic relations with Canberra, and the Soviet Australian Network came to an end.

See also PETROV, VLADIMIR.

FURTHER READING: *Vladimir Petrov and Evdokia Petrov, *Empire of Fear* (1956); Norman Lucas, *The Great Spy Ring* (1966).

Soviet Canadian Network (1941-45)   Russian-directed spy ring operating in Canada during World War II.

After Nazi Germany attacked the Soviet Union in 1941, the Russians began a vast expansion of their espionage, not only against the enemy but also against their allies, the western democracies. In Canada they established what came to be called, after its exposure, the Soviet Canadian Network, which for two years covertly gathered data on strategy, troop movements, new weapons, and the development of chemicals useful in war.

In 1943 this spy ring received a higher priority from Moscow. Russian intelligence knew that Canada, Britain, and the United States were working on the atomic bomb. Soviet physicists were lagging behind in this crucial area, and the quickest way to catch up would be to learn what the three western democracies had already achieved and the direction in which their research was pointing. In Canada, this meant conducting espionage at the Chalk River nuclear installation.

Colonel Nikolai Zabotin arrived in Ottawa in 1943 ostensibly as a military attaché but actually to direct the Soviet Canadian Network, which included an array of Canadians in sensitive positions with access to classified information —scientists, engineers, secretaries, and even a member of the Canadian parliament. The star of the spy ring, however, was British, Alan Nunn May, an atomic scientist who came to Chalk River to add his knowledge and experience to Canada's nuclear research and who was a committed Communist loyal to the Soviet Union. Nunn May, among his other efforts in behalf of the Russians, provided samples of experimental uranium from Chalk River.

The Soviet Canadian Network continued to operate successfully until 1945, when Igor Gouzenko, a code clerk at the Russian Embassy, became disillusioned by the way the Russians were conducting espionage against the Canadians while pretending to be their friends. Gouzenko defected, received political asylum in Canada, and revealed what he knew about Zabotin and the spy ring. The members were arrested (Nunn May in Britain, to which he had returned), and several were given prison sentences after being tried and found guilty of espionage (1946). Zabotin, protected by diplomatic immunity, returned to Moscow, where he received a cold reception and perhaps a jail term. The case created a scandal in Canada and elsewhere. The spies had reported to the Russians on British and American nuclear experiments (Nunn May had participated in British research and been briefed on American research), so the implications were international. Again, the stolen information was of fundamental importance and enabled Soviet scientists to close the research gap and produce an atomic bomb of their own. From the Canadian point of view the appalling thing was how easily Zabotin persuaded Canadian citizens to work for him. Most of the spies had led outwardly respectable lives while betraying their country. The Canadian government appointed a commission to look into the scandal, and as a result of the commission's report, new regulations were drawn up to prevent other groups like the Soviet Canadian Network from operating in Canada.

See also GOUZENKO, IGOR; NUNN MAY, ALAN.

FURTHER READING: *"Report of the Royal Commission Appointed to Investigate the Facts Relating to and the Circumstances Surrounding the Communication by Public Officials and other Persons in Positions of Trust of Secret and Confidential Information to Agents of a Foreign Power* (1946); Bernard Newman, *The Red Spider Web* (1948); Oliver Pilat, *The Atom Spies* (1952); Norman Lucas, *The Great Spy Ring* (1966); H. Montgomery Hyde, *The Atom Bomb Spies* (1980).

Special Branch   A department of Scotland Yard and the arresting arm of British counterespionage.

The Special Branch is the partner of MI5 (Military Intelligence 5, British counterespionage), the security service, in controlling espionage in Britain. The duty of tracking down spies and gathering evidence against them belongs to MI5, which, however, has no arresting power, nor does it usually play a role in trials of accused persons. The reason for this is the need to maintain anonymity in the security service, the successful functioning of which depends on its officers and operatives remaining unknown to the public at large and, therefore, to potential enemies.

The Special Branch, as a department of Scotland Yard, is a public organization concerned with crime. It protects foreign dignitaries during their visits to Britain, and this responsibility includes controlling individuals who might threaten them. This, essentially, is counterespionage, which is concerned not only with spies in the strict sense but also with would-be assassins and other dangerous persons.

The duties of the Special Branch and of MI5 overlap, and the distinction between investigation and arrest allows the two organizations to collaborate. The agents of MI5, having done their work, can vanish into anonymity, while those of the Special Branch appear openly in court as witnesses.

Cooperation was remarkable during World War I, when Basil Thomson was in charge of the Special Branch. He worked with Vernon Kell of MI5 so well that German spies achieved nothing of any significance in Britain throughout the war.

See also THOMSON, BASIL.

FURTHER READING: *"Basil Thomson, *The Story of Scotland Yard* (1935); John Bulloch, *MI5: The Origin and History of the British Counter-Espionage Service* (1963); David Wise and Thomas B. Ross, *The Espionage Establishment* (1967).

Special Operations Executive *(1940-46)*   Undercover organization established by the British to disrupt German control of occupied Europe.

When France collapsed and the British were driven from the Continent in 1940, no Allied forces existed to challenge the victorious German army in battle. Only undercover tactics were possible, and the Special Operations Executive (SOE) was created to implement such tactics. Officially, the SOE was commissioned to encourage hope in the occupied nations, to form spy networks to report on conditions in these nations, and to arm freedom fighters for sabotage and other anti-German measures. Prime Minister Winston

Churchill stated the aim of the SOE more dramatically when he said he wanted the organization to "set Europe ablaze."

The extent of the German conquests during World War II (1939–45) gave the SOE responsibility for clandestine activities from France to Norway to Greece. The minister of economic warfare had ultimate authority, but the executive director had considerable control. It was in the latter capacity that General Colin Gubbins made his reputation. Appointed in 1943, Gubbins ran the SOE in its most critical days.

The London headquarters was located, appropriately enough, in the Baker Street of Sherlock Holmes fame. The divisions of the SOE organized operations by nation; each division was responsible for recruiting and training its own agents—men and women volunteers who spoke the necessary language fluently and could pass for nationals or at least as residents while in the field. These agents reached their target nations surreptitiously by sea (small boats in the English Channel and the Mediterranean), by air (parachutes or secret landings), and by land (over the Pyrenees from Spain). The agents joined or formed active patriotic groups, delivered and received information, and whenever possible reported to London by radio. They accepted as confederates all who would move against the Germans, across the political spectrum from left to right, from republicans to monarchists.

France, the biggest nation under German occupation and the nearest to Britain, was the principal area of SOE activity. Two sections dealt with France —Section F, established in 1940 and purely British-directed, and Section RF, established in 1941, which cooperated with the BCRA, the intelligence service of the Free French in London led by General Charles de Gaulle. Section F was not connected with the French resistance, which played an essential role in the planning and operations of Section RF.

The SOE grew from nothing until it had hundreds of agents, thousands of partisans, and scores of networks in France alone, an enormous apparatus at work under the noses of the occupation forces. Many SOE operatives were captured. Networks were disrupted. In Holland a network was "turned around" in the North Pole operation conducted by the Germans. SOE successes, however, were great, marked by skillful planning and heroism in the field. American General William Donovan copied much of the SOE structure and methods when he organized the OSS (Office of Strategic Services) in 1942, and during the rest of the war the SOE and the OSS cooperated excellently. In 1946, with the war won, the Continent liberated (at least in the west), and no further need for its services, the SOE was disbanded.

See also BCRA; GUBBINS, COLIN; NORTH POLE; OSS.

FURTHER READING: *M. R. D. Foot, *SOE in France: An Account of the Work of the British Special Operations Executive in France, 1940–1944* (1966); Edward Spiro, *Set Europe Ablaze* (1967); Jean Overton Fuller, *The German Penetration of SOE: France, 1941–1944* (1975).

Spy   A person who obtains information about one side for the benefit of a rival.

A spy is a sword, as a counterspy is a shield.

According to the Hague Convention of 1899: "A spy is one who, acting clandestinely, or on false pretenses, obtains, or seeks to obtain, information in the zone of operations of a belligerent, with the intention of communicating it to the hostile party." This old definition refers to military intelligence and is still accurate as far as it goes.

In this age of sensitive monitoring devices, espionage is often detected when little can be done to prevent it. Moreover, spying, like most other forms of activity, tends to become specialized as information and experience accumulate. Strategic intelligence (on the national level) and industrial espionage are two areas of expanding activity by spies.

A spy may simply be an individual who happens to notice something significant and reports on it to those who can exploit the information. Professional spies fall into various classes. First, there are those who stay at headquarters reading documents and examining photographs. Then there are those who remain outside enemy territory but near enough to receive correspondence, meet agents, and question travelers. Some spies make secret reconnaissance trips and return as quickly as possible.

The traditional picture of the spy is of one who remains among the enemy, engages in espionage, and reports covertly to an intelligence organization. Such a spy may be a sleeper, inoperative at the moment but waiting to be activated by an order from headquarters. A spy may be an alien sent across a border, a national recruited by an enemy agent, or a volunteer offering to serve for money or out of ideological commitment. A spy can work individually or belong to an espionage network under a chief (e.g., a resident director, if the network happens to be Russian).

A cut-out is a go-between who makes it unnecessary for members of a network to meet one another. A courier is a messenger who carries documents or other espionage material from one person or place to another. A radio operator often has no responsibility except to broadcast information to headquarters over a clandestine transmitter. One of the recent developments in espionage is the attachment to a network of a member who has a grasp of science and technology and can read blueprints of sophisticated machinery, such as rocket engines, atomic-bomb triggers, and space satellites.

Spies, like counterspies, are subject to international law. Historically, the death penalty has been frequently assessed. This has changed because nations holding enemy spies are concerned about their own spies being held by the enemy. Since World War II spies have largely been exchanged rather than executed. This is the espionage revolution of our time.

See also COUNTERSPY; COURIER; CUT-OUT; ESPIONAGE REVOLUTION; INDUS-TRIAL ESPIONAGE; MOLE; NETWORK; RESIDENT DIRECTOR; STRATEGIC INTELLI-GENCE.

FURTHER READING: *Allen Dulles, *The Craft of Intelligence* (1963); U. S. Department of Defense, Joint Chiefs of Staff Publication No. 1, *Dictionary of Military and Associated Terms* (1972); Miles Copeland, *Without Cloak or Dagger: The Truth about the New Espionage* (1974).

Spy-in-the-Sky   Space satellite equipped for espionage.

The use of outer space for espionage is characteristic of the space age. Orbiting satellites can watch everything on the surface of the earth, from weather to demographic phenomena, and spying by satellites is a natural application of this capability. The two major explorers of space, the United States and the Soviet Union, have maintained spies-in-the-sky almost since it became feasible to do so.

The first thing that made it feasible was the development of a rocket capable of orbiting the earth. The Russians were the first to achieve this, and in 1957 they put Sputnik into orbit. The United States succeeded in 1958 with Vanguard. Since then, rockets have become bigger and more powerful and have carried increasingly sophisticated payloads, among which are the spies-in-the-sky.

The second thing that made this type of espionage feasible was the development of equipment sensitive enough to survey the ground in detail and on a large scale. Today space satellites carry camera and radar equipment that can pinpoint an object two feet long from more than one hundred miles up and can send clear television pictures back to monitoring stations. They can also intercept and record phone calls.

The American Samos ("Satellite and Missile observer") program, using an Atlas-Agena rocket traveling at 18,000 mph, has put hundreds of satellites into orbit. Criss-crossing the Soviet Union, they have reported on nuclear explosions, rocket launchings, troop movements, and even military commands. Samos satellites report from outer space, and while falling back to destruction within the earth's atmosphere, they can eject a capsule over the Pacific to be plucked from the air by a rescue plane or else fished out of the water.

Since espionage always breeds counterespionage, the protection of one's secrets from prying eyes, strategy in outer space includes counterattacks against spies-in-the-sky. In 1980 Congressional committees heard testimony by Pentagon spokesmen that snooping enemy space vehicles could be intercepted by killer satellites much smaller in size and not even carrying an explosive charge. The collision at extreme velocity would destroy both. Most of the research that has been done since then is secret, but clearly both the United States and the Soviet Union are developing counterespionage in outer space.

In one sense, the Russians have an advantage in both espionage and counterespionage. The United States, an open society, puts much more of its research in the public domain than does the Soviet Union, which is therefore able to acquire on the ground the kind of information that the Americans must obtain by way of outer space.

See also INTELLIGENCE, SCIENTIFIC.

FURTHER READING: *John M. Carroll, *Secrets of Electronic Espionage* (1966); Philip J. Klass, *Secret Sentries in Space* (1971).

Standen, Anthony *(1550?-1600?)*   English secret agent on the Continent during the Elizabethan period.

The biography of Standen contains many gaps, but he is known to have been a Catholic by birth who, probably out of patriotism, served Francis Walsingham, the anti-Catholic director of intelligence for Queen Elizabeth. In 1565 Standen went with diplomatic delegations to Scotland and France, after which he traveled on the Continent until he found employment in Florence at the court of the duke of Tuscany.

At least as early as 1582 Standen was sending to Walsingham information picked up from diplomats at the Tuscan court. This was the period when Queen Elizabeth was threatened by a rival for the English throne, Mary Queen of Scots, who had a legitimate claim through her own royal descent and because Elizabeth was childless. Religion intensified the duel of the two queens: Mary was a Catholic and Elizabeth a Protestant. Finally, Mary, having fled from the Protestant rebellion against her in Scotland to presumed sanctuary in England, had become Elizabeth's prisoner.

Many English Catholics, at home and on the Continent, plotted to assassinate Elizabeth and place Mary on the throne. Walsingham's duty as intelligence director was to uncover these plots and to imprison or execute the plotters. To that end, he organized a vast network of spies, of whom Standen was the most effective, not only reporting what he learned himself but also maintaining spies in Spain and France. These spies became of great significance in 1587, the year Elizabeth had Mary executed, for King Philip II of Spain decided to support the English Catholics and avenge Mary by sending a Spanish army to conquer England.

Standen, who used the cover name "Pompeo Pelligrini," was a friend of the Tuscan ambassador to the Spanish court and therefore found it easy to introduce spies into Madrid through the good offices of the ambassador. Before the end of 1587, one of these spies achieved the remarkable coup of obtaining a copy of the report on the armada drawn up by the commanding admiral. Standen also informed Walsingham, correctly, that the armada would not sail before the year was out.

In 1588 Standen went to Spain, from which he wrote directly to London on the sailing of the armada. As the Spanish ships moved northward toward England, Standen's agents reported on their progress from points along the coasts of Spain and France. All of this information became part of the English battle plan, and the armada was defeated.

Standen lapsed back into obscurity after that, but during his brief time in the limelight he produced a masterpiece of espionage.

See also WALSINGHAM, FRANCIS.

FURTHER READING: *Conyers Read, *Mr. Secretary Walsingham and the Policy of Queen Elizabeth* (1925); Garrett Mattingly, *The Armada* (1959); Jean Plaidy, *Mary Queen of Scots: The Fair Devil of Scotland* (1975).

Stashinsky, Bogdan (1931-   ) Russian secret agent for, and defector from the Soviet Union.

Born in the Polish Ukraine, Stashinsky was the son of a farmer. He received a good education while the region was going through political and military convulsions. The Russians assumed control, following the Hitler-Stalin pact of 1939. The Germans overran the region during their attack on Russia in 1941 and began to Nazify it. Then the Russians returned toward the end of the war (1944), and a policy of ruthless Communization followed.

In 1950 the Russians, through the KGB (Committee for State Security, Soviet intelligence), forced Stashinsky to do espionage work for them, and he showed sufficient ability to be given special training and sent to West Germany for two years (1954–56), where he worked mainly as a courier and counterspy reporting on western intelligence, especially on the American CIA (Central Intelligence Agency).

Success brought him a transfer within the KGB to SMERSH, "death to spies," the department specializing in scientific violence. He joined SMERSH in 1957, was trained, and received the difficult assignment of going to Munich and murdering a Ukrainian nationalist. He performed his task by spraying prussic acid from a small tube into the victim's face.

Two years later another Ukrainian nationalist fell to his spray gun, and again Stashinsky got away. But his scruples had been growing, and he decided he could no longer accept such horrible assignments. He confided in his wife, who was horrified to learn what his job was and persuaded him to defect. Biding their time, they reached Berlin and escaped to the American sector of the city in 1961.

The West Germans put him on trial for two murders, but in view of the mitigating circumstances, the court sentenced him to only eight years. Stashinsky served his time, cleared his conscience, and revealed to the West what he knew about the activities of SMERSH. He was one of the most important defectors from the Soviet murder machine that still threatens those who betray its secrets.

See also SMERSH.

FURTHER READING: *Ronald Seth, *The Executioners: The Story of SMERSH* (1967); Karl Anders, *Murder to Order* (1967); John Barron, *KGB: The Secret Work of Soviet Secret Agents* (1974).

Steinhauer, Gustav *(1870?-1930?)*   German spymaster with responsibility for the British Isles during World War I.

Steinhauer, of a middle-class family and anxious for a higher place in life, gained a commission in the German navy in 1889. He had the good fortune, while his ship was berthed in a Greek harbor later that year, to have Kaiser Wilhelm come aboard, tour the vessel, meet Steinhauer, and respond favorably to him. When the royal yacht *Hohenzollern* needed a signals officer, the kaiser named Steinhauer to the post.

Steinhauer made several long voyages aboard the yacht. In 1892, deciding to try something other than a naval career, he went to the United States in search of a job. He worked in vaudeville and in a cigar factory before joining the Pinkerton Detective Agency in Chicago, where he mastered the English language and received training in the techniques of detection and arrest.

He states in his book that he tracked one fugitive to Europe, decided to remain in Germany, and reentered the kaiser's navy. In 1908 he made his first espionage trip to Britain, reporting to German naval intelligence on the British fleet in the North Sea.

The next three years saw him building a spy network of Germans, some nationalized Britons, who lived in England and Scotland. He found, among others, Karl Ernst, a barber willing to be his "letter box" in London and to whom Steinhauer wrote using the cover name "Frau T. Reimers."

Ernst proved to be the Achilles heel of the Steinhauer network, for Vernon Kell of MI5 (Military Intelligence 5, British counterespionage) and Basil Thomson of the Special Branch of Scotland Yard received reports that the barber had many German officers among his customers and that he was the recipient of an inordinate amount of mail from Germany. They began reading Ernst's correspondence surreptitiously and gathered information that enabled them to arrest most of the German spies in Britain on the outbreak of World War I.

Steinhauer's failure was through his own ineptitude. However, to Steinhauer's credit, he did warn Karl Lody of the dangers before Lody crossed the English Channel to spy, was caught, and died before a firing squad.

See also ERNST, KARL; LODY, KARL.

FURTHER READING: *Gustav Steinhauer, *Steinhauer, the Kaiser's Master Spy* (1930); John Bulloch, *MI5: The Origin and History of the British Counter-Espionage Service* (1963); Richard Deacon, *A History of the British Secret Service* (1969).

Stephenson, William *(1896-   )* Canadian coordinator of Anglo-American intelligence during World War II.

Stephenson, the son of an executive in the lumber business, was born at Point Douglas near Winnipeg and educated in a neighborhood elementary school. At the beginning of World War I in 1914, he left high school to enlist in the Royal Canadian Engineers, received a commission as a second lieutenant, saw service in the trench warfare in France, and was invalided to England after being gassed (1915). He transferred to the Royal Flying Corps in 1916, became a flight commander, and scored numerous "kills" in dogfights with German pilots. A French pilot shot him down by mistake toward the end of the war. Captured and interned by the Germans, Stephenson made a daring escape back to France (1918).

After the war, Stephenson went into business, married Mary Simmons of Tennessee, and during his travels on the Continent watched with concern the turmoil of the 1920s. He was in Berlin in 1933 when the Nazis staged their notorious book burning. Three years later, noting the growing military might of Nazi Germany under the leadership of Chancellor Adolf Hitler, Stephenson reported his impressions to Winston Churchill, who, however, was out of power and could not act on the information (other British leaders, led by Prime Minister Stanley Baldwin, would not act on it).

Follwing the outbreak of World War II in 1939, Stephenson, because of his knowledge of German industry, was asked by MI6 (Military Intelligence 6, British espionage) to predict on which Scandinavian sources of iron ore Hitler might rely. His success led MI6 to send him on his first intelligence mission to Washington, where he investigated the possibility of undercover cooperation between MI6 and the FBI (Federal Bureau of Investigation). His talks with J. Edgar Hoover, director of the FBI, were fruitful, and on returning to London he delivered a favorable report. In 1940, following the lightning German conquest of France, Prime Minister Winston Churchill persuaded Stephenson to go back to Washington with the title of chief of British Security Coordination (BSC).

Using the code name "Intrepid" and directing the BSC from his headquarters in Room 3603 of the RCA Building in New York, Stephenson meshed Anglo-American intelligence. This had to be done with special care in 1940, because the United States was not yet in the war. His main success at this time was his employment of Amy Thorpe Pack, who as "Cynthia" penetrated the French Embassy in Washington, which was loyal to the Vichy government of France, a puppet of the Germans. She obtained the Vichy naval ciphers, which allowed the Allies to read Vichy orders before and during the Allied landings in French North Africa in 1942.

When the Americans established an espionage organization, the Central Office of Information (COI) in 1941 under William Donovan, Stephenson assisted Donovan. The COI became the OSS (Office of Strategic Services) in

1942. After the Japanese attack on Pearl Harbor had forced the United States into the war, the two men cooperated on espionage, sabotage, and guerrilla warfare against the Germans and Italians. The pair were different personalities, Donovan the flamboyant "Wild Bill" and Stephenson the "quiet Canadian," were both men of action and they got along well at this time and in the postwar years.

Stephenson had to deal with many factors from his base in New York. He assisted the OSS and its British parallel, the Special Operations Executive (SOE); he also cooperated closely with the FBI. He passed disinformation to the enemy through the mail via Bermuda. Camp X on Lake Ontario in Canada was used to rehearse sabotage missions. All the while, he was dealing with superiors in London and Washington who did not always see eye to eye with him or each other on objectives or methods. He succeeded so notably that King George VI knighted him in 1944, and President Franklin Roosevelt awarded him the Presidential Medal for Merit in 1945. The BSC, like the OSS, was disbanded in 1946.

Stephenson went back to business, some of it in partnership with Donovan, bought a retreat in Jamaica, and became an adviser on industrial development to several governments, including that of his own country, Canada.

See also DONOVAN, WILLIAM; HOOVER, J. EDGAR; PACK, AMY THORPE.

FURTHER READING: *H. Montgomery Hyde, *Room 3603: The Story of the British Intelligence Center in New York during World War II* (1962); William Stevenson, *A Man Called Intrepid: The Secret War* (1976).

Stieber, Wilhelm *(1818-82)*   German spymaster during the era of Otto von Bismarck.

Born in Merseburg, in Saxony, Stieber was the son of a minor church official. He claimed that through his mother he belonged to the English landed gentry. Stieber studied theology at Berlin University but soon switched to law, against the wishes of his father, who disowned him. In order to support himself and continue his studies he worked, by his own account, as a clerk for the Berlin criminal courts and in its police stations. He graduated in 1841 and established a legal practice, putting his knowledge of the criminal mind, gleaned in the course of his police duties, to good use. He quickly gained a reputation for his clever defenses of his clients, most of whom were criminals. However, his experience of police work convinced Stieber that he should join the Berlin force. In 1844 he was appointed a commissioner in its new criminal department.

In 1845, disguised as an artist, Stieber was an *agent provocateur* in Silesia, where socialist ideas were beginning to surface. A devoted royalist himself, he had no scruples about betraying those whose confidence he won, and he soon rounded up many suspects who were subsequently sentenced to jail. In 1848 he gained the favor of the Prussian King, Friedrich Wilhelm IV, by apparently saving him from a socialist mob—an episode that may have been engineered by Stieber himself. The grateful king promoted him to director of the Berlin criminal police and two years later sent him to London and Paris (this time as "Herr Schmidt," an editor) to spy on Karl Marx and his Communist party. The first international Communist trials, which took place in Cologne in 1852, drew on the information gathered by Stieber.

His methods of entrapment raised public protests, but the king supported him. However, in 1858 Friedrich Wilhelm became insane, and his brother, who later became Emperor Wilhelm I, took power. Wilhelm disliked Stieber and allowed his enemies to bring him to trial, accusing him of extreme brutality in his methods of interrogation. In his own defense, Stieber was able to prove—legally and embarrassingly—that all he had done was carry out the king's orders. If he were condemned the mad old king would stand equally condemned. The court therefore acquitted him. Stieber moved vindictively against those who had tried to curb him. Wilhelm dismissed him and ordered him out of Berlin.

During the next five years Stieber helped the Russians reorganize their secret service, in particular the Foreign Branch, concerned with counterespionage. This was disbanded in 1878, but the changes initiated by Stieber were transferred to the Ochrana, which succeeded the Foreign Branch in 1881.

In 1863 Stieber met Bismarck, who had been Prussian ambassador to Russia and was now King Wilhelm's right-hand man. It was the beginning of a long collaboration. After an attack on his life, about which Stieber had warned him, Bismarck asked Stieber to form the Secret Security Police. Its function would be to protect the king, his ministers, and the social establishment. Calling his organization the Central Intelligence Bureau, Stieber soon had his police force in action. Bismarck was already plotting war with Austria, the first step in his program for the aggrandizement of Prussia. He asked Stieber to prepare the way. Disguised as a peddler, his cart filled half with religious statuettes and half with pornographic pictures, Stieber made his way to Austria, where he spent many months judiciously selling his wares and gathering information. He returned to Bismarck in Berlin with a detailed estimate of Austria's military capabilities. Austria was defeated in a matter of weeks by a well-planned blitzkrieg (1866). Stieber rode with the Prussian generals as head of the new Field Security Police, the first official counterespionage unit in the field.

The next year Chancellor Bismarck and his spymaster turned their attention to France. Stieber amassed intelligence to use in the Franco-Prussian War (1870–71). He planted spies and agents in major cities all over France; he knew the layout of virtually every farm, village, and house in the fighting area; and he knew the exact extent to which each could be expected to provide supplies for the invaders. His army of spies in Paris had long been in place when the city was besieged. Nine thousand spies were said to be concentrated at German headquarters in Versailles alone. The peace was signed when Paris fell in January 1871.

After the war Stieber retired to the Central Intelligence Bureau, which grew to unheard of peacetime strength under his control. Many of Stieber's techniques—saturation of an area with spies; subtle manipulation of the press, business, and the banks; military censorship; psychological warfare; terrorism; and the use of women as bait—are now basic in the espionage operations of many nations. One of his least pleasing inventions, the notorious Green House, was a high-class house of prostitution, run by the police and offering every possible form of vice for the benefit of high government officials and foreign diplomats. The girls, said Stieber, were born spies, some of his best. They kept him well supplied with material for blackmail.

Ironically the much decorated "king of sleuthhounds" (Bismarck's name for him) desperately wanted social recognition. He could not get it, so greatly was he detested in the upper reaches of society and government. Then, too, the Prussian generals refused to acknowledge the part he had played in the wars, which detracted from their image. His enemies abroad, the French in particular, were even more reluctant to give him credit for his espionage exploits. A conspiracy of silence settled on the name of Wilhelm Stieber, a spy of malevolent genius who played a key role in the formation of the German empire. His influence is widespread in all modern espionage systems.

FURTHER READING: *J. Auerbach, *Denkwürdigkeiten des Geheimen Regierungsrathes Dr. Stieber aus seinen Hinterlassen Papieren Bearbeitet* (1882), is Stieber's own account; Hamil Grant, *Spies and Secret Service* (1915); Bernard Newman, *Epics of Espionage* (1950); Allen Dulles, *The Craft of Intelligence* (1963), contains a tribute by one spymaster to another; Wilhelm J. Stieber, *The Chancellor's Spy* (Jan Van Heurck, ed., 1980).

Stosch, Philip von *(1691-1757)*   German art collector and spy for the British government during the time of the Jacobite movement.

Stosch came of a noble Brandenburg family, which gave him a baronial title and association with the aristocrats of Europe. Pointed toward the Lutheran ministry by his father, Stosch turned to art instead and became an expert collector. In 1715 he migrated to Italy, a land of art treasures. Here he met Allessandro Albani, and ecclesiastic, an art collector like himself, and soon to become a cardinal and a spy for the British government.

Needing money to indulge his fine tastes, Stosch also became a spy for the British government. London was willing to pay for reports on the Jacobites, the British in exile who supported the "Old Pretender," the son of James II, who wanted to regain the English throne, lost by his father in 1688, at the time of the Glorious Revolution. In the year of Stosch's arrival in Rome, the Old Pretender invaded Great Britain, only to be defeated. In 1721 Stosch joined the British spy network in Rome. He used the cover name "John Walton" and sent weekly reports to Lord Carteret, a member of the British government. Stosch wrote to Carteret in French and put highly confidential messages into cipher.

When the Old Pretender had trouble with his wife in 1725, when he returned to Rome from Bologna in 1726, when he or those around him drew traveling Englishmen into the Jacobite movement in 1729, when a group of English Catholics came to pay their respects to their uncrowned king in 1730, Stosch wrote to London immediately. He kept his eyes and ears open while meeting Jacobites or dealing in art and picked up information from Albani and other ecclesiastics.

But Stosch fell under Jacobite suspicion because of his inquisitiveness. The Old Pretender protested to the pope that Stosch was a spy, and in 1731 Stosch received orders to leave Rome. He settled in Florence, where he met the British resident, who was also a British spymaster, Horace Mann. From then on, Stosch's undercover reports had little significance because he no longer knew first-hand what the Jacobites were doing in Rome. He corresponded with Albani and contrived to make reports to Mann and to London from what Albani told him, but his information was so minor that he had trouble getting the British government to pay for it.

One thing Stosch did for Mann was to provide Florentine gossip that went into Mann's famous correspondence with Horace Walpole in England. One thing Stosch did for himself was to indulge his taste for Florentine art.

See also MANN, HORACE.

FURTHER READING: Dorothy Mackay Quynn, "Philip von Stosch," *Catholic Historical Review* (1941); *Lesley Lewis, *Connoisseurs and Secret Agents in Eighteenth Century Rome* (1961); David Daiches, *Charles Edward Stuart: The Life and Times of Bonnie Prince Charlie* (1973).

Stringer A spy who works on an occasional, freelance basis for an intelligence organization.

See SPY.

Stringfellow, Benjamin Franklin *(1840-1913)* Confederate scout and spy during the American Civil War.

Stringfellow came from a line of planters in Virginia, where he was born at The Retreat, the family estate in Culpeper County. Given a classical education, he became a teacher of Greek and Latin in Mississippi. In 1861 he returned to Virginia to fight for his state when he realized that the secession of the South must be followed by war.

Rejected by the Confederate army because he was not fit enough (he weighed less than 100 pounds), Stringfellow kept applying until he was accepted as a private in the cavalry. He was a mounted courier at the battle of Bull Run (1861), where he so distinguished himself that he received an appointment as an officer on the staff of Confederate General J. E. B. ("Jeb") Stuart.

Stringfellow was a spy as well as a cavalryman. After scouting behind the Union lines in 1862, he accepted from Jeb Stuart in 1863 an undercover mission to Washington. Taking two men with him, Stringfellow crossed the Union lines without being detected and entered the Federal capital in civilian clothes—which meant that all three could be officially considered spies and subject to execution if caught.

Using the cover name "R. M. Franklin," Stringfellow covertly approached Southern sympathizers, not a difficult thing to do, since many remained in Washington and a few were in contact with friends or military commanders in the Confederacy. Stringfellow arranged for a small network of spies close to the Federal War Department to send secret messages to him; he then made his way back to Stuart's headquarters.

In subsequent scouting and espionage operations, he was several times captured by the Federals, each time escaping to his own lines and resuming his activities. He served at Gettysburg on the staff of General Robert E. Lee, who promoted him to command of the scouts of the Army of Northern Virginia, in which capacity Stringfellow became renowned during 1864 and 1865 for his hit-and-run tactics against the forces of Union General Ulysses S. Grant, who was driving on Richmond.

After the Civil War, Stringfellow turned to religion, graduating from the Episcopal seminary in Virginia in 1876. For three decades he was one of the most popular clergymen in the state because he took his own feats of 1861 to 1865 as subjects for his sermons. He left a lasting impression on his grandson, Stringfellow Barr, an educator who in the twentieth century presided over St. John's College in Annapolis, Maryland, and its famous "great books" program.

FURTHER READING: Virgil Carrington Jones, *Gray Ghosts and Rebel Raiders* (1956); *R. Shepard Brown, *Stringfellow of the Fourth* (1960); John Bakeless, *Spies of the Confederacy* (1970).

***Tai Li** (1895-1945)* Director of intelligence for nationalist China through World War II.

Tai Li apparently was born in Chekiang Province, although this, like his family background, is uncertain because in the days of his power he systematically concealed his origins. He supported the nationalists, entered the service of their leader Chiang Kai-shek, and in 1927 was Chiang's captain of military police in Shanghai. K'ang Sheng, the man who would serve Communist leader Mao Tse-tung as Tai Li served Chiang Kai-shek, was organizing Communist cells in Shanghai in the same year, but the two did not meet.

Rising within the nationalist organization, Tai Li in 1942 replaced "Two-Gun" Cohen as Chiang's intelligence chief (Cohen having been jailed by the Japanese). Tai Li, extending Cohen's counterespionage network, relied more than had his predecessor on women, narcotics, and alcohol to trap suspects.

Tai Li also enjoyed the advantage of working with the American OSS (Office of Strategic Services) and at times directly with the head of the OSS, General William Donovan. The cooperation was close, and Donovan recognized in Tai Li a great spymaster. The Americans provided military supplies for the common effort during World War II, while the Chinese network provided information on the Japanese forces in China. Tai-Li and Donovan both had a hand in the final victory, which came with the surrender of Japan in 1945.

This cooperation, however, had one unfortunate outcome. The Americans in China were so convinced of Tai Li's infallibility that they failed to notice his gross underestimation of the Chinese Communists. The Americans believed him when he swore that Chiang Kai-shek could easily handle Mao Tse-tung.

Tai Li was killed in a plane that exploded in mid-air. He evidently fell victim to his rival, K'ang Sheng, who headed Mao's intelligence department.

See also COHEN, TWO-GUN; K'ANG SHENG.

FURTHER READING: Charles Drage, *Two-Gun Cohen* (1954); Oliver J. Caldwell, *A Secret War: Americans in China, 1944–1945* (1972); *Richard Deacon, *The Chinese Secret Service* (1974).

***Tallmadge, Benjamin** (1754-1835)* Spymaster for General George Washington during the American War of Independence.

Tallmadge, a New Yorker, graduated from Yale (1773) and was beginning a career in the Connecticut school system when the American Revolution broke out (1775). He joined Connecticut's armed forces with the rank of lieutenant, received promotions to captain (1776) and major (1777) in the

Continental army, and fought in the battles of Long Island, White Plains, Brandywine, Germantown, and Monmouth.

When the British evacuated Philadelphia and returned to New York City in 1778, the Americans occupied positions up the Hudson and in adjoining areas. General George Washington was determined not to have an intelligence fiasco comparable to that involving Nathan Hale, who in 1776 while on a spy mission in New York City had been captured and executed. Washington ordered Tallmadge to establish an espionage system that would bring reliable information from inside the city. Tallmadge founded the Culper Ring and directed it (under the cover name "John Bolton") in the most successful clandestine operation of the war. He was the opposite number of John André (cover name, "John Anderson"), who from New York City ran the British spy system for his commanding general, Sir Henry Clinton.

Tallmadge's association with André occurred in 1780 at the time of Benedict Arnold's decision to betray West Point to the British. André, stopped by American militiamen while on his way back to New York City after his secret meeting with Arnold up the Hudson, showed a pass made out by Arnold to "John Anderson." His captors, finding plans of West Point in his boot, took him to their commanding officer, who sent André under guard toward Arnold's headquarters. Tallmadge arrived shortly afterward. He had been asked by Arnold to pass "John Anderson" through the lines, was disturbed by the finding of the plans of West Point, became suspicious of Arnold, and persuaded the commanding officer to have the prisoner brought back. André was identified, and Washington, upon being notified, ordered him held for trial.

Tallmadge had custody of André during the latter's captivity, was impressed by him as an officer and a gentleman, and lamented his execution though not dissenting from the judgment of the court-martial, ratified by Washington, that André the spy merited death under the espionage code.

Also in 1780, Tallmadge led a raid on Fort George, on Long Island, and accomplished his mission, which was to destroy a British supply depot. This was the last serious action he saw during the war. From then on his importance to Washington was almost entirely as a spymaster. In 1783 he was breveted a lieutenant general, meaning that he received the honor for meritorious service although he did not hold the command or receive the pay that normally went with the rank.

After the war, Tallmadge became a merchant in Litchfield, Connecticut. He won election to the Congress of the United States in 1801 and served there until 1817, representing the Federalist party, which stood for the policies advocated by his old commanding general, mentor, and friend, the late President George Washington.

See also ANDRÉ, JOHN; CULPER RING; WASHINGTON, GEORGE.

FURTHER READING: Morton Pennypacker, *General Washington's Spies on Long Island and in New York* (1939); Charles Swain Hall, *Benjamin Tallmadge, Revolutionary Soldier and American Businessman* (1943); *Corey Ford, *A Peculiar Service* (1965), is the best book on Tallmadge and the Culper Ring.

Thompson, Benjamin *(1753-1814)*   American Loyalist who spied for the British during the American Revolution before achieving fame as a scientist.

Born in Massachusetts, Thompson had to develop his scientific bent by himself because his family could not afford to send him to school. He worked for businessmen in Salem and Boston as a boy, at which time he became interested in the physics of gunpowder and other explosives. In 1770 he entered into an apprenticeship with a physician in his home town of Woburn, Massachusetts and received training in this branch of science, although never taking a medical degree.

Thompson taught school briefly. Then he married a wealthy widow of Concord, New Hampshire (formerly Rumford, from which he later took his aristocratic title). He belonged to the social circle that included the royal governor, who appointed him an officer in the New Hampshire militia, an experience that made Thompson a convinced Loyalist during the period when the American Revolution was developing, in the early 1770s. By 1773, the year of the Boston Tea Party (when a band of Americans threw a cargo of British tea into Boston harbor), Thompson was covertly watching disaffected Americans and reporting to the governor.

In 1774 Thompson's Loyalist opinions brought him to the attention of the local Committee of Safety, a group of Patriots acting as watchdogs of American rights. Although acquitted of charges that he was acting against the interests of New Hampshire, he retreated to Massachusetts, where he went to Boston to see the British governor, General Thomas Gage.

At this meeting, Thompson agreed to resume his espionage activities on behalf of the British. He returned to Woburn and began to spy on the Patriots. He wrote to Gage in invisible ink between the lines of innocent letters, putting his scientific knowledge to good use by employing a form of tannic acid that became visible when washed with ferrous sulphate.

One report that Thompson delivered in this covert manner in 1775 concerned an American plan to raise 30,000 men in New England. By then the battle of Lexington had taken place, and Gage was shut up in Boston by the Continental army, of which George Washington was the commander in chief. In these circumstances, Thompson, who was spying on the Patriots outside Boston while Paul Revere was spying on the British inside the city, again fell under suspicion. Again he was interrogated by the Committee of Safety, again he was acquitted, and again he fled to Boston. There he wrote a detailed account on "the State of the Rebel Army," which was so accurate that it remains a basic source of our knowledge of Washington's command.

In 1776 Sir William Howe, who had replaced Gage, decided to abandon Boston and launch a campaign in New York. Thompson, afraid to stay in Boston and unwilling to follow the British forces to New York, migrated to London. There he did scientific work, was consulted by the British authorities on conditions in America, and received both political and military appointments. He returned to America with a military commission in 1781, achieved nothing, and left his homeland for good in 1783.

His greatest achievements lay before him, but they were in physics, not espionage. His research on light and heat led to his election to the Royal Society. His theoretical and practical scientific work in the Holy Roman Empire caused the emperor to raise him to the nobility, and he took the title of Count Rumford. At the time of his death, Count Rumford was considered, as he still is, a major figure in the history of science.

FURTHER READING: Edward A. Jones, *Loyalists of Massachusetts* (1930); *Allen French, *General Gage's Informers: New Material Upon Lexington and Concord, Benjamin Thompson as Loyalist and the Treachery of Benjamin Church* (1932); Sanford G. Brown, *Count Rumford* (1962).

Thomson, Basil *(1861-1939)*   Director of the Special Branch of Scotland Yard during World War I.

Thomson began life with a solid place in the British establishment, for his father was archbishop of York, and he himself enjoyed the benefits of an education at Eton and Oxford. Instead of becoming a clergyman or a professor, Thomson went into law enforcement, serving in the prison system and becoming governor of Dartmoor Prison, which housed some of Britain's most notorious criminals.

In 1913 Thomson became head of the Criminal Investigation Department of Scotland Yard, with the Special Branch under his supervision. This brought him into counterespionage, since the Special Branch had, as it still does, the arresting function with regard to spies in Britain. Thomson cooperated closely with Vernon Kell of MI5 (Military Intelligence 5, the investigatory agency of British counterespionage). Thomson also collaborated with Reginald Hall of the Admiralty's Room 40, the cryptology center.

Thomson did his major work during World War I when he helped round up German spies in Britain. He was responsible for taking Franz von Rintelen from a Dutch vessel, ending Rintelen's career as an undercover agent for the kaiser. Thomson also interrogated Mata Hari as she passed through England en route from Spain to Holland. He suspected her of spying for the Germans and advised her to give it up (she rejected his advice) before allowing her to proceed on her way.

Thomson retired after the war and devoted himself to writing about the crime-fighting organizations he had belonged to and the strange men and women whom he had met in the line of duty.

See also SPECIAL BRANCH.

FURTHER READING: *Basil Thomson, *Queer People* (1922); John Bulloch, *MI5: The Origin and History of the British Counter-Espionage Service* (1963); Harry Howe Ransom, *The Intelligence Establishment* (1970).

---

355   Code name of an unidentified woman who spied for the Patriots in New York during the American War of Independence.

See TOWNSEND, ROBERT.

Thurloe, John *(1616-68)*   Antiroyalist spymaster during the English Civil War and the period of the Commonwealth.

Thurloe, the son of a parson in the Church of England, abandoned his father's religious institution after the Great Rebellion, against King Charles I, broke out in 1642 under the leadership of Oliver Cromwell. Thurloe, like Cromwell, became an Independent in religion and a rebel in politics. He took a law degree in 1645, and six years later he was one of an English mission to the Netherlands. Cromwell summoned him into the English government, naming him secretary to the council of state (1652) and a member of the council (1657). During their years of power, Thurloe served as virtual viceroy to Cromwell the dictator.

Charles I was executed in 1649, an act that shocked the English people and led to conspiracies to restore the monarchy in the person of Charles II. Threatened by royalist enemies, Cromwell gave Thurloe the task of counteracting them, provided him with money sufficient to pay for espionage and counterespionage, and allowed him a free hand. Thurloe organized the best spy system in England since the Elizabethan period, a prime support of the Commonwealth with which Cromwell replaced the monarchy.

Thurloe's chief assistant was John Wallis, an Oxford mathematician who specialized in cryptology and was credited with the ability to break any code. Thurloe, as Cromwell's postmaster general, was in a strategic position to censor the mail surreptitiously. He had letters opened and read, and he sent those in cipher to Wallis for decoding. Most information, however, came from Thurloe's spy networks, one with agents throughout England, the other with agents across the Continent and in European colonies of the New World.

Thurloe dispatched his spies to the capitals of Europe fully briefed on their assignments and with orders to report to London every week if possible. His skillful handling of espionage prompted a Venetian ambassador to comment that the English government always knew what other governments planned to do, but that the reverse was not true.

When an English fleet captured a Spanish treasure convoy off the Canary Islands, much of the credit belonged to one of Thurloe's spies in Jamaica who knew about the sailing and reported it. When the Royalist plot called the "sealed knot" became dangerous, Thurloe bribed a member to betray it and would have had Charles II kidnaped from the Continent except that one of Thurloe's agents betrayed him and warned Charles.

After Cromwell died in 1658, Thurloe served his son, "Tumbledown Dick" Cromwell, who lacked the ability to govern. The restoration of Charles II occurred in 1660, and Thurloe was charged with high treason. Released on a promise to serve the king's government, Thurloe wrote analyses of politics and international problems, but he never again held the power he had wielded when Oliver Cromwell ruled England.

FURTHER READING: G. M. Trevelyan, *England under the Stuarts* (1904), covers the period of Cromwell and Thurloe; C. H. Firth, "Secretary Thurloe on the Relations of England and Holland," *English Historical Review* (1906); *Maurice Ashley, *Oliver Cromwell and His World* (1972).

Townsend, Robert *(1754-1838)*   Patriot spy in New York City during the American War of Independence.

Townsend was a merchant from Oyster Bay, on Long Island, who made a living by selling to the stores and markets of Manhattan. As a Patriot, he disliked British attempts to enforce American obedience to the king, but he was also a Quaker, pledged not to engage in violence. These two principles fought for control of his mind and conscience until, like Lydia Darragh, a Philadelphia Quaker, he opted for war and freedom instead of nonviolence and oppression.

In 1778 Townsend was recruited by Abraham Woodhull into the Culper Ring, the Patriot spy network then being organized by Major Benjamin Tallmadge, espionage chief to General George Washington. Woodhull, who farmed at Setauket, on Long Island, lacked a plausible motive to visit Manhattan regularly to spy on the British, who held New York City under the command of Sir Henry Clinton. Townsend, on the contrary, had to go there regularly on business. He could continue to do so without arousing suspicion among the British or the Loyalists in the city. He therefore provided a needed link in the espionage chain that ran from New York City to Woodhull's farm at Setauket and then across Long Island Sound to the Connecticut shore, where Tallmadge waited.

Woodhull's cover name was "Samuel Culper, Senior," and Townsend became "Samuel Culper, Junior." To make his cover more secure, Townsend both served with Loyalist volunteers in New York City and wrote for the *Royal Gazette,* published by James Rivington (a Loyalist editor who, when the wind changed, shifted his allegiance and became a double agent for the Americans). Townsend also joined Rivington in running a Manhattan coffeehouse (1779). That same year, Townsend opened a dry goods store nearby, which gave him another legitimate excuse to be in the city most of the time.

He spied on Clinton's forces, received information from other Patriots, and reported in coded messages, which he gave to Austin Roe, a courier. Roe took them on horseback to Woodhull in Setauket, who gave them to boatman Caleb Brewster, who conveyed them to Tallmadge on the opposite shore of Long Island Sound. A few more individuals belonged to the Culper Ring, including Enoch Hale, brother of Nathan Hale, who had been hanged as a spy by the British in 1776.

Some of Townsend's relatives helped him with information, notably his sister, Sarah. The most intriguing figure has never been identified, a woman known as "355" in the numerical code used by the Culper Ring. She was the mother of Townsend's son, but for some reason, and despite his Quaker scruples, they never married.

Apparently Benedict Arnold knew about and informed on 355, for the British arrested her shortly after Arnold arrived in New York City in 1780, following the collapse of his plot to betray West Point to Clinton. She died on a British prison ship in 1781.

Townsend himself remained a mysterious figure until the 1930s, when Long Island historian Morton Pennypacker uncovered his identity by comparing the handwriting of Samuel Culper, Junior, with that of Townsend, who could then finally be credited with his place in the transmission of a mass of vital intelligence data from Manhattan to Washington's headquarters.

Washington himself, always protective of his espionage agents who needed to remain anonymous, never asked for the real name of Samuel Culper, Junior. In 1783, Tallmadge met Townsend for the only time, when the British were evacuating New York after the peace with Great Britain had been signed. Tallmadge remained silent about him, as did the others who knew the facts.

Townsend retired from the adventures of spying to the placidity of the ancestral home of the Townsends in Oyster Bay. He never talked about his service in the revolution, at least not to outsiders.

See also CULPER RING; TALLMADGE, BENJAMIN.

FURTHER READING: *Morton Pennypacker, *General Washington's Spies on Long Island and in New York* (1939); John Bakeless, *Turncoats, Traitors, and Heroes* (1959), has an account of Townsend; Corey Ford, *A Peculiar Service* (1965), is the best book on Townsend and the Culper Ring.

Tremblay, François Leclerc du *(1577-1638)* French Capuchin friar and undercover agent for Cardinal Richelieu.

Born in Paris, Tremblay was an aristocrat important enough to be invited to the court of King Henry IV in 1595. He forsook the glitter of royalty to enter the Capuchin order, where he rose to become its provincial in the province of Touraine in 1613, a success that brought him back to court during the reign of King Louis XIII. An adviser on ecclesiastical affairs, Tremblay was a strong advocate of the idea of a regenerate France leading crusades to bring the Protestants of Europe back to Catholicism and to convert the adherents of Islam in North Africa and the Near East.

Tremblay himself could not mount crusades. He found a man he considered the necessary leader when he met Armand Jean du Plessis, who would become a renowned statesman as Cardinal Richelieu, first minister to Louis XIII.

Tremblay wanted to reduce the power of Catholic Austria in Europe so that Catholic France could become the principal champion of Catholicism. Richelieu wanted to effect this shift in the power balance for political reasons. The two men therefore agreed on the practical objective, although for different motives. For that reason Tremblay, having the ear of Louis XIII, urged the king to bring Richelieu back into the government after the latter had suffered a temporary eclipse. In 1621 Richelieu was back.

When Richelieu became the King's first minister in 1624, he and Tremblay began to put into practice their ideas on foreign policy. The Thirty Years' War (1618–48) gave them their opportunity, for this was basically a conflict between the Holy Roman Emperor, Ferdinand II, in Vienna and the Protestants of Germany. The Richelieu-Tremblay policy was to support the Protestants and thereby to weaken Austria.

During the 1620s Tremblay, known familiarly as "Father Joseph" and Richelieu's "Gray Eminence," went on secret missions to the smaller German states, encouraging them to oppose the emperor. In 1630 he was at the Diet of Regensburg, where the emperor and the subordinate princes debated the fate of Albrecht von Wallenstein, the best Catholic general of the Thirty Years' War. By artfully playing on the fear of Wallenstein's army, which lived off the country, whether Catholic or Protestant, Tremblay persuaded the princes to demand Wallenstein's dismissal. Ferdinand bowed to the demand.

Meanwhile, Richelieu was subsidizing the Protestant king of Sweden, Gustavus Adolphus, to attack the Catholic forces of the emperor. The victories of Gustavus ensured the success of the Protestant cause in Germany. The emperor in desperation recalled Wallenstein to his command in 1632, but Gustavus defeated Wallenstein in the battle of Lutzen, though the Swedish king was killed. The war dragged on indecisively until the signing of the Treaty of Westphalia (1648), which signaled the rise to preeminence of France and the corresponding decline of Austria.

Richelieu's political objective had been achieved. Tremblay's religious objective never really became a part of French foreign policy.

See also RICHELIEU, CARDINAL.

FURTHER READING: J. W. Thompson and S. K. Padover, *Secret Diplomacy: A Record of Espionage and Double-dealing: 1500–1815* (1937); *Aldous Huxley, *Gray Eminence* (1941), is a biography of Tremblay; G. R. Treasure, *Cardinal Richelieu and the Development of Absolutism* (1972).

Trepper, Leopold (1904-1982) Polish spymaster for the Soviet Union in western Europe during World War II.

Trepper was born in Neumark, Poland. The son of a Jewish shopkeeper, he received much of his education at home, attended a local school, and in his teens managed to gain entry to Krakow University. Forced to drop out for financial reasons, he worked at different jobs, ending as a miner in Galicia. His experience led him to become a Communist, and in 1925 he helped foment a strike at Dombrova, for which he served eight months in jail.

Trepper moved to Palestine in 1926, motivated by a Zionist fervor that took him to a kibbutz where he engaged in communal farming. However, he joined a Communist group, decided that farming was not as satisfying as Communist agitation, was expelled from Palestine by the British in 1928, and went back to Europe. By the early 1930s he was a leader in Rabcors, a French organization working illegally for the Soviet Union. The French authorities broke up Rabcors in 1932 and arrested Trepper. He escaped and reached Moscow in 1933.

Trepper seems to have traveled between Moscow and Paris during the next six years. In 1939, having received thorough espionage training, he arrived in western Europe to replace Soviet spymaster Walter Krivitsky, who had defected from the Soviet Union from disgust with and fear of the Stalinist tyranny. Trepper's orders from Moscow were to coordinate the pro-Soviet spy rings in the west. Trepper's success made him the *grand chef* ("big Chief") of the Red Orchestra of World War II. He operated principally in Belgium and France, although branches of the Red Orchestra existed in Holland, Germany, and Switzerland.

Brussels became his first headquarters. From there he directed the transmission of information by radio to Moscow until his move to Paris in 1940, following the German conquest of France. In 1941 he and his secret agents were ready for action when the Germans invaded Russia, and they responded to Russian appeals for reports on the German armed forces. German counterespionage picked up radio broadcasts of the Red Orchestra and began to track down the sources, finally succeeding in Brussels in 1941. Trepper could have been seized along with the radio operator, for he unsuspectingly appeared at the building at the time of the arrest. He talked his way out of his predicament by posing as a rabbit salesman, according to one report.

In 1942 another Red Orchestra radio operator in Brussels, Johann Wenzel, fell into the hands of the Germans, and they persuaded him to tell what he knew about the clandestine organization. Wenzel informed his captors that the *grand chef* was Trepper, now using the cover name "Jean Gilbert" and hiding in Paris. The Germans traced Trepper through his dentist and arrested him as he sat in the dentist's chair. Trepper, perhaps because of German threats to his family, named some of his agents, who were rounded up. More than that, he was "turned around" and joined a German "playback" campaign, continuing to transmit radio messages to Moscow, but now messages made up by the Germans. However, Moscow demanded detailed information that the Germans decided to withhold, which naturally alerted the Russians to the truth, and the playback campaign came to an end in 1943.

Trepper escaped at about the same time. He remained at liberty until he returned to Moscow in 1945, at the end of the war. The Russians imprisoned him on the charge that he had cooperated with the Germans. Trepper convinced his interrogators that he had been loyal to the Soviet Union all the while and that his radio playback messages for the Germans had been a pretense that fooled them. Allowed to go free, he subsequently turned up at Communist meetings in Poland and survived to publish his autobiography thirty years later.

See also KRIVITSKY, WALTER; RED ORCHESTRA.

FURTHER READING: Heinz Höhne, *Codeword: Direktor: The Story of the Red Orchestra* (1971); *Leopold Trepper, *The Great Game: Memoirs of the Spy Hitler Couldn't Silence* (1977); Paul L. Kesaris (ed.), *The Rote Kapelle: The CIA's History of Soviet Intelligence and Espionage Networks in Western Europe, 1936–1945* (1979).

Trotsky, Leon *(1877-1940)*   Russian revolutionary, founder of the Red Army and Soviet military intelligence, and victim of Stalinist terror.

Trotsky's real name was Lev Bronstein, which he abandoned when he became an underground conspirator against the tsarist regime. He was born in the Ukraine, of a Jewish family. He received a good education and was sent to the University of Odessa, from which he dropped out in 1897 to become a revolutionary. Arrested by the tsarist police and exiled to Siberia in 1900, Trotsky escaped abroad, where he joined Vladimir Ilyich Lenin, leader of the Bolshevik wing of the Russian Communists.

Trotsky differed with Lenin at the time on fundamental questions of Marxism, but later became a devoted Leninist, and when the Bolsheviks seized power in 1917, he became commissar for foreign affairs. He negotiated the World War I Russian surrender to the Germans at Brest-Litovsk. In 1918, as commissar for military and naval affairs, Trotsky founded the Red Army, which was victorious in the civil war against the anti-Communists (1918–20) and which has continued in existence ever since. In 1920 Trotsky established the GRU (Chief Intelligence Directorate of the General Staff of the Red Army, military intelligence).

He published *The Defense of Terrorism* (1921), calling for the use of violence against enemies of the Communist regime, ironic in view of his own fate. When Lenin died in 1924, Trotsky was the apparent successor, but he was outmaneuvered by Joseph Stalin, who exiled him from the USSR in 1929. Trotsky then began a life of wandering from one country to another, all the while sniping at Stalin's dictatorship. In the international Communist movement, small bands of Trotskyites formed most of the opposition to Stalinist majorities.

Trotsky arrived in Mexico City in 1937, by which time Stalin had given orders for him to be murdered. After two secret agents failed in 1940, an assassin who called himself Ramón Mercader got in to see Trotsky, who suspected nothing, and killed him with an icepick. Mercader remains a mystery man, but the prevalent belief is that he was acting on instructions from SMERSH ("death to spies"), the terror department of Soviet intelligence. This theory is consistent with the fact that after serving a jail term Mercader went to Moscow to stay.

See also GRU; SMERSH.

FURTHER READING: *Hugo Dewar, *Assassins at Large: Being a Fully Documented and Hitherto Unpublished Account of Executions Outside Russia Ordered by the GPU* (1951); Isaac Don Levine, *The Mind of an Assassin* (1959); Irving H. Smith (ed.), *Trotsky* (1972).

Turing, Alan *(1912-54)*   British cryptologist of World War II who played a fundamental role in creating the Ultra intelligence system.

Turing, son of a British civil servant in India, was born in London and educated at Sherborne School and Cambridge University, graduating in 1934.

A mathematical logician of recognized genius, he heralded the arrival of computer science in a 1936 paper on computable numbers. This paper described a theoretical machine, later called the "universal Turing machine," capable of imitating the performance of any other computing machine.

During World War II, Turing and his colleague Gordon Welchman in the Government Code and Cypher School at Bletchley Park, near London, working under veteran cryptologist Dillwyn Knox, created a machine capable of unscrambling Germany's top code machine, the Enigma. The team was able to crack Enigma and make available to Allied leaders the vitally important intelligence derived from reading signals sent by the German high command.

When the Germans produced an even more sophisticated code machine, the Bletchley cryptologists, incorporating Turing's 1936 ideas and working with post office engineers, responded with Colossus, the world's first programmed electronic digital computer.

Turing died of a dose of poison in 1954, an apparent suicide, though most of his friends refused to accept that verdict and considered his death an accident.

See also ENIGMA; ULTRA.

FURTHER READING: Sara Turing, *Alan M. Turing* (1959); Anthony Cave Brown, *Bodyguard of Lies* (1975); *Ronald Lewin, *Ultra Goes to War* (1978).

Ultra *(1939-45)*   Intelligence developed by the British in World War II from breaking German ciphers based on the Enigma machine.

Because of the Enigma machine's complexity, the Germans remained convinced throughout World War II that their ciphers could not be broken. British cryptologists, however, with the help before 1940 of their Polish and French counterparts, succeeded in cracking intercepted Enigma signals. The intelligence derived from the decoded German texts was named Ultra (because it was ultra-secret). Eventually the term was used to designate the whole system.

At its best Ultra presented British leaders, later joined by the Americans, with a clear picture of German strategic and tactical plans. It gave the Allies early access to Hitler's directives and allowed them to read German armed forces situation reports, orders of battle, and strength reports and to learn details of the secret weapons with which Hitler hoped to win the war.

This "shadow OKW" (German high command), as it was dubbed, had its headquarters at Station X, or Bletchley Park, an ornate Victorian mansion on the edge of the small railway town of Bletchley, in Buckinghamshire, strategically placed on the main line some 50 miles north of London. Bletchley Park was the war station of the Government Code and Cypher School, where decoding of enemy signals was concentrated. Housed in a clump of army huts on the lawns, a small band of brilliant cryptologists, led by Dillwyn Knox, broke the Enigma ciphers, which they received from radio intercept stations around the country and abroad. To do so, they constructed a machine, sometimes called the "Turing machine," after Alan Turing its main designer. This still-mysterious machine, a kind of data processor, handled the superhuman task of trying all possible solutions against an enciphered text. The cryptological huts were Hut 8, dealing with naval Enigma traffic, and Hut 6, dealing with German army, air force, railway and police traffic. Enigma variations, for example broken ciphers thought to be on Enigma, and ciphers from the Abwehr (Foreign Information and Counterintelligence Department, German intelligence), were dealt with in special sections.

Adjoining the cryptological huts were the Ultra intelligence huts—Hut 3 (German army and air force) and Hut 4 (navy). Halfway through the war the sections were better housed in new brick buildings, but they retained their hut numbers. In Huts 3 and 4 the decoded signals were put into recognizable German, translated, evaluated for content and urgency, and sent on their way stamped "Top Secret Ultra" to a severely limited list of Ultra recipients.

This work was done in Hut 3, the larger of the intelligence huts, by a staff of little more than 100, most of whom worked in three shifts around the clock. Translation was handled by a watch of about a dozen linguists sitting at a horseshoe table. The head of the watch in the center checked all watchkeepers' work. By the end of the war, the original watch had expanded to four watches, two of them staffed entirely by women. Backing these watches were military and air advisers who decided, on the basis of need, which headquarters should receive the decoded information. Relevant indexes, the repositories of all Ultra knowledge of the German army and air force, were built up painstakingly decode by decode. They comprised detailed preferences and cross-references to every aspect of the German armed forces, all taken from the Wehrmacht's own statements. So valuable were the index cards that they were photographed and the copies hidden in the Bodleian Library at Oxford, in case the Germans should one day discover and bomb Bletchley.

In 1943 Ultra ranks were swelled by the arrival of U. S. Army and Air Corps officers who became watch members or military advisers or were trained to be Ultra advisers attached to U.S. commands. The advisers were the American version of British SLUs (Special Liaison Units) set up at all command head-quarters to receive Ultra signals and to ensure their security.

Security was of the essence, since any hint that Enigma had been broken would have caused the Germans to abandon it. A mixture of temporary army, navy, air force, and civilian personnel attached to the foreign office were carefully screened before being appointed to the Ultra staff. Cryptologists were mostly mathematicians drawn from the universities, especially Cambridge. The intelligence specialists all knew German. Almost all were young (25–35), and after the war many went on to high positions in government or elsewhere. Once appointed to Ultra, none could quit until the war ended. Only commands with a "need to know" and at the highest level were in the secret. Within Bletchley Park itself, the Ultra huts were not allowed to discuss their work with Bletchleyites working in other huts. The secret was well kept.

Prime Minister Winston Churchill was one of Ultra's most enthusiastic ad-mirers. Calling the Bletchleyites his "geese that laid the golden eggs and never cackled," he used the knowledge Ultra gave him to strengthen his position at summit conferences and to make his points when dealing with his own generals. With it he could take an active part in strategic planning, and he did.

Ultra was of immense importance in the conduct of the war. Properly used, it won battles. But at first there were significant gaps in its coverage. During the Battle of Britain in 1940 and 1941, Hitler's intended preliminary to the invasion of England, Ultra revealed that a great German air offensive was coming, where the aircraft were being assembled, and what their strength was. It did not, however, pinpoint the exact dates of the offensive. It did help the vastly outnumbered Royal Air Force to dispose its forces strategically and economically, without which disposition, in the face of German air superiority, the battle might have been lost. When Ultra reported that Hitler was disbanding his invasion experts, Churchill knew the British had won the Battle of Britain, and he knew that Operation Sea Lion (the German invasion of England) had been canceled. This knowledge allowed Churchill to send desperately needed tanks and reinforcements to the North African front without further delay.

As early as 1940 Ultra provided information in North Africa. At first this could not be used operationally for lack of men and supplies. But Ultra information later proved invaluable to General Bernard Montgomery at El Alamein and to General Dwight Eisenhower in Tunisia, when it was instrumental in defeating German General Erwin Rommel, the "Desert Fox" (1943).

Some consider Ultra's greatest triumph to have been in the Battle of the Atlantic. After February 1942 Ultra could no longer read U-boat Enigma codes because the Germans had gone to a new version of Enigma. This was a desperate situation, since Allied shipping, especially the vital convoys to and from Russia and America, was being decimated by German submarines. But by December, with the help of an intact machine captured from a U-boat, the new Enigma code had been broken. The Admiralty now knew the whereabouts of and could attack the U-boats causing the havoc. This contribution by Ultra, it was estimated, was equivalent to the winning of a major battle.

Ultra also helped the Allies conceal their strategy. Before the invasion of Sicily, for instance, a network of double agents worked to persuade the Germans that northern Greece and the Balkans, not Sicily, were to be attacked. The British knew through Ultra how the Germans were reacting to the disinformation transmitted by these agents (most were captured German agents who had agreed to cooperate with the Allies). Once the invasion of Sicily had begun, Ultra was again invaluable, supplying the latest enemy orders of battle and information on the locations and movements of units, serviceable aircraft, available tanks, guns, and supplies, and so on.

Ultra played a similar part in Operation Bodyguard, the spectacular deception before D-Day (June 6, 1944), and in Normandy after the Allied invasion. Armies were fabricated to mislead the Germans as to the place of the invasion and to keep their forces defensively deployed along the coast of the Continent from Norway to France. This was largely accomplished by double agents monitored by Ultra.

Ultra figured significantly in the Avranches offensive. Hitler had decided to take command himself and ordered a reluctant General Gunther von Kluge to attack the advancing Americans under General Omar Bradley—only to have Kluge caught in a well-prepared and deadly trap. Ultra had presented the Allied commanders with Hitler's orders three days before the attack.

Ultra was not perfect. Occasionally, for example, the day's code would not break or would not break early enough. Bletchley has been criticized for failing to warn of the German Ardennes offensive (the Battle of the Bulge), when, it has been said, commanders were relying too much on Ultra. But Ultra, as well as other intelligence sources, provided much indirect evidence of German strategy during that offensive, though it failed to pinpoint the attack. At the Arnhem landings, Ultra warned of substantial German forces in the area, a warning that was not heeded. Ultra was always only as good as the use made of it.

See also DOUBLE-CROSS SYSTEM; ENIGMA; LONDON CONTROLLING SECTION; TURING, ALAN.

F. W. Winterbotham, *The Ultra Secret* (1974); Anthony Cave Brown, *Bodyguard of Lies* (1975); *Ronald Lewin, *Ultra Goes to War* (1978); Peter Calvocoressi, *Top Secret Ultra* (1980); F. H. Hinsley (with E. E. Thomas, C. F. G. Ransom, and R. C. Knight), *British Intelligence in the Second World War: Its Influence on Strategy and Operations* (vol. 1, 1979; vol. 2, 1981).

U-2 American high-altitude plane used in espionage missions.

The secrecy behind which the Russians concealed their military exercises and atomic experiments led the American government to decide during the early 1950s that some means must be found to monitor such events in the Soviet Union without asking permission from the Kremlin. The principal means discussed within the CIA (Central Intelligence Agency) was the spy plane. Since the purpose of the plane would be to fly over the Soviet Union, it had to be built to fly above the altitude limits of Russian fighters and rockets. The Lockheed Aircraft Corporation met the challenge by producing the U-2, a plane with a light frame, powered by a single jet engine, and with a wing span of 80 feet. The U-2 could reach an altitude of more than 80,000 feet and had a range of 4,000 miles. It carried a camera capable of photographing objects a foot long on the ground, and its other instruments could track missiles in outer space and check the fallout from atomic explosions. A destruct mechanism enabled the pilot to blow up the aircraft if necessary.

The U-2s went into action in 1956, and for four years carefully chosen pilots flew them between American bases in Norway and Pakistan, crossing over the Soviet Union en route. The Russians knew about the flights (they are said to have called the U-2 the "black lady" of espionage), but there was nothing they could do to stop them until Russian engineers produced a rocket capable of reaching higher altitudes. In 1960, a rocket knocked down a U-2 piloted by Francis Gary Powers. He was captured by the Russians, convicted as a spy, and held in jail until 1962, when he was exchanged for Soviet spy Rudolf Abel. Soviet Premier Nikita Khrushchev made an international scandal of the Powers case, and President Dwight Eisenhower canceled the flights over the Soviet Union.

The U-2s, however, continued in operation elsewhere. A flight over Cuba in 1962 brought back pictures of offensive missiles, which Khrushchev had promised not to send to the island. With this evidence, President John Kennedy forced Khrushchev to remove the missiles. Subsequently the planes were assigned to espionage missions inside West Germany, but high enough to allow observation for fifty miles into East Germany with electronic instruments.

Nothing else, however, has matched the four years of U-2 flights over the

Soviet Union, one of the greatest achievements in the history of espionage. *See also* POWERS, FRANCIS GARY.

FURTHER READING: *Francis Gary Powers (with Curt Gentry), *Operation Overflight: The U-2 Spy Pilot Tells His Story for the First Time* (1970); John W. R. Taylor, *Jane's All the World's Aircraft* (annual).

Van Lew, Elizabeth *(1818-1900)*   Spy and undercover agent for the Union during the American Civil War.

Van Lew was born in Virginia, but her sympathies for the North can be accounted for by the fact that her father came from New York and her mother from Pennsylvania, and she herself was educated in Philadelphia. The family lived in Richmond, where they were known for their strong antislavery stand.

When the Civil War divided the nation in 1861, Elizabeth Van Lew remained openly loyal to the Union, an attitude she got away with by affecting a behavior so odd that her neighbors termed her "Crazy Bet." They did not know that she spied for the North, used her house as a place of concealment for Northerners on the run, and maintained a series of underground relay stations by which they could escape from the South.

Van Lew was the Union's woman in Richmond, now the Capital of the Confederacy, just as Rose Greenhow was the Confederacy's woman in Washington, the Union capital.

Van Lew operated throughout the war. Her greatest disappointment (not failure, for she could have done nothing about it) was the execution in 1862 of Timothy Webster on a charge of being a Union spy. Her greatest triumph came in 1864 when, as Union General Ulysses S. Grant bore down on Richmond, she kept him informed through a stream of couriers (most of them her household servants) about conditions in the city. After entering Richmond, Grant paid a call on Van Lew, thanked her, and stated that her information had been the best available to him during the campaign through Virginia.

After Grant had become president of the United States, he heard that Van Lew was in financial difficulties because of her wartime service to the Union, so he appointed her postmistress of Richmond. She later served in Washington, then returned to Richmond, and suffered in her last years from the animosity of her neighbors, who by then were fully aware of her contribution to their misfortunes in the late war.

See also GREENHOW, ROSE; WEBSTER, TIMOTHY.

FURTHER READING: Harnett T. Kane, *Spies for the Blue and the Gray* (1954); Mary Elizabeth Massey, *Bonnet Brigades* (1966), has a passage on Van Lew; Oscar A. Kinchen, *Women Who Spied for the Blue and the Gray* (1972).

Vardill, John *(1749-1811)*   American clergyman and secret agent for the British government in London during the American Revolution.

The son of a New York ship owner, Vardill received a good elementary education before entering King's College (later Columbia University), where he took his bachelor's degree in 1766 and his master's in theology three years later.

A staunch Loyalist, Vardill wrote against the Patriots during the period leading up to the American Revolution. In particular, he opposed resistance to the British tax on tea that led to the Boston Tea Party (1773), when a band of Americans threw a consignment of tea into Boston harbor.

Vardill went to London in 1774 to be ordained in the Church of England. He would have returned to King's College with a royal appointment as Regius Professor of Divinity, but the revolution cut him off, and he never saw his native land again.

Passionately loyal to King George III, Vardill wrote in defense of British measures regarding the American colonies (1774) and became a secret agent for the British government (1775). He spied on American sympathizers in England, tried to convert to the British cause American visitors to London, and sent agents to work against the American cause on the Continent. His most effective agent was Joseph Hynson, a sailor who obtained a file of dispatches (March-October, 1777) from the American commissioners in Paris to the Continental Congress in Philadelphia. Hynson stole the dispatches from their pouches in Le Havre, substituted blank paper, and resealed the pouches, which were taken aboard ship and transported to America.

Vardill's espionage career lasted until 1781, when the American victory at Yorktown ensured American independence. He then concentrated on his career as a clergyman of the Church of England.

FURTHER READING: *Lewis Einstein, *Divided Loyalties: Americans in England during the War of Independence* (1933); Carl Van Doren, *Secret History of the American Revolution* (1941); Richard B. Morris, *The Peacemakers: The Great Powers and American Independence* (1965).

Vassall, John (1924-   ) British spy for the Soviet Union.

Vassall was a Londoner, the homosexual son of a clergyman in the Church of England.

In 1940 Vassall left his public school to join the British armed forces during World War II. After being rejected by the Royal Air Force as a pilot, he received training as a photographer and served in this capacity throughout the war. Then he went into the civil service; his work took him to the British Embassy in Moscow in 1954, where he became an assistant to the naval attaché.

Agents of the KGB (Committee for State Security, Russian intelligence) noticed, as members of the embassy staff did not, that Vassall was a homosexual. The Russians exploited Vassall by maneuvering him into compromising situations, photographing him, and then using the photographs for blackmail. In 1955, Vassall, trapped and fearful, began stealing classified information for the KGB.

Returning to London in 1956, he remained of interest to the Soviets because he was assigned to the Admiralty. He now photographed documents to which he had access and delivered the microfilm to his Russian contact at secret meetings around London.

In 1961 Vassall lay low for a while as the Portland spy case developed with the revelation that an espionage ring including two Admiralty employees, Harry Houghton and Ethel Gee, had been stealing classified information for the Russians from a major naval research center. In the following year, under Russian pressure, Vassall was back at his espionage work.

Unknown to him, a message from the British Embassy in Moscow warned that the Russians possessed secret information that could have come only from a person inside the Admiralty in London. Suspicion focused on Vassall, who was arrested in 1962, incriminated by government documents found in his room, and sentenced to eighteen years in prison.

See also VASSALL TRIBUNAL.

FURTHER READING: *Rebecca West, *The Vassall Affair* (1963); John Bulloch, *MI5: The Origin and History of the British Counter-Espionage Service* (1963); Norman Lucas, *The Great Spy Ring* (1966); John Vassall, *Vassall: The Autobiography of a Spy* (1975).

Vassall Tribunal *(1962-63)*   British Parliamentary commission appointed to investigate and make recommendations concerning the treason of John Vassall.

The Vassall Tribunal, with Lord Radcliffe as chairman, addressed itself to the question of why no one at the British Embassy in Moscow or at the Admiralty in London had realized that Vassall was a security risk who might be spying for the Russians. As the tribunal assembled, critics demanded a policy of no cover-up, because the previous year had seen the Portland scandal, when another spy for the Soviets, Harry Houghton, had been discovered in the Admiralty, from which he had transmitted copies of secret documents to the Russian spymaster Gordon Lonsdale.

The members of the Vassall Tribunal heard 142 witnesses, some testifying on matters so sensitive that they appeared at meetings held behind closed doors to keep anything damaging to the national security from becoming public. Two newsmen went to jail for refusing to disclose their sources while covering the Vassall story.

Charges that higher-ups had known of a second spy in the Admiralty (Houghton being the first) were shown to be unfounded, as were allegations of collusion to protect Vassall at the British Embassy in Moscow. The tribunal did, however, register two negative judgments on the affair. The first stated that security checks were too lax regarding the selection of government employees for jobs involving classified information. The second stated that Vassall should have come under suspicion because his homosexuality made him vulnerable, and he had more money than his salary could account for.

As a result of this affair, measures were taken to keep unstable personnel from positions in which they could be blackmailed.

See also VASSALL, JOHN.

FURTHER READING: *Report of the Tribunal Appointed to Inquire into the Vassall Case and Related Matters* (1963); Rebecca West, *The Vassall Affair* (1963); John Barron, *KGB: The Secret Work of Soviet Secret Agents* (1974).

Venlo Incident *(1939)*   The capture of British espionage agents by German agents early in World War II.

A principal aim of the Allies in 1939 was to see German Chancellor Adolf Hitler overthrown and replaced by a regime that would make peace. Thus, British intelligence took the bait when informed by a German operative of an anti-Nazi group inside Germany with which London could make a deal. Captain Sigismund Payne Best and Major R. H. Stevens of MI6 (Military Intelligence 6, British espionage) traveled to Zutphen, Holland, to meet "Captain Schaemmel," who really was Major Walter Schellenberg, of Nazi counterespionage.

This meeting satisfied the British agents, and they agreed to another at The Hague. Here an agreement was reached for the arrest of Hitler, an end to the war, and the restoration of the status quo in eastern Europe.

Now very hopeful, Best and Stevens kept in touch with Schaemmel during the following days. They thought they were bringing off a remarkable coup when Schaemmel announced that the leader of the anti-Nazi Germans, a general, wanted to fly to London for talks with the British government. Best and Stevens assured him that a British plane would be standing by at the next meeting place, Venlo, in Holland near the German border.

Up to this point, Schellenberg had not decided what his next move would be, for his superiors had given him no instructions. Then word came to him from Berlin that Hitler wanted the British agents seized on Dutch soil, kidnaped, and carried into the German Reich.

As a result, the scene at Venlo on November 8, 1939, resembled a spy film. Best and Stevens were waiting when a German car came crashing across the border amid gunfire between its occupants and Dutch border guards. The two British agents were quickly overpowered, pushed into the car, and driven into Germany.

For Best and Stevens, this was the end of wartime espionage, and indeed of the war itself. They remained prisoners in the Nazi Reich until the day in 1945 when American soldiers overran the prison area and set them free.

See also SCHELLENBERG, WALTER.

FURTHER READING: Sigismund P. Best, *The Venlo Incident* (1950); *Walter Schellenberg, *The Labyrinth: The Memoirs of Walter Schellenberg* (1956); David Kahn, *Hitler's Spies: German Military Intelligence in World War II* (1978).

Vidocq, François-Eugène **(1775-1857)** French criminal, police spy, detective, and secret agent.

Born in Arras, the son of a baker, Vidocq was put to school with the Franciscans at the age of five. Nine years later, on the outbreak of the French Revolution, he ran away to become a soldier. He deserted the armed forces in 1795 and took up the life of a wandering criminal, living by his wits in the French provinces.

Tired of being on the run when he was not in jail, Vidocq in 1809 became a police spy. He achieved remarkable successes going underground, tracking robbers and murderers, and bringing them back to face trial. He remains perhaps the best practical example of the old adage "set a thief to catch a thief."

Vidocq's success brought him an invitation to join the Paris police force, and in 1812 he founded within it the Sûrêté, which in time would become one of the great crime-fighting organizations of the world. Following his own example, he hired former criminals to handle unsolved cases and to hunt fugitives from justice. He also advanced scientific criminology by keeping comprehensive files on members of the underworld.

Resented by rivals on the police force for his success, his unsavory past, and his employment of dubious characters, Vidocq resigned under pressure in 1827. He was recalled to service by harassed police officials in 1831, but he resigned again in 1833, and a year later he established a private detective agency, the first of its kind and destined to have many imitators. It lasted for ten years, long enough to prove that Vidocq's idea was a good one.

In 1848, when King Louis Philippe was overthrown and fled into exile, the head of the Provisional Government, Alphonse Lamartine, needed a secret agent for a sensitive mission. Prince Louis Napoleon, nephew of the great Napoleon Bonaparte and leader of the Bonapartist faction in French politics, was in London. Lamartine wanted someone to talk to the prince confidentially and estimate his intentions.

Vidocq received this assignment. Traveling to London, he met the prince and held conversations with him. Exactly what was said cannot be determined, but Louis Napoleon was at that moment holding a moderate position, not advising his followers to make overt demonstrations in his behalf for fear of convulsing France with quarrels between Republicans and Bonapartists. Vidocq must have so reported to Lamartine on his return to Paris.

Louis Napoleon waited until he was elected to the National Assembly with strong electoral support from the French people. He returned to Paris, took his seat, and before the year ended was elected president of France. He then maneuvered astutely until he became Napoleon III, ruler of the Second Empire (1852–71).

Vidocq, who had been impressed with Louis Napoleon in London, accepted the regime of Napoleon III, and even worked for it as a secret agent, keeping an eye on anti-Bonapartist movements in Paris and reporting to the ministry of the interior. He remained active in this way until he was nearly eighty and then retired from a field in which he had played so many strenuous roles for so many years.

FURTHER READING: E. A. Brayley Hodgetts, *Vidocq: A Master of Crime* (1928), is a free translation of Vidocq's semifictionalized memoirs; Philip John Stead, *Vidocq: A Biography* (1953); *Samuel Edwards, *The Vidocq Dossier: The Story of the World's First Detective* (1977).

Vogel, Wolfgang *(1924-   )*   East German lawyer and a central figure in the espionage revolution by which spies are exchanged rather than executed.

Vogel was born in Silesia, but he concealed other facts about his early life, apparently because he wanted to divorce himself completely from any association with the Nazi regime of Adolf Hitler. After that regime collapsed in 1945, Vogel entered the University of Jena in the Soviet zone of divided Germany. He studied law at Jena and later at Leipzig, and established a practice in 1954 in East Berlin.

Vogel became involved in the espionage revolution because of the number of Soviet spies captured in the west. In 1962 he negotiated with American lawyer James Donovan regarding Russian spy Rudolf Abel, who had been captured in New York, and American pilot Francis Gary Powers, who was shot down on an espionage flight over the Soviet Union. Vogel and Donovan worked out an exchange of Abel for Powers.

The 1960s produced the Portland spy case in England, when Russian spymaster Gordon Lonsdale was arrested, along with Americans Peter and

Helen Kroger. Since the Russians were holding two British prisoners, Greville Wynne and Gerald Brooke, Vogel was able to arrange two transfers—Wynne for Lonsdale in 1964 and Brooke for the Krogers in 1969.

By then the espionage revolution was established, and Vogel was its foremost practitioner.

See also DONOVAN, JAMES; ESPIONAGE REVOLUTION; LONSDALE, GORDON.

FURTHER READING: James B. Donovan, *Strangers on a Bridge: The Case of Colonel Abel* (1964); David Wise and Thomas B. Ross, *The Espionage Establishment* (1967), has a chapter on the espionage revolution; *E. H. Cookridge, *Spy Trade* (1971).

Walsingham, Francis (1532?-90) English statesman, diplomat, and spymaster during the Elizabethan era.

Descended from a Norfolk family, the son of a lawyer who served King Henry VIII, Walsingham studied at Cambridge, took a law degree in 1552, and spent most of the years 1553 to 1558 on the Continent because he disliked the Catholic policies of Queen Mary. He became interested in codes and ciphers while in Italy, where the art of secret writing had been developing since the early Renaissance.

Walsingham returned to England in 1558, on the accession of Queen Elizabeth to the English throne. He entered Parliament five years later, rising to prominence under the patronage of William Cecil, subsequently Lord Burghley, the trusted adviser of the queen. Walsingham joined the Privy Council in 1573 and was knighted in 1577.

This was the period when England took the side of the Protestant Reformation, as a result of which English Catholics plotted to restore the old religion, and Catholic ambassadors in London were automatically considered spies. The Catholics found a leader in Mary Stuart, queen of Scotland and heiress to the English throne because of her own dynastic claim and because Elizabeth had no children. When Mary fled to England in 1568 to escape the Scottish reformers and was imprisoned by Elizabeth, the Scottish queen became the hope of diehard conspirators who sought to rescue her and place her on Elizabeth's throne.

Some conspirators relied on an invading army to be sent to England by King Philip II of Spain. Catholics and Protestants spied on each other, so that London and Mary's prison (she was moved from place to place for security) became hotbeds of espionage and counterespionage.

Walsingham, who had been Elizabeth's ambassador to France (1570–72) before carrying out diplomatic missions to the Low Countries (1578), France (1580), and Scotland (1583), had the responsibility for seeing to it that none of the pro-Mary plots succeeded. He established the best spy system in Europe, the forerunner of the renowned British secret service, placing his agents not only in Mary's entourage but also at the courts of France, Italy, and Spain. He recruited Christopher Marlowe for undercover work at the Catholic seminary in Rheims, while Anthony Munday reported from the English College in Rome.

Walsingham gathered experts in ciphers into a cryptology department, and one of these men, Gilbert Gifford, posed as a Catholic, gained Mary's confidence, and surreptitiously opened her mail. Gifford decoded the letters that were in cipher and reported the contents to Walsingham in London.

Using espionage and counterespionage, Walsingham discovered in 1583 that Francis Throckmorton was plotting with Mary and the Spanish ambassador in London. The most dangerous conspiracy came to light in 1586, when Walsingham learned of the Babington plot to murder Elizabeth. He ordered his agents to draw Anthony Babington on, incriminating himself as he went, until at the critical moment all the conspirators were arrested. Exposure of this plot enabled Burghley and Walsingham to persuade Elizabeth to sign Mary's death warrant.

That execution in 1587 made King Philip of Spain decide to dispatch his armada for the conquest of England in 1588. Walsingham, surmising that Philip would attack, prepared for the crisis by devising the espionage campaign described in his *Plot for Intelligence out of Spain.* His undercover agents reported to him across the Continent, from Portugal to Poland, on what Spanish diplomats were saying about Philip's intentions and other matters relating to the coming expedition. Anthony Standen, in Florence, was especially successful in gathering information. Occultist John Dee was probably the Walsingham spy in Krakow.

Long before the armada sailed, Walsingham possessed detailed data from his spies in Madrid and in the Spanish seaports about its size, its warships, the army it would carry, the route it would follow, and the strategy for a link-up with a Spanish army in the Netherlands. The English captains, therefore, were able to prepare for the battle knowing the enemy's plans; their victory was substantially the result of good intelligence.

The defeat of the armada was Walsingham's last great achievement as a spymaster. He lived for two more years, but out of office, burdened by debts, and ignored by the queen who owed him so much for his services to her personally and to her realm.

See also BABINGTON, ANTHONY; DEE, JOHN; MARLOWE, CHRISTOPHER; MUNDAY, ANTHONY; STANDEN, ANTHONY.

FURTHER READING: *Conyers Read, *Mr. Secretary Walsingham and the Policy of Queen Elizabeth* (1925); A. G. Smith, *The Babington Plot* (1936); Richard Deacon, *A History of the British Secret Service* (1969), has an account of Walsingham as the original English spymaster.

Washington, George (1732-99) Commander in chief of the Continental army whose adept handling of espionage helped win the American War of Independence.

Washington assumed his military command in 1775 at the siege of Boston. During the siege, some letters were intercepted that showed that his surgeon general, Dr. Benjamin Church, was transmitting information about the Continental army to the British in Boston. The treason of the surgeon general came as a shock to Washington, who dismissed Church from the army and determined to maintain tighter security in the military, with emphasis on better intelligence methods.

When the war shifted from Boston to New York in 1776, and the Continental Army was pushed back from Long Island to Manhattan, Washington asked for a spy to be found who would reconnoiter behind the British lines. Nathan Hale volunteered, but his indiscreet conduct (he seems to have talked about his mission to a relative, who betrayed him) followed by his capture and execution, convinced Washington that American espionage had to be handled in a more professional manner.

After the retreat of the Continental army across New Jersey into Pennsylvania, Washington dealt personally with Patriots who arrived at his headquarters with information about enemy forces in the area. This information indicated that the Hessians in Trenton were off guard and vulnerable to a sudden attack, and that was the logic behind Washington's famous crossing of the Delaware River on Christmas night, 1776, and his decisive victory at the battle of Trenton.

When the British under Sir William Howe occupied Philadelphia in 1777, Washington received intelligence reports from inside the city, but he could not repeat his coup at Trenton because he lacked the military strength. Now he used intelligence methods to defend himself. During the dreadful winter of 1777/78 at Valley Forge, he disguised the desperate condition of his troops by letting a Tory spy obtain deliberately exaggerated estimates of their numbers, equipment, supplies, and morale. The Tory took this misinformation to Howe, who found it another good reason to follow his indolent inclinations and to remain in Philadelphia instead of venturing through the cold and snow to attack Valley Forge.

Sir Henry Clinton, replacing Howe in 1778, marched from Philadelphia, fought with Washington the indecisive battle of Monmouth in New Jersey, and reached New York City. Washington followed and deployed his forces north of the city and in New Jersey and Connecticut.

As the two armies, American and British, faced each other, Washington ordered Major Benjamin Tallmadge to set up an espionage network to report on men and events inside New York City. This was the origin of the celebrated Culper Ring, which proved to be the best organization of its type in the war.

Washington employed his spies to find out what the enemy was doing, and he used counterspies to plant false information about his own activities. Sometimes he met his agents for long conversations in the secrecy of his headquarters. At other times, he avoided knowing who they were so that he might not inadvertently mention their names. His attention to espionage work extended to the paper, ciphers and codes, and invisible inks.

Washington's exploitation of military intelligence was masterly. In 1780 he prevented Clinton from attacking at Newport, Rhode Island, where Jean Baptiste de Vimeur, comte de Rochambeau, had landed with a French army to join the Americans. Washington arranged to have a fake American plan to attack New York fall into the hands of a Tory, who promptly delivered the plan to the British. The apparent threat caused Clinton to cancel his Newport attack in order to defend New York, and Rochambeau had time to muster his troops for the campaign. In 1781 Washington masked his and Rochambeau's move south to trap Cornwallis at Yorktown by leading a Tory spy to believe he was actually headed for Staten Island to take New York from the rear. Again Clinton was immobilized by his own poor espionage and Washington's adept intelligence methods.

A stunning failure of Washington's espionage system occurred in 1780, with the treasonous conspiracy of Benedict Arnold. Washington was so totally uninformed when the case broke that he had to investigate whether any of Arnold's subordinates were involved in the scheme to hand West Point to the British (none was). Washington allowed the execution of Major John André, the captured co-conspirator of the plot, because he considered André a spy to whom the code governing espionage applied in all its rigor.

See also ANDRÉ, JOHN; ARNOLD, BENEDICT; CULPER RING; TALLMADGE, BENJAMIN.

FURTHER READING: Morton Pennypacker, *General Washington's Spies on Long Island and in New York* (1939); *John Bakeless, *Turncoats, Traitors, and Heroes* (1959), is a gallery of secret agents at work during the American Revolution; Burke Davis, *George Washington and the American Revolution* (1975).

Wassmuss, Wilhelm *(1880-1931)*   German diplomat and secret agent in Persia during World War I.

Wassmuss, who was born in Hanover, decided early in life to become a diplomat. His family gave him a good education, and in 1906 he entered the kaiser's foreign service, which sent him to Madagascar. Promoted to consul, he served in Bushire, in Persia (1909), returned to Madagascar, where he spent three years (1910–13) mastering languages and local customs, and then accepted another appointment to Bushire.

In Persia when World War I broke out in 1914, Wassmuss became a secret agent against the British, who sent a military force to try to maintain control of the oil-rich area in the south. He vanished into the rugged countryside beyond Bushire and, plentifully supplied with gold from Berlin, waged an underground campaign to keep the various peoples of Persia loyal to Germany and fighting the British. He flitted from place to place, meeting local leaders clandestinely, encouraging them to wage guerrilla warfare, paying them in gold, and offering promises of future rewards when Germany won the war.

Wassmuss succeeded so well that the British, declaring this lone German in Persia to be worth two army corps, put an enormous price on his head (it was never collected). At the Foreign Office in London, where the course of the fighting in the major theaters of war was plotted on large-scale maps, the map of Persia bore a single word—the name "Wassmuss"—which identified succinctly the nature of the problem facing the British commander in that region.

Military patrols sent to capture Wassmuss or cut him off invariably found that he had slipped away, for he had spies everywhere who kept him informed about his enemies. His marriage to the daughter of a Persian chief strengthened his hand with the people among whom he hid, and he remained at large until the end of the war in 1918.

By then his gold had run out, and with the kaiser in exile and Germany defeated, he could not honor the ringing promises he had made. Demoralized at having to tell the Persians that his pledged word would be broken, he returned to Berlin in 1919 hoping to salvage something from the wreckage. The foreign service informed him that it could do nothing to solve his Persian problem and that he would not be reassigned to Bushire. As a result, he resigned in 1924, went to Persia on his own, and tried to raise money by farming to pay off at least some of the debts he had incurred during the war. All of his attempts failed. Having merely increased the enmity of his Persian creditors by raising and dashing their hopes, he returned to Berlin in 1931 and died shortly afterward.

Wassmuss has been called "the German Lawrence" because, like T. E. Lawrence ("Lawrence of Arabia") he was a European who exercised remarkable leadership among an Islamic people during World War I, partly by making promises in his country's name, and then seeing those promises violated after the war's end. The difference is that Lawrence was on the winning side, Wassmuss on the losing.

FURTHER READING: *Christopher Sykes, *Wassmuss, 'The German Lawrence': His Adventures in Persia during and after the War* (1936); Ferdinand Tuohy, *The Crater of Mars* (n.d.); Richard Wilmer Rowan (with Robert G. Deindorfer), *Secret Service: Thirty-three Centuries of Espionage* (1967), has a passage on Wassmuss.

Watergate Affair *(1972-74)*   Political espionage affair and worst scandal in American history.

Narrowly considered, the Watergate affair was the attempted break-in at the headquarters of the Democratic Party in Washington's Watergate apartment-hotel-office complex during the presidential campaign of 1972. Broadly, the Watergate affair includes the events after the burglars were caught, especially the revelations of fraud and chicanery in the White House that rocked the nation and forced the resignation of President Richard Nixon.

On June 17, 1972, five men were arrested in the Democratic headquarters at the Watergate—James McCord, Bernard Barker, Frank Sturgis, Virgilio Gonzalez, and Eugenio Martinez. Two others, the leaders of the operation, were picked up later—E. Howard Hunt, and G. Gordon Liddy. Three of the seven, McCord, Hunt, and Liddy, were former agents of the CIA (Central Intelligence Agency). McCord and Liddy were working for the Committee to Re-Elect the President (i.e., Nixon). The five burglars carried lockpicks, cameras, bugging equipment, miniature tear-gas devices, and a walkie-talkie for reporting to Hunt and Liddy. The break-in plainly was an espionage mission. The burglars intended to photograph Democratic documents and install a means of listening to conversations between the party's leaders as they laid plans for the coming presidential election.

The seven accused remained silent as they were tried, convicted, and sent to jail (1973). The affair refused to die because the positions of McCord and Liddy at the Committee to Re-Elect the President caused speculation in the news media, among the public, and of course in Congress, where the Democrats, led by the party's candidate for president, Senator George McGovern of South Dakota, demanded a full explanation. This might not have been forthcoming except that some of the convicted demanded money for their silence and executive clemency by President Nixon to get them out of prison. Neither of these demands was met. An angry McCord wrote a letter to Judge John Sirica, who had presided over the trial, charging that a cover-up of the truth surrounding the burglary was being orchestrated by the White House.

The McCord letter cracked the dike holding back the Watergate flood. The Senate established an investigating committee, with Sam Ervin of South Carolina for its chairman. A parade of witnesses, led by McCord, began revealing what they knew about "dirty tricks" by members or employees of the Committee to Re-Elect the President. The Ervin committee heard how some Republicans had employed classical espionage techniques against the Democrats and had broken the law in so doing. They had used illegal entry to gain information about Nixon's opponents that might be construed as derogatory. They had covertly taken photographs and planted bugs. They had sown disinformation (i.e., false reports about certain individuals). They had "laundered" money to keep it from being traced and had passed it by courier from sources to destinations. The system even included drops (hiding-places in public areas where money could be concealed by one person and retrieved by another—one of the oldest spy maneuvers).

A disturbing aspect of the Watergate affair was the possibility that the CIA had been involved in illegalities. A number of factors pointed in that direction. Former members were among the burglars, apparently selected for the undercover mission because of their spy training within the organization. Witnesses before the Ervin committee testified that the White House staff had tried to pressure the CIA into becoming part of a plan to hide the facts about Watergate. Then again, the CIA's sister organization, the FBI (Federal Bureau of Investigation), was proven to have submitted to pressure when its acting director, L. Patrick Gray, destroyed evidence and allowed the White House to misuse FBI files (the revelation forced Gray to end his bid to become director). However, all the subsequent evidence showed that the CIA, under Director Richard Helms, had not been part of either the Watergate burglary or the conspiracy to conceal the truth about it.

The rest of the Watergate affair belongs to politics rather than espionage. Star witness John Dean, former counsel to the President, implicated Nixon and a number of those around him, including his advisers H. R. Haldeman and John Erlichman. Tapes made in the oval office at the White House supported Dean's contention that the President had been the leader in the attempted cover-up following the Watergate burglary. The evidence caused the House Judiciary Committee to approve articles of impeachment against the President. Warned by former supporters in Congress that he would certainly be impeached if he resisted, Nixon resigned from office in 1974, the only chief executive to do so in the history of the United States. He escaped a jail sentence because his successor, Gerald Ford, gave him an executive pardon. Many other Watergate conspirators, not so fortunate, went to prison.

FURTHER READING: *Congressional Quarterly, *Watergate: Chronology of a Crisis* (1973); Carl Bernstein and Bob Woodward, *All the President's Men* (1974); Sam Ervin, Jr., *The Whole Truth: The Watergate Conspiracy* (1980).

Webster, Timothy *(1821-62)* Spy for the Union during the American Civil War.

Born in London and taken to America as a child, Webster grew up in Princeton, New Jersey, became a laborer, and joined the New York police force. Assigned to the World's Fair of 1853, he met Allan Pinkerton, who had founded the Pinkerton National Detective Agency in Chicago in the previous year. Webster joined Pinkerton's organization and had several years of undercover work behind him in 1861, at the beginning of the Civil War.

An experienced and trusted agent, Webster was one of those dispatched by Pinkerton to investigate the plot to assassinate President-elect Abraham Lincoln. After Pinkerton successfully escorted Lincoln to Washington, Webster undertook espionage assignments in the Confederacy, where his method was to pretend to be a Southern sympathizer who could move freely in the North and report back to Richmond. He thus became an effective double agent for the Union.

In 1861 he was in Tennessee and Virginia, delivering disinformation concocted in Washington and taking letters that he would deliver to Southern sympathizers in the North—after Pinkerton or his assistants had read them. Webster was so persuasive in his role that he wangled a passport from Judah P. Benjamin, the Confederate secretary of war, giving him freedom of travel between Richmond and Baltimore.

In 1862 Webster returned to Richmond on an assignment from Pinkerton. He contracted a bad case of rheumatism and was laid up for so long that Pinkerton, alarmed by the silence, sent two agents to find him. The agents were caught, talked to save their own lives, and fatally incriminated Webster, who was tried as a spy, found guilty, and sentenced to death.

At that moment in Richmond, Elizabeth Van Lew was using her house to hide Federal soldiers and partisans before sending them along relay stations to safety in the North. She could, however, do nothing for Webster; nor could anyone else, and he was executed.

See also PINKERTON, ALLAN.

FURTHER READING: Harnett T. Kane, *Spies for the Blue and the Gray* (1954); Philip Van Doren Stern, *Secret Missions of the Civil War* (1959); James D. Horan, *The Pinkertons: The Detective Dynasty That Made History* (1968).

Wellington, Duke of *(1769-1852)*   British general and spymaster during the Napoleonic Wars.

Born in Ireland and named Arthur Wellesley, the future duke of Wellington entered the British army in 1787 and made his first mark as a soldier while serving for six years in India (1799–1805). He received a military command in Portugal and Spain in 1808, while Great Britain was at war with Napoleon, emperor of France. The British were trying to force the French out of the Iberian Peninsula. A year later Wellington received supreme command in the Peninsular War (1808–14).

He developed an espionage system that gave him crucial assistance in his battles with such French generals as Michel Ney and André Masséna. Wellington's spy apparatus benefited from Spanish hatred of the French invaders, for Spanish agents brought the British information and documents pilfered from French headquarters. Wellington paid well for French dispatches as an incentive to Spaniards in a position to waylay French couriers.

He also used British spies attached to his staff. One of these spies stole Masséna's code book, which enabled Wellington's cryptologists to read French messages in cipher. Another British spy, captured by the French and held at French headquarters, sent information to British headquarters by means of Spanish couriers. Wellington's espionage chief, Captain Henry Hardinge, assessed the military situation on a day-to-day basis as fresh reports came in.

One of the oddest events of the Peninsular War brought Wellington aid from far-off Denmark. Napoleon, in an effort to weaken Spain, had coerced the Spaniards into sending part of their military forces to the Danish islands, ostensibly to keep the British out. James Robertson, a Scottish monk and secret agent for the London government, reached the Spanish commander and persuaded him to have his men covertly taken aboard British ships. These men arrived in Spain in time to take part in Wellington's campaign, which drove the French back across the Pyrenees.

Created duke of Wellington in 1814, he again had the expert assistance of Hardinge at Waterloo in 1815. Hardinge learned Napoleon's strategy in advance, a critical factor in the winning of the decisive battle. Wellington later held military and political offices, including that of prime minister (1828–30).

See also HARDINGE, HENRY; ROBERTSON, JAMES.

FURTHER READING: J. W. Thompson and S. K. Padover, *Secret Diplomacy: A Record of Espionage and Double-dealing, 1500–1815* (1937); *Godfrey Davies, *Wellington and His Army* (1954); John Castle, *Wellington* (1969).

Wennerström, Stig (1906-   ) Swedish spy for the Soviet Union.

Wennerström used to say that he "grew up in an ordinary officer's house" in Stockholm, where he was born while his father was in the Swedish navy. Following the family tradition, Wennerström entered the navy as a cadet in 1929. He served at the Swedish Karlskrona naval base (1930–31), where he began to study Russian, feeling, as proved to be the case, that this particular language might be useful to him one day.

Wennerström then switched to the Swedish air force. He qualified as a pilot in 1934, the same year in which he went to Riga as air attaché to the Swedish legation. In 1940 he held the same position at the Swedish Embassy in Moscow. During the years 1941 to 1948 he served in Sweden, rising to the rank of lieutenant-colonel. In all of these posts, he was part of the Swedish intelligence apparatus, reporting especially on the Soviet Union.

In 1949 he went to Moscow again as air attaché at the Swedish Embassy. By that time he had already become a double agent for the Soviets. Transferred to Washington in 1952, he for five years reported to the Russians about the United States and the North Atlantic Treaty Organization, to which the United States belonged. Returning to Stockholm in 1957, he sent to the Soviet Union details on the part of Swedish defense system that was directed against the Soviet Union.

The leaks in Stockholm were traced to Wennerström, but his superiors refused to consider the possibility that so respected an officer could be a traitor. They were staggered when, in 1963, a maid in the Wennerström home, suspicious of her employer, produced films of secret documents she had found in his attic.

Arrested in 1963 and charged with spying against his country, Wennerström broke down and confessed that he had been a double agent working for the Russians for over a decade. Tried in 1964, he received a sentence of life imprisonment. His treason compelled the Swedish military to do their defense planning all over again.

FURTHER READING: N. K. Ronblom, *The Spy without a Country* (1965); *Thomas Whiteside, *An Agent in Place: The Wennerström Affair* (1967).

Wentworth, Paul (1740?-93) American secret agent who spied for the British during the American War of Independence.

Wentworth was a member of a powerful New Hampshire family of that name, so that although a poor relation, he always acted the part of a gentlemen. He became rich himself by manipulating stocks in London and Paris, and by growing sugar and rice in Guiana, in South America, where during the 1760s he ran a plantation. Another American, Edward Bancroft, worked on the plantation in the years 1763 to 1766.

Hopeful of obtaining a British title, Wentworth migrated to London in 1770, where he served as New Hampshire's agent while the troubles between the colonies and the mother country were leading up to the American Revolution. He opposed the rebellion, which he viewed as a case of anarchy leading to despotism, and he offered his services to the London government, to which he reported first on New Hampshire alone and then on the colonies generally.

When William Eden became head of the British secret service in 1776, he gave Wentworth charge of the Paris connection. Wentworth organized a spy ring that included his old friend Edward Bancroft, then confidential secretary to Silas Deane, the American commissioner working for an alliance between France and America. Bancroft sent Wentworth secret messages on everything of importance he learned in Paris, and Wentworth took the information to Eden.

Wentworth cherished the illusion that enough colonial leaders might be bought with pensions and titles to stop the drive toward independence. To that end, he wrote thumbnail sketches of the most important as a guide for the king's ministers. Thus, on George Washington: "He is very jealous of Dr. Franklin and those who are governed by republican principles, from which he is very averse." Wentworth's opinions were not invariably justified by subsequent events.

In 1777 and 1778, Wentworth represented Eden at meetings with the three American commissioners in Paris (Silas Deane, Benjamin Franklin, and Arthur Lee). The talks came to nothing because of British demands that the rebellion cease. Indeed, Franklin used the meetings to alarm the French with fears that a reconciliation might be worked out. The government of King Louis XVI then speeded up the process of negotiating the Franco-American alliance of 1778.

This agreement left Wentworth with little to do in the way of espionage. He never did receive a British title, although in 1780 he held a seat briefly in Parliament. The following decade was one in which he spent most of his time dabbling in stocks and participating in various financial ventures. In 1790 he retired to his plantation in Guiana, where he died.

See also BANCROFT, EDWARD.

FURTHER READING: *Lewis Einstein, *Divided Loyalties: Americans in England during the War of Independence* (1933); Carl Van Doren, *Secret History of the American Revolution* (1941); Richard Deacon, *A History of the British Secret Service* (1969)

Wickham, William *(1761-1840)*   British spymaster on the Continent during the French Revolution.

An upper-class Englishman from Yorkshire, Wickham attended Harrow and Oxford before studying in Geneva, Switzerland, where he took a law degree (1786) and married a Swiss woman (1788), both of much help when he entered the British diplomatic service. Naturally considered an expert on Switzerland, he went there in 1794 to assist the British minister.

In 1795 Wickham became minister himself. His diplomatic work this time was secondary to his real assignment as British spymaster on the Continent, commissioned to act against the French revolutionaries, with whom Great Britain was at war.

The assignment included finding and using spies, plotting invasions of France by royalist forces or foreign powers, fomenting rebellions inside France, and spending money as need be in pursuit of the great objective, which was to defeat the revolution and restore King Louis XVIII, the monarch in exile, to his throne in Paris. British agents elsewhere in Europe reported to Wickham on all these matters.

During Wickham's tenure in Switzerland, the Pichegru affair occurred. It came to Wickham's attention in 1795 that General Charles Pichegru, a victorious French commander in the revolutionary cause, was disillusioned with the violence of the revolution and might be persuaded to change sides. Since Wickham realized that the Pichegru plan would be disrupted should the British appear to have a hand in it, he decided to work through Louis Joseph de Bourbon, prince de Condé, a royalist who maintained an army on the Rhine.

Condé had for a personal agent the comte de Montgaillard, who brought into the plot Louis Fauche-Borel, a Swiss printer and ardent royalist. Fauche-Borel became an intermediary between Pichegru in Strasbourg and Wickham in Berne. Pichegru's first concern was for money to pay his soldiers and buy supplies, and so sanguine was Wickham that he gave Fauche-Borel a draft for 8000 pounds to turn over to Pichegru, an enormous amount at that period. Wickham also entrusted letters for Pichegru to Fauche-Borel.

Unfortunately for Wickham, Pichegru temporized, claimed that the conditions for transferring his loyalty were not right, and never did lead his army into the royalist camp. (Pichegru made his move on behalf of the king in 1804, only to be seized by Napoleon's agents and thrown into a cell, where he was found dead under mysterious circumstances).

Wickham sent voluminous reports to London, where the accuracy of his information gained him a high reputation with his superiors. However, the French knew of his activities through their own spies, and in 1797 they brought such pressure to bear that the Swiss government asked him to resign his post as minister.

Wickham went home, where he was rewarded with the post of undersecretary of state in the British government. The rise of Napoleon to power in France created a fresh need in London for good intelligence on the Continent. Wickham returned to Switzerland and during the years 1799 to 1801 directed another espionage organization, which attempted to make the royalist cause a real alternative to the government in Paris.

The effort collapsed. Again returning home, Wickham was rewarded this time with the post of chief secretary for Ireland (1802). When he retired from politics in 1807, Napoleon ruled France and controlled most of Europe. However, Wickham lived to hear of the emperor's defeat at Waterloo in 1815 and his death on St. Helena in 1821.

See also FAUCHE-BOREL, LOUIS.

FURTHER READING: John Hall, *General Pichegru's Treason* (1915), describes Wickham's strategy with Pichegru; J. W. Thompson and S. K. Padover, *Secret Diplomacy: A Record of Espionage and Double-dealing: 1500–1815* (1937), has an account of Wickham as spymaster; *Harvey Mitchell, *The Underground War against France: The Missions of William Wickham 1794–1800* (1965).

Wiesenthal, Simon *(1908-   )*   Jewish hunter of Nazi war criminals.

Wiesenthal was born in Buczacz, then a part of the Austro-Hungarian empire. His father, a businessman, joined the armed forces during World War I, and was killed in action in 1915. As a result of the German surrender in 1918, Buczacz was transferred to Poland. Thus it was as a Polish Jew that Wiesenthal received his education at the local high school, from which he graduated in 1928. He then studied architecture at the technical university in Lvov (1932–36), took his degree, and opened an office. The Nazi-Soviet agreement of 1939, followed by the conquest and partition of Poland, left Lvov under Soviet control. Then the Germans overran the area in 1941. Wiesenthal, arrested as a Jew, was subjected to forced labor. He moved among Nazi concentration camps during the period 1943 to 1945; he was in the Mauthausen camp when American troops arrived and liberated the inmates.

Wiesenthal vowed that the men and women who had run the murderous Nazi system would be punished. After working with the Americans on this task, in 1947 he opened his Documentation Center in Linz, Austria. Here he gathered information, wrote thousands of file cards bearing the names, identities, and possible whereabouts of former Nazis, and turned evidence over to prosecutors for use in the courts. While at Linz he was instrumental in locating Adolf Eichmann, the director of Hitler's extermination policy, who was living in Buenos Aires. Wiesenthal provided Israel with this information. Israeli agents kidnaped Eichmann in 1960, and he was tried in Israel and executed in 1962.

Wiesenthal moved the Documentation Center to Vienna in 1961 to give his work a broader basis. He traveled widely, lectured on the holocaust, and pressed for the continued prosecution of those responsible. He also headed the Federation of Jewish Victims of the Nazi Regime. However, his concern extended beyond the Jews. He also provided information on former Nazis implicated in the mass murder of gypsies, Poles, Russians, and others.

See also EICHMANN, ADOLF.

FURTHER READING: *Simon Wiesenthal, *The Murderers Among Us: The Simon Wiesenthal Memoirs* (Joseph Wechsberg, ed., 1967); Isser Harel, *The House on Garibaldi Street: The First Account of the Capture of Adolf Eichmann Told by the Former Head of Israel's Secret Service* (1976).

Wolkoff, Anna *(1902-70?)*   Russian spy for Germany in England during World War II.

Born in St. Petersburg (modern-day Leningrad), Wolkoff belonged to the Russian aristocracy. Her father, a naval attaché of the tsar, served in various capitals; thus, she grew up a cosmopolitan whose education included several languages. In 1917, after the fall of the tsar, the family became refugees in London.

Bitterly anti-Communist, Anna Wolkoff became both a British subject and an admirer of Nazi Germany. In 1939 she met Tyler Kent, a code clerk at the United States Embassy in London, whom she persuaded to take classified documents from the code room and to allow her to transcribe the contents. She sent this information to Berlin during 1940, the worst year of World War II for the British.

Her pro-German bias led the Special Bureau of Scotland Yard to keep her under surveillance, and its agents arrested her along with Kent in 1940. It was discovered that she had been using the embassies of Italy and Rumania, neutrals at the time, to transmit her stolen information to the Germans.

Wolkoff went on trial and received a sentence of ten years. Released in 1946, after having been deprived of her British citizenship, she went to the Continent and dropped from view.

See also KENT, TYLER.

FURTHER READING: Kurt Singer, *The World's Greatest Women Spies* (1951); E. H. Cookridge, *Sisters of Delilah: Stories of Famous Women Spies* (1959); *John Holland Snow, *The Case of Tyler Kent* (1962).

Wollweber, Ernst **(1898-1967)** Director of espionage and sabotage for the Soveit Union and the German Democratic Republic.

Wollweber came out of the rough coal and steel region of the Ruhr, where he was born the son of a poverty-stricken miner. Compelled to leave school at an early age, he worked as a longshoreman on the docks of North Sea ports and became a left-wing radical. He joined the kaiser's navy in 1917, served briefly as World War I moved toward its end, and in 1918 was an instigator of the naval mutiny at Kiel that symbolized the German defeat.

Now a full-fledged Communist, Wollweber went to Moscow to express his support for the Bolshevik revolution. After receiving training in espionage and sabotage, he returned to Germany, where as secretary of the International Seamen's Union (Communist dominated) he established a spy network that gathered information for the Russians. During the 1930s, after Adolf Hitler became chancellor of Germany, Wollweber lived in Denmark, posing as a German businessman but operating undercover as a saboteur against the Nazi merchant marine. His agents planted bombs and started fires aboard German ships and otherwise harassed them.

Wollweber escaped from Denmark at the time of the German invasion of 1940. Transferring his secret operations to Sweden, he became more active in his anti-German sabotage in behalf of the Soviet Union following the German invasion of Russia in 1941. Then Swedish counterespionage discovered his undercover activities, arrested him, and broke up his spy ring.

Returning to Germany at the end of the war (1945), Wollweber went to Russian-occupied East Berlin and began to work for the Communist regime. He rose to become in 1953 the minister of state security of the German Democratic Republic (East Germany), which made him the head of the East German intelligence establishment. He had much success with his network of spies and saboteurs in the German Federal Republic (West Germany) until it was discovered that his opposite number in the west, Reinhard Gehlen, had planted a spy named Walter Gramsch in his office. Gramsch, who had been reporting to Gehlen for seven years, escaped to West Berlin. Wollweber survived this blow, regained his credit with the Russians, and remained on the job into the 1960s.

See also GEHLEN, REINHARD; GRAMSCH, WALTER.

FURTHER READING: Charles Wighton, *The World's Greatest Spies* (1962); J. Bernard Hutton, *Struggle in the Dark: How Russian and Other Iron Curtain Spies Operate* (1967); *Heinz Höhne and Hermann Zolling, *The General Was a Spy: The Truth about General Gehlen and His Spy Ring* (1972), has a discussion of Wollweber as Gehlen's antagonist.

Woodhull, Abraham **(1750-1826)** American secret agent on Long Island during the American War of Independence.

Born on the family farm at Setauket on the shore of Long Island Sound across from Connecticut, Woodhull took over the farm from his father and ran it profitably until the outbreak of hostilities between the Americans and the British at Lexington in 1775. The British occupation of New York in the following year brought Long Island within the area of the fighting, and Woodhull felt especially vulnerable because his farm lay open to attack. He remained, nonetheless, a Patriot committed to the American cause.

He was therefore receptive when Major Benjamin Tallmadge, spymaster for General George Washington, approached him in 1778 on the subject of forming an espionage network to report on Sir Henry Clinton and his British forces in New York. Woodhull recruited Robert Townsend, a New York merchant who was in a position to keep the enemy under surveillance. The network included Austin Roe, a courier who carried Townsend's messages from Manhattan to Setauket, and Caleb Brewster, a sailor who ferried them across Long Island Sound to Tallmadge's headquarters on the Connecticut shore.

Woodhull used the cover name "Samuel Culper, Senior," while Townsend was "Samuel Culper, Junior." Their network was therefore known as the Culper Ring, and it became the best espionage group of the war, operating successfully in New York for five years without detection (1778–83).

Woodhull's place in the operation was the more remarkable in that he was a timorous individual who lived in constant fear of being discovered. He repeatedly implored Tallmadge to maintain the tightest secrecy. Roe, arriving in Setauket with coded messages from Townsend in New York, usually did not deliver them directly to Woodhull but hid them in a wooden box buried in one of Woodhull's fields. Woodhull retrieved the papers and passed them on to Brewster.

Woodhull's fears ended with the British evacuation of New York in 1783. Able to farm in peace, he got married, took part in public affairs, and became a judge. Like the other members of the Culper Ring, he maintained to the end a public silence about his wartime espionage activities.

See also CULPER RING; TALLMADGE, BENJAMIN.

FURTHER READING: *Morton Pennypacker, *General Washington's Spies on Long Island and in New York* (1939); John Bakeless, *Turncoats, Traitors, and Heroes* (1959), has an account of Woodhull; Corey Ford, *A Peculiar Service* (1965), is the best book on Woodhull and the Culper Ring.

Wright, Patience *(1725?-86)* American sculptor and spy in London during the American War of Independence.

Patience Lovell Wright, fifth daughter of an eccentric Quaker farmer, was probably born in Oyster Bay, on Long Island. Her father sold his farm in 1729 and moved the family to Bordentown, New Jersey. Patience married Joseph Wright in 1748. Her husband died in 1769, leaving her, at age 44, to support four children, with a fifth on the way.

As children, Mrs. Wright and her sister Rachel had amused themselves by modeling in clay and bread. They now set up studios in Philadelphia and New York and began to model in wax for a living. Patience excelled in creating for her sitters likenesses of astonishing delicacy and truth.

In 1772, bearing a letter from Benjamin Franklin's sister, she sailed for London. There she became an overnight success. Franklin, in London, liked her—perhaps because her forthrightness amused him—and he urged his friends to order their portraits in wax. He himself sat for a bust.

The sculptor's lively, satirical comments and gusty manner, her way of modeling a head in her lap under her apron (to keep the wax pliable) then whipping it out for all to admire, captivated Londoners. They saw in her a free-spirited American original and listened eagerly to her garrulous chatter about her native land.

Soon the talented and powerful frequented the Pall Mall studio of this "Promethean modeller," among them William Pitt, earl of Chatham, and Prime Minister Lord North. King George III brought Queen Caroline, and they sat for their portraits in wax. The royal patronage guaranteed Patience Wright's success.

The American Revolution was not far off. Mrs. Wright, an ardent Patriot with a taste for intrigue, began to worm information out of her famous sitters as she worked—scraps of political news, military appointments, troop or fleet movements. All this she relayed to her friends in America, thus becoming the first American woman to spy for her country abroad.

On the British side, Lord Chatham, for one, supported the protesting colonies, and consulted her about the rights and wrongs of the Boston Tea Party. The reclusive elder stateman was grateful enough for her information to sit for his portrait in wax.

"The fleat is any moment to sail and a new Constructed Cannon, lite, Portable on horse Back, 32 Inches Long, wide muzzel to fire at the Inhabitants and kill many at a shot." So wrote Mrs. Wright on April 6, 1775, thirteen days before the outbreak of the revolution at the battle of Lexington, to John Dickinson, the "farmer statesman," who had drafted the American Declaration of Rights in 1765. At the same time she mentioned to Dickinson "26 men in London who make your affair all their study and are Impatient to be Employed." She claimed to have an informant in the office of Lord Dartmouth, secretary of state for American affairs, and warned Dickinson against Americans in London loyal to the crown. General Sir William Howe, she reported, was bound for New York, not Boston. (However, this was not true, and, it has been suggested, may have been the result of an exercise in deception by the British secret service.)

Letters addressed abroad were now being opened by the British authorities, so she sent her information, destined for the Continental Congress, to her sister Rachel's waxworks in Philadelphia concealed in wax heads.

One of Mrs. Wright's main concerns was to supply Franklin, who in 1776 had been appointed an American commissioner in Paris, with news from London. She kept up a flow of letters in his direction, entrusting them to traveling friends, such as Mrs. Edward Bancroft. Since Edward Bancroft, secretary to the commissioner, was a double agent working for the British, they must have known what she was about.

In 1781 the sculptor went to Paris, where Franklin again sponsored her works. She was not so successful there and returned to London a year later. She longed to go back to "dear America," but died in 1786 while preparing to do so.

Several bas-reliefs attributed to Patience Wright are extant. Her remarkable life-size memorial figure of Pitt, done at the time of his death in 1778, still stands in Westminster Abbey.

FURTHER READING: *The Political Magazine and Parliamentary, Naval, Military and Literary Journal for the Year M, DCC, LXXXVI;* *Charles Coleman Sellers, *Patience Wright, American Artist and Spy in George III's London* (1976); Paul Engle, *Women in the American Revolution* (1976).

Wynne, Greville *(1919-   )*   British businessman and secret agent.

A native of the British Midlands, and the son of a mining engineer, Wynne studied electrical engineering at Nottingham University (1938), a training of which he made good use when he went into the British army as Europe moved toward World War II (1939–45). He was assigned to intelligence work and emerged from the war adept at it.

With the end of the conflict, Wynne went into business, becoming a salesman on the Continent. His travels often took him to eastern Europe, and during the years 1955 to 1959 he reported to British intelligence. In 1960 he went to Moscow to negotiate for a Russian trade delegation to visit London. After some difficulties, the arrangements were agreed on in 1961.

The leader of the delegation was Oleg Penkovskiy, who confessed to Wynne that he felt disillusioned with the Soviet system and desired to work against it. He suggested that Wynne put him in touch with western intelligence. Wynne returned to London, reported to British intelligence, and prepared the way for Penkovskiy when he arrived with the Russian trade delegation. That was how Penkovskiy became a spy for the west.

Penkovskiy and Wynne worked together in espionage during 1961 and 1962, but Soviet counterespionage picked up their trail, and both were arrested, Penkovskiy in Moscow and Wynne in Budapest. Convicted after his trial in 1963, Penkovskiy was said by the Russians to have been executed. Wynne served nearly a year of an eight-year sentence before being exchanged for Gordon Lonsdale, a convicted Soviet spy imprisoned in Britain.

See also PENKOVSKIY, OLEG.

FURTHER READING: *Greville Wynne, *The Man from Moscow* (1967); Fitzroy Maclean, *Take Nine Spies* (1978), has a chapter on Penkovskiy.

Yagoda, Genrikh *(1891-1938)*   Polish director of Soviet espionage and counterespionage.

Born in Lodz, Yagoda was the son of a chemist. The history of his early years has been obscured by his later systematic concealment of it, but he is known to have mastered chemistry and to have participated in left-wing movements in Poland. Yagoda served in the Red Army during the Russian civil war that followed the Communist revolution of 1917, and by 1920 he was closely associated with Communist leader Joseph Stalin.

Yagoda rose with Stalin during the late 1920s, and by 1930 he was in charge of the notorious labor camps of the Soviet Union. In 1934 Stalin appointed him head of the NKVD (People's Commissariat for Internal Affairs, 1934–46; Soviet intelligence). Yagoda established a network of Stalinist spies across the Soviet Union and founded the system of employing mass terror against the

Soviet people. He used drugs and torture, sent secret executioners to assassinate Stalin's enemies abroad, and prepared defendants for their confessions at the Moscow purge trials of the 1930s, where the remaining important opponents of Stalin were condemned to death.

The purge trials were the final achievement of the Soviet spymaster. Stalin, mistrustful of Yagoda's power, had him imprisoned in 1936 and shot two years later.

See also KGB.

FURTHER READING: Robert Conquest, *The Soviet Police System* (1968); *Boris Levytsky, *The Uses of Terror: The Soviet Secret Service, 1917–1970* (1971); Richard Deacon, *History of the Russian Secret Service* (1972).

Yamamoto, Isoroku *(1884-1943)*   Admiral of the Japanese navy who planned the attack on Pearl Harbor.

Born on the island of Nagaoka, Yamamoto belonged to a naval family. He graduated from the academy and took his commission in the imperial navy in time to see service in the Russo-Japanese War (1904–05). The Japanese victory over the Russians gained Japan recognition in the eyes of the world as a great power and opened the way for military adventures in the first half of the twentieth century.

Yamamoto rose through the grades, becoming chief of naval aviation in 1938. Growing militarism combined with Japanese ambitions following the invasion of China created a war fever in Tokyo. Yamamoto was not a warmonger, but as admiral of the First Fleet in 1939 he necessarily became part of the prewar planning at headquarters in Tokyo. He was admiral of the Combined Fleet when the Japanese government decided to attack the United States, so to him fell responsibility for devising the plan and selecting the commanders and ships for the strike at Pearl Harbor (1941).

In 1942 Yamamoto commanded the fleet that challenged the rebuilt American Pacific fleet in the battle of Midway. He lost the battle largely because American cryptologists broke the Japanese naval ciphers and read the messages sent from Tokyo to the ships at sea. American Admiral Chester Nimitz at Pearl Harbor who knew Yamamoto's plans and strength, organized an effective battle fleet in the light of that knowledge. This enabled Admiral Raymond Spruance to win the battle that turned the tide of the war in the Pacific.

Yamamoto did not live to see the defeat of Japan. Setting out on a flying visit to Japanese bases in the South Pacific, he was again victimized by American intelligence, which plotted his route by means of the broken ciphers. The Americans set a trap for him, his plane was shot down, and he died in the crash.

See also PEARL HARBOR.

FURTHER READING: Samuel Eliot Morison, *History of United States Naval Operations in World War II* (vol. 3, 1948); Roberta Wohlstetter, *Pearl Harbor: Warning and Decision* (1962); *Burke Davis, *Get Yamamoto* (1969).

Yardley, Herbert O. *(1889-1958)*   American cryptologist during and after World War I.

Born in Worthington, Indiana, Yardley belonged to an ordinary family of moderate means. After graduating from high school in 1907, he spent some years studying law, playing poker, and solving puzzles. In 1913 he got a job as a telegraph operator with the State Department in Washington, where the handling of messages in code and the fact that he was able to read some of them, aroused his interest in cryptology.

This interest and his persuasiveness brought Yardley a transfer in 1917 to the War Department, for which he developed a special cryptological bureau called MI8 (Military Intelligence, Section 8). MI8 lasted through America's participation in World War I (1917–18), its foremost achievement being the exposure of Lothar Witzke, the only German secret agent to be executed in the United States during that conflict.

Yardley served as a cryptologist at the Paris Peace Conference in 1919, and when he returned to Washington, he persuaded the State and War departments to establish a permanent cryptological organization, one celebrated in espionage history as the American Black Chamber. This organization, under Yardley's direction, broke dozens of codes and read thousands of secret messages during the ten years of its existence (1919–29).

Success ruined the American Black Chamber. Yardley and his men angered friendly nations, especially Japan, by translating their coded documents into plain English, and when President Herbert Hoover took office in 1929, his secretary of state, Henry L. Stimson, decided to close the bureau. Justifying his decision, Stimson, very much a product of the old school, said stiffly: "Gentlemen do not read each other's mail."

Yardley created a scandal two years later when he published *The American Black Chamber.* Most of the contents derived from his official work for the government, a fact that caused him to be denounced in Congress, which passed a bill to prevent similar situations from arising. Signed by President Franklin Roosevelt in 1933, Public Law 37 makes it a crime for anyone to use for personal reasons any material in official codes.

The American Black Chamber brought Yardley a lot of money, as well as fame. He wrote a number of books, including a novel, *The Blonde Countess,* which was made into a Hollywood motion picture. He did some cryptological work for the governments of China (1938) and Canada (1941). He spent most of World War II (1941–45) with the Office of Price Administration in Washington.

His final book, published in the year before his death, concerned one of his oldest interests. He called it *The Education of a Poker Player.*

FURTHER READING: *Herbert O. Yardley, *The American Black Chamber* (1931); Allen Dulles, *The Craft of Intelligence* (1963); David Kahn, *The Codebreakers: The Story of Secret Writing* (1967).

Yeo-Thomas, F. F. E. *(1901-64)* British spy in France during World War II.

Although born in London, Yeo-Thomas spent most of his life in Paris, where his father was a businessman. Yeo-Thomas went to school in France and England, served in the French army toward the end of World War I (1914–18), and was a soldier with the Polish forces that turned back a Russian invasion in the years 1919 and 1920. Captured by the Russians, he escaped during their retreat from Poland. Reaching Paris, he went into business, rising between the wars to be director of a fashion house.

When World War II broke out in 1939, Yeo-Thomas became an interpreter for British forces in France. After the Allied debacle and the French surrender of 1940, he left France for England, where in 1941 he was an interpreter assigned to the Free French forces led by General Charles de Gaulle. The following year Yeo-Thomas was transferred to the Special Operations Executive (SOE), the British organization supporting the resistance in France. He became a liaison man between the SOE and the BCRA (Central Bureau of Intelligence and Operations, de Gaulle's intelligence department) working with the head of the department, "Colonel Passy" in the code terminology, actually André Dewavrin. Yeo-Thomas was called the "White Rabbit" when he and Dewavrin parachuted into France in 1943 to plan strategy with leaders of the French resistance and bring unity to the underground movement against the Germans.

Yeo-Thomas left France aboard a British plane that had picked him up at a secret rendezvous. He soon made a second visit to France as a spy, and on his return to England reported directly to Prime Minister Winston Churchill on the pressing need of the resistance for more agents and more supplies (Churchill promised to see that the need was met). On his third secret mission to France in 1943, Yeo-Thomas was accompanied by Pierre Brossolette of the BCRA. Captured by the Gestapo (German secret police), Brossolette committed suicide. Yeo-Thomas was arrested in Paris, taken to Germany, and held in the Nazi death camp at Buchenwald. In 1945 he escaped from the Germans to safety with the American forces advancing through Germany.

Yeo-Thomas lived to testify against the war criminals of Buchenwald in 1947 and to return to the business of being a fashion designer in Paris..

See also BROSSOLETTE, PIERRE; DEWAVRIN, ANDRÉ; FRENCH RESISTANCE; SPECIAL OPERATIONS EXECUTIVE.

FURTHER READING: *Bruce Marshal, *The White Rabbit* (1952); M. R. D. Foot, *SOE in France: An Account of the Work of the British Special Operations Executive in France, 1940–1944* (1966); David Schoenbrun, *Soldiers of the Night: The Story of the French Resistance* (1980).

Yoshikawa, Takeo (1916-   )   Japanese spy in Hawaii before the attack on Pearl Harbor.

Yoshikawa belonged to a middle-class family, and after leaving school, he joined the Japanese navy. He was an ensign when he arrived in Hawaii in 1941 to serve as a secretary at the Japanese consulate and covertly as a spy whose assignment it was to keep Tokyo informed about the U. S. Navy during the period when the Japanese warlords were planning to attack the United States.

Yoshikawa made many trips through the Hawaiian Islands to gather information, but he concentrated on the warships at the Pearl Harbor naval base. He inspected as much of the base as he could, and he obtained secret information from other sources both legal and illegal (his principal illegal source was a German spy in Hawaii, Bernard Kühn).

Yoshikawa's information was so good that his estimate of the number of American warships at Pearl Harbor very nearly matched the number there when Japanese planes attacked on December 7, 1941.

The American authorities in Hawaii never realized he was a spy. Thinking he was merely a secretary at the consulate, they repatriated him to Japan along with the rest of the Japanese staff.

See also KÜHN, BERNARD; PEARL HARBOR.

FURTHER READING: *Ronald Seth, *Secret Servants: A History of Japanese Espionage* (1957); Roberta Wohlstetter, *Pearl Harbor: Warning and Decision* (1962); David Kahn, *The Code-breakers: The Story of Secret Writing* (1967).

Zimmermann, Arthur *(1864-1940)*   German foreign minister and author of the "Zimmermann telegram" that helped bring the United States into World War I on the side of the Allies.

Zimmermann was born into a middle-class family of East Prussia. He attended the University of Königsberg (modern-day Kaliningrad, in the Soviet Union since the realignment of borders that followed World War II). Entering the consular service, Zimmermann held posts abroad during the years 1896 to 1901. Then he shifted to the diplomatic department in Berlin (1901) and entered the foreign office (1902), rising by 1911 to be undersecretary. In 1914 he drafted a telegram from Berlin to Vienna stating that Germany supported Austria's ultimatum to Serbia following the assassination of the Austrian Archduke Franz Ferdinand at Sarajevo. Zimmermann thus had a part in the events that led to World War I (1914–18).

His part in the war itself became much more significant in 1916 when, named Berlin's foreign minister, he backed the German high command on the decision to begin unrestricted submarine warfare in the Atlantic Ocean. Because of the danger that the Americans would enter the war against Germany, Zimmermann planned to obtain aid from Mexico and Japan against the United States. That was the background to the Zimmermann telegram of 1917, in which the German foreign minister secretly offered to help Mexico to regain the territories of Texas, New Mexico, and Arizona if Mexico would enter the war as a belligerent on the side of Germany. The message also suggested that the president of Mexico invite Japan to join the alliance.

The Zimmermann telegram was intercepted and decoded by British intelligence. Transmitted to Washington and published in the American press on orders from President Woodrow Wilson, Zimmermann's proposal caused a sensation among the American people, who because of it were the more prepared to respond when Wilson called for a declaration of war on Germany. With the truth out in the open, the German foreign minister defended his action by pointing to America's bias toward the Allies. However, in 1917 Zimmermann was removed from office. He never held a high post in the German government again, although he lived into the period of World War II.

See also ZIMMERMANN TELEGRAM.

FURTHER READING: *Barbara W. Tuchman, *The Zimmermann Telegram* (new ed., 1966); Thomas A. Bailey, *Diplomatic History of the American People* (9th ed., 1974), describes the Zimmermann telegram within the context of Wilson's diplomacy.

Zimmermann Telegram *(1917)*   German coded message and the worst diplomatic blunder of World War I.

In 1917 Room 40 of the British Admiralty (naval intelligence) intercepted a telegram in code from the German foreign minister, Arthur Zimmermann, to the German ambassador in Washington. The cryptanalysts of Room 40 decoded the "Zimmermann telegram," which was intended for transmission by the ambassador to the president of Mexico. The United States had not yet entered World War I (1914–18), but Zimmermann was worried about the possibilty that the Americans would join Britain and France against Germany, and his message concerned a proposed German riposte should this happen. The message to the president of Mexico read as follows:

> We intend to begin on the 1st of February unrestricted submarine warfare. We shall endeavour in spite of this to keep the United States of America neutral. In the event of this not succeeding, we make Mexico a proposal of alliance on the following basis: Make war together, make peace together, generous financial support and an understanding on our part that Mexico is to reconquer the lost territory in Texas, New Mexico and Arizona. You will inform the [Mexican] President of the above most secretly as soon as the outbreak of war with the United States is certain and add the suggestion that he should, on his own initiative, invite Japan to immediate adherence.

The Zimmermann telegram thus proposed to reverse the outcome of the Mexican War and to restore the territories acquired by the United States from Mexico in the nineteenth century. The reference to Japan seemed logical to Zimmermann because Japanese ambitions conflicted with American interests in the Far East. He did not indicate in his secret message how his plans were to be executed. The Mexican army plainly could not reconquer the lost lands that were now states of the United States, nor could the German army, tied down by the fighting in Europe, spare any divisions to be transported to Mexico, even supposing that German convoys were able to break through the British naval blockade. Again, the president of Mexico would seem not to have had a persuasive voice in Tokyo. Perhaps Zimmermann's real thought was to prepare for German submarines to use the coast of Mexico for refueling and refitting should America enter the war on the side of the Allies.

London, seeing the usefulness of the Zimmermann telegram, transmitted the contents to Washington. President Woodrow Wilson had the text published, and the resulting storm of protest among the American people strengthened his hand when he went before Congress to ask for a declaration of war against Germany. None of the clauses of Zimmerman's message ever passed from the verbal stage to reality. The Zimmermann telegram proved to be a boomerang that damaged Germany. The boomerang struck the man who launched it. Zimmermann lost his place as foreign minister of the German government because of his blunder in sending the Zimmermann telegram.

See also ROOM 40; ZIMMERMANN, ARTHUR.

FURTHER READING: William F. Friedman and Charles J. Mendelsohn, *The Zimmermann Telegram of January 16, 1917, and Its Cryptographic Background* (1938), was declassified in 1965; *Barbara Tuchman, *The Zimmermann Telegram,* (new ed., 1966).

INDEX